To my best friend

Contents at a Glance

Learn Java for Android Development

Jeff "JavaJeff" Friesen

Apress®

Learn Java for Android Development

ISBN-13 (pbk): 978-1-4302-3156-1

ISBN-13 (electronic): 978-1-4302-3157-8

Printed and bound in the United States of America (POD)

President and Publisher: Paul Manning
Lead Editor: Steve Anglin
Development Editor: Tom Welsh
Technical Reviewer: Paul Connolly
Editorial Board: Steve Anglin, Mark Beckner, Ewan Buckingham, Gary Cornell, Jonathan Gennick, Jonathan Hassell, Michelle Lowman, Matthew Moodie, Jeffrey Pepper, Frank Pohlmann, Douglas Pundick, Ben Renow-Clarke, Dominic Shakeshaft, Matt Wade, Tom Welsh
Coordinating Editor: Debra Kelly
Copy Editor: Bill McManus
Compositor: MacPS, LLC
Indexer: John Collin
Artist: April Milne
Cover Designer: Anna Ishchenko

Distributed to the book trade worldwide by Springer Science+Business Media, LLC., 233 Spring Street, 6th Floor, New York, NY 10013. Phone 1-800-SPRINGER, fax (201) 348-4505, e-mail orders-ny@springer-sbm.com, or visit www.springeronline.com.

For information on translations, please e-mail rights@apress.com, or visit www.apress.com.

Apress and friends of ED books may be purchased in bulk for academic, corporate, or promotional use. eBook versions and licenses are also available for most titles. For more information, reference our Special Bulk Sales–eBook Licensing web page at www.apress.com/info/bulksales.

The source code for this book is available to readers at www.apress.com/book/view/1430231564.

Contents

About the Author

Jeff "JavaJeff" Friesen has been actively involved with Java since the late 1990s. Jeff has worked with Java in various companies, including a healthcare-oriented consulting firm, where he created his own Java/C++ software for working with smart cards. Jeff has written about Java in numerous articles for JavaWorld (www.javaworld.com), informIT (www.informit.com), and java.net (http://java.net), and has authored several books on Java, including *Beginning Java SE 6 Platform: From Novice to Professional* (Apress, 2007; ISBN: 159059830X), which focuses exclusively on Java version 6's new and improved features. Jeff has also taught Java in university and college continuing education classes. He has a Bachelor of Science degree in mathematics and computer science from Brandon University in Brandon, Manitoba, Canada, and currently freelances in Java and other software technologies.

About the Technical Reviewer

 **Paul Connolly** is the Director of Engineering for Atypon Systems' RightSuite product line. RightSuite is an enterprise access-control and commerce solution used by many of the world's largest publishing and media companies. Paul enjoys designing and implementing high-performance, enterprise-class software systems. He is also an active contributor in the open-source community.

Prior to joining Atypon Systems, Paul worked as a senior software engineer at Standard & Poor's where he architected and developed key communications systems. Paul is a Sun Certified Java Programmer, Sun Certified Business Component Developer, and a Sun Certified Web Component Developer. Paul lives in New York City with his wife, Marina.

Acknowledgments

I thank Steve Anglin for contacting me to write this book, Debra Kelly for guiding me through the various aspects of this project, Tom Welsh for helping me with the development of my chapters, Paul Connolly for his diligence in catching various flaws that would otherwise have made it into this book, and Bill McManus and the production team for making the book's content look good.

It has been many years since I started writing about Java, and I also thank the following editors who have helped me share my knowledge with others: Chris Adamson, Bridget Collins, Richard Dal Porto, Sean Dixon, Victoria Elzey, Kevin Farnham, Todd Green, Jennifer Orr, Athen O'Shea, Esther Schindler, Daniel Steinberg, Jill Steinberg, Dustin Sullivan, and Atlanta Wilson.

Introduction

Smartphones and other touch-based mobile devices are all the rage these days. Their popularity is largely due to their ability to run *apps*. Although the iPhone and iPad with their growing collection of Objective-C-based apps are the leaders of the pack, Android-based smartphones with their growing collection of Java-based apps are proving to be a strong competitor.

Not only are many iPhone/iPad developers making money by selling their apps, many Android developers are also making money by selling similar apps. According to tech websites such as *The Register* (www.theregister.co.uk/), some Android developers are making lots of money (www.theregister.co.uk/2010/03/02/android_app_profit/).

In today's tough economic climate, perhaps you would like to try your hand at becoming an Android developer and make some money. If you have good ideas, perseverance, and some artistic talent (or perhaps know some talented individuals), you are already part of the way toward achieving this goal.

Tip: A good reason to consider Android app development over iPhone/iPad app development is the lower startup costs that you will incur with Android. For example, you do not need to purchase a Mac on which to develop Android apps (a Mac is required for developing iPhone/iPad apps); your existing Windows, Linux, or Unix machine will do nicely.

Most importantly, you will need to possess a solid understanding of the Java language and foundational application programming interfaces (APIs) before jumping into Android. After all, Android apps are written in Java and interact with many of the standard Java APIs (such as threading and input/output APIs).

I wrote *Learn Java for Android Development* to give you a solid Java foundation that you can later extend with knowledge of Android architecture, API, and tool specifics. This book will give you a strong grasp of the Java language and many important APIs that are fundamental to Android apps and other Java applications. It will also introduce you to key development tools.

Learn Java for Android Development is organized into ten chapters and one appendix. Each chapter focuses on a collection of related topics and presents a set of exercises that you should complete to get the most benefit from the chapter's content. The appendix provides the solutions to each chapter's exercises.

Note: You can download this book's source code by pointing your web browser to
www.apress.com/book/view/1430231564 and clicking the Source Code link under Book Resources.
Although most of this code is compilable with Java version 6, you will need Java version 7 to compile one
of the applications.

Chapter 1 introduces you to Java by first focusing on Java's dual nature (language and platform). It then briefly introduces you to Sun's/Oracle's Java SE, Java EE, and Java ME editions of the Java development software, as well as Google's Android edition. You next learn how to download and install the Java SE Development Kit (JDK), and learn some Java basics by developing and playing with a pair of simple Java applications. After receiving a brief introduction to the NetBeans and Eclipse IDEs, you learn about application development in the context of *Four of a Kind*, a console-based card game.

Chapter 2 starts you on an in-depth journey of the Java language by focusing on language fundamentals (such as types, expressions, variables, and statements) in the contexts of classes and objects. Because applications are largely based on classes, it is important to learn how to architect classes correctly, and this chapter shows you how to do so.

Chapter 3 adds to Chapter 2's pool of object-based knowledge by introducing you to those language features that take you from object-based applications to object-oriented applications. Specifically, you learn about features related to inheritance, polymorphism, and interfaces. While exploring inheritance, you learn about Java's ultimate superclass. Also, while exploring interfaces, you discover the real reason for their inclusion in the Java language; interfaces are not merely a workaround for Java's lack of support for multiple implementation inheritance, but serve a higher purpose.

Chapter 4 introduces you to four categories of advanced language features: nested types, packages, static imports, and exceptions. While discussing nested types, I briefly introduce the concept of a closure and state that closures will appear in Java version 7 (which many expect to arrive later this year).

Note: I wrote this book several months before Java version 7's expected arrival in the fall of 2010. Although I have tried to present an accurate portrayal of version 7–specific language features, it is possible that feature syntax may differ somewhat from what is presented in this book. Also, I only discuss closures briefly because this feature was still in a state of flux while writing this book. For more information about closures and other functional programming concepts (such as lambdas) being considered for Java version 7, I recommend that you check out articles such as "Functional Programming Concepts in JDK 7" by Alex Collins (http://java.dzone.com/articles/lambdas-closures-jdk-7).

Chapter 5 continues to explore advanced language features by focusing on assertions, annotations, generics, and enums. Although the topic of generics has brought confusion to many developers, I believe that my discussion of this topic will clear up much of the murkiness. Among other items, you learn how to interpret type declarations such as Enum<E extends Enum<E>>.

Chapter 6 begins a trend that focuses more on APIs than language features. This chapter first introduces you to many of Java's math-oriented types (such as Math, StrictMath, BigDecimal, and BigInteger), and also introduces you to Java's strictfp reserved word. It then looks at the Package class, primitive wrapper classes, and the References API.

Chapter 7 continues to explore Java's basic APIs by focusing on reflection, string management, the System class, and threading.

Chapter 8 focuses exclusively on Java's collections framework, which provides you with a solution for organizing objects in lists, sets, queues, and maps.

Chapter 9 continues to explore Java's utility APIs by introducing you to the concurrency utilities, internationalization, preferences, random number generation, and regular expressions.

Chapter 10 is all about input/output (I/O). In this chapter, you explore Java's classic I/O support in terms of its File class, RandomAccessFile class, various stream classes, and various writer/reader classes. My discussion of stream I/O includes coverage of Java's object serialization and deserialization mechanisms.

Note: This book largely discusses APIs that are common to Java SE and Android. However, it diverges from this practice in Chapter 9, where I use the Swing toolkit to provide a graphical user interface for one of this chapter's internationalization examples. (Android does not support Swing.)

After you complete this book, I recommend that you obtain a copy of *Beginning Android 2* by Mark L Murphy (Apress, 2010; ISBN: 1430226293) and start learning how to develop Android apps. In that book, "you'll learn how to develop applications for Android 2.x mobile devices, using simple examples that are ready to run with your copy of the JDK."

Note: Over the next few months, I will make available at my javajeff.mb.ca website six additional PDF-based chapters. These chapters will introduce you to more Java APIs (such as networking and database APIs) that I could not discuss in this book because the book has greatly exceeded its initial 400-page estimate (and the good folks at Apress have been gracious enough to let me do so, but there are limits). I present more information about these PDF files at the end of Chapter 10's "Summary" section.

Thanks for purchasing my book. I hope you find it a helpful preparation for, and I wish you lots of success in achieving, a satisfying and lucrative career as an Android app developer.

Jeff "JavaJeff" Friesen, August 2010

Chapter 1

Getting Started with Java

Android is Google's software stack for mobile devices that includes an operating system and middleware. With help from Java, the OS runs specially designed Java applications known as *Android apps*. Because these apps are based on Java, it makes sense for you to learn about Java before you dive into the world of Android development.

NOTE: This book illustrates Java concepts via non-Android Java applications.

This chapter sets the stage for teaching you the essential Java concepts that you need to understand before you embark on your Android career. I first answer the "What is Java?" question. I next show you how to install the Java SE Development Kit, and introduce you to JDK tools for compiling and running Java applications.

After showing you how to install and use the open source NetBeans and Eclipse IDEs so that you can develop these applications faster, I present an application for playing a card game that I call *Four of a Kind*. This application gives you a significant taste of the Java language, and is the centerpiece of my discussion on developing applications.

What Is Java?

Java is a language and a platform originated by Sun Microsystems. This section briefly describes this language and reveals what it means for Java to be a platform. To meet various needs, Sun organized Java into three main editions: Java SE, Java EE, and Java ME. This section also briefly explores each of these editions, along with Android.

NOTE: Java has an interesting history that dates back to December 1990. At that time, James Gosling, Patrick Naughton, and Mike Sheridan (all employees of Sun Microsystems) were given the task of figuring out the next major trend in computing. They concluded that one trend would involve the convergence of computing devices and intelligent consumer appliances. Thus was born the Green project.

The fruits of Green were *Star7*, a handheld wireless device featuring a five-inch color LCD screen, a SPARC processor, a sophisticated graphics capability, and a version of Unix; and *Oak*, a language developed by James Gosling for writing applications to run on Star7, and which he named after an oak tree growing outside of his office window at Sun. To avoid a conflict with another language of the same name, Dr. Gosling changed this language's name to Java.

Sun Microsystems subsequently evolved the Java language and platform until Oracle acquired Sun in early 2010. Check out http://java.sun.com/ for the latest Java news from Oracle.

Java Is a Language

Java is a language in which developers express *source code* (program text). Java's *syntax* (rules for combining symbols into language features) is partly patterned after the C and C++ languages to shorten the learning curve for C/C++ developers.

The following list identifies a few similarities between Java and C/C++:

- Java and C/C++ share the same single-line and multiline comment styles. Comments let you document source code.

- Many of Java's reserved words are identical to their C/C++ counterparts (for, if, switch, and while are examples) and C++ counterparts (catch, class, public, and try are examples).

- Java also supports character, double precision floating-point, floating-point, integer, long integer, and short integer primitive types, and via the same char, double, float, int, long, and short reserved words.

- Java also supports many of the same operators, including arithmetic (+, -, *, /, and %) and conditional (?:) operators.

- Java also uses brace characters ({ and }) to delimit blocks of statements.

The following list identifies a few differences between Java and C/C++:

- Java supports an additional comment style known as Javadoc. (I will briefly introduce Javadoc later in this chapter.)

- Java provides reserved words not found in C/C++ (extends, strictfp, synchronized, and transient are examples).

- Java supports the byte integer type, does not provided a signed version of the character type, and does not provide unsigned versions of integer, long integer, and short integer. Furthermore, all of Java's primitive types have guaranteed implementation sizes, which is an important part of achieving portability (discussed later). The same cannot be said of equivalent primitive types in C and C++.

- Java provides operators not found in C/C++. These operators include `instanceof` and `>>>` (unsigned right shift).

- Java provides labeled break and continue statements that you will not find in C/C++.

You will learn about single-line and multiline comments in Chapter 2. Also, you will learn about reserved words, primitive types, operators, blocks, and statements (including labeled break and continue) in that chapter.

Java was designed to be a safer language than C/C++. It achieves safety in part by omitting certain C/C++ features. For example, Java does not support *pointers* (variables containing addresses) and does not let you overload operators.

Java also achieves safety by modifying certain C/C++ features. For example, loops must be controlled by Boolean expressions instead of integer expressions where 0 is false and a nonzero value is true. (Chapter 2 discusses loops and expressions.)

Suppose you must code a C/C++ while loop that repeats no more than ten times. Being tired, you specify `while (x) x++;` (assume that x is an integer-based variable initialized to 0—I discuss variables in Chapter 2) where x++ adds 1 to x's value. This loop does not stop when x reaches 10; you have introduced a *bug* (a defect).

This problem is less likely to occur in Java because it complains when it sees `while (x)`. This complaint requires you to recheck your expression, and you will then most likely specify `while (x != 10)`. Not only is safety improved (you cannot specify just x), meaning is also clarified: `while (x != 10)` is more meaningful than `while (x)`.

The aforementioned and other fundamental language features support classes, objects, inheritance, polymorphism, and interfaces. Java also provides advanced features related to nested types, packages, static imports, exceptions, assertions, annotations, generics, enums, and more. Subsequent chapters explore all of these language features.

Java Is a Platform

Java is a platform for executing programs. In contrast to platforms that consist of physical processors (such as an Intel processor) and operating systems (such as Linux), the Java platform consists of a virtual machine and associated execution environment.

The *virtual machine* is a software-based processor that presents its own instruction set. The associated *execution environment* consists of libraries for running programs and interacting with the underlying operating system.

The execution environment includes a huge library of prebuilt classfiles that perform common tasks, such as math operations (trigonometry, for example) and network communications. This library is commonly referred to as the *standard class library*.

A special Java program known as the *Java compiler* translates source code into instructions (and associated data) that are executed by the virtual machine. These instructions are commonly referred to as *bytecode*.

The compiler stores a program's bytecode and data in files having the .class extension. These files are known as *classfiles* because they typically store the compiled equivalent of classes, a language feature discussed in Chapter 2.

A Java program executes via a tool (such as java) that loads and starts the virtual machine, and passes the program's main classfile to the machine. The virtual machine uses a *classloader* (a virtual machine or execution environment component) to load the classfile.

After the classfile has been loaded, the virtual machine's *bytecode verifier* component makes sure that the classfile's bytecode is valid and does not compromise security. The verifier terminates the virtual machine when it finds a problem with the bytecode.

Assuming that all is well with the classfile's bytecode, the virtual machine's *interpreter* interprets the bytecode one instruction at a time. *Interpretation* consists of identifying bytecode instructions and executing equivalent native instructions.

> **NOTE:** *Native instructions* (also known as native code) are the instructions understood by the underlying platform's physical processor.

When the interpreter learns that a sequence of bytecode instructions is executed repeatedly, it informs the virtual machine's *Just In Time (JIT) compiler* to compile these instructions into native code.

JIT compilation is performed only once for a given sequence of bytecode instructions. Because the native instructions execute instead of the associated bytecode instruction sequence, the program executes much faster.

During execution, the interpreter might encounter a request to execute another classfile's bytecode. When that happens, it asks the classloader to load the classfile and the bytecode verifier to verify the bytecode prior to executing that bytecode.

The platform side of Java promotes *portability* by providing an abstraction over the underlying platform. As a result, the same bytecode runs unchanged on Windows-based, Linux-based, Mac OS X–based, and other platforms.

> **NOTE:** Java was introduced with the "write once, run anywhere" slogan. Although Java goes to great lengths to enforce portability, it does not always succeed. Despite being mostly platform independent, certain parts of Java (such as the scheduling of threads, discussed in Chapter 7) vary from underlying platform to underlying platform.

The platform side of Java also promotes *security* by providing a secure environment in which code executes. The goal is to prevent malicious code from corrupting the underlying platform (and possibly stealing sensitive information).

> **NOTE:** Because many developers are not satisfied with the Java language, but believe that the Java platform is important, they have devised additional languages (such as Groovy) that run on the Java platform. Furthermore, Java version 7 includes an enhanced virtual machine that simplifies adapting even more *dynamic programming languages* (languages that require less-rigid coding; you do not have to define a variable's type before using the variable, for example) to this platform.

Java SE, Java EE, Java ME, and Android

Developers use different editions of the Java platform to create Java programs that run on desktop computers, web browsers, web servers, mobile information devices (such as cell phones), and embedded devices (such as television set-top boxes):

- *Java Platform, Standard Edition (Java SE)*: The Java platform for developing *applications*, which are stand-alone programs that run on desktops. Java SE is also used to develop *applets*, which are programs that run in the context of a web browser.

- *Java Platform, Enterprise Edition (Java EE)*: The Java platform for developing enterprise-oriented applications and *servlets*, which are server programs that conform to Java EE's Servlet API. Java EE is built on top of Java SE.

- *Java Platform, Micro Edition (Java ME)*: The Java platform for developing *MIDlets*, which are programs that run on mobile information devices, and *Xlets*, which are programs that run on embedded devices.

Developers also use a special Google-created edition of the Java platform (see `http://developer.android.com/index.html`) to create Android apps that run on Android-enabled devices. This edition is known as the *Android platform*.

Google's Android platform largely consists of Java core libraries (partly based on Java SE) and a virtual machine known as *Dalvik*. This collective software runs on top of a specially modified Linux kernel.

NOTE: Check out Wikipedia's "Android (operating system)" entry
(http://en.wikipedia.org/wiki/Android_%28operating_system%29) to learn more
about the Android OS, and Wikipedia's "Dalvik (software)" entry
(http://en.wikipedia.org/wiki/Dalvik_%28software%29) to learn more about the
Dalvik virtual machine.

In this book, I cover the Java language (supported by Java SE and Android) and Java SE APIs (also supported by Android). Furthermore, I present the source code (typically as code fragments) to Java SE–based applications.

Installing and Exploring the JDK

The *Java Runtime Environment (JRE)* implements the Java SE platform and makes it possible to run Java programs. The public JRE can be downloaded from the Java SE Downloads page (http://java.sun.com/javase/downloads/index.jsp).

However, the public JRE does not make it possible to develop Java programs. For that task, you need to download and install the *Java SE Development Kit (JDK)*, which contains development tools (including the Java compiler) and a private JRE.

NOTE: JDK 1.0 was the first JDK to be released (in May 1995). Until JDK 6 arrived, JDK stood for Java Development Kit (SE was not part of the title). Over the years, numerous JDKs have been released, with JDK 7 set for release in fall or winter 2010.

Each JDK's version number identifies a version of Java. For example, JDK 1.0 identifies Java version 1.0, and JDK 5 identifies Java version 5.0. JDK 5 was the first JDK to also provide an internal version number: 1.5.0.

The Java SE Downloads page also provides access to the current JDK, which is JDK 6 Update 20 at time of writing. Click the Download JDK link to download the current JDK's installer program for your platform.

NOTE: Some of this book's code requires JDK 7, which is only available as a preview release (http://java.sun.com/javase/downloads/ea.jsp) at time of writing.

The JDK installer installs the JDK in a home directory. (It can also install the public JRE in another directory.) On my Windows XP platform, the home directory is C:\Program Files\Java\jdk1.6.0_16—JDK 6 Update 16 was current when I began this book.

> **TIP:** After installing the JDK, you should add the `bin` subdirectory to your platform's PATH environment variable. That way, you will be able to execute JDK tools from any directory in your filesystem.
>
> Finally, you might want to create a `projects` subdirectory of the JDK's home directory to organize your Java projects, and create a separate subdirectory within `projects` for each of these projects.

The home directory contains various files (such as `README.html`, which provides information about the JDK, and `src.zip`, which provides the standard class library source code) and subdirectories, including the following three important subdirectories:

- `bin`: This subdirectory contains assorted JDK tools, including the Java compiler tool. You will discover some of these tools shortly.

- `jre`: This subdirectory contains the JDK's private copy of the JRE, which lets you run Java programs without having to download and install the public JRE.

- `lib`: This subdirectory contains library files that are used by JDK tools. For example, `tools.jar` contains the Java compiler's classfiles—the compiler was written in Java.

You will use only a few of the `bin` subdirectory's tools in this book, specifically `javac` (Java compiler), `java` (Java application launcher), `javadoc` (Java documentation generator), and `jar` (Java archive creator, updater, and extractor).

> **NOTE:** `javac` is not the Java compiler. It is a tool that loads and starts the virtual machine, identifies the compiler's main classfile (located in `tools.jar`) to the virtual machine, and passes the name of the source file being compiled to the compiler's main classfile.

You execute JDK tools at the *command line*, passing *command-line arguments* to a tool. Learn about the command line and arguments via Wikipedia's "Command-line interface" entry (http://en.wikipedia.org/wiki/Command-line_interface).

Now that you have installed the JDK and know something about its tools, you are ready to explore a small `DumpArgs` application that outputs its command-line arguments to the standard output device.

> **NOTE:** The standard output device is part of a mechanism known as *Standard I/O*. This mechanism, which consists of Standard Input, Standard Output, and Standard Error, and which originated with the Unix operating system, makes it possible to read text from different sources (keyboard or file) and write text to different destinations (screen or file).
>
> Text is read from the standard input device, which defaults to the keyboard but can be redirected to a file. Text is output to the standard output device, which defaults to the screen but can be redirected to a file. Error message text is output to the standard error device, which defaults to the screen but can be redirected to a file that differs from the standard output file.

Listing 1–1 presents the DumpArgs application source code.

Listing 1–1. *Dumping command-line arguments via* main() *'s* args *array to the standard output device*

```java
public class DumpArgs
{
   public static void main(String[] args)
   {
      System.out.println("Passed arguments:");
      for (int i = 0; i < args.length; i++)
         System.out.println(args[i]);
   }
}
```

Listing 1–1's DumpArgs application consists of a class named DumpArgs and a method within this class named main(), which is the application's entry point and provides the code to execute. (You will learn about classes and methods in Chapter 2.)

main() is called with an array of *strings* (character sequences) that identify the application's command-line arguments. These strings are stored in String-based array variable args. (I discuss method calling, arrays, and variables in Chapter 2.)

> **NOTE:** Although the array variable is named args, there is nothing special about this name. You could name this variable anything you want.

main() first executes System.out.println("Passed arguments:");, which calls System.out's println() method with the "Passed arguments:" string. This method call outputs Passed arguments: to the standard output device and then terminates the current line so that subsequent output is sent to a new line immediately below the current line. (I discuss System.out in Chapter 7.)

NOTE: `System.out` provides access to a family of `println()` methods and a family of `print()` methods for outputting different kinds of data (such as sequences of characters and integers). Unlike the `println()` methods, the `print()` methods do not terminate the current line; subsequent output continues on the current line.

Each `println()` method terminates a line by outputting a line separator string, which is defined by system property `line.separator`, and which is not necessarily a single newline character (identified in source code via character literal `'\n'`). (I discuss system properties in Chapter 7, `line.separator` in Chapter 10, and character literals in Chapter 2.) For example, on Windows platforms, the line separator string is a carriage return character (whose integer code is 13) followed by a line feed character (whose integer code is 10).

`main()` uses a for loop to repeatedly execute `System.out.println(args[i]);`. The loop executes `args.length` times, which happens to identify the number of strings that are stored in `args`. (I discuss for loops in Chapter 2.)

The `System.out.println(args[i]);` method call reads the string stored in the ith entry of the `args` array—the first entry is located at *index* (location) 0; the last entry is stored at index `args.length - 1`. This method call then outputs this string to standard output.

Assuming that you are familiar with your platform's command-line interface and are at the command line, make DumpArgs your current directory and copy Listing 1–1 to a file named `DumpArgs.java`. Then compile this source file via the following command line:

```
javac DumpArgs.java
```

Assuming that that you have included the `.java` extension, which is required by `javac`, and that `DumpArgs.java` compiles, you should discover a file named `DumpArgs.class` in the current directory. Run this application via the following command line:

```
java DumpArgs
```

If all goes well, you should see the following line of output on the screen:

```
Passed arguments:
```

For more interesting output, you will need to pass command-line arguments to DumpArgs. For example, execute the following command line, which specifies `Curly`, `Moe`, and `Larry` as three arguments to pass to DumpArgs:

```
java DumpArgs Curly Moe Larry
```

This time, you should see the following expanded output on the screen:

```
Passed arguments:
Curly
Moe
Larry
```

You can redirect the output destination to a file by specifying the greater than angle bracket (>) followed by a filename. For example, java DumpArgs Curly Moe Larry >out.txt stores the DumpArgs application's output in a file named out.txt.

> **NOTE:** Instead of specifying System.out.println(), you could specify System.err.println() to output characters to the standard error device. (System.err provides the same families of println() and print() methods as System.out.) However, you should only switch from System.out to System.err when you need to output an error message so that the error messages are displayed on the screen, even when standard output is redirected to a file.

Congratulations on successfully compiling your first application source file and running the application! Listing 1–2 presents the source code to a second application, which echoes text obtained from the standard input device to the standard output device.

Listing 1–2. *Echoing text read from standard input to standard output*

```java
public class EchoText
{
    public static void main(String[] args) throws java.io.IOException
    {
        System.out.println("Please enter some text and press Enter!");
        int ch;
        while ((ch = System.in.read()) != 13)
            System.out.print((char) ch);
        System.out.println();
    }
}
```

After outputting a message that prompts the user to enter some text, main() introduces int variable ch to store each character's integer representation. (You will learn about int and integer in Chapter 2.)

main() now enters a while loop (discussed in Chapter 2) to read and echo characters. The loop first calls System.in.read() to read a character and assign its integer value to ch. The loop ends when this value equals 13 (the integer value of the Enter key).

> **NOTE:** When standard input is not redirected to a file, System.in.read() returns 13 to indicate that the Enter key has been pressed. On platforms such as Windows, a subsequent call to System.in.read() returns integer 10, indicating a line feed character. Whether or not standard input has been redirected, System.in.read() returns -1 when there are no more characters to read.

For any other value in ch, this value is converted to a character via (char), which is an example of Java's cast operator (discussed in Chapter 2). The character is then output via System.out.println(). The final System.out.println(); call terminates the current line without outputting any content.

> **NOTE:** When standard input is redirected to a file and `System.in.read()` is unable to read text from the file (perhaps the file is stored on a removable storage device that has been removed prior to the read operation), `System.in.read()` fails by throwing an object that describes this problem. I acknowledge this possibility by appending `throws java.io.IOException` to the end of the `main()` method header. I discuss `throws` in Chapter 4 and `java.io.IOException` in Chapter 10.

Compile Listing 1–2 via `javac EchoText.java`, and run the application via `java EchoText`. You will be prompted to enter some text. After you input this text and press Enter, the text will be sent to standard output. For example, consider the following output:

```
Please enter some text and press Enter!
Hello Java
Hello Java
```

You can redirect the input source to a file by specifying the less than angle bracket (<) followed by a filename. For example, `java EchoText <EchoText.java` reads its text from `EchoText.java` and outputs this text to the screen.

Run this application and you will only see `EchoText.java`'s first line of text. Each one of this file's lines ends in a carriage return character (13) (followed by a line feed character, 10, on Windows platforms), and `EchoText` terminates after reading a carriage return.

In addition to downloading and installing the JDK, you might want to download the JDK's companion documentation archive file (`jdk-6u18-docs.zip` is the most recent file at time of writing).

After downloading the documentation archive file from the same Java SE Downloads page (`http://java.sun.com/javase/downloads/index.jsp`), unzip this file and move its docs directory to the JDK's home directory.

To access the documentation, point your web browser to the documentation's start page. For example, after moving docs to my JDK's home directory, I point my browser to `C:\Program Files\Java\jdk1.6.0_16\docs\index.html`. See Figure 1–1.

Scroll a bit down the start page and you discover the "API, Language, and Virtual Machine Documentation" section, which presents a Java 2 Platform API Specification link. Click this link and you can access the standard class library's documentation.

> **TIP:** You can read the online documentation by pointing your web browser to a link such as `http://download.java.net/jdk6/archive/b104/docs/`, which provides the online documentation for JDK 6.

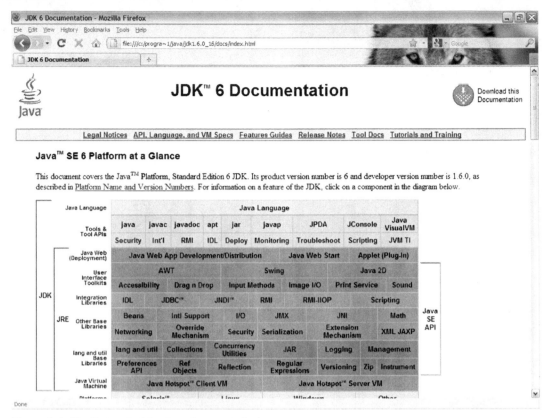

Figure 1–1. *The first part of the Java documentation's start page*

Installing and Exploring Two Popular IDEs

Working with the JDK's tools at the command line is probably okay for small projects. However, this practice is not recommended for large projects, which are hard to manage without the help of an integrated development environment (IDE).

An IDE consists of a project manager for managing a project's files, a text editor for entering and editing source code, a debugger for locating bugs, and other features. Two popular IDEs are NetBeans and Eclipse.

NOTE: For convenience, I use JDK tools throughout this book, except for this section where I use NetBeans IDE and Eclipse IDE.

NetBeans IDE

NetBeans IDE is an open source, Java-based IDE for developing programs in Java and other languages (such as PHP, Ruby, C++, Groovy, and Scala). Version 6.8 is the current version of this IDE at time of writing.

You should download and install NetBeans IDE 6.8 (or a more recent version) to follow along with this section's NetBeans-oriented example. Begin by pointing your browser to `http://netbeans.org/downloads/` and accomplishing the following tasks:

1. Select an appropriate IDE language (such as English).

2. Select an appropriate platform (such as Linux).

3. Click the Download button underneath the leftmost (Java SE) column.

After a few moments, the current page is replaced by another page that gives you the opportunity to download an installer file. I downloaded the approximately 47MB `netbeans-6.8-ml-javase-windows.exe` installer file for my Windows XP platform.

> **NOTE:** According to the "NetBeans IDE 6.8 Installation Instructions" (`http://netbeans.org/community/releases/68/install.html`), you must install JDK 5.0 Update 19 or JDK 6 Update 14 or newer on your platform before installing NetBeans IDE 6.8. If you do not have a JDK installed, you cannot install the NetBeans IDE.

Start the installer file and follow the instructions. You will need to agree to the NetBeans license, and are given the options of providing anonymous usage data and registering your copy of NetBeans when installation finishes.

Assuming that you have installed the NetBeans IDE, start this Java application. You should discover a splash screen identifying this IDE, followed by a main window similar to that shown in Figure 1–2.

The NetBeans user interface is based on a main window that consists of a menu bar, a toolbar, a workspace area, and a status bar. The workspace area initially presents a Start Page tab, which provides NetBeans tutorials as well as news and blogs.

To help you get comfortable with the NetBeans user interface, I will show you how to create a `DumpArgs` project containing a single `DumpArgs.java` source file with Listing 1–1's source code. You will also learn how to compile and run this application.

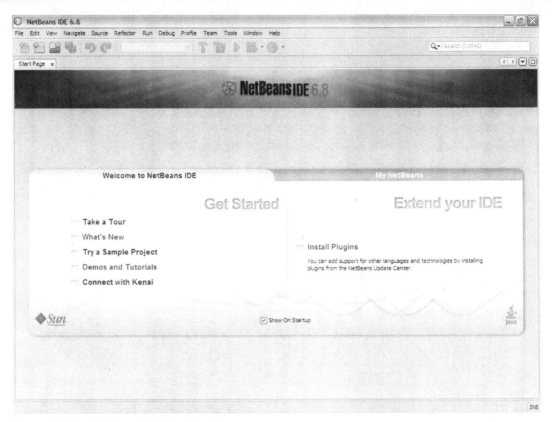

Figure 1–2. *The NetBeans IDE 6.8 main window*

Complete the following steps to create the DumpArgs project:

1. Select New Project from the File menu.

2. On the resulting New Project dialog box's initial pane, make sure that Java is the selected category in the Categories list, and Java Application is the selected project in the Projects list. Click the Next button.

3. On the resulting pane, enter **DumpArgs** in the Project Name text field. You will notice that dumpargs.Main appears in the text field to the right of the Create Main Class check box. Replace dumpargs.Main with **DumpArgs** and click Finish. (dumpargs names a package, discussed in Chapter 4, and Main names a class stored in this package.)

After a few moments, you will see a workspace similar to that shown in Figure 1–3.

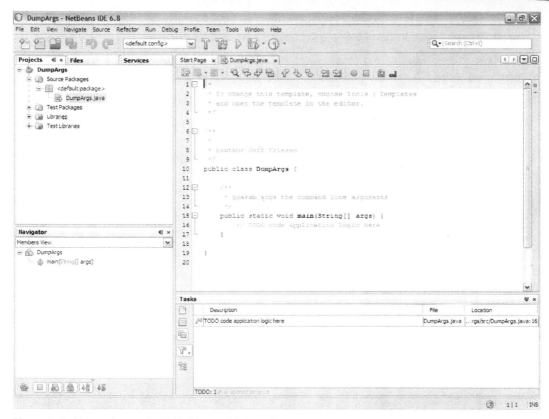

Figure 1-3. *The workspace is divided into multiple work areas.*

After creating the DumpArgs project, you will discover that NetBeans has organized the workspace into four main areas: projects, editor, navigator, and tasks.

The *projects area* helps you manage your projects. This window is divided into Projects, Files, and Services tabs:

- The Projects tab is the main entry point to your project's source and resource files. It presents a logical view of important project contents.

- The Files tab presents a directory-based view of your projects, including any files and folders that are not displayed on the Projects tab.

- The Services tab is the main entry point to runtime resources. It shows a logical view of important runtime resources such as the servers, databases, and web services that are registered with the IDE.

The *editor area* helps you edit a project's source files. Each file has its own tab, labeled with the file's name.

Figure 1-3 reveals a single DumpArgs.java tab, which provides access to skeletal source code. You will shortly replace this source code with Listing 1-1.

The skeletal source code reveals single-line and multiline comments (discussed in Chapter 2) and Javadoc comments (discussed later in this chapter).

The *navigator area* reveals the Navigator tab, which presents a compact view of the currently selected file and simplifies navigation between different parts of the file.

The *tasks area* reveals the Tasks tab, which presents a to-do list of items for the project's various files that need to be resolved.

Replace the skeletal DumpArgs.java source code with Listing 1–1, and select Run Main Project from the Run menu to compile and run this application. Figure 1–4 shows this application's results.

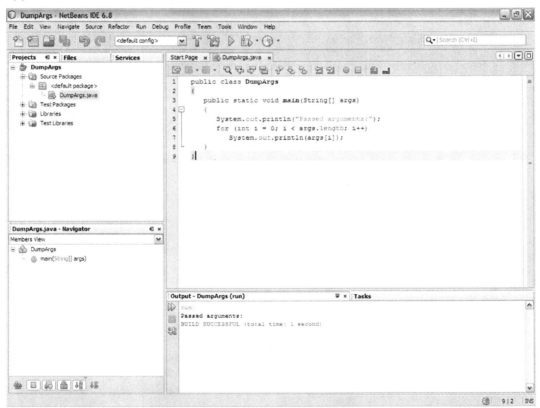

Figure 1–4. *An Output tab appears to the left of the Tasks tab and shows the* DumpArgs *application's output.*

Figure 1–4's Output tab reveals only the result of the System.out.println("Passed arguments:") method call. To see more output, you must pass command-line arguments to DumpArgs. Accomplish this task from within NetBeans IDE 6.8 as follows:

1. Select Project Properties (DumpArgs) from the File menu.

2. In the resulting Project Properties dialog box, select Run in the Categories tree and enter **Curly Moe Larry** in the Arguments text field on the resulting pane. Click the OK button.

Once again, select Run Main Project from the Run menu to run the DumpArgs application. This time, the Output tab should reveal Curly, Moe, and Larry on separate lines below Passed arguments:.

This is all I have to say about the NetBeans IDE. For more information, study the tutorials via the Start Page tab, access IDE help via the Help menu, and explore the NetBeans knowledge base at http://netbeans.org/kb/.

Eclipse IDE

Eclipse IDE is an open source IDE for developing programs in Java and other languages (such as C, COBOL, PHP, Perl, and Python). Eclipse Classic is one distribution of this IDE that is available for download; version 3.5.2 is the current version at time of writing.

You should download and install Eclipse Classic to follow along with this section's Eclipse-oriented example. Begin by pointing your browser to http://www.eclipse.org/downloads/ and accomplishing the following tasks:

1. Scroll down the page until you see an Eclipse Classic entry.

2. Click one of the platform links (such as Linux 32 Bit) to the right of this entry.

3. Select a download mirror from the subsequently displayed page and proceed to download the distribution's archive file.

I downloaded the approximately 163MB eclipse-SDK-3.5.2-win32.zip archive file for my Windows XP platform, unarchived this file, moved the resulting eclipse home directory to another location, and created a shortcut to that directory's eclipse.exe file.

NOTE: Unlike NetBeans IDE 6.8, which requires that a suitable JDK be installed before you can run the installer, a JDK does not have to be installed before running eclipse.exe because the Eclipse IDE comes with its own Java compiler. However, you will need at least JDK 6 Update 16 to run most of this book's code (or JDK 7 to run all of the code).

Assuming that you have installed Eclipse Classic, start this application. You should discover a splash screen identifying this IDE and a dialog box that lets you choose the location of a *workspace* for storing projects, followed by a main window like that shown in Figure 1–5.

The Eclipse user interface is based on a main window that consists of a menu bar, a toolbar, a workbench area, and a status bar. The workbench area initially presents a Welcome tab with icon links for accessing tutorials and more.

To help you get comfortable with the Eclipse user interface, I will show you how to create a DumpArgs project containing a single DumpArgs.java source file with Listing 1–1's source code. You will also learn how to compile and run this application.

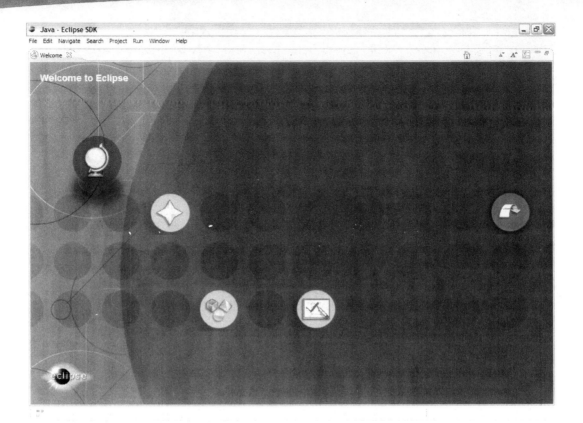

Figure 1–5. *The Eclipse IDE 3.5.2 main window*

Complete the following steps to create the DumpArgs project:

1. Select New from the File menu and Java Project from the resulting pop-up menu.

2. In the resulting New Java Project dialog box, enter **DumpArgs** into the Project name text field. Keep all the other defaults and click the Finish button.

3. Click the rightmost (Workbench) icon link to go to the workbench. Eclipse bypasses the Welcome tab and takes you to the workbench the next time you start this IDE.

> **TIP:** To return to the Welcome tab, select Welcome from the Help menu.

After the final step, you will see a workbench similar to that shown in Figure 1–6.

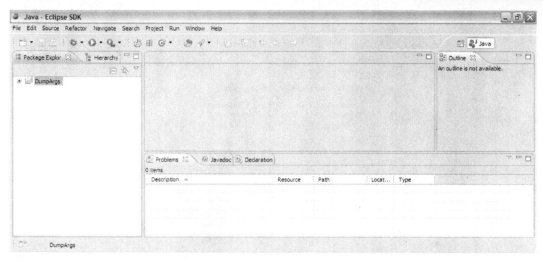

Figure 1–6. *The workbench is divided into multiple work areas.*

On the left side of the workbench, you see a tab titled Package Explorer. This tab identifies the workspace's projects in terms of packages (discussed in Chapter 4). At the moment, only a single DumpArgs entry appears on this tab.

Clicking the + icon to the left of DumpArgs expands this entry to reveal src and JRE System Library items. The src item stores the DumpArgs project's source files, and JRE System Library identifies various JRE files that are used to run this application.

We will now add a new file named DumpArgs.java to src, as follows:

1. Highlight src and select New from the File menu, and File from the resulting pop-up menu.

2. In the resulting New File dialog box, enter **DumpArgs.java** into the File name text field, and click the Finish button.

Eclipse responds by displaying an editor tab titled DumpArgs.java. Copy Listing 1–1 into this tab, and then compile and run this application by selecting Run from the Run menu. Figure 1–7 shows the results.

Figure 1–7. *The Console tab at the bottom of the workbench presents the* DumpArgs *application's output.*

As with the NetBeans IDE, you must pass command-line arguments to DumpArgs to see additional output from this application. Accomplish this task from within Eclipse IDE 3.5.2 as follows:

1. Select Run Configurations from the Run menu.

2. In the resulting Run Configurations dialog box, select the Arguments tab.

3. Enter **Curly Moe Larry** into the Program arguments text area and click the Close button.

Once again, select Run from the Run menu to run the DumpArgs application. This time, the Console tab reveals Curly, Moe, and Larry on separate lines below Passed arguments:.

This is all I have to say about the Eclipse IDE. For more information, study the tutorials via the Welcome tab, access IDE help via the Help menu, and explore the Eclipse documentation at http://www.eclipse.org/documentation/.

Four of a Kind

Application development is not an easy task. If you do not plan carefully before you develop an application, you will probably waste your time and money as you endeavor to create it, and waste your users' time and money if it does not meet their needs.

> **CAUTION:** It is extremely important to carefully test your software. You could face a lawsuit if malfunctioning software causes financial harm to its users.

In this section, I present one technique for developing applications efficiently. I present this technique in the context of a Java application that lets you play a simple card game called *Four of a Kind* against the computer.

Understanding Four of a Kind

Before sitting down at the computer and writing code, we need to fully understand the *problem domain* that we are trying to model via that code. In this case, the problem domain is *Four of a Kind*, and we want to understand how this card game works.

Two to four players play *Four of a Kind* with a standard 52-card deck. The object of the game is to be the first player to put down four cards that have the same rank (four aces, for example), which wins the game.

The game begins by shuffling the deck and placing it face down. Each player takes a card from the top of the deck. The player with the highest ranked card (king is highest) deals four cards to each player, starting with the player to the dealer's left. The dealer then starts his/her turn.

The player examines his/her cards to determine which cards are optimal for achieving four of a kind. The player then throws away the least helpful card on a discard pile and picks up another card from the top of the deck. (If each card has a different rank, the player randomly selects a card to throw away.) If the player has four of a kind, the player puts down these cards (face up) and wins the game.

Modeling Four of a Kind in Pseudocode

Now that we understand how *Four of a Kind* works, we can begin to model this game. We will not model the game in Java source code because we would get bogged down in too many details. Instead, we will use pseudocode for this task.

Pseudocode is a compact and informal high-level description of the problem domain. Unlike the previous description of *Four of a Kind*, the pseudocode equivalent is a step-by-step recipe for solving the problem. Check out Listing 1–3.

Listing 1–3. *Four of a Kind pseudocode for two players (human and computer)*

1. Create a deck of cards and shuffle the deck.
2. Create empty discard pile.
3. Have each of the human and computer players take a card from the top of the deck.
4. Designate the player with the highest ranked card as the current player.
5. Return both cards to the bottom of the deck.
6. The current player deals four cards to each of the two players in alternating fashion, with the first card being dealt to the other player.

7. The current player examines its current cards to see which cards are optimal for achieving four of a kind. The current player throws the least helpful card onto the top of the discard pile.

8. The current player picks up the deck's top card. If the current player has four of a kind, it puts down its cards and wins the game.

9. Designate the other player as the current player.

10. If the deck has no more cards, empty the discard pile to the deck and shuffle the deck.

11. Repeat at step **7**.

Deriving Listing 1–3's pseudocode from the previous description is the first step in achieving an application that implements *Four of a Kind*. This pseudocode performs various tasks, including decision making and repetition.

Despite being a more useful guide to understanding how *Four of a Kind* works, Listing 1–3 is too high level for translation to Java. Therefore, we must refine this pseudocode to facilitate the translation process. Listing 1–4 presents this refinement.

Listing 1–4. *Refined Four of a Kind pseudocode for two players (human and computer)*

```
1. deck = new Deck()
2. deck.shuffle()
3. discardPile = new DiscardPile()
4. hCard = deck.deal()
5. cCard = deck.deal()
6. if hCard.rank() == cCard.rank()
   6.1. deck.putBack(hCard)
   6.2. deck.putBack(cCard)
   6.3. deck.shuffle()
   6.4. Repeat at step 4
7. curPlayer = HUMAN
   7.1. if cCard.rank() > hCard.rank()
        7.1.1. curPlayer = COMPUTER
8. deck.putBack(hCard)
9. deck.putBack(cCard)
10. if curPlayer == HUMAN
    10.1. for i = 0 to 3
          10.1.1. cCards[i] = deck.deal()
          10.1.2. hCards[i] = deck.deal()
    else
    10.2. for i = 0 to 3
          10.2.1. hCards[i] = deck.deal()
          10.2.2. cCards[i] = deck.deal()
11. if curPlayer == HUMAN
    11.01. output(hCards)
    11.02. choice = prompt("Identify card to throw away")
    11.03. discardPile.setTopCard(hCards[choice])
    11.04. hCards[choice] = deck.deal()
    11.05. if isFourOfAKind(hCards)
           11.05.1. output("Human wins!")
           11.05.2. putDown(hCards)
           11.05.3. output("Computer's cards:")
           11.05.4. putDown(cCards)
           11.05.5. End game
    11.06. curPlayer = COMPUTER
```

```
      else
11.07. choice = leastDesirableCard(cCards)
11.08. discardPile.setTopCard(cCards[choice])
11.09. cCards[choice] = deck.deal()
11.10. if isFourOfAKind(cCards)
       11.10.1. output("Computer wins!")
       11.10.2. putDown(cCards)
       11.10.3. End game
11.11. curPlayer = HUMAN
12. if deck.isEmpty()
12.1. if discardPile.topCard() != null
      12.1.1. deck.putBack(discardPile.getTopCard())
      12.1.2. Repeat at step 12.1.
12.2. deck.shuffle()
13. Repeat at step 11.
```

In addition to being longer than Listing 1–3, Listing 1–4 shows the refined pseudocode becoming more like Java. For example, Listing 1–4 reveals Java expressions (such as new Deck(), to create a Deck object), operators (such as ==, to compare two values for equality), and method calls (such as deck.isEmpty(), to call deck's isEmpty() method to return a Boolean value indicating whether [true] or not [false] the deck identified by deck is empty of cards).

Converting Pseudocode to Java Code

Now that you have had a chance to absorb Listing 1–4's Java-like pseudocode, you are ready to examine the process of converting that pseudocode to Java source code. This process consists of a couple of steps.

The first step in converting Listing 1–4's pseudocode to Java involves identifying important components of the game's structure and implementing these components as classes. I will formally introduce classes in Chapter 2.

Apart from the computer player (which is implemented via game logic), the important components are card, deck, and discard pile. I represent these components via Card, Deck, and DiscardPile classes. Listing 1–5 presents Card.

NOTE: Do not be concerned if you find this section's Java source code somewhat hard to follow. After you have read the next few chapters, you should find this code easier to understand.

Listing 1–5. *Merging suits and ranks into cards*

```
/**
 *  Simulating a playing card.
 *
 *  @author Jeff Friesen
 */
public enum Card
{
   ACE_OF_CLUBS(Suit.CLUBS, Rank.ACE),
   TWO_OF_CLUBS(Suit.CLUBS, Rank.TWO),
```

```
THREE_OF_CLUBS(Suit.CLUBS, Rank.THREE),
FOUR_OF_CLUBS(Suit.CLUBS, Rank.FOUR),
FIVE_OF_CLUBS(Suit.CLUBS, Rank.FIVE),
SIX_OF_CLUBS(Suit.CLUBS, Rank.SIX),
SEVEN_OF_CLUBS(Suit.CLUBS, Rank.SEVEN),
EIGHT_OF_CLUBS(Suit.CLUBS, Rank.EIGHT),
NINE_OF_CLUBS(Suit.CLUBS, Rank.NINE),
TEN_OF_CLUBS(Suit.CLUBS, Rank.TEN),
JACK_OF_CLUBS(Suit.CLUBS, Rank.JACK),
QUEEN_OF_CLUBS(Suit.CLUBS, Rank.QUEEN),
KING_OF_CLUBS(Suit.CLUBS, Rank.KING),
ACE_OF_DIAMONDS(Suit.DIAMONDS, Rank.ACE),
TWO_OF_DIAMONDS(Suit.DIAMONDS, Rank.TWO),
THREE_OF_DIAMONDS(Suit.DIAMONDS, Rank.THREE),
FOUR_OF_DIAMONDS(Suit.DIAMONDS, Rank.FOUR),
FIVE_OF_DIAMONDS(Suit.DIAMONDS, Rank.FIVE),
SIX_OF_DIAMONDS(Suit.DIAMONDS, Rank.SIX),
SEVEN_OF_DIAMONDS(Suit.DIAMONDS, Rank.SEVEN),
EIGHT_OF_DIAMONDS(Suit.DIAMONDS, Rank.EIGHT),
NINE_OF_DIAMONDS(Suit.DIAMONDS, Rank.NINE),
TEN_OF_DIAMONDS(Suit.DIAMONDS, Rank.TEN),
JACK_OF_DIAMONDS(Suit.DIAMONDS, Rank.JACK),
QUEEN_OF_DIAMONDS(Suit.DIAMONDS, Rank.QUEEN),
KING_OF_DIAMONDS(Suit.DIAMONDS, Rank.KING),
ACE_OF_HEARTS(Suit.HEARTS, Rank.ACE),
TWO_OF_HEARTS(Suit.HEARTS, Rank.TWO),
THREE_OF_HEARTS(Suit.HEARTS, Rank.THREE),
FOUR_OF_HEARTS(Suit.HEARTS, Rank.FOUR),
FIVE_OF_HEARTS(Suit.HEARTS, Rank.FIVE),
SIX_OF_HEARTS(Suit.HEARTS, Rank.SIX),
SEVEN_OF_HEARTS(Suit.HEARTS, Rank.SEVEN),
EIGHT_OF_HEARTS(Suit.HEARTS, Rank.EIGHT),
NINE_OF_HEARTS(Suit.HEARTS, Rank.NINE),
TEN_OF_HEARTS(Suit.HEARTS, Rank.TEN),
JACK_OF_HEARTS(Suit.HEARTS, Rank.JACK),
QUEEN_OF_HEARTS(Suit.HEARTS, Rank.QUEEN),
KING_OF_HEARTS(Suit.HEARTS, Rank.KING),
ACE_OF_SPADES(Suit.SPADES, Rank.ACE),
TWO_OF_SPADES(Suit.SPADES, Rank.TWO),
THREE_OF_SPADES(Suit.SPADES, Rank.THREE),
FOUR_OF_SPADES(Suit.SPADES, Rank.FOUR),
FIVE_OF_SPADES(Suit.SPADES, Rank.FIVE),
SIX_OF_SPADES(Suit.SPADES, Rank.SIX),
SEVEN_OF_SPADES(Suit.SPADES, Rank.SEVEN),
EIGHT_OF_SPADES(Suit.SPADES, Rank.EIGHT),
NINE_OF_SPADES(Suit.SPADES, Rank.NINE),
TEN_OF_SPADES(Suit.SPADES, Rank.TEN),
JACK_OF_SPADES(Suit.SPADES, Rank.JACK),
QUEEN_OF_SPADES(Suit.SPADES, Rank.QUEEN),
KING_OF_SPADES(Suit.SPADES, Rank.KING);

private Suit suit;
/**
 * Return <code>Card</code>'s suit.
 *
 * @return <code>CLUBS</code>, <code>DIAMONDS</code>, <code>HEARTS</code>,
 * or <code>SPADES</code>
```

```java
     */
    public Suit suit() { return suit; }
    private Rank rank;
    /**
     *  Return <code>Card</code>'s rank.
     *
     *  @return <code>ACE</code>, <code>TWO</code>, <code>THREE</code>,
     *  <code>FOUR</code>, <code>FIVE</code>, <code>SIX</code>,
     *  <code>SEVEN</code>, <code>EIGHT</code>, <code>NINE</code>,
     *  <code>TEN</code>, <code>JACK</code>, <code>QUEEN</code>,
     *  <code>KING</code>.
     */
    public Rank rank() { return rank; }
    Card(Suit suit, Rank rank)
    {
       this.suit = suit;
       this.rank = rank;
    }
    /**
     *  A card's suit is its membership.
     *
     *  @author Jeff Friesen
     */
    public enum Suit
    {
       CLUBS, DIAMONDS, HEARTS, SPADES
    }
    /**
     *  A card's rank is its integer value.
     *
     *  @author Jeff Friesen
     */
    public enum Rank
    {
       ACE, TWO, THREE, FOUR, FIVE, SIX, SEVEN, EIGHT, NINE, TEN, JACK, QUEEN,
       KING
    }
}
```

Listing 1–5 begins with a Javadoc comment that is used to briefly describe the `Card`
class and identify this class's author. I will introduce you to Javadoc comments at the
end of this section.

> **NOTE:** One feature of Javadoc comments is the ability to embed HTML tags. These tags specify
> different kinds of formatting for sections of text within these comments. For example, `<code>`
> and `</code>` specify that their enclosed text is to be formatted as a code listing. Later in this
> chapter, you will learn how to convert these comments into HTML documentation.

`Card` is an example of an enum, which is a special kind of class that I discuss in Chapter
5. For now, think of `Card` as a place to create and store `Card` objects that identify all 52
cards that make up a standard deck.

Card declares a nested Suit enum. (I discuss nesting in Chapter 4.) A card's *suit* denotes its membership. The only legal Suit values are CLUBS, DIAMONDS, HEARTS, and SPADES.

Card also declares a nested Rank enum. A card's *rank* denotes its value: ACE, TWO, THREE, FOUR, FIVE, SIX, SEVEN, EIGHT, NINE, TEN, JACK, QUEEN, and KING are the only legal Rank values.

A Card object is created when Suit and Rank objects are passed to its constructor. (I discuss constructors in Chapter 2.) For example, KING_OF_HEARTS(Suit.HEARTS, Rank.KING) combines Suit.HEARTS and Rank.KING into KING_OF_HEARTS.

Card provides a rank() method for returning a Card's Rank object. Similarly, Card provides a suit() method for returning a Card's Suit object. For example, KING_OF_HEARTS.rank() returns Rank.KING, and KING_OF_HEARTS.suit() returns Suit.HEARTS.

Listing 1–6 presents the Java source code to the Deck class, which implements a deck of 52 cards.

Listing 1–6. *Pick a card, any card*

```java
import java.util.ArrayList;
import java.util.Collections;
import java.util.List;

/**
 *  Simulate a deck of cards.
 *
 *  @author Jeff Friesen
 */
public class Deck
{
   private Card[] cards = new Card[]
   {
      Card.ACE_OF_CLUBS,
      Card.TWO_OF_CLUBS,
      Card.THREE_OF_CLUBS,
      Card.FOUR_OF_CLUBS,
      Card.FIVE_OF_CLUBS,
      Card.SIX_OF_CLUBS,
      Card.SEVEN_OF_CLUBS,
      Card.EIGHT_OF_CLUBS,
      Card.NINE_OF_CLUBS,
      Card.TEN_OF_CLUBS,
      Card.JACK_OF_CLUBS,
      Card.QUEEN_OF_CLUBS,
      Card.KING_OF_CLUBS,
      Card.ACE_OF_DIAMONDS,
      Card.TWO_OF_DIAMONDS,
      Card.THREE_OF_DIAMONDS,
      Card.FOUR_OF_DIAMONDS,
      Card.FIVE_OF_DIAMONDS,
      Card.SIX_OF_DIAMONDS,
      Card.SEVEN_OF_DIAMONDS,
      Card.EIGHT_OF_DIAMONDS,
      Card.NINE_OF_DIAMONDS,
```

```
         Card.TEN_OF_DIAMONDS,
         Card.JACK_OF_DIAMONDS,
         Card.QUEEN_OF_DIAMONDS,
         Card.KING_OF_DIAMONDS,
         Card.ACE_OF_HEARTS,
         Card.TWO_OF_HEARTS,
         Card.THREE_OF_HEARTS,
         Card.FOUR_OF_HEARTS,
         Card.FIVE_OF_HEARTS,
         Card.SIX_OF_HEARTS,
         Card.SEVEN_OF_HEARTS,
         Card.EIGHT_OF_HEARTS,
         Card.NINE_OF_HEARTS,
         Card.TEN_OF_HEARTS,
         Card.JACK_OF_HEARTS,
         Card.QUEEN_OF_HEARTS,
         Card.KING_OF_HEARTS,
         Card.ACE_OF_SPADES,
         Card.TWO_OF_SPADES,
         Card.THREE_OF_SPADES,
         Card.FOUR_OF_SPADES,
         Card.FIVE_OF_SPADES,
         Card.SIX_OF_SPADES,
         Card.SEVEN_OF_SPADES,
         Card.EIGHT_OF_SPADES,
         Card.NINE_OF_SPADES,
         Card.TEN_OF_SPADES,
         Card.JACK_OF_SPADES,
         Card.QUEEN_OF_SPADES,
         Card.KING_OF_SPADES
   };
   private List<Card> deck;
   /**
    *  Create a <code>Deck</code> of 52 <code>Card</code> objects. Shuffle
    *  these objects.
    */
   public Deck()
   {
      deck = new ArrayList<Card>();
      for (int i = 0; i < cards.length; i++)
      {
         deck.add(cards[i]);
         cards[i] = null;
      }
      Collections.shuffle(deck);
   }
   /**
    *  Deal the <code>Deck</code>'s top <code>Card</code> object.
    *
    *  @return the <code>Card</code> object at the top of the
    *  <code>Deck</code>
    */
   public Card deal()
   {
      return deck.remove(0);
   }
   /**
```

```
 *   Return an indicator of whether or not the <code>Deck</code> is empty.
 *
 *   @return true if the <code>Deck</code> contains no <code>Card</code>
 *   objects; otherwise, false
 */
public boolean isEmpty()
{
   return deck.isEmpty();
}
/**
 *   Put back a <code>Card</code> at the bottom of the <code>Deck</code>.
 *
 *   @param card <code>Card</code> object being put back
 */
public void putBack(Card card)
{
   deck.add(card);
}
/**
 *   Shuffle the <code>Deck</code>.
 */
public void shuffle()
{
   Collections.shuffle(deck);
}
}
```

Deck initializes a private cards array to all 52 Card objects. Because it is easier to implement Deck via a list that stores these objects, Deck's constructor creates this list and adds each Card object to the list. (I discuss List and ArrayList in Chapter 8.)

Deck also provides deal(), isEmpty(), putBack(), and shuffle() methods to deal a single Card from the Deck (the Card is physically removed from the Deck), determine whether or not the Deck is empty, put a Card back into the Deck, and shuffle the Deck's Cards.

Listing 1–7 presents the source code to the DiscardPile class, which implements a discard pile on which players can throw away a maximum of 52 cards.

Listing 1–7. *A garbage dump for cards*

```
/**
 *   Simulate a pile of discarded cards.
 *
 *   @author Jeff Friesen
 */
public class DiscardPile
{
   private Card[] cards;
   private int top;
   /**
    *   Create a <code>DiscardPile</code> that can accommodate a maximum of 52
    *   <code>Card</code>s. The <code>DiscardPile</code> is initially empty.
    */
   public DiscardPile()
   {
      cards = new Card[52]; // Room for entire deck on discard pile (should
```

```
                               // never happen).
      top = -1;
   }
   /**
    *  Return the <code>Card</code> at the top of the <code>DiscardPile</code>.
    *
    *  @return <code>Card</code> object at top of <code>DiscardPile</code> or
    *  null if <code>DiscardPile</code> is empty
    */
   public Card gctTopCard()
   {
      if (top == -1)
         return null;
      Card card = cards[top];
      cards[top--] = null;
      return card;
   }
   /**
    *  Set the <code>DiscardPile</code>'s top card to the specified
    *  <code>Card</code> object.
    *
    *  @param card <code>Card</code> object being thrown on top of the
    *  <code>DiscardPile</code>
    */
   public void setTopCard(Card card)
   {
      cards[++top] = card;
   }
   /**
    *  Identify the top <code>Card</code> on the <code>DiscardPile</code>
    *  without removing this <code>Card</code>.
    *
    *  @return top <code>Card</code>, or null if <code>DiscardPile</code> is
    *  empty
    */
   public Card topCard()
   {
      return (top == -1) ? null : cards[top];
   }
}
```

DiscardPile implements a discard pile on which to throw Card objects. It implements the discard pile via a stack metaphor: the last Card object thrown on the pile sits at the top of the pile and is the first Card object to be removed from the pile.

This class stores its stack of Card objects in a private cards array. I found it convenient to specify 52 as this array's storage limit because the maximum number of Cards is 52. (Game play will never result in all Cards being stored in the array.)

Along with its constructor, DiscardPile provides getTopCard(), setTopCard(), and topCard() methods to remove and return the stack's top Card, store a new Card object on the stack as its top Card, and return the top Card without removing it from the stack.

The constructor demonstrates a single-line comment, which starts with the // character sequence. This comment documents that the cards array has room to store the entire Deck of Cards. I will formally introduce single-line comments in Chapter 2.

The second step in converting Listing 1–4's pseudocode to Java involves introducing a FourOfAKind class whose main() method contains the Java code equivalent of this pseudocode. Listing 1–8 presents FourOfAKind.

Listing 1–8. *FourOfAKind application source code*

```java
/**
 *  <code>FourOfAKind</code> implements a card game that is played between two
 *  players: one human player and the computer. You play this game with a
 *  standard 52-card deck and attempt to beat the computer by being the first
 *  player to put down four cards that have the same rank (four aces, for
 *  example), and win.
 *
 *  <p>
 *  The game begins by shuffling the deck and placing it face down. Each
 *  player takes a card from the top of the deck. The player with the highest
 *  ranked card (king is highest) deals four cards to each player starting
 *  with the other player. The dealer then starts its turn.
 *
 *  <p>
 *  The player examines its cards to determine which cards are optimal for
 *  achieving four of a kind. The player then throws away one card on a
 *  discard pile and picks up another card from the top of the deck. If the
 *  player has four of a kind, the player puts down these cards (face up) and
 *  wins the game.
 *
 *  @author Jeff Friesen
 *  @version 1.0
 */
public class FourOfAKind
{
   /**
    *  Human player
    */
   final static int HUMAN = 0;
   /**
    *  Computer player
    */
   final static int COMPUTER = 1;
   /**
    *  Application entry point.
    *
    *  @param args array of command-line arguments passed to this method
    */
   public static void main(String[] args)
   {
      System.out.println("Welcome to Four of a Kind!");
      Deck deck = new Deck(); // Deck automatically shuffled
      DiscardPile discardPile = new DiscardPile();
      Card hCard;
      Card cCard;
      while (true)
      {
         hCard = deck.deal();
         cCard = deck.deal();
         if (hCard.rank() != cCard.rank())
            break;
```

```
      deck.putBack(hCard);
      deck.putBack(cCard);
      deck.shuffle(); // prevent pathological case where every successive
}                     // pair of cards have the same rank
int curPlayer = HUMAN;
if (cCard.rank().ordinal() > hCard.rank().ordinal())
   curPlayer = COMPUTER;
deck.putBack(hCard);
hCard = null;
deck.putBack(cCard);
cCard = null;
Card[] hCards = new Card[4];
Card[] cCards = new Card[4];
if (curPlayer == HUMAN)
   for (int i = 0; i < 4; i++)
   {
      cCards[i] = deck.deal();
      hCards[i] = deck.deal();
   }
else
   for (int i = 0; i < 4; i++)
   {
      hCards[i] = deck.deal();
      cCards[i] = deck.deal();
   }
while (true)
{
   if (curPlayer == HUMAN)
   {
      showHeldCards(hCards);
      int choice = 0;
      while (choice < 'A' || choice > 'D')
      {
         choice = prompt("Which card do you want to throw away (A, B, " +
                         "C, D)? ");
         switch (choice)
         {
            case 'a': choice = 'A'; break;
            case 'b': choice = 'B'; break;
            case 'c': choice = 'C'; break;
            case 'd': choice = 'D';
         }
      }
      discardPile.setTopCard(hCards[choice-'A']);
      hCards[choice-'A'] = deck.deal();
      if (isFourOfAKind(hCards))
      {
         System.out.println();
         System.out.println("Human wins!");
         System.out.println();
         putDown("Human's cards:", hCards);
         System.out.println();
         putDown("Computer's cards:", cCards);
         return; // Exit application by returning from main()
      }
      curPlayer = COMPUTER;
   }
```

```
            else
            {
                int choice = leastDesirableCard(cCards);
                discardPile.setTopCard(cCards[choice]);
                cCards[choice] = deck.deal();
                if (isFourOfAKind(cCards))
                {
                    System.out.println();
                    System.out.println("Computer wins!");
                    System.out.println();
                    putDown("Computer's cards:", cCards);
                    return; // Exit application by returning from main()
                }
                curPlayer = HUMAN;
            }
            if (deck.isEmpty())
            {
                while (discardPile.topCard() != null)
                    deck.putBack(discardPile.getTopCard());
                deck.shuffle();
            }
        }
    }
}
/**
 *  Determine if the <code>Card</code> objects passed to this method all
 *  have the same rank.
 *
 *  @param cards array of <code>Card</code> objects passed to this method
 *
 *  @return true if all <code>Card</code> objects have the same rank;
 *  otherwise, false
 */
static boolean isFourOfAKind(Card[] cards)
{
    for (int i = 1; i < cards.length; i++)
        if (cards[i].rank() != cards[0].rank())
            return false;
    return true;
}
/**
 *  Identify one of the <code>Card</code> objects that is passed to this
 *  method as the least desirable <code>Card</code> object to hold onto.
 *
 *  @param cards array of <code>Card</code> objects passed to this method
 *
 *  @return 0-based rank (ace is 0, king is 13) of least desirable card
 */
static int leastDesirableCard(Card[] cards)
{
    int[] rankCounts = new int[13];
    for (int i = 0; i < cards.length; i++)
        rankCounts[cards[i].rank().ordinal()]++;
    int minCount = Integer.MAX_VALUE;
    int minIndex = -1;
    for (int i = 0; i < rankCounts.length; i++)
        if (rankCounts[i] < minCount && rankCounts[i] != 0)
        {
```

```
                  minCount = rankCounts[i];
                  minIndex = i;
            }
      for (int i = 0; i < cards.length; i++)
            if (cards[i].rank().ordinal() == minIndex)
                  return i;
      return 0; // Needed to satisfy compiler (should never be executed)
}
/**
 *  Prompt the human player to enter a character.
 *
 *  @param msg message to be displayed to human player
 *
 *  @return integer value of character entered by user.
 */
static int prompt(String msg)
{
   System.out.print(msg);
   try
   {
      int ch = System.in.read();
      // Erase all subsequent characters including terminating \n newline
      // so that they do not affect a subsequent call to prompt().
      while (System.in.read() != '\n');
      return ch;
   }
   catch (java.io.IOException ioe)
   {
   }
   return 0;
}
/**
 *  Display a message followed by all cards held by player. This output
 *  simulates putting down held cards.
 *
 *  @param msg message to be displayed to human player
 *  @param cards array of <code>Card</code> objects to be identified
 */
static void putDown(String msg, Card[] cards)
{
   System.out.println(msg);
   for (int i = 0; i < cards.length; i++)
      System.out.println(cards[i]);
}
/**
 *  Identify the cards being held via their <code>Card</code> objects on
 *  separate lines. Prefix each line with an uppercase letter starting with
 *  <code>A</code>.
 *
 *  @param cards array of <code>Card</code> objects to be identified
 */
static void showHeldCards(Card[] cards)
{
   System.out.println();
   System.out.println("Held cards:");
   for (int i = 0; i < cards.length; i++)
      if (cards[i] != null)
```

```
        System.out.println((char) ('A'+i) + ". " + cards[i]);
      System.out.println();
   }
}
```

Listing 1–8 follows the steps outlined by and expands on Listing 1–4's pseudocode. Because of the various comments, I do not have much to say about this listing. However, there are a couple of items that deserve mention:

- Card's nested Rank enum stores a sequence of 13 Rank objects beginning with ACE and ending with KING. These objects cannot be compared directly via > to determine which object has the greater rank. However, their integer-based *ordinal* (positional) values can be compared by calling the Rank object's ordinal() method. For example, Card.ACE_OF_SPADES.rank().ordinal() returns 0 because ACE is located at position 0 within Rank's list of Rank objects, and Card.KING_OF_CLUBS.rank().ordinal() returns 12 because KING is located at the last position in this list.

- The leastDesirableCard() method counts the ranks of the Cards in the array of Card objects passed to this method, and stores these counts in a rankCounts array. For example, given two of clubs, ace of spades, three of clubs, and ace of diamonds, this array identifies one two, two aces, and one three. This method then searches rankCounts from smallest index (representing ace) to largest index (representing king) for the first smallest nonzero count (there might be a tie, as in one two and one three)—a zero count represents no Cards having that rank in the array of Card objects. Finally, the method searches the array of Card objects to identify the object whose rank ordinal matches the index of the smallest nonzero count, and returns the index of this Card object.

   This behavior implies that the least desirable card is always the smallest ranked card. Furthermore, if there are multiple cards of the same rank, and if this rank is smaller than the rank of another card in the array, this method will choose the first (in a left-to-right manner) of the multiple cards having the same rank as the least desirable card. However, if the rank of the multiple cards is greater than the rank of another card, this other card will be chosen as least desirable.

I previously stated that Listing 1–5 begins with a Javadoc comment that describes the Card class and identifies this class's author. A *Javadoc comment* is a documentation item that documents a class, a method, or other program entity.

A Javadoc comment begins with /** and ends with */. Sandwiched between these *delimiters* (a pair of characters that mark the start and stop of some section) are text, HTML tags (such as <p> and <code>), and *Javadoc tags*, which are @-prefixed instructions. The following list identifies three common tags:

- @author identifies the source code's author.

- @param identifies one of a method's parameters (discussed in Chapter 2).

- @return identifies the kind of value that a method returns.

The JDK provides a javadoc tool that extracts all Javadoc comments from one or more source files and generates a set of HTML files containing this documentation in an easy-to-read format. These files serve as the program's documentation.

For example, suppose that the current directory contains Card.java, Deck.java, DiscardPile.java, and FourOfAKind.java. To extract all of the Javadoc comments that appear in these files, specify the following command:

```
javadoc *.java
```

The javadoc tool responds by outputting the following messages:

```
Loading source file Card.java...
Loading source file Deck.java...
Loading source file DiscardPile.java...
Loading source file FourOfAKind.java...
Constructing Javadoc information...
Standard Doclet version 1.6.0_16
Building tree for all the packages and classes...
Generating Card.html...
Generating Card.Rank.html...
Generating Card.Suit.html...
Generating Deck.html...
Generating DiscardPile.html...
Generating FourOfAKind.html...
Generating package-frame.html...
Generating package-summary.html...
Generating package-tree.html...
Generating constant-values.html...
Building index for all the packages and classes...
Generating overview-tree.html...
Generating index-all.html...
Generating deprecated-list.html...
Building index for all classes...
Generating allclasses-frame.html...
Generating allclasses-noframe.html...
Generating index.html...
Generating help-doc.html...
Generating stylesheet.css...
```

Furthermore, it generates a series of files, including the index.html entry-point file. If you point your web browser to this file, you should see a page that is similar to the page shown in Figure 1–8.

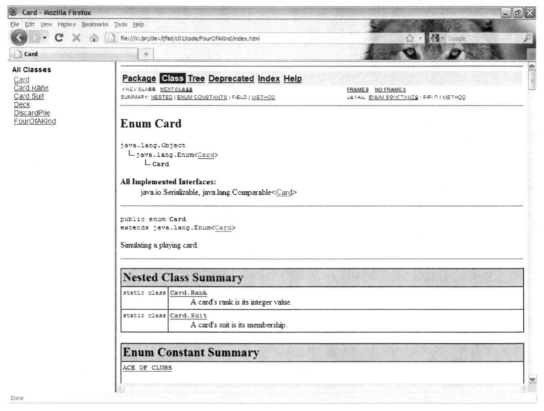

Figure 1–8. *The entry-point page into the generated Javadoc for* FourOfAKind *and supporting classes*

javadoc defaults to generating HTML-based documentation for public classes and public/protected members of classes. You will learn about public classes and public/protected members of classes in Chapter 2.

For this reason, FourOfAKind's documentation reveals only the public main() method. It does not reveal isFourOfAKind() and the other package-private methods. If you want to include these methods in the documentation, you must specify -package with javadoc:

```
javadoc -package *.java
```

> **NOTE:** The standard class library's documentation was also generated by javadoc and adheres to the same format.

Compiling, Running, and Distributing FourOfAKind

Unlike the previous DumpArgs and EchoText applications, which each consist of one source file, FourOfAKind consists of Card.java, Deck.java, DiscardPile.java, and FourOfAKind.java. You can compile all four source files via the following command line:

```
javac FourOfAKind.java
```

The javac tool launches the Java compiler, which recursively compiles the source files of the various classes it encounters during compilation. Assuming successful compilation, you should end up with six classfiles in the current directory.

> **TIP:** You can compile all Java source files in the current directory by specifying `javac *.java`.

After successfully compiling FourOfAKind.java and the other three source files, specify the following command line to run this application:

```
java FourOfAKind
```

In response, you see an introductory message and the four cards that you are holding. The following output reveals a single session:

```
Welcome to Four of a Kind!

Held cards:
A. SIX_OF_CLUBS
B. QUEEN_OF_DIAMONDS
C. SIX_OF_HEARTS
D. SIX_OF_SPADES

Which card do you want to throw away (A, B, C, D)? B

Held cards:
A. SIX_OF_CLUBS
B. NINE_OF_HEARTS
C. SIX_OF_HEARTS
D. SIX_OF_SPADES

Which card do you want to throw away (A, B, C, D)? B

Held cards:
A. SIX_OF_CLUBS
B. FOUR_OF_DIAMONDS
C. SIX_OF_HEARTS
D. SIX_OF_SPADES

Which card do you want to throw away (A, B, C, D)? B

Held cards:
A. SIX_OF_CLUBS
B. KING_OF_HEARTS
C. SIX_OF_HEARTS
D. SIX_OF_SPADES
```

```
Which card do you want to throw away (A, B, C, D)? B

Held cards:
A. SIX_OF_CLUBS
B. QUEEN_OF_CLUBS
C. SIX_OF_HEARTS
D. SIX_OF_SPADES

Which card do you want to throw away (A, B, C, D)? B

Held cards:
A. SIX_OF_CLUBS
B. KING_OF_DIAMONDS
C. SIX_OF_HEARTS
D. SIX_OF_SPADES

Which card do you want to throw away (A, B, C, D)? B

Held cards:
A. SIX_OF_CLUBS
B. TWO_OF_HEARTS
C. SIX_OF_HEARTS
D. SIX_OF_SPADES

Which card do you want to throw away (A, B, C, D)? B

Held cards:
A. SIX_OF_CLUBS
B. FIVE_OF_DIAMONDS
C. SIX_OF_HEARTS
D. SIX_OF_SPADES

Which card do you want to throw away (A, B, C, D)? B

Held cards:
A. SIX_OF_CLUBS
B. JACK_OF_CLUBS
C. SIX_OF_HEARTS
D. SIX_OF_SPADES

Which card do you want to throw away (A, B, C, D)? B

Held cards:
A. SIX_OF_CLUBS
B. TWO_OF_SPADES
C. SIX_OF_HEARTS
D. SIX_OF_SPADES

Which card do you want to throw away (A, B, C, D)? B

Human wins!

Human's cards:
SIX_OF_CLUBS
SIX_OF_DIAMONDS
SIX_OF_HEARTS
```

```
SIX_OF_SPADES

Computer's cards:
SEVEN_OF_HEARTS
TEN_OF_HEARTS
SEVEN_OF_CLUBS
SEVEN_OF_DIAMONDS
```

Although *Four of a Kind* is not much of a card game, you might decide to share the FourOfAKind application with a friend. However, if you forget to include even one of the application's five supporting classfiles, your friend will not be able to run the application.

You can overcome this problem by bundling FourOfAKind's six classfiles into a single *JAR (Java ARchive) file*, which is a ZIP file that contains a special directory and the .jar file extension. You can then distribute this single JAR file to your friend.

The JDK provides the jar tool for working with JAR files. To bundle all six classfiles into a JAR file named FourOfAKind.jar, you could specify the following command line, where c tells jar to create a JAR file and f identifies the JAR file's name:

```
jar cf FourOfAKind.jar *.class
```

After creating the JAR file, try to run the application via the following command line:

```
java -jar FourOfAKind.jar
```

Instead of the application running, you will receive an error message having to do with java not knowing which of the JAR file's six classfiles is the *main classfile* (the file whose class's main() method executes first).

You can provide this knowledge via a text file that is merged into the JAR file's *manifest*, a special file named MANIFEST.MF that stores information about the contents of a JAR file, and which is stored in the JAR file's META-INF directory. Consider Listing 1–9.

Listing 1–9. *Identifying the application's main class*

```
Main-Class: FourOfAKind
```

Listing 1–9 tells java which of the JAR's classfiles is the main class file. (You must leave a blank line after Main-Class: FourOfAKind.)

The following command line, which creates FourOfAKind.jar, includes m and the name of the text file providing manifest content:

```
jar cfm FourOfAKind.jar manifest *.class
```

This time, java -jar FourOfAKind.jar succeeds and the application runs because java is able to identify FourOfAKind as the main classfile.

EXERCISES

The following exercises are designed to test your understanding of what Java means, the JDK, NetBeans, Eclipse, and Java application development:

1. What is Java?

2. What is a virtual machine?

3. What is the purpose of the Java compiler?

4. True or false: A classfile's instructions are commonly referred to as bytecode.

5. What does the virtual machine's interpreter do when it learns that a sequence of bytecode instructions is being executed repeatedly?

6. How does the Java platform promote portability?

7. How does the Java platform promote security?

8. True or false: Java SE is the Java platform for developing servlets.

9. What is the JRE?

10. What is the difference between the public and private JREs?

11. What is the JDK?

12. Which JDK tool is used to compile Java source code?

13. Which JDK tool is used to run Java applications?

14. What is the purpose of the JDK's `jar` tool?

15. What is Standard I/O?

16. What is an IDE?

17. Identify two popular IDEs.

18. What is pseudocode?

19. How would you list `FourOfAKind.jar`'s *table of contents* (list of directories and files contained in the JAR file)?

20. Modify `FourOfAKind` to give each player the option of picking up the top card from the deck or discard pile (assuming that the discard pile is not empty; it is empty when the human player goes first and starts his/her first turn). Display the discard pile's top card for the human player's benefit. (Do not display the deck's top card.)

Summary

Java is a language and a platform. The language is partly patterned after the C and C++ languages to shorten the learning curve for C/C++ developers. The platform consists of a virtual machine and associated execution environment.

Developers use different editions of the Java platform to create Java programs that run on desktop computers, web browsers, web servers, mobile information devices, and embedded devices. These editions are known as Java SE, Java EE, and Java ME.

Developers also use a special Google-created edition of the Java platform to create Android apps that run on Android-enabled devices. This edition, known as the Android platform, largely consists of Java core libraries and a virtual machine known as Dalvik.

The public JRE implements the Java SE platform and makes it possible to run Java programs. The JDK provides tools (including the Java compiler) for developing Java programs and also includes a private copy of the JRE.

Working with the JDK's tools at the command line is not recommended for large projects, which are hard to manage without the help of an integrated development environment. Two popular IDEs are NetBeans and Eclipse.

Application development is not an easy task. All applications except for the most trivial require careful planning or you will probably waste your (and your users') time and money. One way to develop applications efficiently involves using pseudocode.

FourOfAKind gave you a significant taste of the Java language. Although much of its source code is probably hard to understand right now, you will find it much easier to grasp after reading Chapter 2, which introduces you to Java's language fundamentals.

Chapter 2

Learning Language Fundamentals

Aspiring Android developers need to understand the Java language. *Java* is an object-oriented language in which developers use objects to represent *entities* (things that exist, such as vehicles, checking and savings bank accounts, and buttons and other user interface components). Language features supporting this paradigm are the focus of this chapter and Chapter 3. More advanced features are discussed in Chapters 4 and 5. Additional advanced but minor features are more appropriately discussed in later chapters.

Classes

Object-oriented applications represent entities as *objects* (entity abstractions). Each object *encapsulates* (combines into a single unit) an entity's attributes and behaviors. For example, a checking bank account object might encapsulate a balance attribute (with a current value of $50) along with deposit and withdrawal behaviors.

> **NOTE:** Encapsulation exists in stark contrast to the separation of attributes and behaviors in C and other structured programming languages. In such a language, the developer cannot merge an entity's attributes and behaviors into an object. Instead, the developer must separately declare attributes via suitable *data structures* (organizations of data) and behaviors via suitable functions, to which data structure instances that contain attribute values are passed.

Objects do not pop out of thin air; they must be *instantiated* (created) from something. Languages such as C++ and Java refer to this *something* as a *class*, a template for manufacturing objects (also known as *class instances*, or *instances* for short). This section introduces you to Java's language features for architecting classes.

Declaring Classes

Because you cannot instantiate objects from a class that does not exist, you must declare the class. The declaration consists of a header followed by a body. At minimum, the header consists of reserved word `class` followed by a name that identifies the class (so that it can be referred to from elsewhere in the source code). The body starts with an open brace character ({) and ends with a close brace (}). Sandwiched between these *delimiters* (a pair of characters that mark the start and stop of some section) are field, method, and other kinds of declarations. Consider Listing 2–1.

Listing 2–1. *Declaring a skeletal* `CheckingAccount` *class*

```
class CheckingAccount
{
   // field, method, and other member declarations
}
```

Listing 2–1 declares a class named `CheckingAccount`. By convention, a class's name begins with an uppercase letter. Furthermore, the first letter of each subsequent word in a multiword class name is capitalized. This is known as camel-casing.

> **NOTE:** A class declaration is an example of *type*, a template for a set of data values and the operations that can be legally performed on these values.

`CheckingAccount` is one example of an *identifier*, which is a name that identifies a class or other source code entity. Identifiers consist of letters (A-Z, a-z, or equivalent uppercase/lowercase letters in other human languages), digits (0-9 or equivalent digits in other human languages), connecting punctuation characters (such as the underscore), and currency symbols (such as the dollar sign). However, an identifier can only begin with a letter, a currency symbol, or a connecting punctuation character. Also, an identifier's maximum length cannot exceed the length of the line in which it appears.

> **NOTE:** Identifiers are expressed in *Unicode* (http://en.wikipedia.org/wiki/Unicode), a universal character set that encodes the various symbols making up the world's written languages.

Additional examples include `temperature`, `Temperature`, `_class`, `first$name`, and `loopCounter1`. `temperature` and `Temperature` are two different identifiers because Java is a case-sensitive language. In contrast, `6x` and `door^color` are not identifiers because the former character sequence begins with a digit, and the latter character sequence contains an illegal character (^).

You can choose almost any identifier to name classes and other source code entities. However, Java reserves the following identifiers, which are commonly referred to as *reserved words*, for special uses: `abstract, assert, boolean, break, byte, case, catch, char, class, const, continue, default, do, double, enum, else, extends, false, final, finally, float, for, goto, if, implements, import, instanceof, int, interface, long,` native, new, null, package, private, protected, public, return, short, static, strictfp, super, switch, synchronized, this, throw, throws, transient, true, try, void, volatile, and while. Attempting to use any of these reserved words outside of their usage contexts results in compiler error messages.

The class body is currently empty because we have yet to explore fields, methods, and other class members. This fact is pointed out by the *single-line comment*, a line of documentation that begins with //. The compiler ignores everything from // to the end of the line.

Introducing Fields

After declaring a class, you can declare *variables* (memory locations whose values can change) in the class's body. Some of these variables are used in an object context to describe entity attributes. Other variables are used in a class context to describe *class attributes* (attributes that are shared by all created objects, such as a variable that contains a count of all objects created from the class). Regardless of its purpose, a variable that is introduced into a class's body is known as a *field*. This section shows you how to declare fields, how to initialize them to nondefault values, and how to declare read-only fields.

Declaring Fields

You can declare a field within a class's body by minimally specifying a type name, followed by an identifier that names the field, followed by a semicolon character (;). Listing 2–2 presents a pair of field declarations.

Listing 2–2. *Declaring* owner *and* balance *fields in the* CheckingAccount *class*

```
class CheckingAccount
{
    String owner; // name of person who owns this checking account
    int balance; // number of dollars that can be withdrawn
}
```

Listing 2–2 declares two fields named owner and balance. By convention, a field's name begins with a lowercase letter, and the first letter of each subsequent word in a multiword field name is capitalized.

A field's *type* identifies the kind of values that can be assigned to the field. The owner field is of type String, which is one of Java's predefined classes. String objects contain sequences of characters; the character sequence in any String object assigned to owner will contain the name of the account's owner.

The balance field is of type integer, which is implied by reserved word int. (In common practice, we say that balance is of type int.) This field can store the account balance as a whole number without a fraction.

Integer is one of several *primitive types* (types whose values are not objects) that are supported by Java. Table 2–1 describes all of Java's primitive types except for void (discussed later).

Table 2–1. *Primitive Types*

Primitive Type	Reserved Word	Size	Min Value	Max Value
Boolean	`boolean`	--	--	--
Character	`char`	16-bit	Unicode 0	Unicode $2^{16} - 1$
Byte integer	`byte`	8-bit	-128	+127
Short integer	`short`	16-bit	-2^{15}	$+2^{15} - 1$
Integer	`int`	32–bit	-2^{31}	$+2^{31} - 1$
Long integer	`long`	64-bit	-2^{63}	$+2^{63} - 1$
Floating-point	`float`	32–bit	IEEE 754	IEEE 754
Double precision floating-point	`double`	64-bit	IEEE 754	IEEE 754

Table 2–1 expresses primitive type sizes in terms of the number of *bits* (binary digits— each digit is either 0 or 1) that a value of that type occupies in memory. A group of eight bits is known as a *byte*.

Also, Unicode 0 is shorthand for "the first Unicode character," and IEEE 754 (http://en.wikipedia.org/wiki/IEEE_754) refers to a standard for representing floating-point numbers in memory.

Except for Boolean, whose size is implementation dependent (one Java implementation might store a Boolean value in a single bit, whereas another implementation might require an eight-bit byte for performance efficiency), each primitive type's implementation has a specific size.

> **NOTE:** Unlike their C and C++ counterparts, Java's primitive types have the same size in each Java implementation, which partly accounts for the portability of Java applications.

Except for Boolean, whose only values are true and false, each primitive type has a minimum and a maximum value. By studying these limits, you can deduce that the character type is unsigned (all values are positive). In contrast, each numeric type is signed (the type supports positive and negative values).

NOTE: Developers who argue that everything in Java should be an object are not happy about the inclusion of primitive types in the language. However, Java was designed to include primitive types to overcome the speed and memory limitations of early 1990s-era devices, to which Java was originally targeted.

The owner and balance fields are examples of non-array fields because each field can hold only one value—an *array* is a multivalue variable; each *array element* (storage slot) holds one of these values. Java also lets you declare array-based fields, which, as Listing 2–3 reveals, are identified by the presence of square brackets ([and]).

Listing 2–3. *Declaring* cities *and* temperatures *array-based fields in a* WeatherData *class*

```
class WeatherData
{
    String country;
    String[] cities;
    double[][]temperatures;
}
```

Listing 2–3 declares a WeatherData class that holds temperature extremes for a variety of cities in a specific country. The one-dimensional cities array contains the names of these cities; the two-dimensional temperatures array contains the maximum and minimum temperature values for each city.

A *one-dimensional array* is a sequential list of values; it is identified in source code by one pair of square brackets. A *two-dimensional array* is a table of values; it is identified in source code by two pairs of square brackets. These brackets can appear on either side of the field name, but are often shown with the type name. (Java also supports higher-dimensional arrays.)

CheckingAccount's owner and balance fields, and WeatherData's country, cities, and temperatures fields are examples of *instance fields* because they associate with objects. Each CheckingAccount instance is given its own copy of owner and balance when the object is created. Similarly, each WeatherData instance is given its own copy of country, cities, and temperatures when the object is created. Modifying any field's value does not affect the value in any other copy of that field.

In many situations, instance fields are all that you need. However, you might encounter a situation where you need a single copy of a field no matter how many objects are created.

For example, suppose you want to track the number of CheckingAccount objects that have been created, and introduce a counter field (initialized to 0) into this class. You also place code in the class's constructor (which I will present when I discuss constructors) to increase counter's value by 1 when an object is created. However, because each object has its own copy of the counter field, this field's value never advances past 1.

You can solve this problem by declaring `counter` to be a *class field*, a field that associates with a class instead of with that class's objects. Listing 2–4 accomplishes this task by prefixing `counter`'s declaration with the `static` reserved word.

Listing 2–4. *Adding a `counter` class field to `CheckingAccount`*

```
class CheckingAccount
{
   String owner;
   int balance;
   static int counter;
}
```

Listing 2–4's `static` prefix implies that there is only one copy of the `counter` field, not one copy per object. Each time an object is created, `counter` will increase by 1, and you will get an accurate tally of all `CheckingAccount` objects that have been created.

Each of `owner` and `balance` is created when a `CheckingAccount` object is created, and destroyed when the object is destroyed. In contrast, `counter` is created when `CheckingAccount` is loaded into memory, and destroyed when this class is removed from memory (when the application ends). This quality is known as *lifetime*.

Each of `owner` and `balance` can be accessed only from an instance context (such as a constructor). In contrast, `counter` can be accessed from instance and class contexts (such as a class method, discussed later in this chapter). This quality is known as *scope*.

Initializing Fields

Listing 2–4's `owner` and `balance` fields are initialized to default null and 0 values (respectively) when an object is created from the `CheckingAccount` class. The `counter` field is initialized to 0 when this class is loaded into memory.

It is common to initialize an instance field to a (potentially unique) value from within the class's constructor. However, you might want to explicitly assign some reasonable nonunique default value to this field, and give yourself the option of overriding that default value via the constructor. In contrast, you often explicitly initialize class fields.

Regardless of how you initialize a field, the value results from evaluating an *expression*, which is a combination of variables, method *calls* (invocations), *literals* (values specified verbatim), and operators. The expression's type must agree with the field's type when assigning the expression to the field. Otherwise, the compiler reports an error.

Simple Expressions

A *simple expression* is a value expressed as a variable name (value is read from the variable), a method call (value is returned from the method), or a literal in source code.

Java supports several kinds of literals: string, Boolean, character, integer, floating-point, and `null` (which I will discuss later in this chapter).

A *string literal* consists of a sequence of Unicode characters surrounded by a pair of double quotes ("). Example: `"The quick brown fox jumps over the lazy dog."`

A string literal might also contain *escape sequences*, which are special *syntax* (rules for combining symbols into language features) for representing certain printable and nonprintable characters that otherwise cannot appear in the literal. For example, string literal "The quick brown \"fox\" jumps over the lazy dog." uses the \" escape sequence to surround fox with double quotes. Table 2–2 describes all supported escape sequences.

Table 2–2. *Escape Sequences*

Escape Syntax	Description
\\	Backslash
\"	Double quote
\'	Single quote
\b	Backspace
\f	Form feed
\n	Newline (also referred to as linefeed)
\r	Carriage return
\t	Horizontal tab

Finally, a string literal might contain *Unicode escape sequences*, which are special syntax for representing Unicode characters. A Unicode escape sequence begins with \u and continues with four hexadecimal digits (0-9, A-F, a-f) with no intervening space. For example, \u0041 represents capital letter A, and \u20ac represents the European Union's euro currency symbol.

A *Boolean literal* consists of reserved word true or reserved word false.

A *character literal* consists of a single Unicode character surrounded by a pair of single quotes ('A' is an example). You can also represent, as a character literal, an escape sequence ('\'', for example) or a Unicode escape sequence (such as '\u0041').

An *integer literal* consists of a sequence of digits. If the literal is to represent a long integer value, then it must be suffixed with an uppercase L or lowercase l (L is easier to read). If there is no suffix, the literal represents a 32–bit integer (an int).

Integer literals can be specified in the default decimal, hexadecimal, octal, and (starting with Java version 7) binary formats:

- The decimal format is the default format. Example: 255
- The hexadecimal format requires that the literal be prefixed with 0x or 0X and continue with hexadecimal digits (0-9, A-F, a-f). Example: 0xFF

■ The octal format requires that the literal be prefixed with 0 and continue with octal digits (0-7). Example: 077

■ The binary format requires that the literal be prefixed with 0b or 0B and continue with 0s and 1s. Example: 0b11111111

Java version 7 also adds another nice feature where integer literals are concorned: it lets you insert underscores between digits to improve readability. Example: 123_456_789. Although you can insert multiple successive underscores between digits (as in 0b1111__0000), you cannot specify a leading underscore (as in _123) because the compiler would treat the literal as an identifier. Also, you cannot specify a trailing underscore (as in 123_).

Finally, a *floating-point literal* consists of an integer part, a decimal point (represented by the period character (.)), a fractional part, an exponent (starting with letter E or e), and a type suffix (letter D, d, F, or f). Most parts are optional, but enough information must be present to differentiate the floating-point literal from an integer literal. Examples include 0.1 (double precision floating-point), 10F (floating-point), 10D (double precision floating-point), and 3.0E+23 (double precision floating-point).

Suppose you need to create a class whose objects are used to log messages to a specific file. Each instance will have a field that identifies the target file, initialized to a default filename. Listing 2–5 presents this class and shows you how to initialize this field.

Listing 2–5. *Initializing the* Logger *class's* filename *field*

```
class Logger
{
   String filename = "log.txt";
}
```

Listing 2–5 uses simple initialization to initialize a non-array field. You can also use simple initialization with array-based fields. For example, Listing 2–6 shows you how to initialize array-based cities and temperatures fields.

Listing 2–6. *Initializing the* WeatherData *class's fields*

```
class WeatherData
{
   String country = "United States";
   String[] cities = {"Chicago", "New York", "Los Angeles"};
   double[][] temperatures = {{0.0, 0.0}, {0.0, 0.0}, {0.0, 0.0}};
}
```

Listing 2–6's WeatherData class defaults its objects to providing weather data for three American cities. The cities array is initialized to a comma-separated list of three String literals, which are specified between braces; the temperatures array is initialized to a three-row by two-column table of double precision floating-point zeros, which is specified as a three-element row array with each comma-separated element containing a two-element column array.

Compound Expressions

A *compound expression* is a sequence of simple expressions and operators, where an *operator* is a sequence of instructions (symbolically represented in source code) that transforms one or more values, known as *operands*, into another value.

For example, the + symbol denotes the addition or string concatenation operator, depending on the types of its two operands. When this symbol appears between numeric operands (6+4, for example), addition is implied. Similarly, when + appears between string literals (as in "A"+"B"), string concatenation is implied.

Java supplies a wide variety of operators that are classified by the number of operands they take. A *unary operator* takes only one operand, a *binary operator* takes two operands, and Java's single *ternary operator* takes three operands.

These operators are also classified as prefix, postfix, and infix. A *prefix operator* is a unary operator that precedes its operand, a *postfix operator* is a unary operator that trails its operand, and an *infix operator* is a binary or ternary operator that is sandwiched between the binary operator's two or the ternary operator's three operands.

Table 2–3 describes all supported operators. (I will explain precedence after this table.)

Table 2–3. *Operators*

Operator	Symbol	Description	Precedence
Addition	+	Given *operand1* + *operand2*, where each operand must be of character or numeric type, add *operand2* to *operand1* and return the sum.	10
Array index	[ ]	Given *variable*[*index*], where *index* must be of integral type, read value from or store value into *variable*'s storage element at location *index*.	13
Assignment	=	Given *variable* = *operand*, which must be assignment-compatible (their types must agree), store *operand* in *variable*.	0
Bitwise AND	&	Given *operand1* & *operand2*, where each operand must be of character or integer type, bitwise AND their corresponding bits and return the result. A result bit is set to 1 if each operand's corresponding bit is 1. Otherwise, the result bit is set to 0.	6
Bitwise complement	~	Given ~*operand*, where *operand* must be of character or integer type, flip *operand*'s bits (1s to 0s and 0s to 1s) and return the result.	12
Bitwise exclusive OR	^	Given *operand1* ^ *operand2*, where each operand must be of character or integer type, bitwise exclusive OR their corresponding bits and return the result. A result bit is set to 1 if one operand's corresponding bit is 1 and the other operand's corresponding bit is 0. Otherwise, the result bit is set to 0.	5

Operator	Symbol	Description	Precedence
Bitwise inclusive OR	|	Given *operand1* | *operand2*, which must be of character or integer type, bitwise inclusive OR their corresponding bits and return the result. A result bit is set to 1 if either (or both) of the operands' corresponding bits is 1. Otherwise, the result bit is set to 0.	4
Cast	(*type*)	Given (*type*) *operand*, convert *operand* to an equivalent value that can be represented by *type*. For example, you could use this operator to convert a floating-point value to a 32–bit integer value.	12
Compound assignment	+=, -=, *=, /=, %=, &=, |=, ^=, <<=, >>=, >>>=	Given *variable operator operand*, where *operator* is one of the listed compound operator symbols, and where *operand* is assignment-compatible with *variable*, perform the indicated operation using *variable*'s value as *operator*'s left operand value, and store the resulting value in *variable*.	0
Conditional	?:	Given *operand1* ? *operand2* : *operand3*, where *operand1* must be of Boolean type, return *operand2* if *operand1* is true or *operand3* if *operand1* is false. The types of *operand2* and *operand3* must agree.	1
Conditional AND	&&	Given *operand1* && *operand2*, where each operand must be of Boolean type, return true if both operands are true. Otherwise, return false. If *operand1* is false, *operand2* is not examined. This is known as *short-circuiting*.	3
Conditional OR	||	Given *operand1* || *operand2*, where each operand must be of Boolean type, return true if at least one operand is true. Otherwise, return false. If *operand1* is true, *operand2* is not examined. This is known as *short-circuiting*.	2
Division	/	Given *operand1* / *operand2*, where each operand must be of character or numeric type, divide *operand1* by *operand2* and return the quotient.	11
Equality	==	Given *operand1* == *operand2*, where both operands must be comparable (you cannot compare an integer with a string literal, for example), compare both operands for equality. Return true if these operands are equal. Otherwise, return false.	7
Inequality	!=	Given *operand1* != *operand2*, where both operands must be comparable (you cannot compare an integer with a string literal, for example), compare both operands for inequality. Return true if these operands are not equal. Otherwise, return false.	7

Operator	Symbol	Description	Precedence
Left shift	<<	Given *operand1* << *operand2*, where each operand must be of character or integer type, shift *operand1*'s binary representation left by the number of bits that *operand2* specifies. For each shift, a 0 is shifted into the rightmost bit and the leftmost bit is discarded. Only the five low-order bits of *operand2* are used when shifting a 32–bit integer (to prevent shifting more than the number of bits in a 32–bit integer). Only the six low-order bits of *operand2* are used when shifting a 64-bit integer (to prevent shifting more than the number of bits in a 64-bit integer). The shift preserves negative values. Furthermore, it is equivalent to (but faster than) multiplying by a multiple of 2.	9
Logical AND	&	Given *operand1* & *operand2*, where each operand must be of Boolean type, return true if both operands are true. Otherwise, return false. In contrast to conditional AND, logical AND does not perform short-circuiting.	6
Logical complement	!	Given !*operand*, where *operand* must be of Boolean type, flip *operand*'s value (true to false or false to true) and return the result.	12
Logical exclusive OR	^	Given *operand1* ^ *operand2*, where each operand must be of Boolean type, return true if one operand is true and the other operand is false. Otherwise, return false.	5
Logical inclusive OR	|	Given *operand1* | *operand2*, where each operand must be of Boolean type, return true if at least one operand is true. Otherwise, return false. In contrast to conditional OR, logical inclusive OR does not perform short-circuiting.	4
Member access	.	Given *identifier1.identifier2*, access the *identifier2* member of *identifer1*. You will learn about this operator later in this chapter.	13
Method call	()	Given *identifier(argument list)*, call the method identified by *identifier* and matching parameter list. You will learn about calling methods later in this chapter.	13
Multiplication	*	Given *operand1* * *operand2*, where each operand must be of character or numeric type, multiply *operand1* by *operand2* and return the product.	11
Object creation	new	Given new *identifier(argument list)*, allocate memory for object and call constructor specified as *identifier(argument list)*. Given new *identifier[integer size]*, allocate a one-dimensional array of values.	12
Postdecrement	--	Given *variable--*, where *variable* must be of character or numeric type, subtract 1 from *variable*'s value (storing the result in *variable*) and return the original value.	13

Operator	Symbol	Description	Precedence
Postincrement	++	Given *variable*++, where *variable* must be of character or numeric type, add 1 to *variable*'s value (storing the result in *variable*) and return the original value.	13
Predecrement	--	Given --*variable*, where *variable* must be of character or numeric type, subtract 1 from its value, store the result in *variable*, and return this value.	12
Preincrement	++	Given ++*variable*, where *variable* must be of character or numeric type, add 1 to its value, store the result in *variable*, and return this value.	12
Relational greater than	>	Given *operand1* > *operand2*, where each operand must be of character or numeric type, return true if *operand1* is greater than *operand2*. Otherwise, return false.	8
Relational greater than or equal to	>=	Given *operand1* >= *operand2*, where each operand must be of character or numeric type, return true if *operand1* is greater than or equal to *operand2*. Otherwise, return false.	8
Relational less than	<	Given *operand1* < *operand2*, where each operand must be of character or numeric type, return true if *operand1* is less than *operand2*. Otherwise, return false.	8
Relational less than or equal to	<=	Given *operand1* <= *operand2*, where each operand must be of character or numeric type, return true if *operand1* is less than or equal to *operand2*. Otherwise, return false.	8
Relational type checking	instanceof	Given *operand1* instanceof *operand2*, where *operand1* is an object and *operand2* is a class (or other user-defined type), return true if *operand1* is an instance of *operand2*. Otherwise, return false.	8
Remainder	%	Given *operand1* % *operand2*, where each operand must be of character or numeric type, divide *operand1* by *operand2* and return the remainder.	11
Signed right shift	>>	Given *operand1* >> *operand2*, where each operand must be of character or integer type, shift *operand1*'s binary representation right by the number of bits that *operand2* specifies. For each shift, a copy of the sign bit (the leftmost bit) is shifted to the right and the rightmost bit is discarded. Only the five low-order bits of *operand2* are used when shifting a 32–bit integer (to prevent shifting more than the number of bits in a 32–bit integer). Only the six low-order bits of *operand2* are used when shifting a 64-bit integer (to prevent shifting more than the number of bits in a 64-bit integer). The shift preserves negative values. Furthermore, it is equivalent to (but faster than) dividing by a multiple of 2.	9

Operator	Symbol	Description	Precedence
String concatenation	+	Given *operand1* + *operand2*, where at least one operand is of String type, append *operand2*'s string representation to *operand1*'s string representation and return the concatenated result.	10
Subtraction	-	Given *operand1* - *operand2*, where each operand must be of character or numeric type, subtract *operand2* from *operand1* and return the difference.	10
Unary minus	-	Given -*operand*, where *operand* must be of character or numeric type, return *operand*'s arithmetic negative.	12
Unary plus	+	Like its predecessor, but return *operand*. Rarely used.	12
Unsigned right shift	>>>	Given *operand1* >>> *operand2*, where each operand must be of character or integer type, shift *operand1*'s binary representation right by the number of bits that *operand2* specifies. For each shift, a zero is shifted into the leftmost bit and the rightmost bit is discarded. Only the five low-order bits of *operand2* are used when shifting a 32–bit integer (to prevent shifting more than the number of bits in a 32–bit integer). Only the six low-order bits of *operand2* are used when shifting a 64-bit integer (to prevent shifting more than the number of bits in a 64-bit integer). The shift does not preserve negative values. Furthermore, it is equivalent to (but faster than) dividing by a multiple of 2.	9

In Table 2–3's operator descriptions, "integer type" refers to any of the byte integer, short integer, integer, or long integer types, unless integer type is qualified as a 32–bit integer. Also, "numeric type" refers to any of these integer types along with floating-point and double precision floating-point.

Table 2–3's rightmost column presents a value that indicates the operator's *precedence* (level of importance): the higher the number, the higher the precedence. For example, addition's precedence level is 10 and multiplication's precedence level is 11, which means that multiplication is performed before addition when evaluating 40+2*4.

Precedence can be circumvented by introducing open and close parentheses, (and), into the expression, where the innermost pair of nested parentheses is evaluated first. For example, (40+2)*4 results in addition being performed before multiplication, and 40/(2-4) results in subtraction being performed before divison.

During evaluation, operators with the same precedence level (such as addition and subtraction, which both have level 10) are processed according to their *associativity* (a property that determines how operators having the same precedence are grouped when parentheses are missing).

For example, expression 6*3/2 is evaluated as if it was (6*3)/2 because * and / are left-to-right associative operators. In contrast, expression a=b=c=10 is evaluated as if it was a=(b=(c=10))—10 is assigned to c, c's new value (10) is assigned to b, and b's new value (10) is assigned to a—because = is a right-to-left associative operator.

Most of Java's operators are left-to-right associative. Right-to-left associative operators include assignment, bitwise complement, cast, compound assignment, conditional, logical complement, object creation, predecrement, preincrement, unary minus, and unary plus.

Whenever an operator encounters two operands of different types, it attempts to convert one (and possibly both) of the operands to a type that is suitable for performing its operation. For example, if you attempt to add a 16-bit short integer value to a 32–bit integer value, the addition operator will first convert the short integer value to a 32–bit integer value, and then add together both 32–bit integer values.

Similarly, if you attempt to add a 32–bit integer value to a 32–bit floating-point value, the operator will first convert the 32–bit integer value to a 32–bit floating-point value, and then add together both floating-point values. The operator always converts the value with a more limited representation (such as a 16-bit short integer) to an equivalent value in a less limited representation (such as a 32–bit integer).

Sometimes, you need to explicitly perform a conversion, and this is where the cast operator comes into play. For example, suppose your class contains the following field declarations:

```
char c = 'A';
byte b = c;
```

The compiler reports an error about loss of precision when it encounters byte b = c;. The reason is that c can represent any unsigned integer value from 0 through 65535, whereas b can only represent a signed integer value from -128 through +127. Even though 'A' equates to +65, which can fit within b's range, c could just have easily been initialized to '\u0123', which would not fit. Because of the potential for data loss, the compiler complains.

The solution to this problem involves introducing a (byte) cast, which explicitly tells the compiler that the developer is aware of the potential for data loss but wants the conversion to occur:

```
byte b = (byte) c;
```

Not all conversions can be performed. For example, the subtraction operator cannot subtract a string literal from a 32–bit integer. Also, attempting to cast a floating-point value to a String, as in String s = (String) 20.0;, does not work. In these situations, the compiler provides suitable error messages.

The mathematical operators (+, -, *, /, %) can yield values that overflow or underflow the limits of the resulting value's type. For example, multiplying two large positive 32–bit integer values can produce a value that cannot be represented as a 32–bit integer value. Java does not detect overflows and underflows.

Dividing (via / or %) a numeric value by 0 also results in interesting behavior. In the first case, dividing an integer value by integer 0 causes the operator to throw an ArithmeticException object (I briefly discuss ArithmeticException in Chapter 4 when I cover exceptions). Secondly, dividing a floating-point value by 0 causes the operator to return +infinity or -infinity, depending on whether the dividend is positive or negative. Finally, dividing floating-point 0 by 0 causes the operator to return NaN (Not a Number).

Suppose you have created a `ReportWriter` class that outputs reports to the printer. During the testing phase, you want to make sure that reports are properly generated without wasting paper, so you would like the output to be directed to a file. An additional requirement is that you would like to be able to change the file's name or the printer's name from application code. Listing 2–7 presents a possible solution.

Listing 2–7. *Initializing the* `ReportWriter` *class's* `outputDevice` *field with the help of the conditional operator*

```
class ReportWriter
{
    static boolean test = true;
    static String outputDevice = (test) ? "file" : "printer";
}
```

Listing 2–7's `ReportWriter` class satisfies the first requirement by providing a `test` class field. When this class loads, `true` is assigned to `test`, overriding its default false value. The expression assigned to the `outputDevice` class field uses the conditional operator to examine `test`. Finding this field to contain true, the operator subsequently returns string literal `"file"`, which is assigned to `outputDevice`. If `test` is found to contain false, `"printer"` is returned and assigned to `outputDevice`.

To satisfy the second requirement, simply assign the appropriate destination string literal to `outputDevice` from the application's code.

Read-only Fields

Java provides reserved word `final` for declaring that a field is read-only.

Each object receives its own copy of a read-only instance field. This field must be initialized, as part of the field's declaration or in the class's constructor. If initialized in the constructor, the read-only instance field is known as a *blank final* because it does not have a value until one is assigned to it in the constructor. Because a constructor can potentially assign a different value to each object's blank final, these read-only variables are not truly constants.

If you want a true *constant*, which is a single read-only value that is available to all objects, you need to create a read-only class field. You can accomplish this task by including the reserved word `static` with `final` in that field's declaration.

Listing 2–8 shows you how to declare a read-only class field.

Listing 2–8. *Declaring a true constant in the* `Employee` *class*

```
class Employee
{
    final static int RETIREMENT_AGE = 65;
}
```

Listing 2–8's `RETIREMENT_AGE` declaration is an example of a *compile-time constant*. Because there is only one copy of its value (thanks to the `static` reserved word), and because this value will never change (thanks to the `final` reserved word), the compiler is free to optimize the compiled code by inserting the constant value into all calculations where it is used. The code runs faster because it does not have to access a read-only class field.

Introducing Methods

After declaring a class, you can introduce *methods* (named bodies of code) into the class's body. Some of these methods can associate with objects in order to describe entity behaviors. Other methods can associate with classes. This section shows you how to declare methods, how to implement their bodies, and how to overload methods.

Declaring Methods

You can declare a method within a class's body by minimally specifying a return type, followed by an identifier that names the method, followed by a parameter list, followed by a body. Listing 2–9 presents a simple method declaration.

Listing 2–9. *Declaring a* printBalance() *method in the* CheckingAccount *class*

```
class CheckingAccount
{
   String owner;
   int balance;
   static int counter;
   void printBalance()
   {
      // code that outputs the balance field's value
   }
}
```

Listing 2–9 declares a method named `printBalance` in `CheckingAccount`'s body. By convention, a method's name begins with a lowercase letter. Furthermore, the first letter of each subsequent word in a multiword method name is capitalized.

A method's *parameter list* identifies the number, order, and types of values that are passed to the method when the method is called via a parentheses-delimited and comma-separated list of variable declarations. Each value passed to the method is called an *argument*; the variable that receives the argument is called a *parameter*. Because arguments are not passed to `printBalance()`, its parameter list is empty.

> **NOTE:** The method's name and the types of its parameters are known as its *signature*.

The method's body specifies code that is to be executed when the method is called. In this example, I chose to leave the body empty, but have supplied a single-line comment to describe what the body should contain.

Finally, a method's *return type* identifies the kind of values returned by the method. Because `printBalance()` does not return a value, its return type is set to void via reserved word void. (Think of void as a special kind of primitive type, even though variables cannot be declared to be void, which is why I did not include it in Table 2–1.)

Because a CheckingAccount class should also provide methods for making deposits and withdrawals, Listing 2–10 introduces deposit() and withdraw() methods into this class.

Listing 2–10. *Declaring* deposit() *and* withdraw() *methods*

```
class CheckingAccount
{
    String owner;
    int balance;
    static int counter;
    void printBalance()
    {
        // code that outputs the balance field's value
    }
    int deposit(int amount)
    {
        // code that adds the specified amount to balance, and returns the new balance
    }
    int withdraw(int amount)
    {
        /* code that subtracts the specified amount from balance, and returns the new
           balance */
    }
}
```

Listing 2–10's deposit() and withdraw() methods each specify a nonempty parameter list consisting of a single amount parameter. As with any parameter, amount's lifetime ranges from the point where execution enters the method to the point where execution exits the method and returns to the method's *caller* (the code that called the method). Also, amount's scope is the entire method.

The deposit() and withdraw() methods also specify, via their int return types, that they return integer values.

Because we are not yet ready to code these methods' bodies, I have introduced comments to document their tasks. In contrast to printBalance() and deposit(), withdraw() reveals a *multiline comment*, one or more lines of documentation starting with /* and ending with */. The compiler ignores everything from /* through */.

> **CAUTION:** You cannot place a multiline comment inside another multiline comment: /*/*
> Nesting multiline comments is illegal! */*/

CheckingAccount's printBalance(), deposit(), and withdraw() methods are examples of instance methods because they associate with objects. Each method is called with a hidden argument that refers to the current object. The hidden argument allows the method to access the object's instance fields and call other instance methods. Furthermore, instance methods can access class fields and call class methods.

In many situations, instance methods are all that you need. However, when writing an application, you must introduce at least one *class method*, a method that associates with a class instead of with that class's objects, into one of the application's classes.

Specifically, an application must specify `public static void main(String[] args)` to serve as the application's entry point. The `static` reserved word is what makes this method a class method. (I will explain reserved word `public` later in this chapter.)

> **NOTE:** `main()` is called with an array of `String` objects, where each object contains the character representation of a command-line argument.

Because class methods are not called with a hidden argument that refers to the current object, `main()` cannot access an object's instance fields or call its instance methods. This method can only access class fields and call class methods.

Many methods require you to pass a fixed number of arguments when they are called. However, Java also provides the ability to pass a variable number of arguments. To declare a method that takes a variable number of arguments, specify three consecutive periods after the type name of the method's rightmost parameter. For example, Listing 2–11 places these periods after the `double` type name.

Listing 2–11. *Declaring a `sum()` method that takes a variable number of arguments*

```
double sum(double... values)
{
   // code that sums the passed double arguments and returns the sum
}
```

You will shortly learn how to codify this method, along with the methods that were previously introduced. Later on, you will learn how to call all of these methods.

Implementing Methods

Listing 2–10's empty `printBalance()` method accomplishes nothing. Furthermore, its empty `deposit()` and `withdraw()` methods result in compiler errors because these methods have non-void return types and do not return values. To make these methods useful and legal, you must introduce statements into their bodies.

A *statement* is one or more instructions that perform a task. It can be expressed as a simple statement or as a compound statement.

A *simple statement* is a single instruction terminated by a semicolon. In addition to the empty simple statement, Java supplies local variable declaration, assignment, method-call, decision, *loop* (repeated execution), break and continue, and method-return simple statements. (Chapter 4 introduces additional kinds of simple statements.)

A *compound statement* is a (possibly empty) sequence of simple and other compound statements sandwiched between open and close brace delimiters. A method body is an example. Compound statements can appear wherever simple statements appear, and are alternatively referred to as *blocks*.

Empty Statements, Local Variable Declarations, Assignments, and Method Calls

An *empty statement* is nothing followed by a semicolon. Although this kind of statement appears to be useless, it is useful, as I will explain when I discuss loop statements.

A *local variable declaration* introduces a variable into a method's body or other compound statement. This *local variable*'s lifetime and scope range from its point of declaration to the end of the compound statement in which it is declared. Only statements appearing after the declaration can access the local variable.

> **NOTE:** A local variable is similar to a parameter in that both kinds of variables only exist during a method's execution. However, a parameter contains a passed argument, whereas a local variable contains whatever value is necessary to help the method accomplish its task.

This statement is similar to an instance field declaration in that it minimally begins with a type name, continues with an identifier that names the local variable, and ends with a semicolon. By convention, a local variable's name begins with a lowercase letter. Furthermore, the first letter of each subsequent word in a multiword local variable name is capitalized.

> **CAUTION:** You cannot declare multiple local variables with the same name in the same scope because the compiler will report an "already defined" error message.

An *assignment* is a close relative of the local variable declaration statement. Instead of starting with a type, this statement begins with the name of a variable that has already been declared, continues with the assignment operator (=) or a compound assignment operator (such as +=), and concludes with an expression and a semicolon.

A *method call* executes a method, possibly passing arguments and possibly receiving a value in return. Regardless of whether or not a value is returned, a method call is a statement. If you do not assign the method's return value to a variable, the return value is lost. However, you occasionally might be more interested in what the method accomplishes than in what the method returns.

Listing 2–12's `printBalance()` method demonstrates these statements except for empty.

Listing 2–12. *Declaring and using local variables in* `printBalance()`

```
void printBalance()
{
   int magnitude = (balance < 0) ? -balance : balance;
   String balanceRep = (balance < 0) ? "(" : "";
   balanceRep += magnitude;
   balanceRep += (balance < 0) ? ")" : "";
   System.out.println(balanceRep);
}
```

Listing 2–12 introduces several statements into `printBalance()` to create a suitable string-based representation of the `balance` field's value and output this string. If this value is positive, it is represented and printed as is. If this value is negative, its *magnitude* (absolute or positive value) is represented and printed between parentheses.

This listing's first two statements declare a pair of local variables: `magnitude` and `balanceRep`. An expression initializes the magnitude variable to the balance field's magnitude, whereas another expression initializes `balanceRep` to `"("` or `""` (the empty string), depending on whether the `balance` field's value is negative or positive.

Unlike fields, which are initialized to default values, and parameters, which are initialized to arguments, local variables are not implicitly initialized. Before you can read a local variable's value, you must assign a value to the variable. Otherwise, the compiler reports an error about the local variable not having been initialized.

Moving on, two assignment statements follow the local variable declaration statements. These statements append a string representation of the `balance` field's magnitude followed by `")"` or `""` to `balanceRep`. Alternatively, I could have expressed the first of these statements as `balanceRep = balanceRep + magnitude;`.

Listing 2–12 concludes by calling the `System.out.println()` method to output `balanceRep`'s character sequence to the standard output device. (Chapter 1 briefly introduces the concept of standard input/output along with `System.out.println()` and related methods.)

Decisions

Listing 2–12 used the conditional operator to determine whether to assign `-balance` or `balance` to `magnitude`. Although this operator is useful for initializing a variable to one of two values, it cannot be used for choosing between two statements to execute. Java supplies the if-else statement for this purpose.

The if-else statement has the following syntax:

```
if (Boolean expression)
   statement1
else
   statement2
```

This statement consists of reserved word `if`, followed by a Boolean expression in parentheses, followed by a statement to execute (if the Boolean expression evaluates to true), followed by reserved word `else`, followed by another statement to execute (if the Boolean expression evaluates to false).

Listing 2–13 demonstrates if-else.

Listing 2–13. *A revised* `printBalance()` *method*

```
void printBalance()
{
   if (balance < 0)
      System.out.println("(" + -balance + ")");
   else
```

```
      System.out.println(balance);
}
```

Listing 2–13's if-else statement results in the first System.out.println() method call executing if balance's value is less than 0, and the second System.out.println() method call executing if balance's value is greater than or equal to 0.

Each of *statement1* and *statement2* describes another statement to execute. If you do not need the else part in the preceding syntax, you can omit else and *statement2* from the syntax. The resulting statement is called if.

NOTE: When if and if-else are used together, and the source code is not properly indented, it can be difficult to determine which if associates with the else. For example:

```
if (car.door.isOpen())
    if (car.key.isPresent())
        car.start();
else car.door.open();
```

Did the developer intend for the else to match the inner if, but improperly formatted the code to make it appear otherwise? For example:

```
if (car.door.isOpen())
    if (car.key.isPresent())
        car.start();
    else
        car.door.open();
```

If car.door.isOpen() and car.key.isPresent() each return true, car.start() executes. If car.door.isOpen() returns true and car.key.isPresent() returns false, car.door.open(); executes. Attempting to open an open door makes no sense.

The developer must have wanted the else to match the outer if, but forgot that else matches the nearest if. This problem can be fixed by surrounding the inner if with braces, as follows:

```
if (car.door.isOpen())
{
    if (car.key.isPresent())
        car.start();
}
else
    car.door.open();
```

When car.door.isOpen() returns true, the compound statement executes. When this method returns false, car.door.open(); executes, which makes sense.

> Forgetting that else matches the nearest if and using poor indentation to obscure this fact is known as the *dangling-else problem*.

You can chain multiple if-else statements together, resulting in the following syntax:

```
if (Boolean expression1)
   statement1
else
if (Boolean expression2)
   statement2
else
   ...
else
   statementN
```

If the first Boolean expression is true, `statement1` executes. Otherwise, if the second Boolean expression is true, `statement2` executes. This pattern continues until one of these expressions is true and its corresponding statement executes, or the final `else` is reached and `statementN` (the default statement) executes.

Listing 2–14 demonstrates chained if-else.

Listing 2–14. *A revised* `printBalance()` *method using chained if-else*

```
void printBalance()
{
   if (balance < 0)
      System.out.println("(" + -balance + ")");
   else
   if (balance == 0)
      System.out.println("zero balance");
   else
      System.out.println(balance);
}
```

Look closely at Listing 2–14 and you will see that its chained if-else statement is actually an if-else statement, where the statement following the else part (the first `else`) is another if-else statement.

Chaining if-else statements together leads to verbosity that, in some cases, can be made more concise by using a switch statement. This statement lets you write code for choosing one of several statements to execute, and has the following syntax:

```
switch (selector expression)
{
   case value1: statement1 [break;]
   case value2: statement2 [break;]
   ...
   case valueN: statementN [break;]
   [default: statement]
}
```

The switch statement consists of reserved word `switch`, followed by a *selector expression* in parentheses, followed by a body of cases. The selector expression is typically any expression that evaluates to an integral value. For example, it might evaluate to a 32-bit integer or to a 16-bit character.

Each case begins with reserved word `case`, continues with a literal value and a colon character (`:`), continues with a statement to execute, and optionally concludes with a break statement (which I have yet to discuss).

After evaluating the selector expression, switch compares this value with each case's value until it finds a match. If there is a match, the case's statement is executed. For example, if the selector expression's value matches *value1*, *statement1* executes.

The optional break statement (anything placed in square brackets is optional), which consists of reserved word `break` followed by a semicolon, prevents the flow of execution from continuing with the next case's statement. Instead, execution continues with the first statement following switch.

> **NOTE:** You will usually place a break statement after a case's statement. Forgetting to include break can lead to a hard-to-find bug. However, there are situations where you want to group several cases together and have them execute common code. In such a situation, you would omit the break statement from the participating cases.

If none of the cases' values match the selector expression's value, and if a default case (signified by the `default` reserved word followed by a colon) is present, the default case's statement is executed.

Listing 2–15 demonstrates switch.

Listing 2–15. *Using switch to output a compass direction*

```
class Compass
{
   static final int NORTH = 0;
   static final int SOUTH = 1;
   static final int WEST = 2;
   static final int EAST = 3;
   void printDirection(int dir)
   {
      switch (dir)
      {
         case NORTH: System.out.println("You are travelling north."); break;
         case SOUTH: System.out.println("You are travelling south."); break;
         case EAST : System.out.println("You are travelling east."); break;
         case WEST : System.out.println("You are travelling west."); break;
         default   : System.out.println("Unknown direction");
      }
   }
}
```

Listing 2–15's Compass class is an example of an *enumerated type*, a named sequence of related constants. NORTH, SOUTH, EAST, and WEST are Compass's set of constants.

Java version 5 introduced the enum as an improved enumerated type that overcomes problems with the listing's form of enumerated type. This feature includes a change to the switch statement, which I will discuss when I cover enums in Chapter 5.

> **NOTE:** Java version 7 introduces the ability to switch on a string-based selector expression. In this situation, each case's value is a string literal. I will demonstrate this form of the switch statement in the next section.

Loops

It is sometimes necessary to execute a statement repeatedly. This repeated execution is called a *loop*.

Java provides three kinds of loop statements: for, while, and do-while.

The for statement has the following syntax:

```
for ([initialize]; [test]; [update])
    statement
```

This statement consists of reserved word for, followed by a header in parentheses, followed by a statement to execute. The header consists of an optional initialization section, followed by an optional test section, followed by an optional update section. A non-optional semicolon separates each of the first two sections from the next section.

The initialization section consists of a comma-separated list of local variable declarations or variable assignments. Some or all of these variables are typically used to control the loop's duration, and are known as *loop-control variables*.

The test section consists of a Boolean expression that determines how long the loop executes. Execution continues as long as this expression evaluates to true.

Finally, the update section consists of a comma-separated list of expressions that typically modify the loop-control variables.

The for statement is perfect for *iterating* (looping) over an array. Each *iteration* (loop execution) accesses one of the array's elements via an *array*[*index*] expression, where *array* is the array whose element is being accessed, and *index* is the zero-based location of the element being accessed.

Listing 2–16 uses the for statement to iterate over the array of command-line arguments that is passed to the main() method. Each argument is read from the array, and Java version 7's enhanced switch statement uses the argument to determine a course of action.

Listing 2–16. *Using for with switch on a string-based selector expression to process command-line arguments*

```
public static void main(String[] args)
{
   for (int i = 0; i < args.length; i++)
      switch (args[i])
      {
         case "-v":
         case "-V": System.out.println("version 1.0");
                    break;
         default  : showUsage();
      }
}
```

Listing 2–16's for statement presents an initialization section that declares local variable i, a test section that compares i's current value to the length of the args array (every array has a length field that returns the number of elements in the array) to ensure that this value is less than the array's length, and an update section that increments i by 1. The loop continues until i's value equals the array's length.

Each *iteration* (loop execution) accesses one of the array's values via the args[i] expression. This expression returns the array's ith value (which happens to be a String object in this example). The first value is stored in args[0].

The args[i] expression serves as the switch statement's selector expression. If this String object contains -V, the second case is executed, which calls System.out.println() to output a version number message. The subsequent break statement keeps execution from falling into the default case, which calls showUsage() to output usage information when main() is called with unexpected arguments.

If this String object contains -v, the lack of a break statement following the first case causes execution to fall through to the second case, calling System.out.println(). This example demonstrates the occasional need to group cases to execute common code.

The while statement has the following syntax:

```
while (Boolean expression)
   statement
```

This statement consists of reserved word while, followed by a parenthesized Boolean expression header, followed by a statement to repeatedly execute.

The while statement first evaluates the Boolean expression. If it is true, while executes the other statement. Once again, the Boolean expression is evaluated. If it is still true, while re-executes the statement. This cyclic pattern continues.

Prompting the user to enter a specific character is one situation where while is useful. For example, suppose that you want to prompt the user to enter a specific uppercase letter or its lowercase equivalent. Listing 2–17 provides a demonstration.

Listing 2–17. *Prompting the user to enter a specific character via a while statement*

```
int ch = 0;
while (ch != 'C' && ch != 'c')
{
   System.out.println("Press C or c to continue.");
```

```
   ch = System.in.read();
}
```

Listing 2–17 begins by initializing local variable ch. This variable must be initialized; otherwise, the compiler will report an uninitialized variable when it tries to read ch's value in the while statement's Boolean expression.

This expression uses the conditional AND operator (&&) to test ch's value. This operator first evaluates its left operand, which happens to be expression ch != 'C'. (The != operator converts 'C' from 16-bit unsigned char type to 32–bit signed int type, prior to the comparison.)

If ch does not contain C (which it does not at this point—0 was just assigned to ch), this expression evaluates to true.

The && operator next evaluates its right operand, which happens to be expression ch != 'c'. Because this expression also evaluates to true, conditional AND returns true and while executes the compound statement.

The compound statement first outputs, via the System.out.println() method call, a message that prompts the user to press either the C key or the c key. It next reads the entered character via System.in.read() (discussed in Chapter 1), saving the character's integer value in ch.

Following this assignment, the compound statement ends and while reevaluates its Boolean expression.

Suppose ch contains C's integer value. Conditional AND evaluates ch != 'C', which evaluates to false. Seeing that the expression is already false, conditional AND short circuits its evaluation by not evaluating its right operand, and returns false. The while statement subsequently detects this value and terminates.

Suppose ch contains c's integer value. Conditional AND evaluates ch != 'C', which evaluates to true. Seeing that the expression is true, conditional AND evaluates ch != 'c', which evaluates to false. Once again, the while statement terminates.

> **NOTE:** A for statement can be coded as a while statement. For example,
>
> ```
> for (int i = 0; i < 10; i++)
>    System.out.println(i);
> ```
>
> is equivalent to
>
> ```
> int i = 0;
> while (i < 10)
> {
>    System.out.println(i);
>    i++;
> }
> ```

The do-while statement has the following syntax:

```
do
    statement
while(Boolean expression);
```

This statement consists of the do reserved word, followed by a statement to repeatedly execute, followed by the while reserved word, followed by a parenthesized Boolean expression header, followed by a semicolon.

The do-while statement first executes the other statement. It then evaluates the Boolean expression. If it is true, do-while executes the other statement. Once again, the Boolean expression is evaluated. If it is still true, do-while re-executes the statement. This cyclic pattern continues.

Listing 2–18 demonstrates do-while in another example of prompting the user to enter a specific uppercase letter or its lowercase equivalent.

Listing 2–18. *Prompting the user to enter a specific character via a do-while statement*

```
int ch;
do
{
    System.out.println("Press C or c to continue.");
    ch = System.in.read();
}
while (ch != 'C' && ch != 'c');
```

Listing 2–18 is similar to Listing 2–17. This time, however, the compound statement is executed prior to the test. As a result, it is no longer necessary to initialize ch—ch is assigned System.in.read()'s return value prior to the Boolean expression's evaluation.

It is sometimes useful for a loop statement to execute the empty statement repeatedly. The actual work performed by the loop statement takes place in the statement header. Listing 2–19 presents an example.

Listing 2–19. *Reading and outputting lines of text*

```
for (String line; (line = readLine()) != null; System.out.println(line));
```

Listing 2–19 uses for to present a programming idiom for copying lines of text that are read from some source, via the fictitious readLine() method in this example, to some destination, via System.out.println() in this example. Copying continues until readLine() returns null. Note the semicolon (empty statement) at the end of the line.

> **CAUTION:** Be careful with the empty statement because it can introduce subtle bugs into your code. For example, the following code fragment is supposed to output Hello on ten lines. Instead, only one instance of this string appears—the empty statement is executed ten times:
>
> ```
> for (int i = 0; i < 10; i++); // this ; represents the empty statement
>     System.out.println("Hello");
> ```

Break and Continue

What do for(;;);, while(true);, and do;while(true); have in common? Each of these loop statements presents an extreme example of an *infinite loop* (a loop that never ends).

An infinite loop is something that you should avoid because its unending execution causes your application to hang, which is not desirable from the point of view of your application's users.

> **CAUTION:** An infinite loop can also arise from a loop header's Boolean expression comparing a floating-point value against a nonzero value via the equality or inequality operator, because many floating-point values have inexact internal representations. For example, the following code fragment never ends because 0.1 does not have an exact internal representation:
>
> ```
> for (double d = 0.0; d != 1.0; d += 0.1)
>    System.out.println(d);
> ```

However, there are times when it is handy to code a loop as if it were infinite by using one of the aforementioned programming idioms. For example, you might code a while(true) loop that repeatedly prompts for a specific keystroke until the correct key is pressed.

When the correct key is pressed, the loop must end. Java provides the break statement for this purpose.

The break statement transfers execution to the first statement following a switch statement (as discussed earlier) or a loop. In either scenario, this statement consists of reserved word break followed by a semicolon.

Listing 2–20 uses break with an if decision statement to exit a while(true)-based infinite loop when the user presses the C or c key.

Listing 2–20. *Breaking out of an infinite loop*

```
int ch;
while (true)
{
   System.out.println("Press C or c to continue.");
   ch = System.in.read();
   if (ch == 'C' || ch == 'c')
      break;
}
```

The break statement is also useful in the context of a finite loop. For example, consider a scenario where an array of values is searched for a specific value, and you want to exit the loop when this value is found. Listing 2–21 reveals this scenario.

Listing 2–21. *Prematurely breaking out of a for-based loop*

```
int[] employeeIDs = { 123, 854, 567, 912, 224 };
int employeeSearchID = 912;
boolean found = false;
for (int i = 0; i < employeeIDs.length; i++)
   if (employeeSearchID == employeeIDs[i])
   {
      found = true;
      break;
   }
System.out.println((found) ? "employee " + employeeSearchID + " exists"
                           : "no employee ID matches " + employeeSearchID);
```

Listing 2–21 uses for and if to search an array of employee IDs to determine if a specific employee ID exists. If this ID is found, if's compound statement assigns true to found. Because there is no point in continuing the search, it then uses break to quit the loop.

The continue statement skips the remainder of the current loop iteration, reevaluates the header's Boolean expression, and performs another iteration (if true) or terminates the loop (if false). Continue consists of reserved word continue followed by a semicolon.

Consider a while loop that reads lines from a source and processes nonblank lines in some manner. Because it should not process blank lines, while skips the current iteration when a blank line is detected, as demonstrated in Listing 2–22.

Listing 2–22. *Skipping the remainder of the current iteration*

```
String line;
while ((line = readLine()) != null)
{
   if (isBlank(line))
      continue;
   processLine(line);
}
```

Listing 2–22 employs a fictitious isBlank() method to determine if the currently read line is blank. If this method returns true, if executes the continue statement to skip the rest of the current iteration and read the next line whenever a blank line is detected.

Look carefully at Listing 2–22 and you should realize that the continue statement is not needed. Instead, this listing can be shortened via *refactoring* (rewriting source code to improve its readability, organization, or reusability), as demonstrated in Listing 2–23.

Listing 2–23. *A refactored if statement*

```
String line;
while ((line = readLine()) != null)
{
   if (!isBlank(line))
      processLine(line);
}
```

Listing 2–23's refactoring modifies if's Boolean expression to use the logical complement operator (!). Whenever isBlank() returns false, this operator flips this value to true and if executes processLine().

Unlike break, continue does not appear to be a necessary part of the language. As you have just seen, it is possible to remove continue by inverting the Boolean expression. If you find yourself relying too much on continue, perhaps you need to refactor your code.

Java provides labeled versions of break and continue as disciplined versions of *goto*, a statement that transfers execution to a labeled statement. (Many developers hate goto because undisciplined use of this statement results in unreadable/unmaintainable code.)

> **NOTE:** Java reserves the goto identifier so that it cannot be used to name any source code entity. However, GOTO is not reserved, so it seems pointless to reserve goto.

The labeled break statement consists of break, followed by an identifier for which a matching *label* (an identifier followed by a colon) must exist. Furthermore, the label must immediately precede a loop statement.

Labeled break is useful for breaking out of *nested loops* (loops within loops). For example, Listing 2–24 reveals the labeled break statement transferring execution to the first statement that follows the outer for loop.

Listing 2–24. *Breaking out of nested for loops*

```
outer:
for (int i = 0; i < 3; i++)
   for (int j = 0; j < 3; j++)
      if (i == 1 && j == 1)
         break outer;
      else
         System.out.println("i=" + i + ", j=" + j);
System.out.println("Both loops terminated.");
```

When i's value is 1 and j's value is 1, break outer; is executed to terminate both for loops. This statement transfers execution to the first statement after the outer for loop, which happens to be System.out.println("Both loops terminated.");.

The following output is generated:

```
i=0, j=0
i=0, j=1
i=0, j=2
i=1, j=0
Both loops terminated.
```

The labeled continue statement consists of continue, followed by an identifier for which a matching *label* (an identifier followed by a colon) must exist. Furthermore, the label must immediately precede a loop statement.

Labeled continue is useful for terminating the current and future iterations of nested loops and beginning a new iteration of the labeled loop. For example, Listing 2–25 reveals the labeled continue statement terminating the inner for loop's iterations.

Listing 2–25. *Continuing the outer for loop*

```
outer:
for (int i = 0; i < 3; i++)
   for (int j = 0; j < 3; j++)
      if (i == 1 && j == 1)
         continue outer;
      else
         System.out.println("i=" + i + ", j=" + j);
System.out.println("Both loops terminated.");
```

When i's value is 1 and j's value is 1, continue outer; is executed to terminate the inner for loop and continue with the outer for loop at its next value of i. Both loops continue until they finish.

The following output is generated:

```
i=0, j=0
i=0, j=1
i=0, j=2
i=1, j=0
i=2, j=0
i=2, j=1
i=2, j=2
Both loops terminated.
```

Method Return

A void method's execution flows from its first statement to its last statement. However, Java's return statement lets a method exit prior to the last statement. As Listing 2–26 reveals, this statement consists of reserved word return followed by a semicolon.

Listing 2–26. *Returning from a method*

```
class Employee
{
   int salary;
   void setSalary(int empSalary)
   {
      if (empSalary < 0)
      {
         System.out.println("salary cannot be negative");
         return;
      }
      salary = empSalary;
   }
}
```

Listing 2–26's setSalary() method uses an if statement to detect an attempt to assign a negative value to the salary field. In this case, an error message is output and return prematurely exits the method so that the negative value cannot be assigned.

This form of the return statement is not legal in a method that returns a value. For such methods, Java provides a version of return that lets the method return a value (whose type must match the method's return type). Listing 2–27 demonstrates this version.

Listing 2–27. *Returning a value from a method*

```
int deposit(int amount)
{
   if (amount <= 0)
   {
      System.out.println("cannot deposit a negative or zero amount");
      return balance;
   }
   balance += amount;
   return balance;
}
```

Listing 2–27's deposit() method uses an if statement to detect an attempt to assign a negative or zero value to the balance field (of the previously presented CheckingAccount class), and outputs an error message when this attempt is detected. Furthermore, it returns balance's current value. If there is no problem, balance is updated and its new value is returned.

I previously declared a sum() method whose parameter list indicates that this method takes a variable number of arguments. I did not present a body for this method because I had not covered statements (especially return). Now that you have been introduced to the return statement, take a look at Listing 2–28.

Listing 2–28. *Declaring the body of a variable-argument sum() method*

```
double sum(double... values)
{
   int total = 0;
   for (int i = 0; i < values.length; i++)
      total += values[i];
   return total;
}
```

Listing 2–28's implementation totals the number of arguments passed to this method. (Behind the scenes, these arguments are stored in a one-dimensional array, as evidenced by values.length and values[i]). After these values have been totaled, this total is returned via the return statement.

Overloaded Methods

Java lets you introduce methods with the same name but different parameter lists into the same class. This feature is known as *method overloading*. When the compiler encounters a method call, it compares the called method's arguments list with each overloaded method's parameter list as it looks for the correct method to call.

Two same-named methods are overloaded if their parameter lists differ in number or order of parameters. For example, Java's String class provides overloaded public int indexOf(int ch) and public int indexOf(int ch, int fromIndex) methods. These methods differ in parameter counts. (I explore String in Chapter 7.)

Two same-named methods are overloaded if at least one parameter differs in type. For example, Java's Math class provides overloaded public static double abs(double a) and public static int abs(int a) methods. One method's parameter is a double; the other method's parameter is an int. (I explore Math in Chapter 6.)

You cannot overload a method by changing only the return type. For example, double sum(double... values) and int sum(double... values) are not overloaded. These methods are not overloaded because the compiler does not have enough information to choose which method to call when it encounters sum(1.0, 2.0) in source code.

Introducing Constructors

Constructors are named blocks of code, declared in class bodies, for constructing objects by initializing their instance fields and performing other initialization tasks.

A constructor declaration specifies the same name as the class and a (potentially empty) parameter list. However, it does not specify a return type. A return type is not necessary because the result of a constructor call is always a newly created object whose type is the constructor's class. Listing 2–29 shows you how to declare a constructor.

Listing 2–29. *Introducing a constructor into the* CheckingAccount *class*

```
class CheckingAccount
{
   String owner;
   int balance;
   static int counter;
   CheckingAccount(String acctOwner, int acctBalance)
   {
      owner = acctOwner;
      balance = acctBalance;
      counter++; // keep track of created CheckingAccount objects
   }
}
```

Listing 2–29 declares a two-parameter constructor. When this constructor is called during object creation, acctOwner and acctBalance arguments are passed to this constructor's parameters, and subsequently assigned to CheckingAccount's owner and balance instance fields.

> **CAUTION:** You cannot include the reserved word static in a constructor declaration because constructors are used to initialize objects—you can initialize class fields from within a constructor, but assigning an expression to a class field would probably make more sense. You cannot include the reserved word final in a constructor declaration because constructors cannot be inherited. (I discuss inheritance in the next chapter.)

Constructors can be overloaded, just like regular methods. For example, Listing 2–30 reveals a second CheckingAccount constructor.

Listing 2-30. *An overloaded* CheckingAccount *constructor*

```
CheckingAccount(String acctOwner)
{
   owner = acctOwner;
   balance = 100;
   counter++; // keep track of created CheckingAccount objects
}
```

Listing 2-30's constructor declaration specifies a single acctOwner parameter, which is assigned to the owner field. Furthermore, it assigns 100 to balance. (Perhaps this second constructor is called when creating a new checking account, where the initial balance must default to a minimum of $100.)

Instead of duplicating constructor code, you can have the overloaded constructor call a previously declared constructor to reuse existing code. Listing 2-31 provides a demonstration.

Listing 2-31. *Calling a* CheckingAccount *constructor from another* CheckingAccount *constructor*

```
CheckingAccount(String acctOwner)
{
   this(acctOwner, 100);
}
```

Listing 2-31's constructor declaration also specifies a single acctOwner parameter. Furthermore, it uses reserved word this to call the previous constructor with acctOwner's value and 100.

> **CAUTION:** You must use this to call another constructor—you cannot use the class's name, as in CheckingAccount(). The this() constructor call (if present) must be the first statement that is executed within the constructor—this rule prevents you from specifying multiple this() constructor calls in the same constructor. Finally, you cannot specify this() in a non-constructor method—constructors can be called only by other constructors and during object creation.

If a class does not declare a constructor, the class is assigned a default noargument constructor; this constructor is called during object creation. In addition to taking no arguments, this constructor's body is empty: it contains no initialization code for initializing objects. There is no default constructor when a constructor is declared.

Introducing Other Initializers

You previously learned how to initialize fields by assigning expressions to them. These kinds of *initializers* are known as *class field initializers* and *instance field initializers*. You also learned how to use constructors to initialize instance fields. Additionally, Java supports class initializers and instance initializers.

Class Initializers

A *class initializer* is a `static`-prefixed compound statement that is introduced into a class body. It is used to initialize a loaded class via a sequence of statements. For example, I once used a class initializer to load a custom database driver class. Listing 2–32 shows the loading details.

Listing 2–32. *Loading a database driver via a class initializer*

```
class JDBCFilterDriver implements Driver
{
   static private Driver d;
   static
   {
      // Attempt to load JDBC-ODBC Bridge Driver and register that
      // driver.
      try
      {
         Class c = Class.forName("sun.jdbc.odbc.JdbcOdbcDriver");
         d = (Driver) c.newInstance();
         DriverManager.registerDriver(new JDBCFilterDriver());
      }
      catch (Exception e)
      {
         System.out.println(e);
      }
   }
   //...
}
```

Listing 2–32's `JDBCFilterDriver` class uses its class initializer to load and instantiate the class that describes Java's JDBC-ODBC Bridge Driver, and to register a `JDBCFilterDriver` instance with Java's database driver. Although much of this listing is probably meaningless to you right now, it illustrates the usefulness of class initializers.

Instance Initializers

An *instance initializer* is a compound statement that is introduced into a class body, as opposed to being introduced into the body of a method or a constructor. The instance initializer is used to initialize an object via a sequence of statements, as demonstrated in Listing 2–33.

Listing 2–33. *Initializing a pair of arrays via an instance initializer*

```
class Graphics
{
   double[] sines = { 0.0, 0.0, /* ... */ 0.0 };   // should be 360 entries
   double[] cosines = { 0.0, 0.0, /* ... */ 0.0 }; // should be 360 entries
   {
      for (int i = 0; i < sines.length; i++)
      {
         sines[i] = Math.sin(Math.toRadians(i));
         cosines[i] = Math.cos(Math.toRadians(i));
      }
   }
}
```

Listing 2–33's `Graphics` class uses an instance initializer to initialize an object's `sines` and `cosines` arrays to the sines and cosines of angles ranging from 0 through (ideally) 360—not all array elements are present, for brevity. It is faster to read array elements than to repeatedly call `Math.sin()` and `Math.cos()` elsewhere; performance matters.

Because the code in Listing 2–33's instance initializer could just as easily have been placed in a constructor, what is the advantage in using an instance initializer? Apart from possibly clarifying source code, instance initializers are useful in anonymous classes (discussed Chapter 4), which cannot declare constructors.

Initialization Order

A class's body can contain multiple instance field initializers, class field initializers, constructors, instance initializers, and class initializers. Furthermore, class fields and instance fields initialize to default values. Understanding the order in which all of this initialization occurs is important to preventing confusion, so check out Listing 2–34.

Listing 2–34. *A complete initialization demo*

```java
// InitDemo.java

public class InitDemo
{
   static boolean bool1;
   boolean bool2;
   static byte byte1;
   byte byte2;
   static char char1;
   char char2;
   static double double1;
   double double2;
   static float float1;
   float float2;
   static int int1;
   int int2;
   static long long1;
   long long2;
   static short short1;
   short short2;
   static String string1;
   String string2;
   static
   {
      System.out.println("[class] bool1 = " + bool1);
      System.out.println("[class] byte1 = " + byte1);
      System.out.println("[class] char1 = " + char1);
      System.out.println("[class] double1 = " + double1);
      System.out.println("[class] float1 = " + float1);
      System.out.println("[class] int1 = " + int1);
      System.out.println("[class] long1 = " + long1);
      System.out.println("[class] short1 = " + short1);
      System.out.println("[class] string1 = " + string1);
      System.out.println();
   }
   {
```

```
      System.out.println("[instance] bool2 = " + bool2);
      System.out.println("[instance] byte2 = " + byte2);
      System.out.println("[instance] char2 = " + char2);
      System.out.println("[instance] double2 = " + double2);
      System.out.println("[instance] float2 = " + float2);
      System.out.println("[instance] int2 = " + int2);
      System.out.println("[instance] long2 = " + long2);
      System.out.println("[instance] short2 = " + short2);
      System.out.println("[instance] string2 = " + string2);
      System.out.println();
   }
   static
   {
      bool1 = true;
      byte1 = 127;
      char1 = 'A';
      double1 = 1.0;
      float1 = 2.0F;
      int1 = 1000000000;
      long1 = 1000000000000L;
      short1 = 32767;
      string1 = "abc";
   }
   {
      bool2 = true;
      byte2 = 127;
      char2 = 'A';
      double2 = 1.0;
      float2 = 2.0F;
      int2 = 1000000000;
      long2 = 1000000000000L;
      short2 = 32767;
      string2 = "abc";
   }
   InitDemo()
   {
      System.out.println("InitDemo() called");
      System.out.println();
   }
   static double double3 = 10.0;
   double double4 = 10.0;
   static
   {
      System.out.println("[class] double3 = " + double3);
      System.out.println();
   }
   {
      System.out.println("[instance] double4 = " + double3);
      System.out.println();
   }
   public static void main(String[] args)
   {
      System.out.println ("main() started");
      System.out.println();
      System.out.println("[class] bool1 = " + bool1);
      System.out.println("[class] byte1 = " + byte1);
      System.out.println("[class] char1 = " + char1);
```

```
            System.out.println("[class] double1 = " + double1);
            System.out.println("[class] double3 = " + double3);
            System.out.println("[class] float1 = " + float1);
            System.out.println("[class] int1 = " + int1);
            System.out.println("[class] long1 = " + long1);
            System.out.println("[class] short1 = " + short1);
            System.out.println("[class] string1 = " + string1);
            System.out.println();
            for (int i = 0; i < 2; i++)
            {
                System.out.println("About to create InitDemo object");
                System.out.println();
                InitDemo id = new InitDemo();
                System.out.println("id created");
                System.out.println();
                System.out.println("[instance] id.bool2 = " + id.bool2);
                System.out.println("[instance] id.byte2 = " + id.byte2);
                System.out.println("[instance] id.char2 = " + id.char2);
                System.out.println("[instance] id.double2 = " + id.double2);
                System.out.println("[instance] id.double4 = " + id.double4);
                System.out.println("[instance] id.float2 = " + id.float2);
                System.out.println("[instance] id.int2 = " + id.int2);
                System.out.println("[instance] id.long2 = " + id.long2);
                System.out.println("[instance] id.short2 = " + id.short2);
                System.out.println("[instance] id.string2 = " + id.string2);
                System.out.println();
            }
        }
    }
}
```

Listing 2–34's InitDemo class declares one class field and one instance field for each of
the primitive types plus String. It also introduces one explicitly initialized class field, one
explicitly initialized instance field, three class initializers, three instance initializers, and
one constructor. If you compile and run this code, you will observe the following output:

```
[class] bool1 = false
[class] byte1 = 0
[class] char1 =  // A char value defaults to Unicode 0, which cannot be printed.
[class] double1 = 0.0
[class] float1 = 0.0
[class] int1 = 0
[class] long1 = 0
[class] short1 = 0
[class] string1 = null

[class] double3 = 10.0

main() started

[class] bool1 = true
[class] byte1 = 127
[class] char1 = A
[class] double1 = 1.0
[class] double3 = 10.0
[class] float1 = 2.0
[class] int1 = 1000000000
[class] long1 = 1000000000000
```

```
[class] short1 = 32767
[class] string1 = abc

About to create InitDemo object

[instance] bool2 = false
[instance] byte2 = 0
[instance] char2 =
[instance] double2 = 0.0
[instance] float2 = 0.0
[instance] int2 = 0
[instance] long2 = 0
[instance] short2 = 0
[instance] string2 = null

[instance] double4 = 10.0

InitDemo() called

id created

[instance] id.bool2 = true
[instance] id.byte2 = 127
[instance] id.char2 = A
[instance] id.double2 = 1.0
[instance] id.double4 = 10.0
[instance] id.float2 = 2.0
[instance] id.int2 = 1000000000
[instance] id.long2 = 1000000000000
[instance] id.short2 = 32767
[instance] id.string2 = abc

About to create InitDemo object

[instance] bool2 = false
[instance] byte2 = 0
[instance] char2 =
[instance] double2 = 0.0
[instance] float2 = 0.0
[instance] int2 = 0
[instance] long2 = 0
[instance] short2 = 0
[instance] string2 = null

[instance] double4 = 10.0

InitDemo() called

id created

[instance] id.bool2 = true
[instance] id.byte2 = 127
[instance] id.char2 = A
[instance] id.double2 = 1.0
[instance] id.double4 = 10.0
[instance] id.float2 = 2.0
[instance] id.int2 = 1000000000
```

```
[instance] id.long2 = 1000000000000
[instance] id.short2 = 32767
[instance] id.string2 = abc
```

As you study this output, you will discover some interesting facts about initialization:

- Class fields initialize to default values just after a class is loaded.

- All class initialization occurs prior to the `main()` method being called.

- Class initialization is performed in a top-down manner. (Attempting to access a class field prior to its declaration causes the compiler to report an illegal forward reference.)

- Instance fields initialize to default values at the start of object creation.

- All instance initialization occurs prior to a constructor returning.

- Instance initialization is performed in a top-down manner. (Attempting to access an instance field prior to its declaration causes the compiler to report an illegal forward reference.)

Interface Versus Implementation

Every class X exposes an *interface* (a protocol consisting of constructors, methods, and [possibly] fields that are made available to objects created from other classes for use in creating and communicating with X's objects). X also provides an *implementation* (the code within exposed methods along with optional helper methods and optional supporting fields that should not be exposed) that codifies the interface. *Helper methods* are methods that assist exposed methods and should not be exposed.

When designing a class, your goal is to expose a useful interface while hiding details of that interface's implementation. You hide the implementation to prevent developers from accidentally accessing parts of your class that do not belong to the class's interface, so that you are free to change the implementation without breaking client code. Hiding the implementation is often referred to as *information hiding*. Furthermore, many developers consider implementation hiding to be part of encapsulation.

Java supports implementation hiding by providing four levels of access control, where three of these levels are indicated via a reserved word. You can use the following access control levels to control access to fields, methods, and constructors, and two of these levels to control access to classes:

- *Public*: A field, method, or constructor that is declared `public` is accessible from anywhere. Classes can be declared `public` as well.

- *Protected*: A field, method, or constructor that is declared `protected` is accessible from all classes in the same package as the member's class as well as subclasses of that class, regardless of package. (I will discuss packages in Chapter 4.)

- *Private*: A field, method, or constructor that is declared `private` cannot be accessed from beyond the class in which it is declared.

- *Package-private*: In the absence of an access control reserved word, a field, method, or constructor is only accessible to classes within the same package as the member's class. The same is true for non-public classes.

> **NOTE:** A class that is declared `public` must be stored in a file with the same name. For example, a `public` `Employee` class must be stored in `Employee.java`. A source file can only contain one `public` class.

You will often declare your class's instance fields to be `private` and provide special `public` instance methods for setting and getting their values. By convention, methods that set field values have names starting with `set` and are known as *setters*. Similarly, methods that get field values have names with `get` (or `is`, for Boolean fields) prefixes and are known as *getters*. Listing 2–35 demonstrates this pattern in the context of an Employee class declaration.

Listing 2–35. *Separation of interface from implementation*

```
public class Employee
{
    private String name;
    public Employee(String name)
    {
        setName(name);
    }
    public void setName(String empName)
    {
        name = empName; // Assign the empName argument to the name field.
    }
    public String getName()
    {
        return name;
    }
}
```

Listing 2–35 presents an interface consisting of the `public` constructor and `public` setter/getter methods. The implementation consists of the `private` name field and constructor/method code.

It might seem pointless to go to all this bother when you could simply omit `private` and access the name field directly. However, suppose you are told to introduce a new constructor that takes separate first and last name arguments, and new methods that set/get the employee's first and last names into this class. Furthermore, suppose that it has been determined that the first and last names will be accessed more often than the entire name. Listing 2–36 reveals these changes.

Listing 2–36. *Revising implementation without affecting existing interface*

```
class Employee
{
   private String firstName;
   private String lastName;
   Employee(String name)
   {
      setName(name);
   }
   Employee(String firstName, String lastName)
   {
      setName(firstName + " " + lastName);
   }
   void setName(String name)
   {
      // Assume that the first and last names are separated by a
      // single space character. indexOf() locates a character in a
      // string; substring() returns a portion of a string.
      setFirstName(name.substring(0, name.indexOf(' ')));
      setLastName(name.substring(name.indexOf(' ')+1));
   }
   String getName()
   {
      return getFirstName() + " " + getLastName();
   }
   void setFirstName(String empFirstName)
   {
      firstName = empFirstName;
   }
   String getFirstName()
   {
      return firstName;
   }
   void setLastName(String empLastName)
   {
      lastName = empLastName;
   }
   String getLastName()
   {
      return lastName;
   }
}
```

Listing 2–36 reveals that the name field has been removed in favor of new firstName and lastName fields, which were added to improve performance. Because setFirstName() and setLastName() will be called more frequently than setName(), and because getFirstName() and getLastName() will be called more frequently than getName(), it is faster (in each case) to have the first two methods set/get firstName's and lastName's values rather than having to merge either value into/extract this value from name's value.

Listing 2–36 also reveals setName() calling setFirstName() and setLastName(), and getName() calling getFirstName() and getLastName(), rather than directly accessing the firstName and lastName fields. Although avoiding direct access to these fields is not necessary in this example, imagine another implementation change that adds more code to `setFirstName()`, `setLastName()`, `getFirstName()`, and `getLastName()`; not calling these methods will result in the new code not executing.

Client code (code that instantiates and uses a class, such as `Employee`) will not break when `Employee`'s implementation changes from that shown in Listing 2–35 to that shown in Listing 2–36, because the original interface remains intact, although the interface has been extended. This lack of breakage results from hiding Listing 2–35's implementation, especially the name field.

> **TIP:** Get into the habit of developing useful interfaces while hiding implementations because it will save you much trouble when maintaining your classes.

Objects

You previously learned that objects are instantiated from classes. You also discovered Java's `new` operator in Table 2–3, and observed brief examples of this operator's usage in Listings 2–32 and 2–34. This section explores object and array creation via `new`, and also focuses on accessing fields, calling methods, and garbage collection.

Creating Objects and Arrays

The `new` operator is used to create, from a class that has already been loaded into memory, an object whose instance fields default to zero values, which you interpret as literal value `false`, `'\u0000'`, 0, 0L, 0.0, 0.0F, or `null` (depending on field type). Furthermore, this operator calls the specified constructor to initialize instance fields to appropriate nondefault values and perform other kinds of initialization. For example, `new Employee("John", "Doe")` creates an object from Listing 2–36's `Employee` class, and calls its `Employee(String firstName, String lastName)` constructor to initialize this object's instance fields to the employee's first and last names.

The `new` operator creates the object in a special region of memory known as the *heap*. Furthermore, `new` returns this object's *reference* (a value that helps the Java virtual machine locate the heap-based object). One virtual machine implementation might implement references as physical memory addresses, whereas another implementation might use *handles* (numeric identifiers that are used to locate object addresses). It does not matter how the reference is implemented because it cannot be directly accessed. About the only thing you can do with a reference is to use `==`/`!=` to compare it with `null`, a special literal value that does not refer to any object.

> **NOTE:** The reference that is returned by `new` is represented literally by reserved word `this`. Wherever `this` appears in source code, it represents the current object.

References are lost unless they are stored in fields or local variables, or passed as arguments to a method. For example, Employee emp = new Employee("John", "Doe"); stores the Employee reference that new returns in Employee variable emp (the reference and variable types must agree). This variable is known as a *reference variable*.

> **NOTE:** The String class is treated specially by Java. For example, you have previously learned that you can assign a string literal to a String variable, as in String s = "abc";. Behind the scenes, however, Java treats this statement as a shorthand for String s = new String("abc");, in which a reference to a String object is assigned to s. (I will say more about this topic when I discuss String in Chapter 7.)

The new operator is also used to create a one-dimensional array of values in the heap. When creating the array, specify new, followed by a name that identifies the type of the values that are stored in the array, followed by an integral expression between a pair of square brackets that specifies the size of the array (the number of elements).

> **NOTE:** An array is implemented as a special Java object whose read-only length field contains the array's size.

For example, you can use new to create a one-dimensional array of object references, as demonstrated in Listing 2–37.

Listing 2–37. *Creating a one-dimensional array of Employee object references*

```
Employee[] empArray = new Employee[10];
```

When you create a one-dimensional array, new zeros the bits in each array element's storage location, which you interpret as literal value false, '\u0000', 0, 0L, 0.0, 0.0F, or null (depending on element type). In the previous example, each of empArray's elements is initialized to null.

You cannot access objects via this array until you assign nonnull object references to its elements, which Listing 2–38 demonstrates.

Listing 2–38. *Storing Employee object references in a one-dimensional array*

```
for (int i = 0; i < empArray.length; i++)
    empArray[i] = new Employee("John Doe #" + i);
```

> **NOTE:** You can combine new with the array initialization syntax if desired. For example, Employee[] empArray = new Employee[] {new Employee ("John Doe")}; creates a single-element Employee array initialized to a single Employee object reference.

Suppose you want to use new to create a two-dimensional array, perhaps to assign to the temperatures field in Listing 2–3's WeatherData class. The way you accomplish this task in Java is to first create a one-dimensional row array (the outer array), and then create a one-dimensional column array (the inner array) for each row, as shown in Listing 2–39.

Listing 2–39. *Creating a two-dimensional array*

```
// Create the row array.
double[][] temperatures = new double[3][]; // Note the extra empty pair of brackets.
// Create a column array for each row.
for (int row = 0; row < temperatures.length; row++)
   temperatures[row] = new double[2]; // 2 columns per row
```

When creating the row array, you must specify an extra pair of empty brackets as part of the expression following new. (For a three-dimensional array—a one-dimensional array of tables, where this array's elements contain row arrays—you must specify two pairs of empty brackets as part of the expression following new.)

After creating a two-dimensional array, you will want to populate its elements with suitable values. For example, Listing 2–40 initializes each temperatures element, which is accessed as temperatures[row][col], to a random temperature value.

Listing 2–40. *Initializing a two-dimensional array*

```
for (int row = 0; row < temperatures.length; row++)
   for (int col = 0; col < temperatures[row].length; col++)
      temperatures[row][col] = Math.round(Math.random()*100);
```

You can subsequently output these values in a tabular format by calling Listing 2–41's for loop (this listing makes no attempt to align the temperature values in perfect columns).

Listing 2–41. *Outputting a two-dimensional array's values*

```
for (int row = 0; row < temperatures.length; row++)
{
   for (int col = 0; col < temperatures[row].length; col++)
      System.out.print(temperatures[row][col] + " ");
   System.out.println();
}
```

Accessing Fields

When you codify a class, you can often specify the field's name as is in an expression. For example, Listing 2–12's printBalance() instance method specifies the name of CheckingAccount's balance instance field in statement int magnitude = (balance < 0) ? -balance : balance;.

However, you cannot always access a field by simply specifying its name. For example, you cannot access a class field from another class in this manner. Also, you cannot access a field that is hidden from you. For example, you cannot access a private field from another class.

The following rules will help you learn how to access fields in different contexts, and even if such access is possible:

- Specify the name of a class field as is from anywhere within the same class as the class field. Example: `counter`

- Specify the name of the class field's class, followed by the member access operator (.), followed by the name of the class field from outside the class provided that its access control permits this form of access—the field is `public`, for example. Example: `CheckingAccount.counter`

- Specify the name of an instance field as is from any instance method, constructor, or instance initializer in the same class as the instance field. Example: `balance`

- Specify an object reference, followed by the member access operator, followed by the name of the instance field from any class method or class initializer within the same class as the instance field, or from outside the class provided that its access control permits this form of access. Example: `CheckingAccount ca = new CheckingAccount(); int bal = ca.balance;`

> **CAUTION:** Accessing an instance field (such as `ca.balance`) is usually not a good idea because the field exposes implementation details. However, if the class is declared as a private member of another class (a topic discussed in Chapter 4), and if its fields are frequently accessed by its enclosing class's methods, performance is often improved if these fields are accessed directly rather than being accessed via getter method calls. Although direct access opens up implementation details to the enclosing class, this is not a problem because these details are hidden to clients of the enclosing class.

Although the latter rule might seem to imply that you can access an instance field from a class context, this is not the case. Instead, you access the field from an object context.

The previous access rules are not exhaustive because there exist two more access scenarios to consider: declaring a local variable (or even a parameter) with the same name as an instance field or as a class field. In either scenario, the local variable/parameter is said to *shadow* (hide or mask) the field.

If you find that you have declared a local variable or parameter that shadows a field, you can rename the local variable/parameter, or you can use the member access operator with reserved word `this` (instance field) or class name (class field) to explicitly identify the field. Listing 2–42 uses `this` to qualify an instance field name.

Listing 2–42. *Qualifying the name field to circumvent shadowing by a same-named parameter*

```
class Employee
{
    String name;
    void setName(String name)
    {
        this.name = name; // Assign the name argument to the name field.
```

```
    }
}
```

Listing 2–42's `setName()` method uses `this.name` to refer to the `name` field, not to `setName()`'s `name` parameter.

Calling Methods

When you codify a class, you can often specify the method's name as is in a method-call statement. For example, the constructor in Listing 2–35's **Employee** class specifies the name of **Employee**'s `setName()` method in method-call statement `setName(name);`.

However, you cannot always call a method by simply specifying its name. For example, you cannot call a class method from another class in this manner. Also, you cannot call a method that is hidden from you. For example, you cannot call a private method from another class.

The following rules will help you learn how to call methods in different contexts, and even if such calling is possible:

- Specify the name of a class method as is from anywhere within the same class as the class method. Example: `main(new String[0]); // No arguments are passed`

- Specify the name of the class method's class, followed by the member access operator, followed by the name of the class method from outside the class provided that its access control permits this form of access — the method is declared `public`, for example. Example: `Math.sin(Math.toRadians(45));`

- Specify the name of an instance method as is from any instance method, constructor, or instance initializer in the same class as the instance field. Example: `processLine(line);`

- Specify an object reference, followed by the member access operator, followed by the name of the instance method from any class method or class initializer within the same class as the instance method, or from outside the class provided that its access control permits this form of access. Example: `CheckingAccount ca = new CheckingAccount("John Doe"); ca.printBalance();`

Although the latter rule might seem to imply that you can call an instance method from a class context, this is not the case. Instead, you call the method from an object context.

> **NOTE:** Field access and method call rules are combined in statement `System.out.println();`, where the leftmost member access operator accesses the `out` class field (of type `PrintStream`) in the `System` class, and where the rightmost member access operator calls this field's `println()` method.

Method-Call Stack

Method calls require a special area of memory known as the *method-call stack*. You can think of the method-call stack as a simulation of a pile of clean trays in a cafeteria—you *pop* (remove) the clean tray off of the top of the pile and the dishwasher will *push* (insert) the next clean tray onto the top of the pile.

When a method is called, the virtual machine pushes its arguments and the address of the first statement to execute following the called method onto the method-call stack. The virtual machine also allocates stack space for the method's local variables. When the method returns, the virtual machine removes local variable space, pops the address and arguments off of the stack, and transfers execution to the statement at this address.

Recursive Calls

A method normally executes statements that may include calls to other methods. However, it is occasionally convenient to have a method call itself. This scenario is known as *recursion*.

For example, suppose you need to write a method that returns a *factorial* (the product of all the positive integers up to and including a specific integer). For example, 3! (the ! is the mathematical symbol for factorial) equals 3×2×1 or 6.

Your first approach to writing this method might consist of the code presented in Listing 2–43.

Listing 2–43. *A nonrecursive approach to obtaining a factorial*

```
int factorial(int n)
{
   int product = 1;
   for (int i = 2; i <= n; i++)
      product *= i;
   return product;
}
```

Although this code accomplishes its task, factorial() could also be written in Listing 2–44's recursive style.

Listing 2–44. *A recursive approach to obtaining a factorial*

```
int factorial(int n)
{
   if (n == 1)
      return 1; // base problem
   else
      return n*factorial(n-1);
}
```

The recursive approach takes advantage of being able to express a problem in simpler terms of itself. According to Listing 2–44, the simplest problem, which is also known as the *base problem*, is 1! (1).

When an argument greater than 1 is passed to factorial(), this method breaks the problem into a simpler problem by calling itself with the next smaller argument value. Eventually, the base problem will be reached.

For example, calling factorial(4) results in the following stack of expressions:

```
4*factorial(3)
3*factorial(2)
2*factorial(1)
```

This last expression is at the top of the stack. When factorial(1) returns 1, these expressions are evaluated as the stack begins to unwind:

2*factorial(1) now becomes 2*1 (2)

3*factorial(2) now becomes 3*2 (6)

4*factorial(3) now becomes 4*6 (24)

Recursion provides an elegant way to express many problems. Additional examples include searching tree-based data structures for specific values and, in a hierarchical file system, outputting the names of all files that contain specific text.

> **CAUTION:** Recursion consumes stack space, so make sure that your recursion eventually ends in a base problem; otherwise, you will run out of stack space and your application will terminate.

Argument Passing

A method call includes a list of (potentially no) arguments being passed to the method. Arguments are passed using a style of argument passing that is known as *pass-by-value*, which is demonstrated in Listing 2–45.

Listing 2–45. *A demonstration of pass-by-value*

```
Employee emp = new Employee("John Doe");
int recommendedAnnualSalaryIncrease = 1000;
printReport(emp, recommendAnnualSalaryIncrease);
printReport(new Employee("Jane Doe"), 1500);
```

Pass-by-value passes the value of a variable (the reference value stored in emp or the 1000 value stored in recommendedAnnualSalaryIncrease, for example) or the value of some other expression (such as new Employee("Jane Doe") or 1500) to the method.

Because of pass-by-value, you cannot assign a different Employee object's reference to emp from inside printReport() via the printReport() parameter for this argument. After all, you have only passed a copy of emp's value to the method.

Chained Instance Method Calls

Two or more instance method calls can be chained together via the member access operator. For example, new CheckingAccount().deposit(1000).printBalance();. This capability lets you express code more compactly, and is also quite readable. However, you have to re-architect your methods somewhat differently, as Listing 2–46 reveals.

Listing 2–46. *Implementing instance methods so that calls to these methods can be chained together*

```
class CheckingAccount
{
   int balance;
   CheckingAccount deposit(int amount)
   {
      balance += amount;
      return this;
   }
   CheckingAccount printBalance()
   {
      int magnitude = (balance < 0) ? -balance : balance;
      String balanceRep = (balance < 0) ? "(" : "";
      balanceRep += magnitude;
      balanceRep += (balance < 0) ? ")" : "";
      System.out.println(balanceRep);
      return this;
   }
}
```

According to Listing 2–46, you must specify the name of the class as the method's return type. For example, each of deposit() and printBalance() must specify CheckingAccount as the return type. Also, you must specify return this; (return a reference to the current object) as the instance method's last statement.

Garbage Collection

Objects are created via reserved word new, but how are they destroyed? Without some way to destroy objects, they will eventually fill up the heap's available space and the application will not be able to continue.

Java solves this problem by using a *garbage collector*, code that runs in the background and checks for unreferenced objects. When it discovers an unreferenced object, the garbage collector removes it from the heap, making more heap space available.

An *unreferenced object* is an object that cannot be accessed from anywhere within an application. For example, new Employee("John", "Doe"); is an unreferenced object because the Employee reference returned by new is thrown away.

In contrast, a *referenced object* is an object where the application stores at least one reference. For example, Employee emp = new Employee("John", "Doe"); is a referenced object because variable emp contains a reference to the Employee object.

A referenced object becomes unreferenced when the application removes its last stored reference. For example, if emp is a local variable that contains the only reference to an Employee object, this object becomes unreferenced when emp's method terminates.

An application can remove a stored reference by assigning null to its reference variable. For example, emp = null; removes the reference to the Employee object that was previously stored in emp.

Java's garbage collector eliminates a form of memory leakage in C++ implementations that do not rely on a garbage collector. In these implementations, the developer must destroy dynamically created objects before they go out of scope. If they vanish before destruction, they remain in the heap. Eventually, the heap fills and the application halts.

Although this form of memory leakage is not a problem in Java, a related form of leakage is problematic: continually creating objects and forgetting to remove even one reference to each object causes the heap to fill up and the application to eventually come to a halt.

This form of memory leakage is a major problem for applications that run for lengthy periods of time—a web server is one example. For shorter-lived applications, you will normally not notice this form of memory leakage. However, it is a good habit to assign null to reference variables when their referenced objects are no longer required.

EXERCISES

The following exercises are designed to test your understanding of Java's language fundamentals:

1. What does a class declaration contain?

2. Is transient a reserved word? Is delegate a reserved word?

3. What is a variable?

4. Identify Java's only unsigned primitive type.

5. What is the difference between an instance field and a class field?

6. What is an array?

7. How do you declare a one-dimensional array variable? How do you declare a two-dimensional array variable?

8. Define scope.

9. Is string literal "The quick brown fox \jumps\ over the lazy dog." legal or illegal? Why?

10. What is the purpose of the cast operator?

11. Which operator is used to create an object?

12. Can you nest multiline comments?

13. True or false: When declaring a method that takes a variable number of arguments, you must specify the three consecutive periods just after the rightmost parameter's type name.

14. Given a two-dimensional array x, what does x.length return?

15. What is the difference between the while and do-while statements?

16. Initialize the sines and cosines array declarations using the new syntax.

17. Why is it okay for an expression assigned to an instance field to access a class field that is declared after the instance field? In contrast, it is not okay for the expression to access another instance field that is declared after the instance field.

18. What is required to create an array of objects?

19. How do you prevent a field from being shadowed?

20. How do you chain together instance method calls?

21. The factorial() method provides an example of *tail recursion*, a special case of recursion in which the method's last statement contains a recursive call, which is known as the *tail call*. Provide another example of tail recursion.

22. Merge the various CheckingAccount code fragments into a complete application.

Summary

Before you can write applications, you need to understand the fundamentals of the Java language. These fundamentals revolve around the concepts of class and object, where a class is nothing more than a template from which objects are created.

Classes are declared with reserved word class and a name. The class declaration's brace-delimited body is populated with a combination of field, method, and constructor declarations.

A field is a variable that stores a value. It initializes to a default value, although you can explicitly initialize it to a value with the help of an expression, which is a combination of variables, method calls, literals, and operators.

There are two kinds of fields: instance and class. Instance fields are used to describe entity attributes, whereas class fields are used to describe class attributes. A class field is differentiated from an instance field by being declared static.

A method is a named block of code that is called with an optional list of arguments, and possibly returns a value. Arguments are passed to parameters, which are another kind of variable. Parameters only exist while the method executes.

A method uses statements to perform tasks. A statement can be a simple statement, such as empty, local variable declaration, assignment, method-call, decision, loop, break and continue, and method-return.

A statement can be a compound statement, which contains simple and other compound statements that are placed between braces. A compound statement is also known as a block and can appear anywhere that a simple statement can appear.

A constructor is a named body of code (it is named after its class) that constructs objects by initializing their instance fields and performing other initialization tasks. Unlike methods, constructors do not have return types because they do not return anything.

Constructors (and methods) can be overloaded: they have the same names but different parameter lists. Constructors use this() to call other constructors in the same class. A class that does not declare a constructor is assigned a default noargument constructor.

In addition to letting you initialize fields by assigning expressions to them, and providing constructors for initializing objects, Java provides instance and class initializers to perform object initialization (when a constructor is not available) and class initialization.

Certain initialization rules are followed when multiple field initializers, constructors, instance initializers, and class initializers are mixed together in a class. For example, class initialization occurs prior to instance initialization.

Every class exposes an interface and also provides an implementation that codifies that interface. When designing a class, your goal is to expose a useful interface while hiding details of that interface's implementation. Hiding details is known as information hiding.

Java supports implementation hiding by providing four levels of access control: public, protected, private, and package-private. Except for package-private, each access control level is indicated via a same-named reserved word.

An object encapsulates an entity's attributes and behaviors as initialized fields and methods. The new operator creates an object from a class and calls its constructor to initialize these fields and perform other kinds of initialization.

The new operator creates the object in a special region of memory known as the heap. Furthermore, new returns this object's reference. Virtual machine implementations can implement references as physical memory addresses or as handles.

The new operator also creates a one-dimensional array of values in the heap. To create a two-dimensional array, create a one-dimensional row array and then, for each row array element, create a one-dimensional column array and assign its reference to the element.

There are rules for accessing fields. For example, to access a public class field from outside the class, you must specify the name of the class field's class, followed by the member access operator, followed by the class field's name.

A local variable or parameter shadows a field when it has the same name as the field. To access the field, either rename the local variable/parameter, or use the member access operator with reserved word this (instance field) or the class name (class field).

There are also rules for calling methods. For example, to call a public class method from outside the class, you must specify the name of a class method's class, followed by the member access operator, followed by the class method's name and argument list.

Method calls require a special area of memory known as the method-call stack. When a method is called, the virtual machine pushes its arguments and the address of the first statement to execute following the called method onto the method-call stack.

A method normally executes statements that may include calls to other methods. However, it is occasionally convenient to have a method call itself. This scenario is known as recursion.

A method call includes a list of (potentially no) arguments being passed to the method. Arguments are passed using a style of argument passing that is known as pass-by-value.

Two or more instance method calls can be chained together via the member access operator. Accomplish this task by having each method specify its class name as the method's return type, and by having the method return this.

Java uses a garbage collector to destroy objects. When it discovers an unreferenced object, the garbage collector removes it from the heap, making more heap space available.

Although the garbage collector eliminates the need to explicitly destroy objects, all references to objects that are no longer needed must be nullified, or else they will remain in the heap. This scenario is known as a memory leak.

Now that you know how to architect classes and work with objects, you are ready to write object-based applications. However, this knowledge is not enough to write object-oriented applications. To acquire that knowledge, you need to proceed to Chapter 3.

Chapter 3

Learning Object-Oriented Language Features

An *object-based language* encapsulates attributes and behaviors in objects. To be known as an *object-oriented language*, the language must also support inheritance and polymorphism. This chapter introduces you to Java's language features that support these twin pillars of object orientation. Furthermore, the chapter introduces you to interfaces, Java's ultimate abstract type mechanism.

Inheritance

Inheritance is a hierarchical relationship between entity categories in which one category inherits attributes and behaviors from at least one other category. For example, tiger inherits from animal (tiger is a kind of animal), car inherits from vehicle (car is a kind of vehicle), and checking account inherits from bank account (checking account is a kind of bank account). Animal, vehicle, and bank account are more generic categories; and tiger, car, and checking account are more specific categories.

Java supports *implementation inheritance* (class extension) by providing language features for declaring and initializing classes that are extensions of existing classes. After showing you how to use these features, this section introduces you to a special class that sits at the top of Java's class hierarchy. The section then introduces you to composition, an alternative to implementation inheritance for reusing code. Lastly, I will show you how composition can overcome problems with implementation inheritance.

> **NOTE:** Java also supports another kind of inheritance called interface inheritance. Later in this chapter, while discussing Java's interfaces language feature, I discuss interface inheritance.

Extending Classes

Java provides the reserved word extends for specifying a hierarchical relationship between two classes. For example, suppose you have a Vehicle class and want to introduce a Car class as a kind of Vehicle. Listing 3–1 uses extends to cement this relationship.

Listing 3–1. *Relating two classes via* extends

```
class Vehicle
{
   // member declarations
}
class Car extends Vehicle
{
   // member declarations
}
```

Listing 3–1 codifies a relationship that is known as an "is-a" relationship: a car is a kind of vehicle. In this relationship, Vehicle is known as the *base class*, *parent class*, or *superclass*; and Car is known as the *derived class*, *child class*, or *subclass*.

CAUTION: You cannot extend a final class. For example, if you declared Vehicle as final class Vehicle, the compiler would report an error upon encountering class Car extends Vehicle. Developers declare their classes final when they do not want these classes to be subclassed (for security or other reasons).

In addition to being capable of providing its own member declarations, Car is capable of inheriting member declarations from its Vehicle superclass. As Listing 3–2 shows, inherited members become accessible to members of the Car class.

Listing 3–2. *Inheriting members*

```
class Vehicle
{
   private String make;
   private String model;
   private int year;
   Vehicle(String make, String model, int year)
   {
      this.make = make;
      this.model = model;
      this.year = year;
   }
   String getMake()
   {
      return make;
   }
   String getModel()
   {
      return model;
   }
   int getYear()
```

```
    {
        return year;
    }
}
class Car extends Vehicle
{
    private int numWheels;
    Car(String make, String model, int year, int numWheels)
    {
        super(make, model, year);
        this.numWheels = numWheels;
    }
    public static void main(String[] args)
    {
        Car car = new Car("Ford", "Fiesta", 2009, 4);
        System.out.println("Make = " + car.getMake());
        System.out.println("Model = " + car.getModel ());
        System.out.println("Year = " + car.getYear ());
        // Normally, you cannot access a private field via an object
        // reference. However, numWheels is being accessed from
        // within a method (main()) that is part of the Car class.
        System.out.println("Number of wheels = "+car.numWheels);
    }
}
```

Listing 3–2's Vehicle class declares private fields that store a vehicle's make, model, and year; a constructor that initializes these fields to passed arguments; and getter methods that retrieve these fields' values.

The Car subclass provides a private numWheels field, a constructor that initializes a Car object's Vehicle and Car layers, and a main() class method for test-driving this application.

Car's constructor uses reserved word super to call Vehicle's constructor with Vehicle-oriented arguments, and then initializes Car's numWheels instance field. The super() call is analogous to specifying this() to call another constructor in the same class.

> **CAUTION:** The super() call can only appear in a constructor. Furthermore, it must be the first code that is specified in the constructor.
>
> If super() is not specified, and if the superclass does not have a noargument constructor, the compiler will report an error because the subclass constructor must call a noargument superclass constructor when super() is not present.

Car's main() method creates a Car object, initializing this object to a specific make, model, year, and number of wheels. Four System.out.println() method calls subsequently output this information.

The first three System.out.println() method calls retrieve their pieces of information by calling the Car instance's inherited getMake(), getModel(), and getYear() methods. The final System.out.println() method call accesses the instance's numWheels field directly.

> **NOTE:** A class whose instances cannot be modified is known as an *immutable class*. Vehicle is an example. If Car's main() method, which can directly read or write numWheels, was not present, Car would also be an example of an immutable class.
>
> A class cannot inherit constructors, nor can it inherit private fields and methods. Car does not inherit Vehicle's constructor, nor does it inherit Vehicle's private make, model, and year fields.

A subclass can *override* (replace) an inherited method so that the subclass's version of the method is called instead. Listing 3–3 shows you that the overriding method must specify the same name, parameter list, and return type as the method being overridden.

Listing 3–3. *Overriding a method*

```
class Vehicle
{
   private String make;
   private String model;
   private int year;
   Vehicle(String make, String model, int year)
   {
      this.make = make;
      this.model = model;
      this.year = year;
   }
   void describe()
   {
      System.out.println(year + " " + make + " " + model);
   }
}
class Car extends Vehicle
{
   private int numWheels;
   Car(String make, String model, int year, int numWheels)
   {
      super(make, model, year);
   }
   void describe()
   {
      System.out.print("This car is a "); // Print without newline - see Chapter 1.
      super.describe();
   }
   public static void main(String[] args)
   {
      Car car = new Car("Ford", "Fiesta", 2009, 4);
      car.describe();
   }
}
```

Listing 3–3's Car class declares a describe() method that overrides Vehicle's describe() method to output a car-oriented description. This method uses reserved word super to call Vehicle's describe() method via super.describe();.

NOTE: You call a superclass method from the overriding subclass method by prefixing the method's name with reserved word `super` and the member access operator. If you do not do this, you end up recursively calling the subclass's overriding method.

You can also use `super` and the member access operator to access non-`private` superclass fields from subclasses that replace these fields by declaring same-named fields.

If you were to compile and run Listing 3–3, you would discover that Car's overriding `describe()` method executes instead of Vehicle's overridden `describe()` method, and outputs `This car is a 2009 Ford Fiesta`.

CAUTION: You cannot override a `final` method. For example, if Vehicle's `describe()` method was declared as `final void describe()`, the compiler would report an error upon encountering an attempt to override this method in the Car class. Developers declare their methods `final` when they do not want these methods to be overridden (for security or other reasons).

Also, you cannot make an overriding method less accessible than the method it overrides. For example, if Car's `describe()` method was declared as `private void describe()`, the compiler would report an error because private access is less accessible than the default package access. However, `describe()` could be made more accessible by declaring it `public`, as in `public void describe()`.

Suppose you happened to replace Listing 3–3's `describe()` method with the method shown in Listing 3–4.

Listing 3–4. *Incorrectly overriding a method*

```
void describe(String owner)
{
    System.out.print("This car, which is owned by " + owner + ", is a ");
    super.describe();
}
```

The modified Car class now has two `describe()` methods, the explicitly declared method in Listing 3–4 and the method inherited from Vehicle. Listing 3–4 does not override Vehicle's `describe()` method. Instead, it overloads this method.

The Java compiler helps you detect an attempt to overload instead of override a method at compile time by letting you prefix a subclass's method header with the @Override annotation, as shown in Listing 3–5. (I will discuss annotations in Chapter 5.)

Listing 3–5. *Annotating an overriding method*

```
@Override void describe()
{
    System.out.print("This car is a ");
    super.describe();
}
```

Specifying @Override tells the compiler that the method overrides another method. If you overload the method instead, the compiler reports an error. Without this annotation, the compiler would not report an error because method overloading is a valid feature.

> **TIP:** Get into the habit of prefixing overriding methods with the @Override annotation. This habit will help you detect overloading mistakes much sooner.

Chapter 2 discussed the initialization order of classes and objects, where you learned that class members are always initialized first, and in a top-down order (the same order applies to instance members). Implementation inheritance adds a couple more details:

- A superclass's class initializers always execute before a subclass's class initializers.

- A subclass's constructor always calls the superclass constructor to initialize an object's superclass layer, and then initializes the subclass layer.

Java lets you extend a single class, which is commonly referred to as *single inheritance*. However, Java does not permit you to extend multiple classes, which is known as *multiple implementation inheritance*, because it leads to ambiguities.

For example, suppose Java supported multiple implementation inheritance, and you decided to model a *tiglon* (a cross between a tiger and a lioness) via the class structure shown in Listing 3–6.

Listing 3–6. *Modeling a tiglon*

```
class Tiger
{
   void describe()
   {
      // Code that outputs a description of the tiger's appearance and behaviors.
   }
}
class Lioness
{
   void describe()
   {
      // Code that outputs a description of the lioness's appearance and behaviors.
   }
}
class Tiglon extends Tiger, Lioness
{
   // Which describe() method does Tiglon inherit?
}
```

Listing 3–6 shows an ambiguity resulting from each of Tiger and Lioness possessing a describe() method. Which of these methods does Tiglon inherit? A related ambiguity arises from same-named fields, possibly of different types. Which field is inherited?

The Ultimate Superclass

A class that does not explicitly extend another class implicitly extends Java's `Object` class (located in the `java.lang` package—I will discuss packages in the next chapter). For example, Listing 3–1's `Vehicle` class extends `Object`, whereas `Car` extends `Vehicle`.

`Object` is Java's ultimate superclass because it serves as the ancestor of every other class, but does not itself extend any other class. `Object` provides a common set of methods that other classes inherit. Table 3–1 describes these methods.

Table 3–1. *Object's Methods*

Method	Description
`Object clone()`	Create and return a copy of the current object.
`boolean equals(Object obj)`	Determine if the current object is equal to the object identified by `obj`.
`void finalize()`	Finalize the current object.
`Class<?> getClass()`	Return the current object's `Class` object.
`int hashCode()`	Return the current object's hash code.
`void notify()`	Wake up one of the threads that are waiting on the current object's monitor.
`void notifyAll()`	Wake up all threads that are waiting on the current object's monitor.
`String toString()`	Return a string representation of the current object.
`void wait()`	Cause the current thread to wait on the current object's monitor until it is woken up via `notify()` or `notifyAll()`.
`void wait(long timeout)`	Cause the current thread to wait on the current object's monitor until it is woken up via `notify()` or `notifyAll()`, or until the specified `timeout` value (in milliseconds) has elapsed, whichever comes first.
`void wait` `(long timeout, int nanos)`	Cause the current thread to wait on the current object's monitor until it is woken up via `notify()` or `notifyAll()`, or until the specified `timeout` value (in milliseconds) plus nanos value (in nanoseconds) has elapsed, whichever comes first.

I will discuss getClass(), notify(), notifyAll(), and the wait() methods in Chapter 7.

Cloning

The clone() method *clones* (duplicates) an object without calling a constructor. It copies each primitive or reference field's value to its counterpart in the clone, a task known as *shallow copying* or *shallow cloning*. Listing 3–7 demonstrates this behavior.

Listing 3–7. *Shallowly cloning an* Employee *object*

```
class Employee implements Cloneable
{
   String name;
   int age;
   Employee(String name, int age)
   {
      this.name = name;
      this.age = age;
   }
   public static void main(String[] args) throws CloneNotSupportedException
   {
      Employee e1 = new Employee("John Doe", 46);
      Employee e2 = (Employee) e1.clone();
      System.out.println(e1 == e2); // Output: false
      System.out.println(e1.name == e2.name); // Output: true
   }
}
```

Listing 3–7 declares an Employee class with name and age instance fields, and a constructor for initializing these fields. The main() method uses this constructor to initialize a new Employee object's copies of these fields to John Doe and 46.

> **NOTE:** A class must implement the Cloneable interface or its instances cannot be shallowly cloned via Object's clone() method—this method performs a runtime check to see if the class implements Cloneable. (I will discuss interfaces later in this chapter.) If a class does not implement Cloneable, clone() throws CloneNotSupportedException. (Because CloneNotSupportedException is a checked exception, it is necessary for Listing 3–7 to satisfy the compiler by appending throws CloneNotSupportedException to the main() method's header. I will discuss exceptions in the next chapter.) String is an example of a class that does not implement Cloneable; hence, String objects cannot be shallowly cloned.

After assigning the Employee object's reference to local variable e1, main() calls the clone() method on this variable to duplicate the object, and then assigns the resulting reference to variable e2. The (Employee) cast is needed because clone() returns Object.

To prove that the objects whose references were assigned to e1 and e2 are different, main() next compares these references via == and outputs the Boolean result, which happens to be false.

To prove that the Employee object was shallowly cloned, main() next compares the references in both Employee objects' name fields via == and outputs the Boolean result, which happens to be true.

NOTE: Object's clone() method was originally specified as a public method, which meant that any object could be cloned from anywhere. For security reasons, this access was later changed to protected, which means that only code within the same package as the class whose clone() method is to be called, or code within a subclass of this class (regardless of package), can call clone().

Shallow cloning is not always desirable because the original object and its clone refer to the same object via their equivalent reference fields. For example, each of Listing 3–7's two Employee objects refers to the same String object via its name field.

Although not a problem for String, whose instances are immutable, changing a mutable object via the clone's reference field results in the original (noncloned) object seeing the same change via its equivalent reference field.

For example, suppose you add a reference field named hireDate to Employee. This field is of type Date with year, month, and day fields. Because Date is mutable, you can change the contents of these fields in the Date instance assigned to hireDate.

Now suppose you plan to change the clone's date, but want to preserve the original Employee object's date. You cannot do this with shallow cloning because the change is also visible to the original Employee object.

To solve this problem, you must modify the cloning operation so that it assigns a new Date reference to the Employee clone's hireDate field. This task, which is known as *deep copying* or *deep cloning*, is demonstrated in Listing 3–8.

Listing 3–8. *Deeply cloning an* Employee *object*

```
class Date
{
   int year, month, day;
   Date(int year, int month, int day)
   {
      this.year = year;
      this.month = month;
      this.day = day;
   }
}
class Employee implements Cloneable
{
   String name;
   int age;
   Date hireDate;
   Employee(String name, int age, Date hireDate)
   {
      this.name = name;
      this.age = age;
      this.hireDate = hireDate;
   }
   @Override protected Object clone() throws CloneNotSupportedException
   {
      Employee emp = (Employee) super.clone();
```

```
    if (hireDate != null) // no point cloning a null object (one that does not exist)
        emp.hireDate = new Date(hireDate.year, hireDate.month, hireDate.day);
    return emp;
    }
    public static void main(String[] args) throws CloneNotSupportedException
    {
        Employee e1 = new Employee("John Doe", 46, new Date(2000, 1, 20));
        Employee e2 = (Employee) e1.clone();
        System.out.println(e1 == e2); // Output: false
        System.out.println(e1.name == e2.name); // Output: true
        System.out.println(e1.hireDate == e2.hireDate); // Output: false
        System.out.println(e2.hireDate.year + " " + e2.hireDate.month + " " +
                           e2.hireDate.day); // Output: 2000 1 20
    }
}
```

Listing 3–8 declares Date and Employee classes. The Date class declares year, month, and day fields and a constructor. (You can declare a comma-separated list of variables on one line provided that these variables all share the same type, which is int in this case.)

The Employee class overrides the clone() method to deeply clone the hireDate field. This method first calls the Object superclass's clone() method to shallowly clone the current Employee instance's fields, and then stores the new instance's reference in emp.

The clone() method next assigns a new Date instance to emp's hireDate field, where this instance's fields are initialized to the same values as those in the original Employee object's hireDate instance.

At this point, you have an Employee clone with shallowly cloned name and age fields, and a deeply cloned hireDate field. The clone() method finishes by returning this Employee clone.

> **NOTE:** If you are not calling Object's clone() method from an overridden clone() method (because you prefer to deeply clone reference fields and do your own shallow copying of non-reference fields), it is not necessary for the class containing the overridden clone() method to implement Cloneable, but it should implement this interface for consistency. String does not override clone(), so String objects cannot be deeply cloned.

Equality

The == and != operators compare two primitive values (such as integers) for equality (==) or inequality (!=). These operators also compare two references to see if they refer to the same object or not. This latter comparison is known as an *identity check*.

You cannot use == and != to determine if two objects are logically the same (or not). For example, two Car objects with the same field values are logically equivalent. However, == reports them as unequal because of their different references.

NOTE: Because == and != perform the fastest possible comparisons, and because string comparisons need to be performed quickly (especially when sorting a huge number of strings), the String class contains special support that allows literal strings and string-valued constant expressions to be compared via == and !=. (I will discuss this support when I present String in Chapter 7.) The following statements demonstrate these comparisons:

```
System.out.println("abc" == "abc"); // Output: true
System.out.println("abc" == "a" + "bc"); // Output: true
System.out.println("abc" == "Abc"); // Output: false
System.out.println("abc" != "def"); // Output: true
System.out.println("abc" == new String("abc")); // Output: false
```

Recognizing the need to support logical equality in addition to reference equality, Java provides an equals() method in the Object class. Because this method defaults to comparing references, you need to override equals() to compare object contents.

Before overriding equals(), make sure that this is necessary. For example, Java's StringBuffer class does not override equals(). Perhaps this class's designers did not think it necessary to determine if two StringBuffer objects are logically equivalent.

You cannot override equals() with arbitrary code. Doing so will probably prove disastrous to your applications. Instead, you need to adhere to the contract that is specified in the Java documentation for this method, and which I present next.

The equals() method implements an equivalence relation on nonnull object references:

- *It is reflexive*: For any nonnull reference value x, x.equals(x) returns true.

- *It is symmetric*: For any nonnull reference values x and y, x.equals(y) returns true if and only if y.equals(x) returns true.

- *It is transitive*: For any nonnull reference values x, y, and z, if x.equals(y) returns true and y.equals(z) returns true, then x.equals(z) returns true.

- *It is consistent*: For any nonnull reference values x and y, multiple invocations of x.equals(y) consistently return true or consistently return false, provided no information used in equals() comparisons on the objects is modified.

- For any nonnull reference value x, x.equals(null) returns false.

Although this contract probably looks somewhat intimidating, it is not that difficult to satisfy. For proof, take a look at the implementation of the equals() method in Listing 3–9's Point class.

Listing 3–9. *Logically comparing* Point *objects*

```
class Point
{
   private int x, y;
   Point(int x, int y)
   {
      this.x = x;
      this.y = y;
   }
   int getX()
   {
      return x;
   }
   int getY()
   {
      return y;
   }
   @Override public boolean equals(Object o)
   {
      if (!(o instanceof Point))
         return false;
      Point p = (Point) o;
      return p.x == x && p.y == y;
   }
   public static void main(String[] args)
   {
      Point p1 = new Point(10, 20);
      Point p2 = new Point(20, 30);
      Point p3 = new Point(10, 20);
      // Test reflexivity
      System.out.println(p1.equals(p1)); // Output: true
      // Test symmetry
      System.out.println(p1.equals(p2)); // Output: false
      System.out.println(p2.equals(p1)); // Output: false
      // Test transitivity
      System.out.println(p2.equals(p3)); // Output: false
      System.out.println(p1.equals(p3)); // Output: true
      // Test nullability
      System.out.println(p1.equals(null)); // Output: false
      // Extra test to further prove the instanceof operator's usefulness.
      System.out.println(p1.equals("abc")); // Output: false
   }
}
```

Listing 3–9's overriding equals() method begins with an if statement that uses the instanceof operator to determine if the argument passed to parameter o is an instance of the Point class. If not, the if statement executes return false;.

The o instanceof Point expression satisfies the last portion of the contract: For any nonnull reference value *x*, *x*.equals(null) returns false. Because null is not an instance of any class, passing this value to equals() causes the expression to evaluate to false.

The o instanceof Point expression also prevents a ClassCastException instance from being thrown via expression (Point) o in the event that you pass an object other than a Point object to equals(). (I will discuss exceptions in the next chapter.)

Following the cast, the contract's reflexivity, symmetry, and transitivity requirements are met by only allowing `Points` to be compared with other `Points`, via expression `p.x == x && p.y == y`.

The final contract requirement, consistency, is met by making sure that the `equals()` method is deterministic. In other words, this method does not rely on any field value that could change from method call to method call.

> **TIP:** You can optimize the performance of a time-consuming `equals()` method by first using `==` to determine if o's reference identifies the current object. Simply specify `if (o == this) return true;` as the `equals()` method's first statement. This optimization is not necessary in Listing 3–9's `equals()` method, which has satisfactory performance.

It is important to always override the `hashCode()` method when overriding `equals()`. I did not do so in Listing 3–9 because I have yet to formally introduce `hashCode()`.

Finalization

Finalization refers to cleanup. The `finalize()` method's Java documentation states that `finalize()` is "called by the garbage collector on an object when garbage collection determines that there are no more references to the object. A subclass overrides the `finalize()` method to dispose of system resources or to perform other cleanup."

`Object`'s version of `finalize()` does nothing; you must override this method with any needed cleanup code. Because the virtual machine might never call `finalize()` before an application terminates, you should provide an explicit cleanup method, and have `finalize()` call this method as a safety net in case the method is not otherwise called.

> **CAUTION:** Never depend on `finalize()` for releasing limited resources such as graphics contexts or file descriptors. For example, if an application object opens files, expecting that its `finalize()` method will close them, the application might find itself unable to open additional files when a tardy virtual machine is slow to call `finalize()`. What makes this problem worse is that `finalize()` might be called more frequently on another virtual machine, resulting in this too-many-open-files problem not revealing itself. The developer might falsely believe that the application behaves consistently across different virtual machines.

If you decide to override `finalize()`, your object's subclass layer must give its superclass layer an opportunity to perform finalization. You can accomplish this task by specifying `super.finalize();` as the last statement in your method, which Listing 3–10 demonstrates.

Listing 3–10. *A properly coded* finalize() *method for a subclass*

```
protected void finalize() throws Throwable
{
   try
   {
      // Perform subclass cleanup.
   }
   finally
   {
      super.finalize();
   }
}
```

Listing 3–10's finalize() declaration appends throws Throwable to the method header because the cleanup code might throw an exception. If an exception is thrown, execution leaves the method and, in the absence of try-finally, super.finalize(); never executes. (I will discuss exceptions and try-finally in Chapter 4.)

To guard against this possibility, the subclass's cleanup code executes in a compound statement that follows reserved word try. If an exception is thrown, Java's exception-handling logic executes the compound statement following the finally reserved word, and super.finalize(); executes the superclass's finalize() method.

Hash Codes

The hashCode() method returns a 32-bit integer that identifies the current object's *hash code*, a small value that results from applying a mathematical function to a potentially large amount of data. The calculation of this value is known as *hashing*.

You must override hashCode() when overriding equals(), and in accordance with the following contract, which is specified in hashCode()'s Java documentation:

- Whenever it is invoked on the same object more than once during an execution of a Java application, the hashCode() method must consistently return the same integer, provided no information used in equals(Object) comparisons on the object is modified. This integer need not remain consistent from one execution of an application to another execution of the same application.

- If two objects are equal according to the equals(Object) method, then calling the hashCode() method on each of the two objects must produce the same integer result.

- It is not required that if two objects are unequal according to the equals(Object) method, then calling the hashCode() method on each of the two objects must produce distinct integer results. However, the programmer should be aware that producing distinct integer results for unequal objects might improve the performance of hash tables.

Fail to obey this contract and your class's instances will not work properly with Java's hash-based collections, such as HashMap. (I will discuss collections in Chapter 8.)

If you override `equals()` but not `hashCode()`, you most importantly violate the second item in the contract: The hash codes of equal objects must also be equal. This violation can lead to serious consequences, as demonstrated in Listing 3–11.

Listing 3–11. *The problem of not overriding* `hashCode()`

```
java.util.Map map = new java.util.HashMap();
map.put(p1, "first point");
System.out.println(map.get(p1)); // Output: first point
System.out.println(map.get(new Point(10, 20))); // Output: null
```

Assume that Listing 3–11's statements are appended to Listing 3–9's `main()` method. After `main()` creates its `Point` objects and calls its `System.out.println()` methods, it executes Listing 3–11's statements, which perform the following tasks:

- The first statement instantiates the `HashMap` class, which is located in the `java.util` package. (I will discuss packages in the next chapter.)

- The second statement calls `HashMap`'s `put()` method to store Listing 3–9's `p1` object key and the `"first point"` value in the hashmap.

- The third statement retrieves the value of the hashmap entry whose `Point` key is logically equal to `p1` via `HashMap`'s `get()` method.

- The fourth statement is equivalent to the third statement, but returns the null reference instead of `"first point"`.

Although objects `p1` and `Point(10, 20)` are logically equivalent, these objects have different hash codes, resulting in each object referring to a different entry in the hashmap. If an object is not stored (via `put()`) in that entry, `get()` returns null.

Correcting this problem requires that `hashCode()` be overridden in order to return the same integer value for logically equivalent objects. I will show you how to accomplish this task when I discuss `HashMap` in Chapter 8.

String Representation

The `toString()` method returns a string-based representation of the current object. This representation defaults to the object's class name, followed by the @ symbol, followed by a hexadecimal representation of the object's hash code.

For example, if you were to execute `System.out.println(p1);` to output Listing 3–9's `p1` object, you would see a line of output similar to `Point@3e25a5`. (`System.out.println()` calls `p1`'s inherited `toString()` method behind the scenes.)

You should strive to override `toString()` so that it returns a concise but meaningful description of the object. For example, you might declare, in Listing 3–9's `Point` class, a `toString()` method that is similar to Listing 3–12's `toString()` method.

Listing 3–12. *Returning a meaningful string-based representation of a* `Point` *object*

```
public String toString()
{
   return "(" + x + ", " + y + ")";
}
```

This time, executing System.out.println(p1); results in more meaningful output, such as (10, 20).

Composition

Implementation inheritance and composition offer two different approaches to reusing code. As you have learned, implementation inheritance is concerned with extending a class with a new class, which is based upon an "is-a" relationship between them: a Car is a Vehicle, for example.

On the other hand, *composition* is concerned with composing classes out of other classes, which is based upon a "has-a" relationship between them. For example, a Car has an Engine, Wheels, and a SteeringWheel.

You have already seen examples of composition in Chapter 2 and this chapter. For example, Chapter 2's CheckingAccount class included a String owner field. Listing 3–13's Car class provides another example of composition.

Listing 3–13. *A Car class whose instances are composed of other objects*

```
class Car extends Vehicle
{
   private Engine engine;
   private Wheel[] wheels;
   private SteeringWheel steeringWheel;
}
```

Listing 3–13 demonstrates that composition and implementation inheritance are not mutually exclusive. Although not shown, Car inherits various members from its Vehicle superclass, in addition to providing its own engine, wheels, and steeringwheel fields.

The Trouble with Implementation Inheritance

Implementation inheritance is potentially dangerous, especially when the developer does not have complete control over the superclass, or when the superclass is not designed and documented with extension in mind.

The problem is that implementation inheritance breaks encapsulation. The subclass relies on implementation details in the superclass. If these details change in a new version of the superclass, the subclass might break, even if the subclass is not touched.

For example, suppose you have purchased a library of Java classes, and one of these classes describes an appointment calendar. Although you do not have access to this class's source code, assume that Listing 3–14 describes part of its code.

Listing 3–14. *An appointment calendar class*

```
public class ApptCalendar
{
   private final static int MAX_APPT = 1000;
   private Appt[] appts;
   private int size;
```

```
      public ApptCalendar()
      {
         appts = new Appt[MAX_APPT];
         size = 0; // redundant because field automatically initialized to 0
                   // adds clarity, however
      }
      public void addAppt(Appt appt)
      {
         if (size == appts.length)
            return; // array is full
         appts[size++] = appt;
      }
      public void addAppts(Appt[] appts)
      {
         for (int i = 0; i < appts.length; i++)
            addAppt(appts[i]);
      }
   }
```

Listing 3–14's ApptCalendar class stores an array of appointments, with each appointment described by an Appt instance. For this discussion, the details of Appt are irrelevant.

Suppose you want to log each appointment in a file. Because a logging capability is not provided, you extend ApptCalendar with Listing 3–15's LoggingApptCalendar class, which adds logging behavior in overriding addAppt() and addAppts() methods.

Listing 3–15. *Extending the appointment calendar class*

```
public class LoggingApptCalendar extends ApptCalendar
{
   // A constructor is not necessary because the Java compiler will add a
   // noargument constructor that calls the superclass's noargument
   // constructor by default.
   @Override public void addAppt(Appt appt)
   {
      Logger.log(appt.toString());
      super.addAppt(appt);
   }
   @Override public void addAppts(Appt[] appts)
   {
      for (int i = 0; i < appts.length; i++)
         Logger.log(appts[i].toString());
      super.addAppts(appts);
   }
}
```

Listing 3–15's LoggingApptCalendar class relies on a Logger class whose log() class method logs a string to a file (the details are unimportant). Notice the use of toString() to convert an Appt object to a String object, which is then passed to log().

Although this class looks okay, it does not work as you might expect. Suppose you instantiate this class and add a few Appt instances to this instance via addAppts(), as demonstrated in Listing 3–16.

Listing 3–16. *Demonstrating the logging appointment calendar*

```
LoggingApptCalendar lapptc = new LoggingApptCalendar();
lapptc.addAppts(new Appt[] {new Appt(), new Appt(), new Appt()});
```

If you also add a `System.out.println()` method call to `Logger`'s `log()` method, to output this method's argument, you will discover that `log()` outputs a total of six messages; each of the expected three messages (one per `Appt` object) is duplicated.

When `LoggingApptCalendar`'s `addAppts()` method is called, it first calls `Logger.log()` for each `Appt` instance in the `appts` array that is passed to `addAppts()`. This method then calls `ApptCalendar`'s `addAppts()` method via `super.addAppts(appt);`.

`ApptCalendar`'s `addAppts()` method calls `LoggingApptCalendar`'s overriding `addAppt()` method for each `Appt` instance in its `appts` array argument. `addAppt()` calls `Logger.log()` to log its `appt` argument, and you end up with three additional logged messages.

If you did not override the `addAppts()` method, this problem would go away. However, the subclass would be tied to an implementation detail: `ApptCalendar`'s `addAppts()` method calls `addAppt()`.

It is not a good idea to rely on an implementation detail when the detail is not documented. (I previously stated that you do not have access to `ApptCalendar`'s source code.) When a detail is not documented, it can change in a new version of the class.

Because a base class change can break a subclass, this problem is known as the *fragile base class problem*. A related cause of fragility that also has to do with overriding methods occurs when new methods are added to a superclass in a subsequent release.

For example, suppose a new version of the library introduces a new `public void addAppt(Appt appt, boolean unique)` method into the `ApptCalendar` class. This method adds the `appt` instance to the calendar when `unique` is false, and, when `unique` is true, adds the `appt` instance only if it has not previously been added.

Because this method has been added after the `LoggingApptCalendar` class was created, `LoggingApptCalendar` does not override the new `addAppt()` method with a call to `Logger.log()`. As a result, `Appt` instances passed to the new `addAppt()` method are not logged.

Here is another problem: You introduce a method into the subclass that is not also in the superclass. A new version of the superclass presents a new method that matches the subclass method signature and return type. Your subclass method now overrides the superclass method, and probably does not fulfill the superclass method's contract.

There is a way to make these problems disappear. Instead of extending the superclass, create a private field in a new class, and have this field reference an instance of the superclass. This task demonstrates composition because you are forming a has-a relationship between the new class and the superclass.

Additionally, have each of the new class's instance methods call the corresponding superclass method via the superclass instance that was saved in the private field, and also return the called method's return value. This task is known as *forwarding*, and the new methods are known as *forwarding methods*.

Listing 3–17 presents an improved LoggingApptCalendar class that uses composition and forwarding to forever eliminate the fragile base class problem and the additional problem of unanticipated method overriding.

Listing 3–17. *A composed logging appointment calendar class*

```
public class LoggingApptCalendar
{
   private ApptCalendar apptCal;
   public LoggingApptCalendar(ApptCalendar apptCal)
   {
      this.apptCal = apptCal;
   }
   public void addAppt(Appt appt)
   {
      Logger.log(appt.toString());
      apptCal.addAppt(appt);
   }
   public void addAppts(Appt[] appts)
   {
      for (int i = 0; i < appts.length; i++)
         Logger.log(appts[i].toString());
      apptCal.addAppts(appts);
   }
}
```

Listing 3–17's LoggingApptCalendar class does not depend upon implementation details of the ApptCalendar class. You can add new methods to ApptCalendar and they will not break LoggingApptCalendar.

> **NOTE:** LoggingApptCalendar is an example of a *wrapper class*, a class whose instances wrap other instances. Each LoggingApptCalendar instance wraps an ApptCalendar instance.
>
> LoggingApptCalendar is also an example of the *Decorator design pattern*, which is presented on page 175 of *Design Patterns: Elements of Reusable Object-Oriented Software* by Erich Gamma, Richard Helm, Ralph Johnson, and John Vlissides (Addison-Wesley, 1995; ISBN: 0201633612).

When should you extend a class and when should you use a wrapper class? Extend a class when an is-a relationship exists between the superclass and the subclass, and either you have control over the superclass or the superclass has been designed and documented for class extension. Otherwise, use a wrapper class.

What does "design and document for class extension" mean? Design means provide protected methods that hook into the class's inner workings (to support writing efficient subclasses), and ensure that constructors and the clone() method never call overridable methods. Document means clearly state the impact of overriding methods.

CAUTION: Wrapper classes should not be used in a *callback framework*, an object framework in which an object passes its own reference to another object (via `this`) so that the latter object can call the former object's methods at a later time. This "calling back to the former object's method" is known as a *callback*. Because the wrapped object does not know of its wrapper class, it passes only its reference (via `this`), and resulting callbacks do not involve the wrapper class's methods.

Polymorphism

Polymorphism is the ability to change forms. Examples of polymorphism abound in nature. For example, water is naturally a liquid, but it changes to a solid when frozen, and it changes to a gas when heated to its boiling point.

Java supports several kinds of polymorphism:

- *Coercion*: An operation serves multiple types through implicit type conversion. For example, division lets you divide an integer by another integer, or divide a floating-point value by another floating-point value. If one operand is an integer and the other operand is a floating-point value, the compiler *coerces* (implicitly converts) the integer to a floating-point value, to prevent a type error. (There is no division operation that supports an integer operand and a floating-point operand.) Passing a subclass object reference to a method's superclass parameter is another example of coercion polymorphism. The compiler coerces the subclass type to the superclass type, to restrict operations to those of the superclass.

- *Overloading*: The same operator symbol or method name can be used in different contexts. For example, + can be used to perform integer addition, floating-point addition, or string concatenation, depending on the types of its operands. Also, multiple methods having the same name can appear in a class (through declaration and/or inheritance).

- *Parametric*: Within a class declaration, a field name can associate with different types and a method name can associate with different parameter and return types. The field and method can then take on different types in each class instance. For example, a field might be of type `Integer` and a method might return an `Integer` in one class instance, and the same field might be of type `String` and the same method might return a `String` in another class instance. Java supports parametric polymorphism via generics, which I will discuss in Chapter 5.

■ *Subtype*: A type can serve as another type's subtype. When a subtype instance appears in a supertype context, executing a supertype operation on the subtype instance results in the subtype's version of that operation executing. For example, suppose that `Circle` is a subclass of `Point`, and that both classes contain a `draw()` method. Assigning a `Circle` instance to a variable of type `Point`, and then calling the `draw()` method via this variable, results in `Circle`'s `draw()` method being called.

Many developers do not regard coercion and overloading as valid kinds of polymorphism. They see coercion and overloading as nothing more than type conversions and *syntactic sugar* (syntax that simplifies a language, making it "sweeter" to use). In contrast, parametric and subtype are regarded as valid polymorphisms.

This section focuses on subtype polymorphism by first examining upcasting and late binding. The section then introduces you to abstract classes and abstract methods, downcasting and runtime type identification, and covariant return types.

Upcasting and Late Binding

Listing 3–9's Point class represents a point as an x-y pair. Because a circle (in this example) is an x-y pair denoting its center, and has a radius denoting its extent, you can extend Point with a Circle class that introduces a radius field. Check out Listing 3–18.

Listing 3–18. *A Circle class extending the Point class*

```
class Circle extends Point
{
   private int radius;
   Circle(int x, int y, int radius)
   {
      super(x, y);
      this.radius = radius;
   }
   int getRadius()
   {
      return radius;
   }
}
```

The fact that Circle is really a Point with a radius implies that you can treat a Circle instance as if it was a Point instance. Accomplish this task by assigning the Circle instance to a Point variable, as demonstrated in Listing 3–19.

Listing 3–19. *Upcasting from Circle to Point*

```
Circle c = new Circle(10, 20, 30);
Point p = c;
```

The cast operator is not needed to convert from Circle to Point because access to a Circle instance via Point's interface is legal. After all, a Circle is at least a Point. This assignment is known as *upcasting* because you are implicitly casting up the type hierarchy (from the Circle subclass to the Point superclass).

After upcasting `Circle` to `Point`, you cannot call `Circle`'s `getRadius()` method because this method is not part of `Point`'s interface. Losing access to subtype features after narrowing it to a superclass seems useless, but is necessary for achieving subtype polymorphism.

In addition to upcasting the subclass instance to a variable of the superclass type, subtype polymorphism involves declaring a method in the superclass and overriding this method in the subclass.

For example, suppose `Point` and `Circle` are to be part of a graphics application, and you need to introduce a `draw()` method into each class to draw a point and a circle, respectively. You end with the class structure shown in Listing 3–20.

Listing 3–20. *Declaring a graphics application's* `Point` *and* `Circle` *classes*

```
class Point
{
    private int x, y;
    Point(int x, int y)
    {
        this.x = x;
        this.y = y;
    }
    int getX()
    {
        return x;
    }
    int getY()
    {
        return y;
    }
    @Override public String toString()
    {
        return "(" + x + ", " + y + ")";
    }
    void draw()
    {
        System.out.println("Point drawn at " + toString ());
    }
}
class Circle extends Point
{
    private int radius;
    Circle(int x, int y, int radius)
    {
        super(x, y);
        this.radius = radius;
    }
    int getRadius()
    {
        return radius;
    }
    @Override public String toString()
    {
        return "" + radius;
    }
}
```

```
@Override void draw()
{
    System.out.println("Circle drawn at " + super.toString() +
                       " with radius " + toString());
}
}
```

Although the draw() methods will ultimately draw graphics shapes, simulating their behaviors via System.out.println() method calls is sufficient during the early testing phase of the graphics application.

Now that you have temporarily finished with Point and Circle, you want to test their draw() methods in a simulated version of the graphics application. To achieve this objective, you write Listing 3–21's Graphics class.

Listing 3–21. *A* Graphics *class for testing* Point*'s and* Circle*'s* draw() *methods*

```
class Graphics
{
    public static void main(String[] args)
    {
        Point[] points = new Point[] {new Point(10, 20), new Circle(10, 20, 30)};
        for (int i = 0; i < points.length; i++)
            points[i].draw();
    }
}
```

Listing 3–21's main() method first declares an array of Points. Upcasting is demonstrated by first having the array's initializer instantiate the Circle class, and then by assigning this instance's reference to the second element in the points array.

Moving on, main() uses a for loop to call each Point element's draw() method. Because the first iteration calls Point's draw() method, whereas the second iteration calls Circle's draw() method, you observe the following output:

```
Point drawn at (10, 20)
Circle drawn at (10, 20) with radius 30
```

How does Java "know" that it must call Circle's draw() method on the second loop iteration? Should it not call Point's draw() method because Circle is being treated as a Point thanks to the upcast?

At compile time, the compiler does not know which method to call. All it can do is verify that a method exists in the superclass, and verify that the method call's arguments list and return type match the superclass's method declaration.

In lieu of knowing which method to call, the compiler inserts an instruction into the compiled code that, at runtime, fetches and uses whatever reference is in points[1] to call the correct draw() method. This task is known as *late binding*.

Late binding is used for calls to non-final instance methods. For all other method calls, the compiler knows which method to call, and inserts an instruction into the compiled code that calls the method associated with the variable's type (not its value). This task is known as *early binding*.

Abstract Classes and Abstract Methods

Suppose new requirements dictate that your graphics application must include a Rectangle class. Furthermore, this class must include a draw() method, and this method must be tested in a manner similar to that shown in Listing 3–21's Graphics class.

In contrast to Circle, which is a Point with a radius, it does not make sense to think of a Rectangle as a being a Point with a width and height. Rather, a Rectangle instance would probably be composed of a Point (indicating its origin) and a width and height.

Because circles, points, and rectangles are examples of shapes, it makes more sense to declare a Shape class with its own draw() method than to specify class Rectangle extends Point. Listing 3–22 presents Shape's declaration.

Listing 3–22. *Declaring a Shape class*

```
class Shape
{
   void draw() {}
}
```

You can now refactor Point to extend Listing 3–22's Shape class, leave Circle as is, and introduce a Rectangle class that extends Shape. You can then refactor Listing 3–21's Graphics class's main() method to take Shape into account. Check out Listing 3–23.

Listing 3–23. *A new main() method for the Graphics class takes Shape into account*

```
public static void main(String[] args)
{
   Shape[] shapes = new Shape[] {new Point(10, 20), new Circle(10, 20, 30),
                                 new Rectangle(20, 30, 15, 25)};
   for (int i = 0; i < shapes.length; i++)
      shapes[i].draw();
}
```

Because Point and Rectangle directly extend Shape, and because Circle indirectly extends Shape by extending Point, Listing 3–23's main() method will call the appropriate subclass's draw() method in response to shapes[i].draw();.

Although the introduction of Shape makes our code more flexible, there is a problem. What is to stop us from instantiating Shape and adding this meaningless instance to the shapes array, as Listing 3–24 demonstrates?

Listing 3–24. *A useless instantiation*

```
Shape[] shapes = new Shape[] {new Point(10, 20), new Circle(10, 20, 30),
                              new Rectangle(20, 30, 15, 25), new Shape()};
```

What does it mean to instantiate Shape? Because this class describes an abstract concept, what does it mean to draw a generic shape? Fortunately, Java provides a solution to this problem, which is demonstrated in Listing 3–25.

Listing 3–25. *Abstracting the Shape class*

```
abstract class Shape
{
   abstract void draw(); // semicolon is required
}
```

Listing 3–25 uses Java's `abstract` reserved word to declare a class that cannot be instantiated. The compiler reports an error should you try to instantiate this class.

> **TIP:** Get into the habit of declaring classes that describe generic categories (such as shape, animal, vehicle, and account) `abstract`. This way, you will not inadvertently instantiate them.

The `abstract` reserved word is also used to declare a method without a body. The `draw()` method does not need a body because it cannot draw an abstract shape.

> **CAUTION:** The compiler reports an error if you attempt to declare a class that is both abstract and final. For example, `abstract final class` Shape is an error because an abstract class cannot be instantiated and a final class cannot be extended.
>
> The compiler also reports an error if you declare a method to be abstract but do not declare its class to be abstract. For example, removing `abstract` from the Shape class's header in Listing 3–25 results in an error. This removal is an error because a non-`abstract` (concrete) class cannot be instantiated if it contains an abstract method.
>
> When you extend an abstract class, the extending class must override all of the abstract class's abstract methods, or else the extending class must itself be declared to be abstract; otherwise, the compiler will report an error.

An abstract class can contain non-`abstract` methods in addition to or instead of abstract methods. For example, Listing 3–2's Vehicle class could have been declared abstract. The constructor would still be present, to initialize private fields, even though you could not instantiate the resulting class.

Downcasting and Runtime Type Identification

Moving up the type hierarchy via upcasting results in loss of access to subtype features. For example, assigning a Circle instance to Point variable p means that you cannot use p to call Circle's getRadius() method.

However, it is possible to once again access the Circle instance's getRadius() method by performing an explicit cast operation; for example, Circle c = (Circle) p;. This assignment is known as *downcasting* because you are explicitly moving down the type hierarchy (from the Point superclass to the Circle subclass).

Although an upcast is always safe (the superclass's interface is a subset of the subclass's interface), the same cannot be said of a downcast. Listing 3–26 shows you what kind of trouble you can get into when downcasting is used incorrectly.

Listing 3–26. *The trouble with downcasting*

```
class A
{
}
class B extends A
{
    void d() {}
}
class C
{
    public static void main(String[] args)
    {
        A a = new A();
        B b = (B) a;
        b.d();
    }
}
```

Listing 3–26 presents a class hierarchy consisting of a superclass named A and a subclass named B. Although A does not declare any members, B declares a single d() method.

A third class named C provides a main() method that first instantiates A, and then tries to downcast this instance to B and assign the result to variable b. The compiler will not complain because downcasting from a superclass to a subclass in the same type hierarchy is legal.

However, if the assignment is allowed, the application will undoubtedly crash when it tries to execute b.d();. The crash happens because the virtual machine will attempt to call a method that does not exist—class A does not have a d() method.

Fortunately, this scenario will never happen because the virtual machine verifies that the cast is legal. Because it detects that A does not have a d() method, it does not permit the cast by throwing an instance of the ClassCastException class.

The virtual machine's cast verification illustrates *runtime type identification* (or RTTI, for short). Cast verification performs RTTI by examining the type of the cast operator's operand to see if the cast should be allowed. Clearly, the cast should not be allowed.

A second form of RTTI involves the instanceof operator. This operator checks the left operand to see if it is an instance of the right operand, and returns true if this is the case. Listing 3–27 introduces instanceof to Listing 3–26 to prevent the ClassCastException.

Listing 3–27. *Preventing a ClassCastException*

```
if(a instanceof B)
{
    B b = (B) a;
    b.d();
}
```

The instanceof operator detects that variable a's instance was not created from B and returns false to indicate this fact. As a result, the code that performs the illegal cast will not execute. (Overuse of instanceof probably indicates poor software design.)

Because a subtype is a kind of supertype, `instanceof` will return true when its left operand is a subtype instance or a supertype instance of its right operand supertype. Listing 3–28 provides a demonstration.

Listing 3–28. *Subtype and supertype instances of a supertype*

```
A a = new A();
B b = new B();
System.out.println(b instanceof A); // Output: true
System.out.println(a instanceof A); // Output: true
```

Listing 3–28, which assumes the class structure shown in Listing 3–26, instantiates superclass A and subclass B. The first `System.out.println()` method call outputs true because b's reference identifies an instance of a subclass of A; the second `System.out.println()` method call outputs true because a's reference identifies an instance of superclass A.

So far, you have encountered two forms of RTTI. Java also supports a third form that is known as reflection. I will introduce you to this form of RTTI when I cover reflection in Chapter 7.

Covariant Return Types

A *covariant return type* is a method return type that, in the superclass's method declaration, is the supertype of the return type in the subclass's overriding method declaration. Listing 3–29 provides a demonstration of this language feature.

Listing 3–29. *A demonstration of covariant return types*

```
class Zip
{
   ZipFile getArchive(String name) throws IOException
   {
      return new ZipFile(name); // ZipFile is located in the java.util.zip package
   }
}
class Jar extends Zip
{
   @Override JarFile getArchive(String name) throws IOException
   {
      return new JarFile(name); // JarFile is located in the java.util.jar package
   }
}
class Archive
{
   public static void main(String[] args) throws IOException
   {
      if (args.length == 2 && args[0].equals("-zip"))
      {
         ZipFile zf = new Zip().getArchive(args[1]);
      }
      else
      if (args.length == 2 && args[0].equals("-jar"))
      {
         JarFile jf = new Jar().getArchive(args[1]);
```

```
        }
      }
    }
```

Listing 3–29 declares a Zip superclass and a Jar subclass; each class declares a getArchive() method. Zip's method has its return type set to ZipFile, whereas Jar's overriding method has its return type set to JarFile, a subclass of ZipFile.

Covariant return types minimize upcasting and downcasting. For example, Jar's getArchive() method does not need to upcast its JarFile instance to its JarFile return type. Furthermore, this instance does not need to be downcast to JarFile when assigning to variable jf.

In the absence of covariant return types, you would end up with Listing 3–30.

Listing 3–30. *Upcasting and downcasting in the absence of covariant return types*

```java
class Zip
{
   ZipFile getArchive(String name) throws IOException
   {
      return new ZipFile(name);
   }
}
class Jar extends Zip
{
   @Override ZipFile getArchive(String name) throws IOException
   {
      return new JarFile(name);
   }
}
class Archive2
{
   public static void main(String[] args) throws IOException
   {
      if (args.length == 2 && args[0].equals("-zip"))
      {
         ZipFile zf = new Zip().getArchive(args[1]);
      }
      else
      if (args.length == 2 && args[0].equals("-jar"))
      {
         JarFile jf = (JarFile) new Jar().getArchive(args[1]);
      }
   }
}
```

In Listing 3–30, the first bolded code reveals an upcast from JarFile to ZipFile, and the second bolded code uses the required (JarFile) cast operator to downcast from ZipFile to jf, which is of type JarFile.

Interfaces

In Chapter 2, I stated that every class *X* exposes an *interface*, which is a protocol or contract consisting of constructors, methods, and (possibly) fields that are made available to objects created from other classes for use in creating and communicating with *X*'s objects.

> **NOTE:** A *contract* is an agreement between two parties. In this case, those parties are a class and *clients* (external constructors, methods, class initializers, and instance initializers) that communicate with the class's instances by calling constructors and methods, and by accessing fields (typically `public static final` fields, or constants). The essence of the contract is that the class promises to not change its interface, which would break clients that depend upon the interface.

Java formalizes the interface concept by providing reserved word `interface`, which is used to introduce a type without implementation. Java also provides language features to declare, implement, and extend interfaces. After looking at interface declaration, implementation, and extension, this section explains the rationale for using interfaces.

Declaring Interfaces

An interface declaration consists of a header followed by a body. At minimum, the header consists of reserved word `interface` followed by a name that identifies the interface. The body starts with an open brace character and ends with a close brace. Sandwiched between these delimiters are constant and method header declarations. Consider Listing 3–31.

Listing 3–31. *Declaring a* Drawable *interface*

```
interface Drawable
{
   int RED = 1;    // For simplicity, integer constants are used. These constants are
   int GREEN = 2; // not that descriptive, as you will see.
   int BLUE = 3;
   int BLACK = 4;
   void draw(int color);
}
```

Listing 3–31 declares an interface named `Drawable`. By convention, an interface's name begins with an uppercase letter. Furthermore, the first letter of each subsequent word in a multiword interface name is capitalized.

> **NOTE:** Many interface names end with the `able` suffix. For example, the Java's standard class library includes interfaces named `Adjustable`, `Callable`, `Comparable`, `Cloneable`, `Iterable`, `Runnable`, and `Serializable`. It is not mandatory to use this suffix. For example, the standard class library also provides interfaces named `CharSequence`, `Collection`, `Composite`, `Executor`, `Future`, `Iterator`, `List`, `Map`, and `Set`.

`Drawable` declares four fields that identify color constants. `Drawable` also declares a `draw()` method that must be called with one of these constants to specify the color used to draw something.

> **NOTE:** As with a class declaration, you can precede `interface` with `public`, to make your interface accessible to code outside of its package. (I will discuss packages in the next chapter). Otherwise, the interface is only accessible to other types in its package.
>
> You can also precede `interface` with `abstract`, to emphasize that an interface is abstract. Because an interface is already abstract, it is redundant to specify `abstract` in the interface's declaration.
>
> An interface's fields are implicitly declared `public`, `static`, and `final`. It is therefore redundant to declare them with these reserved words. Because these fields are constants, they must be explicitly initialized; otherwise, the compiler reports an error.
>
> An interface's methods are implicitly declared `public` and `abstract`. Therefore, it is redundant to declare them with these reserved words. Because these methods must be instance methods, do not declare them `static` or the compiler will report errors.

`Drawable` identifies a type that specifies what to do (draw something) but not how to do it. Implementation details are left up to classes that implement this interface. Instances of such classes are known as *drawables* because they know how to draw themselves.

> **NOTE:** An interface that declares no members is known as a *marker interface* or a *tagging interface*. It associates metadata with a class. For example, the `Cloneable` marker/tagging interface states that instances of its implementing class can be shallowly cloned.
>
> RTTI is used to detect that an object's class implements a marker/tagging interface. For example, when `Object`'s `clone()` method detects, via RTTI, that the calling instance's class implements `Cloneable`, it shallowly clones the object.

Implementing Interfaces

By itself, an interface is useless. To be of any benefit to an application, the interface needs to be implemented by a class. Java provides the `implements` reserved word for this task. This reserved word is demonstrated in Listing 3–32.

Listing 3–32. *Implementing the Drawable interface*

```java
class Point implements Drawable
{
    private int x, y;
    Point(int x, int y)
    {
        this.x = x;
        this.y = y;
    }
    int getX()
    {
        return x;
    }
    int getY()
    {
        return y;
    }
    @Override public String toString()
    {
        return "(" + x + ", " + y + ")";
    }
    @Override public void draw(int color)
    {
        System.out.println("Point drawn at " + toString () + " in color " + color);
    }
}
class Circle extends Point implements Drawable
{
    private int radius;
    Circle(int x, int y, int radius)
    {
        super(x, y);
        this.radius = radius;
    }
    int getRadius()
    {
        return radius;
    }
    @Override public String toString()
    {
        return "" + radius;
    }
    @Override public void draw(int color)
    {
        System.out.println("Circle drawn at " + super.toString() +
                            " with radius " + toString() + " in color " + color);
    }
}
```

Listing 3–32 retrofits Listing 3–20's class hierarchy to take advantage of Listing 3–31's Drawable interface. You will notice that each of classes Point and Circle implements this interface by attaching the implements Drawable clause to its class header.

To implement an interface, the class must specify, for each interface method header, a method whose header has the same signature and return type as the interface's method header, and a code body to go with the method header.

> **CAUTION:** When implementing a method, do not forget that the interface's methods are implicitly declared public. If you forget to include public in the implemented method's declaration, the compiler will report an error because you are attempting to assign weaker access to the implemented method.

When a class implements an interface, the class inherits the interface's constants and method headers, and overrides the method headers by providing implementations (hence the @Override annotation). This is known as *interface inheritance*.

It turns out that Circle's header does not need the implements Drawable clause. If this clause is not present, Circle inherits Point's draw() method, and is still considered to be a Drawable, whether it overrides this method or not.

An interface specifies a type whose data values are the objects whose classes implement the interface, and whose behaviors are those specified by the interface. This fact implies that you can assign an object's reference to a variable of the interface type, provided that the object's class implements the interface. Listing 3–33 provides a demonstration.

Listing 3–33. *Exercising the Drawable interface*

```
public static void main(String[] args)
{
   Drawable[] drawables = new Drawable[] {new Point(10, 20), new Circle(10, 20, 30)};
   for (int i = 0; i < drawables.length; i++)
      drawables[i].draw(Drawable.RED);
}
```

Because Point and Circle instances are drawables by virtue of these classes implementing the Drawable interface, it is legal to assign Point and Circle instance references to variables (including array elements) of type Drawable.

When you run this method, it generates the following output:

```
Point drawn at (10, 20) in color 1
Circle drawn at (10, 20) with radius 30 in color 1
```

Listing 3–31's Drawable interface is useful for drawing a shape's outline. Suppose you also need to fill a shape's interior. You might attempt to satisfy this requirement by declaring Listing 3–34's Fillable interface.

Listing 3–34. *Declaring a* `Fillable` *interface*

```
interface Fillable
{
   int RED = 1;
   int GREEN = 2;
   int BLUE = 3;
   int BLACK = 4;
   void fill(int color);
}
```

You can declare that the Point and Circle classes implement both interfaces by specifying `class Point implements Drawable, Fillable` and `class Circle implements Drawable, Fillable`.

> **TIP:** You can list as many interfaces as you need to implement by specifying a comma-separated list of interface names after `implements`.

Implementing multiple interfaces can lead to name collisions, and the compiler will report errors. For example, suppose that you attempt to compile Listing 3–35's interface and class declarations.

Listing 3–35. *Colliding interfaces*

```
interface A
{
   int X = 1;
   void foo();
}
interface B
{
   int X = 1;
   int foo();
}
class C implements A, B
{
   public void foo();
   public int foo() { return X; }
}
```

Each of interfaces A and B declares a constant named X. Despite each constant having the same type and value, the compiler will report an error when it encounters X in C's second foo() method because it does not know which X is being inherited.

Speaking of foo(), the compiler reports an error when it encounters C's second foo() declaration because foo() has already been declared. You cannot overload a method by changing only its return type.

The compiler will probably report additional errors. For example, the Java version 6 update 16 compiler has this to say when told to compile Listing 3–35:

```
X.java:14: foo() is already defined in C
    public int foo() { return X; }
              ^
```

```
X.java:11: C is not abstract and does not override abstract method foo() in B
class C implements A, B
^
X.java:13: foo() in C cannot implement foo() in B; attempting to use incompatible↩
 return type
found    : void
required: int
   public void foo();
                ^
X.java:14: reference to X is ambiguous, both variable X in A and variable X in B match
   public int foo() { return X; }
                             ^
4 errors
```

Extending Interfaces

Just as a subclass can extend a superclass via reserved word extends, you can use this reserved word to have a subinterface extend a superinterface. This is known as *interface inheritance*.

For example, the duplicate color constants in Drawable and Fillable lead to name collisions when you specify their names by themselves in an implementing class. To avoid these name collisions, prefix a name with its interface name and the member access operator, or place these constants in their own interface, and have Drawable and Fillable extend this interface, as demonstrated in Listing 3–36.

Listing 3–36. *Extending the Colors interface*

```
interface Colors
{
   int RED = 1;
   int GREEN = 2;
   int BLUE = 3;
   int BLACK = 4;
}
interface Drawable extends Colors
{
   void draw(int color);
}
interface Fillable extends Colors
{
   void fill(int color);
}
```

The fact that Drawable and Fillable each inherit constants from Colors is not a problem for the compiler. There is only a single copy of these constants (in Colors) and no possibility of a name collision, and so the compiler is satisfied.

If a class can implement multiple interfaces by declaring a comma-separated list of interface names after implements, it seems that an interface should be able to extend multiple interfaces in a similar way. This feature is demonstrated in Listing 3–37.

Listing 3–37. *Extending a pair of interfaces*

```
interface A
{
    int X = 1;
}
interface B
{
    double X = 2.0;
}
interface C extends A, B
{
}
```

Listing 3–37 will compile even though C inherits two same-named constants X with different return types and initializers. However, if you implement C and then try to access X, as in Listing 3–38, you will run into a name collision.

Listing 3–38. *Discovering a name collision*

```
class D implements C
{
    public void output()
    {
        System.out.println(X); // Which X is accessed?
    }
}
```

Suppose you introduce a void foo(); method header declaration into interface A, and an int foo(); method header declaration into interface B. This time, the compiler will report an error when you attempt to compile the modified Listing 3–37.

Why Use Interfaces?

Now that the mechanics of declaring, implementing, and extending interfaces are out of the way, we can focus on the rationale for using them. Unfortunately, newcomers to Java's interfaces feature are often told that this feature was created as a workaround to Java's lack of support for multiple implementation inheritance. While interfaces are useful in this capacity, this is not their reason for existence. Instead, **Java's interfaces feature was created to give developers the utmost flexibility in designing their applications, by decoupling interface from implementation.**

If you are an adherent to *agile software development* (a group of software development methodologies based on iterative development that emphasizes keeping code simple, testing frequently, and delivering functional pieces of the application as soon as they are deliverable), you know the importance of flexible coding. You know that you cannot afford to tie your code to a specific implementation because a change in requirements for the next iteration could result in a new implementation, and you might find yourself rewriting significant amounts of code, which wastes time and slows development.

Interfaces help you achieve flexibility by decoupling interface from implementation. For example, Listing 3–23's main() method creates an array of objects from classes that subclass the Shape class, and then iterates over these objects, calling each object's draw() method. The only objects that can be drawn are those that subclass Shape.

Suppose you also have a hierarchy of classes that model resistors, transistors, and other electronic components. Each component has its own symbol that allows the component to be shown in a schematic diagram of an electronic circuit. Perhaps you want to add a drawing capability to each class that draws that component's symbol.

You might consider specifying Shape as the superclass of the electronic component class hierarchy. However, electronic components are not shapes so it makes no sense to place these classes in a class hierarchy rooted in Shape.

However, you can make each component class implement the Drawable interface, which lets you add expressions that instantiate these classes to Listing 3–33's drawables array (so you can draw their symbols). This is legal because these instances are drawables.

Wherever possible, you should strive to specify interfaces instead of classes in your code, to keep your code adaptable to change. This is especially true when working with Java's collections framework, which I will discuss at length in Chapter 8.

For now, consider a simple example that consists of the collections framework's List interface, and its ArrayList and LinkedList classes. Listing 3–39 shows you an example of inflexible code based on the ArrayList class.

Listing 3–39. *Hardwiring the ArrayList class into source code*

```
ArrayList<String> arrayList = new ArrayList<String>();
void dump(ArrayList<String> arrayList)
{
   // suitable code to dump out the arrayList
}
```

Listing 3–39 uses the generics-based parameterized type language feature (which I will discuss in Chapter 5) to identify the kind of objects stored in an ArrayList instance. In this example, String objects are stored.

Listing 3–39 is inflexible because it hardwires the ArrayList class into multiple locations. This hardwiring focuses the developer into thinking specifically about array lists instead of generically about lists.

Lack of focus is problematic when a requirements change, or perhaps a performance issue brought about by *profiling* (analyzing a running application to check its performance), suggests that the developer should have used LinkedList.

Listing 3–39 only requires a minimal number of changes to satisfy the new requirement. In contrast, a larger code base might need many more changes. Although you only need to change ArrayList to LinkedList, to satisfy the compiler, consider changing arrayList to linkedList, to keep *semantics* (meaning) clear—you might have to change multiple occurrences of names that refer to an ArrayList instance throughout the source code.

The developer is bound to lose time while refactoring the code to adapt to LinkedList. Instead, time could have been saved by writing Listing 3–39 to use the equivalent of constants. In other words, Listing 3–39 could have been written to rely on interfaces, and to only specify `ArrayList` in one place. Listing 3–40 shows you what the resulting code would look like.

Listing 3–40. *Using* `List` *to minimize referrals to the* `ArrayList` *implementation class*

```
List<String> list = new ArrayList<String>();
void dump(List<String> list)
{
    // suitable code to dump out the list
}
```

Listing 3–40 is much more flexible than Listing 3–39. If a requirements or profiling change suggests that `LinkedList` should be used instead of `ArrayList`, simply replace Array with Linked and you are done. You do not even have to change the parameter name.

> **NOTE:** Java provides interfaces and abstract classes for describing *abstract types* (types that cannot be instantiated). Abstract types represent abstract concepts (drawable and shape, for example), and instances of such types would be meaningless.
>
> Interfaces promote flexibility through lack of implementation—`Drawable` and `List` illustrate this flexibility. They are not tied to any single class hierarchy, but can be implemented by any class in any hierarchy.
>
> Abstract classes support implementation, but can be genuinely abstract (Listing 3–25's abstract `Shape` class, for example). However, they are limited to appearing in the upper levels of class hierarchies.
>
> Interfaces and abstract classes can be used together. For example, the collections framework provides `List`, `Map`, and `Set` interfaces; and `AbstractList`, `AbstractMap`, and `AbstractSet` abstract classes that provide skeletal implementations of these interfaces.
>
> The skeletal implementations make it easy for you to create your own interface implementations, to address your unique requirements. If they do not meet your needs, you can optionally have your class directly implement the appropriate interface.

EXERCISES

The following exercises are designed to test your understanding of Java's object-oriented language features:

1. What is implementation inheritance?

2. How does Java support implementation inheritance?

3. Can a subclass have two or more superclasses?

4. How do you prevent a class from being subclassed?

5. True or false: The super() call can appear in any method.

6. If a superclass declares a constructor with one or more parameters, and if a subclass constructor does not use super() to call that constructor, why does the compiler report an error?

7. What is an immutable class?

8. True or false: A class can inherit constructors.

9. What does it mean to override a method?

10. What is required to call a superclass method from its overriding subclass method?

11. How do you prevent a method from being overridden?

12. Why can you not make an overriding subclass method less accessible than the superclass method it is overriding?

13. How do you tell the compiler that a method overrides another method?

14. Why does Java not support multiple implementation inheritance?

15. What is the name of Java's ultimate superclass?

16. What is the purpose of the clone() method?

17. When does Object's clone() method throw CloneNotSupportedException?

18. Explain the difference between shallow copying and deep copying.

19. Can the == operator be used to determine if two objects are logically equivalent? Why or why not?

20. What does Object's equals() method accomplish?

21. Does expression "abc" == "a" + "bc" return true or false?

22. How can you optimize a time-consuming equals() method?

23. What is the purpose of the finalize() method?

24. Should you rely on finalize() for closing open files? Why or why not?

25. What is a hash code?

26. True or false: You should override the hashCode() method whenever your override the equals() method.

27. What does Object's toString() method return?

28. Why should you override toString()?

29. What is composition?

30. True or false: Composition is used to implement is-a relationships and implementation inheritance is used to describe has-a relationships.

31. Identify the fundamental problem of implementation inheritance. How do you fix this problem?

32. What is subtype polymorphism?

33. How is subtype polymorphism accomplished?

34. Why would you use abstract classes and abstract methods?

35. Can an abstract class contain concrete methods?

36. What is the purpose of downcasting?

37. List the three forms of RTTI.

38. What is a covariant return type?

39. How do you formally declare an interface?

40. True or false: You can precede an interface declaration with the `abstract` reserved word.

41. What is a marker interface?

42. What is interface inheritance?

43. How do you implement an interface?

44. What problem might you encounter when you implement multiple interfaces?

45. How do you form a hierarchy of interfaces?

46. Why is Java's interfaces feature so important?

47. What do interfaces and abstract classes accomplish?

48. How do interfaces and abstract classes differ?

49. Model part of an animal hierarchy by declaring `Animal`, `Bird`, `Fish`, `AmericanRobin`, `DomesticCanary`, `RainbowTrout`, and `SockeyeSalmon` classes:

- `Animal` is public and abstract, declares private String-based `kind` and `appearance` fields, declares a public constructor that initializes these fields to passed-in arguments, declares public and abstract `eat()` and `move()` methods that take no arguments and whose return type is void, and overrides the `toString()` method to output the contents of `kind` and `appearance`.

- `Bird` is public and abstract, extends `Animal`, declares a public constructor that passes its `kind` and `appearance` parameter values to its superclass constructor, overrides its `eat()` method to output `eats seeds and insects` (via `System.out.println()`), and overrides its `move()` method to output `flies through the air`.

- `Fish` is public and abstract, extends `Animal`, declares a public constructor that passes its `kind` and `appearance` parameter values to its superclass constructor, overrides its `eat()` method to output `eats krill, algae, and insects`, and overrides its `move()` method to output `swims through the water`.

- AmericanRobin is public, extends Bird, and declares a public noargument constructor that passes "americanrobin" and "red breast" to its superclass constructor.

- DomesticCanary is public, extends Bird, and declares a public noargument constructor that passes "domesticcanary" and "yellow, orange, black, brown, white, red" to its superclass constructor.

- RainbowTrout is public, extends Fish, and declares a public noargument constructor that passes "rainbowtrout" and "bands of brilliant speckled multicolored stripes running nearly the whole length of its body" to its superclass constructor.

- SockeyeSalmon is public, extends Fish, and declares a public noargument constructor that passes "sockeyesalmon" and "bright red with a green head" to its superclass constructor.

For brevity, I have omitted from the Animal hierarchy abstract Robin, Canary, Trout, and Salmon classes that generalize robins, canaries, trout, and salmon. Perhaps you might want to include these classes in the hierarchy.

Although this exercise illustrates the accurate modeling of a natural scenario using inheritance, it also reveals the potential for class explosion—too many classes may be introduced to model a scenario, and it might be difficult to maintain all of these classes. Keep this in mind when modeling with inheritance.

50. Continuing from the previous exercise, declare an Animals class with a main() method. This method first declares an animals array that is initialized to AmericanRobin, RainbowTrout, DomesticCanary, and SockeyeSalmon objects. The method then iterates over this array, first outputting animals[i] (which causes toString() to be called), and then calling each object's eat() and move() methods (demonstrating subtype polymorphism).

51. Continuing from the previous exercise, declare a public Countable interface with a String getID() method. Modify Animal to implement Countable and have this method return kind's value. Modify Animals to initialize the animals array to AmericanRobin, RainbowTrout, DomesticCanary, SockeyeSalmon, RainbowTrout, and AmericanRobin objects. Also, introduce code that computes a census of each kind of animal. This code will use the Census class that is declared in Listing 3–41.

Listing 3–41. *The Census class stores census data on four kinds of animals*

```
public class Census
{
   public final static int SIZE = 4;
   private String[] IDs;
   private int[] counts;
   public Census()
   {
      IDs = new String[SIZE];
      counts = new int[SIZE];
   }
   public String get(int index)
   {
      return IDs[index] + " " + counts[index];
```

```
   }
   public void update(String ID)
   {
      for (int i = 0; i < IDs.length; i++)
      {
         // If ID not already stored in the IDs array (which is indicated by
         // the first null entry that is found), store ID in this array, and
         // also assign 1 to the associated element in the counts array, to
         // initialize the census for that ID.
         if (IDs[i] == null)
         {
            IDs[i] = ID;
            counts[i] = 1;
            return;
         }

         // If a matching ID is found, increment the associated element in
         // the counts array to update the census for that ID.
         if (IDs[i].equals(ID))
         {
            counts[i]++;
            return;
         }
      }
   }
}
```

Summary

An understanding of Java's fundamental language features must take inheritance and polymorphism into account. Java supports two forms of inheritance: implementation via class extension, and interface via interface implementation or interface extension.

Java supports four kinds of polymorphism: coercion, overloading, parametric, and subtype. Subtype polymorphism is used to invoke subclass methods via references to subclass objects that are stored in variables of the superclass type.

Java's interfaces feature is essential for writing extremely flexible code. It achieves this flexibility by decoupling interface from implementation. Classes that implement an interface provide their own implementations.

You now have enough language knowledge to write interesting Java applications, but Java's advanced language features related to nested types, packages, static imports, and exceptions help simplify this task. Chapter 4 focuses on these feature categories.

Chapter 4

Mastering Advanced Language Features Part 1

Chapters 2 and 3 laid a foundation for learning the Java language. Chapter 4 builds onto this foundation by introducing you to some of Java's more advanced language features, specifically those features related to nested types, packages, static imports, and exceptions. Additional advanced language features are covered in Chapter 5.

Nested Types

Classes that are declared outside of any class are known as *top-level classes*. Java also supports *nested classes*, which are classes declared as members of other classes or scopes. Nested classes help you implement top-level class architecture.

There are four kinds of nested classes: static member classes, nonstatic member classes, anonymous classes, and local classes. The latter three categories are known as *inner classes*.

This section introduces you to static member classes and inner classes. For each kind of nested class, I provide you with a brief introduction, an abstract example, and a more practical example. The section then briefly examines the topic of nesting interfaces within classes.

Static Member Classes

A *static member class* is a `static` member of an enclosing class. Although enclosed, it does not have an enclosing instance of that class, and cannot access the enclosing class's instance fields and call its instance methods. However, it can access or call `static` members of the enclosing class, even those members that are declared `private`.

Listing 4–1 presents a static member class declaration.

Listing 4–1. *Declaring a static member class*

```
public class EnclosingClass
{
   private static int i;
   private static void m1()
   {
      System.out.println(i); // Output: 1
   }
   public static void m2()
   {
      EnclosedClass.accessEnclosingClass();
   }
   public static class EnclosedClass
   {
      public static void accessEnclosingClass()
      {
         i = 1;
         m1();
      }
      public void accessEnclosingClass2()
      {
         m2();
      }
   }
}
```

Listing 4–1 declares a top-level class named EnclosingClass with class field i, class methods m1() and m2(), and static member class EnclosedClass. Also, EnclosedClass declares class method accessEnclosingClass() and instance method accessEnclosingClass2().

Because accessEnclosingClass() is declared static, m2() must prefix this method's name with EnclosedClass and the member access operator to call this method. Also, EnclosingClass must be part of the prefix when calling this method from beyond this class. For example, EnclosingClass.EnclosedClass.accessEnclosingClass();.

Because accessEnclosingClass2() is nonstatic, it must be called from an instance of EnclosedClass. For example, when calling this method from beyond EnclosingClass, you might specify EnclosingClass.EnclosedClass ec = new EnclosingClass.EnclosedClass(); ec.accessEnclosingClass2();.

Static member classes have their uses. For example, Listing 4–2's Double and Float static member classes provide different implementations of their enclosing Rectangle class. The Float version occupies less memory because of its 32-bit float fields, and the Double version provides greater accuracy because of its 64–bit double fields.

Listing 4–2. *Using static member classes to declare multiple implementations of their enclosing class*

```
public abstract class Rectangle
{
   public abstract double getX();
   public abstract double getY();
   public abstract double getWidth();
   public abstract double getHeight();
   public static class Double extends Rectangle
```

```
{
   private double x, y, width, height;
   public Double(double x, double y, double width, double height)
   {
      this.x = x;
      this.y = y;
      this.width = width;
      this.height = height;
   }
   public double getX() { return x; }
   public double getY() { return y; }
   public double getWidth() { return width; }
   public double getHeight() { return height; }
}
public static class Float extends Rectangle
{
   private float x, y, width, height;
   public Float(float x, float y, float width, float height)
   {
      this.x = x;
      this.y = y;
      this.width = width;
      this.height = height;
   }
   public double getX() { return x; }
   public double getY() { return y; }
   public double getWidth() { return width; }
   public double getHeight() { return height; }
}
// Prevent subclassing. Use the type-specific Double and Float
// implementation subclass classes to instantiate.
private Rectangle() {}
public boolean contains(double x, double y)
{
   return (x >= getX() && x < getX()+getWidth()) &&
          (y >= getY() && y < getY()+getHeight());
}
}
```

Listing 4–2's Rectangle class demonstrates nested subclasses. Each of the Double and Float static member classes subclass the abstract Rectangle class, providing private floating-point or double precision floating-point fields, and overriding Rectangle's abstract methods to return these fields' values as doubles.

Rectangle is abstract because it makes no sense to instantiate this class. Because it also makes no sense to directly extend Rectangle with new implementations (the Double and Float nested subclasses should be sufficient), its default constructor is declared private. Instead, you must instantiate Rectangle.Float (to save memory) or Rectangle.Double (when accuracy is required). Check out Listing 4–3.

Listing 4–3. *Creating and using different Rectangle implementations*

```
public static void main(String[] args)
{
   Rectangle r = new Rectangle.Double(10.0, 10.0, 20.0, 30.0);
   System.out.println("x = " + r.getX());
   System.out.println("y = " + r.getY());
```

```
        System.out.println("width = " + r.getWidth());
        System.out.println("height = " + r.getHeight());
        System.out.println("contains(15.0, 15.0) = " + r.contains(15.0, 15.0));
        System.out.println("contains(0.0, 0.0) = " + r.contains(0.0, 0.0));
        System.out.println();
        r = new Rectangle.Float(10.0f, 10.0f, 20.0f, 30.0f);
        System.out.println("x = " + r.getX());
        System.out.println("y = " + r.getY());
        System.out.println("width = " + r.getWidth());
        System.out.println("height = " + r.getHeight());
        System.out.println("contains(15.0, 15.0) = " + r.contains(15.0, 15.0));
        System.out.println("contains(0.0, 0.0) = " + r.contains(0.0, 0.0));
   }
```

This method generates the following output:

```
x = 10.0
y = 10.0
width = 20.0
height = 30.0
contains(15.0, 15.0) = true
contains(0.0, 0.0) = false

x = 10.0
y = 10.0
width = 20.0
height = 30.0
contains(15.0, 15.0) = true
contains(0.0, 0.0) = false
```

Java's class library contains many static member classes. For example, the Character class (in the java.lang package) encloses a static member class named Subset whose instances represent subsets of the Unicode character set. AbstractMap.SimpleEntry, ObjectInputStream.GetField, and KeyStore.PrivateKeyEntry are other examples.

NOTE: When you compile an enclosing class that contains a static member class, the compiler creates a classfile for the static member class whose name consists of its enclosing class's name, a dollar-sign character, and the static member class's name. For example, compile Listing 4–1 and you will discover EnclosingClass$EnclosedClass.class in addition to EnclosingClass.class. This format also applies to nonstatic member classes.

Nonstatic Member Classes

A *nonstatic member class* is a non-static member of an enclosing class. Each instance of the nonstatic member class implicitly associates with an instance of the enclosing class. The nonstatic member class's instance methods can call instance methods in the enclosing class and access the enclosing class instance's nonstatic fields.

Listing 4–4 presents a nonstatic member class declaration.

Listing 4–4. *Declaring a nonstatic member class*

```
public class EnclosingClass
{
   private int i;
   private void m1()
   {
      System.out.println(i); // Output: 1
   }
   public class EnclosedClass
   {
      public void accessEnclosingClass()
      {
         i = 1;
         m1();
      }
   }
}
```

Listing 4–4 declares a top-level class named EnclosingClass with instance field i, instance method m1(), and nonstatic member class EnclosedClass. Furthermore, EnclosedClass declares instance method accessEnclosingClass().

Because accessEnclosingClass() is nonstatic, EnclosedClass must be instantiated before this method can be called. This instantiation must take place via an instance of EnclosingClass. Listing 4–5 accomplishes these tasks.

Listing 4–5. *Calling a nonstatic member class's instance method*

```
public class NSMCDemo
{
   public static void main(String[] args)
   {
      EnclosingClass ec = new EnclosingClass();
      ec.new EnclosedClass().accessEnclosingClass();
   }
}
```

Listing 4–5's main() method first instantiates EnclosingClass and saves its reference in local variable ec. Then, main() uses this reference as a prefix to the new operator, to instantiate EnclosedClass, whose reference is then used to call accessEnclosingClass().

NOTE: Prefixing new with a reference to the enclosing class is rare. Instead, you will typically call an enclosed class's constructor from within a constructor or an instance method of its enclosing class.

Suppose you need to maintain a to-do list of items, where each item consists of a name and a description. After some thought, you create Listing 4–6's ToDo class to implement these items.

Listing 4–6. *Implementing to-do items as name-description pairs*

```
public class ToDo
{
   private String name;
```

```
   private String desc;
   public ToDo(String name, String desc)
   {
      this.name = name;
      this.desc = desc;
   }
   public String getName()
   {
      return name;
   }
   public String getDesc()
   {
      return desc;
   }
   public String toString()
   {
      return "Name = " + getName() + ", Desc = " + getDesc();
   }
}
```

You next create a ToDoList class to store ToDo instances. ToDoList uses its ToDoArray
nonstatic member class to store ToDo instances in a growable array—you do not know
how many instances will be stored, and Java arrays have fixed lengths. See Listing 4–7.

Listing 4–7. *Storing a maximum of two ToDo instances in a ToDoArray instance*

```
public class ToDoList
{
   private ToDoArray toDoArray;
   private int index = 0;
   public ToDoList()
   {
      toDoArray = new ToDoArray(2);
   }
   public boolean hasMoreElements()
   {
      return index < toDoArray.size();
   }
   public ToDo nextElement()
   {
      return toDoArray.get(index++);
   }
   public void add(ToDo item)
   {
      toDoArray.add(item);
   }
   private class ToDoArray
   {
      private ToDo[] toDoArray;
      private int index = 0;
      ToDoArray(int initSize)
      {
         toDoArray = new ToDo[initSize];
      }
      void add(ToDo item)
      {
         if (index >= toDoArray.length)
         {
```

```
            ToDo[] temp = new ToDo[toDoArray.length*2];
            for (int i = 0; i < toDoArray.length; i++)
               temp[i] = toDoArray[i];
            toDoArray = temp;
         }
         toDoArray[index++] = item;
      }
      ToDo get(int i)
      {
         return toDoArray[i];
      }
      int size()
      {
         return index;
      }
   }
}
```

In addition to providing an add() method to store ToDo instances in the ToDoArray instance, ToDoList provides hasMoreElements() and nextElement() methods to iterate over and return the stored instances. Listing 4–8 demonstrates these methods.

Listing 4–8. *Creating a list of* ToDo *instances and iterating over this list*

```
public static void main(String[] args)
{
   ToDoList toDoList = new ToDoList();
   toDoList.add(new ToDo("#1", "Do laundry."));
   toDoList.add(new ToDo("#2", "Buy groceries."));
   toDoList.add(new ToDo("#3", "Vacuum apartment."));
   toDoList.add(new ToDo("#4", "Write report."));
   toDoList.add(new ToDo("#5", "Wash car."));
   while (toDoList.hasMoreElements())
      System.out.println(toDoList.nextElement());
}
```

This method generates the following output:

```
Name = #1, Desc = Do laundry.
Name = #2, Desc = Buy groceries.
Name = #3, Desc = Vacuum apartment.
Name = #4, Desc = Write report.
Name = #5, Desc = Wash car.
```

Java's class library presents many examples of nonstatic member classes. For example, the java.util package's HashMap class declares private HashIterator, ValueIterator, KeyIterator, and EntryIterator classes for iterating over a hashmap's values, keys, and entries. (I will discuss HashMap in Chapter 8.)

NOTE: Code within an enclosed class can obtain a reference to its enclosing class instance by qualifying reserved word this with the enclosing class's name and the member access operator. For example, if code within accessEnclosingClass() needed to obtain a reference to its EnclosingClass instance, it would specify EnclosingClass.this.

Anonymous Classes

An *anonymous class* is a class without a name. Furthermore, it is not a member of its enclosing class. Instead, an anonymous class is simultaneously declared (as an anonymous extension of a class or as an anonymous implementation of an interface) and instantiated any place where it is legal to specify an expression.

Listing 4–9 demonstrates an anonymous class declaration and instantiation.

Listing 4–9. *Declaring and instantiating an anonymous class that extends a class*

```
abstract class Speaker
{
   abstract void speak();
}
public class ACDemo
{
   public static void main(final String[] args)
   {
      new Speaker()
      {
         String msg = (args.length == 1) ? args[0] : "nothing to say";
         void speak()
         {
            System.out.println(msg);
         }
      }
      .speak();
   }
}
```

Listing 4–9 introduces an abstract class named Speaker and a concrete class named ACDemo. The latter class's main() method declares an anonymous class that extends Speaker and overrides its speak() method. When this method is called, it outputs main()'s first command-line argument or a default message if there are no arguments.

An anonymous class does not have a constructor (because the anonymous class does not have a name). However, its classfile does contain a hidden method that performs instance initialization. This method calls the superclass's noargument constructor (prior to any other initialization), which is the reason for specifying Speaker() after new.

Anonymous class instances should be able to access the surrounding scope's local variables and parameters. However, an instance might outlive the method in which it was conceived (as a result of storing the instance's reference in a field), and try to access local variables and parameters that no longer exist after the method returns.

Because Java cannot allow this illegal access, which would most likely crash the virtual machine, it lets an anonymous class instance only access local variables and parameters that are declared final. Upon encountering a final local variable/parameter name in an anonymous class instance, the compiler does one of two things:

- If the variable's type is primitive (int or double, for example), the compiler replaces its name with the variable's read-only value.

- If the variable's type is reference (String, for example), the compiler introduces, into the classfile, a *synthetic variable* (a manufactured variable) and code that stores the local variable's/parameter's reference in the synthetic variable.

Listing 4–10 demonstrates an alternative anonymous class declaration and instantiation.

Listing 4–10. *Declaring and instantiating an anonymous class that implements an interface*

```
interface Speakable
{
   void speak();
}
public class ACDemo
{
   public static void main(final String[] args)
   {
      new Speakable()
      {
         String msg = (args.length == 1) ? args[0] : "nothing to say";
         public void speak()
         {
            System.out.println(msg);
         }
      }
      .speak();
   }
}
```

Listing 4–10 is very similar to Listing 4–9. However, instead of subclassing a Speaker class, this listing's anonymous class implements an interface named Speakable. Apart from the hidden method calling Object() (interfaces have no constructors), Listing 4–10 behaves like Listing 4–9.

Although an anonymous class does not have a constructor, you can provide an instance initializer to handle complex initialization. For example, new Office() {{addEmployee(new Employee("John Doe"));}}; instantiates an anonymous subclass of Office and adds one Employee object to this instance by calling Office's addEmployee() method.

You will often find yourself creating and instantiating anonymous classes for their convenience. For example, suppose you need to return a list of all filenames having the .java suffix. Listing 4–11 shows you how an anonymous class simplifies using the java.io package's File and FilenameFilter classes to achieve this objective.

Listing 4–11. *Using an anonymous class instance to return a list of files with .java extensions*

```
String[] list = new File(directory).list(new FilenameFilter()
               {
                  public boolean accept(File f, String s)
                  {
                     return s.endsWith(".java");
                  }
               });
```

> **NOTE:** An instance of an anonymous class is similar to a *closure*, which is a first-class *function* (a method not declared in a class) with free variables that are bound in the *lexical environment* (surrounding scope). A *first-class function* is a function that can be passed as an argument to or returned from a method. A *free variable* is a variable referred to in a function that is not a local variable or a parameter. Think of this variable as a placeholder.
>
> Despite their similarity, there are two key differences between these language features. First, anonymous classes are more syntactically verbose than closures. Second, an anonymous class instance does not really close over its surrounding scope, because Java cannot allow the anonymous class instance to access non-`final` local variables and parameters.
>
> Java version 7 will introduce closures, although the exact syntax and implementation are unknown at the time of writing. However, Baptiste Wicht revealed Oracle's first attempt at implementing closures via his May 29, 2010 blog post "Java 7: Oracle pushes a first version of closures" (`http://www.baptiste-wicht.com/2010/05/oracle-pushes-a-first-version-of-closures/`).

Local Classes

A *local class* is a class that is declared anywhere that a local variable is declared. Furthermore, it has the same scope as a local variable. Unlike an anonymous class, a local class has a name and can be reused. Like anonymous classes, local classes only have enclosing instances when used in nonstatic contexts.

A local class instance can access the surrounding scope's local variables and parameters. However, the local variables and parameters that are accessed must be declared `final`. For example, Listing 4–12's local class declaration accesses a final parameter and a final local variable.

Listing 4–12. *Declaring a local class*

```
public class EnclosingClass
{
   public void m(final int x)
   {
      final int y = x*2;
      class LocalClass
      {
         int a = x;
         int b = y;
      }
      LocalClass lc = new LocalClass();
      System.out.println(lc.a);
      System.out.println(lc.b);
   }
}
```

Listing 4–12 declares EnclosingClass with its instance method m() declaring a local class named LocalClass. This local class declares a pair of instance fields (a and b) that are initialized to the values of final parameter x and final local variable y when LocalClass is instantiated: new EnclosingClass().m(10);, for example.

Local classes help improve code clarity because they can be moved closer to where they are needed. For example, Listing 4–13 declares an Iterator interface and a ToDoList class whose iterator() method returns an instance of its local Iter class as an Iterator instance (because Iter implements Iterator).

Listing 4–13. *The* Iterator *interface and the* ToDoList *class*

```
public interface Iterator
{
   boolean hasMoreElements();
   Object nextElement();
}
public class ToDoList
{
   private ToDo[] toDoList;
   private int index = 0;
   public ToDoList(int size)
   {
      toDoList = new ToDo[size];
   }
   public Iterator iterator()
   {
      class Iter implements Iterator
      {
         int index = 0;
         public boolean hasMoreElements()
         {
            return index < toDoList.length;
         }
         public Object nextElement()
         {
            return toDoList[index++];
         }
      }
      return new Iter();
   }
   public void add(ToDo item)
   {
      toDoList[index++] = item;
   }
}
```

Because each of Iterator and ToDoList is declared public, these types need to be stored in separate source files.

Listing 4–14's main() method demonstrates this revised ToDoList class, Listing 4–6's ToDo class, and Iterator.

Listing 4–14. *Creating a list of ToDo instances and iterating over this list*

```
public static void main(String[] args)
{
   ToDoList toDoList = new ToDoList(5);
   toDoList.add(new ToDo("#1", "Do laundry."));
   toDoList.add(new ToDo("#2", "Buy groceries."));
   toDoList.add(new ToDo("#3", "Vacuum apartment."));
   toDoList.add(new ToDo("#4", "Write report."));
   toDoList.add(new ToDo("#5", "Wash car."));
   Iterator iter = toDoList.iterator();
   while (iter.hasMoreElements())
      System.out.println(iter.nextElement());
}
```

The Iterator instance that is returned from iterator() returns ToDo items in the same order as when they were added to the list. Although you can only use the returned Iterator once, you can call iterator() whenever you need a new Iterator. This capability is a big improvement over the one-shot iterator presented in Listing 4–7.

Interfaces Within Classes

Interfaces can be nested within classes. Once declared, an interface is considered to be static, even if it is not declared static. For example, Listing 4–15 declares an enclosing class named X along with two nested static interfaces named A and B.

Listing 4–15. *Declaring a pair of interfaces within a class*

```
class X
{
   interface A
   {
   }
   static interface B
   {
   }
}
```

As with nested classes, nested interfaces help to implement top-level class architecture by being implemented by nested classes. Collectively, these types are nested because they cannot (as in Listing 4–13's Iter local class) or need not appear at the same level as a top-level class and pollute its package namespace.

> **NOTE:** The previous chapter's introduction to interfaces showed you how to declare constants and method headers in the body of an interface. You can also declare interfaces and classes in an interface's body. Because there does not appear to be a good reason to do this, it is probably best to avoid nesting interfaces and/or classes within interfaces.

Packages

Hierarchical structures organize items in terms of hierarchical relationships that exist between those items. For example, a filesystem might contain a taxes directory with multiple year subdirectories, where each subdirectory contains tax information pertinent to that year. Also, an enclosing class might contain multiple nested classes that only make sense in the context of the enclosing class.

Hierarchical structures also help to avoid name conflicts. For example, two files cannot have the same name in a nonhierarchical filesystem (which consists of a single directory). In contrast, a hierarchical filesystem lets same-named files exist in different directories. Similarly, two enclosing classes can contain same-named nested classes. Name conflicts do not exist because items are partitioned into different *namespaces*.

Java also supports the partitioning of top-level types into multiple namespaces, to better organize these types and to also prevent name conflicts. Java uses packages to accomplish these tasks.

This section introduces you to packages. After defining this term and explaining why package names must be unique, the section presents the package and import statements. It next explains how the virtual machine searches for packages and types, and then presents an example that shows you how to work with packages. This section closes by showing you how to encapsulate a package of classfiles into JAR files.

What Are Packages?

A *package* is a unique namespace that can contain a combination of top-level classes, other top-level types, and subpackages. Only types that are declared public can be accessed from outside the package. Furthermore, the constants, constructors, methods, and nested types that describe a class's interface must be declared public to be accessible from beyond the package.

Every package has a name, which must be a nonreserved identifier. The member access operator separates a package name from a subpackage name, and separates a package or subpackage name from a type name. For example, the two member access operators in graphics.shapes.Circle separate package name graphics from the shapes subpackage name, and separate subpackage name shapes from the Circle type name.

> **NOTE:** Each of Java SE's standard class library and Android's class library organizes its many classes and other top-level types into multiple packages. Many of these packages are subpackages of the standard java package. Examples include java.io (types related to input/output operations), java.lang (language-oriented types), java.lang.reflect (reflection-oriented language types), java.net (network-oriented types), and java.util (utility types).

Package Names Must Be Unique

Suppose you have two different graphics.shapes packages, and suppose that each shapes subpackage contains a Circle class with a different interface. When the compiler encounters System.out.println(new Circle(10.0, 20.0, 30.0).area()); in the source code, it needs to verify that the area() method exists.

The compiler will search all accessible packages until it finds a graphics.shapes package that contains a Circle class. If the found package contains the appropriate Circle class with an area() method, everything is fine. Otherwise, if the Circle class does not have an area() method, the compiler will report an error.

This scenario illustrates the importance of choosing unique package names. Specifically, the top-level package name must be unique. The convention in choosing this name is to take your Internet domain name and reverse it. For example, I would choose ca.mb.javajeff as my top-level package name because javajeff.mb.ca is my domain name. I would then specify ca.mb.javajeff.graphics.shapes.Circle to access Circle.

> **NOTE:** Reversed Internet domain names are not always valid package names. One or more of its component names might start with a digit (6.com), contain a hyphen (-) or other illegal character (aq-x.com), or be one of Java's reserved words (int.com). Convention dictates that you prefix the digit with an underscore (com._6), replace the illegal character with an underscore (com.aq_x), and suffix the reserved word with an underscore (com.int_).

The Package Statement

The package statement identifies the package in which a source file's types are located. This statement consists of reserved word package, followed by a member access operator–separated list of package and subpackage names, followed by a semicolon.

For example, package graphics; specifies that the source file's types locate in a package named graphics, and package graphics.shapes; specifies that the source file's types locate in the graphics package's shapes subpackage.

By convention, a package name is expressed in lowercase. If the name consists of multiple words, each word except for the first word is capitalized.

Only one package statement can appear in a source file. When it is present, nothing apart from comments must precede this statement.

> **CAUTION:** Specifying multiple package statements in a source file or placing anything apart from comments above a package statement causes the compiler to report an error.

Java implementations map package and subpackage names to same-named directories. For example, an implementation would map graphics to a directory named graphics, and would map graphics.shapes to a shapes subdirectory of graphics. The Java compiler stores the classfiles that implement the package's types in the corresponding directory.

> **NOTE:** If a source file does not contain a package statement, the source file's types are said to belong to the *unnamed package*. This package corresponds to the current directory.

The Import Statement

Imagine having to repeatedly specify ca.mb.javajeff.graphics.shapes.Circle or some other lengthy package-qualified type name for each occurrence of that type in source code. Java provides an alternative that lets you avoid having to specify package details. This alternative is the import statement.

The import statement imports types from a package by telling the compiler where to look for unqualified type names during compilation. This statement consists of reserved word import, followed by a member access operator–separated list of package and subpackage names, followed by a type name or * (asterisk), followed by a semicolon.

The * symbol is a wildcard that represents all unqualified type names. It tells the compiler to look for such names in the import statement's specified package, unless the type name is found in a previously searched package.

For example, import ca.mb.javajeff.graphics.shapes.Circle; tells the compiler that an unqualified Circle class exists in the ca.mb.javajeff.graphics.shapes package. Similarly, import ca.mb.javajeff.graphics.shapes.*; tells the compiler to look in this package if it encounters a Rectangle class, a Triangle class, or even an Employee class (if Employee has not already been found).

> **TIP:** You should avoid using the * wildcard so that other developers can easily see which types are used in source code.

Because Java is case sensitive, package and subpackage names specified in an import statement must be expressed in the same case as that used in the package statement.

When import statements are present in source code, only a package statement and comments can precede them.

> **CAUTION:** Placing anything other than a package statement, import/static import statements, and comments above an import statement causes the compiler to report an error.

You can run into name conflicts when using the wildcard version of the import statement because any unqualified type name matches the wildcard. For example, you have graphics.shapes and geometry packages that each contain a Circle class, the source code begins with import geometry.*; and import graphics.shape.*; statements, and it also contains an unqualified occurrence of Circle. Because the compiler does not know if Circle refers to geometry's Circle class or graphics.shape's Circle class, it reports an error. You can fix this problem by qualifying Circle with the correct package name.

NOTE: The compiler automatically imports the String class and other types from the java.lang package, which is why it is not necessary to qualify String with java.lang.

Searching for Packages and Types

Newcomers to Java who first start to work with packages often become frustrated by "no class definition found" and other errors. This frustration can be partly avoided by understanding how the virtual machine searches for packages and types.

This section explains how the search process works. To understand this process, you need to realize that the compiler is a special Java application that runs under the control of the virtual machine. Furthermore, there are two different forms of search.

Compile-Time Search

When the compiler encounters a type expression (such as a method call) in source code, it must locate that type's declaration to verify that the expression is legal (a method exists in the type's class whose parameter types match the types of the arguments passed in the method call, for example).

The compiler first searches the Java platform packages (which contain class library types). It then searches extension packages (for extension types). If the -sourcepath command-line option was specified when starting the virtual machine (via javac), the compiler searches the indicated path's source files.

NOTE: Java platform packages are stored in rt.jar and a few other important JAR files. Extension packages are stored in a special extensions directory named ext.

Otherwise, it searches the user classpath (in left-to-right order) for the first user classfile or source file containing the type. If no user classpath is present, the current directory is searched. If no package matches or the type still cannot be found, the compiler reports an error. Otherwise, the compiler records the package information in the classfile.

NOTE: The user classpath is specified via the -classpath option used to start the virtual machine or, if not present, the CLASSPATH environment variable.

Runtime Search

When the compiler or any other Java application runs, the virtual machine will encounter types and must load their associated classfiles via special code known as a *classloader*. It will use the previously stored package information that is associated with the encountered type in a search for that type's classfile.

The virtual machine searches the Java platform packages, followed by extension packages, followed by the user classpath (in left-to-right order) for the first classfile that contains the type. If no user classpath is present, the current directory is searched. If no package matches or the type cannot be found, a "no class definition found" error is reported. Otherwise, the classfile is loaded into memory.

> **NOTE:** Whether you use the -classpath option or the CLASSPATH environment variable to specify a user classpath, there is a specific format that must be followed. Under Windows, this format is expressed as path1;path2;..., where path1, path2, and so on are the locations of package directories. Under Unix and Linux, this format changes to path1:path2:....

Playing with Packages

Suppose your application needs to log messages to the console, to a file, or to another destination (perhaps to an application running on another computer). Furthermore, suppose the application needs to perform some combination of these tasks.

To demonstrate packages, this section presents a simple and reusable logging library. This library consists of an interface named Logger, an abstract class named LoggerFactory, and a pair of package-private classes named Console and File.

> **NOTE:** The logging library is an example of the *Abstract Factory design pattern*, which is presented on page 87 of *Design Patterns: Elements of Reusable Object-Oriented Software* by Erich Gamma, Richard Helm, Ralph Johnson, and John Vlissides (Addison-Wesley, 1995; ISBN: 0201633612).

Listing 4–16 presents the Logger interface, which describes objects that log messages.

Listing 4–16. *Describing objects that log messages via the Logger interface*

```
package logging;

public interface Logger
{
    boolean connect();
    boolean disconnect();
    boolean log(String msg);
}
```

Each of the connect(), disconnect(), and log() methods returns true upon success, and false upon failure. (Later in this chapter, you will discover a better technique for dealing with failure.)

Listing 4–17 presents the LoggerFactory abstract class.

Listing 4-17. *Obtaining a logger for logging messages to a specific destination*

```
package logging;

public abstract class LoggerFactory
{
   public final static int CONSOLE = 0;
   public final static int FILE = 1;

   public static Logger newLogger(int dstType, String...dstName)
   {
      switch (dstType)
      {
         case CONSOLE: return new Console(dstName.length == 0 ? null
                                                              : dstName[0]);
         case FILE   : return new File(dstName.length == 0 ? null
                                                           : dstName[0]);
         default     : return null;
      }
   }
}
```

newLogger() returns a Logger for logging messages to an appropriate destination. It uses the variable arguments feature to optionally accept an extra String argument for those destination types that require the argument. For example, FILE requires a filename.

Listing 4–18 presents the package-private Console class.

Listing 4-18. *Logging messages to the console*

```
package logging;

class Console implements Logger
{
   private String dstName;
   Console(String dstName)
   {
      this.dstName = dstName;
   }
   public boolean connect()
   {
      return true;
   }
   public boolean disconnect()
   {
      return true;
   }
   public boolean log(String msg)
   {
      System.out.println(msg);
      return true;
   }
}
```

Console's package-private constructor saves its argument, which most likely will be null because there is no need for a String argument. Perhaps a future version of Console will use this argument to identify one of multiple console windows.

Listing 4–19 presents the package-private File class.

Listing 4–19. *Logging messages to a file (eventually)*

```
package logging;

class File implements Logger
{
    private String dstName;
    File(String dstName)
    {
        this.dstName = dstName;
    }
    public boolean connect()
    {
        if (dstName == null)
            return false;
        System.out.println("opening file " + dstName);
        return true;
    }
    public boolean disconnect()
    {
        if (dstName == null)
            return false;
        System.out.println("closing file " + dstName);
        return true;
    }
    public boolean log(String msg)
    {
        if (dstName == null)
            return false;
        System.out.println("writing " + msg + " to file " + dstName);
        return true;
    }
}
```

Unlike Console, File requires a nonnull argument. Each method first verifies that this argument is not null. If the argument is null, the method returns false to signify failure. (In Chapter 10, I refactor File to incorporate appropriate file-writing code.)

The logging library allows us to introduce portable logging code into an application. Apart from a call to newLogger(), this code will remain the same regardless of the logging destination. Listing 4–20 presents an application that tests this library.

Listing 4–20. *Testing the logging library*

```
import logging.*;

public class TestLogger
{
    public static void main(String[] args)
    {
        Logger logger = LoggerFactory.newLogger(LoggerFactory.CONSOLE);
        if (logger.connect())
```

```
   {
      logger.log("test message #1");
      logger.disconnect();
   }
   else
      System.out.println("cannot connect to console-based logger");

   logger = LoggerFactory.newLogger(LoggerFactory.FILF, "x.txt");
   if (logger.connect())
   {
      logger.log("test message #2");
      logger.disconnect();
   }
   else
      System.out.println("cannot connect to file-based logger");

   logger = LoggerFactory.newLogger(LoggerFactory.FILE);
   if (logger.connect())
   {
      logger.log("test message #3");
      logger.disconnect();
   }
   else
      System.out.println("cannot connect to file-based logger");
   }
}
```

Follow the steps (which assume that the JDK has been installed) to create the `logging` package and `TestLogger` application, and to run this application:

1. Create a new directory and make this directory current.

2. Create a `logging` directory in the current directory.

3. Copy Listing 4–16 to a file named `Logger.java` in the `logging` directory.

4. Copy Listing 4–17 to a file named `LoggerFactory.java` in the `logging` directory.

5. Copy Listing 4–18 to a file named `Console.java` in the `logging` directory.

6. Copy Listing 4–19 to a file named `File.java` in the `logging` directory.

7. Copy Listing 4–20 to a file named `TestLogger.java` in the current directory.

8. Execute `javac TestLogger.java`, which also compiles `logger`'s source files.

9. Execute `java TestLogger`.

After completing the previous step, you should observe the following output from the `TestLogger` application:

```
test message #1
opening file x.txt
writing test message #2 to file x.txt
closing file x.txt
cannot connect to file-based logger
```

What happens when `logging` is moved to another location? For example, move `logging` to the root directory and run `TestLogger`. You will now observe an error message about the virtual machine not finding the `logging` package and its `LoggerFactory` classfile.

You can solve this problem by specifying `-classpath` when running the `java` tool, or by adding the location of the `logging` package to the `CLASSPATH` environment variable. For example, I chose to use `-classpath` in the following Windows-specific command line:

```
java -classpath \;. TestLogger
```

The backslash represents the root directory in Windows. (I could have specified a forward slash as an alternative.) Also, the period represents the current directory. If it is missing, the virtual machine complains about not finding the `TestLogger` classfile.

> **TIP:** If you discover an error message where the virtual machine reports that it cannot find an application classfile, try appending a period character to the classpath. Doing so will probably fix the problem.

Packages and JAR Files

Chapter 1 introduced you to the Java SDK's `jar` tool, which is used to archive classfiles in JAR files, and is also used to extract a JAR file's classfiles. It probably comes as no surprise that you can store packages in JAR files, which greatly simplify the distribution of your package-based class libraries.

> **NOTE:** Java version 7 will introduce *modules* as a replacement to JAR files. Modules address JAR file problems such as a lack of versioning support; no reliable way to express, resolve, and enforce one JAR file's dependency on another JAR file; and having to specify a JAR file as part of the classpath. Because the JAR file's location might change during deployment, developers are forced to correct all references to the JAR file. This new feature will probably include a new reserved word named `module`.

To show you how easy it is to store a package in a JAR file, we will create a `logger.jar` file that contains the `logging` package's four classfiles (`Logger.class`, `LoggerFactory.class`, `Console.class`, and `File.class`). Complete the following steps to accomplish this task:

1. Make sure that the current directory contains the previously created `logging` directory with its four classfiles.

2. Execute `jar cf logger.jar logging\*.class`. You could alternatively execute `jar cf logger.jar logging/*.class`.

You should now find a `logger.jar` file in the current directory. To prove to yourself that this file contains the four classfiles, execute `jar tf logger.jar`.

You can run `TestLogger.class` by adding `logger.jar` to the classpath. For example, you can run `TestLogger` under Windows via `java -classpath logger.jar;. TestLogger`.

Static Imports

An interface should only be used to declare a type. However, some developers violate this principle by using interfaces to only export constants. Such interfaces are known as *constant interfaces*, and Listing 4–21 presents an example.

Listing 4–21. *Declaring a constant interface*

```
public interface Directions
{
   int NORTH = 0;
   int SOUTH = 1;
   int EAST = 2;
   int WEST = 3;
}
```

Developers who resort to constant interfaces do so to avoid having to prefix a constant's name with the name of its class (as in `Math.PI`, where `PI` is a constant in the `java.lang.Math` class). They do this by implementing the interface—see Listing 4–22.

Listing 4–22. *Implementing a constant interface*

```
public class TrafficFlow implements Directions
{
   public static void main(String[] args)
   {
      showDirection((int)(Math.random()*4));
   }
   private static void showDirection(int dir)
   {
      switch (dir)
      {
         case NORTH: System.out.println("Moving north"); break;
         case SOUTH: System.out.println("Moving south"); break;
         case EAST : System.out.println("Moving east"); break;
         case WEST : System.out.println("Moving west");
      }
   }
}
```

Listing 4–22's `TrafficFlow` class implements `Directions` for the sole purpose of not having to specify `Directions.NORTH`, `Directions.SOUTH`, `Directions.EAST`, and `Directions.WEST`.

This is an appalling misuse of an interface. These constants are nothing more than an implementation detail that should not be allowed to leak into the class's exported *interface*, because they might confuse the class's users (what is the purpose of these constants?). Also, they represent a future commitment: even when the class no longer uses these constants, the interface must remain to ensure binary compatibility.

Java version 5 introduced an alternative that satisfies the desire for constant interfaces while avoiding their problems. This static imports feature lets you import a class's `static` members so that you do not have to qualify them with their class names. It is implemented via a small modification to the import statement, as follows:

```
import static packagespec . classname . ( staticmembername | * );
```

The static import statement specifies `static` after `import`. It then specifies a member access operator–separated list of package and subpackage names, which is followed by the member access operator and a class's name. Once again, the member access operator is specified, followed by a single static member name or the asterisk wildcard.

> **CAUTION:** Placing anything apart from a package statement, import/static import statements, and comments above a static import statement causes the compiler to report an error.

You specify a single static member name to import only that name:

```
import static java.lang.Math.PI; // Import the PI static field only.
import static java.lang.Math.cos; // Import the cos() static method only.
```

In contrast, you specify the wildcard to import all static member names:

```
import static java.lang.Math.*;   // Import all static members from Math.
```

You can now refer to the static member(s) without having to specify the class name:

```
System.out.println(cos(PI));
```

Using multiple static import statements can result in name conflicts, which causes the compiler to report errors. For example, suppose your geom package contains a `Circle` class with a static member named PI. Now suppose you specify `import static java.lang.Math.*;` and `import static geom.Circle.*;` at the top of your source file. Finally, suppose you specify `System.out.println(PI);` somewhere in that file's code. The compiler reports an error because it does not know if PI belongs to `Math` or `Circle`.

Exceptions

In an ideal world, nothing bad ever happens when an application runs. For example, a file always exists when the application needs to open the file, the application is always able to connect to a remote computer, and the virtual machine never runs out of memory when the application needs to instantiate objects.

In contrast, real-world applications occasionally attempt to open files that do not exist, attempt to connect to remote computers that are unable to communicate with them, and require more memory than the virtual machine can provide. Your goal is to write code that properly responds to these and other exceptional situations (exceptions).

This section introduces you to exceptions. After defining this term, the section looks at representing exceptions in source code. It then examines the topics of throwing and handling exceptions, and concludes by discussing how to perform cleanup tasks before a method returns, whether or not an exception has been thrown.

What Are Exceptions?

An *exception* is a divergence from an application's normal behavior. For example, the application attempts to open a nonexistent file for reading. The normal behavior is to successfully open the file and begin reading its contents. However, the file cannot be read if the file does not exist.

This example illustrates an exception that cannot be prevented. However, a workaround is possible. For example, the application can detect that the file does not exist and take an alternate course of action, which might include telling the user about the problem. Unpreventable exceptions where workarounds are possible must not be ignored.

Exceptions can occur because of poorly written code. For example, an application might contain code that accesses each element in an array. Because of careless oversight, the array-access code might attempt to access a nonexistent array element, which leads to an exception. This kind of exception is preventable by writing correct code.

Finally, an exception might occur that cannot be prevented, and for which there is no workaround. For example, the virtual machine might run out of memory, or perhaps it cannot find a classfile. This kind of exception, known as an *error*, is so serious that it is impossible (or at least inadvisable) to work around; the application must terminate, presenting a message to the user that states why it is terminating.

Representing Exceptions in Source Code

An exception can be represented via error codes or objects. This section discusses each kind of representation and explains why objects are superior. It then introduces you to Java's exception and error class hierarchy, emphasizing the difference between checked and runtime exceptions. It closes by discussing custom exception classes.

Error Codes Versus Objects

One way to represent exceptions in source code is to use error codes. For example, a method might return true on success and false when an exception occurs. Alternatively, a method might return 0 on success and a nonzero integer value that identifies a specific kind of exception.

Developers traditionally designed methods to return error codes; I demonstrated this tradition in each of the three methods in Listing 4–16's Logger interface. Each method returns true on success, or returns false to represent an exception (unable to connect to the logger, for example).

Although a method's return value must be examined to see if it represents an exception, error codes are all too easy to ignore. For example, a lazy developer might ignore the return code from Logger's connect() method and attempt to call log(). Ignoring error codes is one reason why a new approach to dealing with exceptions has been invented.

This new approach is based on objects. When an exception occurs, an object representing the exception is created by the code that was running when the exception occurred. Details describing the exception's surrounding context are stored in the object. These details are later examined to work around the exception.

The object is then *thrown*, or handed off to the virtual machine to search for a *handler*, code that can handle the exception. (If the exception is an error, the application should not provide a handler.) When a handler is located, its code is executed to provide a workaround. Otherwise, the virtual machine terminates the application.

Apart from being too easy to ignore, an error code's Boolean or integer value is less meaningful than an object name. For example, fileNotFound is self-evident, but what does false mean? Also, an object can contain information about what led to the exception. These details can be helpful to a suitable workaround.

The Throwable Class Hierarchy

Java provides a hierarchy of classes that represent different kinds of exceptions. These classes are rooted in java.lang.Throwable, the ultimate superclass for all *throwables* (exception and error objects—exceptions and errors, for short—that can be thrown). Table 4–1 identifies and describes most of Throwable's constructors and methods.

Table 4–1. *Throwable's Constructors and Methods*

Method	Description
Throwable()	Create a throwable with a null detail message and cause.
Throwable(String message)	Create a throwable with the specified detail message and a null cause.
Throwable(String message, Throwable cause)	Create a throwable with the specified detail message and cause.
Throwable(Throwable cause)	Create a throwable whose detail message is the string representation of a nonnull cause, or null.
Throwable getCause()	Return the cause of this throwable. If there is no cause, null is returned.
String getMessage()	Return this throwable's detail message, which might be null.
StackTraceElement[] getStackTrace()	Provide programmatic access to the stack trace information printed by printStackTrace() as an array of stack trace elements, each representing one stack frame.

Method	Description
`Throwable initCause(Throwable cause)`	Initialize the cause of this throwable to the specified value.
`void printStackTrace()`	Print this throwable and its backtrace of stack frames to the standard error stream.

It is not uncommon for a class's public methods to call helper methods that throw various exceptions. A public method will probably not document exceptions thrown from a helper method because they are implementation details that often should not be visible to the public method's caller.

However, because this exception might be helpful in diagnosing the problem, the public method can wrap the lower-level exception in a higher-level exception that is documented in the public method's contract interface. The wrapped exception is known as a *cause* because its existence causes the higher-level exception to be thrown.

When an exception is thrown, it leaves behind a stack of unfinished method calls. Each stack entry is represented by an instance of the `java.lang.StackTraceElement` class. This class's methods provide access to information about a stack entry. For example, `public String getMethodName()` returns the name of an unfinished method.

Moving down the throwable hierarchy, you encounter the `java.lang.Exception` and `java.lang.Error` classes, which respectively represent exceptions and errors. Each class offers four constructors that pass their arguments to their `Throwable` counterparts, but provides no methods apart from those that are inherited from `Throwable`.

`Exception` is itself subclassed by `java.lang.CloneNotSupportedException` (discussed in Chapter 3), `java.lang.IOException` (discussed in Chapter 10), and other classes. Similarly, `Error` is itself subclassed by `java.lang.AssertionError` (discussed in Chapter 5), `java.lang.OutOfMemoryError`, and other classes.

> **CAUTION:** Never instantiate `Throwable`, `Exception`, or `Error`. The resulting objects are meaningless because they are too generic.

Checked Exceptions Versus Runtime Exceptions

A *checked exception* is an exception that represents a problem with the possibility of recovery, and for which the developer must provide a workaround. The developer checks (examines) the code to ensure that the exception is handled in the method where it is thrown, or is explicitly identified as being handled elsewhere.

`Exception` and all subclasses except for `RuntimeException` (and its subclasses) describe checked exceptions. For example, the aforementioned `CloneNotSupportedException` and `IOException` classes describe checked exceptions. (`CloneNotSupportedException` should not be checked because there is no runtime workaround for this kind of exception.)

A *runtime exception* is an exception that represents a coding mistake. This kind of exception is also known as an *unchecked exception* because it does not need to be handled or explicitly identified—the mistake must be fixed. Because these exceptions can occur in many places, it would be burdensome to be forced to handle them.

RuntimeException and its subclasses describe unchecked exceptions. For example, java.lang.ArithmeticException describes arithmetic problems such as integer division by zero. Another example is java.lang.ArrayIndexOutOfBoundsException. (In hindsight, RuntimeException should have been named UncheckedException because all exceptions occur at runtime.)

> **NOTE:** Many developers are not happy with checked exceptions because of the work involved in having to handle them. This problem is made worse by libraries providing methods that throw checked exceptions when they should throw unchecked exceptions. As a result, many modern languages support only unchecked exceptions.

Custom Exception Classes

You can declare your own exception classes. Before doing so, ask yourself if an existing exception class in Java's class library meets your needs. If you find a suitable class, you should reuse it. (Why reinvent the wheel?) Other developers will already be familiar with the existing class, and this knowledge will make your code easier to learn.

If no existing class meets your needs, think about whether to subclass Exception or RuntimeException. In other words, will your exception class be checked or unchecked? As a rule of thumb, your class should subclass RuntimeException if you think that it will describe a coding mistake.

> **TIP:** When you name your class, follow the convention of providing an Exception suffix. This suffix clarifies that your class describes an exception.

Suppose you are creating a Media class whose static methods perform various media-oriented utility tasks. For example, one method converts files in non-MP3 media formats to MP3 format. This method will be passed source file and destination file arguments, and will convert the source file to the format implied by the destination file's extension.

Before performing the conversion, the method needs to verify that the source file's format agrees with the format implied by its file extension. If there is no agreement, an exception must be thrown. Furthermore, this exception must store the expected and existing media formats so that a handler can identify them in a message to the user.

Because Java's class library does not provide a suitable exception class, you decide to introduce a class named InvalidMediaFormatException. Detecting an invalid media format is not the result of a coding mistake, and so you also decide to extend Exception to indicate that the exception is checked. Listing 4–23 presents this class's declaration.

Listing 4–23. *Declaring a custom exception class*

```
public class InvalidMediaFormatException extends Exception
{
   private String expectedFormat;
   private String existingFormat;
   public InvalidMediaFormatException(String expectedFormat,
                                      String existingFormat)
   {
      super("Expected format: " + expectedFormat + ", Existing format: " +
         existingFormat);
      this.expectedFormat = expectedFormat;
      this.existingFormat = existingFormat;
   }
   public String getExpectedFormat()
   {
      return expectedFormat;
   }
   public String getExistingFormat()
   {
      return existingFormat;
   }
}
```

InvalidMediaFormatException provides a constructor that calls Exception's public
Exception(String message) constructor with a detail message that includes the expected
and existing formats. It is wise to capture such details in the detail message because the
problem that led to the exception might be hard to reproduce.

InvalidMediaFormatException also provides getExpectedFormat() and
getExistingFormat() methods that return these formats. Perhaps a handler will present
this information in a message to the user. Unlike the detail message, this message might be
localized, expressed in the user's language (French, German, English, and so on).

Throwing Exceptions

Now that you have created an InvalidMediaFormatException class, you can declare the
Media class and begin to code its convert() method. The initial version of this method
validates its arguments, and then verifies that the source file's media format agrees with the
format implied by its file extension. Check out Listing 4–24.

Listing 4–24. *Throwing exceptions from the* convert() *method*

```
public static void convert(String srcName, String dstName)
   throws InvalidMediaFormatException
{
   if (srcName == null)
      throw new NullPointerException("the source name is null");
   if (dstName == null)
      throw new NullPointerException("the destination name is null");
   // Code to access source file and verify that its format matches the
   // format implied by its file extension.
   //
   // Assume that the source file's extension is RM (for Real Media) and
   // that the file's internal signature suggests that its format is
```

```
   // Microsoft WAVE.
   String expectedFormat = "RM";
   String existingFormat = "WAVE";
   throw new InvalidMediaFormatException(expectedFormat, existingFormat);
}
```

Listing 4–24 demonstrates a throws clause, which consists of reserved word throws followed by a comma-separated list of checked exception class names, and which is appended to a method header. This clause identifies all checked exceptions that are thrown out of the method, and which must be handled by some other method.

Listing 4–24 also demonstrates the throw statement, which consists of reserved word throw followed by an instance of Throwable or a subclass. (You typically instantiate an Exception subclass.) This statement throws the instance to the virtual machine, which then searches for a suitable handler to handle the exception.

The first use of the throw statement is to throw a java.lang.NullPointerException instance when a null reference is passed as the source or destination filename. This unchecked exception is commonly thrown to indicate that a contract has been violated via a passed null reference. For example, you cannot pass null filenames to convert().

The second use of the throw statement is to throw an InvalidMediaFormatException instance when the expected media format does not match the existing format. In the contrived example, the exception is thrown because the expected format is RM and the existing format is WAVE.

Unlike InvalidMediaFormatException, NullPointerException is not listed in convert()'s throws clause because NullPointerException instances are unchecked. They can occur so frequently that it is too big a burden to force the developer to properly handle these exceptions. Instead, the developer should write code that minimizes their occurrences.

NullPointerException is one kind of exception that is thrown when an argument proves to be invalid. The java.lang.IllegalArgumentException class generalizes the illegal argument scenario to include other kinds of illegal arguments. For example, Listing 4–25 throws an IllegalArgumentException instance when a numeric argument is negative.

Listing 4–25. *Throwing an* IllegalArgumentException *instance when* x *is negative (you can't calculate a negative number's square root)*

```
public static double sqrt(double x)
{
   if (x < 0)
      throw new IllegalArgumentException(x + " is negative");
   // Calculate the square root of x.
}
```

There are a few additional items to keep in mind when working with throws clauses and throw statements:

- You can append a throws clause to a constructor and throw an exception from the constructor when something goes wrong while the constructor is executing. The resulting object will not be created.

- When an exception is thrown out of an application's `main()` method, the virtual machine terminates the application and calls the exception's `printStackTrace()` method to print, to the console, the sequence of nested method calls that was awaiting completion when the exception was thrown.

- If a superclass method declares a throws clause, the overriding subclass method does not have to declare a throws clause. However, if it does declare a throws clause, the clause must not include the names of exception classes that are not also included in the superclass method's throws clause.

- A checked exception class name does not need to appear in a throws clause when the name of its superclass appears.

- The compiler reports an error when a method throws a checked exception and does not also handle the exception or list the exception in its throws clause.

- Do not include the names of unchecked exception classes in a throws clause. These names are not required because such exceptions should never occur. Furthermore, they only clutter source code, and possibly confuse someone who is trying to understand that code.

- You can declare a checked exception class name in a method's throws clause without throwing an instance of this class from the method. Perhaps the method has yet to be fully coded.

Handling Exceptions

A method indicates its intention to handle one or more exceptions by specifying a try statement and one or more appropriate catch clauses. The try statement consists of reserved word `try` followed by a brace-delimited body. You place code that throws exceptions into this body.

A catch clause consists of reserved word `catch`, followed by a round bracket–delimited single-parameter list that specifies an exception class name, followed by a brace-delimited body. You place code that handles exceptions whose types match the type of the catch clause's parameter list's exception class parameter in this body.

A catch clause is specified immediately after a try statement's body. When an exception is thrown, the virtual machine searches for a handler by first examining the catch clause to see if its parameter type matches or is the superclass type of the exception that has been thrown.

If the catch clause is found, its code executes and the exception is handled. Otherwise, the virtual machine proceeds up the method-call stack, looking for the first method whose try statement contains an appropriate catch clause. This process continues unless a catch clause is found or execution leaves the `main()` method.

Listing 4–26 illustrates try and catch.

Listing 4–26. *Handling a thrown exception*

```
public static void main(String[] args)
{
   if (args.length != 2)
   {
      System.err.println("usage: java Converter srcfile dstfile");
      return;
   }
   try
   {
      Media.convert(args[0], args[1]);
   }
   catch (InvalidMediaFormatException imfe)
   {
      System.out.println("Unable to convert " + args[0] + " to " + args[1]);
      System.out.println("Expecting " + args[0] + " to conform to " +
                         imfe.getExpectedFormat() + " format.");
      System.out.println("However, " + args[0] + " conformed to " +
                         imfe.getExistingFormat() + " format.");
   }
}
```

Media's convert() method is placed in a try statement's body because this method is capable of throwing an instance of the checked InvalidMediaFormatException class—checked exceptions must be handled or be declared to be thrown via a throws clause that is appended to the method.

A catch clause immediately follows try's body. This clause presents a parameter list whose single parameter matches the type of the InvalidMediaFormatException object thrown from convert(). When the object is thrown, the virtual machine will transfer execution to the statements within this clause.

TIP: You might want to name your catch clause parameters using the abbreviated style shown in Listing 4–26. Not only does this convention result in more meaningful exception-oriented parameter names (imfe indicates that an InvalidMediaFormatException has been thrown), it will probably reduce compiler errors.

It is common practice to name a catch clause's parameter e, for convenience. (Why type a long name?) However, the compiler will report an error when a previously declared local variable or parameter also uses e as its name—multiple same-named local variables and parameters cannot exist in the same scope.

The catch clause's statements are designed to provide a descriptive error message to the user. A more sophisticated application would localize these names so that the user could read the message in the user's language. The developer-oriented detail message is not output because it is not necessary in this trivial application.

NOTE: A developer-oriented detail message is typically not localized. Instead, it is expressed in the developer's language. Users should never see detail messages.

You can specify multiple catch clauses after try's body. For example, a later version of convert() will also throw java.io.FileNotFoundException when it cannot open the source file or create the destination file, and IOException when it cannot read from the source file or write to the destination file. All of these exceptions must be handled.

Listing 4–27 illustrates multiple catch clauses.

Listing 4–27. *Handling more than one thrown exception*

```
try
{
   Media.convert(args[0], args[1]);
}
catch (InvalidMediaFormatException imfe)
{
   System.out.println("Unable to convert " + args[0] + " to " + args[1]);
   System.out.println("Expecting " + args[0] + " to conform to " +
                      imfe.getExpectedFormat() + " format.");
   System.out.println("However, " + args[0] + " conformed to " +
                      imfe.getExistingFormat() + " format.");
}
catch (FileNotFoundException fnfe)
{
}
catch (IOException ioe)
{
}
```

Listing 4–27 assumes that convert() also throws IOException and FileNotFoundException. Although this assumption suggests that both classes need to be listed in convert()'s throws clause, only IOException needs to be listed because it is the superclass of FileNotFoundException.

CAUTION: The compiler reports an error when you specify two or more catch clauses with the same parameter type after a try body. Example: try {} catch (IOException ioe1) {} catch (IOException ioe2) {}. You must merge these catch clauses into one clause.

Catch clauses often can be specified in any order. However, the compiler restricts this order when one catch clause's parameter is a supertype of another catch clause's parameter. The subtype parameter catch clause must precede the supertype parameter catch clause; otherwise, the subtype parameter catch clause will never be called.

For example, the FileNotFoundException catch clause must precede the IOException catch clause. If the compiler allowed the IOException catch clause to be specified first, the FileNotFoundException catch clause would never execute because a FileNotFoundException instance is also an instance of its IOException superclass.

NOTE: Java version 7 introduces a catch clause improvement known as *multicatch*, which lets you place common exception-handling code in a single catch clause. For example, `catch (InvalidMediaFormatException | UnsupportedMediaFormatException ex) { /* common code */ }` handles `InvalidMediaFormatException` and a similar `UnsupportedMediaFormatException` in one place.

Multicatch is not always necessary. For example, you do not need to specify `catch (FileNotFoundException | IOException exc) { /* suitable common code */ }` to handle `FileNotFoundException` and `IOException` because `catch (IOException ioe)` accomplishes the same task, by catching `FileNotFoundException` as well as `IOException`.

The empty `FileNotFoundException` and `IOException` catch clauses illustrate the often-seen problem of leaving catch clauses empty because they are inconvenient to code. Unless you have a good reason, do not create an empty catch clause. It swallows exceptions and you do not know that the exceptions were thrown.

CAUTION: Do not code empty catch clauses. Because they swallow exceptions, you will probably find it more difficult to debug a faulty application.

While discussing the `Throwable` class, I discussed wrapping lower-level exceptions in higher-level exceptions. This activity will typically take place in a catch clause, and is illustrated in Listing 4–28.

Listing 4–28. *Throwing a new exception that contains a wrapped exception*

```
catch (IOException ioe)
{
    throw new ReportCreationException(ioe);
}
```

This example assumes that a helper method has just thrown a generic `IOException` as the result of trying to create a report. The public method's contract states that `ReportCreationException` is thrown in this case. To satisfy the contract, the latter exception is thrown. To satisfy the developer who is responsible for debugging a faulty application, the `IOException` instance is wrapped inside the `ReportCreationException` instance that is thrown to the public method's caller.

Sometimes, a catch clause might not be able to fully handle an exception. Perhaps it needs access to information provided by some ancestor method in the method-call stack. However, the catch clause might be able to partly handle the exception. In this case, it should partly handle the exception, and then rethrow the exception so that a handler in the ancestor method can finish handling the exception. This scenario is demonstrated in Listing 4–29.

Listing 4–29. *Rethrowing an exception*

```
catch (FileNotFoundException fnfe)
{
    // Provide code to partially handle the exception here.
    throw fnfe; // Rethrow the exception here.
}
```

> **NOTE:** Java version 7 introduces a catch clause improvement known as *final rethrow*, which lets you declare a catch clause parameter `final` in order to throw only those checked exception types that were thrown in the try body, are a subtype of the catch parameter type, and are not caught in preceding catch clauses. For example, suppose you declare the following method:
>
> ```
> void method() throws Exc1, Exc2 // Exc1 and Exc2 extend Exception
> {
>     try
>     {
>         /* Code that can throw Exc1,Exc2 */
>     }
>     catch (Exception exc)
>     {
>         logger.log(exc);
>         throw exc; // Attempt to throw caught exception as an Exception
>     }
> }
> ```
>
> The compiler would report an error when asked to compile this method because you are trying to rethrow an exception that is first upcasted to `Exception`, but `Exception` is not listed in `method()`'s throws clause. However, if you change the catch clause header to `catch (final Exception exc)`, the compiler will not report an error because you are rethrowing `Exc1` or `Exc2` exceptions without the upcasting.

Performing Cleanup

In some situations, you might want to prevent an exception from being thrown out of a method before the method's cleanup code is executed. For example, you might want to close a file that was opened, but could not be written, possibly because of insufficient disk space. Java provides the finally clause for this situation.

The finally clause consists of reserved word `finally` followed by a body, which provides the cleanup code. A finally clause follows either a catch clause or a try body. In the former case, the exception is handled (and possibly rethrown) before finally executes. In the latter case, finally executes before the exception is thrown and handled.

Listing 4–30 demonstrates the finally clause in the context of a file-copying application's main() method.

Listing 4–30. *Cleaning up after handling a thrown exception*

```
public static void main(String[] args)
{
    if (args.length != 2)
    {
        System.err.println("usage: java Copy srcfile dstfile");
        return;
    }
    FileInputStream fis = null;
    try
    {
        fis = new FileInputStream(args[0]);
        FileOutputStream fos = null;
        try
        {
            fos = new FileOutputStream(args[1]);
            int b; // I chose b instead of byte because byte is a reserved word.
            while ((b = fis.read()) != -1)
                fos.write(b);
        }
        catch (FileNotFoundException fnfe)
        {
            String msg = args[1] + " could not be created, possibly because " +
                        "it might be a directory";
            System.err.println(msg);
        }
        catch (IOException ioe)
        {
            String msg = args[0] + " could not be read, or " + args[1] +
                        " could not be written";
            System.err.println(msg);
        }
        finally
        {
            if (fos != null)
                try
                {
                    fos.close();
                }
                catch (IOException ioe)
                {
                    System.err.println("unable to close " + args[1]);
                }
        }
    }
    catch (FileNotFoundException fnfe)
    {
        String msg = args[0] + " could not be found or might be a directory";
        System.err.println(msg);
    }
    finally
    {
        if (fis != null)
            try
```

```
         {
             fis.close();
         }
         catch (IOException ioe)
         {
             System.err.println("unable to close " + args[0]);
         }
      }
}
```

> **NOTE:** Do not be concerned if you find this listing's file-oriented code difficult to grasp; I will formally introduce I/O and the listing's file-oriented types in Chapter 10. I'm presenting this code here because file copying provides a perfect example of the finally clause.

Listing 4–30 presents an application that copies bytes from a source file to a destination file via a nested pair of try bodies. The outer try body uses a FileInputStream object to open the source file for reading; the inner try body uses a FileOutputStream object to create the destination file for writing, and also contains the file-copying code.

If the fis = new FileInputStream(args[0]); expression throws FileNotFoundException, execution flows into the outer try statement's catch (FileNotFoundException fnfe) clause, which outputs a suitable message to the user. Execution then enters the outer try statement's finally clause.

The outer try statement's finally clause closes an open source file. However, when FileNotFoundException is thrown, the source file is not open—no reference was assigned to fis. The finally clause uses if (fis != null) to detect this situation, and does not attempt to close the file.

If fis = new FileInputStream(args[0]); succeeds, execution flows into the inner try statement, whose body executes fos = new FileOutputStream(args[1]);. If this expression throws FileNotFoundException, execution moves into the inner try's catch (FileNotFoundException fnfe) clause, which outputs a suitable message to the user.

This time, execution continues with the inner try statement's finally clause. Because the destination file was not created, no attempt is made to close this file. In contrast, the open source file must be closed, and this is accomplished when execution moves from the inner finally clause to the outer finally clause.

FileInputStream's and FileOutputStream's close() methods throw IOException when a file is not open. Because IOException is checked, these exceptions must be handled; otherwise, it would be necessary to append a throws IOException clause to the main() method header.

You can specify a try statement with only a finally clause. You would do so when you are not prepared to handle an exception in the enclosing method (or enclosing try statement, if present), but need to perform cleanup before the thrown exception causes execution to leave the method. Listing 4–31 provides a demonstration.

Listing 4–31. *Cleaning up before handling a thrown exception*

```java
public static void main(String[] args)
{
   if (args.length != 2)
   {
      System.err.println("usage: java Copy srcfile dstfile");
      return;
   }
   try
   {
      copy(args[0], args[1]);
   }
   catch (FileNotFoundException fnfe)
   {
      String msg = args[0] + " could not be found or might be a directory," +
                   " or " + args[1] + " could not be created, " +
                   "possibly because " + args[1] + " is a directory";
      System.err.println(msg);
   }
   catch (IOException ioe)
   {
      String msg = args[0] + " could not be read, or " + args[1] +
                   " could not be written";
      System.err.println(msg);
   }
}
static void copy(String srcFile, String dstFile) throws IOException
{
   FileInputStream fis = new FileInputStream(srcFile);
   try
   {
      FileOutputStream fos = new FileOutputStream(dstFile);
      try
      {
         int b;
         while ((b = fis.read()) != -1)
            fos.write(b);
      }
      finally
      {
         try
         {
            fos.close();
         }
         catch (IOException ioe)
         {
            System.err.println("unable to close " + dstFile);
         }
      }
   }
   finally
   {
      try
      {
         fis.close();
      }
```

```
      catch (IOException ioe)
      {
         System.err.println("unable to close " + srcFile);
      }
   }
}
```

Listing 4–31 provides an alternative to Listing 4–30 that attempts to be more readable. It accomplishes this task by introducing a copy() method that uses a nested pair of try-finally constructs to perform the file-copy operation, and also close each open file whether an exception is or is not thrown.

If the FileInputStream fis = new FileInputStream(srcFile); expression results in a thrown FileNotFoundException, execution leaves copy() without entering the outer try statement. This statement is only entered after the FileInputStream object has been created, indicating that the source file was opened.

If the FileOutputStream fos = new FileOutputStream(dstFile); expression results in a thrown FileNotFoundException, execution leaves copy() without entering the inner try statement. However, execution leaves copy() only after entering the finally clause that is mated with the outer try statement. This clause closes the open source file.

If the read() or write() method in the inner try statement's body throws an IOException object, the finally clause associated with the inner try statement is executed. This clause closes the open destination file. Execution then flows into the outer finally clause, which closes the open source file, and continues on out of copy().

> **CAUTION:** If the body of a try statement throws an exception, and if the finally clause results in another exception being thrown, this new exception replaces the previous exception, which is lost.

Despite Listing 4–31 being somewhat more readable than Listing 4–30, there is still too much boilerplate thanks to each finally clause requiring a try statement to close a file. This boilerplate is necessary; its removal results in a new IOException possibly being thrown from the catch clause, which would mask a previously thrown IOException.

> **NOTE:** Java version 7 introduces *automatic resource management* to eliminate the boilerplate associated with closing files and other resources. Furthermore, this feature can eliminate bugs that arise from masking thrown exceptions with other exceptions.
>
> Automatic resource management consists of a new Disposable interface that resource classes (such as FileInputStream) implement, and syntactic sugar that associates a semicolon-separated list of resource class instantiations with try.
>
> For example, automatic resource management can turn Listing 4–31's copy() method into the following shorter method:

```
static void copy(String srcFile, String dstFile) throws IOException
{
   try (FileInputStream fis = new FileInputStream(srcFile);
       FileOutputStream fos = new FileOutputStream(dstFile))
   {
      int b;
      while ((b = fis.read()) != -1)
         fos.write(b);
   }
}
```

EXERCISES

The following exercises are designed to test your understanding of nested types, packages, static imports, and exceptions:

1. What is a nested class?

2. Identify the four kinds of nested classes.

3. Which nested classes are also known as inner classes?

4. True or false: A static member class has an enclosing instance.

5. How do you instantiate a nonstatic member class from beyond its enclosing class?

6. When is it necessary to declare local variables and parameters `final`?

7. True or false: An interface can be declared within a class or within another interface.

8. What is a package?

9. How do you ensure that package names are unique?

10. What is a package statement?

11. True or false: You can specify multiple package statements in a source file.

12. What is an import statement?

13. How do you indicate that you want to import multiple types via a single import statement?

14. During a runtime search, what happens when the virtual machine cannot find a classfile?

15. How do you specify the user classpath to the virtual machine?

16. What is a constant interface?

17. Why are constant interfaces used?

18. Why are constant interfaces bad?

19. What is a static import statement?

20. How do you specify a static import statement?

21. What is an exception?

22. In what ways are objects superior to error codes for representing exceptions?

23. What is a throwable?

24. What does the getCause() method return?

25. What is the difference between Exception and Error?

26. What is a checked exception?

27. What is a runtime exception?

28. Under what circumstance would you introduce your own exception class?

29. True or false: You use a throw statement to identify exceptions that are thrown from a method by appending this statement to a method's header.

30. What is the purpose of a try statement, and what is the purpose of a catch clause?

31. What is the purpose of a finally clause?

32. A 2D graphics package supports two-dimensional drawing and transformations (rotation, scaling, translation, and so on). These transformations require a 3-by-3 matrix (a table). Declare a G2D class that encloses a private Matrix nonstatic member class. Instantiate Matrix within G2D's noargument constructor, and initialize the Matrix instance to the *identity matrix* (a matrix where all entries are 0 except for those on the upper-left to lower-right diagonal, which are 1).

33. Extend the logging package to support a null device in which messages are thrown away.

34. Modify the logging package so that Logger's connect() method throws CannotConnectException when it cannot connect to its logging destination, and the other two methods each throw NotConnectedException when connect() was not called or when it threw CannotConnectException.

35. Modify TestLogger to respond appropriately to thrown CannotConnectException and NotConnectedException objects.

Summary

Classes that are declared outside of any class are known as top-level classes. Java also supports nested classes, which are classes declared as members of other classes or scopes.

There are four kinds of nested classes: static member classes, nonstatic member classes, anonymous classes, and local classes. The latter three categories are known as inner classes.

Java supports the partitioning of top-level types into multiple namespaces, to better organize these types and to also prevent name conflicts. Java uses packages to accomplish these tasks.

The package statement identifies the package in which a source file's types are located. The import statement imports types from a package by telling the compiler where to look for unqualified type names during compilation.

An exception is a divergence from an application's normal behavior. Although it can be represented by an error code or object, Java uses objects because error codes are meaningless and cannot contain information about what led to the exception.

Java provides a hierarchy of classes that represent different kinds of exceptions. These classes are rooted in Throwable. Moving down the throwable hierarchy, you encounter the Exception and Error classes, which represent nonerror exceptions and errors.

Exception and its subclasses, except for RuntimeException (and its subclasses), describe checked exceptions. They are checked because you must check the code to ensure that an exception is handled where thrown or identified as being handled elsewhere.

RuntimeException and its subclasses describe unchecked exceptions. You do not have to handle these exceptions because they represent coding mistakes (fix the mistakes). Although the names of their classes can appear in throws clauses, doing so adds clutter.

The throw statement throws an exception to the virtual machine, which searches for an appropriate handler. If the exception is checked, its name must appear in the method's throws clause, unless the name of the exception's superclass is listed in this clause.

A method handles one or more exceptions by specifying a try statement and appropriate catch clauses. A finally clause can be included to execute cleanup code whether an exception is thrown or not, and before a thrown exception leaves the method.

Now that you have mastered the advanced language features related to nested types, packages, static imports, and exceptions, you can leverage this knowledge in Chapter 5, where you explore features related to assertions, annotations, generics, and enums.

Chapter 5

Mastering Advanced Language Features Part 2

Chapters 2 and 3 laid a foundation for learning the Java language, and Chapter 4 built onto this foundation by introducing some of Java's more advanced language features. Chapter 5 continues to cover advanced language features by focusing on those features related to assertions, annotations, generics, and enums.

Assertions

Writing source code is not an easy task. All too often, *bugs* (defects) are introduced into the code. When a bug is not discovered before compiling the source code, it makes it into runtime code, which will probably fail unexpectedly. At this point, the cause of failure can be very difficult to determine.

Developers often make assumptions about application correctness, and some developers think that specifying comments that state their beliefs about what they think is true at the comment locations is sufficient for determining correctness. However, comments are useless for preventing bugs because the compiler ignores them.

Many languages address this problem by providing an assertions language feature that lets the developer codify assumptions about application correctness. When the application runs, if an assertion fails, the application terminates with a message that helps the developer diagnose the failure's cause.

This section introduces you to Java's assertions language feature. After defining this term, showing you how to declare assertions, and providing examples, the section looks at using and avoiding assertions. Finally, you learn how to selectively enable and disable assertions via the Java SE 6u16 `javac` compiler tool's command-line arguments.

Declaring Assertions

An *assertion* is a statement that lets you express an assumption of program correctness via a Boolean expression. If this expression evaluates to true, execution continues with the next statement. Otherwise, an error that identifies the cause of failure is thrown.

There are two forms of the assertion statement, with each form beginning with reserved word assert:

```
assert expression1 ;
assert expression1 : expression2 ;
```

In both forms of this statement, *expression1* is the Boolean expression. In the second form, *expression2* is any expression that returns a value. It cannot be a call to a method whose return type is void.

When *expression1* evaluates to false, this statement instantiates the AssertionError class. The first statement form calls this class's noargument constructor, which does not associate a message identifying failure details with the AssertionError instance.

The second form calls an AssertionError constructor whose type matches the type of *expression2*'s value. This value is passed to the constructor and its string representation is used as the error's detail message.

When the error is thrown, the name of the source file and the number of the line from where the error was thrown are output to the console as part of the thrown error's stack trace. In many situations, this information is sufficient for identifying what led to the failure, and the first form of the assertion statement should be used.

Listing 5–1 demonstrates the first form of the assertion statement.

Listing 5–1. *Throwing an assertion error without a detail message*

```
public class AssertionDemo
{
    public static void main(String[] args)
    {
        int x = 1;
        assert x == 0;
    }
}
```

When assertions are enabled (I discuss this task later), running the previous application results in the following output:

```
Exception in thread "main" java.lang.AssertionError
        at AssertionDemo.main(AssertionDemo.java:6)
```

In other situations, more information is needed to help diagnose the cause of failure. For example, suppose *expression1* compares variables x and y, and throws an error when x's value exceeds y's value. Because this should never happen, you would probably use the second statement form to output these values so you could diagnose the problem.

Listing 5–2 demonstrates the second form of the assertion statement.

Listing 5–2. *Throwing an assertion error with a detail message*

```
public class AssertionDemo
{
   public static void main(String[] args)
   {
      int x = 1;
      assert x == 0: x;
   }
}
```

Once again, it is assumed that assertions are enabled. Running the previous application results in the following output:

```
Exception in thread "main" java.lang.AssertionError: 1
        at AssertionDemo.main(AssertionDemo.java:6)
```

The value in x is appended to the end of the first output line, which is somewhat cryptic. To make this output more meaningful, you might want to specify an expression that also includes the variable's name: assert x == 0: "x = " + x;, for example.

Using Assertions

There are many situations where assertions should be used. These situations organize into internal invariant, control-flow invariant, and design-by-contract categories. An *invariant* is something that does not change.

Internal Invariants

An *internal invariant* is expression-oriented behavior that is not expected to change. For example, Listing 5–3 introduces an internal invariant by way of chained if-else statements that output the state of water based on its temperature.

Listing 5–3. *Discovering that an internal invariant can vary*

```
public class IIDemo
{
   public static void main(String[] args)
   {
      double temperature = 50.0; // Celsius
      if (temperature < 0.0)
         System.out.println("water has solidified");
      else
      if (temperature >= 100.0)
         System.out.println("water is boiling into a gas");
      else
      {
         // temperature > 0.0 and temperature < 100.0
         assert(temperature > 0.0 && temperature < 100.0): temperature;
         System.out.println("water is remaining in its liquid state");
      }
   }
}
```

A developer might specify only a comment stating an assumption as to what expression causes the final `else` to be reached. Because the comment might not be enough to detect the lurking < 0.0 expression bug, an assertion statement is necessary.

Another example of an internal invariant concerns a switch statement with no default case. The default case is avoided because the developer believes that all paths have been covered. However, this is not always true, as Listing 5–4 demonstrates.

Listing 5–4. *Another buggy internal invariant*

```
public class IIDemo
{
   final static int NORTH = 0;
   final static int SOUTH = 1;
   final static int EAST = 2;
   final static int WEST = 3;
   public static void main(String[] args)
   {
      int direction = (int)(Math.random()*5);
      switch (direction)
      {
         case NORTH: System.out.println("travelling north"); break;
         case SOUTH: System.out.println("travelling south"); break;
         case EAST : System.out.println("travelling east"); break;
         case WEST : System.out.println("travelling west"); break;
         default   : assert false;
      }
   }
}
```

Listing 5–4 assumes that the expression tested by switch will only evaluate to one of four integer constants. However, `(int)(Math.random()*5)` can also return 4, causing the default case to execute `assert false;`, which always throws AssertionError. (You might have to run this application a few times to see the assertion error, but first you need to learn how to enable assertions, which I discuss later in this chapter.)

> **TIP:** When assertions are disabled, `assert false;` does not execute and the bug goes undetected. To always detect this bug, replace `assert false;` with `throw new AssertionError(direction);`.

Control-Flow Invariants

A *control-flow invariant* is a flow of control that is not expected to change. For example, Listing 5–4 uses an assertion to test an assumption that switch's default case will not execute. Listing 5–5, which fixes Listing 5–4's bug, provides another example.

Listing 5–5. *A buggy control-flow invariant*

```
public class CFDemo
{
   final static int NORTH = 0;
   final static int SOUTH = 1;
```

```
final static int EAST = 2;
final static int WEST = 3;
public static void main(String[] args)
{
   int direction = (int)(Math.random()*4);
   switch (direction)
   {
      case NORTH: System.out.println("travelling north"); break;
      case SOUTH: System.out.println("travelling south"); break;
      case EAST : System.out.println("travelling east"); break;
      case WEST : System.out.println("travelling west");
      default   : assert false;
   }
}
}
```

Because the original bug has been fixed, the default case should never be reached. However, the omission of a break statement that terminates case WEST causes execution to reach the default case. This control-flow invariant has been broken. (Again, you might have to run this application a few times to see the assertion error, but first you need to learn how to enable assertions, which I discuss later in this chapter.)

> **CAUTION:** Be careful when using an assertion statement to detect code that should never be executed. If the assertion statement cannot be reached according to the rules set forth in *The Java Language Specification, Third Edition,* by James Gosling, Bill Joy, Guy Steele, and Gilad Bracha (Addison-Wesley, 2005; ISBN: 0321246780) (also available at `http://java.sun.com/docs/books/jls/third_edition/html/j3TOC.html`), the compiler will report an error. For example, `for(;;); assert false;` causes the compiler to report an error because the infinite for loop prevents the assertion statement from executing.

Design-by-Contract

Design-by-Contract is a way to design software based on preconditions, postconditions, and invariants (internal, control-flow, and class). Assertion statements support an informal design-by-contract style of development.

Preconditions

A *precondition* is something that must be true when a method is called. Assertion statements are often used to satisfy a helper method's preconditions by checking that its arguments are legal. Listing 5–6 provides an example.

Listing 5–6. *Verifying a precondition*

```
public class Lotto649
{
   public static void main(String[] args)
   {
      // Lotto 649 requires that six unique numbers be chosen.
```

```java
int[] selectedNumbers = new int[6];

// Assign a unique random number from 1 to 49 (inclusive) to each slot
// in the selectedNumbers array.
for (int slot = 0; slot < selectedNumbers.length; slot++)
{
    int num;

    // Obtain a random number from 1 to 49. That number becomes the
    // selected number if it has not previously been chosen.
    try_again:
    do
    {
        num = rnd(49)+1;
        for (int i = 0; i < slot; i++)
            if (selectedNumbers[i] == num)
                continue try_again;
        break;
    }
    while (true);

    // Assign selected number to appropriate slot.
    selectedNumbers[slot] = num;
}

// Sort all selected numbers into ascending order and then print these
// numbers.
sort(selectedNumbers);
for (int i = 0; i < selectedNumbers.length; i++)
    System.out.print(selectedNumbers[i] + " ");
}
private static int rnd(int limit)
{
    // This method returns a random number (actually, a pseudorandom number)
    // ranging from 0 through limit-1 (inclusive).
    assert limit > 1: "limit = " + limit;
    return (int)(Math.random()*limit);
}
private static void sort(int[] x)
{
    // This method sorts the integers in the passed array into ascending
    // order.
    for (int pass = 0; pass < x.length-1; pass++)
        for (int i = x.length-1; i > pass; i--)
            if (x[i] < x[pass])
            {
                int temp = x[i];
                x[i] = x[pass];
                x[pass] = temp;
            }
}
}
```

Listing 5–6's application simulates Lotto 6/49, one of Canada's national lottery games.
The rnd() helper method returns a randomly chosen integer between 0 and limit-1. An
assertion statement verifies the precondition that limit's value must be 2 or higher.

NOTE: The sort() helper method *sorts* (orders) the selectedNumbers array's integers into ascending order by implementing an *algorithm* (a recipe for accomplishing some task) called *Bubble Sort.*

Bubble Sort works by making multiple passes over the array. During each pass, various comparisons and swaps ensure that the next smallest element value "bubbles" toward the top of the array, which would be the element at index 0.

Bubble Sort is not efficient, but is more than adequate for sorting a six-element array. Although I could have used one of the efficient sort() methods located in the java.util package's Arrays class (for example, Arrays.sort(selectedNumbers); accomplishes the same objective as Listing 5–6's sort(selectedNumbers); method call, but does so more efficiently), I chose to use Bubble Sort because I prefer to wait until Chapter 8 before getting into the Arrays class.

Postconditions

A *postcondition* is something that must be true after a method successfully completes. Assertion statements are often used to satisfy a helper method's postconditions by checking that its result is legal. Listing 5–7 provides an example.

Listing 5–7. *Verifying a postcondition in addition to preconditions*

```java
public class MergeArrays
{
   public static void main(String[] args)
   {
      int[] x = { 1, 2, 3, 4, 5 };
      int[] y = { 1, 2, 7, 9 };
      int[] result = merge(x, y);
      for (int i = 0; i < result.length; i++)
         System.out.println(result[i]);
   }
   public static int[] merge(int[] a, int[] b)
   {
      if (a == null)
         throw new NullPointerException("a is null");
      if (b == null)
         throw new NullPointerException("b is null");
      int[] result = new int[a.length+b.length];
      // Precondition
      assert result.length == a.length+b.length: "length mismatch";
      for (int i = 0; i < a.length; i++)
         result[i] = a[i];
      for (int i = 0; i < b.length; i++)
         result[a.length+i-1] = b[i];
      // Postcondition
      assert containsAll(result, a, b): "value missing from array";
      return result;
   }
```

```
    private static boolean containsAll(int[] result, int[] a, int[] b)
    {
       for (int i = 0; i < a.length; i++)
          if (!contains(result, a[i]))
             return false;
       for (int i = 0; i < b.length; i++)
          if (!contains(result, b[i]))
             return false;
       return true;
    }
    private static boolean contains(int[] a, int val)
    {
       for (int i = 0; i < a.length; i++)
          if (a[i] == val)
             return true;
       return false;
    }
}
```

Listing 5–7 uses an assertion statement to verify the postcondition that all of the values in the two arrays being merged are present in the merged array. The postcondition is not satisfied, however, because this listing contains a bug.

Listing 5–7 also shows preconditions and postconditions being used together. The solitary precondition verifies that the merged array length equals the lengths of the arrays being merged prior to the merge logic.

Class Invariants

A *class invariant* is a kind of internal invariant that applies to every instance of a class at all times, except when an instance is transitioning from one consistent state to another.

For example, suppose instances of a class contain arrays whose values are sorted in ascending order. You might want to include an isSorted() method in the class that returns true if the array is still sorted, and verify that each constructor and method that modifies the array specifies assert isSorted(); prior to exit, to satisfy the assumption that the array is still sorted when the constructor/method exists.

Avoiding Assertions

Although there are many situations where assertions should be used, there also are situations where they should be avoided. For example, you should not use assertions to check the arguments that are passed to public methods, for the following reasons:

▪ Checking a public method's arguments is part of the contract that exists between the method and its caller. If you use assertions to check these arguments, and if assertions are disabled, this contract is violated because the arguments will not be checked.

- Assertions also prevent appropriate exceptions from being thrown. For example, when an illegal argument is passed to a public method, it is common to throw `IllegalArgumentException` or `NullPointerException`. However, `AssertionError` is thrown instead.

You should also avoid using assertions to perform work required by the application to function correctly. This work is often performed as a side effect of the assertion's Boolean expression. When assertions are disabled, the work is not performed.

For example, suppose you have a list of `Employee` objects and a few null references that are also stored in this list, and you want to remove all of the null references. It would not be correct to remove these references via the following assertion statement:

```
assert employees.removeAll(null);
```

Although the assertion statement will not throw `AssertionError` because there is at least one null reference in the `employees` list, the application that depends upon this statement executing will fail when assertions are disabled.

Instead of depending on the former code to remove the null references, you would be better off using code similar to the following:

```
boolean allNullsRemoved = employees.removeAll(null);
assert allNullsRemoved;
```

This time, all null references are removed regardless of whether assertions are enabled or disabled, and you can still specify an assertion to verify that nulls were removed.

Enabling and Disabling Assertions

The compiler records assertions in the classfile. However, assertions are disabled at runtime because they can affect performance. An assertion might call a method that takes awhile to complete, and this would impact the running application's performance.

You must enable the classfile's assertions before you can test assumptions about the behaviors of your classes. Accomplish this task by specifying the -enableassertions or -ea command-line option when running the java application launcher tool.

The -enableassertions and -ea command-line options let you enable assertions at various granularities based upon one of the following arguments (except for the noargument scenario, you must use a colon to separate the option from its argument):

- *No argument*: Assertions are enabled in all classes except system classes.

- *PackageName*...: Assertions are enabled in the specified package and its subpackages by specifying the package name followed by ....

- ...: Assertions are enabled in the unnamed package, which happens to be whatever directory is current.

- *ClassName*: Assertions are enabled in the named class by specifying the class name.

For example, you can enable all assertions except system assertions when running the `MergeArrays` application via java `-ea MergeArrays`. Also, you could enable any assertions in Chapter 4's `logging` package by specifying java `-ea:logging TestLogger`.

Assertions can be disabled, and also at various granularities, by specifying either of the `-disableassertions` or `–da` command-line options. These options take the same arguments as `-enableassertions` and `-ea`. For example, java `-ea –da:loneclass mainclass` enables all assertions except for those in *loneclass*. (*loneclass* and *mainclass* are placeholders for the actual classes that you specify.)

The previous options apply to all classloaders. Except when taking no arguments, they also apply to system classes. This exception simplifies the enabling of assertion statements in all classes except for system classes, which is often desirable.

To enable system assertions, specify either `-enablesystemassertions` or `-esa`; for example, java `-esa –ea:logging TestLogger`. Specify either `-disablesystemassertions` or `-dsa` to disable system assertions.

Annotations

While developing a Java application, you might want to *annotate*, or associate *metadata* (data that describes other data) with, various application elements. For example, you might want to identify methods that are not fully implemented so that you will not forget to implement them. Java's annotations language feature lets you accomplish this task.

This section introduces you to annotations. After defining this term and presenting three kinds of compiler-supported annotations as examples, the section shows you how to declare your own annotation types and use these types to annotate source code. Finally, you discover how to process your own annotations to accomplish useful tasks.

> **NOTE:** Java has always supported ad hoc annotation mechanisms. For example, the `java.lang.Cloneable` interface identifies classes whose instances can be shallowly cloned via `Object`'s `clone()` method, the `transient` reserved word marks fields that are to be ignored during serialization, and the `@deprecated javadoc` tag documents methods that are no longer supported. In contrast, the annotations feature is a standard for annotating code.

Discovering Annotations

An *annotation* is an instance of an annotation type and associates metadata with an application element. It is expressed in source code by prefixing the type name with the @ symbol. For example, `@Readonly` is an annotation and `Readonly` is its type.

NOTE: You can use annotations to associate metadata with constructors, fields, local variables, methods, packages, parameters, and types (annotation, class, enum, and interface).

Beginning with Java version 7, annotations can appear on any use of a type. For example, you might declare Employee[@Readonly] emps; to indicate that emps is an unmodifiable one-dimensional array of *mutable* (modifiable) Employee instances.

The compiler supports the Override, Deprecated, and SuppressWarnings annotation types. These types are located in the java.lang package.

@Override annotations are useful for expressing that a subclass method overrides a method in the superclass, and does not overload that method instead. Listing 5–8 reveals that this annotation prefixes the overriding method.

Listing 5–8. *Annotating an overriding method*

```
@Override
public void draw(int color)
{
    // drawing code
}
```

NOTE: In Chapter 3, I presented @Override on the same line as the method header. In Listing 5–8, I present this annotation on a separate line above the method header.

It is common practice to place annotations on separate lines above the application elements that they annotate, unless they are being used to annotate parameters. In that case, an annotation must appear on the same line as and in front of the parameter's name.

@Deprecated annotations are useful for indicating that the marked application element is *deprecated* (phased out) and should no longer be used. The compiler warns you when a deprecated application element is accessed by nondeprecated code.

In contrast, the @deprecated javadoc tag and associated text warns you against using the deprecated item, and tells you what to use instead. Listing 5–9 demonstrates that @Deprecated and @deprecated can be used together.

Listing 5–9. *Deprecating a method via @Deprecated and @deprecated*

```
/**
 * Allocates a <code>Date</code> object and initializes it so that
 * it represents midnight, local time, at the beginning of the day
 * specified by the <code>year</code>, <code>month</code>, and
 * <code>date</code> arguments.
 *
 * @param    year    the year minus 1900.
 * @param    month   the month between 0-11.
 * @param    date    the day of the month between 1-31.
 * @see      java.util.Calendar
 * @deprecated As of JDK version 1.1,
```

```
 * replaced by <code>Calendar.set(year + 1900, month, date)</code>
 * or <code>GregorianCalendar(year + 1900, month, date)</code>.
 */
@Deprecated
public Date(int year, int month, int date)
{
    this(year, month, date, 0, 0, 0);
}
```

Listing 5–9 excerpts one of the constructors in Java's Date class (located in the java.util package). This constructor has been deprecated in favor of using the set() method in the Calendar class (also located in the java.util package).

The compiler suppresses warnings if a compilation unit (typically a class or interface) refers to a deprecated class, method, or field. This feature lets you modify legacy APIs without generating deprecation warnings, and is demonstrated in Listing 5–10.

Listing 5–10. *Referencing a deprecated field from within the same class declaration*

```
public class Employee
{
    /**
     * Employee's name
     * @deprecated New version uses firstName and lastName fields.
     */
    @Deprecated
    String name;
    String firstName;
    String lastName;
    public static void main(String[] args)
    {
        Employee emp = new Employee();
        emp.name = "John Doe";
    }
}
```

Listing 5–10 declares an Employee class with a name field that has been deprecated. Although Employee's main() method refers to name, the compiler will suppress a deprecation warning because the deprecation and reference occur in the same class.

Suppose you refactor Listing 5–10 by introducing a new UseEmployee class and moving Employee's main() method to this class. Listing 5–11 presents the resulting class structure.

Listing 5–11. *Referencing a deprecated field from within another class declaration*

```
class Employee
{
    /**
     * Employee's name
     * @deprecated New version uses firstName and lastName fields.
     */
    @Deprecated
    String name;
    String firstName;
    String lastName;
}
```

```
public class UseEmployee
{
   public static void main(String[] args)
   {
      Employee emp = new Employee();
      emp.name = "John Doe";
   }
}
```

If you attempt to compile this source code via Java SE 6u16's javac compiler tool, you will discover the following messages:

```
Note: Employee.java uses or overrides a deprecated API.
Note: Recompile with -Xlint:deprecation for details.
```

You will need to specify -Xlint:deprecation as one of javac's command-line arguments to discover the deprecated item and the code that refers to this item:

```
Employee.java:17: warning: [deprecation] name in Employee has been deprecated
      emp.name = "John Doe";
          ^
1 warning
```

@SuppressWarnings annotations are useful for suppressing deprecation or unchecked warnings via a "deprecation" or an "unchecked" argument. (Unchecked warnings occur when mixing code that uses generics with pre-generics legacy code.)

For example, Listing 5–12 uses @SuppressWarnings with a "deprecation" argument to suppress the compiler's deprecation warnings when code within the UseEmployee class's main() method accesses the Employee class's name field.

Listing 5–12. *Suppressing the previous deprecation warning*

```
public class UseEmployee
{
   @SuppressWarnings("deprecation")
   public static void main(String[] args)
   {
      Employee emp = new Employee();
      emp.name = "John Doe";
   }
}
```

Declaring Annotation Types and Annotating Source Code

Before you can annotate source code, you need annotation types that can be instantiated. Java supplies many annotation types in addition to Override, Deprecated, and SuppressWarnings. Java also lets you declare your own types.

You declare an annotation type by specifying the @ symbol, immediately followed by reserved word interface, followed by the type's name, followed by a body. For example, Listing 5–13 uses @interface to declare an annotation type named Stub.

Listing 5–13. *Declaring the Stub annotation type*

```
public @interface Stub
```

```
{
}
```

Instances of annotation types that supply no data apart from a name—their bodies are empty—are known as *marker annotations* because they mark application elements for some purpose. As Listing 5–14 reveals, @Stub is used to mark empty methods (stubs).

Listing 5–14. *Annotating a stubbed-out method*

```
public class Deck // Describes a deck of cards.
{
   @Stub
   public void shuffle()
   {
      // This method is empty and will presumably be filled in with appropriate
      // code at some later date.
   }
}
```

Listing 5–14's Deck class declares an empty shuffle() method. This fact is indicated by instantiating Stub and prefixing shuffle()'s method header with the resulting @Stub annotation.

> **NOTE:** Although marker interfaces (discussed in Chapter 3) appear to have been replaced by marker annotations, this is not the case, because marker interfaces have advantages over marker annotations. One advantage is that a marker interface specifies a type that is implemented by a marked class, which lets you catch problems at compile time. For example, if a class does not implement the Cloneable interface, its instances cannot be shallowly cloned via Object's clone() method. If Cloneable had been implemented as a marker annotation, this problem would not be detected until runtime.

Although marker annotations are useful (@Override and @Deprecated are good examples), you will typically want to enhance an annotation type so that you can store metadata via its instances. You accomplish this task by adding elements to the type.

An *element* is a method header that appears in the annotation type's body. It cannot have parameters or a throws clause, and its return type must be a primitive type (such as int), String, Class, an enum, an annotation type, or an array of the preceding types. However, it can have a default value.

Listing 5–15 adds three elements to Stub.

Listing 5–15. *Adding three elements to the Stub annotation type*

```
public @interface Stub
{
   int id(); // A semicolon must terminate an element declaration.
   String dueDate();
   String developer() default "unassigned";
}
```

The id() element specifies a 32-bit integer that identifies the stub. The dueDate() element specifies a String-based date that identifies when the method stub is to be implemented. Finally, developer() specifies the String-based name of the developer responsible for coding the method stub.

Unlike id() and dueDate(), developer() is declared with a default value, "unassigned". When you instantiate Stub and do not assign a value to developer() in that instance, as is the case with Listing 5–16, this default value is assigned to developer().

Listing 5–16. *Initializing a Stub instance's elements*

```
public class Deck
{
    @Stub
    (
       id = 1,
       dueDate = "10/21/2010"
    )
    public void shuffle()
    {
    }
}
```

Listing 5–16 reveals one @Stub annotation that initializes its id() element to 1 and its dueDate() element to "10/21/2010". Each element name does not have a trailing (), and the comma-separated list of two element initializers appears between (and).

Suppose you decide to replace Stub's id(), dueDate(), and developer() elements with a single String value() element whose string specifies comma-separated ID, due date, and developer name values. Listing 5–17 shows you two ways to initialize value.

Listing 5–17. *Initializing each Stub instance's value() element*

```
public class Deck
{
    @Stub(value = "1,10/21/2010,unassigned")
    public void shuffle()
    {
    }
    @Stub("2,10/21/2010,unassigned")
    public Card[] deal(int ncards)
    {
       return null;
    }
}
```

This listing reveals special treatment for the value() element. When it is an annotation type's only element, you can omit value()'s name and = from the initializer. I used this fact to specify @SuppressWarnings("deprecation") in Listing 5–12.

Using Meta-Annotations in Annotation Type Declarations

Each of the Override, Deprecated, and SuppressWarnings annotation types is itself annotated with *meta-annotations* (annotations that annotate annotation types). For example, Listing 5–18 shows you that the SuppressWarnings annotation type is annotated with two meta-annotations.

Listing 5–18. *The annotated SuppressWarnings type declaration*

```
@Target(value={TYPE,FIELD,METHOD,PARAMETER,CONSTRUCTOR,LOCAL_VARIABLE})
@Retention(value=SOURCE)
public @interface SuppressWarnings
```

The Target annotation type, which is located in the java.lang.annotation package, identifies the kinds of application elements to which an annotation type applies. @Target indicates that @SuppressWarnings annotations can be used to annotate types, fields, methods, parameters, constructors, and local variables.

Each of TYPE, FIELD, METHOD, PARAMETER, CONSTRUCTOR, and LOCAL_VARIABLE is a member of the ElementType enum, which is also located in the java.lang.annotation package.

The { and } characters surrounding the comma-separated list of values assigned to Target's value() element signify an array—value()'s return type is String[]. Although these braces are necessary (unless the array consists of one item), value= could be omitted when initializing @Target because Target declares only a value() element.

The Retention annotation type, which is located in the java.lang.annotation package, identifies the retention (also known as lifetime) of an annotation type's annotations. @Retention indicates that @SuppressWarnings annotations have a lifetime that is limited to source code—they do not exist after compilation.

SOURCE is one of the members of the RetentionPolicy enum (located in the java.lang.annotation package). The other members are CLASS and RUNTIME. These three members specify the following retention policies:

- CLASS: The compiler records annotations in the classfile, but the virtual machine does not retain them (to save memory space). This policy is the default.

- RUNTIME: The compiler records annotations in the classfile, and the virtual machine retains them so that they can be read via the Reflection API (discussed in Chapter 7) at runtime.

- SOURCE: The compiler discards annotations after using them.

There are two problems with the Stub annotation type shown in Listings 5–13 and 5–15. First, the lack of an @Target meta-annotation means that you can annotate any application element @Stub. However, this annotation only makes sense when applied to methods and constructors. Check out Listing 5–19.

Listing 5–19. *Annotating undesirable application elements*

```
@Stub("1,10/21/2010,unassigned")
public class Deck
{
   @Stub("2,10/21/2010,unassigned")
   private Card[] cardsRemaining;
   @Stub("3,10/21/2010,unassigned")
   public Deck()
   {
   }
   @Stub("4,10/21/2010,unassigned")
   public void shuffle()
   {
   }
   @Stub("5,10/21/2010,unassigned")
   public Card[] deal(@Stub("5,10/21/2010,unassigned") int ncards)
   {
      return null;
   }
}
```

Listing 5–19 uses @Stub to annotate the Deck class, the cardsRemaining field, and the ncards parameter in addition to annotating the constructor and the two methods. The first three application elements are inappropriate to annotate because they are not stubs.

You can fix this problem by prefixing the Stub annotation type declaration with @Target({ElementType.METHOD, ElementType.CONSTRUCTOR}) so that Stub only applies to methods and constructors. After doing this, the Java SE 6u16 javac compiler tool will output the following error messages when you attempt to compile Listing 5–19:

```
Deck.java:1: annotation type not applicable to this kind of declaration
@Stub("1,10/21/2010,unassigned")
^
Deck.java:4: annotation type not applicable to this kind of declaration
   @Stub("2,10/21/2010,unassigned")
   ^
Deck.java:15: annotation type not applicable to this kind of declaration
   public Card[] deal(@Stub("5,10/21/2010,unassigned") int ncards)
                      ^
3 errors
```

The second problem is that the default CLASS retention policy makes it impossible to process @Stub annotations at runtime. You can fix this problem by prefixing the Stub type declaration with @Retention(RetentionPolicy.RUNTIME).

Listing 5–20 presents the Stub annotation type with the desired @Target and @Retention meta-annotations.

Listing 5–20. *A revamped Stub annotation type*

```
@Target({ElementType.METHOD, ElementType.CONSTRUCTOR})
@Retention(RetentionPolicy.RUNTIME)
public @interface Stub
{
   String value();
}
```

> **NOTE:** Java also provides Documented and Inherited meta-annotation types in the java.lang.annotation package. Instances of @Documented-annotated annotation types are to be documented by javadoc and similar tools.
>
> Instances of @Inherited-annotated annotation types are automatically inherited. According to Inherited's Java documentation, if "the user queries the annotation type on a class declaration, and the class declaration has no annotation for this type, then the class's superclass will automatically be queried for the annotation type. This process will be repeated until an annotation for this type is found, or the top of the class hierarchy (Object) is reached. If no superclass has an annotation for this type, then the query will indicate that the class in question has no such annotation."

Processing Annotations

It is not enough to declare an annotation type and use that type to annotate source code. Unless you do something specific with those annotations, they remain dormant. One way to accomplish something specific is to write an application that processes the annotations. Listing 5–21's StubFinder application does just that.

Listing 5–21. *The StubFinder application*

```
import java.lang.reflect.*;

public class StubFinder
{
   public static void main(String[] args) throws Exception
   {
      if (args.length != 1)
      {
         System.err.println("usage: java StubFinder classfile");
         return;
      }
      Method[] methods = Class.forName(args[0]).getMethods();
      for (int i = 0; i < methods.length; i++)
         if (methods[i].isAnnotationPresent(Stub.class))
         {
            Stub stub = methods[i].getAnnotation(Stub.class);
            String[] components = stub.value().split(",");
            System.out.println("Stub ID = " + components[0]);
            System.out.println("Stub Date = " + components[1]);
            System.out.println("Stub Developer = " + components[2]);
            System.out.println();
         }
   }
}
```

StubFinder loads a classfile whose name is specified as a command-line argument, and outputs the metadata associated with each @Stub annotation that precedes each public method header. These annotations are instances of Listing 5–20's Stub annotation type.

StubFinder next uses a special class named Class and its forName() class method to load a classfile. Class also provides a getMethods() method that returns an array of Method objects describing the loaded class's public methods.

For each loop iteration, a Method object's isAnnotationPresent() method is called to determine if the method is annotated with the annotation described by the Stub class (referred to as Stub.class).

If isAnnotationPresent() returns true, Method's getAnnotation() method is called to return the annotation Stub instance. This instance's value() method is called to retrieve the string stored in the annotation.

Next, String's split() method is called to split the string's comma-separated list of ID, date, and developer values into an array of String objects. Each object is then output along with descriptive text.

Class's forName() method is capable of throwing various exceptions that must be handled or explicitly declared as part of a method's header. For simplicity, I chose to append a throws Exception clause to the main() method's header.

> **CAUTION:** There are two problems with throws Exception. First, it is better to handle the exception and present a suitable error message than to "pass the buck" by throwing it out of main(). Second, Exception is generic—it hides the names of the kinds of exceptions that are thrown. However, it is convenient to specify throws Exception in a throwaway utility.

Do not be concerned if you do not understand Class, forName(), getMethods(), Method, isAnnotationPresent(), .class, getAnnotation(), and split(). You will learn about these items in Chapter 7.

After compiling StubFinder (javac StubFinder.java), Stub (javac Stub.java), and Listing 5-17's Deck class (javac Deck.java), run StubFinder with Deck as its single command-line argument (java StubFinder Deck). You will observe the following output:

```
Stub ID = 2
Stub Date = 10/21/2010
Stub Developer = unassigned

Stub ID = 1
Stub Date = 10/21/2010
Stub Developer = unassigned
```

If you expected the output to reflect the order of appearance of @Stub annotations in Deck.java, you are probably surprised by the output's unsorted order. This lack of order is caused by getMethods(). According to this method's Java documentation, "the elements in the array returned are not sorted and are not in any particular order."

> **NOTE:** Java version 5 introduced an `apt` tool for processing annotations. This tool's functionality has been integrated into the compiler beginning with Java version 6—`apt` is being phased out. My "Processing Annotations in Java SE 6" article (`http://javajeff.mb.ca/cgi-hin/mp.cgi?a=/java/javase/articles/paijse6`) provides a tutorial on using the Java version 6 compiler to process annotations.

Generics

Java version 5 introduced *generics*, language features for declaring and using type-agnostic classes and interfaces. When working with Java's collections framework (which I introduce in Chapter 8), these features help you avoid `java.lang.ClassCastExceptions`.

> **NOTE:** Although the main use for generics is the collections framework, Java's class library also contains *generified* (retrofitted to make use of generics) classes that have nothing to do with this framework: `java.lang.Class`, `java.lang.ThreadLocal`, and `java.lang.ref.WeakReference` are three examples.

This section introduces you to generics. You first learn how generics promote type safety in the context of the collections classes, and then you explore generics in the contexts of generic types and generic methods.

Collections and the Need for Type Safety

Java's collections framework makes it possible to store objects in various kinds of containers (known as collections) and later retrieve those objects. For example, you can store objects in a list, a set, or a map. You can then retrieve a single object, or iterate over the collection and retrieve all objects.

Before Java version 5 overhauled the collections framework to take advantage of generics, there was no way to prevent a collection from containing objects of mixed types. The compiler did not check an object's type to see if it was suitable before it was added to a collection, and this lack of static type checking led to `ClassCastExceptions`.

Listing 5–22 demonstrates how easy it is to generate a `ClassCastException`.

Listing 5–22. *Lack of type safety leading to a* `ClassCastException` *at runtime*

```
public static void main(String[] args)
{
    List employees = new ArrayList();
    employees.add(new Employee("John Doe"));
    employees.add(new Employee("Jane Doe"));
    employees.add("Doe Doe");
    Iterator iter = employees.iterator();
    while (iter.hasNext())
```

```
   {
      Employee emp = (Employee) iter.next();
      System.out.println(emp.getName());
   }
}
```

After instantiating ArrayList, main() uses this list collection object's reference to add a pair of Employee objects to the list. It then adds a String object, which violates the implied contract that ArrayList is supposed to store only Employee objects.

Moving on, main() obtains an Iterator for iterating over the list of Employees. As long as Iterator's hasNext() method returns true, its next() method is called to return an object stored in the ArrayList.

The Object that next() returns must be downcast to Employee so that the Employee object's getName() method can be called to return the employee's name. The string that this method returns is then output to the standard output device via System.out.println().

The (Employee) cast checks the type of each object returned by next() to make sure that it is an Employee. Although this is true of the first two objects, it is not true of the third object. Attempting to cast "Doe Doe" to Employee results in a ClassCastException.

The ClassCastException occurs because of an assumption that a list is *homogenous*. In other words, a list stores only objects of a single type or a family of related types. In reality, the list is *heterogeneous* in that it can store any Object.

Listing 5–23's generics-based homogenous list avoids ClassCastException.

Listing 5–23. *Lack of type safety leading to a compiler error*

```
public static void main(String[] args)
{
   List<Employee> employees = new ArrayList<Employee>();
   employees.add(new Employee("John Doe"));
   employees.add(new Employee("Jane Doe"));
   employees.add("Doe Doe");
   Iterator<Employee> iter = employees.iterator();
   while (iter.hasNext())
   {
      Employee emp = iter.next();
      System.out.println(emp.getName());
   }
}
```

Three of Listing 5–23's bolded code fragments illustrate the central feature of generics, which is the *parameterized type* (a class or interface name followed by an angle bracket–delimited type list identifying what kinds of objects are legal in that context).

For example, List<Employee> indicates only Employee objects can be stored in the List. The <Employee> designation must be repeated with ArrayList, which is the collection implementation that stores the Employees.

> **NOTE:** Java version 7 introduces the diamond operator (<>) to save you from having to repeat a parameterized type. For example, you could use this operator to specify List<Employee> employees = new ArrayList<>();.

Also, Iterator<Employee> indicates that iterator() returns an Iterator whose next() method returns only Employee objects. It is not necessary to cast iter.next()'s returned value to Employee because the compiler inserts the cast on your behalf.

If you attempt to compile this listing, the compiler will report an error when it encounters employees.add("Doe Doe");. The error message will tell you that the compiler cannot find an add(java.lang.String) method in the java.util.List<Employee> interface.

Unlike in the pre-generics List interface, which declares an add(Object) method, the generified List interface's add() method parameter reflects the interface's parameterized type name. For example, List<Employee> implies add(Employee).

Listing 5–22 revealed that the unsafe code causing the ClassCastException (employees.add("Doe Doe");) and the code that triggers the exception ((Employee) iter.next()) are quite close. However, they are often farther apart in larger applications.

Rather than having to deal with angry clients while hunting down the unsafe code that ultimately led to the ClassCastException, you can rely on the compiler saving you this frustration and effort by reporting an error when it detects this code during compilation. Detecting type safety violations at compile time is the benefit of using generics.

Generic Types

A *generic type* is a class or interface that introduces a family of parameterized types by declaring a *formal type parameter list* (a comma-separated list of *type parameter* names between angle brackets). This syntax is expressed as follows:

```
class identifier<formal_type_parameter_list> {}
interface identifier<formal_type_parameter_list> {}
```

For example, List<E> is a generic type, where List is an interface and type parameter E identifies the list's element type. Similarly, Map<K, V> is a generic type, where Map is an interface and type parameters K and V identify the map's key and value types.

> **NOTE:** When declaring a generic type, it is conventional to specify single uppercase letters as type parameter names. Furthermore, these names should be meaningful. For example, E indicates element, T indicates type, K indicates key, and V indicates value. If possible, you should avoid choosing a type parameter name that is meaningless where it is used. For example, List<E> means list of elements, but what does List<S> mean?

Parameterized types instantiate generic types. Each parameterized type replaces the generic type's type parameters with type names. For example, List<Employee> (List of

Employee) and List<String> (List of String) are examples of parameterized types based on List<E>. Similarly, Map<String, Employee> is an example of a parameterized type based on Map<K, V>.

The type name that replaces a type parameter is known as an *actual type argument*. Generics supports five kinds of actual type arguments:

- *Concrete type*: The name of a class or interface is passed to the type parameter. For example, List<Employee> employees; specifies that the list elements are Employee instances.

- *Concrete parameterized type*: The name of a parameterized type is passed to the type parameter. For example, List<List<String>> nameLists; specifies that the list elements are lists of strings.

- *Array type*: An array is passed to the type parameter. For example, List<String[]> countries; specifies that the list elements are arrays of Strings, possibly city names.

- *Type parameter*: A type parameter is passed to the type parameter. For example, given class declaration class X<E> { List<E> queue; }, X's type parameter E is passed to List's type parameter E.

- *Wildcard*: The ? is passed to the type parameter. For example, List<?> list; specifies that the list elements are unknown. You will learn about this type parameter later in the chapter, in "The Need for Wildcards" section.

A generic type also identifies a *raw type*, which is a generic type without its type parameters. For example, List<Employee>'s raw type is List. Raw types are nongeneric and can hold any Object.

> **NOTE:** Java allows raw types to be intermixed with generic types to support the vast amount of legacy code that was written prior to the arrival of generics. However, the compiler outputs a warning message whenever it encounters a raw type in source code.

Declaring and Using Your Own Generic Types

It is not difficult to declare your own generic types. In addition to specifying a formal type parameter list, your generic type specifies its type parameter(s) throughout its implementation. For example, Listing 5–24 declares a Queue<E> generic type.

Listing 5–24. *Declaring and using a Queue<E> generic type*

```java
public class Queue<E>
{
    private E[] elements;
    private int head, tail;
    @SuppressWarnings("unchecked")
    public Queue(int size)
```

```
   {
      elements = (E[]) new Object[size];
      head = 0;
      tail = 0;
   }
   public void insert(E element)
   {
      if (isFull()) // insert() should throw an exception when full. I did
         return;    // not implement insert() to do so for brevity.
      elements[tail] = element;
      tail = (tail+1)%elements.length;
   }
   public E remove()
   {
      if (isEmpty())
         return null;
      E element = elements[head];
      head = (head+1)%elements.length;
      return element;
   }
   public boolean isEmpty()
   {
      return head == tail;
   }
   public boolean isFull()
   {
      return (tail+1)%elements.length == head;
   }
   public static void main(String[] args)
   {
      Queue<String> queue = new Queue<String>(5);
      System.out.println(queue.isEmpty());
      queue.insert("A");
      queue.insert("B");
      queue.insert("C");
      queue.insert("D");
      queue.insert("E");
      System.out.println(queue.isFull());
      System.out.println(queue.remove());
      queue.insert("F");
      while (!queue.isEmpty())
         System.out.println(queue.remove());
      System.out.println(queue.isEmpty());
      System.out.println(queue.isFull());
   }
}
```

Queue implements a *queue*, a data structure that stores elements in first-in, first-out order. An element is inserted at the *tail* and removed at the *head*. The queue is empty when the head equals the tail, and full when the tail is one less than the head.

Notice that Queue<E>'s E type parameter appears throughout the source code. For example, E appears in the elements array declaration to denote the array's element type. E is also specified as the type of insert()'s parameter and as remove()'s return type.

E also appears in `elements = (E[]) new Object[size];`. (I will explain later why I specified this expression instead of specifying the more compact `elements = new E[size];` expression.)

The `E[]` cast results in the compiler warning about this cast being unchecked. The compiler is concerned that downcasting from `Object[]` to `E[]` might result in a violation of type safety because any kind of object can be stored in `Object[]`.

The compiler's concern is not justified in this example. There is no way that a non-E object can appear in the `E[]` array. Because the warning is meaningless in this context, it is suppressed by prefixing the constructor with `@SuppressWarnings("unchecked")`.

> **CAUTION:** Be careful when suppressing an unchecked warning. You must first prove that a `ClassCastException` cannot occur, and then you can suppress the warning.

When you run this application, it generates the following output:

```
true
true
A
B
C
D
F
true
false
```

Type Parameter Bounds

`List<E>`'s E type parameter and `Map<K, V>`'s K and V type parameters are examples of unbounded type parameters. You can pass any actual type argument to an unbounded type parameter.

It is sometimes necessary to restrict the kinds of actual type arguments that can be passed to a type parameter. For example, you might want to declare a class whose instances can only store instances of classes that subclass an abstract `Shape` class.

To restrict actual type arguments, you can specify an *upper bound*, a type that serves as an upper limit on the types that can be chosen as actual type arguments. The upper bound is specified via reserved word extends followed by a type name.

For example, `ShapesList<E extends Shape>` identifies Shape as an upper bound. You can specify `ShapesList<Circle>`, `ShapesList<Rectangle>`, and even `ShapesList<Shape>`, but not `ShapesList<String>` because String is not a subclass of Shape.

You can assign more than one upper bound to a type parameter, where the first bound is a class or interface, and where each additional upper bound is an interface, by using the ampersand character (&) to separate bound names. Consider Listing 5–25.

Listing 5–25. *Assigning multiple upper bounds to a type parameter*

```
abstract class Shape
{
}
class Circle extends Shape implements Comparable<Circle>
{
   private double x, y, radius;
   Circle(double x, double y, double radius)
   {
      this.x = x;
      this.y = y;
      this.radius = radius;
   }
   @Override
   public int compareTo(Circle circle)
   {
      if (radius < circle.radius)
         return -1;
      else
      if (radius > circle.radius)
         return 1;
      else
         return 0;
   }
   @Override
   public String toString()
   {
      return "(" + x + ", " + y + ", " + radius + ")";
   }
}
class SortedShapesList<S extends Shape & Comparable<S>>
{
   @SuppressWarnings("unchecked")
   private S[] shapes = (S[]) new Shape[2];
   private int index = 0;
   void add(S shape)
   {
      shapes[index++] = shape;
      if (index < 2)
         return;
      System.out.println("Before sort: " + this);
      sort();
      System.out.println("After sort: " + this);
   }
   private void sort()
   {
      if (index == 1)
         return;
      if (shapes[0].compareTo(shapes[1]) > 0)
      {
         S shape = (S) shapes[0];
         shapes[0] = shapes[1];
         shapes[1] = shape;
      }
   }
   @Override
   public String toString()
```

```
    {
        return shapes[0].toString() + " " + shapes[1].toString();
    }
}
public class SortedShapesListDemo
{
    public static void main(String[] args)
    {
        SortedShapesList<Circle> ssl = new SortedShapesList<Circle>();
        ssl.add(new Circle(100, 200, 300));
        ssl.add(new Circle(10, 20, 30));
    }
}
```

Listing 5–25's Circle class extends Shape and implements the java.lang.Comparable interface, which is used to specify the *natural ordering* of Circle objects. The interface's compareTo() method implements this ordering by returning a value to reflect the order:

- A negative value is returned if the current object should precede the object passed to compareTo() in some fashion.

- A zero value is returned if the current and argument objects are the same.

- A positive value is returned if the current object should succeed the argument object.

Circle's overriding compareTo() method compares two Circle objects based on their radii. This method orders a Circle instance with the smaller radius before a Circle instance with a larger radius.

The SortedShapesList class specifies <S extends Shape & Comparable<S>> as its parameter list. The actual type argument passed to the S parameter must subclass Shape, and it must also implement the Comparable interface.

Circle satisfies both criteria: it subclasses Shape and implements Comparable. As a result, the compiler does not report an error when it encounters the main() method's SortedShapesList<Circle> ssl = new SortedShapesList<Circle>(); statement.

An upper bound offers extra static type checking that guarantees that a parameterized type adheres to its bounds. This assurance means that the upper bound's methods can be called safely. For example, sort() can call Comparable's compareTo() method.

If you run this application, you will discover the following output, which shows that the two Circle objects are sorted in ascending order of radius:

```
Before sort: (100.0, 200.0, 300.0) (10.0, 20.0, 30.0)
After sort: (10.0, 20.0, 30.0) (100.0, 200.0, 300.0)
```

You can also restrict actual type arguments by specifying a *lower bound*, a type that serves as a lower limit on the types that can be chosen as actual type arguments. The lower bound is specified via the wildcard, reserved word super, and a type name.

Because lower bounds are used exclusively with the wildcard type argument, I will have more to say about lower bounds when I discuss the need for wildcards.

Type Parameter Scope

A type parameter's *scope* (visibility) is its generic type, which includes the formal type parameter list of which the type parameter is a member. For example, the scope of S in SortedShapesList<S extends Shape & Comparable<S>> is all of SortedShapesList and the formal type parameter list.

> **NOTE:** A type parameter bound that includes the type parameter is known as a *recursive type bound*. For example, Comparable<S> in <S extends Shape & Comparable<S>> is a recursive type bound. Recursive type bounds are rare and typically show up in conjunction with the Comparable interface, for specifying a type's natural ordering.

It is possible to mask a type parameter by declaring a same-named type parameter in a nested type's formal type parameter list. For example, Listing 5–26 masks an enclosing class's T type parameter.

Listing 5–26. *Masking a type variable*

```
class EnclosingClass<T>
{
   static class EnclosedClass<T extends Comparable<T>>
   {
   }
}
```

EnclosingClass's T type parameter is masked by EnclosedClass's T type parameter, which specifies an upper bound where only those types that implement the Comparable interface can be passed to EnclosedClass.

If masking is undesirable, it is best to choose a different name for the type parameter. For example, you might specify EnclosedClass<U extends Comparable<U>>. Although U is not as meaningful a name as T, this situation justifies this choice.

The Need for Wildcards

In Chapter 3, you learned that a subtype is a kind of supertype. For example, Circle is a kind of Shape and String is a kind of Object. This polymorphic behavior also applies to related parameterized types with the same type parameters (List<Object> is a kind of Collection<Object>, for example).

However, this polymorphic behavior does not apply to multiple parameterized types that differ only in regard to one type parameter being a subtype of another type parameter. For example, List<String> is not a kind of List<Object>. Listing 5–27 reveals why parameterized types differing only in type parameters are not polymorphic.

Listing 5–27. *Proving that parameterized types differing only in type parameters are not polymorphic*

```
public static void main(String[] args)
{
   List<String> ls = new ArrayList<String>();
   List<Object> lo = ls;
```

```
    lo.add(new Employee());
    String s = ls.get(0);
}
```

If Listing 5–27 compiled, a ClassCastException would be thrown at runtime. After instantiating a List of String and upcasting its reference to a List of Object, main() adds a new Employee object to the List of Object. The Employee object is then returned via get() and the List of String reference variable. The ClassCastException is thrown because of the implicit cast to String—an Employee is not a String.

> **NOTE:** Although you cannot upcast List<String> to List<Object>, you can upcast List<String> to the raw type List in order to interoperate with legacy code.

This example can be generalized into the following rule: for a given subtype *x* of type *y*, and given *G* as a raw type declaration, *G*<*x*> is not a subtype of *G*<*y*>. Listing 5–28 shows you how easy it is to run afoul of this rule.

Listing 5–28. *Attempting to output a list of string*

```
public static void main(String[] args)
{
    List<String> ls = new ArrayList<String>();
    ls.add("first");
    ls.add("second");
    ls.add("third");
    outputList(ls);
}
static void outputList(List<Object> list)
{
    for (int i = 0; i < list.size(); i++)
        System.out.println(list.get(i));
}
```

Listing 5–28 will not compile because it assumes that List of String is also a List of Object, which you have just learned is not true because it violates type safety. The outputList() method can only output a list of objects, which makes it useless.

The wildcard type argument (?) provides a typesafe workaround to this problem because it accepts any actual type argument. Simply change List<Object> list to List<?> list and Listing 5–28 will compile.

However, you cannot add elements to a List<?> because doing so would violate type safety. For example, Listing 5–29 presents a copyList() method that attempts to copy one List<?> to another List<?>.

Listing 5–29. *Attempting to copy one List<?> to another List<?>*

```
public static void main(String[] args)
{
    List<String> ls1 - new ArrayList<String>();
    ls1.add("first");
    ls1.add("second");
    ls1.add("third");
    List<String> ls2 = new ArrayList<String>();
```

```
      copyList(ls1, ls2);
}
static void copyList(List<?> list1, List<?> list2)
{
   for (int i = 0; i < list1.size(); i++)
      list2.add(list1.get(i));
}
```

Listing 5–29 will not compile. Instead, the compiler reports the following error message when it encounters `list2.add(list1.get(i));`:

```
x.java:13: cannot find symbol
symbol  : method add(java.lang.Object)
location: interface java.util.List<capture#469 of ?>
      list2.add(list1.get(i));
           ^
1 error
```

The error message reflects that although list1's elements (which can be of any type) can be assigned to Object, list2's element type is unknown. If this type is anything other than Object (such as String), type safety is violated. One solution to this problem is to specify `static void copyList(List<String> list1, List<String> list2)`.

A second solution to this problem requires that copyList()'s first type parameter be specified as ? extends String and its second parameter be specified as ? super String. Listing 5–30 reveals the same copyList() method with these upper and lower bounds.

Listing 5–30. *Using bounded wildcards to successfully copy one list to another*

```
public static void main(String[] args)
{
   List<String> ls1 = new ArrayList<String>();
   ls1.add("first");
   ls1.add("second");
   ls1.add("third");
   List<String> ls2 = new ArrayList<String>();
   copyList(ls1, ls2);
}
static void copyList(List<? extends String> list1, List<? super String> list2)
{
   for (int i = 0; i < list1.size(); i++)
      list2.add(list1.get(i));
}
```

Listing 5–30's copyList() method reveals that the list1 parameter accepts String or any subclass. Because String is declared final, no subclasses can be passed as actual type arguments. In contrast, the list2 parameter accepts String and its Object superclass—a subclass is a kind of superclass.

Although Listing 5–30 compiles and runs, its version of the copyList() header is little better than specifying `static void copyList(List<String> list1, List<String> list2)`. You can only copy a List of String to a List of String or a List of Object. You will shortly discover that generic methods offer a much better solution.

Reification and Erasure

Reification is the process or result of treating the abstract as if it was concrete. For example, 0xa000000 is an abstract hexadecimal integer literal that is treated as if it was the concrete 32-bit memory address that it represents.

Java arrays are reified. Because they are aware of their element types, they can enforce these types at runtime. Attempting to store an invalid element in an array (see Listing 5–31) results in a `java.lang.ArrayStoreException`.

Listing 5–31. *How an* `ArrayStoreException` *occurs*

```
class Point
{
   int x, y;
}
class ColoredPoint extends Point
{
   int color;
}
public class ReificationDemo
{
   public static void main(String[] args)
   {
      ColoredPoint[] cptArray = new ColoredPoint[1];
      Point[] ptArray = cptArray;
      ptArray[0] = new Point();
   }
}
```

Listing 5–31 demonstrates that arrays are *covariant* in that an array of supertype references is a supertype of an array of subtype references. A subtype array can be assigned to a supertype variable; for example, `Point[] ptArray = cptArray;`.

Covariance can be dangerous. For example, an `ArrayStoreException` is thrown when `ptArray[0] = new Point();` tries to store a `Point` object in the `ColoredPoint` array via the `ptArray` intermediary. The exception occurs because a `Point` is not a `ColoredPoint`.

In contrast to arrays, a generic type's type parameters are not reified. In other words, they are not available at runtime. Instead, these type parameters are discarded following compilation. This throwing away of type parameters is known as *erasure*.

Erasure also involves replacing uses of other type variables by the upper bound of the type variable (such as `Object`) and inserting casts to the appropriate type when the resulting code is not type correct.

Although erasure makes it possible for generic types to interoperate with raw types, it does have consequences. For example, you cannot create an array of a generic type: `new List<E>[10]`, `new E[size]`, and `new Map<String, String>[100]` are illegal.

The compiler reports a "generic array creation" error when it encounters an attempt to create an array of a generic type. It does so because the attempt is not typesafe. If allowed, compiler-inserted casts could trigger `ClassCastExceptions`—see Listing 5–32.

Listing 5–32. *Why creating an array of a generic type is not a good idea*

```
List<Employee>[] empListArray = new List<Employee>[1];
List<String> strList = new ArrayList<String>(); strList.add("string");
Object[] objArray = empListArray;
objArray[0] = strList;
Fmployee e = empListArray[0].get(0);
```

Let us assume that Listing 5–32 is legal. The first line creates a one-element array where this element stores a List of Employee. The second line creates a List of String and stores a single String in this list.

The third line assigns empListArray to objArray. This assignment is legal because arrays are covariant. The fourth line stores the List of String into objArray[0], which works because of erasure. An ArrayStoreException does not occur because List<String>'s runtime type is List and List<Employee>[]'s runtime type is List[].

However, there is a problem. A List<String> instance has been stored in an array that can only hold List<Employee> instances. When the compiler-inserted cast operator attempts to cast empListArray[0].get(0)'s return value ("string") to Employee, the cast operator throws a ClassCastException object.

Another consequence of erasure is that the instanceof operator cannot be used with parameterized types apart from unbounded wildcard types. For example, List<String> ls = null; if (ls instanceof LinkedList<String>) {} is illegal. Instead you must change the instanceof expression to either of the following expressions:

```
ls instanceof LinkedList<?> // legal to use with unbounded wildcard type
ls instanceof LinkedList    // legal to use with raw type (the preferred use)
```

Generic Methods

A *generic method* is a static or non-static method with a type-generalized implementation. A formal type parameter list precedes the method's return type, uses the same syntax, and has the same meaning as the generic type's formal type parameter list. This syntax is expressed as follows:

```
<formal_type_parameter_list> return_type identifier(parameter_list)
{
}
```

The collections framework provides many examples of generic methods. For example, the Collections class provides a public static <T extends Object & Comparable<? super T>> T min(Collection<? extends T> coll) method for returning the minimum element in the given collection according to the natural ordering of its elements.

Listing 5–33 converts the aforementioned copyList() method into a generic method so that it can copy a list of an arbitrary type to another list of the same type.

Listing 5–33. *Declaring and using a copyList() generic method*

```
class Circle
{
    private double x, y, radius;
```

```
      Circle(double x, double y, double radius)
      {
         this.x = x;
         this.y = y;
         this.radius = radius;
      }
      @Override
      public String toString()
      {
         return "(" + x + ", " + y + ", " + radius + ")";
      }
}
public class CopyList
{
   public static void main(String[] args)
   {
      List<String> ls = new ArrayList<String>();
      ls.add("A");
      ls.add("B");
      ls.add("C");
      outputList(ls);
      List<String> lsCopy = new ArrayList<String>();
      copyList(ls, lsCopy);
      outputList(lsCopy);
      List<Circle> lc = new ArrayList<Circle>();
      lc.add(new Circle(10.0, 20.0, 30.0));
      lc.add(new Circle (5.0, 4.0, 16.0));
      outputList(lc);
      List<Circle> lcCopy = new ArrayList<Circle>();
      copyList(lc, lcCopy);
      outputList(lcCopy);
   }
   static <T> void copyList(List<T> c1, List<T> c2)
   {
      for (int i = 0; i < c1.size(); i++)
         c2.add(c1.get(i));
   }
   static void outputList(List<?> l)
   {
      for (int i = 0; i < l.size(); i++)
         System.out.println (l.get(i));
      System.out.println();
   }
}
```

The generic method's type parameters are inferred from the context in which the method was invoked. For example, the compiler determines that copyList(ls, lsCopy); copies a List of String to another List of String. Similarly, it determines that copyList(lc, lcCopy); copies a List of Circle to another List of Circle.

When you run this application, it generates the following output:

```
A
B
C

A
B
C

(10.0, 20.0, 30.0)
(5.0, 4.0, 16.0)

(10.0, 20.0, 30.0)
(5.0, 4.0, 16.0)
```

Enums

An *enumerated type* is a type that specifies a named sequence of related constants as its legal values. The months in a calendar, the coins in a currency, and the days of the week are examples of enumerated types.

Java developers have traditionally used sets of named integer constants to represent enumerated types. Because this form of representation has proven to be problematic, Java version 5 introduced the enum alternative.

This section introduces you to enums. After discussing the problems with traditional enumerated types, the section presents the enum alternative. It then introduces you to the Enum class, from which enums originate.

The Trouble with Traditional Enumerated Types

Listing 5–34 declares a Coin enumerated type whose set of constants identifies different kinds of coins in a currency.

Listing 5–34. *An enumerated type identifying coins*

```
public class Coin
{
   public final static int PENNY = 0;
   public final static int NICKEL = 1;
   public final static int DIME = 2;
   public final static int QUARTER = 3;
}
```

Listing 5–35 declares a Weekday enumerated type whose set of constants identifies the days of the week.

Listing 5–35. *An enumerated type identifying weekdays*

```
public class Weekday
{
   public final static int SUNDAY = 0;
   public final static int MONDAY = 1;
```

```
    public final static int TUESDAY = 2;
    public final static int WEDNESDAY = 3;
    public final static int THURSDAY = 4;
    public final static int FRIDAY = 5;
    public final static int SATURDAY = 6;
}
```

Listing 5–34's and 5–35's approach to representing an enumerated type is problematic, where the biggest problem is the lack of compile-time type safety. For example, you can pass a coin to a method that requires a weekday and the compiler will not complain.

You can also compare coins to weekdays, as in `Coin.NICKEL == Weekday.MONDAY`, and specify even more meaningless expressions, such as `Coin.DIME+Weekday.FRIDAY-1/Coin.QUARTER`. The compiler does not complain because it only sees ints.

Applications that depend upon enumerated types are brittle. Because the type's constants are compiled into an application's classfiles, changing a constant's int value requires you to recompile dependent applications or risk them behaving erratically.

Another problem with enumerated types is that int constants cannot be translated into meaningful string descriptions. For example, what does 4 mean when debugging a faulty application? Being able to see THURSDAY instead of 4 would be more helpful.

NOTE: You could circumvent the previous problem by using `String` constants. For example, you might specify `public final static String THURSDAY = "THURSDAY";`. Although the constant value is more meaningful, `String`-based constants can impact performance because you cannot use `==` to efficiently compare just any old strings (as you will discover in Chapter 7). Other problems related to `String`-based constants include hard-coding the constant's value ("THURSDAY") instead of the constant's name (THURSDAY) into source code, which makes it very difficult to change the constant's value at a later time; and misspelling a hard-coded constant ("THURZDAY"), which compiles correctly but is problematic at runtime.

The Enum Alternative

Java version 5 introduced enums as a better alternative to traditional enumerated types. An *enum* is an enumerated type that is expressed via reserved word enum. Listing 5–36 uses enum to declare Listing 5–34's and 5–35's enumerated types.

Listing 5–36. *Improved enumerated types for coins and weekdays*

```
public enum Coin { PENNY, NICKEL, DIME, QUARTER }
public enum Weekday { SUNDAY, MONDAY, TUESDAY, WEDNESDAY, THURSDAY, FRIDAY,
SATURDAY }
```

Despite their similarity to the int-based enumerated types found in C++ and other languages, Listing 5–36's enums are classes. Each constant is a public static final field that represents an instance of its enum class.

Because constants are final, and because you cannot call an enum's constructors to create more constants, you can use == to compare constants efficiently and (unlike string constant comparisons) safely. For example, you can specify c == Coin.NICKEL.

Enums promote compile-time type safety by preventing you from comparing constants in different enums. For example, the compiler will report an error when it encounters Coin.PENNY == Weekday.SUNDAY.

The compiler also frowns upon passing a constant of the wrong enum kind to a method. For example, you cannot pass Weekday.FRIDAY to a method whose parameter type is Coin.

Applications depending upon enums are not brittle because the enum's constants are not compiled into an application's classfiles. Also, the enum provides a toString() method for returning a more useful description of a constant's value.

Because enums are so useful, Java version 5 enhanced the switch statement to support them. Listing 5–37 demonstrates this statement switching on one of the constants in Listing 5–36's Coin enum.

Listing 5–37. *Using the switch statement with an enum*

```
public class EnhancedSwitch
{
   private enum Coin { PENNY, NICKEL, DIME, QUARTER }
   public static void main(String[] args)
   {
      Coin coin = Coin.NICKEL;
      switch (coin)
      {
         case PENNY   : System.out.println("1 cent"); break;
         case NICKEL  : System.out.println("5 cents"); break;
         case DIME    : System.out.println("10 cents"); break;
         case QUARTER : System.out.println("25 cents"); break;
         default      : assert false;
      }
   }
}
```

Listing 5–37 demonstrates switching on an enum's constants. This enhanced statement only allows you to specify the name of a constant as a case label. If you prefix the name with the enum, as in case Coin.DIME, the compiler reports an error.

Enhancing an Enum

You can add fields, constructors, and methods to an enum—you can even have the enum implement interfaces. For example, Listing 5–38 adds a field, a constructor, and two methods to Coin to associate a denomination value with a Coin constant (such as 1 for penny and 5 for nickel) and convert pennies to the denomination.

Listing 5–38. *Enhancing the* Coin *enum*

```
public enum Coin
{
    PENNY(1),
    NICKEL(5),
    DIME(10),
    QUARTER(25);

    private final int denomValue;
    Coin(int denomValue)
    {
        this.denomValue = denomValue;
    }
    public int denomValue()
    {
        return denomValue;
    }
    public int toDenomination(int numPennies)
    {
        return numPennies/denomValue;
    }
}
```

Listing 5–38's constructor accepts a denomination value, which it assigns to a `private` blank final field named denomValue—all fields should be declared `final` because constants are immutable. Notice that this value is passed to each constant during its creation (PENNY(1), for example).

> **CAUTION:** When the comma-separated list of constants is followed by anything other than an enum's closing brace, you must terminate the list with a semicolon or the compiler will report an error.

Furthermore, this listing's denomValue() method returns denomValue, and its toDenomination() method returns the number of coins of that denomination that are contained within the number of pennies passed to this method as its argument. For example, 3 nickels are contained in 16 pennies.

Listing 5–39 shows you how to use the enhanced Coin enum.

Listing 5–39. *Exercising the enhanced* Coin *enum*

```
public static void main(String[] args)
{
    if (args.length == 1)
    {
        int numPennies = Integer.parseInt(args[0]);
        System.out.println(numPennies + " pennies is equivalent to:");
        int numQuarters = Coin.QUARTER.toDenomination(numPennies);
        System.out.println(numQuarters + " " + Coin.QUARTER.toString() +
                          (numQuarters != 1 ? "s," : ","));
        numPennies -= numQuarters*Coin.QUARTER.denomValue();
        int numDimes = Coin.DIME.toDenomination(numPennies);
        System.out.println(numDimes + " " + Coin.DIME.toString() +
```

```
                           (numDimes != 1 ? "s, " : ","));
        numPennies -= numDimes*Coin.DIME.denomValue();
        int numNickels = Coin.NICKEL.toDenomination(numPennies);
        System.out.println(numNickels + " " + Coin.NICKEL.toString() +
                           (numNickels != 1 ? "s, " : ", and"));
        numPennies -= numNickels*Coin.NICKEL.denomValue();
        System.out.println(numPennies + " " + Coin.PENNY.toString() +
                           (numPennies != 1 ? "s" : ""));
      }
      System.out.println();
      System.out.println("Denomination values:");
      for (int i = 0; i < Coin.values().length; i++)
         System.out.println(Coin.values()[i].denomValue());
   }
```

Listing 5–39 describes an application that converts its solitary "pennies" command-line argument to an equivalent amount expressed in quarters, dimes, nickels, and pennies. In addition to calling a Coin constant's denomValue() and toDenomValue() methods, the application calls toString() to output a string representation of the coin.

Another called enum method is values(). This method returns an array of all Coin constants that are declared in the Coin enum (value()'s return type, in this example, is Coin[]). This array is useful when you need to iterate over these constants. For example, Listing 5–39 calls this method to output each coin's denomination.

When you run this application with 119 as its command-line argument, it generates the following output:

```
119 pennies is equivalent to:
4 QUARTERs,
1 DIME,
1 NICKEL, and
4 PENNYs

Denomination values:
1
5
10
25
```

The output shows that toString() returns a constant's name. It is sometimes useful to override this method to return a more meaningful value. For example, a method that extracts *tokens* (named character sequences) from a string might use a Token enum to list token names and, via an overriding toString() method, values—see Listing 5–40.

Listing 5–40. *Overriding* toString() *to return a* Token *constant's value*

```
public enum Token
{
   IDENTIFIER("ID"),
   INTEGER("INT"),
   LPAREN("("),
   RPAREN(")"),
   COMMA(",");

   private final String tokValue;
   Token(String tokValue)
```

```
    {
        this.tokValue = tokValue;
    }
    @Override
    public String toString()
    {
        return tokValue;
    }
    public static void main(String[] args)
    {
        System.out.println("Token values:");
        for (int i = 0; i < Token.values().length; i++)
            System.out.println(Token.values()[i].name() + " = " +
                               Token.values()[i]);
    }
}
```

This application calls values() to return the array of Token constants. For each constant,
it calls the constant's name() method to return the constant's name, and implicitly calls
toString() to return the constant's value. If you were to run this application, you would
observe the following output:

```
Token values:
IDENTIFIER = ID
INTEGER = INT
LPAREN = (
RPAREN = )
COMMA = ,
```

Another way to enhance an enum is to assign a different behavior to each constant. You
can accomplish this task by introducing an abstract method into the enum and
overriding this method in an anonymous subclass of the constant. Listing 5–41's
TempConversion enum demonstrates this technique.

Listing 5–41. *Using anonymous subclasses to vary the behaviors of enum constants*

```
public enum TempConversion
{
    C2F("Celsius to Fahrenheit")
    {
        @Override
        public double convert(double value)
        {
            return value*9.0/5.0+32.0;
        }
    },
    F2C("Fahrenheit to Celsius")
    {
        @Override
        public double convert(double value)
        {
            return (value-32.0)*5.0/9.0;
        }
    };

    TempConversion(String desc)
    {
```

```
        this.desc = desc;
    }
    private String desc;
    @Override
    public String toString()
    {
        return desc;
    }
    public abstract double convert(double value);
    public static void main(String[] args)
    {
        System.out.println(C2F + " for 100.0 degrees = " +
                        C2F.convert(100.0));
        System.out.println(F2C + " for 98.6 degrees = " +
                        F2C.convert(98.6));
    }
}
```

When you run this application, it generates the following output:

```
Celsius to Fahrenheit for 100.0 degrees = 212.0
Fahrenheit to Celsius for 98.6 degrees = 37.0
```

The Enum Class

The compiler regards enum as syntactic sugar. When it encounters an enum type declaration (enum Coin {}), it generates a class whose name (Coin) is specified by the declaration, and which also subclasses the abstract Enum class (in the java.lang package), the common base class of all Java language–based enumeration types.

If you examine Enum's Java documentation, you will discover that it overrides Object's clone(), equals(), finalize(), hashCode(), and toString() methods:

- clone() is overridden to prevent constants from being cloned so that there is never more than one copy of a constant; otherwise, constants could not be compared via ==.

- equals() is overridden to compare constants via their references— constants with the same identities (==) must have the same contents (equals()), and different identities imply different contents.

- finalize() is overridden to ensure that constants cannot be finalized.

- hashCode() is overridden because equals() is overridden.

- toString() is overridden to return the constant's name.

Except for toString(), all of the overridden methods are declared final so that they cannot be overridden in a subclass.

Enum also provides its own methods. These methods include the final compareTo(), (Enum implements Comparable), getDeclaringClass(), name(), and ordinal() methods:

- compareTo() compares the current constant with the constant passed as an argument to see which constant precedes the other constant in the enum, and returns a value indicating their order. This method makes it possible to sort an array of unsorted constants.

- getDeclaringClass() returns the Class object corresponding to the current constant's enum. For example, the Class object for Coin is returned when calling Coin.PENNY.getDeclaringClass() for Listing 5–36's Coin enum. Also, TempConversion is returned when calling TempConversion.C2F.getDeclaringClass() for Listing 5–41's TempConversion enum. The compareTo() method uses Class's getClass() method and Enum's getDeclaringClass() method to ensure that only constants belonging to the same enum are compared. Otherwise, a ClassCastException is thrown. (I will discuss Class in Chapter 7.)

- name() returns the constant's name. Unless overridden to return something more descriptive, toString() also returns the constant's name.

- ordinal() returns a zero-based *ordinal*, an integer that identifies the position of the constant within the enum type. compareTo() compares ordinals.

Enum also provides the static valueOf(Class<T>enumType, String name) method for returning the enum constant from the specified enum with the specified name:

- enumType identifies the Class object of the enum from which to return a constant.

- name identifies the name of the constant to return.

For example, Coin penny = Enum.valueOf(Coin.class, "PENNY"); assigns the Coin constant whose name is PENNY to penny.

You will not discover a values() method in Enum's Java documentation because the compiler *synthesizes* (manufactures) this method while generating the class.

Extending the Enum Class

Enum's generic type is Enum<E extends Enum<E>>. Although the formal type parameter list looks ghastly, it is not that hard to understand. But first, take a look at Listing 5–42.

Listing 5–42. *The Coin class as it appears from the perspective of its classfile*

```
public final class Coin extends Enum<Coin>
{
   public static final Coin PENNY = new Coin("PENNY", 0);
   public static final Coin NICKEL = new Coin("NICKEL", 1);
   public static final Coin DIME = new Coin("DIME", 2);
   public static final Coin QUARTER = new Coin("QUARTER", 3);
   private static final Coin[] $VALUES = { PENNY, NICKEL, DIME, QUARTER };
   public static Coin[] values()
```

```
    {
        return Coin.$VALUES.clone();
    }
    public static Coin valueOf(String name)
    {
        return Enum.valueOf(Coin.class, "Coin");
    }
    private Coin(String name, int ordinal)
    {
        super(name, ordinal);
    }
}
```

Behind the scenes, the compiler converts Listing 5–36's Coin enum declaration into a class declaration that is similar to Listing 5–42.

The following rules show you how to interpret Enum<E extends Enum<E>> in the context of Coin extends Enum<Coin>:

- Any subclass of Enum must supply an actual type argument to Enum. For example, Coin's header specifies Enum<Coin>.

- The actual type argument must be a subclass of Enum. For example, Coin is a subclass of Enum.

- A subclass of Enum (such as Coin) must follow the idiom that it supplies its own name (Coin) as an actual type argument.

The third rule allows Enum to declare methods—compareTo(), getDeclaringClass(), and valueOf()—whose parameter and/or return types are specified in terms of the subclass (Coin), and not in terms of Enum.

The rationale for doing this is to avoid having to specify casts. For example, you do not need to cast valueOf()'s return value to Coin in Coin penny = Enum.valueOf(Coin.class, "PENNY");.

> **NOTE:** You cannot compile Listing 5–42 because the compiler will not compile any class that extends Enum. It will also complain about super(name, ordinal);.

EXERCISES

The following exercises are designed to test your understanding of assertions, annotations, generics, and enums:

1. What is an assertion?

2. When would you use assertions?

3. True or false: Specifying the -ea command-line option with no argument enables all assertions, including system assertions.

4. What is an annotation?

5. What kinds of application elements can be annotated?

6. Identify the three compiler-supported annotation types.

7. How do you declare an annotation type?

8. What is a marker annotation?

9. What is an element?

10. How do you assign a default value to an element?

11. What is a meta-annotation?

12. Identify Java's four meta-annotation types.

13. Define generics.

14. Why would you use generics?

15. What is the difference between a generic type and a parameterized type?

16. Which one of the nonstatic member class, local class, and anonymous class inner class categories cannot be generic?

17. Identify the five kinds of actual type arguments.

18. True or false: You cannot specify a primitive type name (such as double or int) as an actual type argument.

19. What is a raw type?

20. When does the compiler report an unchecked warning message and why?

21. How do you suppress an unchecked warning message?

22. True or false: List<E>'s E type parameter is unbounded.

23. How do you specify a single upper bound?

24. True or false: MyList<E super Circle> specifies that the E type parameter has a lower bound of Circle.

25. What is a recursive type bound?

26. Why are wildcard type arguments necessary?

27. What is reification?

28. True or false: Type parameters are reified.

29. What is erasure?

30. What is a generic method?

31. In Listing 5–43, which overloaded method does the methodCaller() generic method call?

Listing 5–43. *Which someOverloadedMethod() is called?*

```java
import java.util.Date;

public class CallOverloadedNGMethodFromGMethod
{
```

```
    public static void someOverloadedMethod(Object o)
    {
        System.out.println("call to someOverloadedMethod(Object o)");
    }
    public static void someOverloadedMethod(Date d)
    {
        System.out.println("call to someOverloadedMethod(Date d)");
    }
    public static <T> void methodCaller(T t)
    {
        someOverloadedMethod(t);
    }
    public static void main(String[] args)
    {
        methodCaller(new Date());
    }
}
```

32. What is an enumerated type?

33. Identify three problems that can arise when you use enumerated types whose constants are `int`-based.

34. What is an enum?

35. How do you use the switch statement with an enum?

36. In what ways can you enhance an enum?

37. What is the purpose of the abstract Enum class?

38. What is the difference between Enum's `name()` and `toString()` methods?

39. True or false: Enum's generic type is `Enum<E extends Enum<E>>`.

40. Declare a ToDo marker annotation type that annotates only type elements, and that also uses the default retention policy.

41. Rewrite the `StubFinder` application to work with Listing 5–15's Stub annotation type (with appropriate `@Target` and `@Retention` annotations) and Listing 5–16's Deck class.

42. Implement a stack in a manner that is similar to Listing 5–24's Queue class. `Stack` must be generic, it must declare `push()`, `pop()`, and `isEmpty()` methods (it could also declare an `isFull()` method but that method is not necessary in this exercise), `push()` must throw a `StackFullException` instance when the stack is full, and `pop()` must throw a `StackEmptyException` instance when the stack is empty. (You must create your own package-private `StackFullException` and `StackEmptyException` helper classes because they are not provided for you in Java's class library.) Declare a similar `main()` method, and insert two assertions into this method that validate your assumptions about the stack being empty immediately after being created and immediately after popping the last element.

NOTE: A *stack* is a data structure that stores elements in a last-in, first-out order. Elements are added to the stack via an operation known as *push*. They are removed from the stack via an operation known as *pop*. The last element pushed onto the stack is the first element popped off of the stack.

43. Declare a `Compass` enum with `NORTH`, `SOUTH`, `EAST`, and `WEST` members. Declare a `UseCompass` class whose `main()` method randomly selects one of these constants and then switches on that constant. Each of the switch statement's cases should output a message such as `heading north`.

Summary

An assertion is a statement that lets you express an assumption of application correctness via a Boolean expression. If this expression evaluates to true, execution continues with the next statement. Otherwise, an error that identifies the cause of failure is thrown.

There are many situations where assertions should be used. These situations organize into internal invariant, control-flow invariant, and design-by-contract categories. An invariant is something that does not change.

Although there are many situations where assertions should be used, there also are situations where they should be avoided. For example, you should not use assertions to check the arguments that are passed to public methods.

The compiler records assertions in the classfile. However, assertions are disabled at runtime because they can affect performance. You must enable the classfile's assertions before you can test assumptions about the behaviors of your classes.

Annotations are instances of annotation types and associate metadata with application elements. They are expressed in source code by prefixing their type names with @ symbols. For example, `@Readonly` is an annotation and `Readonly` is its type.

Java supplies a wide variety of annotation types, including the compiler-oriented `Override`, `Deprecated`, and `SuppressWarnings` types. However, you can also declare your own annotation types by using the `@interface` syntax.

Annotation types can be annotated with meta-annotations that identify the application elements they can target (such as constructors, methods, or fields), their retention policies, and other characteristics.

Annotations whose types are assigned a runtime retention policy via `@Retention` annotations can be processed at runtime using custom applications or Java's apt tool, whose functionality has been integrated into the compiler starting with Java version 6.

Java version 5 introduced generics, language features for declaring and using type-agnostic classes and interfaces. When working with Java's collections framework, these features help you avoid `ClassCastException`s.

A generic type is a class or interface that introduces a family of parameterized types by declaring a formal type parameter list. A generic method is a `static` or non-`static` method with a type-generalized implementation.

An enumerated type is a type that specifies a named sequence of related constants as its legal values. Java developers have traditionally used sets of named integer constants to represent enumerated types.

Because sets of named integer constants have proven to be problematic, Java version 5 introduced the enum alternative. An enum is an enumerated type that is expressed via reserved word enum.

You can add fields, constructors, and methods to an enum—you can even have the enum implement interfaces. Also, you can override `toString()` to provide a more useful description of a constant's value, and subclass constants to assign different behaviors.

The compiler regards enum as syntactic sugar for a class that subclasses `Enum`. This abstract class overrides various `Object` methods to provide default behaviors (usually for safety reasons), and provides additional methods for various purposes.

This chapter largely completes our tour of the Java language. However, there are a few more advanced language features to explore. You will encounter one of these minor features in Chapter 6, which begins a multichapter exploration of various types that are located in Java SE's/Android's standard class library.

Exploring the Basic APIs Part 1

Aspiring Android developers need to acquire a solid understanding of foundational Java APIs. You have already encountered a few of these APIs, such as the Object and String classes and the Throwable class hierarchy. This chapter introduces you to additional language-oriented (basic) APIs pertaining to math, packages, primitive types, and the garbage collector.

> **NOTE:** Chapter 6 explores basic API classes and interfaces that are located in the java.lang, java.lang.ref, and java.math packages.

Math APIs

Chapter 2 presented Java's +, -, *, /, and % operators for performing basic arithmetic on primitive type values. Java also provides classes for performing trigonometry and other advanced math operations, representing monetary values accurately, and supporting extremely long integers for use in RSA encryption (http://en.wikipedia.org/wiki/RSA) and other contexts.

Math and StrictMath

The java.lang.Math class declares double constants E and PI that represent the natural logarithm base value (2.71828...) and the ratio of a circle's circumference to its diameter (3.14159...). E is initialized to 2.718281828459045 and PI is initialized to 3.141592653589793. Math also declares assorted class methods to perform various math operations. Table 6–1 describes many of these methods.

Table 6–1. *Math Methods*

Method	Description
double abs(double d)	Return the absolute value of d. There are four special cases: abs(-0.0) = +0.0, abs(+infinity) = +infinity, abs(-infinity) = +infinity, and abs(NaN) = NaN.
float abs(float f)	Return the absolute value of f. There are four special cases: abs(-0.0) = +0.0, abs(+infinity) = +infinity, abs(-infinity) = +infinity, and abs(NaN) = NaN.
int abs(int i)	Return the absolute value of i. There is one special case: the absolute value of Integer.MIN_VALUE is Integer.MIN_VALUE.
long abs(long l)	Return the absolute value of l. There is one special case: the absolute value of Long.MIN_VALUE is Long.MIN_VALUE.
double acos(double d)	Return angle d's arc cosine within the range 0 through PI. There are three special cases: acos(anything > 1) = NaN, acos(anything < -1) = NaN, and acos(NaN) = NaN.
double asin(double d)	Return angle d's arc sine within the range -PI/2 through PI/2. There are three special cases: asin(anything > 1) = NaN, asin(anything < -1) = NaN, and asin(NaN) = NaN.
double atan(double d)	Return angle d's arc tangent within the range -PI/2 through PI/2. There are five special cases: atan(+0.0) = +0.0, atan(-0.0) = -0.0, atan(+infinity) = +PI/2, atan(-infinity) = -PI/2, and atan(NaN) = NaN.
double ceil(double d)	Return the smallest value (closest to negative infinity) that is not less than d and is equal to an integer. There are six special cases: ceil(+0.0) = +0.0, ceil(-0.0) = -0.0, ceil(anything > -1.0 and < 0.0) = -0.0, ceil(+infinity) = +infinity, ceil(-infinity) = -infinity, and ceil(NaN) = NaN.
double cos(double d)	Return the cosine of angle d (expressed in radians). There are three special cases: cos(+infinity) = NaN, cos(-infinity) = NaN, and cos(NaN) = NaN.
double exp(double d)	Return Euler's number e raised to the power d. There are three special cases: exp(+infinity) = +infinity, exp(-infinity) = +0.0, and exp(NaN) = NaN.
double floor(double d)	Return the largest value (closest to positive infinity) that is not greater than d and is equal to an integer. There are five special cases: floor(+0.0) = +0.0, floor(-0.0) = -0.0, floor(+infinity) = +infinity, floor(-infinity) = -infinity, and floor(NaN) = NaN.

Method	Description
double log(double d)	Return the natural logarithm (base e) of d. There are six special cases: log(+0.0) = -infinity, log(-0.0) = -infinity, log(anything < 0) = NaN, log(+infinity) = +infinity, log(-infinity) = NaN, and log(NaN) = NaN.
double log10(double d)	Return the base 10 logarithm of d. There are six special cases: log10(+0.0) = -infinity, log10(-0.0) = -infinity, log10(anything < 0) = NaN, log10(+infinity) = +infinity, log10(-infinity) = NaN, and log10(NaN) = NaN.
double max(double d1, double d2)	Return the most positive (closest to positive infinity) of d1 and d2. There are four special cases: max(NaN, anything) = NaN, max(anything, NaN) = NaN, max(+0.0, -0.0) = +0.0, and max(-0.0, +0.0) = +0.0.
float max(float f1, float f2)	Return the most positive (closest to positive infinity) of f1 and f2. There are four special cases: max(NaN, anything) = NaN, max(anything, NaN) = NaN, max(+0.0, -0.0) = +0.0, and max(-0.0, +0.0) = +0.0.
int max(int i1, int i2)	Return the most positive (closest to positive infinity) of i1 and i2.
long max(long l1, long l2)	Return the most positive (closest to positive infinity) of l1 and l2.
double min(double d1, double d2)	Return the most negative (closest to negative infinity) of d1 and d2. There are four special cases: min(NaN, anything) = NaN, min(anything, NaN) = NaN, min(+0.0, -0.0) = -0.0, and min(-0.0, +0.0) = -0.0.
float min(float f1, float f2)	Return the most negative (closest to negative infinity) of f1 and f2. There are four special cases: min(NaN, anything) = NaN, min(anything, NaN) = NaN, min(+0.0, -0.0) = -0.0, and min(-0.0, +0.0) = -0.0.
int min(int i1, int i2)	Return the most negative (closest to negative infinity) of i1 and i2.
long min(long l1, long l2)	Return the most negative (closest to negative infinity) of l1 and l2.
double random()	Return a pseudorandom number between 0.0 (inclusive) and 1.0 (exclusive).
long round(double d)	Return the result of rounding d to a long integer. The result is equivalent to (long) Math.floor(d+0.5). There are seven special cases: round(+0.0) = +0.0, round(-0.0) = +0.0, round(anything > Long.MAX_VALUE) = Long.MAX_VALUE, round(anything < Long.MIN_VALUE) = Long.MIN_VALUE, round(+infinity) = Long.MAX_VALUE, round(-infinity) = Long.MIN_VALUE, and

Method	Description
	round(+infinity) = Long.MAX_VALUE, round(-infinity) = Long.MIN_VALUE, and round(NaN) = +0.0.
int round(float f)	Return the result of rounding f to an integer. The result is equivalent to (int) Math.floor(f+0.5). There are seven special cases: round(+0.0) = +0.0, round(-0.0) = +0.0, round(anything > Integer.MAX_VALUE) = Integer.MAX_VALUE, round(anything < Integer.MIN_VALUE) = Integer.MIN_VALUE, round(+infinity) = Integer.MAX_VALUE, round(-infinity) = Integer.MIN_VALUE, and round(NaN) = +0.0.
double signum(double d)	Return the sign of d as -1.0 (d less than 0.0), 0.0 (d equals 0.0), and 1.0 (d greater than 0.0). There are five special cases: signum(+0.0) = +0.0, signum(-0.0) = -0.0, signum(+infinity) = +1.0, signum(-infinity) = -1.0, and signum(NaN) = NaN.
float signum(float f)	Return the sign of f as -1.0 (f less than 0.0), 0.0 (f equals 0.0), and 1.0 (f greater than 0.0). There are five special cases: signum(+0.0) = +0.0, signum(-0.0) = -0.0, signum(+infinity) = +1.0, signum(-infinity) = -1.0, and signum(NaN) = NaN.
double sin(double d)	Return the sine of angle d (expressed in radians). There are five special cases: sin(+0.0) = +0.0, sin(-0.0) = -0.0, sin(+infinity) = NaN, sin(-infinity) = NaN, and sin(NaN) = NaN.
double sqrt(double d)	Return the square root of d. There are five special cases: sqrt(+0.0) = +0.0, sqrt(-0.0) = -0.0, sqrt(anything < 0) = NaN, sqrt(+infinity) = +infinity, and sqrt(NaN) = NaN.
double tan(double d)	Return the tangent of angle d (expressed in radians). There are five special cases: tan(+0.0) = +0.0, tan(-0.0) = -0.0, tan(+infinity) = NaN, tan(-infinity) = NaN, and tan(NaN) = NaN.
double toDegrees (double angrad)	Convert angle angrad from radians to degrees via expression angrad*180/PI. There are five special cases: toDegrees(+0.0) = +0.0, toDegrees(-0.0) = -0.0, toDegrees(+infinity) = +infinity, toDegrees(-infinity) = -infinity, and toDegrees(NaN) = NaN.
double toRadians (angdeg)	Convert angle angdeg from degrees to radians via expression angdeg/180*PI. There are five special cases: toRadians(+0.0) = +0.0, toRadians(-0.0) = -0.0, toRadians(+infinity) = +infinity, toRadians(-infinity) = -infinity, and toRadians(NaN) = NaN.

Table 6–1 reveals a wide variety of useful math-oriented methods. For example, each abs() method returns its argument's *absolute value* (number without regard for sign).

abs(double) and abs(float) are useful for comparing double precision floating-point and floating-point values safely. For example, 0.3 == 0.1+0.1+0.1 evaluates to false because 0.1 has no exact representation. However, you can compare these expressions with abs() and a tolerance value, which indicates an acceptable range of error. For example, Math.abs(0.3-(0.1+0.1+0.1)) < 0.1 returns true because the absolute difference between 0.3 and 0.1+0.1+0.1 is less than a 0.1 tolerance value.

Previous chapters demonstrated other Math methods. For example, Chapter 2 demonstrated Math's sin(), toRadians(), cos(), round(double), and random() methods.

As Chapter 5's Lotto649 application revealed, random() (which returns a number that appears to be randomly chosen but is actually chosen by a predictable math calculation, and hence is *pseudorandom*) is useful in simulations, games, and wherever an element of chance is needed, but first its return value (0.0 to almost 1.0) must somehow be transformed into a more useful range, perhaps 0 through 49, or maybe -100 through 100. You will find Listing 6–1's rnd() method useful for making these transformations.

Listing 6–1. *Converting* random() *'s return value into something more useful*

```
public static int rnd(int limit)
{
   return (int) (Math.random()*limit);
}
```

rnd() transforms random()'s 0.0 to almost 1.0 double precision floating-point range to a 0 through limit - 1 integer range. For example, rnd(50) returns an integer ranging from 0 through 49. Also, -100+rnd(201) transforms 0.0 to almost 1.0 into -100 through 100 by adding a suitable offset and passing an appropriate limit value.

> **CAUTION:** Do not specify (int) Math.random()*limit because this expression always evaluates to 0. The expression first casts random()'s double precision floating-point fractional value (0.0 through 0.99999. . .) to integer 0 by truncating the fractional part, and then multiplies 0 by limit, which results in 0.

Table 6–1 also reveals some curiosities beginning with +infinity, -infinity, +0.0, -0.0, and NaN (Not a Number).

Java's floating-point calculations are capable of returning +infinity, -infinity, +0.0, -0.0, and NaN because Java largely conforms to IEEE 754 (http://en.wikipedia.org/wiki/IEEE_754), a standard for floating-point calculations. The following are the circumstances under which these special values arise:

- +infinity returns from attempting to divide a positive number by 0.0. For example, System.out.println(1.0/0.0); outputs Infinity.

- -infinity returns from attempting to divide a negative number by 0.0. For example, System.out.println(-1.0/0.0); outputs -Infinity.

- NaN returns from attempting to divide 0.0 by 0.0, attempting to calculate the square root of a negative number, and attempting other strange operations. For example, `System.out.println(0.0/0.0);` and `System.out.println(Math.sqrt(-1.0));` each output NaN.

- +0.0 results from attempting to divide a positive number by +infinity. For example, `System.out.println(1.0/(1.0/0.0));` outputs +0.0.

- -0.0 results from attempting to divide a negative number by +inflnily. For example, `System.out.println(-1.0/(1.0/0.0));` outputs -0.0.

Once an operation yields +infinity, -infinity, or NaN, the rest of the expression usually equals that special value. For example, `System.out.println(1.0/0.0*20.0);` outputs `Infinity`. Also, an expression that first yields +infinity or -infinity might devolve into NaN. For example, `1.0/0.0*0.0` yields +infinity (`1.0/0.0`) and then NaN (+infinity*0.0).

Another curiosity is `Integer.MAX_VALUE`, `Integer.MIN_VALUE`, `Long.MAX_VALUE`, and `Long.MIN_VALUE`. Each of these items is a primitive wrapper class constant that identifies the maximum or minimum value that can be represented by the class's associated primitive type.

Finally, you might wonder why the `abs()`, `max()`, and `min()` overloaded methods do not include byte and short versions, as in `byte abs(byte b)` and `short abs(short s)`. There is no need for these methods because the limited ranges of bytes and short integers make them unsuitable in calculations. If you need such a method, check out Listing 6–2.

Listing 6–2. *Overloaded* `byte abs(byte b)` *and* `short abs(short s)` *methods*

```
public static byte abs(byte b)
{
    return (b < 0) ? (byte) -b : b;
}
public static short abs(short s)
{
    return (s < 0) ? (short) -s : s;
}
public static void main(String[] args)
{
    byte b = -2;
    System.out.println(abs(b)); // Output: 2
    short s = -3;
    System.out.println(abs(s)); // Output: 3
}
```

The (byte) and (short) casts are necessary because -b converts b's value from a byte to an int, and -s converts s's value from a short to an int. In contrast, these casts are not needed with (b < 0) and (s < 0), which automatically cast b's and s's values to an int before comparing them with int-based 0.

TIP: Their absence from Math suggests that byte and short are not very useful in method declarations. However, these types are useful when declaring arrays whose elements store small values (such as a binary file's byte values). If you declared an array of int or long to store such values, you would end up wasting heap space (and might even run out of memory).

While searching through the Java documentation for the java.lang package, you will probably encounter a class named StrictMath. Apart from a longer name, this class appears to be identical to Math. The differences between these classes can be summed up as follows:

- StrictMath's methods return exactly the same results on all platforms. In contrast, some of Math's methods might return values that vary ever so slightly from platform to platform.

- Because StrictMath cannot utilize platform-specific features such as an extended-precision math coprocessor, an implementation of StrictMath might be less efficient than an implementation of Math.

For the most part, Math's methods call their StrictMath counterparts. Two exceptions are toDegrees() and toRadians(). Although these methods have identical code bodies in both classes, StrictMath's implementations include reserved word strictfp in the method headers:

```
public static strictfp double toDegrees(double angrad)
public static strictfp double toRadians(double angdeg)
```

Wikipedia's "strictfp" entry (http://en.wikipedia.org/wiki/Strictfp) mentions that strictfp restricts floating-point calculations to ensure portability. This reserved word accomplishes portability in the context of intermediate floating-point representations and overflows/underflows (generating a value too large or small to fit a representation).

NOTE: The previously cited "strictfp" article states that Math contains public static strictfp double abs(double); and other strictfp methods. If you check out this class's source code under Java version 6 update 16, you will not find strictfp anywhere in the source code. However, many Math methods (such as sin()) call their StrictMath counterparts, which are implemented in a platform-specific library, and the library's method implementations are strict.

Without strictfp, an intermediate calculation is not limited to the IEEE 754 32-bit and 64-bit floating-point representations that Java supports. Instead, the calculation can take advantage of a larger representation (perhaps 128 bits) on a platform that supports this representation.

An intermediate calculation that overflows/underflows when its value is represented in 32/64 bits might not overflow/underflow when its value is represented in more bits.

Because of this discrepancy, portability is compromised. strictfp levels the playing field by requiring all platforms to use 32/64 bits for intermediate calculations.

When applied to a method, strictfp ensures that all floating-point calculations performed in that method are in strict compliance. However, strictfp can be used in a class header declaration (as in public strictfp class FourierTransform) to ensure that all floating-point calculations performed in that class are strict.

> **NOTE:** Math and StrictMath are declared final so that they cannot be extended. Also, they declare private empty noargument constructors so that they cannot be instantiated.
>
> Math and StrictMath are examples of *utility classes* because they exist as placeholders for utility constants and utility (static) methods.

BigDecimal

In Chapter 2, I introduced a CheckingAccount class with a balance field. I declared this field to be of type int, and included a comment stating that balance represents the number of dollars that can be withdrawn. Alternatively, I could have stated that balance represents the number of pennies that can be withdrawn.

Perhaps you are wondering why I did not declare balance to be of type double or float. That way, balance could store values such as 18.26 (18 dollars in the whole number part and 26 pennies in the fraction part). I did not declare balance to be a double or float for the following reasons:

- Not all floating-point values that can represent monetary amounts (dollars and cents) can be stored exactly in memory. For example, 0.1 (which you might use to represent 10 cents), has no exact storage representation. If you executed double total = 0.1; for (int i = 0; i < 50; i++) total += 0.1; System.out.println(total);, you would observe 5.099999999999998 instead of the correct 5.1 as the output.

- The result of each floating-point calculation needs to be rounded to the nearest cent. Failure to do so introduces tiny errors that can cause the final result to differ from the correct result. Although Math supplies a pair of round() methods that you might consider using to round a calculation to the nearest cent, these methods round to the nearest integer (dollar).

Listing 6–3's InvoiceCalc application demonstrates both problems. However, the first problem is not serious because it contributes very little to the inaccuracy. The more serious problem occurs from failing to round to the nearest cent after performing a calculation.

Listing 6–3. *Floating-point-based invoice calculations leading to confusing results*

```
import java.text.NumberFormat;

class InvoiceCalc
{
   final static double DISCOUNT_PERCENT = 0.1; // 10%
   final static double TAX_PERCENT = 0.05; // 5%
   public static void main(String[] args)
   {
      double invoiceSubtotal = 285.36;
      double discount = invoiceSubtotal*DISCOUNT_PERCENT;
      double subtotalBeforeTax = invoiceSubtotal-discount;
      double salesTax = subtotalBeforeTax*TAX_PERCENT;
      double invoiceTotal = subtotalBeforeTax+salesTax;
      NumberFormat currencyFormat = NumberFormat.getCurrencyInstance();
      System.out.println("Subtotal: " + currencyFormat.format(invoiceSubtotal));
      System.out.println("Discount: " + currencyFormat.format(discount));
      System.out.println("SubTotal after discount: " +
                          currencyFormat.format(subtotalBeforeTax));
      System.out.println("Sales Tax: " + currencyFormat.format(salesTax));
      System.out.println("Total: " + currencyFormat.format(invoiceTotal));
   }
}
```

Listing 6–3 relies on the NumberFormat class (located in the java.text) package and its format() method to format a double precision floating-point value into a currency—I will discuss NumberFormat in Chapter 9. When you run InvoiceCalc, you will discover the following output:

```
Subtotal: $285.36
Discount: $28.54
SubTotal after discount: $256.82
Sales Tax: $12.84
Total: $269.67
```

This output reveals the correct subtotal, discount, subtotal after discount, and sales tax. In contrast, it incorrectly reveals 269.67 instead of 269.66 as the final total. The customer will not appreciate paying an extra penny, even though 269.67 is the correct value according to the floating-point calculations:

```
Subtotal: 285.36
Discount: 28.536
SubTotal after discount: 256.824
Sales Tax: 12.8412
Total: 269.6652
```

The problem arises from not rounding the result of each calculation to the nearest cent before performing the next calculation. As a result, the 0.024 in 256.824 and 0.0012 in 12.84 contribute to the final value, causing NumberFormat's format() method to round this value to 269.67.

Java provides a solution to both problems in the form of a java.math.BigDecimal class. This immutable class (a BigDecimal instance cannot be modified) represents a signed decimal number (such as 23.653) of arbitrary *precision* (number of digits) with an associated *scale* (an integer that specifies the number of digits after the decimal point).

BigDecimal declares three convenience constants: ONE, TEN, and ZERO. Each constant is the BigDecimal equivalent of 1, 10, and 0 with a zero scale.

> **CAUTION:** BigDecimal declares several ROUND_-prefixed constants. These constants are largely obsolete and should be avoided, along with the public BigDecimal divide(BigDecimal divisor, int scale, int roundingMode) and public BigDecimal setScale(int newScale, int roundingMode) methods, which are still present so that dependent legacy code continues to compile.

BigDecimal also declares a variety of useful constructors and methods. A few of these constructors and methods are described in Table 6–2.

Table 6–2. *BigDecimal Constructors and Methods*

Method	Description
BigDecimal(int val)	Initialize the BigDecimal instance to val's digits. Set the scale to 0.
BigDecimal(String val)	Initialize the BigDecimal instance to the decimal equivalent of val. Set the scale to the number of digits after the decimal point, or 0 if no decimal point is specified. This constructor throws java.lang.NullPointerException when val is null, and java.lang.NumberFormatException when val's string representation is invalid (contains letters, for example).
BigDecimal abs()	Return a new BigDecimal instance that contains the absolute value of the current instance's value. The resulting scale is the same as the current instance's scale.
BigDecimal add(BigDecimal augend)	Return a new BigDecimal instance that contains the sum of the current value and the argument value. The resulting scale is the maximum of the current and argument scales. This method throws NullPointerException when augend is null.
BigDecimal divide(BigDecimal divisor)	Return a new BigDecimal instance that contains the quotient of the current value divided by the argument value. The resulting scale is the difference of the current and argument scales. It might be adjusted when the result requires more digits. This method throws NullPointerException when divisor is null, or java.lang.ArithmeticException when divisor represents 0 or the result cannot be represented exactly.
BigDecimal max(BigDecimal val)	Return either this or val, whichever BigDecimal instance contains the larger value. This method throws NullPointerException when val is null.

Method	Description
BigDecimal min(BigDecimal val)	Return either this or val, whichever BigDecimal instance contains the smaller value. This method throws NullPointerException when val is null.
BigDecimal multiply(BigDecimal multiplicand)	Return a new BigDecimal instance that contains the product of the current value and the argument value. The resulting scale is the sum of the current and argument scales. This method throws NullPointerException when multiplicand is null.
BigDecimal negate()	Return a new BigDecimal instance that contains the negative of the current value. The resulting scale is the same as the current scale.
int precision()	Return the precision of the current BigDecimal instance.
BigDecimal remainder(BigDecimal divisor)	Return a new BigDecimal instance that contains the remainder of the current value divided by the argument value. The resulting scale is the difference of the current scale and the argument scale. It might be adjusted when the result requires more digits. This method throws NullPointerException when divisor is null, or ArithmeticException when divisor represents 0.
int scale()	Return the scale of the current BigDecimal instance.
BigDecimal setScale(int newScale, RoundingMode roundingMode)	Return a new BigDecimal instance with the specified scale and rounding mode. If the new scale is greater than the old scale, additional zeros are added to the unscaled value. In this case no rounding is necessary. If the new scale is smaller than the old scale, trailing digits are removed. If these trailing digits are not zero, the remaining unscaled value has to be rounded. For this rounding operation, the specified rounding mode is used. This method throws NullPointerException when roundingMode is null, and ArithmeticException when roundingMode is set to RoundingMode.ROUND_UNNECESSARY but rounding is necessary based on the current scale.
BigDecimal subtract(BigDecimal subtrahend)	Return a new BigDecimal instance that contains the current value minus the argument value. The resulting scale is the maximum of the current and argument scales. This method throws NullPointerException when subtrahend is null.
String toString()	Return a string representation of this BigDecimal. Scientific notation is used when necessary.

Table 6–2 refers to RoundingMode, which is an enum containing various rounding mode constants. These constants are described in Table 6–3.

Table 6–3. *RoundingMode Constants*

Constant	Description
CEILING	Round toward positive infinity.
DOWN	Round toward zero
FLOOR	Round toward negative infinity.
HALF_DOWN	Round toward the "nearest neighbor" unless both neighbors are equidistant, in which case round down.
HALF_EVEN	Round toward the "nearest neighbor" unless both neighbors are equidistant, in which case round toward the even neighbor.
HALF_UP	Round toward "nearest neighbor" unless both neighbors are equidistant, in which case round up. (This is the rounding mode commonly taught at school.)
UNNECESSARY	Rounding is not necessary because the requested operation produces the exact result.
UP	Positive values are rounded toward positive infinity and negative values are rounded toward negative infinity.

The best way to get comfortable with BigDecimal is to try it out. Listing 6–4 uses this class to correctly perform the invoice calculations that were presented in Listing 6–3.

Listing 6–4. *BigDecimal-based invoice calculations not leading to confusing results*

```
class InvoiceCalc
{
   public static void main(String[] args)
   {
      BigDecimal invoiceSubtotal = new BigDecimal("285.36");
      BigDecimal discountPercent = new BigDecimal("0.10");
      BigDecimal discount = invoiceSubtotal.multiply(discountPercent);
      discount = discount.setScale(2, RoundingMode.HALF_UP);
      BigDecimal subtotalBeforeTax = invoiceSubtotal.subtract(discount);
      subtotalBeforeTax = subtotalBeforeTax.setScale(2, RoundingMode.HALF_UP);
      BigDecimal salesTaxPercent = new BigDecimal("0.05");
      BigDecimal salesTax = subtotalBeforeTax.multiply(salesTaxPercent);
      salesTax = salesTax.setScale(2, RoundingMode.HALF_UP);
      BigDecimal invoiceTotal = subtotalBeforeTax.add(salesTax);
      invoiceTotal = invoiceTotal.setScale(2, RoundingMode.HALF_UP);
      System.out.println("Subtotal: " + invoiceSubtotal);
      System.out.println("Discount: " + discount);
      System.out.println("SubTotal after discount: " + subtotalBeforeTax);
      System.out.println("Sales Tax: " + salesTax);
      System.out.println("Total: " + invoiceTotal);
   }
}
```

Listing 6–4's main() method first creates BigDecimal objects invoiceSubtotal and discountPercent that are initialized to 285.36 and 0.10, respectively. It multiplies invoiceSubtotal by discountPercent and assigns the BigDecimal result to discount.

At this point, discount contains 28.5360. Apart from the trailing zero, this value is the same as that generated by invoiceSubtotal*DISCOUNT_PERCENT in Listing 6–3. The value that should be stored in discount is 28.54. To correct this problem before performing another calculation, main() calls discount's setScale() method with these arguments:

- 2: Two digits after the decimal point
- RoundingMode.HALF_UP: The conventional approach to rounding

After setting the scale and proper rounding mode, main() subtracts discount from invoiceSubtotal, and assigns the resulting BigDecimal instance to subtotalBeforeTax. main() calls setScale() on subtotalBeforeTax to properly round its value before moving on to the next calculation.

main() next creates a BigDecimal object named salesTaxPercent that is initialized to 0.05. It then multiplies subtotalBeforeTax by salesTaxPercent, assigning the result to salesTax, and calls setScale() on this BigDecimal object to properly round its value.

Moving on, main() adds salesTax to subtotalBeforeTax, saving the result in invoiceTotal, and rounds the result via setScale(). The values in these objects are sent to the standard output device via System.out.println(), which calls their toString() methods to return string representations of the BigDecimal values.

When you run this new version of InvoiceCalc, you will discover the following output:

```
Subtotal: 285.36
Discount: 28.54
SubTotal after discount: 256.82
Sales Tax: 12.84
Total: 269.66
```

> **CAUTION:** BigDecimal declares a public BigDecimal(double val) constructor that you should avoid using if at all possible. This constructor initializes the BigDecimal instance to the value stored in val, making it possible for this instance to reflect an invalid representation when the double cannot be stored exactly. For example, BigDecimal(0.1) results in 0.1000000000000000055511151231257827021181583404541015625 being stored in the instance. In contrast, BigDecimal("0.1") stores 0.1 exactly.

BigInteger

BigDecimal stores a signed decimal number as an unscaled value with a 32-bit integer scale. The unscaled value is stored in an instance of the java.math.BigInteger class.

BigInteger is an immutable class that represents a signed integer of arbitrary precision. It stores its value in *two's complement format* (all bits are flipped—1s to 0s and 0s to

1s—and 1 is added to the result to be compatible with the two's complement format used by Java's byte integer, short integer, integer, and long integer types).

> **NOTE:** Check out Wikipedia's "Two's complement" entry
> (http://en.wikipedia.org/wiki/Two%27s_complement) to learn more about two's complement.

BigInteger declares three convenience constants: ONE, TEN, and ZERO. Each constant is the BigInteger equivalent of 1, 10, and 0.

BigInteger also declares a variety of useful constructors and methods. A few of these constructors and methods are described in Table 6–4.

Table 6–4. *BigInteger Constructors and Methods*

Method	Description
BigInteger(byte[] val)	Initialize the BigInteger instance to the integer that is stored in the val array, with val[0] storing the integer's most significant (leftmost) eight bits. This constructor throws NullPointerException when val is null, and NumberFormatException when val.length equals 0.
BigInteger(String val)	Initialize the BigInteger instance to the integer equivalent of val. This constructor throws NullPointerException when val is null, and NumberFormatException when val's string representation is invalid (contains letters, for example).
BigInteger abs()	Return a new BigInteger instance that contains the absolute value of the current instance's value.
BigInteger add(BigInteger augend)	Return a new BigInteger instance that contains the sum of the current value and the argument value. This method throws NullPointerException when augend is null.
BigInteger divide(BigInteger divisor)	Return a new BigInteger instance that contains the quotient of the current value divided by the argument value. This method throws NullPointerException when divisor is null, and ArithmeticException when divisor represents 0 or the result cannot be represented exactly.
BigInteger max(BigInteger val)	Return either this or val, whichever BigInteger instance contains the larger value. This method throws NullPointerException when val is null.
BigInteger min(BigInteger val)	Return either this or val, whichever BigInteger instance contains the smaller value. This method throws NullPointerException when val is null.

Method	Description
BigInteger multiply(BigInteger multiplicand)	Return a new BigInteger instance that contains the product of the current value and the argument value. This method throws NullPointerException when multiplicand is null.
BigInteger negate()	Return a new BigInteger instance that contains the negative of the current value.
BigInteger remainder(BigInteger divisor)	Return a new BigInteger instance that contains the remainder of the current value divided by the argument value. This method throws NullPointerException when divisor is null, and ArithmeticException when divisor represents 0.
BigInteger subtract(BigInteger subtrahend)	Return a new BigInteger instance that contains the current value minus the argument value. This method throws NullPointerException when subtrahend is null.
String toString()	Return a string representation of this BigInteger.

The best way to get comfortable with BigInteger is to try it out. Listing 6–5 uses this class in a factorial() method comparison context.

Listing 6–5. *Comparing factorial() methods*

```
class FactComp
{
   public static void main(String[] args)
   {
      System.out.println(factorial(12));
      System.out.println();
      System.out.println(factorial(20L));
      System.out.println();
      System.out.println(factorial(170.0));
      System.out.println();
      System.out.println(factorial(new BigInteger("170")));
      System.out.println();
      System.out.println(factorial(25.0));
      System.out.println();
      System.out.println(factorial(new BigInteger("25")));
   }
   public static int factorial(int n)
   {
      if (n == 0)
         return 1;
      else
         return n*factorial(n-1);
   }
   public static long factorial(long n)
   {
      if (n == 0)
         return 1;
      else
         return n*factorial(n-1);
```

```
    }
    public static double factorial(double n)
    {
        if (n == 1.0)
            return 1.0;
        else
            return n*factorial(n-1);
    }
    public static BigInteger factorial(BigInteger n)
    {
        if (n.equals(BigInteger.ZERO))
            return BigInteger.ONE;
        else
            return n.multiply(factorial(n.subtract(BigInteger.ONE)));
    }
}
```

Listing 6–5 compares four versions of the recursive factorial() method. This comparison reveals the largest argument that can be passed to each of the first three methods before the returned factorial value becomes meaningless, because of limits on the range of values that can be accurately represented by the numeric type.

The first version is based on int and has a useful argument range of 0 through 12. Passing any argument greater than 12 results in a factorial that cannot be represented accurately as an int.

You can increase the useful range of factorial(), but not by much, by changing the parameter and return types to long. After making these changes, you will discover that the upper limit of the useful range is 20.

To further increase the useful range, you might create a version of factorial() whose parameter and return types are double. This is possible because whole numbers can be represented exactly as doubles. However, the largest useful argument that can be passed is 170.0. Anything higher than this value results in factorial() returning +infinity.

It is possible that you might need to calculate a higher factorial value, perhaps in the context of calculating a statistics problem involving combinations or permutations. The only way to accurately calculate this value is to use a version of factorial() based on BigInteger.

When you run the previous application, it generates the following output:
479001600

2432902008176640000

7.257415615307994E306

725741561530799896739672822111292631147169916812964513765435777989005618434017061578523507492426174595114909912378385207766660225654427530253289007732075109024004302800582956039666125996582571043985582942575689663134396122625710949468067112055688804571933402126614528000000000000000000000000000000000000000000000000

1.5511210043330986E25

15511210043330985984000000

The first three values represent the highest factorials that can be returned by the int-based, long-based, and double-based factorial() methods. The fourth value represents the BigInteger equivalent of the highest double factorial.

Notice that the double method fails to accurately represent 170! (! is the math symbol for factorial). Its precision is simply too small. Although the method attempts to round the smallest digit, rounding does not always work—the number ends in 7994 instead of 7998. Rounding is only accurate up to argument 25.0, as the last two output lines reveal.

NOTE: RSA encryption, BigDecimal, and factorial are practical examples of BigInteger's usefulness. However, you can also use BigInteger in unusual ways. For example, my February 2006 *JavaWorld* article titled "Travel Through Time with Java" (http://www.javaworld.com/javaworld/jw-02-2006/jw-0213-funandgames.html), a part of my Java Fun and Games series, used BigInteger to store an image as a very large integer. The idea was to experiment with BigInteger methods to look for images of people and places that existed in the past, will exist in the future, or might never exist. If this craziness appeals to you, check out my article.

Package Information

The java.lang.Package class provides access to information about a package (see Chapter 4 for an introduction to packages). This information includes version information about the implementation and specification of a Java package, the name of the package, and an indication of whether or not the package has been *sealed* (all classes that are part of the package are archived in the same JAR file).

NOTE: Chapter 1 introduces JAR files.

Table 6–5 describes some of Package's methods.

Table 6–5. *Package Methods*

Method	Description
String getImplementationTitle()	Return the title of this package's implementation, which might be null. The format of the title is unspecified.
String getImplementationVendor()	Return the name of the vendor or organization that provides this package's implementation. This name might be null. The format of the name is unspecified.
String getImplementationVersion()	Return the version number of this package's implementation, which might be null. This version string must be a sequence of positive decimal integers separated by periods and might have leading zeros.

Method	Description
String getName()	Return the name of this package in standard dot notation; for example, java.lang.
static Package getPackage(String packageName)	Return the Package object that is associated with the package identified as packageName, or null when the package identified as packageName cannot be found. This method throws NullPointerException when packageName is null.
static Package[] getPackages()	Return an array of all Package objects that are accessible to this method's caller.
String getSpecificationTitle()	Return the title of this package's specification, which might be null. The format of the title is unspecified.
String getSpecificationVendor()	Return the name of the vendor or organization that provides the specification that is implemented by this package. This name might be null. The format of the name is unspecified.
String getSpecificationVersion()	Return the version number of the specification of this package's implementation, which might be null. This version string must be a sequence of positive decimal integers separated by periods, and might have leading zeros.
boolean isCompatibleWith(String desired)	Check this package to determine if it is compatible with the specified version string, by comparing this package's specification version with the desired version. Return true when this package's specification version number is greater than or equal to the desired version number (this package is compatible); otherwise, return false. This method throws NullPointerException when desired is null, and NumberFormatException when this package's version number or the desired version number is not in dotted form.
boolean isSealed()	Return true when this package has been sealed; otherwise, return false.

I have created a PackageInfo application that demonstrates most of Table 6–5's Package methods. Listing 6–6 presents this application's source code.

Listing 6–6. *Obtaining information about a package*

```
public class PackageInfo
{
   public static void main(String[] args)
   {
      if (args.length == 0)
      {
         System.err.println("usage: java PackageInfo packageName [version]");
         return;
      }
```

```
         Package pkg = Package.getPackage(args[0]);
         if (pkg == null)
         {
            System.err.println(args[0] + " not found");
            return;
         }
         System.out.println("Name: " + pkg.getName());
         System.out.println("Implementation title: " +
                            pkg.getImplementationTitle());
         System.out.println("Implementation vendor: " +
                            pkg.getImplementationVendor());
         System.out.println("Implementation version: " +
                            pkg.getImplementationVersion());
         System.out.println("Specification title: " +
                            pkg.getSpecificationTitle());
         System.out.println("Specification vendor: " +
                            pkg.getSpecificationVendor());
         System.out.println("Specification version: " +
                            pkg.getSpecificationVersion());
         System.out.println("Sealed: " + pkg.isSealed());
         if (args.length > 1)
            System.out.println("Compatible with " + args[1] + ": " +
                               pkg.isCompatibleWith(args[1]));
   }
}
```

To use this application, specify at least a package name on the command line. For example, java PackageInfo java.lang returns the following output under Java version 6:

```
Name: java.lang
Implementation title: Java Runtime Environment
Implementation vendor: Sun Microsystems, Inc.
Implementation version: 1.6.0_16
Specification title: Java Platform API Specification
Specification vendor: Sun Microsystems, Inc.
Specification version: 1.6
Sealed: false
```

PackageInfo also lets you determine if the package's specification is compatible with a specific version number. A package is compatible with its predecessors.

For example, java PackageInfo java.lang 1.6 outputs Compatible with 1.6: true, whereas java PackageInfo java.lang 1.8 outputs Compatible with 1.8: false.

You can also use PackageInfo with your own packages, which you learned to create in Chapter 4. For example, that chapter presented a logging package.

Copy PackageInfo.class into the directory containing the logging package directory (which contains the compiled classfiles), and execute java PackageInfo logging.

PackageInfo responds by displaying the following output:

```
logging not found
```

This error message is presented because getPackage() requires at least one classfile to be loaded from the package before it returns a Package object describing that package.

The only way to eliminate the previous error message is to load a class from the package. Accomplish this task by merging Listing 6–7 into Listing 6–6.

Listing 6–7. *Dynamically loading a class from a classfile*

```
if (args.length == 3)
try
{
   Class.forName(args[2]);
}
catch (ClassNotFoundException cnfe)
{
   System.err.println("cannot load " + args[2]);
   return;
}
```

This code fragment, which must precede Package pkg = Package.getPackage(args[0]);, loads the classfile named by the revised PackageInfo application's third command-line argument.

Run the new PackageInfo application via java PackageInfo logging 1.5 logging.File and you will observe the following output—this command line identifies logging's File class as the class to load:

```
Name: logging
Implementation title: null
Implementation vendor: null
Implementation version: null
Specification title: null
Specification vendor: null
Specification version: null
Sealed: false
Exception in thread "main" java.lang.NumberFormatException: Empty version
 string
        at java.lang.Package.isCompatibleWith(Unknown Source)
        at PackageInfo.main(PackageInfo.java:43)
```

It is not surprising to see all of these null values because no package information has been added to the logging package. Also, NumberFormatException is thrown from isCompatibleWith() because the logging package does not contain a specification version number in dotted form (it is null).

Perhaps the simplest way to place package information into the logging package is to create a logging.jar file in a similar manner to the example shown in Chapter 4. But first, you must create a small text file that contains the package information. You can choose any name for the file. Listing 6–8 reveals my choice of manifest.mf.

Listing 6–8. *manifest.mf containing the package information*

```
Implementation-Title: Logging Implementation
Implementation-Vendor: Jeff Friesen
Implementation-Version: 1.0a
Specification-Title: Logging Specification
Specification-Vendor: Jeff "JavaJeff" Friesen
Specification-Version: 1.0
Sealed: true
```

NOTE: Make sure to press the Return/Enter key at the end of the final line (Sealed: true). Otherwise, you will probably observe Sealed: false in the output because this entry will not be stored in the logging package by the JDK's jar tool—jar is a bit quirky.

Execute the following command line to create a JAR file that includes logging and its files, and whose *manifest*, a special file named MANIFEST.MF that stores information about the contents of a JAR file, contains the contents of Listing 6–8:

```
jar cfm logging.jar manifest.mf logging
```

This command line creates a JAR file named logging.jar (via the c [create] and f [file] options). It also merges the contents of manifest.mf (via the m [manifest] option) into MANIFEST.MF, which is stored in the package's META-INF directory.

NOTE: To learn more about a JAR file's manifest, read the "JAR Manifest" section of the JDK documentation's "JAR File Specification" page (http://java.sun.com/javase/6/docs/technotes/guides/jar/jar.html#JAR%20Manifest).

Assuming that the jar tool presents no error messages, execute the following Windows-oriented command line (or a command line suitable for your platform) to run PackageInfo and extract the package information from the logging package:

```
java -cp logging.jar;. PackageInfo logging 1.0 logging.File
```

This time, you should see the following output:

```
Name: logging
Implementation title: Logging Implementation
Implementation vendor: Jeff Friesen
Implementation version: 1.0a
Specification title: Logging Specification
Specification vendor: Jeff "JavaJeff" Friesen
Specification version: 1.0
Sealed: true
Compatible with 1.0: true
```

Primitive Wrapper Classes

The java.lang package includes Boolean, Byte, Character, Double, Float, Integer, Long, and Short. These classes are known as *primitive wrapper classes* because their instances wrap themselves around values of primitive types.

NOTE: The primitive wrapper classes are also known as *value classes*.

Java provides these eight primitive wrapper classes for two reasons:

- The collections framework (discussed Chapter 8) provides lists, sets, and maps that can only store objects; they cannot store primitive values. You store a primitive value in a primitive wrapper class instance and store the instance in the collection.

- These classes provide a good place to associate useful constants (such as MAX_VALUE and MIN_VALUE) and class methods (such as Integer's parseInt() methods and Character's isDigit(), isLetter(), and toUpperCase() methods) with the primitive types.

This section introduces you to each of these primitive wrapper classes and a class named Number.

Boolean

Boolean is the smallest of the primitive wrapper classes. This class declares three constants, including TRUE and FALSE, which denote precreated Boolean objects.

Boolean also declares a pair of constructors for initializing a Boolean object:

- Boolean(boolean value) initializes the Boolean object to value.

- Boolean(String s) converts s's text to a true or false value and stores this value in the Boolean object.

The second constructor compares s's value with true. Because the comparison is case-insensitive, any combination of these four letters (such as true, TRUE, or tRue) results in true being stored in the object. Otherwise, the constructor stores false in the object.

Boolean's constructors are complemented by boolean booleanValue(), which returns the wrapped Boolean value.

Boolean also declares or overrides the following methods:

- int compareTo(Boolean b) compares the current Boolean object with b to determine their relative order. The method returns 0 when the current object contains the same Boolean value as b, a positive value when the current object contains true and b contains false, and a negative value when the current object contains false and b contains true.

- boolean equals(Object o) compares the current Boolean object with o and returns true when o is not null, o is of type Boolean, and both objects contain the same Boolean value.

- static boolean getBoolean(String name) returns true when a system property (discussed in Chapter 7) identified by name exists and is equal to true.

- int hashCode() returns a suitable hash code that allows Boolean objects to be used with hash-based collections (discussed in Chapter 8).

- static boolean parseBoolean(String s) parses s, returning true if s equals "true", "TRUE", "True", or any other combination of these letters. Otherwise, this method returns false. (*Parsing* breaks a sequence of characters into meaningful components, known as *tokens*.)

- String toString() returns "true" when the current Boolean instance contains true; otherwise, this method returns "false".

- static String toString(boolean b) returns "true" when b contains true; otherwise, this method returns "false".

- static Boolean valueOf(boolean b) returns TRUE when b contains true or FALSE when b contains false.

- static Boolean valueOf(String s) returns TRUE when s equals "true", "TRUE", "True", or any other combination of these letters. Otherwise, this method returns FALSE.

CAUTION: Newcomers to the Boolean class often think that getBoolean() returns a Boolean object's true/false value. However, getBoolean() returns the value of a Boolean-based system property—I discuss system properties in Chapter 7. If you need to return a Boolean object's true/false value, use the booleanValue() method instead.

It is often better to use TRUE and FALSE than to create Boolean objects. For example, suppose you need a method that returns a Boolean object containing true when the method's double argument is negative, or false when this argument is zero or positive. You might declare your method like the isNegative() method shown in Listing 6–9.

Listing 6–9. *An* isNegative() *method with unnecessary Boolean object creation*

```
public Boolean isNegative(double d)
{
   return new Boolean(d < 0);
}
```

Although this method is concise, it unnecessarily creates a Boolean object. When the method is called frequently, many Boolean objects are created that consume heap space. When heap space runs low, the garbage collector runs and slows down the application, which impacts performance.

Listing 6–10 reveals a better way to code isNegative().

Listing 6–10. *A refactored* isNegative() *method not creating Boolean objects*

```
public Boolean isNegative(double d)
{
   return (d < 0) ? Boolean.TRUE : Boolean.FALSE;
}
```

This method avoids creating Boolean objects by returning either the precreated TRUE or FALSE object.

> **TIP:** You should strive to create as few objects as possible. Not only will your applications have smaller memory footprints, they will perform better because the garbage collector will not be required to run as often.

Character

Character is the largest of the primitive wrapper classes, containing many constants, a constructor, many methods, and a pair of nested classes (Subset and UnicodeBlock).

> **NOTE:** Character's complexity derives from Java's support for Unicode (http://en.wikipedia.org/wiki/Unicode). For brevity, I ignore much of Character's Unicode-related complexity, which is beyond the scope of this chapter.

Character declares a single Character(char value) constructor, which you use to initialize a Character object to value. This constructor is complemented by char charValue(), which returns the wrapped character value.

When you start writing applications, you might codify expressions such as ch >= '0' && ch <= '9' (test ch to see if it contains a digit) and ch >= 'A' && ch <= 'Z' (test ch to see if it contains an uppercase letter). You should avoid doing so for three reasons:

- It is too easy to introduce a bug into the expression. For example, ch > '0' && ch <= '9' introduces a subtle bug that does not include '0' in the comparison.

- The expressions are not very descriptive of what they are testing.

- The expressions are biased toward Latin digits (0–9) and letters (A–Z and a–z). They do not take into account digits and letters that are valid in other languages. For example, '\u0beb' is a character literal representing one of the digits in the Tamil language.

Character declares several comparison and conversion utility methods that address these concerns. These methods include the following:

- static boolean isDigit(char ch) returns true when ch contains a digit (typically 0 through 9, but also digits in other languages).

- static boolean isLetter(char ch) returns true when ch contains a letter (typically A–Z or a–z, but also letters in other languages).

- static boolean isLetterOrDigit(char ch) returns true when ch contains a letter or digit (typically A–Z, a–z, or 0–9, but also letters or digits in other languages).

- static boolean isLowerCase(char ch) returns true when ch contains a lowercase letter.

- static boolean isUpperCase(char ch) returns true when ch contains an uppercase letter.

- static boolean isWhitespace(char ch) returns true when ch contains a whitespace character (typically a space, a horizontal tab, a carriage return, or a line feed).

- static char toLowerCase(char ch) returns the lowercase equivalent of ch's uppercase letter; otherwise, this method returns ch's value.

- static char toUpperCase(char ch) returns the uppercase equivalent of ch's lowercase letter; otherwise, this method returns ch's value.

For example, isDigit(ch) is preferable to ch >= '0' && ch <= '9' because it avoids a source of bugs, is more readable, and returns true for non-Latin digits (such as '\u0beb') as well as Latin digits.

Float and Double

Float and Double store floating-point and double precision floating-point values in Float and Double objects, respectively. These classes declare the following constants:

- MAX_VALUE identifies the maximum value that can be represented as a float or double.

- MIN_VALUE identifies the minimum value that can be represented as a float or double.

- NaN represents 0.0F/0.0F as a float and 0.0/0.0 as a double.

- NEGATIVE_INFINITY represents -infinity as a float or double.

- POSITIVE_INFINITY represents +infinity as a float or double.

Float and Double also declare the following constructors for initializing their objects:

- Float(float value) initializes the Float object to value.

- Float(double value) initializes the Float object to the float equivalent of value.

- Float(String s) converts s's text to a floating-point value and stores this value in the Float object.

- Double(double value) initializes the Double object to value.

- Double(String s) converts s's text to a double precision floating-point value and stores this value in the Double object.

Float's constructors are complemented by float floatValue(), which returns the wrapped floating-point value. Similarly, Double's constructors are complemented by double doubleValue(), which returns the wrapped double precision floating-point value.

Float declares several utility methods in addition to floatValue(). These methods include the following:

- static int floatToIntBits(float value) converts value to a 32-bit integer.

- static boolean isInfinite(float f) returns true when f's value is +infinity or -infinity. A related public boolean isInfinite() method returns true when the current Float object's value is +infinity or -infinity.

- static boolean isNaN(float f) returns true when f's value is NaN. A related public boolean isNaN() method returns true when the current Float object's value is NaN.

- static float parseFloat(String s) parses s, returning the floating-point equivalent of s's textual representation of a floating-point value or throwing NumberFormatException when this representation is invalid (contains letters, for example).

Double declares several utility methods in addition to doubleValue(). These methods include the following:

- static long doubleToLongBits(double value) converts value to a long integer.

- static boolean isInfinite(double d) returns true when d's value is +infinity or -infinity. A related boolean isInfinite() method returns true when the current Double object's value is +infinity or -infinity.

- static boolean isNaN(double d) returns true when d's value is NaN. A related public boolean isNaN() method returns true when the current Double object's value is NaN.

- static double parseDouble(String s) parses s, returning the double precision floating-point equivalent of s's textual representation of a double precision floating-point value or throwing NumberFormatException when this representation is invalid.

The floatToIntBits() and doubleToIntBits() methods are used in implementations of the equals() and hashCode() methods that must take float and double fields into account. floatToIntBits() and doubleToIntBits() allow equals() and hashCode() to respond properly to the following situations:

- equals() must return true when f1 and f2 contain Float.NaN (or d1 and d2 contain Double.NaN). If equals() was implemented in a manner similar to f1.floatValue() == f2.floatValue() (or d1.doubleValue() == d2.doubleValue()), this method would return false because NaN is not equal to anything, including itself.

- equals() must return false when f1 contains +0.0 and f2 contains -0.0 (or vice versa), or d1 contains +0.0 and d2 contains -0.0 (or vice versa). If equals() was implemented in a manner similar to f1.floatValue() == f2.floatValue() (or d1.doubleValue() == d2.doubleValue()), this method would return true because +0.0 == -0.0 returns true.

These requirements are needed for hash-based collections (discussed in Chapter 8) to work properly. Listing 6–11 shows how they impact Float's and Double's equals() methods.

Listing 6–11. *Demonstrating Float's equals() method in a NaN context and Double's equals() method in a +/-0.0 context*

```
public static void main(String[] args)
{
   Float f1 = new Float(Float.NaN);
   System.out.println(f1.floatValue());
   Float f2 = new Float(Float.NaN);
   System.out.println(f2.floatValue());
   System.out.println(f1.equals(f2));
   System.out.println(Float.NaN == Float.NaN);
   System.out.println();
   Double d1 = new Double(+0.0);
   System.out.println(d1.doubleValue());
   Double d2 = new Double(-0.0);
   System.out.println(d2.doubleValue());
   System.out.println(d1.equals(d2));
   System.out.println(+0.0 == -0.0);
}
```

Run this application. The following output proves that Float's equals() method properly handles NaN and Double's equals() method properly handles +/-0.0:

```
NaN
NaN
true
false

0.0
-0.0
false
true
```

> **TIP:** If you want to test a float or double value for equality with +infinity or -infinity (but not both), do not use isInfinite(). Instead, compare the value with NEGATIVE_INFINITY or POSITIVE_INFINITY via ==. For example, f == Float.NEGATIVE_INFINITY.

You will find parseFloat() and parseDouble() useful in many contexts. For example, Listing 6–12 uses parseDouble() to parse command-line arguments into doubles.

Listing 6–12. *Parsing command-line arguments into double precision floating-point values*

```
public static void main(String[] args)
{
    if (args.length != 3)
    {
        System.err.println("usage: java Calc value1 op value2");
        System.err.println("op is one of +, -, *, or /");
        return;
    }
    try
    {
        double value1 = Double.parseDouble(args[0]);
        double value2 = Double.parseDouble(args[2]);
        if (args[1].equals("+"))
            System.out.println(value1+value2);
        else
        if (args[1].equals("-"))
            System.out.println(value1-value2);
        else
        if (args[1].equals("*"))
            System.out.println(value1*value2);
        else
        if (args[1].equals("/"))
            System.out.println(value1/value2);
        else
            System.err.println("invalid operator: " + args[1]);
    }
    catch (NumberFormatException nfe)
    {
        System.err.println("Bad number format: " + nfe.getMessage());
    }
}
```

Specify java Calc 10E+3 + 66.0 to try out the Calc application. This application responds by outputting 10066.0. If you specified java Calc 10E+3 + A instead, you would observe Bad number format: For input string: "A" as the output, which is in response to the second parseDouble() method call's throwing of a NumberFormatException object.

Although NumberFormatException describes an unchecked exception, and although unchecked exceptions are often not handled because they represent coding mistakes, NumberFormatException does not fit this pattern in this example. The exception does not arise from a coding mistake; it arises from someone passing an illegal numeric argument to the application, which cannot be avoided through proper coding.

Integer, Long, Short, and Byte

Integer, Long, Short, and Byte store 32-bit, 64-bit, 16–bit, and 8-bit integer values in Integer, Long, Short, and Byte objects, respectively.

Each class declares MAX_VALUE and MIN_VALUE constants that identify the maximum and minimum values that can be represented by its associated primitive type.

These classes also declare the following constructors for initializing their objects:

- Integer(int value) initializes the Integer object to value.

- Integer(String s) converts s's text to a 32-bit integer value and stores this value in the Integer object.

- Long(long value) initializes the Long object to value.

- Long(String s) converts s's text to a 64-bit integer value and stores this value in the Long object.

- Short(short value) initializes the Short object to value.

- Short(String s) converts s's text to a 16–bit integer value and stores this value in the Short object.

- Byte(byte value) initializes the Byte object to value.

- Byte(String s) converts s's text to an 8-bit integer value and stores this value in the Byte object.

Integer's constructors are complemented by int intValue(), Long's constructors are complemented by long longValue(), Short's constructors are complemented by short shortValue(), and Byte's constructors are complemented by byte byteValue(). These methods return wrapped integers.

These classes declare various useful integer-oriented methods. For example, Integer declares the following class methods for converting a 32-bit integer to a String according to a specific representation (binary, hexadecimal, octal, and decimal):

- static String toBinaryString(int i) returns a String object containing i's binary representation. For example, Integer.toBinaryString(255) returns a String object containing 11111111.

- static String toHexString(int i) returns a String object containing i's hexadecimal representation. For example, Integer.toHexString(255) returns a String object containing ff.

- static String toOctalString(int i) returns a String object containing i's octal representation. For example, toOctalString(64) returns a String object containing 377.

- static String toString(int i) returns a String object containing i's decimal representation. For example, toString(255) returns a String object containing 255.

It is often convenient to prepend zeros to a binary string so that you can align multiple binary strings in columns. For example, you might want to create an application that displays the following aligned output:

```
11110001
+
00000111
--------
11111000
```

Unfortunately, toBinaryString() does not let you accomplish this task. For example, Integer.toBinaryString(7) returns a String object containing 111 instead of 00000111. Listing 6–13's toAlignedBinaryString() method addresses this oversight.

Listing 6–13. *Aligning binary strings*

```
public static void main(String[] args)
{
   System.out.println(toAlignedBinaryString(7, 8));
   System.out.println(toAlignedBinaryString(255, 16));
   System.out.println(toAlignedBinaryString(255, 7));
}
static String toAlignedBinaryString(int i, int numBits)
{
   String result = Integer.toBinaryString(i);
   if (result.length() > numBits)
      return null; // cannot fit result into numBits columns
   int numLeadingZeros = numBits-result.length();
   String zerosPrefix = "";
   for (int j = 0; j < numLeadingZeros; j++)
      zerosPrefix += "0";
   return zerosPrefix + result;
}
```

The toAlignedBinaryString() method takes two arguments: the first argument specifies the 32-bit integer that is to be converted into a binary string, and the second argument specifies the number of bit columns in which to fit the string.

After calling toBinaryString() to return i's equivalent binary string without leading zeros, toAlignedBinaryString() verifies that the string's digits can fit into the number of bit columns specified by numBits. If they do not fit, this method returns null. (You will learn about length() and other String methods in Chapter 7.)

Moving on, toAlignedBinaryString() calculates the number of leading "0"s to prepend to result, and then uses a for loop to create a string of leading zeros. This method ends by returning the leading zeros string prepended to the result string.

Although using the compound string concatenation with assignment operator (+=) in a loop to build a string looks okay, it is very inefficient because intermediate String objects are created and thrown away. However, I employed this inefficient code so that I can contrast it with the more efficient code that I present in Chapter 7.

When you run this application, it generates the following output:

```
00000111
0000000011111111
null
```

Number

Each of `Float`, `Double`, `Integer`, `Long`, `Short`, and `Byte` provides the other classes' *x*Value() methods in addition to its own *x*Value() method. For example, `Float` provides `doubleValue()`, `intValue()`, `longValue()`, `shortValue()`, and `byteValue()` in addition to `floatValue()`.

All six methods are members of `java.lang.Number`, which is the abstract superclass of `Float`, `Double`, `Integer`, `Long`, `Short`, and `Byte`—Number's `floatValue()`, `doubleValue()`, `intValue()`, and `longValue()` methods are abstract. `Number` is also the superclass of `BigDecimal` and `BigInteger` (and some concurrency-related classes; see Chapter 9).

`Number` exists to simplify iterating over a collection of `Number` subclass objects. For example, you can declare a variable of `List<Number>` type and initialize it to an instance of `ArrayList<Number>`. You can then store a mixture of `Number` subclass objects in the collection, and iterate over this collection by calling a subclass method polymorphically.

References API

Chapter 2 introduced you to garbage collection, where you learned that the garbage collector removes an object from the heap when there are no more references to the object.

Chapter 3 introduced you to `Object`'s `finalize()` method, where you learned that the garbage collector calls this method before removing an object from the heap. This method gives the object an opportunity to perform cleanup.

This section continues from where Chapters 2 and 3 left off by introducing you to Java's References API. This API makes it possible for an application to interact with the garbage collector in limited ways.

The section first acquaints you with some basic terminology. It then introduces you to the API's `Reference` and `ReferenceQueue` classes, followed by the API's `SoftReference`, `WeakReference`, and `PhantomReference` classes.

Basic Terminology

When an application runs, its execution reveals a *root set of references*, a collection of local variables, parameters, class fields, and instance fields that currently exist and that contain (possibly null) references to objects. This root set changes over time as the application runs. For example, parameters disappear after a method returns.

Many garbage collectors identify this root set when they run. They use the root set to determine if an object is *reachable* (referenced, also known as *live*) or *unreachable* (not referenced). The garbage collector cannot collect reachable objects. Instead, it can only collect objects that, starting from the root set of references, cannot be reached.

> **NOTE:** Reachable objects include objects that are indirectly reachable from root-set variables, which means objects that are reachable through live objects that are directly reachable from those variables. An object that is unreachable by any path from any root-set variable is eligible for garbage collection.

Beginning with Java version 1.2, reachable objects were classified as strongly reachable, softly reachable, weakly reachable, and phantom reachable. Unlike strongly reachable objects, softly, weakly, and phantom reachable objects can be garbage collected.

The following list describes these four kinds of reachability in terms of reference strength, from strongest to weakest:

- An object is *strongly reachable* when it is reachable by a thread without the thread having to traverse References API objects—the thread follows a *strong reference* in a root-set variable. A newly created object (such as the object referenced by d in Double d = new Double(1.0);) is strongly reachable by the thread that created it. (I discuss threads in Chapter 7.)

- An object is *softly reachable* when it is not strongly reachable but can be reached by traversing a *soft reference* (a reference to the object where the reference is stored in a SoftReference object). The strongest reference to this object is a soft reference. When heap memory runs low, the garbage collector typically clears the soft references of the oldest softly reachable objects and removes those objects after finalizing them (by calling finalize()).

- An object is *weakly reachable* when it is not strongly or softly reachable but can be reached by traversing a *weak reference* (a reference to the object where the reference is stored in a WeakReference object). The strongest reference to this object is a weak reference. The garbage collector clears weak references to weakly reachable objects and throws away these objects (after finalizing them) the next time it runs, even when memory is plentiful.

- An object is *phantom reachable* when it is neither strongly, softly, nor weakly reachable, it has been finalized, and the garbage collector is ready to reclaim its memory. Furthermore, it is referred to by some *phantom reference* (a reference to the object where the reference is stored in a PhantomReference object). The strongest reference to this object is a phantom reference.

> **NOTE:** Apart from the garbage collector being less eager to clean up the softly reachable object, a soft reference is exactly like a weak reference. Also, a weak reference is not strong enough to keep an object in memory.

The object whose reference is stored in a SoftReference, WeakReference, or PhantomReference object is known as a *referent*.

Reference and ReferenceQueue

The References API consists of five classes located in the java.lang.ref package. Central to this package are Reference and ReferenceQueue.

Reference is the abstract superclass of this package's concrete SoftReference, WeakReference, and PhantomReference subclasses.

ReferenceQueue is a concrete class whose instances describe queue data structures. When you associate a ReferenceQueue instance with a Reference subclass object (Reference object, for short), the Reference object is added to the queue when the referent to which its encapsulated reference refers becomes garbage.

> **NOTE:** You associate a ReferenceQueue object with a Reference object by passing the ReferenceQueue object to an appropriate Reference subclass constructor.

Reference is declared as generic type Reference<T>, where T identifies the referent's type. This class provides the following methods:

- void clear() assigns null to the stored reference; the Reference object on which this method is called is not *enqueued* (inserted) into its associated reference queue (if there is an associated reference queue). (The garbage collector clears references directly; it does not call clear(). Instead, this method is called by applications.)

- boolean enqueue() adds the Reference object on which this method is called to the associated reference queue. This method returns true when this Reference object has become enqueued; otherwise, this method returns false—this Reference object was already enqueued or was not associated with a queue when created. (The garbage collector enqueues Reference objects directly; it does not call enqueue(). Instead, this method is called by applications.)

- T get() returns this Reference object's stored reference. The return value is null when the stored reference has been cleared, either by the application or by the garbage collector.

- boolean isEnqueued() returns true when this Reference object has been enqueued, either by the application or by the garbage collector. Otherwise, this method returns false—this Reference object was not associated with a queue when created.

> **NOTE:** Reference also declares constructors. Because these constructors are package-private, only classes in the java.lang.ref package can subclass Reference. This restriction is necessary because instances of Reference's subclasses must work closely with the garbage collector.

ReferenceQueue is declared as generic type ReferenceQueue<T>, where T identifies the referent's type. This class declares the following constructor and methods:

- ReferenceQueue() initializes a new ReferenceQueue instance.

- Reference<? extends T> poll() polls this queue to check for an available Reference object. If one is available, the object is removed from the queue and returned. Otherwise, this method returns immediately with a null value.

- Reference<? extends T> remove() removes the next Reference object from the queue and returns this object. This method waits indefinitely for a Reference object to become available, and throws java.lang.InterruptedException when this wait is interrupted.

- Reference<? extends T> remove(long timeout) removes the next Reference object from the queue and returns this object. This method waits until a Reference object becomes available or until timeout milliseconds have elapsed—passing 0 to timeout causes the method to wait indefinitely. If timeout's value expires, the method returns null. This method throws java.lang.IllegalArgumentException when timeout's value is negative, or InterruptedException when this wait is interrupted.

SoftReference

The SoftReference class describes a Reference object whose referent is softly reachable. In addition to inheriting Reference's methods and overriding get(), this generic class provides the following constructors for initializing a SoftReference object:

- SoftReference(T r) encapsulates r's reference. The SoftReference object behaves as a soft reference to r. No ReferenceQueue object is associated with this SoftReference object.

- `SoftReference(T r, ReferenceQueue<? super T> q)` encapsulates r's reference. The `SoftReference` object behaves as a soft reference to r. The `ReferenceQueue` object identified by q is associated with this `SoftReference` object. Passing `null` to q indicates a soft reference without a queue.

`SoftReference` is useful for implementing caches, such as a cache of images. An image cache keeps images in memory (because it takes time to load them from disk) and ensures that duplicate (and possibly very large) images are not stored in memory.

The image cache contains references to image objects that are already in memory. If these references were strong, the images would remain in memory. You would then need to figure out which images are no longer needed and remove them from memory so that they can be garbage collected.

Having to manually remove images duplicates the work of a garbage collector. However, if you wrap the references to the image objects in `SoftReference` objects, the garbage collector will determine when to remove these objects (typically when heap memory runs low) and perform the removal on your behalf.

Listing 6–14 shows how you might use `SoftReference` to maintain a cache of images.

Listing 6–14. *Maintaining a cache of images*

```
class Image
{
   private byte[] image;
   private Image(String name)
   {
      image = new byte[1024*100];
   }
   static Image getImage(String name)
   {
      return new Image(name);
   }
}
public class ImageCache
{
   final static int NUM_IMAGES = 200;
   @SuppressWarnings("unchecked")
   public static void main(String[] args)
   {
      String[] imageNames = new String[NUM_IMAGES];
      for (int i = 0; i < imageNames.length; i++)
         imageNames[i] = new String("image" + i + ".gif");

      SoftReference<Image>[] cache = new SoftReference[imageNames.length];
      for (int i = 0; i < cache.length; i++)
         cache[i] = new SoftReference<Image>(Image.getImage(imageNames[i]));

      for (int i = 0; i < cache.length; i++)
      {
         Image im = cache[i].get();
         if (im == null)
         {
```

```
                      System.out.println(imageNames[i] + " not in cache");
                      im = Image.getImage(imageNames[i]);
                      cache[i] = new SoftReference<Image>(im);
                   }
                   System.out.println("Drawing image");
                   im = null; // Remove strong reference to image.
                }
             }
          }
```

This listing declares an Image class that simulates a loaded image. Each instance is created by calling the getImage() class method, and the instance's private image array occupies 100KB of memory.

The main() method first creates an array of String objects that contain image filenames. The technique employed in creating this array is inefficient. You will discover an efficient alternative in Chapter 7.

main() next creates an array of SoftReference objects that serves as a cache for Image objects. This array is initialized to SoftReference objects; each SoftReference object is initialized to an Image object's reference.

main() now enters the application's main loop. It iterates over the cache, retrieving each Image object or null when the garbage collector has cleared the soft reference to the Image object (so that it can make room in the heap).

If the reference assigned to im is not null, the Image object has not been made unreachable and subsequent code can draw the image on the screen. The im = null; assignment removes the strong reference to the Image object from the im root-set variable.

> **NOTE:** The im = null; assignment is not necessary in this application because either im is immediately overwritten by get()'s return value in the next loop iteration, or the loop and the application ends. Because im's value might hang around for a while in a refactored and longer-lived version of this application, and the garbage collector would not be able to remove the associated Image object from the heap because that object would be strongly reachable, I've included this assignment to show you how to get rid of im's value.

When the reference assigned to im is null, the Image object has been made unreachable and has probably been removed from the heap. In this case, the Image object must be re-created and stored in a new SoftReference object that is stored in the cache.

Here is a small portion of the output that I observed—you may have to adjust the application's code to observe similar output:

```
image162.gif not in cache
Drawing image
image163.gif not in cache
Drawing image
Drawing image
```

Regarding the last line of output, its Drawing image message implies that image164.gif is still in the cache. In other words, the associated Image object is still reachable.

> **NOTE:** If you observe an unending repetition of the Drawing image message, perhaps your Java virtual machine's heap space is larger than the heap space used by my virtual machine when I ran this application on my Windows XP platform. If your virtual machine's heap space is large enough, soft references will not be cleared and you will end up with an infinite loop of output. To correct this situation, you might want to increase the size of Image's image array (perhaps from 1024*100 to 1024*500) and (possibly) assign a larger value to NUM_IMAGES (perhaps 500).

WeakReference

The WeakReference class describes a Reference object whose referent is weakly reachable. In addition to inheriting Reference's methods, this generic class provides the following constructors for initializing a WeakReference object:

- WeakReference(T r) encapsulates r's reference. The WeakReference object behaves as a weak reference to r. No ReferenceQueue object is associated with this WeakReference object.

- WeakReference(T r, ReferenceQueue<? super T> q) encapsulates r's reference. The WeakReference object behaves as a weak reference to r. The ReferenceQueue object identified by q is associated with this WeakReference object. Passing null to q indicates a weak reference without a queue.

WeakReference is useful for preventing memory leaks related to hashmaps. A memory leak occurs when you keep adding objects to a hashmap and never remove them. The objects remain in memory because the hashmap stores strong references to them.

Ideally, the objects should only remain in memory when they are strongly referenced from elsewhere in the application. When an object's last strong reference (apart from hashmap strong references) disappears, the object should be garbage collected.

This situation can be remedied by storing weak references to hashmap entries so they are discarded when no strong references to their keys exist. Java's WeakHashmap class (discussed in Chapter 8) accomplishes this task.

PhantomReference

The PhantomReference class describes a Reference object whose referent is phantom reachable. In addition to inheriting Reference's methods and overriding get(), this generic class provides a single constructor for initializing a PhantomReference object:

■ `PhantomReference(T r, ReferenceQueue<? super T> q)` encapsulates r's reference. The `PhantomReference` object behaves as a phantom reference to r. The `ReferenceQueue` object identified by q is associated with this `PhantomReference` object. Passing `null` to q makes no sense because `get()` is overridden to return null and the `PhantomReference` object will never be enqueued.

Unlike `WeakReference` and `SoftReference` objects, which are enqueued onto their reference queues when their referents become weakly reachable (before finalization), or sometime after their referents become softly reachable (before finalization), `PhantomReference` objects are enqueued after their referents have been reclaimed.

Although you cannot access a `PhantomReference` object's referent (its `get()` method returns null), this class is useful because enqueuing the `PhantomReference` object tells you exactly when the referent has been removed. Perhaps you want to delay creating a large object until another large object has been removed (to avoid a thrown `java.lang.OutOfMemoryError` object).

`PhantomReference` is also useful as a substitute for *resurrection* (making an unreachable object reachable). Because there is no way to access the referent (`get()` returns null), which is no longer in memory when the `PhantomReference` object is enqueued, the object can be cleaned up during the first garbage collection cycle in which that object was discovered to be phantom reachable. You can then clean up related resources after receiving notification via the `PhantomReference` object's reference queue.

> **NOTE:** Resurrection occurs in the `finalize()` method when you assign `this` to a root-set variable. For example, you might specify `r = this;` within `finalize()` to assign the unreachable object identified as `this` to a class field named `r`.

In contrast, the garbage collector requires at least two garbage collection cycles to determine if an object that overrides `finalize()` can be garbage collected. When the first cycle detects that the object is eligible for garbage collection, it calls `finalize()`. Because this method might have resurrected the object, a second garbage collection cycle is needed to determine if resurrection has happened.

> **CAUTION:** Resurrection has been used to implement object pools that recycle the same objects when these objects are expensive (time-wise) to create (database connection objects are an example). Because resurrection exacts a severe performance penalty, and because the `PhantomReference` class makes resurrection unnecessary, you should avoid using resurrection in your applications.

Listing 6–15 shows how you might use `PhantomReference` to detect the removal of a large object.

Listing 6–15. *Detecting a large object's removal*

```
class LargeObject
{
   private byte[] memory = new byte[1024*1024*50]; // 50 megabytes
}
public class LargeObjectDemo
{
   public static void main(String[] args)
   {
      ReferenceQueue<LargeObject> rq;
      rq = new ReferenceQueue<LargeObject>();
      PhantomReference<LargeObject> pr;
      pr = new PhantomReference<LargeObject>(new LargeObject(), rq);
      int counter = 0;
      int[] x;
      while (rq.poll() == null)
      {
         System.out.println("waiting for large object to be removed");
         if (counter++ == 10)
            x = new int[1024*1024];
      }
      System.out.println("large object removed");
   }
}
```

Listing 6–15 declares a LargeObject class whose private memory array occupies 50MB. If your Java implementation throws OutOfMemoryError when you run this application, you might need to reduce the size of this array.

The main() method first creates a ReferenceQueue object that describes a queue onto which a subsequently created PhantomReference object that contains a LargeObject reference will be enqueued.

main() next creates the PhantomReference object, passing a reference to a newly created LargeObject object and a reference to the previously created ReferenceQueue object to the constructor.

After initializing a counter variable (which determines how many loop iterations pass before another large object is created), and after introducing a local variable named x that will hold a strong reference to another large object, main() enters a polling loop.

The polling loop begins by calling poll() to detect the removal of the LargeObject object from memory. As long as this method returns null, meaning that the LargeObject object is still in memory, the loop outputs a message and increments counter.

When counter's value reaches 10, x is assigned an int-based array containing one million integer elements. Because the reference stored in x is strong, this array will not be garbage collected (before the application ends).

On my platform, assigning this array's reference to x is sufficient for the garbage collector to destroy the LargeObject object. Its PhantomReference object is enqueued onto the rq-referenced ReferenceQueue; poll() returns the PhantomReference object.

Depending on your implementation of the virtual machine, you might or might not observe the large object removed message. If you do not see this message, you might need to increase the size of array x, making sure that OutOfMemoryError is not thrown.

When I run this application on my platform, I observe the following output—you may have to adjust the application's code to observe similar output:

```
waiting for large object to be removed
waiting for large object to be removed
waiting for large object to be removed
waiting for large object to be removed
waiting for large object to be removed
waiting for large object to be removed
waiting for large object to be removed
waiting for large object to be removed
waiting for large object to be removed
waiting for large object to be removed
waiting for large object to be removed
large object removed
```

NOTE: For a more useful example of PhantomReference, and for more in-depth knowledge of garbage collection, check out Keith D Gregory's "Java Reference Objects" blog post (http://www.kdgregory.com/index.php?page=java.refobj).

EXERCISES

The following exercises are designed to test your understanding of Java's basic APIs:

1. What constants does Math declare?

2. Why is Math.abs(Integer.MIN_VALUE) equal to Integer.MIN_VALUE?

3. What does Math's random() method accomplish?

4. Identify the five special values that can arise during floating-point calculations.

5. How do Math and StrictMath differ?

6. What is the purpose of strictfp?

7. What is BigDecimal and why might you use this class?

8. Which RoundingMode constant describes the form of rounding commonly taught at school?

9. What is BigInteger?

10. What is the purpose of Package's isSealed() method?

11. True or false: getPackage() requires at least one classfile to be loaded from the package before it returns a Package object describing that package.

12. Identify the two main uses of the primitive wrapper classes.

13. Why should you avoid coding expressions such as ch `>= '0' && ch <= '9'` (test ch to see if it contains a digit) or ch `>= 'A' && ch <= 'Z'` (test ch to see if it contains an uppercase letter)?

14. Identify the four kinds of reachability.

15. What is a referent?

16. Which of the References API's classes is the equivalent of Object's `finalize()` method?

17. Before the era of graphics screens, developers sometimes used a text-based screen to display graphics shapes. For example, a circle might be displayed as follows:

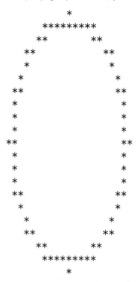

> **NOTE:** This shape appears elliptical instead of circular because each asterisk's displayed height is greater than its displayed width. If the height and width matched, the shape would appear circular.

Create a `Circle` application that generates and displays the previous circle shape. Start by creating a two-dimensional `screen` array of 22 rows by 22 columns. Initialize each array element to the space character (indicating a clear screen). For each integer angle from 0 to 360, compute the x and y coordinates by multiplying a radius value of 10 by each of the cosine and sine of the angle. Add 11 to the x value and 11 to the y value to center the circle shape within the `screen` array. Assign an asterisk to the array at the resulting (x, y) coordinates. After the loop completes, output the array to the standard output device.

18. A *prime number* is a positive integer greater than 1 that is evenly divisible only by 1 and itself. Create a `PrimeNumberTest` application that determines if its solitary integer argument is prime or not prime, and outputs a suitable message. For example, `java PrimeNumberTest 289` should output the message `289 is not prime`. A simple way to check for primality is to loop from 2 through the square root of the integer argument, and use the remainder operator in the loop to determine if the argument is divided evenly by the loop index. For example, because 6%2 yields a remainder of 0 (2 divides evenly into 6), integer 6 is not a prime number.

Summary

The java.lang.Math class supplements the basic math operations (+, -, *, /, and %) with advanced operations (such as trigonometry). The companion java.lang.StrictMath class ensures that all of these operations yield the same values on all platforms.

Money must never be represented by floating-point and double precision floating-point variables because not all monetary values can be represented exactly. In contrast, the java.math.BigDecimal class lets you accurately represent and manipulate these values.

BigDecimal relies on the java.math.BigInteger class for representing its unscaled value. A BigInteger instance describes an integer value that can be of arbitrary length (subject to the limits of the virtual machine's memory).

The java.lang.Package class provides access to package information. This information includes version information about the implementation and specification of a Java package, the package's name, and an indication of whether the package is sealed or not.

Instances of the java.lang package's Boolean, Byte, Character, Double, Float, Integer, Long, and Short primitive wrapper classes wrap themselves around values of primitive types. These classes are useful for storing primitive values in collections.

The References API makes it possible for an application to interact with the garbage collector in limited ways. This API's java.lang.ref package contains classes Reference, ReferenceQueue, SoftReference, WeakReference, and PhantomReference.

SoftReference is useful for implementing image caches, WeakReference is useful for preventing memory leaks related to hashmaps, and PhantomReference is useful for learning when an object has died so its resources can be cleaned up.

Your exploration of Java's basic APIs is far from finished. Chapter 7 continues to focus on basic APIs by discussing the Reflection API, string management, the System class, and the low-level Threading API.

Chapter **7**

Exploring the Basic APIs
Part 2

Chapter 7 continues to explore Java's basic (language-oriented) APIs by introducing APIs that let you use reflection to obtain type information at runtime and more, manage strings, perform system activities (such as retrieving a system property value and obtaining the current time), and use threads to improve application performance.

> **NOTE:** Chapter 7 explores basic API classes and interfaces that are located in the `java.lang` and `java.lang.reflect` packages.

Reflection API

Chapter 3 referred to *reflection* as a third form of runtime type identification (RTTI). Java's Reflection API lets applications learn about loaded classes, interfaces, enums (a kind of class), and annotation types (a kind of interface). The API also lets applications instantiate classes, call methods, access fields, and perform other tasks reflectively.

Chapter 5 presented a `StubFinder` application that used part of the Reflection API to load a class and identify all of the loaded class's public methods that are annotated with `@Stub` annotations. This tool is one example where using reflection is beneficial. Another example is the *class browser*, a tool that enumerates the members of a class.

> **CAUTION:** Reflection should not be used indiscriminately. Application performance suffers because it takes longer to perform operations with reflection than without reflection. Also, reflection-oriented code can be harder to read, and the absence of compile-time type checking can result in runtime failures.

The java.lang package's Class class is the entry point into the Reflection API. Class is generically declared as Class<T>, where T identifies the class, interface, enum, or annotation type that is being modeled by the Class object. T can be replaced by ? (as in Class<?>) when the type being modeled is unknown.

Table 7–1 describes some of Class's methods.

Table 7–1. *Class Methods*

Method	Description
static Class<?> forName(String typename)	Return the Class object that is associated with typename, which must include the type's qualified package name when the type is part of a package (java.lang.String, for example). If the class or interface type has not been loaded into memory, this method takes care of *loading* (reading the classfile's contents into memory), *linking* (taking these contents and combining them into the runtime state of the virtual machine so that they can be executed), and *initializing* (setting class fields to default values, running class initializers, and performing other class initialization) prior to returning the Class object. This method throws java.lang.ClassNotFoundException when the type cannot be found, java.lang.LinkageError when an error occurs during linkage, and java.lang.ExceptionInInitializerError when an exception occurs during a class's static initialization.
Annotation[] getAnnotations()	Return a possibly empty array containing all annotations that are declared for the class represented by this Class object.
Constructor[] getConstructors()	Return an array containing Constructor objects representing all the public constructors of the class represented by this Class object. An array of length zero is returned when the represented class has no public constructors, this Class object represents an array class, or this Class object represents a primitive type or void.
Annotation[] getDeclaredAnnotations()	Return an array containing all annotations that are directly declared on the class represented by this Class object—inherited annotations are not included. The returned array might be empty.
Constructor[] getDeclaredConstructors()	Return an array of Constructor objects representing all the constructors declared by the class represented by this Class object. These are public, protected, default (package) access, and private constructors. The elements in the returned array are not sorted and are not in any particular order. If the class has a default constructor, it is included in the returned array. This method returns an array of length zero when this Class object represents an interface, a primitive type, an array class, or void.

Method	Description
`Field[] getDeclaredFields()`	Return an array of `Field` objects representing all the fields declared by the class or interface represented by this `Class` object. This array includes public, protected, default (package) access, and private fields, but excludes inherited fields. The elements in the returned array are not sorted and are not in any particular order. This method returns an array of length zero when the class or interface declares no fields, or when this `Class` object represents a primitive type, an array class, or void.
`Method[] getDeclaredMethods()`	Return an array of `Method` objects representing all the methods declared by the class or interface represented by this `Class` object. This array includes public, protected, default (package) access, and private methods, but excludes inherited methods. The elements in the returned array are not sorted and are not in any particular order. This method returns an array of length zero when the class or interface declares no methods, or when this `Class` object represents a primitive type, an array class, or void.
`Field[] getFields()`	Return an array containing `Field` objects representing all the public fields of the class or interface represented by this `Class` object, including those public fields inherited from superclasses and superinterfaces. The elements in the returned array are not sorted and are not in any particular order. This method returns an array of length zero when this `Class` object represents a class or interface that has no accessible public fields, or when this `Class` object represents an array class, a primitive type, or void.
`Method[] getMethods()`	Return an array containing `Method` objects representing all the public methods of the class or interface represented by this `Class` object, including those public methods inherited from superclasses and superinterfaces. Array classes return all the public member methods inherited from the `Object` class. The elements in the returned array are not sorted and are not in any particular order. This method returns an array of length zero when this `Class` object represents a class or interface that has no public methods, or when this `Class` object represents a primitive type or void.
`String getName()`	Return the name of the class represented by this `Class` object.
`Package getPackage()`	Return a `Package` object that describes the package in which the class represented by this `Class` object is located, or null when the class is a member of the unnamed package.

Method	Description
Class<? super T> getSuperclass()	Return the Class object representing the superclass of the entity (class, interface, primitive type, or void) represented by this Class object. When the Class object on which this method is called represents the Object class, an interface, a primitive type, or void, null is returned. When this object represents an array class, the Class object representing the Object class is returned.
T newInstance()	Create and return a new instance of the class represented by this Class object. The class is instantiated as if by a new expression with an empty argument list. The class is initialized when it has not already been initialized. This method throws java.lang.IllegalAccessException when the class or its noargument constructor is not accessible; java.lang.InstantiationException when this Class object represents an abstract class, an interface, an array class, a primitive type, or void, or when the class does not have a noargument constructor (or when instantiation fails for some other reason); and ExceptionInInitializerError when initialization fails because the object threw an exception during initialization.

Table 7–1's description of the forName() method reveals one way to obtain a Class object. This method loads, links, and initializes a class or interface that is not in memory and returns a Class object that represents the class or interface. Listing 7–1 demonstrates forName() and additional methods described in this table.

Listing 7–1. *Using reflection to identify a class's name, package, public fields, constructors, and methods*

```
import java.lang.reflect.Constructor;
import java.lang.reflect.Field;
import java.lang.reflect.Method;

public class ExploreType
{
   public static void main(String[] args)
   {
      if (args.length != 1)
      {
         System.err.println("usage: java ExploreType pkgAndTypeName");
         return;
      }
      try
      {
         Class<?> clazz = Class.forName(args[0]);
         System.out.println("NAME: " + clazz.getName());
         System.out.println("PACKAGE: " + clazz.getPackage().getName());
         System.out.println("FIELDS");
         Field[] fields = clazz.getDeclaredFields();
         for (int i = 0; i < fields.length; i++)
            System.out.println(fields[i]);
```

```
        System.out.println("CONSTRUCTORS");
        Constructor[] constructors = clazz.getDeclaredConstructors();
        for (int i = 0; i < constructors.length; i++)
            System.out.println(constructors[i]);
        System.out.println("METHODS");
        Method[] methods = clazz.getDeclaredMethods();
        for (int i = 0; i < methods.length; i++)
            System.out.println(methods[i]);
      }
      catch (ClassNotFoundException cnfe)
      {
         System.err.println("could not locate " + args[0]);
      }
   }
}
```

Listing 7–1 presents an application that uses the Reflection API to explore a class or
interface by outputting its name, package, fields, constructors (classes only), and
methods. Only fields, constructors, and methods that are declared in the class, or fields
and methods that are declared in the interface, are output.

After verifying that one command-line argument has been passed to this application,
main() calls forName() to try to return a Class object representing the class or interface
identified by this argument. If successful, the returned object's reference is assigned to
clazz—I cannot name this variable class because class is a reserved word.

forName() throws an instance of the checked ClassNotFoundException class when it
cannot locate the class's classfile (perhaps the classfile was erased prior to executing
the application). It also throws LinkageError when a class's classfile is malformed, and
ExceptionInInitializerError when a class's static initialization fails.

> **NOTE:** ExceptionInInitializerError is often thrown as the result of a class initializer
> throwing an unchecked exception. For example, the class initializer in the following
> FailedInitialization class results in ExceptionInInitializerError because
> someMethod() throws NullPointerException:
>
> ```
> public class FailedInitialization
> {
>    static
>    {
>       someMethod(null);
>    }
>    public static void someMethod(String s)
>    {
>       int len = s.length(); // s contains null
>       System.out.println(s + "'s length is " + len + " characters");
>    }
> }
> ```

When you run this application, you must include the package specification when the class or interface is located in a package. For example, specifying java ExploreType java.lang.Boolean to output the fields, constructors, and methods declared in the java.lang package's Boolean class results in the following output:

```
NAME: java.lang.Boolean
PACKAGE: java.lang
FIELDS
public static final java.lang.Boolean java.lang.Boolean.TRUE
public static final java.lang.Boolean java.lang.Boolean.FALSE
public static final java.lang.Class java.lang.Boolean.TYPE
private final boolean java.lang.Boolean.value
private static final long java.lang.Boolean.serialVersionUID
CONSTRUCTORS
public java.lang.Boolean(java.lang.String)
public java.lang.Boolean(boolean)
METHODS
public int java.lang.Boolean.hashCode()
public boolean java.lang.Boolean.equals(java.lang.Object)
public int java.lang.Boolean.compareTo(java.lang.Boolean)
public int java.lang.Boolean.compareTo(java.lang.Object)
public static boolean java.lang.Boolean.getBoolean(java.lang.String)
public static java.lang.String java.lang.Boolean.toString(boolean)
public java.lang.String java.lang.Boolean.toString()
public static java.lang.Boolean java.lang.Boolean.valueOf(java.lang.String)
public static java.lang.Boolean java.lang.Boolean.valueOf(boolean)
public boolean java.lang.Boolean.booleanValue()
public static boolean java.lang.Boolean.parseBoolean(java.lang.String)
private static boolean java.lang.Boolean.toBoolean(java.lang.String)
```

Table 7-1's descriptions of the getAnnotations() and getDeclaredAnnotations() methods reveal that each method returns an array of Annotation, an interface that is located in the java.lang.annotation package. Annotation is the superinterface of Override, SuppressWarnings, and all other annotation types.

Table 7-1's method descriptions also refer to Constructor, Field, and Method. Instances of these classes (which are members of the java.lang.reflect package) represent a class's constructors and a class's or an interface's fields and methods.

Constructor represents a constructor and is generically declared as Constructor<T>, where T identifies the class in which the constructor represented by Constructor is declared. Constructor declares various methods, including the following methods:

- Annotation[] getDeclaredAnnotations() returns an array of all annotations declared on the constructor. The returned array has zero length when there are no annotations.

- Class<T> getDeclaringClass() returns a Class object that represents the class in which the constructor is declared.

- Class[]<?> getExceptionTypes() returns an array of Class objects representing the types of exceptions listed in the constructor's throws clause. The returned array has zero length when there is no throws clause.

- String getName() returns the constructor's name.

- Class[]<?> getParameterTypes() returns an array of Class objects representing the constructor's parameters. The returned array has zero length when the constructor does not declare parameters.

Field represents a field and declares various methods, including the following methods:

- Object get(Object object) returns the value of the field for the specified object.

- boolean getBoolean(Object object) returns the value of the Boolean field for the specified object.

- byte getByte(Object object) returns the value of the byte integer field for the specified object.

- char getChar(Object object) returns the value of the character field for the specified object.

- double getDouble(Object object) returns the value of the double precision floating-point field for the specified object.

- float getFloat(Object object) returns the value of the floating-point field for the specified object.

- int getInt(Object object) returns the value of the integer field for the specified object.

- long getLong(Object object) returns the value of the long integer field for the specified object.

- short getShort(Object object) returns the value of the short integer field for the specified object.

get() returns the value of any type of field. In contrast, the other listed methods return the values of specific types of fields. All of these methods throw NullPointerException when object is null and the field is an instance field, IllegalArgumentException when object is not an instance of the class or interface declaring the underlying field (or not an instance of a subclass or interface implementor), and IllegalAccessException when the underlying field cannot be accessed (it is private, for example).

Method represents a method and declares various methods, including the following methods:

- `int getModifiers()` returns a 32-bit integer whose bit fields identify the method's reserved word modifiers (such as `public`, `abstract`, or `static`). These bit fields must be interpreted via the `java.lang.reflect.Modifier` class. For example, you might specify `(method.getModifiers() & Modifier.ABSTRACT) == Modifier.ABSTRACT` to find out if the method (represented by the `Method` object whose reference is stored in `method`) is abstract—this expression evaluates to true when the method is abstract.

- `Class<?> getReturnType()` returns a `Class` object that represents the method's return type.

- `Object invoke(Object receiver, Object... args)` calls the method on the object identified by `receiver` (which is ignored when the method is a class method), passing the variable number of arguments identified by `args` to the called method. The `invoke()` method throws `NullPointerException` when `receiver` is `null` and the method being called is an instance method, `IllegalAccessException` when the method is not accessible (it is private, for example), `IllegalArgumentException` when an incorrect number of arguments are passed to the method (and other reasons), and `java.lang.reflect.InvocationTargetException` when an exception is thrown from the called method.

- `boolean isVarArgs()` returns true when the method is declared to receive a variable number of arguments.

The `java.lang.reflect.AccessibleObject` class is the superclass of `Constructor`, `Field`, and `Method`. This superclass provides methods for reporting a constructor's, field's, or method's accessibility (is it private?) and making an inaccessible constructor, field, or method accessible. `AccessibleObject`'s methods include the following:

- `T getAnnotation(Class<T> annotationType)` returns the constructor's, field's, or method's annotation of the specified type when such an annotation is present; otherwise, null returns.

- `boolean isAccessible()` returns true when the constructor, field, or method is accessible.

- `boolean isAnnotationPresent(Class<? extends Annotation> annotationType)` returns true when an annotation of the type specified by `annotationType` has been declared on the constructor, field, or method. This method takes inherited annotations into account.

- `void setAccessible(boolean flag)` attempts to make an inaccessible constructor, field, or method accessible when `flag` is `true`.

> **NOTE:** The `java.lang.reflect` package also includes an `Array` class whose class methods make it possible to reflectively create and access Java arrays.

Another way to obtain a `Class` object is to call `Object`'s `getClass()` method on an object reference; for example, `Employee e = new Employee(); Class<? extends Employee> clazz = e.getClass();`. The `getClass()` method does not throw an exception because the class from which the object was created is already present in memory.

There is one more way to obtain a `Class` object, and that is to employ a *class literal*, which is an expression consisting of a class name, followed by a period separator, followed by reserved word `class`. Examples of class literals include `Class<Employee> clazz = Employee.class;` and `Class<String> clazz = String.class`.

Perhaps you are wondering about how to choose between `forName()`, `getClass()`, and a class literal. To help you make your choice, the following list compares each competitor:

- `forName()` is very flexible in that you can dynamically specify any reference type by its package-qualified name. If the type is not in memory, it is loaded, linked, and initialized. However, lack of compile-time type safety can lead to runtime failures.

- `getClass()` returns a `Class` object describing the type of its referenced object. If called on a superclass variable containing a subclass instance, a `Class` object representing the subclass type is returned. Because the class is in memory, type safety is assured.

- A class literal returns a `Class` object representing its specified class. Class literals are compact and the compiler enforces type safety by refusing to compile the source code when it cannot locate the literal's specified class.

> **NOTE:** You can use class literals with primitive types, including void. Examples include `int.class`, `double.class`, and `void.class`. The returned `Class` object represents the class identified by a primitive wrapper class's TYPE field or `java.lang.Void.TYPE`. For example, each of `int.class == Integer.TYPE` and `void.class == Void.TYPE` evaluates to true.
>
> You can also use class literals with primitive type–based arrays. Examples include `int[].class` and `double[].class`. For these examples, the returned `Class` objects represent `Class<int[]>` and `Class<double[]>`.

String Management

Many computer languages implement the concept of a *string*, a sequence of characters treated as a single unit (and not as individual characters). For example, the C language implements a string as an array of characters terminated by the null character (`'\0'`). In contrast, Java implements a string via the `java.lang.String` class.

String objects are immutable: you cannot modify a String object's string. The various String methods that appear to modify the String object actually return a new String object with modified string content instead. Because returning new String objects is often wasteful, Java provides the java.lang.StringBuffer class as a workaround.

This section introduces you to String and StringBuffer.

String

String represents a string as a sequence of characters. Unlike C strings, this sequence is not terminated by a null character. Instead, its length is stored separately.

The Java language provides syntactic sugar that simplifies working with strings. For example, the compiler recognizes String favLanguage = "Java"; as the assignment of string literal "Java" to String variable favLanguage. Without this sugar, you would have to specify String favLanguage = new String("Java");.

Table 7–2 describes some of String's constructors and methods for initializing String objects and working with strings.

Table 7–2. *String Constructors and Methods*

Method	Description
String(char[] data)	Initialize this String object to the characters in the data array. Modifying data after initializing this String object has no effect on the object.
String(String s)	Initialize this String object to s's string.
char charAt(int index)	Return the character located at the zero-based index in this String object's string. This method throws java.lang.IndexOutOfBoundsException when index is less than 0 or greater than or equal to the length of the string.
String concat(String s)	Return a new String object containing this String object's string followed by the s argument's string.
boolean endsWith(String suffix)	Return true when this String object's string ends with the characters in the suffix argument, when suffix is empty (contains no characters), or when suffix contains the same character sequence as this String object's string. This method performs a case-sensitive comparison (a is not equal to A, for example), and throws NullPointerException when suffix is null.
boolean equals(Object object)	Return true when object is of type String and this argument's string contains the same characters (and in the same order) as this String object's string.

Method	Description
boolean equalsIgnoreCase(String s)	Return true when s and this String object contain the same characters (ignoring case). This method returns false when the character sequences differ or when null is passed to s.
int indexOf(int c)	Return the zero-based index of the first occurrence (from the start of the string to the end of the string) of the character represented by c in this String object's string. Return -1 when this character is not present.
int indexOf(String s)	Return the zero-based index of the first occurrence (from the start of the string to the end of the string) of s's character sequence in this String object's string. Return -1 when s is not present. This method throws NullPointerException when s is null.
String intern()	Search an internal table of String objects for an object whose string is equal to this String object's string. This String object's string is added to the table when not present. Return the object contained in the table whose string is equal to this String object's string. The same String object is always returned for strings that are equal.
int lastIndexOf(int c)	Return the zero-based index of the last occurrence (from the start of the string to the end of the string) of the character represented by c in this String object's string. Return -1 when this character is not present.
int lastIndexOf(String s)	Return the zero-based index of the last occurrence (from the start of the string to the end of the string) of s's character sequence in this String object's string. Return -1 when s is not present. This method throws NullPointerException when s is null.
int length()	Return the number of characters in this String object's string.
String replace(char oldChar, char newChar)	Return a new String object whose string matches this String object's string except that all occurrences of oldChar have been replaced by newChar.
String[] split(String expr)	Split this String object's string into an array of String objects using the regular expression (a string whose pattern [template] is used to search a string for substrings that match the pattern) specified by expr as the basis for the split. This method throws NullPointerException when expr is null and java.util.regex.PatternSyntaxException when expr's syntax is invalid.

Method	Description
boolean startsWith(String prefix)	Return true when this String object's string starts with the characters in the prefix argument, when prefix is empty (contains no characters), or when prefix contains the same character sequence as this String object's string. This method performs a case-sensitive comparison (a is not equal to A, for example), and throws NullPointerException when prefix is null.
String substring(int start)	Return a new String object whose string contains this String object's characters beginning with the character located at start. This method throws IndexOutOfBoundsException when start is negative or greater than the length of this String object's string.
char[] toCharArray()	Return a character array that contains the characters in this String object's string.
String toLowerCase()	Return a new String object whose string contains this String object's characters where uppercase letters have been converted to lowercase. This String object is returned when it contains no uppercase letters to convert.
String toUpperCase()	Return a new String object whose string contains this String object's characters where lowercase letters have been converted to uppercase. This String object is returned when it contains no lowercase letters to convert.
String trim()	Return a new String object that contains this String object's string with *whitespace characters* (characters whose Unicode values are 32 or less) removed from the start and end of the string, or this String object if no leading/trailing whitespace.

Table 7–2 reveals a couple of interesting items about String. First, this class's public String(String s) constructor does not initialize a String object to a string literal. Instead, it initializes the String object to the contents of another String object. This behavior suggests that a string literal is more than what it appears to be.

In reality, a string literal is a String object. You can prove this to yourself by executing System.out.println("abc".length()); and System.out.println("abc" instanceof String);. The first method call outputs 3, which is the length of the "abc" String object's string, and the second method call outputs true ("abc" is a String object).

The second interesting item is the intern() method, which *interns* (stores a unique copy of) a String object in an internal table of String objects. intern() makes it possible to compare strings via their references and == or !=. These operators are the fastest way to compare strings, which is especially valuable when sorting a huge number of strings.

By default, String objects denoted by literal strings ("abc") and string-valued constant expressions ("a" + "bc") are interned in this table, which is why `System.out.println("abc" == "a" + "bc");` outputs true. However, String objects created via String constructors are not interned, which is why `System.out.println("abc" == new String("abc"));` outputs false. In contrast, `System.out.println("abc" == new String("abc").intern());` outputs true.

Table 7–2 also reveals `split()`, a method that I employed in Chapter 5's StubFinder application to split a string's comma-separated list of values into an array of String objects. This method uses a regular expression that identifies a sequence of characters around which the string is split. (I will discuss regular expressions in Chapter 9.)

> **TIP:** The `charAt()` and `length()` methods are useful for iterating over a string's characters. For example, `String s = "abc"; for (int i = 0; i < s.length(); i++) System.out.println(s.charAt(i));` returns each of s's a, b, and c characters and outputs each character on a separate line.

StringBuffer

StringBuffer provides an internal character array for building a string efficiently. After creating a StringBuffer object, you call various methods to append, delete, and insert the character representations of various values to, from, and into the array. You then call `toString()` to convert the array's content to a String object and return this object.

> **CAUTION:** Divulging a class's internal implementation typically is not a good idea because doing so violates information hiding. Furthermore, the internal implementation might change, which voids the description of the previous implementation. However, I believe that divulging StringBuffer's internal array adds value to my discussion of this class. Furthermore, it is highly unlikely that StringBuffer will ever use anything other than a character array.

Table 7–3 describes some of StringBuffer's constructors and methods for initializing StringBuffer objects and working with string buffers.

Table 7–3. *StringBuffer Constructors and Methods*

Method	Description
StringBuffer()	Initialize this StringBuffer object to an empty array with an initial capacity of 16 characters.
StringBuffer(int capacity)	Initialize this StringBuffer object to an empty array with an initial capacity of capacity characters. This constructor throws java.lang.NegativeArraySizeException when capacity is negative.
StringBuffer(String s)	Initialize this StringBuffer object to an array containing s's characters. This object's initial capacity is 16 plus the length of s. This constructor throws NullPointerException when s is null.
StringBuffer append(boolean b)	Append "true" to this StringBuffer object's array when b is true and "false" to the array when b is false, and return this StringBuffer object.
StringBuffer append(char ch)	Append ch's character to this StringBuffer object's array, and return this StringBuffer object.
StringBuffer append(char[] chars)	Append the characters in the chars array to this StringBuffer object's array, and return this StringBuffer object. This method throws NullPointerException when chars is null.
StringBuffer append(double d)	Append the string representation of d's double precision floating-point value to this StringBuffer object's array, and return this StringBuffer object.
StringBuffer append(float f)	Append the string representation of f's floating-point value to this StringBuffer object's array, and return this StringBuffer object.
StringBuffer append(int i)	Append the string representation of i's integer value to this StringBuffer object's array, and return this StringBuffer object.
StringBuffer append(long l)	Append the string representation of l's long integer value to this StringBuffer object's array, and return this StringBuffer object.
StringBuffer append(Object obj)	Call obj's toString() method and append the returned string's characters to this StringBuffer object's array. Append "null" to the array when null is passed to obj. Return this StringBuffer object.
StringBuffer append(String s)	Append s's string to this StringBuffer object's array. Append "null" to the array when null is passed to s. Return this StringBuffer object.

Method	Description
int capacity()	Return the current capacity of this StringBuffer object's array.
char charAt(int index)	Return the character located at index in this StringBuffer object's array. This method throws IndexOutOfBoundsException when index is negative or greater than or equal to this StringBuffer object's length.
void ensureCapacity(int min)	Ensure that this StringBuffer object's capacity is at least that specified by min. If the current capacity is less than min, a new internal array is created with greater capacity. The new capacity is set to the larger of min and the current capacity multiplied by 2, with 2 added to the result. No action is taken when min is negative or zero.
int length()	Return the number of characters stored in this StringBuffer object's array.
StringBuffer reverse()	Return this StringBuffer object with its array contents reversed.
void setCharAt(int index, char ch)	Replace the character at index with ch. This method throws IndexOutOfBoundsException when index is negative or greater than or equal to the length of this StringBuffer object's array.
void setLength(int length)	Set the length of this StringBuffer object's array to length. If the length argument is less than the current length, the array's contents are truncated. If the length argument is greater than or equal to the current length, sufficient null characters ('\u0000') are appended to the array. This method throws IndexOutOfBoundsException when length is negative.
String substring(int start)	Return a new String object that contains all characters in this StringBuffer object's array starting with the character located at start. This method throws IndexOutOfBoundsException when start is less than 0 or greater than or equal to the length of this StringBuffer object's array.
String toString()	Return a new String object whose string equals the contents of this StringBuffer object's array.

A StringBuffer object's internal array is associated with the concepts of capacity and length. *Capacity* refers to the maximum number of characters that can be stored in the array before the array grows to accommodate additional characters. *Length* refers to the number of characters that are already stored in the array.

Chapter 6's Listing 6-13 declared a toAlignedBinaryString() method whose implementation included the following inefficient loop:

```
int numLeadingZeroes = 3;
```

```
String zeroesPrefix = "";
for (int j = 0; j < numLeadingZeroes; j++)
   zeroesPrefix += "0";
```

This loop is inefficient because each of the iterations creates a StringBuffer object and a String object. The compiler transforms this code fragment into the following fragment:

```
int numLeadingZeroes = 3;
String zeroesPrefix = "";
for (int j = 0; j < numLeadingZeroes; j++)
   zeroesPrefix = new StringBuffer().append(zeroesPrefix).append("0").toString();
```

> **NOTE:** Starting with Java version 5, the compiler uses the more performant but otherwise identical java.lang.StringBuilder class instead of StringBuffer.

A more efficient way to code the previous loop involves creating a StringBuffer object prior to entering the loop, calling the appropriate append() method in the loop, and calling toString() after the loop. The following code fragment demonstrates this more efficient scenario:

```
int numLeadingZeroes = 3;
StringBuffer sb = new StringBuffer();
for (int j = 0; j < numLeadingZeroes; j++)
   sb.append('0');
String zeroesPrefix = sb.toString();
```

> **TIP:** When performance matters, and where you are not using multiple threads (discussed later in this chapter), use the StringBuilder class instead of StringBuffer. StringBuilder provides the same methods as StringBuffer, but its methods are not synchronized (discussed later in this chapter). This lack of synchronization results in StringBuilder methods executing faster than their StringBuffer counterparts under most (if not all) Java implementations.

System

The java.lang.System class provides access to system-oriented resources, including standard input, standard output, and standard error.

System declares in, out, and err class fields that support standard input, standard output, and standard error, respectively. The first field is of type java.io.InputStream, and the last two fields are of type java.io.PrintStream. (I will formally introduce these classes in Chapter 10.)

System also declares a variety of utility methods, including those methods that are described in Table 7–4.

Table 7–4. *System Methods*

Method	Description
static void arraycopy(Object src, int srcPos, Object dest, int destPos, int length)	Copy the number of elements specified by length from the src array starting at zero-based offset srcPos into the dest array starting at zero-based offset destPos. This method throws NullPointerException when src or dest is null, IndexOutOfBoundsException when copying causes access to data outside array bounds, and java.lang.ArrayStoreException when an element in the src array could not be stored into the dest array because of a type mismatch.
static long currentTimeMillis()	Return the current system time in milliseconds since January 1, 1970 00:00:00 UTC.
static void gc()	Inform the virtual machine that now would be a good time to run the garbage collector. This is only a hint; there is no guarantee that the garbage collector will run.
static String getProperty(String prop)	Return the value of the *system property* (platform-specific attribute, such as a version number) identified by prop or null if such a property does not exist. System properties recognized by Android include java.vendor.url, java.class.path, user.home, java.class.version, os.version, java.vendor, user.dir, user.timezone, path.separator, os.name, os.arch, line.separator, file.separator, user.name, java.version, and java.home.
static void runFinalization()	Inform the virtual machine that now would be a good time to perform any outstanding object finalizations. This is only a hint; there is no guarantee that outstanding object finalizations will be performed.

Listing 7–2 demonstrates the arraycopy(), currentTimeMillis(), and getProperty() methods.

Listing 7–2. *Experimenting with System methods*

```
public class SystemTasks
{
   public static void main(String[] args)
   {
      int[] grades = { 86, 92, 78, 65, 52, 43, 72, 98, 81 };
      int[] gradesBackup = new int[grades.length];
      System.arraycopy(grades, 0, gradesBackup, 0, grades.length);
      for (int i = 0; i < gradesBackup.length; i++)
         System.out.println(gradesBackup[i]);
      System.out.println("Current time: " + System.currentTimeMillis());
      String[] propNames =
      {
         "java.vendor.url",
         "java.class.path",
         "user.home",
```

```
                    "java.class.version",
                    "os.version",
                    "java.vendor",
                    "user.dir",
                    "user.timezone",
                    "path.separator",
                    "os.name",
                    "os.arch",
                    "line.separator",
                    "file.separator",
                    "user.name",
                    "java.version",
                    "java.home"
              };
              for (int i = 0; i < propNames.length; i++)
                  System.out.println(propNames[i] + ": " +
                                    System.getProperty(propNames[i]));

    }
}
```

Listing 7–2's `main()` method begins by demonstrating `arraycopy()`. It uses this method to copy the contents of a grades array to a gradesBackup array.

> **TIP:** The `arraycopy()` method is the fastest portable way to copy one array to another. Also, when you write a class whose methods return a reference to an internal array, you should use `arraycopy()` to create a copy of the array, and then return the copy's reference. That way, you prevent clients from directly manipulating (and possibly screwing up) the internal array.

`main()` next calls `currentTimeMillis()` to return the current time as a milliseconds value. Because this value is not human-readable, you might want to use the `java.util.Date` class (discussed in Chapter 9). The `Date()` constructor calls `currentTimeMillis()` and its `toString()` method converts this value to a readable date and time.

`main()` concludes by demonstrating `getProperty()` in a for loop. This loop iterates over all of Table 7–4's property names, outputting each name and value.

When I run this application on my platform, it generates the following output:

```
86
92
78
65
52
43
72
98
81
Current time: 1274895119343
java.vendor.url: http://java.sun.com/
java.class.path: .
user.home: C:\Documents and Settings\Jeff Friesen
java.class.version: 50.0
os.version: 5.1
```

```
java.vendor: Sun Microsystems Inc.
user.dir: C:\prj\dev\ljfad\c06\code\SYSTEM~1
user.timezone:
path.separator: ;
os.name: Windows XP
os.arch: x86
line.separator:

file.separator: \
user.name: Jeff Friesen
java.version: 1.6.0_16
java.home: C:\Program Files\Java\jre6
```

NOTE: `line.separator` stores the actual line separator character/characters, not its/their representation (such as \r\n), which is why a blank line appears after `line.separator:`.

Threading API

Applications execute via *threads*, which are independent paths of execution through an application's code. When multiple threads are executing, each thread's path can differ from other thread paths. For example, a thread might execute one of a switch statement's cases, and another thread might execute another of this statement's cases.

NOTE: Applications use threads to improve performance. Some applications can get by with only the default main thread to carry out their tasks, but other applications need additional threads to perform time-intensive tasks in the background, so that they remain responsive to their users.

The virtual machine gives each thread its own method-call stack to prevent threads from interfering with each other. Separate stacks let threads keep track of their next instructions to execute, which can differ from thread to thread. The stack also provides a thread with its own copy of method parameters, local variables, and return value.

Java supports threads via its Threading API. This API consists of one interface (Runnable) and four classes (Thread, ThreadGroup, ThreadLocal, and InheritableThreadLocal) in the java.lang package. After exploring Runnable and Thread (and mentioning ThreadGroup during this exploration), this section explores thread synchronization, ThreadLocal, and InheritableThreadLocal.

NOTE: Java version 5 introduced the `java.util.concurrent` package as a high-level alternative to the low-level Threading API. (I will discuss this package in Chapter 9.) Although `java.util.concurrent` is the preferred API for working with threads, you should also be somewhat familiar with Threading because it is helpful in simple threading scenarios. Also, you might have to analyze someone else's source code that depends on Threading.

Runnable and Thread

Java provides the Runnable interface to identify those objects that supply code for threads to execute via this interface's solitary public void run() method—a thread receives no arguments and returns no value. Classes implement Runnable to supply this code, and one of these classes is Thread.

Thread provides a consistent interface to the underlying operating system's threading architecture. (The operating system is typically responsible for creating and managing threads.) Thread makes it possible to associate code with threads, as well as start and manage those threads. Each Thread instance associates with a single thread.

Thread declares several constructors for initializing Thread objects. Some of these constructors take Runnable arguments: you can supply code to run without having to extend Thread. Other constructors do not take Runnable arguments: you must extend Thread and override its run() method to supply the code to run.

For example, Thread(Runnable runnable) initializes a new Thread object to the specified runnable whose code is to be executed. In contrast, Thread() does not initialize Thread to a Runnable argument. Instead, your Thread subclass provides a constructor that calls Thread(), and the subclass also overrides Thread's run() method.

In the absence of an explicit name argument, each constructor assigns a unique default name (starting with Thread-) to the Thread object. Names make it possible to differentiate threads. In contrast to the previous two constructors, which choose default names, Thread(String threadName) lets you specify your own thread name.

Thread also declares methods for starting and managing threads. Table 7–5 describes many of the more useful methods.

Table 7–5. *Thread Methods*

Method	Description
static Thread currentThread()	Return the Thread object associated with the thread that calls this method.
String getName()	Return the name associated with this Thread object.
Thread.State getState()	Return the state of the thread associated with this Thread object. The state is identified by the Thread.State enum as one of BLOCKED (waiting to acquire a lock, discussed later), NEW (created but not started), RUNNABLE (executing), TERMINATED (the thread has died), TIMED_WAITING (waiting for a specified amount of time to elapse), or WAITING (waiting indefinitely).
void interrupt()	Set the interrupt status flag in this Thread object. If the associated thread is blocked or waiting, clear this flag and wake up the thread by throwing an instance of the checked InterruptedException class.

Method	Description
`static boolean interrupted()`	Return true when the thread associated with this `Thread` object has a pending interrupt request. Clear the interrupt status flag.
`boolean isAlive()`	Return true to indicate that this `Thread` object's associated thread is alive and not dead. A thread's lifespan ranges from just before it is actually started within the `start()` method to just after it leaves the `run()` method, at which point it dies.
`boolean isDaemon()`	Return true when the thread associated with this `Thread` object is a *daemon thread*, a thread that acts as a helper to a *user thread* (nondaemon thread) and dies automatically when the application's last nondaemon thread dies so the application can exit.
`boolean isInterrupted()`	Return true when the thread associated with this `Thread` object has a pending interrupt request.
`void join()`	The thread that calls this method on this `Thread` object waits for the thread associated with this object to die. This method throws `InterruptedException` when this `Thread` object's `interrupt()` method is called.
`void join(long millis)`	The thread that calls this method on this `Thread` object waits for the thread associated with this object to die, or until `millis` milliseconds have elapsed, whichever happens first. This method throws `InterruptedException` when this `Thread` object's `interrupt()` method is called.
`void setDaemon(boolean isDaemon)`	Mark this `Thread` object's associated thread as a daemon thread when `isDaemon` is true. This method throws `java.lang.IllegalThreadStateException` when the thread has not yet been created and started.
`void setName(String threadName)`	Assign `threadName`'s value to this `Thread` object as the name of its associated thread.
`static void sleep(long time)`	Pause the thread associated with this `Thread` object for `time` milliseconds. This method throws `InterruptedException` when this `Thread` object's `interrupt()` method is called while the thread is sleeping.
`void start()`	Create and start this `Thread` object's associated thread. This method throws `IllegalThreadStateException` when the thread was previously started and is running or has died.

Listing 7–3 introduces you to the Threading API via a `main()` method that demonstrates Runnable, `Thread(Runnable runnable)`, `currentThread()`, `getName()`, and `start()`.

Listing 7–3. *A pair of counting threads*

```java
public class CountingThreads
{
    public static void main(String[] args)
    {
        Runnable r = new Runnable()
                    {
                        @Override
                        public void run()
                        {
                            String name = Thread.currentThread().getName();
                            int count = 0;
                            while (true)
                                System.out.println(name + ": " + count++);
                        }
                    };
        Thread thdA = new Thread(r);
        Thread thdB = new Thread(r);
        thdA.start();
        thdB.start();
    }
}
```

The default main thread that executes main() first instantiates an anonymous class that implements Runnable. It then creates two Thread objects, initializing each object to the runnable, and calls Thread's start() method to create and start both threads. After completing these tasks, the main thread exits main() and dies.

Each of the two started threads executes the runnable's run() method. It calls Thread's currentThread() method to obtain its associated Thread instance, uses this instance to call Thread's getName() method to return its name, initializes count to 0, and enters an infinite loop where it outputs name and count and increments count on each iteration.

> **TIP:** To stop an application that does not end, press the Ctrl and C keys simultaneously.

I observe both threads alternating in their execution when I run this application on the Windows XP platform. Partial output from one run appears here:

```
Thread-0: 0
Thread-0: 1
Thread-0: 2
Thread-0: 3
Thread-0: 4
Thread-0: 5
Thread-0: 6
Thread-0: 7
Thread-1: 0
Thread-1: 1
Thread-1: 2
Thread-1: 3
Thread-1: 4
Thread-1: 5
Thread-1: 6
```

```
Thread-1: 7
Thread-1: 8
Thread-1: 9
Thread-1: 10
Thread-1: 11
Thread-1: 12
Thread-1: 13
Thread-1: 14
Thread-1: 15
Thread-0: 8
Thread-0: 9
```

When a computer has enough processors and/or processor cores, the computer's operating system assigns a separate thread to each processor or core so the threads execute *concurrently* (at the same time). When a computer does not have enough processors and/or cores, a thread must wait its turn to use the shared processor/core.

The operating system uses a *scheduler* (http://en.wikipedia.org/wiki/Scheduling_%28computing%29) to determine when a waiting thread executes. The following list identifies three different schedulers:

- Linux 2.6 through 2.6.22 uses the O(1) scheduler (http://en.wikipedia.org/wiki/O%281%29_scheduler).

- Linux 2.6.23 uses the Completely Fair Scheduler (http://en.wikipedia.org/wiki/Completely_Fair_Scheduler).

- Windows NT-based operating systems (NT, XP, and Vista) use a multilevel feedback queue scheduler (http://en.wikipedia.org/wiki/Multilevel_feedback_queue).

The previous output from the counting threads application resulted from running this application via Windows XP's *multilevel feedback queue* scheduler. Because of this scheduler, both threads take turns executing.

> **CAUTION:** Although this output indicates that the first thread starts executing, never assume that the thread associated with the Thread object whose start() method is called first is the first thread to execute. While this might be true of some schedulers, it might not be true of others.

A multilevel feedback queue and many other thread schedulers take the concept of *priority* (thread relative importance) into account. They often combine *preemptive scheduling* (higher priority threads *preempt*—interrupt and run instead of—lower priority threads) with *round robin scheduling* (equal priority threads are given equal slices of time, which are known as *time slices*, and take turns executing).

Thread supports priority via its void setPriority(int priority) method (set the priority of this Thread object's thread to priority, which ranges from Thread.MIN_PRIORITY to Thread.MAX_PRIORITY—Thread.NORMAL_PRIORITY identifies the default priority) and int getPriority() method (return the current priority).

> **CAUTION:** Using the `setPriority()` method can impact an application's portability across platforms because different schedulers can handle a priority change in different ways. For example, one platform's scheduler might delay lower priority threads from executing until higher priority threads finish. This delaying can lead to *indefinite postponement* or *starvation* because lower priority threads "starve" while waiting indefinitely for their turn to execute, and this can seriously hurt the application's performance. Another platform's scheduler might not indefinitely delay lower priority threads, improving application performance.

Listing 7–4 refactors Listing 7–3's `main()` method to give each thread a nondefault name, and to put each thread to sleep after outputting name and count.

Listing 7–4. *A pair of counting threads revisited*

```java
public static void main(String[] args)
{
    Runnable r = new Runnable()
                 {
                     @Override
                     public void run()
                     {
                         String name = Thread.currentThread().getName();
                         int count = 0;
                         while (true)
                         {
                             System.out.println(name + ": " + count++);
                             try
                             {
                                 Thread.sleep(100);
                             }
                             catch (InterruptedException ie)
                             {
                             }
                         }
                     }
                 };
    Thread thdA = new Thread(r);
    thdA.setName("A");
    Thread thdB = new Thread(r);
    thdB.setName("B");
    thdA.start();
    thdB.start();
}
```

Threads A and B execute `Thread.sleep(100);` to sleep for 100 milliseconds. This sleep results in each thread executing more frequently, as the following partial output reveals:

```
A: 0
B: 0
A: 1
B: 1
A: 2
B: 2
A: 3
```

```
B: 3
A: 4
B: 4
A: 5
B: 5
```

A thread will occasionally start another thread to perform a lengthy calculation, download a large file, or perform some other time-consuming activity. After finishing its other tasks, the thread that started the worker thread is ready to process the results of the worker thread and waits for the worker thread to finish and die.

It is possible to wait for the worker thread to die by using a while loop that repeatedly calls Thread's isAlive() method on the worker thread's Thread object and sleeps for a certain length of time when this method returns true. However, Listing 7–5 demonstrates a less verbose alternative: the join() method.

Listing 7–5. *Joining the default main thread with a background thread*

```
public static void main(String[] args)
{
   Runnable r = new Runnable()
                {
                    @Override
                    public void run()
                    {
                        System.out.println("Worker thread is simulating " +
                                           "work by sleeping for 5 seconds.");
                        try
                        {
                            Thread.sleep(5000);
                        }
                        catch (InterruptedException ie)
                        {
                        }
                        System.out.println("Worker thread is dying");
                    }
                };
   Thread thd = new Thread(r);
   thd.start();
   System.out.println("Default main thread is doing work.");
   try
   {
      Thread.sleep(2000);
   }
   catch (InterruptedException ie)
   {
   }
   System.out.println("Default main thread has finished its work.");
   System.out.println("Default main thread is waiting for worker thread " +
                      "to die.");
   try
   {
      thd.join();
   }
   catch (InterruptedException ie)
   {
   }
```

```
      System.out.println("Main thread is dying");
}
```

This listing demonstrates the default main thread starting a worker thread, performing some work, and then waiting for the worker thread to die by calling join() via the worker thread's thd object. When you run this application, you will discover output similar to the following (message order might differ somewhat):

```
Default main thread is doing work.
Worker thread is simulating work by sleeping for 5 seconds.
Default main thread has finished its work.
Default main thread is waiting for worker thread to die.
Worker thread is dying
Main thread is dying
```

Every Thread object belongs to some ThreadGroup object; Thread declares a ThreadGroup getThreadGroup() method that returns this object. You should ignore thread groups because they are not that useful. If you need to logically group Thread objects, you should use an array or collection instead.

> **CAUTION:** Various ThreadGroup methods are flawed. For example, int enumerate(Thread[] threads) will not include all active threads in its enumeration when its threads array argument is too small to store their Thread objects. Although you might think that you could use the return value from the int activeCount() method to properly size this array, there is no guarantee that the array will be large enough because activeCount()'s return value fluctuates with the creation and death of threads.

However, you should still know about ThreadGroup because of its contribution in handling exceptions that are thrown while a thread is executing. Listing 7–6 sets the stage for learning about exception handling by presenting a run() method that attempts to divide an integer by 0, which results in a thrown ArithmeticException instance.

Listing 7–6. *Throwing an exception from the run() method*

```
public static void main(String[] args)
{
   Runnable r = new Runnable()
               {
                  @Override
                  public void run()
                  {
                     int x = 1/0; // Line 8
                  }
               };
   Thread thd = new Thread(r);
   thd.start();
}
```

Run this application and you will see an exception trace that identifies the thrown ArithmeticException:

```
Exception in thread "Thread-0" java.lang.ArithmeticException: / by zero
```

```
   at ExceptionThread$1.run(ExceptionThread.java:8)
   at java.lang.Thread.run(Unknown Source)
```

When an exception is thrown out of the run() method, the thread terminates and the following activities take place:

- The virtual machine looks for an instance of Thread.UncaughtExceptionHandler installed via Thread's void setUncaughtExceptionHandler(Thread.UncaughtExceptionHandler eh) method. When this handler is found, it passes execution to the instance's void uncaughtException(Thread t, Throwable e) method, where t identifies the Thread object of the thread that threw the exception, and e identifies the thrown exception or error—perhaps an OutOfMemoryError instance was thrown. If this method throws an exception/error, the exception/error is ignored by the virtual machine.

- Assuming that setUncaughtExceptionHandler() was not called to install a handler, the virtual machine passes control to the associated ThreadGroup object's uncaughtException(Thread t, Throwable e) method. Assuming that ThreadGroup was not extended, and that its uncaughtException() method was not overridden to handle the exception, uncaughtException() passes control to the parent ThreadGroup object's uncaughtException() method when a parent ThreadGroup is present. Otherwise, it checks to see if a default uncaught exception handler has been installed (via Thread's static void setDefaultUncaughtExceptionHandler (Thread.UncaughtExceptionHandler handler) method.) If a default uncaught exception handler has been installed, its uncaughtException() method is called with the same two arguments. Otherwise, uncaughtException() checks its Throwable argument to determine if it is an instance of java.lang.ThreadDeath. If so, nothing special is done. Otherwise, as Listing 7–6's exception message shows, a message containing the thread's name, as returned from the thread's getName() method, and a stack backtrace, using the Throwable argument's printStackTrace() method, is printed to the standard error stream.

Listing 7–7 demonstrates Thread's setUncaughtExceptionHandler() and setDefaultUncaughtExceptionHandler() methods.

Listing 7–7. *Demonstrating uncaught exception handlers*

```java
public static void main(String[] args)
{
   Runnable r = new Runnable()
              {
                  @Override
                  public void run()
                  {
                      int x = 1/0;
                  }
              };
```

```
        Thread thd = new Thread(r);
        Thread.UncaughtExceptionHandler uceh;
        uceh = new Thread.UncaughtExceptionHandler()
              {
                 public void uncaughtException(Thread t, Throwable e)
                 {
                    System.out.println("Caught throwable " + e + " for thread "
                                       + t);
                 }
              };
        thd.setUncaughtExceptionHandler(uceh);
        uceh = new Thread.UncaughtExceptionHandler()
              {
                 public void uncaughtException(Thread t, Throwable e)
                 {
                    System.out.println("Default uncaught exception handler");
                    System.out.println("Caught throwable " + e + " for thread "
                                       + t);
                 }
              };
        thd.setDefaultUncaughtExceptionHandler(uceh);
        thd.start();
}
```

When you run this application, you will observe the following output:

```
Caught throwable java.lang.ArithmeticException: / by zero for thread↵
 Thread[Thread-0,5,main]
```

You will not also see the default uncaught exception handler's output because the default handler is not called. To see that output, you must comment out `thd.setUncaughtExceptionHandler(uceh);`. If you also comment out `thd.setDefaultUncaughtExceptionHandler(uceh);`, you will see Listing 7–6's output.

> **CAUTION:** Thread declares several deprecated methods, including `stop()` (stop an executing thread). These methods have been deprecated because they are unsafe. Do *not* use these deprecated methods. (I will show you how to safely stop a thread later in this chapter.)
>
> Also, you should avoid the `static void yield()` method, which is intended to switch execution from the current thread to another thread, because it can affect portability and hurt application performance. Although `yield()` might switch to another thread on some platforms (which can improve performance), `yield()` might only return to the current thread on other platforms (which hurts performance because the `yield()` call has only wasted time).

Thread Synchronization

Throughout its execution, each thread is isolated from other threads because it has been given its own method-call stack. However, threads can still interfere with each other when they access and manipulate shared data. This interference can corrupt the shared data, and this corruption can cause an application to fail.

For example, consider a checking account in which a husband and wife have joint access. Suppose that the husband and wife decide to empty this account at the same time without knowing that the other is doing the same thing. Listing 7–8 demonstrates this scenario.

Listing 7–8. *A problematic checking account*

```java
public class CheckingAccount
{
    private int balance;
    public CheckingAccount(int initialBalance)
    {
        balance = initialBalance;
    }
    public boolean withdraw(int amount)
    {
        if (amount <= balance)
        {
            try
            {
                Thread.sleep((int)(Math.random()*200));
            }
            catch (InterruptedException ie)
            {
            }
            balance -= amount;
            return true;
        }
        return false;
    }
    public static void main(String[] args)
    {
        final CheckingAccount ca = new CheckingAccount(100);
        Runnable r = new Runnable()
                     {
                         public void run()
                         {
                             String name = Thread.currentThread().getName();
                             for (int i = 0; i < 10; i++)
                                 System.out.println (name + " withdraws $10: " +
                                                     ca.withdraw(10));
                         }
                     };
        Thread thdHusband = new Thread(r);
        thdHusband.setName("Husband");
        Thread thdWife = new Thread(r);
        thdWife.setName("Wife");
        thdHusband.start();
        thdWife.start();
    }
}
```

This application lets more money be withdrawn than is available in the account. For example, the following output reveals $110 being withdrawn when only $100 is available:

```
Wife withdraws $10: true
```

```
Wife withdraws $10: true
Husband withdraws $10: true
Wife withdraws $10: true
Husband withdraws $10: true
Wife withdraws $10: true
Husband withdraws $10: true
Husband withdraws $10: true
Husband withdraws $10: true
Husband withdraws $10: true
Husband withdraws $10: false
Husband withdraws $10: false
Husband withdraws $10: false
Husband withdraws $10: false
Wife withdraws $10: true
Wife withdraws $10: false
Wife withdraws $10: false
Wife withdraws $10: false
Wife withdraws $10: false
Wife withdraws $10: false
```

The reason why more money is withdrawn than is available for withdrawal is that a race condition exists between the husband and wife threads.

> **NOTE:** A *race condition* is a scenario in which multiple threads update the same object at the same time or nearly at the same time. Part of the object stores values written to it by one thread, and another part of the object stores values written to it by another thread.

The race condition exists because the actions of checking the amount for withdrawal to ensure that it is less than what appears in the balance and deducting the amount from the balance are not *atomic* (indivisible) operations. (Although atoms are divisible, *atomic* is commonly used to refer to something being indivisible.)

> **NOTE:** The Thread.sleep() method call that sleeps for a variable amount of time (up to a maximum of 199 milliseconds) is present so that you can observe more money being withdrawn than is available for withdrawal. Without this method call, you might have to execute the application hundreds of times (or more) to witness this problem, because the scheduler might rarely pause a thread between the amount <= balance expression and the balance -= amount; expression statement—the code executes rapidly.

Consider the following scenario:

- The Husband thread executes withdraw()'s amount <= balance expression, which returns true. The scheduler pauses the Husband thread and lets the Wife thread execute.

- The Wife thread executes withdraw()'s amount <= balance expression, which returns true.

- The Wife thread performs the withdrawal. The scheduler pauses the Wife thread and lets the Husband thread execute.

- The Husband thread performs the withdrawal.

This problem can be corrected by synchronizing access to `withdraw()` so that only one thread at a time can execute inside this method. You synchronize access at the method level by adding reserved word `synchronized` to the method header prior to the method's return type; for example, `public synchronized boolean withdraw(int amount)`.

As I demonstrate later, you can also synchronize access to a block of statements by specifying `synchronized(object) { /* synchronized statements */ }`, where *object* is an arbitrary object reference. No thread can enter a synchronized method or block until execution leaves the method/block; this is known as *mutual exclusion*.

Synchronization is implemented in terms of monitors and locks. A *monitor* is a concurrency construct for controlling access to a *critical section*, a region of code that must execute atomically. It is identified at the source code level as a synchronized method or a synchronized block.

A *lock* is a token that a thread must acquire before a monitor allows that thread to execute inside a monitor's critical section. The token is released automatically when the thread exits the monitor, to give another thread an opportunity to acquire the token and enter the monitor.

> **NOTE:** A thread that has acquired a lock does not release this lock when it calls one of `Thread`'s `sleep()` methods.

A thread entering a synchronized instance method acquires the lock associated with the object on which the method is called. A thread entering a synchronized class method acquires the lock associated with the class's `Class` object. Finally, a thread entering a synchronized block acquires the lock associated with the block's controlling object.

> **TIP:** `Thread` declares a `public static boolean holdsLock(Object o)` method that returns true when the calling thread holds the monitor lock on object o. You will find this method handy in assertion statements, such as `assert Thread.holdsLock(o);`.

The need for synchronization is often subtle. For example, Listing 7–9's ID utility class declares a `getNextID()` method that returns a unique `long`-based ID, perhaps to be used when generating unique filenames. Although you might not think so, this method can cause data corruption and return duplicate values.

Listing 7–9. *A utility class for returning unique IDs*

```
public class ID
{
   private static long nextID = 0;
   public static long getNextID()
```

```
{
    return nextID++;
    }
}
```

There are two lack-of-synchronization problems with getNextID(). Because 32-bit virtual machine implementations require two steps to update a 64-bit long integer, adding 1 to nextID is not atomic: the scheduler could interrupt a thread that has only updated half of nextID, which corrupts the contents of this variable.

> **NOTE:** Variables of type long and double are subject to corruption when being written to in an unsynchronized context on 32-bit virtual machines. This problem does not occur with variables of type boolean, byte, char, float, int, or short; each type occupies 32 bits or less.

Assume that multiple threads call getNextID(). Because postincrement (++) reads and writes the nextID field in two steps, multiple threads might retrieve the same value. For example, thread A executes ++, reading nextID but not incrementing its value before being interrupted by the scheduler. Thread B now executes and reads the same value.

Both problems can be corrected by synchronizing access to nextID so that only one thread can execute this method's code. All that is required is to add synchronized to the method header prior to the method's return type; for example, public static synchronized int getNextID().

Synchronization is also used to communicate between threads. For example, you might design your own mechanism for stopping a thread (because you cannot use Thread's unsafe stop() methods for this task). Listing 7–10 shows how you might accomplish this task.

Listing 7–10. *Attempting to stop a thread*

```java
public static void main(String[] args)
{
    class StoppableThread extends Thread
    {
        private boolean stopped = false;
        @Override
        public void run()
        {
            while(!stopped)
                System.out.println("running");
        }
        public void stopThread()
        {
            stopped = true;
        }
    }
    StoppableThread thd = new StoppableThread();
    thd.start();
    try
    {
        Thread.sleep(1000); // sleep for 1 second
```

```
      }
      catch (InterruptedException ie)
      {
      }
      thd.stopThread();
   }
```

Listing 7–10 introduces a `main()` method with a local class named `StoppableThread` that subclasses Thread. `StoppableThread` declares a `stopped` field initialized to `false`, a `stopThread()` method that sets this field to `true`, and a `run()` method whose infinite loop checks `stopped` on each loop iteration to see if its value has changed to `true`.

After instantiating `StoppableThread`, the default main thread starts the thread associated with this Thread object. It then sleeps for one second and calls `StoppableThread`'s `stop()` method before dying. When you run this application on a single-processor/single-core machine, you will probably observe the application stopping.

You might not see this stoppage when the application runs on a multiprocessor machine or a uniprocessor machine with multiple cores. For performance reasons, each processor or core probably has its own cache with its own copy of `stopped`. When one thread modifies its copy of this field, the other thread's copy of `stopped` is not changed.

Listing 7–11 refactors Listing 7–10 to guarantee that the application will run correctly on all kinds of machines.

Listing 7–11. *Guaranteed stoppage on a multiprocessor/multicore machine*

```java
public static void main(String[] args)
{
   class StoppableThread extends Thread
   {
      private boolean stopped = false;
      @Override
      public void run()
      {
         while(!isStopped())
            System.out.println("running");
      }
      public synchronized void stopThread()
      {
         stopped = true;
      }
      private synchronized boolean isStopped()
      {
         return stopped;
      }
   }
   StoppableThread thd = new StoppableThread();
   thd.start();
   try
   {
      Thread.sleep(1000); // sleep for 1 second
   }
   catch (InterruptedException ie)
   {
   }
```

```
        thd.stopThread();
}
```

Listing 7–11's stopThread() and isStopped() methods are synchronized to support thread communication (between the default main thread that calls stopThread() and the started thread that executes inside run()). When a thread enters one of these methods, it is guaranteed to access a single shared copy of the stopped field (not a cached copy).

Synchronization is necessary to support mutual exclusion or mutual exclusion combined with thread communication. However, there exists an alternative to synchronization when the only purpose is to communicate between threads. This alternative is reserved word volatile, which Listing 7–12 demonstrates.

Listing 7–12. *The* volatile *alternative to synchronization for thread communication*

```
public static void main(String[] args)
{
    class StoppableThread extends Thread
    {
        private volatile boolean stopped = false;
        @Override
        public void run()
        {
            while(!stopped)
                System.out.println("running");
        }
        public void stopThread()
        {
            stopped = true;
        }
    }
    StoppableThread thd = new StoppableThread();
    thd.start();
    try
    {
        Thread.sleep(1000); // sleep for 1 second
    }
    catch (InterruptedException ie)
    {
    }
    thd.stopThread();
}
```

Listing 7–12 declares stopped to be volatile; threads that access this field will always access a single shared copy (not cached copies on multiprocessor/multicore machines). In addition to generating code that is less verbose, volatile might offer improved performance over synchronization.

> **CAUTION:** You should only use `volatile` in the context of thread communication. Also, you can only use this reserved word in the context of field declarations. Although you can declare `double` and `long` fields `volatile`, you should avoid doing so on 32-bit virtual machines because it takes two operations to access a `double` or `long` variable's value, and mutual exclusion via synchronization is required to access their values safely.

Object's `wait()`, `notify()`, and `notifyAll()` methods support a form of thread communication where a thread voluntarily waits for some *condition* (a prerequisite for continued execution) to arise, at which time another thread notifies the waiting thread that it can continue. `wait()` causes its calling thread to wait on an object's monitor, and `notify()` and `notifyAll()` wake up one or all threads waiting on the monitor.

> **CAUTION:** Because the `wait()`, `notify()`, and `notifyAll()` methods depend on a lock, they cannot be called from outside of a synchronized method or synchronized block. If you fail to heed this warning, you will encounter a thrown instance of the `java.lang.IllegalMonitorStateException` class. Also, a thread that has acquired a lock releases this lock when it calls one of Object's `wait()` methods.

A classic example of thread communication involving conditions is the relationship between a producer thread and a consumer thread. The producer thread produces data items to be consumed by the consumer thread. Each produced data item is stored in a shared variable.

Imagine that the threads are not communicating and are running at different speeds. The producer might produce a new data item and record it in the shared variable before the consumer retrieves the previous data item for processing. Also, the consumer might retrieve the contents of the shared variable before a new data item is produced.

To overcome those problems, the producer thread must wait until it is notified that the previously produced data item has been consumed, and the consumer thread must wait until it is notified that a new data item has been produced. Listing 7–13 shows you how to accomplish this task via `wait()` and `notify()`.

Listing 7–13. *The producer-consumer relationship*

```
public class PC
{
   public static void main(String[] args)
   {
      Shared s = new Shared();
      new Producer(s).start();
      new Consumer(s).start();
   }
}
class Shared
{
   private char c = '\u0000';
```

```java
        private boolean writeable = true;
        synchronized void setSharedChar(char c)
        {
            while (!writeable)
                try
                {
                    wait();
                }
                catch (InterruptedException e) {}
            this.c = c;
            writeable = false;
            notify();
        }
        synchronized char getSharedChar()
        {
            while (writeable)
                try
                {
                    wait();
                }
                catch (InterruptedException e) {}
            writeable = true;
            notify();
            return c;
        }
    }
    class Producer extends Thread
    {
        private Shared s;
        Producer(Shared s)
        {
            this.s = s;
        }
        @Override
        public void run()
        {
            for (char ch = 'A'; ch <= 'Z'; ch++)
            {
                synchronized(s)
                {
                    s.setSharedChar(ch);
                    System.out.println(ch + " produced by producer.");
                }
            }
        }
    }
    class Consumer extends Thread
    {
        private Shared s;
        Consumer(Shared s)
        {
            this.s = s;
        }
        @Override
        public void run()
        {
            char ch;
```

```
        do
        {
           synchronized(s)
           {
              ch = s.getSharedChar();
              System.out.println(ch + " consumed by consumer.");
           }
        }
        while (ch != 'Z');
     }
  }
```

The application creates a Shared object and two threads that get a copy of the object's reference. The producer calls the object's setSharedChar() method to save each of 26 uppercase letters; the consumer calls the object's getSharedChar() method to acquire each letter.

The writeable instance field tracks two conditions: the producer waiting on the consumer to consume a data item, and the consumer waiting on the producer to produce a new data item. It helps coordinate execution of the producer and consumer. The following scenario, where the consumer executes first, illustrates this coordination:

1. The consumer executes s.getSharedChar() to retrieve a letter.

2. Inside of that synchronized method, the consumer calls wait() because writeable contains true. The consumer now waits until it receives notification from the producer.

3. The producer eventually executes s.setSharedChar(ch);.

4. When the producer enters that synchronized method (which is possible because the consumer released the lock inside of the wait() method prior to waiting), the producer discovers writeable's value to be true and does not call wait().

5. The producer saves the character, sets writeable to false (which will cause the producer to wait on the next setSharedChar() call when the consumer has not consumed the character by that time), and calls notify() to awaken the consumer (assuming the consumer is waiting).

6. The producer exits setSharedChar(char c).

7. The consumer wakes up (and reacquires the lock), sets writeable to true (which will cause the consumer to wait on the next getSharedChar() call when the producer has not produced a character by that time), notifies the producer to awaken that thread (assuming the producer is waiting), and returns the shared character.

Although the synchronization works correctly, you might observe output (on some platforms) that shows multiple producing messages before a consuming message. For example, you might see A produced by producer., followed by B produced by producer., followed by A consumed by consumer., at the beginning of the application's output.

This strange output order is caused by the call to setSharedChar() followed by its companion System.out.println() method call not being atomic, and by the call to getSharedChar() followed by its companion System.out.println() method call not being atomic. The output order is corrected by wrapping each of these method call pairs in a synchronized block that synchronizes on the Shared object referenced by s.

When you run this application, its output should always appear in the same alternating order, as shown next (only the first few lines are shown for brevity):

```
A produced by producer.
A consumed by consumer.
B produced by producer.
B consumed by consumer.
C produced by producer.
C consumed by consumer.
D produced by producer.
D consumed by consumer.
```

> **CAUTION:** Never call wait() outside of a loop. The loop tests the condition (!writeable or writeable in the previous example) before and after the wait() call. Testing the condition before calling wait() ensures *liveness*. If this test was not present, and if the condition held and notify() had been called prior to wait() being called, it is unlikely that the waiting thread would ever wake up. Retesting the condition after calling wait() ensures *safety*. If retesting did not occur, and if the condition did not hold after the thread had awakened from the wait() call (perhaps another thread called notify() accidentally when the condition did not hold), the thread would proceed to destroy the lock's protected invariants.

Too much synchronization can be problematic. If you are not careful, you might encounter a situation where locks are acquired by multiple threads, neither thread holds its own lock but holds the lock needed by some other thread, and neither thread can enter and later exit its critical section to release its held lock because some other thread holds the lock to that critical section. Listing 7–14's atypical example demonstrates this scenario, which is known as *deadlock*.

Listing 7–14. *A pathological case of deadlock*

```java
public class Deadlock
{
    private Object lock1 = new Object();
    private Object lock2 = new Object();
    public void instanceMethod1()
    {
        synchronized(lock1)
        {
            synchronized(lock2)
            {
                System.out.println("first thread in instanceMethod1");
                // critical section guarded first by
```

```
            // lock1 and then by lock2
        }
    }
}
public void instanceMethod2()
{
    synchronized(lock2)
    {
        synchronized(lock1)
        {
            System.out.println("second thread in instanceMethod2");
            // critical section guarded first by
            // lock2 and then by lock1
        }
    }
}
public static void main(String[] args)
{
    final Deadlock dl = new Deadlock();
    Runnable r1 = new Runnable()
                {
                    @Override
                    public void run()
                    {
                        while(true)
                            dl.instanceMethod1();
                    }
                };
    Thread thdA = new Thread(r1);
    Runnable r2 = new Runnable()
                {
                    @Override
                    public void run()
                    {
                        while(true)
                            dl.instanceMethod2();
                    }
                };
    Thread thdB = new Thread(r2);
    thdA.start();
    thdB.start();
    }
}
```

Listing 7–14's thread A and thread B call instanceMethod1() and instanceMethod2(), respectively, at different times. Consider the following execution sequence:

1. Thread A calls instanceMethod1(), obtains the lock assigned to the lock1-referenced object, and enters its outer critical section (but has not yet acquired the lock assigned to the lock2-referenced object).

2. Thread B calls instanceMethod2(), obtains the lock assigned to the lock2-referenced object, and enters its outer critical section (but has not yet acquired the lock assigned to the lock1-referenced object).

3. Thread A attempts to acquire the lock associated with lock2. The virtual machine forces the thread to wait outside of the inner critical section because thread B holds that lock.

4. Thread B attempts to acquire the lock associated with lock1. The virtual machine forces the thread to wait outside of the inner critical section because thread A holds that lock.

5. Neither thread can proceed because the other thread holds the needed lock. We have a deadlock situation and the program (at least in the context of the two threads) freezes up.

Although the previous example clearly identifies a deadlock state, it is often not that easy to detect deadlock. For example, your code might contain the following circular relationship among various classes (in several source files):

- Class A's synchronized method calls class B's synchronized method.

- Class B's synchronized method calls class C's synchronized method.

- Class C's synchronized method calls class A's synchronized method.

If thread A calls class A's synchronized method and thread B calls class C's synchronized method, thread B will block when it attempts to call class A's synchronized method and thread A is still inside of that method. Thread A will continue to execute until it calls class C's synchronized method, and then block. Deadlock results.

NOTE: Neither the Java language nor the virtual machine provides a way to prevent deadlock, and so the burden falls on you. The simplest way to prevent deadlock from happening is to avoid having either a synchronized method or a synchronized block call another synchronized method/block. Although this advice prevents deadlock from happening, it is impractical because one of your synchronized methods/blocks might need to call a synchronized method in a Java API, and the advice is overkill because the synchronized method/block being called might not call any other synchronized method/block, so deadlock would not occur.

You will sometimes want to associate per-thread data (such a user ID) with a thread. Although you can accomplish this task with a local variable, you can only do so while the local variable exists. You could use an instance field to keep this data around longer, but then you would have to deal with synchronization. Thankfully, Java supplies ThreadLocal as a simple alternative.

Each instance of the ThreadLocal class describes a *thread-local variable*, which is a variable that provides a separate storage slot to each thread that accesses the variable. You can think of a thread-local variable as a multislot variable in which each thread can store a different value in the same variable. Each thread sees only its value and is unaware of other threads having their own values in this variable.

ThreadLocal is generically declared as ThreadLocal<T>, where T identifies the type of value that is stored in the variable. This class declares the following constructor and methods:

- ThreadLocal() creates a new thread-local variable.

- T get() returns the value in the calling thread's storage slot. If an entry does not exist when the thread calls this method, get() calls initialValue().

- T initialValue() creates the calling thread's storage slot and stores an initial (default) value in this slot. The initial value defaults to null. You must subclass ThreadLocal and override this protected method to provide a more suitable initial value.

- void remove() removes the calling thread's storage slot. If this method is followed by get() with no intervening set(), get() calls initialValue().

- void set(T value) sets the value of the calling thread's storage slot to value.

Listing 7–15 shows you how to use ThreadLocal to associate a different user ID with each of two threads.

Listing 7–15. *Different user IDs for different threads*

```
private static volatile ThreadLocal<String> userID =
    new ThreadLocal<String>();
public static void main(String[] args)
{
    Runnable r = new Runnable()
                 {
                     @Override
                     public void run()
                     {
                         String name = Thread.currentThread().getName();
                         if (name.equals("A"))
                             userID.set("foxtrot");
                         else
                             userID.set("charlie");
                         System.out.println(name + " " + userID.get());
                     }
                 };
    Thread thdA = new Thread(r);
    thdA.setName("A");
    Thread thdB = new Thread(r);
    thdB.setName("B");
    thdA.start();
    thdB.start();
}
```

After instantiating ThreadLocal and assigning the reference to a volatile class field named userID (the field is volatile because it is accessed by different threads, which might execute on a multiprocessor/multicore machine), the default main thread creates two more threads that store different String objects in userID and output their objects.

When you run this application, you will observe the following output (possibly not in this order):

```
A foxtrot
B charlie
```

Values stored in thread-local variables are not related. When a new thread is created, it gets a new storage slot containing initialValue()'s value. Perhaps you would prefer to pass a value from a *parent thread*, a thread that creates another thread, to a *child thread*, the created thread. You accomplish this task with InheritableThreadLocal.

InheritableThreadLocal is a subclass of ThreadLocal. In addition to declaring a public InheritableThreadLocal() constructor, this class declares the following protected method:

- T childValue(T parentValue) calculates the child's initial value as a function of the parent's value at the time the child thread is created. This method is called from the parent thread before the child thread is started. The method returns the argument passed to parentValue and should be overridden when another value is desired.

Listing 7–16 shows you how to use InheritableThreadLocal to pass a parent thread's Integer object to a child thread.

Listing 7–16. *Passing an object from parent thread to child thread*

```
private static volatile InheritableThreadLocal<Integer> intVal =
  new InheritableThreadLocal<Integer>();
public static void main(String[] args)
{
    Runnable rP = new Runnable()
                {
                    @Override
                    public void run()
                    {
                        intVal.set(new Integer(10));
                        Runnable rC = new Runnable()
                                {
                                    public void run()
                                    {
                                        Thread thd;
                                        thd = Thread.currentThread();
                                        String name = thd.getName();
                                        System.out.println(name + " " +
                                                            intVal.get());
                                    }
                                };
                        Thread thdChild = new Thread(rC);
                        thdChild.setName("Child");
                        thdChild.start();
                    }
                };
    new Thread(rP).start();
}
```

After instantiating `InheritableThreadLocal` and assigning it to a volatile class field named `intVal`, the default main thread creates a parent thread, which stores an `Integer` object containing 10 in `intVal`. The parent thread creates a child thread, which accesses `intVal` and retrieves its parent thread's `Integer` object.

When you run this application, you will observe the following output:

```
Child 10
```

EXERCISES

The following exercises are designed to test your understanding of this chapter's additional basic APIs:

1. What is reflection?

2. What is the difference between `Class`'s `getDeclaredFields()` and `getFields()` methods?

3. How would you determine if the method represented by a `Method` object is abstract?

4. Identify the three ways of obtaining a `Class` object.

5. True or false: A string literal is a `String` object.

6. What is the purpose of `String`'s `intern()` method?

7. How do `String` and `StringBuffer` differ?

8. How do `StringBuffer` and `StringBuilder` differ?

9. What does `System`'s `arraycopy()` method accomplish?

10. What is a thread?

11. What is the purpose of the `Runnable` interface?

12. What is the purpose of the `Thread` class?

13. True or false: A `Thread` object associates with multiple threads.

14. What is a race condition?

15. What is synchronization?

16. How is synchronization implemented?

17. How does synchronization work?

18. True or false: Variables of type `long` or `double` are not atomic on 32-bit virtual machines.

19. What is the purpose of reserved word `volatile`?

20. True or false: `Object`'s `wait()` methods can be called from outside of a synchronized method or block.

21. What is deadlock?

22. What is the purpose of the `ThreadLocal` class?

23. How does InheritableThreadLocal differ from ThreadLocal?

24. In Chapter 6, Listing 6-14's demonstration of the SoftReference class includes the following array declaration and inefficient loop:

```
String[] imageNames = new String[NUM_IMAGES];
for (int i = 0; i < imageNames.length; i++)
    imageNames[i] = new String("image" + i + ".gif");
```

Rewrite this loop to use StringBuffer.

25. Class declares boolean isAnnotation(), boolean isEnum(), and boolean isInterface() methods that return true when the Class object represents an annotation type, an enum, or an interface, respectively. Create a Classify application that uses Class's forName() method to load its single command-line argument, which will represent an annotation type, enum, interface, or class (the default). Use a chained if-else statement along with the aforementioned methods to output Annotation, Enum, Interface, or Class.

26. The output from Listing 7–1's ExploreType application does not look like a class declaration for the Boolean class. Improve this application so that java ExploreType java.lang.Boolean generates the following output:

```
public class java.lang.Boolean
{
    // FIELDS
    public static final java.lang.Boolean java.lang.Boolean.TRUE
    public static final java.lang.Boolean java.lang.Boolean.FALSE
    public static final java.lang.Class java.lang.Boolean.TYPE
    private final boolean java.lang.Boolean.value
    private static final long java.lang.Boolean.serialVersionUID

    // CONSTRUCTORS
    public java.lang.Boolean(java.lang.String)
    public java.lang.Boolean(boolean)

    // METHODS
    public int java.lang.Boolean.hashCode()
    public boolean java.lang.Boolean.equals(java.lang.Object)
    public int java.lang.Boolean.compareTo(java.lang.Boolean)
    public int java.lang.Boolean.compareTo(java.lang.Object)
    public static boolean java.lang.Boolean.getBoolean(java.lang.String)
    public static java.lang.String java.lang.Boolean.toString(boolean)
    public java.lang.String java.lang.Boolean.toString()
    public static java.lang.Boolean java.lang.Boolean.valueOf(java.lang.String)
    public static java.lang.Boolean java.lang.Boolean.valueOf(boolean)
    public boolean java.lang.Boolean.booleanValue()
    public static boolean java.lang.Boolean.parseBoolean(java.lang.String)
    private static boolean java.lang.Boolean.toBoolean(java.lang.String)
}
```

27. Modify Listing 7–3's CountingThreads application by marking the two started threads as daemon threads. What happens when you run the resulting application?

28. Modify Listing 7–3's CountingThreads application by adding logic to stop both counting threads when the user presses the Enter key. The default main thread should call System.in.read() prior to terminating, and assign true to a variable named stopped after this method call returns. Each counting thread should test this variable to see if it contains true at the start of each loop iteration, and only continue the loop when the variable contains false.

Summary

The Reflection API lets applications learn about loaded classes, interfaces, enums, and annotation types. The API also lets applications instantiate classes, call methods, access fields, and perform other tasks reflectively.

The entry point into the Reflection API is a special java.lang class named Class. Additional classes are located in the java.lang.reflect package, and include Constructor, Field, Method, AccessibleObject, and Array.

The java.lang.String class represents a string as a sequence of characters. Because instances of this class are immutable, Java provides java.lang.StringBuffer for building a string more efficiently.

The java.lang.System class provides access to standard input, standard output, and standard error, and other system-oriented resources. For example, System provides the arraycopy() method as the fastest portable way to copy one array to another.

Finally, Java supports threads via its Threading API. This API consists of one interface (Runnable) and four classes (Thread, ThreadGroup, ThreadLocal, and InheritableThreadLocal) in the java.lang package.

This chapter completes my coverage of Java's basic APIs. Chapter 8 continues to explore Java's foundational APIs by focusing on its utility APIs. Specifically, Chapter 8 introduces you to the collections framework.

Chapter 8

Discovering the Collections Framework

Java's standard class library includes various utility APIs. An important category of utility APIs is the collections framework, which lets applications manage groups of objects. After presenting an overview of this framework, this chapter introduces you to the framework's core interfaces, implementation classes, and utility classes. Chapter 8 ends by discussing Java's classic collections classes.

> **NOTE:** Unless otherwise noted, Chapter 8 explores classes and interfaces that are located in the `java.util` package.

Framework Overview

A *collection* is a group of objects that are stored in an instance of a class designed for this purpose. You could create your own collections classes, but why should you waste time "reinventing the wheel" when you could spend that time focusing on your applications? For this and other reasons, Java provides the *collections framework*, which is a standardized architecture for representing and manipulating collections.

The collections framework largely consists of three components:

- *Core interfaces*: The framework employs core interfaces for manipulating collections independently of their implementations.

- *Implementation classes*: The framework employs classes that provide different implementations of the core interfaces to address performance and other requirements.

- *Utility classes*: The framework provides utility classes whose methods let you sort arrays, obtain synchronized collections, and more.

The collections framework's core interfaces include Iterable, Collection, List, Set, SortedSet, Queue, Map, and SortedMap. Collection extends Iterable; List, Set, and Queue each extend Collection; SortedSet extends Set; and SortedMap extends Map.

Figure 8–1 illustrates the core interfaces hierarchy (arrows point to parent interfaces).

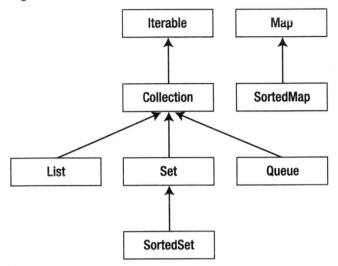

Figure 8–1. *A hierarchy of core interfaces*

The framework's implementation classes include ArrayList, LinkedList, TreeSet, HashSet, LinkedHashSet, EnumSet, PriorityQueue, TreeMap, HashMap, LinkedHashMap, IdentityHashMap, WeakHashMap, and EnumMap. The name of each concrete class ends in a core interface name, identifying the core interface on which it is based.

NOTE: Additional implementation classes are part of the concurrency utilities (see Chapter 9).

The framework's implementation classes also include the abstract AbstractCollection, AbstractList, AbstractSequentialList, AbstractSet, AbstractQueue, and AbstractMap classes. These classes offer skeletal implementations of the core interfaces to facilitate the creation of concrete implementation classes.

Finally, the framework provides two utility classes: Arrays and Collections.

Comparable Versus Comparator

A collection implementation stores its elements in some *order* (arrangement). This order may be unsorted, or it may be sorted according to some criterion (such as alphabetical, numerical, or chronological).

A sorted collection implementation defaults to storing its elements according to their *natural ordering*. For example, the natural ordering of String objects is *lexicographic* or *dictionary* (also known as alphabetical) order.

A collection cannot rely on equals() to dictate natural ordering because this method can only determine if two elements are equivalent. Instead, element classes must implement the java.lang.Comparable<T> interface and its int compareTo(T o) method.

> **NOTE:** According to Comparable's JDK documentation, this interface is considered to be part of the collections framework, even though it is a member of the java.lang package.

A sorted collection uses compareTo() to determine the natural ordering of this method's element argument o in a collection. compareTo() compares argument o with the current element (which is the element on which compareTo() was called) and does the following:

- It returns a negative value when the current element should precede o.

- It returns a zero value when the current element and o are the same.

- It returns a positive value when the current element should succeed o.

When you need to implement Comparable's compareTo() method, there are some rules that you must follow. These rules, listed next, are similar to those shown in Chapter 3 for implementing the equals() method:

- *compareTo() must be reflexive*: For any nonnull reference value *x*, *x*.compareTo(*x*) must return 0.

- *compareTo() must be symmetric*: For any nonnull reference values *x* and *y*, *x*.compareTo(*y*) == -*y*.compareTo(*x*) must hold.

- *compareTo() must be transitive*: For any nonnull reference values *x*, *y*, and *z*, if *x*.compareTo(*y*) > 0 is true, and if *y*.compareTo(*z*) > 0 is true, then *x*.compareTo(*z*) > 0 must also be true.

Also, compareTo() should throw NullPointerException when the null reference is passed to this method. However, you do not need to check for null because this method throws NullPointerException when it attempts to access a null reference's members.

> **NOTE:** Prior to Java version 5 and its introduction of generics, compareTo()'s argument was of type Object and had to be cast to the appropriate type before the comparison could be made. The cast operator would throw a java.lang.ClassCastException instance when the argument's type was not compatible with the cast.

You might occasionally need to store in a collection objects that are sorted in some order that differs from their natural ordering. In this case, you would supply a comparator to provide that ordering.

A *comparator* is an object whose class implements the Comparator interface. This interface, whose generic type is Comparator<T>, provides the following pair of methods:

- int compare(T o1, T o2) compares both arguments for order. This method returns 0 when o1 equals o2, a negative value when o1 is less than o2, and a positive value when o1 is greater than o2.

- boolean equals(Object o) returns true when o "equals" this Comparator in that o is also a Comparator and imposes the same ordering. Otherwise, this method returns false.

> **NOTE:** Comparator declares equals() because this interface places an extra condition on this method's contract. *Additionally, this method can return true only if the specified object is also a comparator and it imposes the same ordering as this comparator.* You do not have to override equals(), but doing so *may improve performance by allowing programs to determine that two distinct comparators impose the same order.*

Chapter 5 provided an example that illustrated implementing Comparable, and you will discover an additional example later in this chapter. Also, this chapter will present examples of implementing Comparator.

Iterable and Collection

Most of the core interfaces are rooted in Iterable and its Collection subinterface. Their generic types are Iterable<T> and Collection<E>.

Iterable describes any object that can return its contained objects in some sequence. This interface declares an Iterator<T> iterator() method that returns an Iterator instance for iterating over all of the contained objects.

Collection represents a collection of objects that are known as *elements*. This interface provides methods that are common to the Collection subinterfaces on which many collections are based. Table 8–1 describes these methods.

Table 8–1. *Collection Methods*

Method	Description
boolean add(E e)	Add element e to this collection. Return true if this collection was modified as a result; otherwise, return false. (Attempting to add e to a collection that does not permit duplicates and already contains a same-valued element results in e not being added.) This method throws java.lang.UnsupportedOperationException when add() is not supported, ClassCastException when e's class is not appropriate for this collection, java.lang.IllegalArgumentException when some property of e prevents it from being added to this collection, and java.lang.NullPointerException when e contains the null reference and this collection does not support null elements.

Method	Description
`boolean addAll(Collection<? extends E> c)`	Add all elements of collection c to this collection. Return true if this collection was modified as the result; otherwise, return false. This method throws `UnsupportedOperationException` when this collection does not support `addAll()`, `ClassCastException` when the class of one of c's elements is inappropriate for this collection, `IllegalArgumentException` when some property of an element prevents it from being added to this collection, and `NullPointerException` when c contains the null reference or when one of its elements is null and this collection does not support null elements.
`void clear()`	Remove all elements from this collection. This method throws `UnsupportedOperationException` when this collection does not support `clear()`.
`boolean contains (Object o)`	Return true when this collection contains o; otherwise, return false. This method throws `ClassCastException` when the class of o is inappropriate for this collection, and `NullPointerException` when o contains the null reference and this collection does not support null elements.
`boolean containsAll (Collection<?> c)`	Return true when this collection contains all of the elements that are contained in the collection specified by c; otherwise, return false. This method throws `ClassCastException` when the class of one of c's elements is inappropriate for this collection, and `NullPointerException` when c contains the null reference or when one of its elements is null and this collection does not support null elements.
`boolean equals (Object o)`	Compare o with this collection and return true when o equals this collection; otherwise, return false.
`int hashCode()`	Return this collection's hash code. Equal collections have equal hash codes.
`boolean isEmpty()`	Return true when this collection contains no elements; otherwise, return false.
`Iterator<E> iterator()`	Return an `Iterator` instance for iterating over all of the elements contained in this collection. This `Iterable` method is redeclared in `Collection` for convenience.
`boolean remove (Object o)`	Remove the element identified as o from this collection. Return true when the element is removed; otherwise, return false. This method throws `UnsupportedOperationException` when this collection does not support `remove()`, `ClassCastException` when the class of o is inappropriate for this collection, and `NullPointerException` when o contains the null reference and this collection does not support null elements.

Method	Description
boolean removeAll (Collection<?> c)	Remove all of the elements from this collection that are also contained in collection c. Return true when this collection is modified by this operation; otherwise, return false. This method throws UnsupportedOperationException when this collection does not support removeAll(), ClassCastFxception when the class of one of c's elements is inappropriate for this collection, and NullPointerException when c contains the null reference or when one of its elements is null and this collection does not support null elements.
boolean retainAll (Collection<?> c)	Retain all of the elements in this collection that are also contained in collection c. Return true when this collection is modified by this operation; otherwise, return false. This method throws UnsupportedOperationException when this collection does not support retainAll(), ClassCastException when the class of one of c's elements is inappropriate for this collection, and NullPointerException when c contains the null reference or when one of its elements is null and this collection does not support null elements.
int size()	Return the number of elements contained in this collection, or Integer.MAX_VALUE when there are more than Integer.MAX_VALUE elements contained in the collection.
Object[] toArray()	Return an array containing all of the elements stored in this collection. If this collection makes any guarantees as to what order its elements are returned in by its iterator, this method returns the elements in the same order. The returned array is "safe" in that no references to it are maintained by this collection. (In other words, this method allocates a new array even when this collection is backed by an array.) The caller can safely modify the returned array.
<T> T[] toArray(T[] a)	Return an array containing all of the elements in this collection; the runtime type of the returned array is that of the specified array. If the collection fits in the specified array, it is returned in the array. Otherwise, a new array is allocated with the runtime type of the specified array and the size of this collection. This method throws NullPointerException when null is passed to a, and java.lang.ArrayStoreException when a's runtime type is not a supertype of the runtime type of every element in this collection.

Table 8–1 reveals three exceptional things about various Collection methods. First, some methods can throw instances of the UnsupportedOperationException class. For example, add() throws UnsupportedOperationException when you attempt to add an object to an *immutable* (unmodifiable) collection (discussed later in this chapter).

Second, some of `Collection`'s methods can throw instances of the `ClassCastException` class. For example, `remove()` throws `ClassCastException` when you attempt to remove an entry (also known as mapping) from a tree-based map whose keys are `Strings`, but specify a non-`String` key instead.

Finally, `Collection`'s `add()` and `addAll()` methods throw `IllegalArgumentException` instances when some *property* (attribute) of the element to be added prevents it from being added to this collection. For example, a third-party collection class's `add()` and `addAll()` methods might throw this exception when they detect negative `Integer` values.

> **NOTE:** Perhaps you are wondering why `remove()` is declared to accept any `Object` argument instead of accepting only objects whose types are those of the collection. In other words, why is `remove()` not declared as `boolean remove(E e)`? Also, why are `containsAll()`, `removeAll()`, and `retainAll()` not declared with an argument of type `Collection<? extends E>`, to ensure that the collection argument only contains elements of the same type as the collection on which these methods are called? The answer to these questions is the need to maintain backward compatibility. The collections framework was introduced prior to Java version 5 and its introduction of generics. To let legacy code written before version 5 continue to compile, these four methods were declared with weaker type constraints.

Iterator and the Enhanced For Loop Statement

By extending `Iterable`, `Collection` inherits that interface's `iterator()` method, which makes it possible to iterate over a collection. `iterator()` returns an instance of a class that implements the `Iterator` interface, whose generic type is expressed as `Iterator<E>` and which declares the following three methods:

- `boolean hasNext()` returns true when this `Iterator` instance has more elements to return; otherwise, this method returns false.

- `E next()` returns the next element from the collection associated with this `Iterator` instance, or throws `NoSuchElementException` when there are no more elements to return.

- `void remove()` removes the last element returned by `next()` from the collection associated with this `Iterator` instance. This method can be called only once per `next()` call. The behavior of an `Iterator` instance is unspecified when the underlying collection is modified while iteration is in progress in any way other than by calling `remove()`. This method throws `UnsupportedOperationException` when it is not supported by this `Iterator`, and `java.lang.IllegalStateException` when `remove()` has been called without a previous call to `next()` or when multiple `remove()` calls occur with no intervening `next()` calls.

Listing 8–1 shows you how to iterate over a collection after calling `iterator()` to return an `Iterator` instance. The while loop repeatedly calls the iterator's `hasNext()` method to determine whether or not iteration should continue, and (if it should continue) the `next()` method to return the next element from the associated collection.

Listing 8–1. *Classic collection iteration via the while loop idiom*

```
Collection<String> col = ... // This code does not compile because of the ...
// Add elements to col.
Iterator iter = col.iterator();
while (iter.hasNext())
   System.out.println(iter.next());
```

Because this idiom is commonly used, Java version 5 introduced syntactic sugar to the for loop statement to simplify iteration in terms of the idiom. This sugar makes this statement appear like the foreach statement found in languages such as Perl, and is revealed in Listing 8–2's simplified equivalent of Listing 8–1.

Listing 8–2. *Simplified collection iteration via the enhanced for loop statement*

```
Collection<String> col = ... // This code does not compile because of the ...
// Add elements to col.
for (String s: col)
   System.out.println(s);
```

This sugar hides `col.iterator()`, a method call that returns an `Iterator` instance for iterating over col's elements. It also hides calls to `Iterator`'s `hasNext()` and `next()` methods on this instance. You interpret this sugar to read as follows: "for each `String` object in col, assign this object to s at the start of the loop iteration."

> **NOTE:** The enhanced for loop statement is also useful in an arrays context, in which it hides the array index variable. Consider the following code fragment:
>
> ```
> String[] verbs = { "run", "walk", "jump" };
> for (String verb: verbs)
>     System.out.println (verb);
> ```
>
> This code fragment, which reads as "for each `String` object in the verbs array, assign that object to verb at the start of the loop iteration," is equivalent to the following code fragment:
>
> ```
> String[] verbs = { "run", "walk", "jump" };
> for (int i = 0; i < verbs.length; i++)
>     System.out.println (verbs[i]);
> ```

The enhanced for loop statement is limited in that you cannot use this statement where access to the iterator is required to remove an element from a collection. Also, it is not usable where you must replace elements in a collection/array during a traversal, and it cannot be used where you must iterate over multiple collections or arrays in parallel.

Autoboxing and Unboxing

Developers who believe that Java should support only reference types have complained about Java's support for primitive types. One area where the dichotomy of Java's type system is clearly seen is the collections framework: you can store objects but not primitive type–based values in collections.

Although you cannot directly store a primitive type–based value in a collection, you can indirectly store this value by first wrapping it in an object created from a primitive wrapper class such as `Integer`, and then storing this primitive wrapper class instance in the collection—see Listing 8–3. (Chapter 6 discusses Java's primitive wrapper classes.)

Listing 8–3. *Wrapping an* int *in an* Integer, *which is then stored in the collection*

```
Collection<Integer> col = ...; // This code does not compile because of the ...
int x = 27;
col.add(new Integer(x)); // Indirectly store int value 27 via an Integer object.
```

The reverse situation is also tedious. When you want to retrieve the `int` from `col`, you must invoke `Integer`'s `intValue()` method (which, if you recall, is inherited from `Integer`'s `Number` superclass). Continuing on from Listing 8–3, you would specify `int y = col.iterator().next().intValue();` to assign the stored 32-bit integer to y.

To alleviate this tedium, Java version 5 introduced autoboxing and unboxing, which are a pair of complementary syntactic sugar–based language features that make primitive values appear more like objects. (This "sleight of hand" is not complete because you cannot specify expressions such as `27.doubleValue()`.)

Autoboxing automatically *boxes* (wraps) a primitive value in an object of the appropriate primitive wrapper class type whenever a primitive type is specified but a reference is required. For example, you could change Listing 8–3's third line to `col.add(x);` and have the compiler box x into an `Integer` object.

Unboxing automatically *unboxes* (unwraps) a primitive value from its wrapper object whenever a reference is specified but a primitive type is required. For example, you could specify `int y = col.iterator().next();` and have the compiler unbox the returned `Integer` object to int value 27 prior to the assignment.

Although autoboxing and unboxing were introduced to simplify working with primitive values in a collections context, these language features can be used in other contexts, and this arbitrary use can lead to a problem that is difficult to understand without knowledge of what is happening behind the scenes. For example, consider Listing 8–4.

Listing 8–4. *The trouble with autoboxing and unboxing*

```
public static void main(String[] args)
{
    Integer i1 = 127;
    Integer i2 = 127;
    System.out.println(i1 == i2); // Output: true
    System.out.println(i1 < i2); // Output: false
    System.out.println(i1 > i2); // Output: false
    System.out.println(i1 + i2); // Output: 254
    i1 = 30000;
```

```
   i2 = 30000;
   System.out.println(i1 == i2); // Output: false
   System.out.println(i1 < i2); // Output: false
   System.out.println(i1 > i2); // Output: false
   i2 = 30001;
   System.out.println(i1 < i2); // Output: true
   System.out.println(i1 + i2); // Output: 60001
}
```

With one exception, this listing's output is as expected. The exception is the i1 == i2 comparison where each of i1 and i2 contains 30000. Instead of returning true, as is the case where each of i1 and i2 contains 127, i1 == i2 returns false. What is causing this problem?

Examine the generated code and you will discover that Integer i1 = 127; is converted to Integer i1 = Integer.valueOf(127); and Integer i2 = 127; is converted to Integer i2 = Integer.valueOf(127);. According to valueOf()'s Java documentation, this method takes advantage of caching to improve performance.

> **NOTE:** valueOf() is also used when adding a primitive value to a collection. For example, col.add(27) is converted to col.add(Integer.valueOf(27)).

Integer maintains an internal cache of unique Integer objects over a small range of values. The low bound of this range is -128, and the high bound defaults to 127. However, you can change the high bound by assigning a different value to system property java.lang.Integer.IntegerCache.high (via the System class's String setProperty(String prop, String value) method—I demonstrated this method's getProperty() counterpart in Chapter 7).

> **NOTE:** Each of Byte, Long, and Short also maintains an internal cache of unique Byte, Long, and Short objects, respectively.

Because of the cache, each Integer.valueOf(127) call returns the same Integer object reference, which is why i1 == i2 (which compares references) evaluates to true. Because 30000 lies outside of the default range, each Integer.valueOf(30000) call returns a reference to a new Integer object, which is why i1 == i2 evaluates to false.

In contrast to == and !=, which do not unbox the boxed values prior to the comparison, operators such as <, >, and + unbox these values before performing their operations. As a result, i1 < i2 is converted to i1.intValue() < i2.intValue() and i1 + i2 is converted to i1.intValue() + i2.intValue().

> **CAUTION:** Do not assume that autoboxing and unboxing are used in the context of the == and != operators.

List

A *list* is an ordered collection, which is also known as a *sequence*. Elements can be stored in and accessed from specific locations via integer indexes. Some of these elements may be duplicates or null (when the list's implementation allows null elements). Lists are described by the List interface, whose generic type is List<E>.

List extends Collection and redeclares its inherited methods, partly for convenience. It also redeclares iterator(), add(), remove(), equals(), and hashCode() to place extra conditions on their contracts. For example, List's contract for add() specifies that it appends an element to the end of the list, rather than adding the element to the collection.

List also declares Table 8–2's list-specific methods.

Table 8–2. *List-specific Methods*

Method	Description
void add(int index, E e)	Insert element e into this list at position index. Shift the element currently at this position (if any) and any subsequent elements to the right. This method throws UnsupportedOperationException when this list does not support add(), ClassCastException when e's class is inappropriate for this list, IllegalArgumentException when some property of e prevents it from being added to this list, NullPointerException when e contains the null reference and this list does not support null elements, and java.lang.IndexOutOfBoundsException when index is less than 0 or index is greater than size().
boolean addAll (int index, Collection<? extends E> c)	Insert all of c's elements into this list starting at position index. Shift the element currently at this position (if any) and any subsequent elements to the right. The new elements appear in this list in the order in which they are returned by c's iterator. This method throws UnsupportedOperationException when this list does not support addAll(), ClassCastException when the class of one of c's elements is inappropriate for this list, IllegalArgumentException when some property of an element prevents it from being added to this list, NullPointerException when c contains the null reference or when one of its elements is null and this list does not support null elements, and IndexOutOfBoundsException when index is less than 0 or index is greater than size().
E get(int index)	Return the element stored in this list at position index. This method throws IndexOutOfBoundsException when index is less than 0 or index is greater than or equal to size().
int indexOf (Object o)	Return the index of the first occurrence of element o in this list, or -1 when this list does not contain the element. This method throws ClassCastException when o's class is inappropriate for this list, and NullPointerException when o contains the null reference and this list does not support null elements.

Method	Description
int lastIndexOf (Object o)	Return the index of the last occurrence of element o in this list, or -1 when this list does not contain the element. This method throws ClassCastException when o's class is inappropriate for this list, and NullPointerException when o contains the null reference and this list does not support null elements.
ListIterator<E> listIterator()	Return a list iterator over the elements in this list. The elements are returned in the same order as they appear in the list.
ListIterator<E> listIterator(int index)	Return a list iterator over the elements in this list starting with the element located at index. The elements are returned in the same order as they appear in the list. This method throws IndexOutOfBoundsException when index is less than 0 or index is greater than size().
E remove(int index)	Remove the element at position index from this list and return this element. This method throws UnsupportedOperationException when this list does not support remove(), and IndexOutOfBoundsException when index is less than 0 or index is greater than or equal to size().
E set(int index, E e)	Replace the element at position index in this list with element e and return the element previously stored at this position. This method throws UnsupportedOperationException when this list does not support set(), ClassCastException when e's class is inappropriate for this list, IllegalArgumentException when some property of e prevents it from being added to this list, NullPointerException when e contains the null reference and this list does not support null elements, and IndexOutOfBoundsException when index is less than 0 or index is greater than or equal to size().
List<E> subList (int fromIndex, int toIndex)	Return a view (discussed later) of the portion of this list between fromIndex (inclusive) and toIndex (exclusive). (If fromIndex and toIndex are equal, the returned list is empty.) The returned list is backed by this list, so nonstructural changes in the returned list are reflected in this list and vice versa. The returned list supports all of the optional list methods (those methods that can throw UnsupportedOperationException) supported by this list. This method throws IndexOutOfBoundsException when fromIndex is less than 0, toIndex is greater than size(), or fromIndex is greater than toIndex.

Table 8–2 refers to the ListIterator interface, which is more flexible than its Iterator superinterface in that ListIterator provides methods for iterating over a list in either direction, modifying the list during iteration, and obtaining the iterator's current position in the list.

NOTE: The Iterator and ListIterator instances that are returned by the iterator() and listIterator() methods in the ArrayList and LinkedList List implementation classes are *fail-fast*: when a list is structurally modified (by calling the implementation's add() method to add a new element, for example) after the iterator is created, in any way except through the iterator's own add() or remove() methods, the iterator throws java.lang.ConcurrentModificationException. Therefore, in the face of concurrent modification, the iterator fails quickly and cleanly, rather than risking arbitrary, nondeterministic behavior at an undetermined time in the future.

ListIterator declares the following methods:

- void add(E e) inserts e into the list being iterated over. This element is inserted immediately before the next element that would be returned by next(), if any, and after the next element that would be returned by previous(), if any. This method throws UnsupportedOperationException when this list does not support add(), ClassCastException when e's class is inappropriate for this list, and IllegalArgumentException when some property of e prevents it from being added to this list.

- boolean hasNext() returns true when this list iterator has more elements when traversing the list in the forward direction.

- boolean hasPrevious() returns true when this list iterator has more elements when traversing the list in the reverse direction.

- E next() returns the next element in this list. This method throws NoSuchElementException when there is no next element.

- int nextIndex() returns the index of the element that would be returned by a subsequent call to next(), or the size of the list when at the end of the list.

- E previous() returns the previous element in this list. This method throws NoSuchElementException when there is no previous element.

- int previousIndex() returns the index of the element that would be returned by a subsequent call to previous(), or -1 when at the beginning of the list.

- void remove() removes from this list the last element that was returned by next() or previous(). This call can be made only once per call to next() or previous(). Furthermore, it can be made only when add() has not been called after the last call to next() or previous(). This method throws UnsupportedOperationException when this list does not support remove(), and IllegalStateException when neither next() nor previous() has been called, or remove() or add() has already been called after the last call to next() or previous().

- void set(E e) replaces the last element returned by next() or previous() with element e. This call can be made only when neither remove() nor add() has been called after the last call to next() or previous(). This method throws UnsupportedOperationException when this list does not support set(), ClassCastException when e's class Is inappropriate for this list, IllegalArgumentException when some property of e prevents it from being added to this lIst, and IllegalStateException when neither next() nor previous() has been called, or remove() or add() has already been called after the last call to next() or previous().

A ListIterator instance does not have the concept of a current element. Instead, it has the concept of a *cursor* for navigating through a list. The nextIndex() and previousIndex() methods return the *cursor position*, which always lies between the element that would be returned by a call to previous() and the element that would be returned by a call to next(). A list iterator for a list of length *n* has *n*+1 possible cursor positions, as illustrated by each caret (^) below:

```
                    Element(0)   Element(1)   Element(2)   ... Element(n-1)
cursor positions:  ^             ^            ^            ^                ^
```

> **NOTE:** You can mix calls to next() and previous() as long as you are careful. Keep in mind that the first call to previous() returns the same element as the last call to next(). Furthermore, the first call to next() following a sequence of calls to previous() returns the same element as the last call to previous().

Table 8–2's description of the subList() method refers to the concept of a *view*, which is a list that is backed by another list. Changes that are made to the view are reflected in this backing list. The view can cover the entire list or, as subList()'s name implies, only part of the list.

The subList() method is useful for performing *range-view* operations over a list in a compact manner. For example, list.subList(fromIndex, toIndex).clear(); removes a range of elements from list where the first element is located at fromIndex and the last element is located at toIndex-1.

> **CAUTION:** A view's meaning becomes undefined when changes are made to the backing list. Therefore, you should only use subList() temporarily, whenever you need to perform a sequence of range operations on the backing list.

ArrayList

The ArrayList class provides a list implementation that is based on an internal array. As a result, access to the list's elements is fast. However, because elements must be moved to open a space for insertion or to close a space after deletion, insertions and deletions of elements is slow.

> **NOTE:** Refer to Chapter 2 for an introduction to arrays.

ArrayList supplies three constructors:

- ArrayList() creates an empty array list with an initial *capacity* (storage space) of ten elements. Once this capacity is reached, a larger array is allocated, elements from the current array are copied into the larger array, and the larger array becomes the new current array. This process repeats as additional elements are added to the array list.

- ArrayList(Collection<? extends E> collection) creates an array list containing collection's elements in the order in which they are returned by the collection's iterator.

- ArrayList(int capacity) creates an empty array list with an initial capacity of capacity elements.

Listing 8–5 demonstrates an array list.

Listing 8–5. *A demonstration of an array-based list*

```java
import java.util.ArrayList;
import java.util.List;

public class ArrayListDemo
{
   public static void main(String[] args)
   {
      List<String> ls = new ArrayList<String>();
      String[] weekDays = {"Sun", "Mon", "Tue", "Wed", "Thu", "Fri", "Sat"};
      for (String weekDay: weekDays)
         ls.add(weekDay);
      dump("ls:", ls);
      ls.set(ls.indexOf("Wed"), "Wednesday");
      dump("ls:", ls);
      ls.remove(ls.lastIndexOf("Fri"));
      dump("ls:", ls);
   }
   static void dump(String title, List<String> ls)
   {
      System.out.print(title + " ");
      for (String s: ls)
         System.out.print(s + " ");
      System.out.println();
   }
}
```

The dump() method's enhanced for loop statement uses iterator(), hasNext(), and next() behind the scenes.

When you run this application, it generates the following output:

```
ls: Sun Mon Tue Wed Thu Fri Sat
ls: Sun Mon Tue Wednesday Thu Fri Sat
ls: Sun Mon Tue Wednesday Thu Sat
```

LinkedList

The LinkedList class provides a list implementation that is based on linked nodes. Because links must be traversed, access to the list's elements is slow. However, because only node references need to be changed, insertions and deletions of elements are fast.

WHAT IS A NODE?

A *node* is a fixed sequence of value and link memory locations. Unlike an array, where each slot stores a single value of the same primitive type or reference supertype, a node can store multiple values of different types. It can also store *links* (references to other nodes).

Consider the following simple Node class:

```
class Node
{
   // value field
   String name;
   // link field
   Node next;
}
```

Node describes simple nodes where each node consists of a single name value field and a single next link field. Notice that next is of the same type as the class in which it is declared. This arrangement lets a node instance store a reference to another node instance (which is the next node) in this field. The resulting nodes are *linked* together.

The following code fragment creates a couple of Node objects and links the second Node object to the first Node object. This fragment also demonstrates how to traverse this *linked list* by following each Node object's next field. Node traversal stops when the traversal code discovers that next contains the null reference, which signifies the end of the list.

```
Node first = new Node();
first.name = "First node";
Node last = new Node();
last.name = "Last node";
last.next = null;
first.next = last;
Node temp = first;
while (temp != null)
{
   System.out.println(temp.name);
   temp = temp.next;
}
```

The code first builds a linked list of two Nodes, and then assigns first to local variable temp in order to traverse the list without losing the reference to the first node that is stored in first. While temp is not null, the loop outputs the name field. It also navigates to the next Node object in the list via the temp = temp.next; statement.

If you convert this code into an application and run the application, you will discover the following output:

```
First node
Last node
```

LinkedList supplies two constructors:

- LinkedList() creates an empty linked list.

- LinkedList(Collection<? extends E> collection) creates a linked list containing collection's elements in the order in which they are returned by the collection's iterator.

Listing 8–6 demonstrates a linked list.

Listing 8–6. *A demonstration of a list of linked nodes*

```java
import java.util.LinkedList;
import java.util.List;
import java.util.ListIterator;

public class LinkedListDemo
{
   public static void main(String[] args)
   {
      List<String> ls = new LinkedList<String>();
      String[] weekDays = {"Sun", "Mon", "Tue", "Wed", "Thu", "Fri", "Sat"};
      for (String weekDay: weekDays)
         ls.add(weekDay);
      dump("ls:", ls);
      ls.add(1, "Sunday");
      ls.add(3, "Monday");
      ls.add(5, "Tuesday");
      ls.add(7, "Wednesday");
      ls.add(9, "Thursday");
      ls.add(11, "Friday");
      ls.add(13, "Saturday");
      dump("ls:", ls);
      ListIterator<String> li = ls.listIterator(ls.size());
      while (li.hasPrevious())
         System.out.print(li.previous() + " ");
      System.out.println();
   }
   static void dump(String title, List<String> ls)
   {
      System.out.print(title + " ");
      for (String s: ls)
         System.out.print(s + " ");
      System.out.println();
   }
}
```

This application demonstrates that each successive add() method call must increase its index by 2 to account for the previously added element when adding longer weekday names to the list. It also shows you how to output a list in reverse order: return a list iterator with its cursor initialized past the end of the list and repeatedly call previous().

When you run this application, it generates the following output:

```
ls: Sun Mon Tue Wed Thu Fri Sat
ls: Sun Sunday Mon Monday Tue Tuesday Wed Wednesday Thu Thursday Fri Friday Sat Saturday
Saturday Sat Friday Fri Thursday Thu Wednesday Wed Tuesday Tue Monday Mon Sunday Sun
```

Set

A *set* is a collection that contains no duplicate elements. In other words, a set contains no pair of elements *e1* and *e2* such that *e1*.equals(*e2*) returns true. Furthermore, a set can contain at most one null element. Sets are described by the Set interface, whose generic type is Set<E>.

Set extends Collection and redeclares its inherited methods, for convenience and also to add stipulations to the contracts for add(), equals(), and hashCode(), to address how they behave in a set context. Also, Set's documentation states that all constructors of implementation classes must create sets that contain no duplicate elements.

Set does not introduce new methods.

TreeSet

The TreeSet class provides a set implementation that is based on a tree data structure. As a result, elements are stored in sorted order. However, accessing these elements is somewhat slower than with the other Set implementations (which are not sorted) because links must be traversed.

> **NOTE:** Check out Wikipedia's "Tree (data structure)" entry (http://en.wikipedia.org/wiki/Tree_%28data_structure%29) to learn about trees.

TreeSet supplies four constructors:

- TreeSet() creates a new, empty tree set that is sorted according to the natural ordering of its elements. All elements inserted into the set must implement the Comparable interface.

- TreeSet(Collection<? extends E> collection) creates a new tree set containing collection's elements, sorted according to the natural ordering of its elements. All elements inserted into the new set must implement the Comparable interface. This constructor throws ClassCastException when collection's elements do not implement Comparable or are not mutually comparable, and NullPointerException when collection contains the null reference.

- TreeSet(Comparator<? super E> comparator) creates a new, empty tree set that is sorted according to the specified comparator. Passing null to comparator implies that natural ordering will be used.

- TreeSet(SortedSet<E> sortedSet) creates a new tree set containing the same elements and using the same ordering as sortedSet. (I discuss sorted sets later in this chapter.) This constructor throws NullPointerException when sortedSet contains the null reference.

Listing 8–7 demonstrates a tree set.

Listing 8–7. *A demonstration of a tree set with* String *elements sorted according to their natural ordering*

```
import java.util.Set;
import java.util.TreeSet;

public class TreeSetDemo
{
   public static void main(String[] args)
   {
      Set<String> ss = new TreeSet<String>();
      String[] fruits = {"apples", "pears", "grapes", "bananas", "kiwis"};
      for (String fruit: fruits)
         ss.add(fruit);
      dump("ss:", ss);
   }
   static void dump(String title, Set<String> ss)
   {
      System.out.print(title + " ");
      for (String s: ss)
         System.out.print(s + " ");
      System.out.println();
   }
}
```

Because String implements Comparable, it is legal for this application to use the TreeSet() constructor to insert the contents of the fruits array into the set.

When you run this application, it generates the following output:

```
ss: apples bananas grapes kiwis pears
```

HashSet

The HashSet class provides a set implementation that is backed by a hashtable data structure (implemented as a HashMap instance, discussed later, which provides a quick way to determine if an element has already been stored in this structure). Although this class provides no ordering guarantees for its elements, HashSet is much faster than TreeSet. Furthermore, HashSet permits the null reference to be stored in its instances.

> **NOTE:** Check out Wikipedia's "Hash table" entry
> (http://en.wikipedia.org/wiki/Hash_table) to learn about hashtables.

HashSet supplies four constructors:

- HashSet() creates a new, empty hashset where the backing HashMap instance has an initial capacity of 16 and a load factor of 0.75. You will learn what these items mean when I discuss HashMap later in this chapter.

- HashSet(Collection<? extends E> collection) creates a new hashset containing collection's elements. The backing HashMap has an initial capacity sufficient to contain collection's elements and a load factor of 0.75. This constructor throws NullPointerException when collection contains the null reference.

- HashSet(int initialCapacity) creates a new, empty hashset where the backing HashMap instance has the capacity specified by initialCapacity and a load factor of 0.75. This constructor throws IllegalArgumentException when initialCapacity's value is less than 0.

- HashSet(int initialCapacity, float loadFactor) creates a new, empty hashset where the backing HashMap instance has the capacity specified by initialCapacity and the load factor specified by loadFactor. This constructor throws IllegalArgumentException when initialCapacity is less than 0 or when loadFactor is less than or equal to 0.

Listing 8–8 demonstrates a hashset.

Listing 8–8. *A demonstration of a hashset with* String *elements unordered*

```
import java.util.HashSet;
import java.util.Set;

public class HashSetDemo
{
   public static void main(String[] args)
   {
      Set<String> ss = new HashSet<String>();
      String[] fruits = {"apples", "pears", "grapes", "bananas", "kiwis",
                         "pears", null};
      for (String fruit: fruits)
         ss.add(fruit);
      dump("ss:", ss);
   }
   static void dump(String title, Set<String> ss)
   {
      System.out.print(title + " ");
      for (String s: ss)
         System.out.print(s + " ");
      System.out.println();
   }
}
```

In Listing 8–7's TreeSetDemo application, I did not add null to the fruits array because TreeSet throws NullPointerException when it detects an attempt to add this element. In contrast, HashSet permits null to be added, which is why Listing 8–8 includes null in HashSetDemo's fruits array.

When you run this application, it generates unordered output such as the following:

```
ss: null grapes bananas kiwis pears apples
```

Suppose you want to add instances of your classes to a hashset. As with String, your classes must override equals() and hashCode(); otherwise, duplicate class instances can be stored in the hashset. For example, Listing 8–9 presents the source code to an application whose Planet class overrides equals() but fails to also override hashCode().

Listing 8–9. *A custom Planet class not overriding hashCode()*

```java
import java.util.HashSet;
import java.util.Set;

public class CustomClassAndHashSet
{
    public static void main(String[] args)
    {
        Set<Planet> sp = new HashSet<Planet>();
        sp.add(new Planet("Mercury"));
        sp.add(new Planet("Venus"));
        sp.add(new Planet("Earth"));
        sp.add(new Planet("Mars"));
        sp.add(new Planet("Jupiter"));
        sp.add(new Planet("Saturn"));
        sp.add(new Planet("Uranus"));
        sp.add(new Planet("Neptune"));
        sp.add(new Planet("Fomalhaut b"));
        Planet p1 = new Planet("51 Pegasi b");
        sp.add(p1);
        Planet p2 = new Planet("51 Pegasi b");
        sp.add(p2);
        System.out.println(p1.equals(p2));
        System.out.println(sp);
    }
}
class Planet
{
    private String name;
    Planet(String name)
    {
        this.name = name;
    }
    @Override
    public boolean equals(Object o)
    {
        if (!(o instanceof Planet))
            return false;
        Planet p = (Planet) o;
        return p.name.equals(name);
    }
    String getName()
    {
        return name;
```

```
    }
    @Override
    public String toString()
    {
        return name;
    }
}
```

Listing 8–9's Planet class declares a single name field of type String. Although it might seem pointless to declare Planet with a single String field because I could refactor this listing to remove Planet and work with String, I might want to introduce additional fields to Planet (perhaps to store a planet's mass and other characteristics) in the future.

> **NOTE:** equals() relies on a little known fact about the Java language: one instance's private members can be accessed from another instance of the same class. For example, equals() can specify p.name to access p's private name field. Directly accessing an instance's private members in this manner is legal because encapsulation is not violated.

When you run this application, it generates unordered output such as the following:

```
true
[Jupiter, Fomalhaut b, Neptune, Uranus, Venus, Earth, Mercury, 51 Pegasi b, Mars,↵
Saturn, 51 Pegasi b]
```

This output reveals two 51 Pegasi b elements in the hashset. Although these elements are equal from the perspective of the overriding equals() method (the first output line, true, proves this point), overriding equals() is not enough to avoid duplicate elements being stored in a hashset: you must also override hashCode().

The easiest way to override hashCode() in Listing 8–9's Planet class is to have the overriding method call the name field's hashCode() method and return its value. (This technique only works with a class whose single reference field's class provides a valid hashCode() method.) Listing 8–10 presents this overriding hashCode() method.

Listing 8–10. *Handing over hash code calculation to another hashCode() method*

```
@Override
public int hashCode()
{
    return name.hashCode();
}
```

Introduce this method into the previous Planet class and run the application. You will observe output (similar to that shown below) that reveals no duplicate elements:

```
true
[Saturn, Earth, Uranus, Fomalhaut b, 51 Pegasi b, Venus, Jupiter, Mercury, Mars,↵
 Neptune]
```

> **NOTE:** LinkedHashSet is a subclass of HashSet that uses a linked list to store its elements. As a result, LinkedHashSet's iterator returns elements in the order in which they were inserted. For example, if Listing 8–8 had specified Set<String> ss = new LinkedHashSet<String>();, the application's output would have been ss: apples pears grapes bananas kiwis null. Also, LinkedHashSet offers slower performance than HashSet and faster performance than TreeSet.

EnumSet

Chapter 5 introduced you to traditional enumerated types and their enum replacement. (An *enum* is an enumerated type that is expressed via reserved word enum.) Listing 8–11 presents an example of a traditional enumerated type.

Listing 8–11. *An enumerated type of weekday constants*

```
public static final int SUNDAY = 1;
public static final int MONDAY = 2;
public static final int TUESDAY = 4;
public static final int WEDNESDAY = 8;
public static final int THURSDAY = 16;
public static final int FRIDAY = 32;
public static final int SATURDAY = 64;
```

Although the enum has many advantages over the traditional enumerated type, the traditional enumerated type is less awkward to use when combining constants into a set; for example, public static final int DAYS_OFF = SUNDAY | MONDAY;.

DAYS_OFF is an example of an integer-based, fixed-length *bitset*, which is a set of bits where each bit indicates that its associated member belongs to the set when the bit is set to 1, and is absent from the set when the bit is set to 0.

> **NOTE:** An int-based bitset cannot contain more than 32 members because int has a size of 32 bits. Similarly, a long-based bitset cannot contain more than 64 members because long has a size of 64 bits.

This bitset is formed by bitwise inclusive ORing the traditional enumerated type's integer constants together via the bitwise inclusive OR operator (|): you could also use +. Each constant must be a unique power of two (starting with one) because otherwise it is impossible to distinguish between the members of this bitset.

To determine if a constant belongs to the bitset, create an expression that involves the bitwise AND operator (&). For example, ((DAYS_OFF & MONDAY) == MONDAY) bitwise ANDs DAYS_OFF (3) with MONDAY (2), which results in 2. This value is compared via == with MONDAY (2), and the result of the expression is true: MONDAY is a member of the DAYS_OFF bitset.

You can accomplish the same task with an enum by instantiating an appropriate Set implementation class and calling the add() method multiple times to store the constants in the set. Listing 8–12 illustrates this more awkward alternative.

Listing 8–12. *Creating the Set equivalent of DAYS_OFF*

```
import java.util.Set;
import java.util.TreeSet;

enum Weekday
{
    SUNDAY, MONDAY, TUESDAY, WEDNESDAY, THURSDAY, FRIDAY, SATURDAY
}
class DaysOff
{
    public static void main(String[] args)
    {
        Set<Weekday> daysOff = new TreeSet<Weekday>();
        daysOff.add(Weekday.SUNDAY);
        daysOff.add(Weekday.MONDAY);
        System.out.println(daysOff);
    }
}
```

When you run this application, it generates the following output:

```
[SUNDAY, MONDAY]
```

> **NOTE:** The constants' ordinals and not their names are stored in the tree set, which is why the names appear unordered even though the constants are stored in sorted order of their ordinals.

In addition to being more awkward to use (and verbose) than the bitset, the Set alternative requires more memory to store each constant and is not as fast. Because of these problems, EnumSet was introduced.

The EnumSet class provides a Set implementation that is based on a bitset. Its elements are constants that must come from the same enum, which is specified when the enum set is created. Null elements are not permitted; any attempt to store a null element results in a thrown NullPointerException.

Listing 8–13 demonstrates EnumSet.

Listing 8–13. *Creating the EnumSet equivalent of DAYS_OFF*

```
import java.util.EnumSet;
import java.util.Iterator;
import java.util.Set;

enum Weekday
{
    SUNDAY, MONDAY, TUESDAY, WEDNESDAY, THURSDAY, FRIDAY, SATURDAY
}
public class EnumSetDemo
{
    public static void main(String[] args)
```

```
    {
        Set<Weekday> daysOff = EnumSet.of(Weekday.SUNDAY, Weekday.MONDAY);
        Iterator<Weekday> iter = daysOff.iterator();
        while (iter.hasNext())
            System.out.println(iter.next());
    }
}
```

EnumSet, whose generic type is EnumSet<E extends Enum<E>>, provides a variety of utility methods for conveniently constructing enum sets. For example, <E extends Enum<E>> EnumSet<E> of(E e1, E e2) returns an EnumSet instance consisting of elements e1 and e2. In this example, those elements are Weekday.SUNDAY and Weekday.MONDAY.

When you run this application, it generates the following output:

```
SUNDAY
MONDAY
```

> **NOTE:** In addition to providing several overloaded of() methods, EnumSet provides other methods for conveniently creating enum sets. For example, allOf() returns an EnumSet instance that contains all of an enum's constants, where this method's solitary argument is a class literal that identifies the enum:
>
> ```
> Set<Weekday> allWeekDays = EnumSet.allOf(Weekday.class);
> ```
>
> Similarly, range() returns an EnumSet instance containing a range of an enum's elements (with the range's limits as specified by this method's two arguments):
>
> ```
> for (WeekDay wd : EnumSet.range(WeekDay.MONDAY, WeekDay.FRIDAY))
>     System.out.println(wd);
> ```

SortedSet

TreeSet is an example of a *sorted set*, which is a set that maintains its elements in ascending order, sorted according to their natural ordering or according to a comparator that is supplied when the sorted set is created. Sorted sets are described by the SortedSet interface.

SortedSet, whose generic type is SortedSet<E>, extends Set. With two exceptions, the methods it inherits from Set behave identically on sorted sets as on other sets:

- The Iterator instance returned from iterator() traverses the sorted set in order.

- The array returned by toArray() contains the sorted set's elements in order.

> **NOTE:** Although not guaranteed, the `toString()` methods of `SortedSet` implementations in the collections framework (such as `TreeSet`) return a string containing all of the sorted set's elements in order.

SortedSet's documentation requires that an Implementation must provide the four standard constructors that I presented in my discussion of `TreeSet`. Furthermore, implementations of this interface must implement the methods that are described in Table 8–3.

Table 8–3. *SortedSet-specific Methods*

Method	Description
Comparator<? super E> comparator()	Return the comparator used to order the elements in this set, or null when this set uses the natural ordering of its elements.
E first()	Return the first (lowest) element currently in this set, or throw a NoSuchElementException instance when this set is empty.
SortedSet<E> headSet(E toElement)	Return a view of that portion of this set whose elements are strictly less than toElement. The returned set is backed by this set, so changes in the returned set are reflected in this set and vice versa. The returned set supports all optional set operations that this set supports. This method throws ClassCastException when toElement is not compatible with this set's comparator (or, when the set has no comparator, when toElement does not implement Comparable), NullPointerException when toElement is null and this set does not permit null elements, and IllegalArgumentException when this set has a restricted range and toElement lies outside of this range's bounds.
E last()	Return the last (highest) element currently in this set, or throw a NoSuchElementException instance when this set is empty.
SortedSet<E> subSet(E fromElement, E toElement)	Return a view of the portion of this set whose elements range from fromElement, inclusive, to toElement, exclusive. (When fromElement and toElement are equal, the returned set is empty.) The returned set is backed by this set, so changes in the returned set are reflected in this set and vice versa. The returned set supports all optional set operations that this set supports. This method throws ClassCastException when fromElement and toElement cannot be compared to one another using this set's comparator (or, when the set has no comparator, using natural ordering), NullPointerException when fromElement or toElement is null and this set does not permit null elements, and IllegalArgumentException when fromElement is greater than toElement or when this set has a restricted range and fromElement or toElement lies outside of this range's bounds.

Method	Description
`SortedSet<E> tailSet(E fromElement)`	Return a view of that portion of this set whose elements are greater than or equal to `fromElement`. The returned set is backed by this set, so changes in the returned set are reflected in this set and vice versa. The returned set supports all optional set operations that this set supports. This method throws `ClassCastException` when `fromElement` is not compatible with this set's comparator (or, when the set has no comparator, when `fromElement` does not implement `Comparable`), `NullPointerException` when `fromElement` is null and this set does not permit null elements, and `IllegalArgumentException` when this set has a restricted range and `fromElement` lies outside of the range's bounds.

The set-based range views returned from `headSet()`, `subSet()`, and `tailSet()` are analogous to the list-based range view returned from `List`'s `subList()` method except that a set-based range view remains valid even when the backing sorted set is modified. As a result, a set-based range view can be used for a lengthy period of time.

> **NOTE:** Unlike a list-based range view whose endpoints are elements in the backing list, the endpoints of a set-based range view are absolute points in element space, allowing a set-based range view to serve as a window onto a portion of the set's element space. Any changes made to the set-based range view are written back to the backing sorted set and vice versa.

Each range view returned by `headSet()`, `subSet()`, or `tailSet()` is *half open* because it does not include its high endpoint (`headSet()` and `subSet()`) or its low endpoint (`tailSet()`). For the first two methods, the high endpoint is specified by argument `toElement`; for the last method, the low endpoint is specified by argument `fromElement`.

> **NOTE:** You could also regard the returned range view as being *half closed* because it includes only one of its endpoints.

Listing 8–14 demonstrates a sorted set based on a tree set.

Listing 8–14. *A sorted set of fruit and vegetable names*

```java
import java.util.SortedSet;
import java.util.TreeSet;

public class SortedSetDemo
{
   public static void main(String[] args)
   {
      SortedSet<String> sss = new TreeSet<String>();
      String[] fruitAndVeg =
      {
         "apple", "potato", "turnip", "banana", "corn", "carrot", "cherry",
         "pear", "mango", "strawberry", "cucumber", "grape", "banana",
         "kiwi", "radish", "blueberry", "tomato", "onion", "raspberry",
```

```
            "lemon", "pepper", "squash", "melon", "zucchini", "peach", "plum",
            "turnip", "onion", "nectarine"
      };
      System.out.println("Array size = " + fruitAndVeg.length);
      for (String fruitVeg: fruitAndVeg)
         sss.add(fruitVeg);
      dump("sss:", sss);
      System.out.println("Sorted set size = " + sss.size());
      System.out.println("First element = " + sss.first());
      System.out.println("Last element = " + sss.last());
      System.out.println("Comparator = " + sss.comparator());
      dump("hs:", sss.headSet("n"));
      dump("ts:", sss.tailSet("n"));
      System.out.println("Count of p-named fruits & vegetables = " +
                        sss.subSet("p", "q").size());
      System.out.println("Incorrect count of c-named fruits & vegetables = " +
                        sss.subSet("carrot", "cucumber").size());
      System.out.println("Correct count of c-named fruits & vegetables = " +
                        sss.subSet("carrot", "cucumber\0").size());
   }
   static void dump(String title, SortedSet<String> sss)
   {
      System.out.print(title + " ");
      for (String s: sss)
         System.out.print(s + " ");
      System.out.println();
   }
}
```

When you run this application, it generates the following output:

```
Array size = 29
ss: apple banana blueberry carrot cherry corn cucumber grape kiwi lemon mango melon
 nectarine onion peach pear pepper plum potato radish raspberry squash strawberry
 tomato turnip zucchini
Sorted set size = 26
First element = apple
Last element = zucchini
Comparator = null
hs: apple banana blueberry carrot cherry corn cucumber grape kiwi lemon mango melon
ts: nectarine onion peach pear pepper plum potato radish raspberry squash strawberry
 tomato turnip zucchini
Count of p-named fruits & vegetables = 5
Incorrect count of c-named fruits & vegetables = 3
Correct count of c-named fruits & vegetables = 4
```

This output reveals that the sorted set's size is less than the array's size because a set cannot contain duplicate elements: the duplicate banana, turnip, and onion elements are not stored in the sorted set.

The comparator() method returns null because the sorted set was not created with a comparator. Instead, the sorted set relies on the natural ordering of String elements to store them in sorted order.

The headSet() and tailSet() methods are called with argument "n" to return, respectively, a set of elements whose names begin with a letter that is strictly less than n, and a letter that is greater than or equal to n.

Finally, the output shows you that you must be careful when passing an upper limit to subSet(). As you can see, ss.subSet("carrot", "cucumber") does not include cucumber in the returned range view because cucumber is subSet()'s high endpoint.

To include cucumber in the range view, you need to form a *closed range* or *closed interval* (both endpoints are included). With String objects, you accomplish this task by appending \0 to the string. For example, ss.subSet("carrot", "cucumber\0") includes cucumber because it is less than cucumber\0.

This same technique can be applied wherever you need to form an *open range* or *open interval* (neither endpoint is included). For example, ss.subSet("carrot\0", "cucumber") does not include carrot because it is less than carrot\0. Furthermore, it does not include high endpoint cucumber.

> **NOTE:** When you want to create closed and open ranges for elements created from your own classes, you need to provide some form of predecessor() and successor() methods that return an element's predecessor and successor.

You need to be careful when designing classes that work with sorted sets. For example, the class must implement Comparable when you plan to store the class's instances in a sorted set where these elements are sorted according to their natural ordering. Consider Listing 8–15.

Listing 8–15. *A custom Employee class not implementing* Comparable

```java
import java.util.SortedSet;
import java.util.TreeSet;

public class CustomClassAndSortedSet
{
    public static void main(String[] args)
    {
        SortedSet<Employee> sse = new TreeSet<Employee>();
        sse.add(new Employee("Sally Doe"));
        sse.add(new Employee("Bob Doe")); // ClassCastException thrown here
        sse.add(new Employee("John Doe"));
        System.out.println(sse);
    }
}
class Employee
{
    private String name;
    Employee(String name)
    {
        this.name = name;
    }
    @Override
    public String toString()
```

```
    {
        return name;
    }
}
```

When you run this application, it generates the following output:

```
Exception in thread "main" java.lang.ClassCastException: Employee cannot be cast to
 java.lang.Comparable
        at java.util.TreeMap.put(Unknown Source)
        at java.util.TreeSet.add(Unknown Source)
        at CustomClassAndSortedSet.main(CustomClassAndSortedSet.java:10)
```

The ClassCastException instance is thrown during the second add() method call because the sorted set implementation, an instance of TreeSet, is unable to call the second Employee element's compareTo() method, because Employee does not implement Comparable.

The solution to this problem is to have the class implement Comparable, which is exactly what is revealed in Listing 8–16.

Listing 8–16. *Making Employee elements comparable*

```
import java.util.SortedSet;
import java.util.TreeSet;

public class CustomClassAndSortedSet
{
    public static void main(String[] args)
    {
        SortedSet<Employee> sse = new TreeSet<Employee>();
        sse.add(new Employee("Sally Doe"));
        sse.add(new Employee("Bob Doe"));
        Employee e1 = new Employee("John Doe");
        Employee e2 = new Employee("John Doe");
        sse.add(e1);
        sse.add(e2);
        System.out.println(sse);
        System.out.println(e1.equals(e2));
    }
}
class Employee implements Comparable<Employee>
{
    private String name;
    Employee(String name)
    {
        this.name = name;
    }
    @Override
    public int compareTo(Employee e)
    {
        return name.compareTo(e.name);
    }
    @Override
    public String toString()
    {
        return name;
    }
}
```

Listing 8–16's `main()` method differs from Listing 8–15 in that it also creates two Employee objects initialized to "John Doe", adds these objects to the sorted set, and compares these objects for equality via `equals()`. Furthermore, Listing 8–16 declares Employee to implement Comparable, introducing a `compareTo()` method into Employee.

When you run this application, it generates the following output:

```
[Bob Doe, John Doe, Sally Doe]
false
```

This output shows that only one "John Doe" Employee object is stored in the sorted set. After all, a set cannot contain duplicate elements. However, the `false` value (resulting from the `equals()` comparison) also shows that the sorted set's natural ordering is inconsistent with `equals()`, which violates SortedSet's contract:

The ordering maintained by a sorted set (whether or not an explicit comparator is provided) must be consistent with equals() if the sorted set is to correctly implement the Set interface. This is so because the Set interface is defined in terms of the equals() operation, but a sorted set performs all element comparisons using its compareTo() (or compare()) method, so two elements that are deemed equal by this method are, from the standpoint of the sorted set, equal.

Because the application works correctly, why should SortedSet's contract matter? Although the contract does not appear to matter with respect to the TreeSet implementation of SortedSet, perhaps it will matter in the context of a third-party class that implements this interface.

Listing 8–17 shows you how to correct this problem and make Employee instances work with any implementation of a sorted set.

Listing 8–17. *A contract-compliant Employee class*

```java
class Employee implements Comparable<Employee>
{
    private String name;
    Employee(String name)
    {
        this.name = name;
    }
    @Override
    public int compareTo(Employee e)
    {
        return name.compareTo(e.name);
    }
    @Override
    public boolean equals(Object o)
    {
        if (!(o instanceof Employee))
            return false;
        Employee e = (Employee) o;
        return e.name.equals(name);
    }
    @Override
    public String toString()
    {
```

```
        return name;
    }
}
```

Listing 8–17 corrects the SortedSet contract violation by overriding equals(). If you replace Listing 8–16's Employee class with Listing 8–17, and run the resulting application, you will observe [Bob Doe, John Doe, Sally Doe] as the first line of output and true as the second line: the sorted set's natural ordering is now consistent with equals().

> **NOTE:** Although it is important to override hashCode() whenever you override equals(), I did not override hashCode() (although I overrode equals()) in Listing 8–17's Employee class to emphasize that tree-based sorted sets ignore hashCode().

Queue

A *queue* is a collection in which elements are stored and retrieved in a specific order. Most queues are categorized as one of the following:

- *First-in, first-out (FIFO) queue*: Elements are inserted at the queue's *tail* and removed at the queue's *head*.

- *Last-in, first-out (LIFO) queue*: Elements are inserted and removed at one end of the queue such that the last element inserted is the first element retrieved. This kind of queue behaves as a *stack*.

- *Priority queue*: Elements are inserted according to their natural ordering, or according to a comparator that is supplied to the queue implementation.

Queue, whose generic type is Queue<E>, extends Collection, redeclaring add() to adjust its contract (insert the specified element into this queue if it is possible to do so immediately without violating capacity restrictions), and inheriting the other methods from Collection. Table 8–4 describes add() and the other Queue-specific methods.

Table 8–4. *Queue-specific Methods*

Method	Description
boolean add(E e)	Insert element e into this queue if it is possible to do so immediately without violating capacity restrictions. Return true on success; otherwise, throw IllegalStateException when the element cannot be added at this time because of a capacity restriction. This method also throws ClassCastException when e's class prevents e from being added to this queue, NullPointerException when e contains the null reference and this queue does not permit null elements to be added, and IllegalArgumentException when some property of e prevents it from being added to this queue.

Method	Description
E element()	Return but do not also remove the element at the head of this queue. This method throws NoSuchElementException when this queue is empty.
boolean offer(E e)	Insert element e into this queue if it is possible to do so immediately without violating capacity restrictions. Return true on success; otherwise, return false when the element cannot be added at this time because of a capacity restriction. This method throws ClassCastException when e's class prevents e from being added to this queue, NullPointerException when e contains the null reference and this queue does not permit null elements to be added, and IllegalArgumentException when some property of e prevents it from being added to this queue.
E peek()	Return but do not also remove the element at the head of this queue. This method returns null when this queue is empty.
E poll()	Return and also remove the element at the head of this queue. This method returns null when this queue is empty.
E remove()	Return and also remove the element at the head of this queue. This method throws NoSuchElementException when this queue is empty. This is the only difference between remove() and poll().

Table 8–4 reveals two sets of methods: in one set, a method (such as add()) throws an exception when an operation fails; in the other set, a method (such as offer()) returns a special value (false or null) in the presence of failure. The methods that return a special value are useful in the context of capacity-restricted Queue implementations where failure is a normal occurrence.

Note: The offer() method is generally preferable to add() when using a capacity-restricted queue because offer() does not throw IllegalStateException.

Java supplies many Queue implementation classes, where most of these classes are members of the java.util.concurrent package: LinkedBlockingQueue and SynchronousQueue are examples. In contrast, the java.util package provides LinkedList and PriorityQueue as its Queue implementation classes.

CAUTION: Many Queue implementation classes do not allow null elements to be added. However, some classes (such as LinkedList) permit null elements. You should avoid adding a null element because null is used as a special return value by the peek() and poll() methods to indicate that a queue is empty.

PriorityQueue

The PriorityQueue class provides an implementation of a *priority queue*, which is a queue that orders its elements according to their natural ordering or by a comparator provided when the queue is instantiated. Priority queues do not permit null elements, and do not permit insertion of non-Comparable objects when relying on natural ordering.

The element at the head of the priority queue is the least element with respect to the specified ordering. If multiple elements are tied for least element, one of those elements is arbitrarily chosen as the least element. Similarly, the element at the tail of the priority queue is the greatest element, which is arbitrarily chosen when there is a tie.

Priority queues are unbounded, but have a capacity that governs the size of the internal array that is used to store the priority queue's elements. The capacity value is at least as large as the queue's length, and grows automatically as elements are added to the priority queue.

PriorityQueue (whose generic type is PriorityQueue<E>) supplies six constructors:

- ▧ PriorityQueue() creates a PriorityQueue instance with an initial capacity of 11 elements, and which orders its elements according to their natural ordering.

- ▧ PriorityQueue(Collection<? extends E> collection) creates a PriorityQueue instance containing collection's elements. If collection is a SortedSet or PriorityQueue instance, this priority queue will be ordered according to the same ordering. Otherwise, this priority queue will be ordered according to the natural ordering of its elements. This constructor throws ClassCastException when collection's elements cannot be compared to one another according to the priority queue's ordering, and NullPointerException when collection or any of its elements contain the null reference.

- ▧ PriorityQueue(int initialCapacity) creates a PriorityQueue instance with the specified initialCapacity, and which orders its elements according to their natural ordering. This constructor throws IllegalArgumentException when initialCapacity is less than 1.

- ▧ PriorityQueue(int initialCapacity, Comparator<? super E> comparator) creates a PriorityQueue instance with the specified initialCapacity, and which orders its elements according to the specified comparator. Natural ordering is used when comparator contains the null reference. This constructor throws IllegalArgumentException when initialCapacity is less than 1.

- PriorityQueue(PriorityQueue<? extends E> priorityQueue) creates a PriorityQueue instance containing priorityQueue's elements. This priority queue will be ordered according to the same ordering as priorityQueue. This constructor throws ClassCastException when priorityQueue's elements cannot be compared to one another according to priorityQueue's ordering, and NullPointerException when priorityQueue or any of its elements contains the null reference.

- PriorityQueue(SortedSet<? extends E> sortedSet) creates a PriorityQueue instance containing sortedSet's elements. This priority queue will be ordered according to the same ordering as sortedSet. This constructor throws ClassCastException when sortedSet's elements cannot be compared to one another according to sortedSet's ordering, and NullPointerException when sortedSet or any of its elements contains the null reference.

Listing 8–18 demonstrates a priority queue.

Listing 8–18. *Adding randomly generated integers to a priority queue*

```
import java.util.PriorityQueue;
import java.util.Queue;

public class PriorityQueueDemo
{
   public static void main(String[] args)
   {
      Queue<Integer> qi = new PriorityQueue<Integer>();
      for (int i = 0; i < 15; i++)
         qi.add((int) (Math.random()*100));
      while (!qi.isEmpty())
         System.out.print(qi.poll() + " ");
      System.out.println();
   }
}
```

After creating a priority queue, the main thread adds 15 randomly generated integers (ranging from 0 through 99) to this queue. It then enters a while loop that repeatedly polls the priority queue for the next element and outputs that element until the queue is empty.

When you run this application, it outputs a line of 15 integers in ascending numerical order from left to right. For example, I observed the following output from one run:

```
5 10 12 13 33 36 40 41 44 55 62 63 64 71 91
```

Because poll() returns null when there are no more elements, I could have coded this loop as follows:

```
Integer i;
while ((i = qi.poll()) != null)
   System.out.print(i + " ");
```

Suppose you want to reverse the order of the previous example's output so that the largest element appears on the left and the smallest element appears on the right. As

Listing 8–19 demonstrates, you can achieve this task by passing a comparator to the appropriate PriorityQueue constructor.

Listing 8–19. *Using a comparator with a priority queue*

```
import java.util.Comparator;
import java.util.PriorityQueue;
import java.util.Queue;

public class PriorityQueueDemo
{
    final static int NELEM = 15;
    public static void main(String[] args)
    {
        Comparator<Integer> cmp;
        cmp = new Comparator<Integer>()
            {
                public int compare(Integer e1, Integer e2)
                {
                    return e2-e1;
                }
            };
        Queue<Integer> qi = new PriorityQueue<Integer>(NELEM, cmp);
        for (int i = 0; i < NELEM; i++)
            qi.add((int) (Math.random()*100));
        while (!qi.isEmpty())
            System.out.print(qi.poll() + " ");
        System.out.println();
    }
}
```

Listing 8–19 is similar to Listing 8–18, but there are some differences. First, I have declared an NELEM constant so that I can easily change both the priority queue's initial capacity and the number of elements inserted into the priority queue by specifying the new value in one place.

Second, Listing 8–19 declares and instantiates an anonymous class that implements Comparator. Its compareTo() method subtracts element e2 from element e1 to achieve descending numerical order. The compiler handles the task of unboxing e2 and e1 by converting e2-e1 to e2.intValue()-e1.intValue().

Finally, Listing 8–19 passes an initial capacity of NELEM elements and the instantiated comparator to the PriorityQueue(int initialCapacity, Comparator<? super E> comparator) constructor. The priority queue will use this comparator to order these elements.

Run this application and you will now see a single output line of 15 integers shown in descending numerical order from left to right. For example, I observed this output line:

91 90 80 72 71 69 67 65 53 38 33 25 8 8 7

Map

A *map* is a group of key/value pairs (also known as *entries*). Because the *key* identifies an entry, a map cannot contain duplicate keys. Furthermore, each key can map to at most one value. Maps are described by the Map interface, which has no parent interface, and whose generic type is Map<K,V> (K is the key's type; V is the value's type).

Table 8–5 describes Map's methods.

Table 8–5. *Map Methods*

Method	Description
void clear()	Remove all elements from this map, leaving it empty. This method throws UnsupportedOperationException when clear() is not supported.
boolean containsKey (Object key)	Return true when this map contains an entry for the specified key; otherwise, return false. This method throws ClassCastException when key is of an inappropriate type for this map, and NullPointerException when key contains the null reference and this map does not permit null keys.
boolean containsValue(Object value)	Return true when this map maps one or more keys to value. This method throws ClassCastException when value is of an inappropriate type for this map, and NullPointerException when value contains the null reference and this map does not permit null values.
Set<Map.Entry<K,V>> entrySet()	Return a Set view of the entries contained in this map. Because the view is backed by this map, changes that are made to the map are reflected in the set and vice versa.
boolean equals(Object o)	Compare o with this map for equality. Return true when o is also a map and the two maps represent the same entries; otherwise, return false.
V get(Object key)	Return the value to which key is mapped, or null when this map contains no entry for key. If this map permits null values, then a return value of null does not necessarily indicate that the map contains no entry for key; it is also possible that the map explicitly maps key to the null reference. The containsKey() method may be used to distinguish between these two cases. This method throws ClassCastException when key is of an inappropriate type for this map, and NullPointerException when key contains the null reference and this map does not permit null keys.

Method	Description
int hashCode()	Return the hash code for this map. A map's hash code is defined to be the sum of the hash codes for the entries in the map's entrySet() view.
boolean isEmpty()	Return true when this map contains no entries; otherwise, return false.
Set<K> keySet()	Return a Set view of the keys contained in this map. Because the view is backed by this map, changes that are made to the map are reflected in the set and vice versa.
V put(K key,V value)	Associate value with key in this map. If the map previously contained an entry for key, the old value is replaced by value. This method returns the previous value associated with key, or null when there was no entry for key. (The null return value can also indicate that the map previously associated the null reference with key, if the implementation supports null values.) This method throws UnsupportedOperationException when put() is not supported, ClassCastException when key's or value's class is not appropriate for this map, IllegalArgumentException when some property of key or value prevents it from being stored in this map, and NullPointerException when key or value contains the null reference and this map does not permit null keys or values.
void putAll(Map<? extends K,? extends V> m)	Copy all of the entries from map m to this map. The effect of this call is equivalent to that of calling put(k, v) on this map once for each mapping from key k to value v in map m. This method throws UnsupportedOperationException when putAll() is not supported, ClassCastException when the class of a key or value in map m is not appropriate for this map, IllegalArgumentException when some property of a key or value in map m prevents it from being stored in this map, and NullPointerException when m contains the null reference or when m contains null keys or values and this map does not permit null keys or values.
V remove(Object key)	Remove key's entry from this map if it is present. This method returns the value to which this map previously associated with key, or null when the map contained no mapping for key. If this map permits null values, then a return value of null does not necessarily indicate that the map contained no entry for key; it is also possible that the map explicitly mapped key to null. This map will not contain an entry for key once the call returns. This method throws UnsupportedOperationException when remove() is not supported, ClassCastException when the class of key is not appropriate for this map, and NullPointerException when key contains the null reference and this map does not permit null keys.

Method	Description
`int size()`	Return the number of key/value entries in this map. If the map contains more than `Integer.MAX_VALUE` entries, this method returns `Integer.MAX_VALUE`.
`Collection<V> values()`	Return a `Collection` view of the values contained in this map. Because the view is backed by this map, changes that are made to the map are reflected in the collection and vice versa.

Unlike `List`, `Set`, and `Queue`, `Map` does not extend `Collection`. However, it is possible to view a map as a `Collection` instance by calling `Map`'s `keySet()`, `values()`, and `entrySet()` methods, which respectively return a `Set` of keys, a `Collection` of values, and a `Set` of key/value pair entries.

> **NOTE:** The `values()` method returns `Collection` instead of `Set` because multiple keys can map to the same value, and `values()` would then return multiple copies of the same value.

The `Collection` views returned by these methods (recall that a `Set` is a `Collection` because `Set` extends `Collection`) provide the only means to iterate over a `Map`. For example, suppose you declare Listing 8–20's `Color` enum with its three `Color` constants, RED, GREEN, and BLUE.

Listing 8–20. *A colorful enum*

```
enum Color
{
   RED(255, 0, 0),
   GREEN(0, 255, 0),
   BLUE(0, 0, 255);
   private int r, g, b;
   private Color(int r, int g, int b)
   {
      this.r = r;
      this.g = g;
      this.b = b;
   }
   @Override
   public String toString()
   {
      return "r = " + r + ", g = " + g + ", b = " + b;
   }
}
```

Listing 8–21's code fragment declares a map of `String` keys and `Color` values, adds several entries to the map, and iterates over the keys and values.

Listing 8–21. *Iterating over a map's `String`-based keys and `Color`-based values*

```
Map<String, Color> colorMap = …; // … represents the creation of a Map implementation
colorMap.put("red", Color.RED);
colorMap.put("blue", Color.BLUE);
```

```
colorMap.put("green", Color.GREEN);
colorMap.put("RED", Color.RED);
for (String colorKey: colorMap.keySet())
    System.out.println(colorKey);
Collection<Color> colorValues = colorMap.values();
for (Iterator<Color> it = colorValues.iterator(); it.hasNext();)
    System.out.println(it.next());
```

When running this code fragment against a hashmap implementation (discussed later) of colorMap, you should observe output similar to the following:

```
red
blue
green
RED
r = 255, g = 0, b = 0
r = 0, g = 0, b = 255
r = 0, g = 255, b = 0
r = 255, g = 0, b = 0
```

The first four output lines identify the map's keys; the second four output lines identify the map's values.

The entrySet() method returns a Set of Map.Entry objects. Each of these objects describes a single entry as a key/value pair and is an instance of a class that implements the Map.Entry interface, where Entry is a nested interface of Map. Table 8–6 describes Map.Entry's methods.

> **NOTE:** In Chapter 4, I mentioned that there does not appear to be a good reason to declare interfaces and classes in an interface's body. Although I have yet to find a good reason to nest a class within an interface, Map.Entry proves that it is occasionally useful to nest an interface within another interface.

Table 8–6. *Map.Entry Methods*

Method	Description
boolean equals(Object o)	Compare o with this entry for equality. Return true when o is also a map entry and the two entries have the same key and value.
K getKey()	Return this entry's key. This method optionally throws IllegalStateException when this entry has previously been removed from the backing map.
V getValue()	Return this entry's value. This method optionally throws IllegalStateException when this entry has previously been removed from the backing map.
int hashCode()	Return this entry's hash code.

Method	Description
V setValue(V value)	Replace this entry's value with value. The backing map is updated with the new value. This method throws UnsupportedOperationException when setValue() is not supported, ClassCastException when value's class prevents it from being stored in the backing map, NullPointerException when value contains the null reference and the backing map does not permit null, IllegalArgumentException when some property of value prevents it from being stored in the backing map, and (optionally) IllegalStateException when this entry has previously been removed from the backing map.

Continuing from the previous example, Listing 8–22 shows you how you might iterate over the map's entries.

Listing 8–22. *Iterating over a map's entries*

```
for (Map.Entry<String, Color> colorEntry: colorMap.entrySet())
    System.out.println(colorEntry.getKey() + ": " + colorEntry.getValue());
```

When running Listing 8–22's code fragment against the previously mentioned hashmap implementation, you would observe the following output:

```
red: r = 255, g = 0, b = 0
blue: r = 0, g = 0, b = 255
green: r = 0, g = 255, b = 0
RED: r = 255, g = 0, b = 0
```

TreeMap

The TreeMap class provides a map implementation that is based on a red-black tree. As a result, entries are stored in sorted order of their keys. However, accessing these entries is somewhat slower than with the other Map implementations (which are not sorted) because links must be traversed.

> **NOTE:** Check out Wikipedia's "Red-black tree" entry (http://en.wikipedia.org/wiki/Red-black_tree) to learn about red-black trees.

TreeMap supplies four constructors:

- TreeMap() creates a new, empty tree map that is sorted according to the natural ordering of its keys. All keys inserted into the map must implement the Comparable interface.

- TreeMap(Comparator<? super K> comparator) creates a new, empty tree map that is sorted according to the specified comparator. Passing null to comparator implies that natural ordering will be used.

■ TreeMap(Map<? extends K, ? extends V> map) creates a new tree map containing map's entries, sorted according to the natural ordering of its keys. All keys inserted into the new map must implement the Comparable interface. This constructor throws ClassCastException when map's keys do not implement Comparable or are not mutually comparable, and NullPointerException when map contains the null reference.

■ TreeMap(SortedMap<K, ? extends V> sortedMap) creates a new tree map containing the same entries and using the same ordering as sortedMap. (I discuss sorted maps later in this chapter.) This constructor throws NullPointerException when sortedMap contains the null reference.

Listing 8–23 demonstrates a tree map.

Listing 8–23. *Sorting a map's entries according to the natural ordering of their* String*-based keys*

```
import java.util.Map;
import java.util.TreeMap;

public class TreeMapDemo
{
   public static void main(String[] args)
   {
      Map<String, Integer> msi = new TreeMap<String, Integer>();
      String[] fruits = {"apples", "pears", "grapes", "bananas", "kiwis"};
      int[] quantities = {10, 15, 8, 17, 30};
      for (int i = 0; i < fruits.length; i++)
         msi.put(fruits[i], quantities[i]);
      for (Map.Entry<String, Integer> entry: msi.entrySet())
         System.out.println(entry.getKey() + ": " + entry.getValue());
   }
}
```

When you run this application, it generates the following output:

```
apples: 10
bananas: 17
grapes: 8
kiwis: 30
pears: 15
```

HashMap

The HashMap class provides a map implementation that is based on a hashtable data structure. This implementation supports all Map operations, and permits null keys and null values. It makes no guarantees on the order in which entries are stored.

A hashtable maps keys to integer values with the help of a *hash function*. Java provides this function in the form of Object's hashCode() method, which classes override to provide appropriate hash codes.

A *hash code* identifies one of the hashtable's array elements, which is known as a *bucket* or *slot*. For some hashtables, the bucket may store the value that is associated with the key. Figure 8–2 illustrates this kind of hashtable.

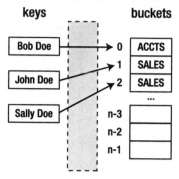

hash function

Figure 8–2. *A simple hashtable of buckets*

The hash function hashes Bob Doe to 0, which identifies the first bucket. This bucket contains ACCTS, which is Bob Doe's employee type. The hash function also hashes John Doe and Sally Doe to 1 and 2 (respectively) whose buckets contain SALES.

A perfect hash function hashes each key to a unique integer value. However, this ideal is very difficult to meet. In practice, some keys will hash to the same integer value. This nonunique mapping is referred to as a *collision*.

To address collisions, most hashtables associate a linked list of entries with a bucket. Instead of containing a value, the bucket contains the address of the first node in the linked list, and each node contains one of the colliding entries. See Figure 8–3.

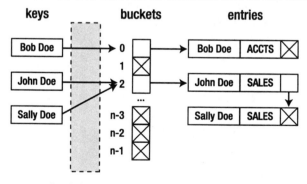

hash function

Figure 8–3. *A complex hashtable of buckets and linked lists (X indicates a null reference)*

When storing a value in a hashtable, the hashtable uses the hash function to hash the key to its hash code, and then searches the appropriate linked list to see if an entry with a matching key exists. If there is an entry, its value is updated with the new value.

Otherwise, a new node is created, populated with the key and value, and appended to the list.

When retrieving a value from a hashtable, the hashtable uses the hash function to hash the key to its hash code, and then searches the appropriate linked list to see if an entry with a matching key exists. If there is an entry, its value is returned. Otherwise, the hashtable may return a special value to indicate that there is no entry, or it might throw an exception.

The number of buckets is known as the hashtable's *capacity*. The ratio of the number of stored entries divided by the number of buckets is known as the hashtable's *load factor*. Choosing the right load factor is important for balancing performance with memory use:

- As the load factor approaches 1, the probability of collisions and the cost of handling them (by searching lengthy linked lists) increase.

- As the load factor approaches 0, the hashtable's size in terms of number of buckets increases with little improvement in search cost.

- For many hashtables, a load factor of 0.75 is close to optimal. This value is the default for HashMap's hashtable implementation.

HashMap supplies four constructors:

- HashMap() creates a new, empty hashmap with an initial capacity of 16 and a load factor of 0.75.

- HashMap(int initialCapacity) creates a new, empty hashmap with a capacity specified by initialCapacity and a load factor of 0.75. This constructor throws IllegalArgumentException when initialCapacity's value is less than 0.

- HashMap(int initialCapacity, float loadFactor) creates a new, empty hashmap with a capacity specified by initialCapacity and a load factor specified by loadFactor. This constructor throws IllegalArgumentException when initialCapacity is less than 0 or when loadFactor is less than or equal to 0.

- HashMap(Map<? extends K, ? extends V> map) creates a new hashmap containing map's entries. This constructor throws NullPointerException when map contains the null reference.

Listing 8–24 demonstrates a hashmap.

Listing 8–24. *Using a hashmap to count command-line arguments*

```java
import java.util.HashMap;
import java.util.Map;

public class HashMapDemo
{
   public static void main(String[] args)
   {
      Map<String, Integer> argMap = new HashMap<String, Integer>();
      for (String arg: args)
```

```
    {
        Integer count = argMap.get(arg);
        argMap.put(arg, (count == null) ? 1 : count+1);
    }
    System.out.println(argMap);
    System.out.println("Number of distinct arguments = " + argMap.size());
    }
}
```

HashMapDemo creates a hashmap of String keys and Integer values. Each key is one of the command-line arguments passed to this application, and its value is the number of occurrences of that argument on the command line.

For example, java HashMapDemo how much wood could a woodchuck chuck if a woodchuck could chuck wood generates the following output:

```
{wood=2, could=2, how=1, if=1, chuck=2, a=2, woodchuck=2, much=1}
Number of distinct arguments = 8
```

Because the String class overrides equals() and hashCode(), Listing 8–24 can use String objects as keys in a hashmap. When you create a class whose instances are to be used as keys, you must ensure that you override both methods.

Listing 8–10 showed you that a class's overriding hashCode() method can call a reference field's hashCode() method and return its value, provided that the class declares a single reference field (and no primitive type fields).

More commonly, classes declare multiple fields, and a better implementation of the hashCode() method is required. The implementation should try to generate hash codes that minimize collisions.

There is no rule on how to best implement hashCode(), and various *algorithms* (recipes for accomplishing tasks) have been created. My favorite algorithm appears in *Effective Java, Second Edition*, by Joshua Bloch (Addison-Wesley, 2008; ISBN: 0321356683).

The following algorithm, which assumes the existence of an arbitrary class that is referred to as *X*, closely follows Bloch's algorithm, but is not identical:

1. Initialize int variable hashCode (the name is arbitrary) to an arbitrary nonzero integer value, such as 19. This variable is initialized to a nonzero value to ensure that it takes into account any initial fields whose hash codes are zeros. If you initialize hashCode to 0, the final hash code will be unaffected by such fields and you run the risk of increased collisions.

2. For each field f that is also used in *X*'s equals() method, calculate f's hash code and assign it to int variable hc as follows:

    a. If f is of Boolean type, calculate hc = f?1:0.

    b. If f is of byte integer, character, integer, or short integer type, calculate hc = (int) f. The integer value is the hash code.

c. If f is of long integer type, calculate hc = (int) (f^(f>>>32)). This expression exclusive ORs the long integer's least significant 32 bits with its most significant 32 bits.

d. If f is of type floating-point, calculate hc = Float.floatToIntBits(f). This method takes +infinity, -infinity, and NaN into account.

e. If f is of type double precision floating-point, calculate long l = Double.doubleToLongBits(f); hc = (int) (l^(l>>>32)).

f. If f is a reference field with a null reference, calculate hc = 0.

g. If f is a reference field with a nonnull reference, and if X's equals() method compares the field by recursively calling equals() (as in Listing 8–17's Employee class), calculate hc = f.hashCode(). However, if equals() employs a more complex comparison, create a *canonical* (simplest possible) representation of the field and call hashCode() on this representation.

h. If f is an array, treat each element as a separate field by applying this algorithm recursively and combining the hc values as shown in the next step.

3. Combine hc with hashCode as follows: hashCode = hashCode*31+hc. Multiplying hashCode by 31 makes the resulting hash value dependent on the order in which fields appear in the class, which improves the hash value when a class contains multiple fields that are similar (several ints, for example). I chose 31 to be consistent with the String class's hashCode() method.

4. Return hashCode from hashCode().

> **TIP:** Instead of using this or another algorithm to create a hash code, you might find it easier to work with the HashCodeBuilder class (see http://commons.apache.org/lang/api-2.4/org/apache/commons/lang/builder/HashCodeBuilder.html for an explanation of this class). This class, which follows Bloch's rules, is part of the Apache Commons Lang component, which you can download from http://commons.apache.org/lang/.

In Chapter 3, Listing 3-9's Point class overrides equals() but does not override hashCode(). Listing 3-11 presents a small code fragment that must be appended to Point's main() method to demonstrate the problem of not overriding hashCode(). I restate this problem here:

Although objects p1 and Point(10, 20) are logically equivalent, these objects have different hash codes, resulting in each object referring to a different entry in the hashmap. If an object is not stored (via put()) in that entry, get() returns null.

Listing 8–25 modifies Listing 3-9's Point class by declaring a hashCode() method. This method uses the aforementioned algorithm to ensure that logically equivalent Point objects hash to the same entry.

Listing 8–25. *Overriding hashCode() to return proper hash codes for Point objects*

```java
import java.util.HashMap;
import java.util.Map;

class Point
{
   private int x, y;
   Point(int x, int y)
   {
      this.x = x;
      this.y = y;
   }
   int getX()
   {
      return x;
   }
   int getY()
   {
      return y;
   }
   @Override
   public boolean equals(Object o)
   {
      if (!(o instanceof Point))
         return false;
      Point p = (Point) o;
      return p.x == x && p.y == y;
   }
   @Override
   public int hashCode()
   {
      int hashCode = 19;
      int hc = x;
      hashCode = hashCode*31+hc;
      hc = y;
      hashCode = hashCode*31+hc;
      return hc;
   }
   public static void main(String[] args)
   {
      Point p1 = new Point(10, 20);
      Point p2 = new Point(20, 30);
      Point p3 = new Point(10, 20);
      // Test reflexivity
      System.out.println(p1.equals(p1)); // Output: true
      // Test symmetry
      System.out.println(p1.equals(p2)); // Output: false
      System.out.println(p2.equals(p1)); // Output: false
      // Test transitivity
      System.out.println(p2.equals(p3)); // Output: false
      System.out.println(p1.equals(p3)); // Output: true
      // Test nullability
```

```
        System.out.println(p1.equals(null)); // Output: false
        // Extra test to further prove the instanceof operator's usefulness.
        System.out.println(p1.equals("abc")); // Output: false
        Map<Point, String> map = new HashMap<Point, String>();
        map.put(p1, "first point");
        System.out.println(map.get(p1)); // Output: first point
        System.out.println(map.get(new Point(10, 20))); // Output: null
    }
}
```

The hashCode() method is a little verbose in that it assigns each of x and y to local variable hc, rather than directly using these fields in the hash code calculation. However, I decided to follow this approach to more closely mirror the hash code algorithm.

When you run this application, its last two lines of output are of the most interest. Instead of presenting first point followed by null on two separate lines, the application now correctly presents first point followed by first point on these lines.

> **NOTE:** LinkedHashMap is a subclass of HashMap that uses a linked list to store its entries. As a result, LinkedHashMap's iterator returns entries in the order in which they were inserted. For example, if Listing 8–24 had specified Map<String, Integer> argMap = new LinkedHashMap<String, Integer>();, the application's output for java HashMapDemo how much wood could a woodchuck chuck if a woodchuck could chuck wood would have been {how=1, much=1, wood=2, could=2, a=2, woodchuck=2, chuck=2, if=1} followed by Number of distinct arguments = 8.

IdentityHashMap

The IdentityHashMap class provides a Map implementation that uses reference equality (==) instead of object equality (equals()) when comparing keys and values. This is an intentional violation of Map's general contract, which mandates the use of equals() when comparing elements.

IdentityHashMap obtains hash codes via System's static int identityHashCode(Object x) method instead of via each key's hashCode() method. identityHashCode() returns the same hash code for x as returned by Object's hashCode() method, whether or not x's class overrides hashCode(). The hash code for the null reference is zero.

These characteristics give IdentityHashMap a performance advantage over other Map implementations. Also, IdentityHashMap supports *mutable keys* (objects used as keys and whose hash codes change when their field values change while in the map). Listing 8–26 contrasts IdentityHashMap with HashMap where mutable keys are concerned.

Listing 8–26. *Contrasting IdentityHashMap with HashMap in a mutable key context*

```
import java.util.IdentityHashMap;
import java.util.HashMap;
import java.util.Map;
```

```java
public class IdentityHashMapDemo
{
   public static void main(String[] args)
   {
      Map<Employee, String> map1 = new IdentityHashMap<Employee, String>();
      Map<Employee, String> map2 = new HashMap<Employee, String>();
      Employee e1 = new Employee("John Doe", 28);
      map1.put(e1, "SALES");
      System.out.println(map1);
      Employee e2 = new Employee("Jane Doe", 26);
      map2.put(e2, "MGMT");
      System.out.println(map2);
      System.out.println("map1 contains key e1 = " + map1.containsKey(e1));
      System.out.println("map2 contains key e2 = " + map2.containsKey(e2));
      e1.setAge(29);
      e2.setAge(27);
      System.out.println(map1);
      System.out.println(map2);
      System.out.println("map1 contains key e1 = " + map1.containsKey(e1));
      System.out.println("map2 contains key e2 = " + map2.containsKey(e2));
   }
}
class Employee
{
   private String name;
   private int age;
   Employee(String name, int age)
   {
      this.name = name;
      this.age = age;
   }
   @Override
   public boolean equals(Object o)
   {
      if (!(o instanceof Employee))
         return false;
      Employee e = (Employee) o;
      return e.name.equals(name) && e.age == age;
   }
   @Override
   public int hashCode()
   {
      int hashCode = 19;
      hashCode = hashCode*31+name.hashCode();
      hashCode = hashCode*31+age;
      return hashCode;
   }
   void setAge(int age)
   {
      this.age = age;
   }
   void setName(String name)
   {
      this.name = name;
   }
   @Override
   public String toString()
```

```
    {
        return name + " " + age;
    }
}
```

Listing 8–26's main() method creates IdentityHashMap and HashMap instances that each store an entry consisting of an Employee key and a String value. Because Employee instances are mutable (because of setAge() and setName()), main() changes their ages while these keys are stored in their maps. These changes result in the following output:

```
{John Doe 28=SALES}
{Jane Doe 26=MGMT}
map1 contains key e1 = true
map2 contains key e2 = true
{John Doe 29=SALES}
{Jane Doe 27=MGMT}
map1 contains key e1 = true
map2 contains key e2 = false
```

The last four lines show that the changed entries remain in their maps. However, map2's containsKey() method reports that its HashMap instance no longer contains its Employee key (which should be Jane Doe 27), whereas map1's containsKey() method reports that its IdentityHashMap instance still contains its Employee key, which is now John Doe 29.

NOTE: IdentityHashMap's documentation states that "a typical use of this class is topology-preserving object graph transformations, such as serialization or deep copying." (I discuss serialization in Chapter 10.) It also states that "another typical use of this class is to maintain proxy objects." Also, developers responding to stackoverflow's "Use Cases for Identity HashMap" topic (http://stackoverflow.com/questions/838528/use-cases-for-identity-hashmap) mention that it is much faster to use IdentityHashMap than HashMap when the keys are Class objects.

WeakHashMap

The WeakHashMap class provides a Map implementation that is based on weakly reachable keys. Because each key object is stored indirectly as the referent of a weak reference, the key is automatically removed from the map only after the garbage collector clears all weak references to the key (inside and outside of the map).

NOTE: Check out Chapter 6's "References API" section to learn about weakly reachable and weak references.

In contrast, value objects are stored via strong references. These objects should not strongly refer to their own keys, either directly or indirectly, because doing so prevents their associated keys from being discarded. When a key is removed from a map, its associated value object is also removed.

Listing 8–27 provides a simple demonstration of the WeakHashMap class.

Listing 8–27. *Automatically removing a* String *value object from a weak hashmap when the strong reference to its associated* LargeObject *key object is nullified*

```
import java.util.Map;
import java.util.WeakHashMap;

class LargeObject
{
    private byte[] memory = new byte[1024*1024*50]; // 50 megabytes
}
public class WeakHashMapDemo
{
    public static void main(String[] args)
    {
        Map<LargeObject, String> map = new WeakHashMap<LargeObject, String>();
        LargeObject lo = new LargeObject();
        map.put(lo, "Large Object");
        System.out.println(map);
        lo = null;
        while (!map.isEmpty())
        {
            System.gc();
            new LargeObject();
        }
        System.out.println(map);
    }
}
```

Listing 8–27's main() method stores a 50MB LargeObject key and a String value in the weak hashmap, and then removes the key's strong reference by assigning null to lo. main() next enters a while loop that executes until the map is empty (map.isEmpty() returns true).

Each loop iteration begins with a System.gc() method call, which may or may not cause a garbage collection to take place (depending upon platform). To encourage a garbage collection, the iteration then creates a LargeObject object and throws away its reference. This activity should eventually cause the garbage collector to run and remove the map's solitary entry.

When I run this application on my Windows XP platform, I observe the following output—you might need to modify the code if you find that the application is in an infinite loop:

```
{LargeObject@addbf1=Large Object}
{}
```

> **NOTE:** WeakHashMap is useful for avoiding memory leaks, as explained in Brian Goetz's article "Java Theory and Practice: Plugging Memory Leaks with Weak References" (http://www.ibm.com/developerworks/java/library/j-jtp11225/).

EnumMap

The EnumMap class provides a Map implementation whose keys are the members of the same enum. Null keys are not permitted; any attempt to store a null key results in a thrown NullPointerException. Because an enum map is represented internally as an array, an enum map approaches an array in terms of performance.

EnumMap supplies the following constructors:

- EnumMap(Class<K> keyType) creates an empty enum map with the specified keyType. This constructor throws NullPointerException when keyType contains the null reference.

- EnumMap(EnumMap<K,? extends V> map) creates an enum map with the same key type as map, and with map's entries. This constructor throws NullPointerException when map contains the null reference.

- EnumMap(Map<K,? extends V> map) creates an enum map initialized with map's entries. If map is an EnumMap instance, this constructor behaves like the previous constructor. Otherwise, map must contain at least one entry in order to determine the new enum map's key type. This constructor throws NullPointerException when map contains the null reference, and IllegalArgumentException when map is not an EnumMap instance and is empty.

Listing 8–28 demonstrates EnumMap.

Listing 8–28. *An enum map of* Coin *constants*

```
import java.util.EnumMap;
import java.util.Map;

enum Coin
{
   PENNY, NICKEL, DIME, QUARTER
}
public class EnumMapDemo
{
   public static void main(String[] args)
   {
      Map<Coin, Integer> map = new EnumMap<Coin, Integer>(Coin.class);
      map.put(Coin.PENNY, 1);
      map.put(Coin.NICKEL, 5);
      map.put(Coin.DIME, 10);
      map.put(Coin.QUARTER, 25);
      System.out.println(map);
      Map<Coin,Integer> mapCopy = new EnumMap<Coin, Integer>(map);
      System.out.println(mapCopy);
   }
}
```

When you run this application, it generates the following output:

```
{PENNY=1, NICKEL=5, DIME=10, QUARTER=25}
{PENNY=1, NICKEL=5, DIME=10, QUARTER=25}
```

SortedMap

TreeMap is an example of a *sorted map*, which is a map that maintains its entries in ascending order, sorted according to the keys' natural ordering or according to a comparator that is supplied when the sorted map is created. Sorted maps are described by the SortedMap interface.

SortedMap, whose generic type is SortedMap<K, V>, extends Map. With two exceptions, the methods it inherits from Map behave identically on sorted maps as on other maps:

- The Iterator instance returned by the iterator() method on any of the sorted map's Collection views traverses the collections in order.

- The arrays returned by the Collection views' toArray() methods contain the keys, values, or entries in order.

> **NOTE:** Although not guaranteed, the toString() methods of the Collection views of SortedSet implementations in the collections framework (such as TreeMap) return a string containing all of the view's elements in order.

SortedMap's documentation requires that an implementation must provide the four standard constructors that I presented in my discussion of TreeMap. Furthermore, implementations of this interface must implement the methods that are described in Table 8–7.

Table 8–7. *SortedMap-specific Methods*

Method	Description
Comparator<? super K> comparator()	Return the comparator used to order the keys in this map, or null when this map uses the natural ordering of its keys.
Set<Map.Entry<K,V>> entrySet()	Return a Set view of the mappings contained in this map. The set's iterator returns these entries in ascending key order. Because the view is backed by this map, changes that are made to the map are reflected in the set and vice versa.
K firstKey()	Return the first (lowest) key currently in this map, or throw a NoSuchElementException instance when this map is empty.
SortedMap<K, V> headMap (K toKey)	Return a view of that portion of this map whose keys are strictly less than toKey. Because the returned map is backed by this map, changes in the returned map are reflected in this map and vice versa. The returned map supports all optional map operations that this map supports. This method throws ClassCastException when toKey is not compatible with this map's comparator (or, when the map has no comparator, when toKey does not implement Comparable), NullPointerException when toKey is null and this map does not permit null keys, and IllegalArgumentException when this map has a restricted range and toKey lies outside of this range's bounds.

Method	Description
Set<K> keySet()	Return a Set view of the keys contained in this map. The set's iterator returns the keys in ascending order. Because the view is backed by this map, changes that are made to the map are reflected in the set and vice versa.
K lastKey()	Return the last (highest) key currently in this map, or throw a NoSuchElementException instance when this map is empty.
SortedMap<K, V> subMap (K fromKey, K toKey)	Return a view of the portion of this map whose keys range from fromKey, inclusive, to toKey, exclusive. (When fromKey and toKey are equal, the returned map is empty.) Because the returned map is backed by this map, changes in the returned map are reflected in this map and vice versa. The returned map supports all optional map operations that this map supports. This method throws ClassCastException when fromKey and toKey cannot be compared to one another using this map's comparator (or, when the map has no comparator, using natural ordering), NullPointerException when fromKey or toKey is null and this map does not permit null keys, and IllegalArgumentException when fromKey is greater than toKey or when this map has a restricted range and fromKey or toKey lies outside of this range's bounds.
SortedMap<K, V> tailMap (K fromKey)	Return a view of that portion of this map whose keys are greater than or equal to fromKey. Because the returned map is backed by this map, changes in the returned map are reflected in this map and vice versa. The returned map supports all optional map operations that this map supports. This method throws ClassCastException when fromKey is not compatible with this map's comparator (or, when the map has no comparator, when fromKey does not implement Comparable), NullPointerException when fromKey is null and this map does not permit null elements, and IllegalArgumentException when this map has a restricted range and fromKey lies outside of the range's bounds.
Collection<V> values()	Return a Collection view of the values contained in this map. The collection's iterator returns the values in ascending order of the corresponding keys. Because the collection is backed by the map, changes that are made to the map are reflected in the collection and vice versa.

Listing 8–29 demonstrates a sorted map based on a tree map.

Listing 8–29. *A sorted map of office supply names and quantities*

```
import java.util.Comparator;
import java.util.SortedMap;
import java.util.TreeMap;

public class SortedMapDemo
```

```
{
    public static void main(String[] args)
    {
        SortedMap<String, Integer> smsi = new TreeMap<String, Integer>();
        String[] officeSupplies =
        {
            "pen", "pencil", "legal pad", "CD", "paper"
        };
        int[] quantities =
        {
            20, 30, 5, 10, 20
        };
        for (int i = 0; i < officeSupplies.length; i++)
            smsi.put(officeSupplies[i], quantities[i]);
        System.out.println(smsi);
        System.out.println(smsi.headMap("pencil"));
        System.out.println(smsi.headMap("paper"));
        SortedMap<String, Integer> smsiCopy;
        Comparator<String> cmp;
        cmp = new Comparator<String>()
                {
                    public int compare(String key1, String key2)
                    {
                        return key2.compareTo(key1); // descending order
                    }
                };
        smsiCopy = new TreeMap<String, Integer>(cmp);
        smsiCopy.putAll(smsi);
        System.out.println(smsiCopy);
    }
}
```

When you run this application, it generates the following output:

```
{CD=10, legal pad=5, paper=20, pen=20, pencil=30}
{CD=10, legal pad=5, paper=20, pen=20}
{CD=10, legal pad=5}
{pencil=30, pen=20, paper=20, legal pad=5, CD=10}
```

Utilities

The collections framework would not be complete without its Arrays and Collections utility classes. Each class supplies various utility (static) methods that implement useful algorithms in the contexts of arrays and collections.

Following is a sampling of the Arrays class's array-oriented utility methods:

- static <T> List<T> asList(T... array) returns a fixed-size list backed by the specified array. (Changes to the returned list "write through" to the array.) For example, List<String> birds = Arrays.asList("Robin", "Oriole", "Bluejay"); converts the three-element array of Strings (recall that a variable sequence of arguments is implemented as an array) to a List whose reference is assigned to birds.

- `static int binarySearch(int[] array, int key)` searches array for entry key using the binary search algorithm (explained following this list). The array must be sorted before calling this method; otherwise, the results are undefined. This method returns the index of the search key, if it is contained in the array; otherwise, (-(insertion point) - 1) is returned. The insertion point is the point at which key would be inserted into the array (the index of the first element greater than key, or array.length if all elements in the array are less than key) and guarantees that the return value will be greater than or equal to 0 if and only if key is found. For example, `Arrays.binarySearch(new String[] {"Robin", "Oriole", "Bluejay"}, "Oriole")` returns 1, "Oriole"'s index.

- `static void fill(char[] array, char character)` stores character in each element of the specified character array. For example, `Arrays.fill(screen[i], ' ');` fills the ith row of a 2D screen array with spaces.

- `static void sort(long[] array)` sorts the elements in the long integer array into ascending numerical order; for example, `long lArray = new long[] { 20000L, 89L, 66L, 33L}; Arrays.sort(lArray);`.

- `static <T> void sort(T[] array, Comparator<? super T> comparator)` sorts the elements in array using comparator to order them. For example, when given `Comparator<String> cmp = new Comparator<String>() { public int compare(String e1, String e2) { return e2.compareTo(e1); } }; String[] innerPlanets = { "Mercury", "Venus", "Earth", "Mars" };,` `Arrays.sort(innerPlanets, cmp);` uses cmp to help in sorting innerPlanets into descending order of its elements: Venus, Mercury, Mars, Earth is the result.

There are two common algorithms for searching an array for a specific element. *Linear search* searches the array element by element from index 0 to the index of the searched for element or the end of the array. On average, half of the elements must be searched; larger arrays take longer to search. However, the arrays do not need to be sorted.

In contrast, *binary search* searches ordered array a's n items for element e in a much faster amount of time. It works by recursively performing the following steps:

1. Set low index to 0.

2. Set high index to n-1.

3. If low index > high index, then Print "Unable to find " e. End.

4. Set middle index to (low index+high index)/2.

5. If $e > a$[middle index], then set low index to middle index+1. Go to 3.

6. If $e < a$[middle index], then set high index to middle index-1. Go to 3.

7. Print "Found " *e* "at index " middle index.

The algorithm is similar to optimally looking for a name in a phone book. Start by opening the book to the exact middle. If the name is not on that page, proceed to open the book to the exact middle of the first half or the second half, depending on in which half the name occurs. Repeat until you find the name (or not).

Applying a linear search to 4,000,000,000 elements results in approximately 2,000,000,000 comparisons (on average), which takes time. In contrast, applying a binary search to 4,000,000,000 elements results in a maximum of 32 comparisons. This is why `Arrays` contains `binarySearch()` methods and not also `linearSearch()` methods.

Following is a sampling of the `Collections` class's collection-oriented utility methods:

- `static <T extends Object & Comparable<? super T>> T min(Collection<? extends T> collection)` returns the minimum element of collection `collection` according to the natural ordering of its elements. For example, `System.out.println(Collections.min(Arrays.asList(10, 3, 18, 25)));` outputs 3. All of collection's elements must implement the `Comparable` interface. Furthermore, all elements must be mutually comparable. This method throws `NoSuchElementException` when `collection` is empty.

- `static void reverse(List<?> list)` reverses the order of list's elements. For example, `List<String> birds = Arrays.asList("Robin", "Oriole", "Bluejay"); Collections.reverse(birds); System.out.println(birds);` results in `[Bluejay, Oriole, Robin]` as the output.

- `static <T> List<T> singletonList(T o)` returns an immutable list containing only object o. For example, `list.removeAll(Collections.singletonList(null));` removes all null elements from `list`.

- `static <T> Set<T> synchronizedSet(Set<T> set)` returns a synchronized (thread-safe) set backed by the specified set; for example, `Set<String> ss = Collections.synchronizedSet(new HashSet<String>());`. In order to guarantee serial access, it is critical that all access to the backing set is accomplished through the returned set.

- `static <K,V> Map<K,V> unmodifiableMap(Map<? extends K,? extends V> map)` returns an unmodifiable view of the specified map; for example, `Map<String, Integer> msi = Collections.synchronizedMap(new HashMap<String, Integer>());`. Query operations on the returned map "read through" to the specified map, and attempts to modify the returned map, whether direct or via its collection views, result in an `UnsupportedOperationException`.

NOTE: For performance reasons, collections implementations are unsynchronized—unsynchronized collections have better performance than synchronized collections. To use a collection in a multithreaded context, however, you need to obtain a synchronized version of that collection. You obtain that version by calling a method such as `synchronizedSet()`.

Classic Collections Classes

Java version 1.2 introduced the collections framework. Prior to the framework's inclusion in Java, developers had two choices where collections were concerned: create their own frameworks, or use the `Vector`, `Enumeration`, `Stack`, `Dictionary`, `Hashtable`, `Properties`, and `BitSet` types, which were introduced by Java version 1.0.

`Vector` is a concrete class that describes a growable array, much like `ArrayList`. Unlike an `ArrayList` instance, a `Vector` instance is synchronized. `Vector` has been generified and also retrofitted to support the collections framework, which makes statements such as `List<String> list = new Vector<String>();` legal.

The collections framework provides `Iterator` for iterating over a collection's elements. In contrast, `Vector`'s `elements()` method returns an instance of a class that implements the `Enumeration` interface for *enumerating* (iterating over and returning) a `Vector` instance's elements via `Enumeration`'s `hasMoreElements()` and `nextElement()` methods.

`Vector` is subclassed by the concrete `Stack` class, which represents a LIFO data structure. `Stack` provides an `E push(E item)` method for pushing an object onto the stack, an `E pop()` method for popping an item off the top of the stack, and a few other methods, such as `boolean empty()` for determining whether or not the stack is empty.

`Stack` is a good example of bad API design. By inheriting from `Vector`, it is possible to call `Vector`'s `void add(int index, E element)` method to add an element anywhere you wish, and violate a `Stack` instance's integrity. In hindsight, `Stack` should have used composition in its design: use a `Vector` instance to store a `Stack` instance's elements.

`Dictionary` is an abstract superclass for subclasses that map keys to values. The concrete `Hashtable` class is `Dictionary`'s only subclass. As with `Vector`, `HashTable` instances are synchronized, `HashTable` has been generified, and `HashTable` has been retrofitted to support the collections framework.

`Hashtable` is subclassed by `Properties`, a concrete class representing a persistent set of *properties* (String-based key/value pairs that identify application settings). `Properties` provides `Object setProperty(String key, String value)` for storing a property, and `public String getProperty(String key)` for returning a property's value.

> **NOTE:** Applications use properties for various purposes. For example, if your application has a graphical user interface, you might persist its main window's screen location and size to a file via a `Properties` object so that the application can restore the window's location and size when it next runs.

`Properties` is another good example of bad API design. By inheriting from `Hashtable`, you can call `Hashtable`'s `V put(K key, V value)` method to store an entry with a non-`String` key and/or a non-`String` value. In hindsight, `Properties` should have leveraged composition: store a `Properties` instance's elements in a `Hashtable` instance.

> **NOTE:** Chapter 3 discusses wrapper classes, which is how `Stack` and `Properties` should have been implemented.

Finally, `BitSet` is a concrete class that describes a variable-length set of bits. This class's ability to represent bitsets of arbitrary length contrasts with the previously described integer-based, fixed-length bitset that is limited to a maximum number of members: 32 members for an `int`-based bitset, or 64 members for a `long`-based bitset.

`BitSet` provides a pair of constructors for initializing a `BitSet` instance: `BitSet()` initializes the instance to initially store an implementation-dependent number of bits, whereas `BitSet(int nbits)` initializes the instance to initially store `nbits` bits. `BitSet` also provides various methods, including the following:

- ▓ `void and(BitSet bs)` bitwise ANDs this bitset with `bs`. This bitset is modified such that a bit is set to 1 when it and the bit at the same position in `bs` are 1.

- ▓ `void andNot(BitSet bs)` sets all of the bits in this bitset to 0 whose corresponding bits are set to 1 in `bs`.

- ▓ `void clear()` sets all of the bits in this bitset to 0.

- ▓ `Object clone()` clones this bitset to produce a new bitset. The clone has exactly the same bits set to one as this bitset.

- ▓ `boolean get(int bitIndex)` returns the value of this bitset's bit, as a Boolean true/false value (true for 1, false for 0) at the zero-based `bitIndex`. This method throws `IndexOutOfBoundsException` when `bitIndex` is less than 0.

- ▓ `int length()` returns the "logical size" of this bitset, which is the index of the highest 1 bit plus 1, or 0 if this bitset contains no 1 bits.

- ▓ `void or(BitSet bs)` bitwise inclusive ORs this bitset with `bs`. This bitset is modified such that a bit is set to 1 when it or the bit at the same position in `bs` is 1, or when both bits are 1.

- void set(int bitIndex, boolean value) sets the bit at the zero-based bitIndex to value (true is converted to 1; false is converted to 0). This method throws IndexOutOfBoundsException when bitIndex is less than 0.

- int size() returns the number of bits that are being used by this bitset to represent bit values.

- String toString() returns a string representation of this bitset in terms of the positions of bits that are 1; for example, {4, 5, 9, 10}.

- void xor(BitSet set) bitwise exclusive ORs this bitset with bs. This bitset is modified such that a bit is set to 1 when either it or the bit at the same position in bs (but not both) is 1.

Listing 8–30 presents an application that demonstrates some of these methods, and gives you more insight into how the bitwise AND (&), bitwise inclusive OR (|), and bitwise exclusive OR (^) operators work.

Listing 8–30. *Working with variable-length bitsets*

```
import java.util.BitSet;

public class BitSetDemo
{
   public static void main(String[] args)
   {
      BitSet bs1 = new BitSet();
      bs1.set(4, true);
      bs1.set(5, true);
      bs1.set(9, true);
      bs1.set(10, true);
      BitSet bsTemp = (BitSet) bs1.clone();
      dumpBitset("          ", bs1);
      BitSet bs2 = new BitSet();
      bs2.set(4, true);
      bs2.set(6, true);
      bs2.set(7, true);
      bs2.set(9, true);
      dumpBitset("          ", bs2);
      bs1.and(bs2);
      dumpSeparator(Math.min(bs1.size(), 16));
      dumpBitset("AND (&) ", bs1);
      System.out.println();
      bs1 = bsTemp;
      dumpBitset("          ", bs1);
      dumpBitset("          ", bs2);
      bsTemp = (BitSet) bs1.clone();
      bs1.or(bs2);
      dumpSeparator(Math.min(bs1.size(), 16));
      dumpBitset("OR (|)   ", bs1);
      System.out.println();
      bs1 = bsTemp;
      dumpBitset("          ", bs1);
      dumpBitset("          ", bs2);
      bsTemp = (BitSet) bs1.clone();
```

```java
      bs1.xor(bs2);
      dumpSeparator(Math.min(bs1.size(), 16));
      dumpBitset("XOR (^) ", bs1);
   }
   static void dumpBitset(String preamble, BitSet bs)
   {
      System.out.print(preamble);
      for (int i = 0; i < Math.min(bs.size(), 16); i++)
         System.out.print(bs.get(i) ? "1" : "0");
      System.out.print(" size(" + bs.size() + "), length(" + bs.length() + ")");
      System.out.println();
   }
   static void dumpSeparator(int len)
   {
      System.out.print("              ");
      for (int i = 0; i < len; i++)
         System.out.print("-");
      System.out.println();
   }
}
```

Why did I specify Math.min(bs.size(), 16) in dumpBitset(), and pass a similar expression to dumpSeparator()? I wanted to display exactly 16 bits and 16 dashes (for aesthetics), and needed to account for a bitset's size being less than 16. Although this does not happen with the JDK's BitSet class, it might happen with a non-JDK variant.

When you run this application, it generates the following output:

```
          0000110001100000  size(64), length(11)
          0000101101000000  size(64), length(10)
          ----------------
AND (&) 0000100001000000  size(64), length(10)

          0000110001100000  size(64), length(11)
          0000101101000000  size(64), length(10)
          ----------------
OR (|)  0000111101100000  size(64), length(11)

          0000110001100000  size(64), length(11)
          0000101101000000  size(64), length(10)
          ----------------
XOR (^) 0000011100100000  size(64), length(11)
```

> **CAUTION:** Unlike Vector and Hashtable, BitSet is not synchronized. You must externally synchronize access to this class when using BitSet in a multithreaded context.

The collections framework has made Vector, Enumeration, Stack, Dictionary, and Hashtable obsolete. These types continue to be part of the standard class library to support legacy code. Also, the Preferences API (see Chapter 9) has made Properties largely obsolete. Because BitSet is still relevant, this class continues to be improved.

NOTE: It is not surprising that BitSet is being improved (as recently as Java version 6 at time of writing) when you realize the usefulness of variable-length bitsets. Because of their compactness and other advantages, variable-length bitsets are often used to implement an operating system's priority queues and facilitate memory page allocation. Unix-oriented file systems also use bitsets to facilitate the allocation of *inodes* (information nodes) and disk sectors. And bitsets are useful in *Huffman coding*, a data-compression algorithm for achieving lossless data compression.

EXERCISES

The following exercises are designed to test your understanding of the collections framework:

1. What is a collection?
2. What is the collections framework?
3. The collections framework largely consists of what components?
4. What is a comparable?
5. When would you have a class implement the Comparable interface?
6. What is a comparator and what is its purpose?
7. True or false: A collection uses a comparator to define the natural ordering of its elements.
8. What does the Iterable interface describe?
9. What does the Collection interface represent?
10. Identify a situation where Collection's add() method would throw an instance of the UnsupportedOperationException class.
11. Iterable's iterator() method returns an instance of a class that implements the Iterator interface. What methods does this interface provide?
12. What is the purpose of the enhanced for loop statement?
13. How is the enhanced for loop statement expressed?
14. True or false: The enhanced for loop works with arrays.
15. What is autoboxing?
16. What is unboxing?
17. What is a list?

18. What does a `ListIterator` instance use to navigate through a list?

19. What is a view?

20. Why would you use the `subList()` method?

21. What does the `ArrayList` class provide?

22. What does the `LinkedList` class provide?

23. What is a node?

24. True or false: `ArrayList` provides faster element insertions and deletions than `LinkedList`.

25. What is a set?

26. What does the `TreeSet` class provide?

27. What does the `HashSet` class provide?

28. True or false: To avoid duplicate elements in a hashset, your own classes must correctly override `equals()` and `hashCode()`.

29. What is the difference between `HashSet` and `LinkedHashSet`?

30. What does the `EnumSet` class provide?

31. What is a sorted set?

32. True or false: `HashSet` is an example of a sorted set.

33. Why would a sorted set's `add()` method throw `ClassCastException` when you attempt to add an element to the sorted set?

34. What is a queue?

35. True or false: `Queue`'s `element()` method throws `NoSuchElementException` when it is called on an empty queue.

36. What does the `PriorityQueue` class provide?

37. What is a map?

38. What does the `TreeMap` class provide?

39. What does the `HashMap` class provide?

40. What does a hashtable use to map keys to integer values?

41. Continuing from the previous question, what are the resulting integer values called, and what do they accomplish?

42. What is a hashtable's capacity?

43. What is a hashtable's load factor?

44. What is the difference between HashMap and LinkedHashMap?

45. What does the IdentityHashMap class provide?

46. What does the WeakHashMap class provide?

47. What does the EnumMap class provide?

48. What is a sorted map?

49. True or false: TreeMap is an example of a sorted map.

50. What is the purpose of the Arrays class's static <T> List<T> asList(T... array) method?

51. True or false: Binary search is slower than linear search.

52. Which Collections method would you use to return a synchronized variation of a hashset?

53. Identify the seven legacy collections-oriented types.

54. As an example of array list usefulness, create a JavaQuiz application that presents a multiple-choice-based quiz on Java features. The JavaQuiz class's main() method first populates the array list with the entries in the following QuizEntry array:

```
static QuizEntry[] quizEntries =
{
   new QuizEntry("What was Java's original name?",
             new String[] { "Oak", "Duke", "J", "None of the above" },
             'A'),
   new QuizEntry("Which of the following reserved words is also a literal?",
             new String[] { "for", "long", "true", "enum" },
             'C'),
   new QuizEntry("The conditional operator (?:) resembles which statement?",
             new String[] { "switch", "if-else", "if", "while" },
             'B')
};
```

Each QuizEntry instance consists of a question, four possible answers, and the letter (A, B, C, or D) of the correct answer.

main() then uses the array list's iterator() method to return an Iterator instance, and this instance's hasNext() and next() methods to iterate over the list. Each of the iterations outputs the question and four possible answers, and then prompts the user to enter the correct choice. After the user enters A, B, C, or D, main() outputs a message stating whether or not the user made the correct choice.

55. Why is (int) (f^(f>>>32)) used instead of (int) (f^(f>>32)) in the hash code generation algorithm?

56. Collections provides the `static int frequency(Collection<?> collection, Object o)` method to return the number of collection elements that are equal to o. Create a `FrequencyDemo` application that reads its command-line arguments and stores all arguments except for the last argument in a list, and then calls `frequency()` with the list and last command-line argument as this method's arguments. It then outputs this method's return value (the number of occurrences of the last command-line argument in the previous command-line arguments). For example, `java FrequencyDemo` should output `Number of occurrences of null = 0`, and `java FrequencyDemo how much wood could a woodchuck chuck if a woodchuck could chuck wood wood` should output `Number of occurrences of wood = 2`.

Summary

A collection is a group of objects that are stored in an instance of a class designed for this purpose. To save you from having to create your own collections classes, Java provides the standardized collections framework for representing and manipulating collections.

The collections framework largely consists of core interfaces, implementation classes, and the `Arrays` and `Collections` utility classes. The core interfaces make it possible to manipulate collections independently of their implementations.

The collections framework's core interfaces include `Iterable`, `Collection`, `List`, `Set`, `SortedSet`, `Queue`, `Map`, and `SortedMap`. `Collection` extends `Iterable`; `List`, `Set`, and `Queue` each extend `Collection`; `SortedSet` extends `Set`; and `SortedMap` extends `Map`.

The framework's implementation classes include the concrete `ArrayList`, `LinkedList`, `TreeSet`, `HashSet`, `LinkedHashSet`, `EnumSet`, `PriorityQueue`, `TreeMap`, `HashMap`, `LinkedHashMap`, `IdentityHashMap`, `WeakHashMap`, and `EnumMap` classes.

The framework's implementation classes also include the abstract `AbstractCollection`, `AbstractList`, `AbstractSequentialList`, `AbstractSet`, `AbstractQueue`, and `AbstractMap` classes, which offer skeletal implementations of the core interfaces.

The collections framework would not be complete without its `Arrays` and `Collections` utility classes. Each class supplies various utility (`static`) methods that implement useful algorithms in the contexts of arrays and collections.

Prior to Java version 1.2's introduction of the collections framework, developers could create their own frameworks, or use the `Vector`, `Enumeration`, `Stack`, `Dictionary`, `Hashtable`, `Properties`, and `BitSet` types, which were introduced by Java version 1.0.

The collections framework has made Vector, Enumeration, Stack, Dictionary, and Hashtable obsolete. Also, the Preferences API (see Chapter 9) has made Properties largely obsolete. Because BitSet is still relevant, this class continues to be improved.

Your exploration of Java's utility APIs is far from finished. Chapter 9 continues to focus on utility APIs by discussing the concurrency utilities, the internationalization APIs, the Preferences API, Random, and the Regular Expressions API.

Discovering Additional Utility APIs

Chapter 9 continues to explore Java's utility APIs by introducing APIs that help you work with threads in an easier way, internationalize your applications to reach a wider audience, save configuration preferences in persistent storage, obtain random numbers in a more flexible manner, and quickly search and parse strings.

> **NOTE:** Chapter 9 explores utility API classes and interfaces that are located in the `java.text` and `java.util` packages, and `java.util`'s concurrent, prefs, and regex subpackages.

Concurrency Utilities

Java version 5 introduced the *concurrency utilities*, classes and interfaces that simplify the development of *concurrent* (multithreaded) applications. These types are located in the `java.util.concurrent` package and in its `java.util.concurrent.atomic` and `java.util.concurrent.locks` subpackages.

The concurrency utilities leverage the low-level Threading API (see Chapter 7) in their implementations and provide higher-level building blocks (such as locking idioms) to make it easier to create multithreaded applications. These utilities are organized into executor, synchronizer, concurrent collection, lock, and atomic variable categories.

Executors

Chapter 7 introduced the Threading API, which lets you execute runnable tasks via expressions such as `new Thread(new RunnableTask()).start();`. These expressions tightly couple task submission with the task's execution mechanics (run on the current thread, a new thread, or a thread arbitrarily chosen from a *pool* [group] of threads).

> **NOTE:** A *task* is an object whose class implements the `java.lang.Runnable` interface (a runnable task) or the `java.util.concurrent.Callable` interface (a callable task).

The concurrency utilities provide executors as a high-level alternative to low-level Threading API expressions for executing runnable tasks. An *executor* is an object whose class directly or indirectly implements the `java.util.concurrent.Executor` interface, which decouples task submission from task-execution mechanics.

> **NOTE:** The executor framework's use of interfaces to decouple task submission from task-execution mechanics is analogous to the collections framework's use of core interfaces to decouple lists, sets, queues, and maps from their implementations. Decoupling results in flexible code that is easier to maintain.

Executor declares a solitary void `execute(Runnable runnable)` method that executes the runnable task named runnable at some point in the future. `execute()` throws `java.lang.NullPointerException` when runnable is null, and `java.util.concurrent.RejectedExecutionException` when it cannot execute runnable.

> **NOTE:** `RejectedExecutionException` can be thrown when an executor is shutting down and does not want to accept new tasks. Also, this exception can be thrown when the executor does not have enough room to store the task (perhaps the executor uses a bounded blocking queue to store tasks and the queue is full—I discuss blocking queues later in this chapter).

Listing 9–1 presents the Executor equivalent of the aforementioned new `Thread(new RunnableTask()).start();` expression.

Listing 9–1. *Decoupling runnable task submission from task-execution mechanics*

```
Executor executor = ...; //  ... represents some executor creation
executor.execute(new RunnableTask());
```

Although Executor is easy to use, this interface is limited in various ways:

- Executor focuses exclusively on Runnable. Because Runnable's run() method does not return a value, there is no convenient way for a runnable task to return a value to its caller.
- Executor does not provide a way to track the progress of executing runnable tasks, cancel an executing runnable task, or determine when the runnable task finishes execution.
- Executor cannot execute a collection of runnable tasks.
- Executor does not provide a way for an application to shut down an executor (much less to properly shut down an executor).

These limitations are addressed by the java.util.concurrent.ExecutorService interface, which extends Executor, and whose implementation is typically a thread pool. Table 9–1 describes ExecutorService's methods.

Table 9–1. *ExecutorService Methods*

Method	Description
boolean awaitTermination (long timeout, TimeUnit unit)	Block (wait) until all tasks have finished after a shutdown request, the timeout (measured in unit time units) expires, or the current thread is interrupted, whichever happens first. Return true when this executor has terminated, and false when the timeout elapses before termination. This method throws java.lang.InterruptedException when interrupted.
<T> List<Future<T>> invokeAll(Collection<? extends Callable<T>> tasks)	Execute each callable task in the tasks collection, and return a List of Future instances that hold task statuses and results when all tasks complete—a task completes through normal termination or by throwing an exception. The List of Futures is in the same sequential order as the sequence of tasks returned by tasks' iterator. This method throws InterruptedException when it is interrupted while waiting, in which case unfinished tasks are canceled, NullPointerException when tasks or any of its elements is null, and RejectedExecutionException when any one of tasks' tasks cannot be scheduled for execution.
<T> List<Future<T>> invokeAll(Collection<? extends Callable<T>> tasks, long timeout, TimeUnit unit)	Execute each callable task in the tasks collection, and return a List of Future instances that hold task statuses and results when all tasks complete—a task completes through normal termination or by throwing an exception—or the timeout (measured in unit time units) expires. Tasks that are not completed at expiry are canceled. The List of Futures is in the same sequential order as the sequence of tasks returned by tasks' iterator. This method throws InterruptedException when it is interrupted while waiting, in which case unfinished tasks are canceled, NullPointerException when tasks or any of its elements is null, and RejectedExecutionException when any one of tasks' tasks cannot be scheduled for execution.
<T> T invokeAny (Collection<? extends Callable<T>> tasks)	Execute the given tasks, returning the result of an arbitrary task that has completed successfully (i.e., without throwing an exception), if any does. Upon normal or exceptional return, tasks that have not completed are canceled. This method throws InterruptedException when it is interrupted while waiting, NullPointerException when tasks or any of its elements is null, java.lang.IllegalArgumentException when tasks is empty, java.util.concurrent.ExecutionException when no task completes successfully, and RejectedExecutionException when none of the tasks can be scheduled for execution.

Method	Description
`<T> T invokeAny` `(Collection<? extends` `Callable<T>> tasks, long` `timeout, TimeUnit unit)`	Execute the given tasks, returning the result of an arbitrary task that has completed successfully (i.e., without throwing an exception), if any does before the timeout (measured in unit time units) expires—tasks that are not completed at expiry are canceled. Upon normal or exceptional return, tasks that have not completed are canceled. This method throws InterruptedException when it is interrupted while waiting, NullPointerException when tasks or any of its elements is null, IllegalArgumentException when tasks is empty, java.util.concurrent.TimeoutException when the timeout elapses before any task successfully completes, ExecutionException when no task completes successfully, and RejectedExecutionException when none of the tasks can be scheduled for execution.
`boolean isShutdown()`	Return true when this executor has been shut down; otherwise, return false.
`boolean isTerminated()`	Return true when all tasks have completed following shutdown; otherwise, return false. This method will never return true prior to shutdown() or shutdownNow() being called.
`void shutdown()`	Initiate an orderly shutdown in which previously submitted tasks are executed, but no new tasks will be accepted. Calling this method has no effect after the executor has shut down.
`List<Runnable>` `shutdownNow()`	Attempt to stop all actively executing tasks, halt the processing of waiting tasks, and return a list of the tasks that were awaiting execution. There are no guarantees beyond best-effort attempts to stop processing actively executing tasks. For example, typical implementations will cancel via Thread.interrupt(), so any task that fails to respond to interrupts may never terminate.
`<T> Future<T> submit` `(Callable<T> task)`	Submit a callable task for execution and return a Future instance representing task's pending results. The Future instance's get() method returns task's result upon successful completion. This method throws RejectedExecutionException when task cannot be scheduled for execution, and NullPointerException when task is null.
`Future<?> submit` `(Runnable task)`	Submit a runnable task for execution and return a Future instance whose get() method returns the null reference upon successful completion. This method throws RejectedExecutionException when task cannot be scheduled for execution, and NullPointerException when task is null.
`<T> Future<T> submit` `(Runnable task, T result)`	Submit a runnable task for execution and return a Future instance whose get() method returns result upon successful completion. This method throws RejectedExecutionException when task cannot be scheduled for execution, and NullPointerException when task is null.

Table 9–1 refers to java.util.concurrent.TimeUnit, an enum that represents time durations at given units of granularity: DAYS, HOURS, MICROSECONDS, MILLISECONDS, MINUTES, NANOSECONDS, and SECONDS. Furthermore, TimeUnit declares methods for converting across units, and for performing timing and delay operations in these units.

Table 9–1 also refers to callable tasks, which are analogous to runnable tasks. Unlike Runnable, whose void run() method cannot throw checked exceptions, Callable<V> declares a V call() method that returns a value, and which can throw checked exceptions because call() is declared with a throws Exception clause.

Finally, Table 9–1 refers to the java.util.concurrent.Future interface, which represents the result of an asynchronous computation. Future, whose generic type is Future<V>, provides methods for canceling a task, for returning a task's value, and for determining whether or not the task has finished. Table 9–2 describes Future's methods.

Table 9–2. *Future Methods*

Method	Description
boolean cancel(boolean mayInterruptIfRunning)	Attempt to cancel execution of this task, and return true when the task was cancelled; otherwise, return false (perhaps the task completed normally before this method was called).
	The cancellation attempt fails when the task has completed, has already been cancelled, or could not be cancelled for some other reason. If successful and this task had not started when cancel() was called, the task should never run. If the task has already started, then mayInterruptIfRunning determines whether the thread executing this task should be interrupted (true) or not (false) in an attempt to stop the task. After this method returns, subsequent calls to isDone() always return true. Subsequent calls to isCancelled() always return true when cancel() returns true.
V get()	Wait if necessary for the task to complete and then return the result. This method throws java.util.concurrent.CancellationException when the task was cancelled prior to this method being called, ExecutionException when the task threw an exception, and InterruptedException when the current thread was interrupted while waiting.
V get(long timeout, TimeUnit unit)	Wait at most timeout units (as specified by unit) for the task to complete and then return the result. This method throws CancellationException when the task was cancelled prior to this method being called, ExecutionException when the task threw an exception, InterruptedException when the current thread was interrupted while waiting, and TimeoutException when this method's timeout value expires (the wait times out).
boolean isCancelled()	Return true when this task was cancelled before it completed normally.
boolean isDone()	Return true when this task completed. Completion may be due to normal termination, an exception, or cancellation—this method returns true in all of these cases.

Suppose you intend to write an application whose graphical user interface lets the user enter a word. Once the user enters the word, the application presents this word to several online dictionaries and obtains each dictionary's entry. These entries are subsequently displayed to the user.

Because online access can be slow, and because the user interface should remain responsive (perhaps the user might want to end the application), you offload the "obtain word entries" task to an executor that runs this task on a separate thread. Listing 9–2 employs ExecutorService, Callable, and Future to accomplish this objective.

Listing 9–2. *An executor-based skeletal framework for obtaining word entries from online dictionaries*

```
ExecutorService executor = ...; //  ... represents some executor creation
Future<String[]> taskFuture = executor.submit(new Callable<String[]>()
                                   {
                                       public String[] call()
                                       {
                                           String[] entries = ...;
                                           // Access online dictionaries
                                           // with search word and populate
                                           // entries with their resulting
                                           // entries.
                                           return entries;
                                       }
                                   });
// Do stuff.
String entries = taskFuture.get();
```

After obtaining an executor in some manner (you will learn how shortly), Listing 9–2's main thread submits a callable task to the executor. The submit() method immediately returns with a reference to a Future object for controlling task execution and accessing results. The main thread ultimately calls this object's get() method to get these results.

> **NOTE:** The java.util.concurrent.ScheduledExecutorService interface extends ExecutorService and describes an executor that lets you schedule tasks to run once or to execute periodically after a given delay.

Although you could create your own Executor, ExecutorService, and ScheduledExecutorService implementations (such as class DirectExecutor implements Executor { public void execute(Runnable r) { r.run(); } }—run executor directly on the calling thread), the concurrency utilities offer a simpler alternative: Executors.

> **TIP:** If you intend to create your own ExecutorService implementations, you will find it helpful to work with the java.util.concurrent.AbstractExecutorService and java.util.concurrent.FutureTask classes.

The java.util.concurrent.Executors utility class declares several static methods that return instances of various ExecutorService and ScheduledExecutorService implementations (and other kinds of instances). This class's utility methods accomplish the following tasks:

- Create and return an ExecutorService instance that is configured with commonly used configuration settings.

- Create and return a ScheduledExecutorService instance that is configured with commonly used configuration settings.

- Create and return a "wrapped" ExecutorService or ScheduledExecutorService instance, and disable reconfiguration of the executor service by making implementation-specific methods inaccessible.

- Create and return a java.util.concurrent.ThreadFactory instance for creating new threads.

- Create and return a Callable instance out of other closure-like forms (such as a Runnable instance) so that they can be used in execution methods (such as ExecutorService's submit(Callable) method) that require Callable arguments.

For example, static ExecutorService newFixedThreadPool(int nThreads) creates a thread pool that reuses a fixed number of threads operating off of a shared unbounded queue. At most, nThreads threads are actively processing tasks. If additional tasks are submitted when all threads are active, they wait in the queue for an available thread.

If any thread terminates because of a failure during execution before the executor shuts down, a new thread will take its place when needed to execute subsequent tasks. The threads in the pool will exist until the executor is explicitly shut down. This method throws IllegalArgumentException when you pass zero or a negative value to nThreads.

> **NOTE:** Thread pools are used to eliminate the overhead from having to create a new thread for each submitted task. Thread creation is not cheap, and having to create many threads could severely impact an application's performance.

You would commonly use executors, runnables, callables, and futures in an input/output context. (I discuss input/output in Chapter 10.) Performing a lengthy calculation offers another scenario where you could use these types. For example, Listing 9–3 uses an executor, a callable, and a future in a calculation context of Euler's number e (2.71828...).

Listing 9–3. *Calculating Euler's number e*

```
import java.math.BigDecimal;
import java.math.MathContext;
import java.math.RoundingMode;

import java.util.concurrent.Callable;
```

```java
import java.util.concurrent.ExecutionException;
import java.util.concurrent.ExecutorService;
import java.util.concurrent.Executors;
import java.util.concurrent.Future;

public class CalculateE
{
   final static int LASTITER = 17;
   public static void main(String[] args)
   {
      ExecutorService executor = Executors.newFixedThreadPool(1);
      Callable<BigDecimal> callable;
      callable = new Callable<BigDecimal>()
               {
                  public BigDecimal call()
                  {
                     MathContext mc = new MathContext(100,
                                                RoundingMode.HALF_UP);
                     BigDecimal result = BigDecimal.ZERO;
                     for (int i = 0; i <= LASTITER; i++)
                     {
                        BigDecimal factorial = factorial(new BigDecimal (i));
                        BigDecimal res = BigDecimal.ONE.divide(factorial, mc);
                        result = result.add(res);
                     }
                     return result;
                  }
                  public BigDecimal factorial(BigDecimal n)
                  {
                     if (n.equals(BigDecimal.ZERO))
                        return BigDecimal.ONE;
                     else
                        return n.multiply(factorial(n.subtract(BigDecimal.ONE)));
                  }
               };
      Future<BigDecimal> taskFuture = executor.submit(callable);
      try
      {
         while (!taskFuture.isDone())
            System.out.println("waiting");
         System.out.println(taskFuture.get());
      }
      catch(ExecutionException ee)
      {
         System.err.println("task threw an exception");
         System.err.println(ee);
      }
      catch(InterruptedException ie)
      {
         System.err.println("interrupted while waiting");
      }
      executor.shutdownNow();
   }
}
```

The main thread first obtains an executor by calling `Executors`' `newFixedThreadPool()` method. It then instantiates an anonymous class that implements `Callable` and submits this task to the executor, receiving a `Future` instance in response.

After submitting a task, a thread typically does some other work until it needs to obtain the task's result. I have chosen to simulate this work by having the main thread repeatedly output a waiting message until the `Future` instance's `isDone()` method returns true. (In a realistic application, I would avoid this looping.) At this point, the main thread calls the instance's `get()` method to obtain the result, which is then output.

> **CAUTION:** It is important to shut down the executor after it completes; otherwise, the application might not end. The executor accomplishes this task by calling `shutdownNow()`.

The callable's `call()` method calculates e by evaluating the mathematical power series e = 1/0!+1/1!+1/2!+…. This series can be evaluated by summing $1/n!$, where n ranges from 0 to infinity.

`call()` first instantiates `java.math.MathContext` to encapsulate a *precision* (number of digits) and a rounding mode. I chose 100 as an upper limit on e's precision, and I also chose `HALF_UP` as the rounding mode.

> **TIP:** Increase the precision as well as `LASTITER`'s value to converge the series to a lengthier and more accurate approximation of e.

`call()` next initializes a `BigDecimal` local variable named `result` to `BigDecimal.ZERO`. It then enters a loop that calculates a factorial, divides `BigDecimal.ONE` by the factorial, and adds the division result to `result`.

The `divide()` method takes the `MathContext` instance as its second argument to ensure that the division does not result in a nonterminating decimal expansion, which throws `java.lang.ArithmeticException`, which the executor rethrows as `ExecutionException`.

When you run this application, you should observe output similar to the following:

```
waiting
waiting
waiting
waiting
waiting
waiting
waiting
2.718281828459045070516047795848605061178979635251032698900735004065225042504843314055↵
8879743442457417300394540627 11
```

Synchronizers

The Threading API offers synchronization primitives for synchronizing thread access to critical sections. Because it can be difficult to correctly write synchronized code that is based on these primitives, the concurrency utilities include *synchronizers*, classes that facilitate common forms of synchronization.

Four commonly used synchronizers are countdown latches, cyclic barriers, exchangers, and semaphores:

- A *countdown latch* lets one or more threads wait at a "gate" until another thread opens this gate, at which point these other threads can continue. The java.util.concurrent.CountDownLatch class implements this synchronizer.

- A *cyclic barrier* lets a group of threads wait for each other to reach a common barrier point. The java.util.concurrent.CyclicBarrier class implements this synchronizer, and makes use of the java.util.concurrent.BrokenBarrierException class.

- An *exchanger* lets a pair of threads exchange objects at a synchronization point. The java.util.concurrent.Exchanger class implements this synchronizer.

- A *semaphore* maintains a set of permits for restricting the number of threads that can access a limited resource. The java.util.concurrent.Semaphore class implements this synchronizer.

Consider the CountDownLatch class. Each of its instances is initialized to a nonzero count. A thread calls one of CountDownLatch's await() methods to block until the count reaches zero. Another thread calls CountDownLatch's countDown() method to decrement the count. Once the count reaches zero, the waiting threads are allowed to continue.

> **NOTE:** Once waiting threads are released, subsequent calls to await() return immediately. Also, because the count cannot be reset, a CountDownLatch instance can be used only once. When repeated use is a requirement, use the CyclicBarrier class instead.

We can use CountDownLatch to ensure that threads start working at approximately the same time. For example, check out Listing 9–4.

Listing 9–4. *Using a countdown latch to trigger a coordinated start*

```
import java.util.concurrent.CountDownLatch;
import java.util.concurrent.ExecutorService;
import java.util.concurrent.Executors;

public class CountDownLatchDemo
{
   final static int NTHREADS = 3;
   public static void main(String[] args)
```

```
    {
        final CountDownLatch enterLatch = new CountDownLatch(NTHREADS);
        Runnable r = new Runnable()
                        {
                            public void run()
                            {
                                try
                                {
                                    report("entered run()");
                                    enterLatch.countDown();
                                    enterLatch.await();
                                    report("doing work");
                                }
                                catch (InterruptedException ie)
                                {
                                    System.err.println(ie);
                                }
                            }
                            void report(String s)
                            {
                                System.out.println(System.currentTimeMillis() + ": " +
                                                   Thread.currentThread() + ": " + s);
                            }
                        };
        ExecutorService executor = Executors.newFixedThreadPool(NTHREADS);
        for (int i = 0; i < NTHREADS; i++)
            executor.execute(r);
        try
        {
            Thread.sleep(3000); // Sleep for 3 seconds.
        }
        catch (InterruptedException ie)
        {
            System.err.println(ie);
        }
        executor.shutdownNow();
    }
}
```

Listing 9–4's main thread first creates a countdown latch with a count initialized to the number of threads that must start working at approximately the same time. It then creates a runnable whose run() method is executed by subsequently created threads.

The runnable's run() method first outputs an initial message and then calls the latch instance's countDown() method to decrement the count. It next calls await() to wait for the latch's count to reach zero, at which time it can output its work message.

After obtaining an executor that is based on a thread pool of NTHREADS threads, the main thread calls the executor's execute() method NTHREADS times, passing the runnable to each of the NTHREADS pool-based threads.

The main thread then sleeps for three seconds to give these threads a chance to demonstrate the countdown latch before the main thread shuts down the executor by calling shutdownNow().

When you run this application, you will observe output similar to the following:

```
1279656117609: Thread[pool-1-thread-1,5,main]: entered run()
1279656117609: Thread[pool-1-thread-2,5,main]: entered run()
1279656117609: Thread[pool-1-thread-3,5,main]: entered run()
1279656117609: Thread[pool-1-thread-1,5,main]: doing work
1279656117609: Thread[pool-1-thread-2,5,main]: doing work
1279656117609: Thread[pool-1-thread-3,5,main]: doing work
```

> **NOTE:** For brevity, I have avoided examples that demonstrate CyclicBarrier, Exchanger, and Semaphore. Instead, I refer you to the Java documentation for these classes. Each class's documentation provides an example that shows you how to use the class.

Concurrent Collections

The java.util.concurrent package includes several interfaces and classes that are concurrency-oriented extensions to the collections framework (see Chapter 8):

■ BlockingQueue is a subinterface of java.util.Queue that describes a first-in, first-out (FIFO) data structure. It provides additional operations that wait for the queue to become nonempty before retrieving an element, and wait for space to become available in the queue before storing an element. Each of the ArrayBlockingQueue, LinkedBlockingQueue, PriorityBlockingQueue, and SynchronousQueue classes implements this interface.

■ ConcurrentMap is a subinterface of java.util.Map that declares additional atomic putIfAbsent(), remove(), and replace() methods. The ConcurrentHashMap class (the concurrent equivalent of java.util.HashMap) implements this interface.

■ ConcurrentLinkedQueue is an unbounded thread-safe FIFO implementation of the Queue interface.

Listing 9–5 uses BlockingQueue and ArrayBlockingQueue in an alternative to Listing 7-13's producer-consumer application (PC).

Listing 9–5. *The blocking queue equivalent of Listing 7-13's PC application*

```java
import java.util.concurrent.ArrayBlockingQueue;
import java.util.concurrent.BlockingQueue;
import java.util.concurrent.ExecutorService;
import java.util.concurrent.Executors;

public class PC
{
   public static void main(String[] args)
   {
      final BlockingQueue<Character> bq;
      bq = new ArrayBlockingQueue<Character>(26);
      final ExecutorService executor = Executors.newFixedThreadPool(2);
      Runnable producer;
      producer = new Runnable()
```

```
                {
                    public void run()
                    {
                        for (char ch = 'A'; ch <= 'Z'; ch++)
                        {
                            try
                            {
                                bq.put(ch);
                                System.out.println(ch + " produced by producer.");
                            }
                            catch (InterruptedException ie)
                            {
                                assert false;
                            }
                        }
                    }
                };
        executor.execute(producer);
        Runnable consumer;
        consumer = new Runnable()
                {
                    public void run()
                    {
                        char ch = '\0';
                        do
                        {
                            try
                            {
                                ch = bq.take();
                                System.out.println(ch + " consumed by consumer.");
                            }
                            catch (InterruptedException ie)
                            {
                                assert false;
                            }
                        }
                        while (ch != 'Z');
                        executor.shutdownNow();
                    }
                };
        executor.execute(consumer);
    }
}
```

Listing 9–5 uses BlockingQueue's put() and take() methods, respectively, to put an object on the blocking queue and to remove an object from the blocking queue. put() blocks when there is no room to put an object; take() blocks when the queue is empty.

Although BlockingQueue ensures that a character is never consumed before it is produced, this application's output may indicate otherwise. For example, here is a portion of the output from one run:

```
Y consumed by consumer.
Y produced by producer.
Z consumed by consumer.
Z produced by producer.
```

Chapter 7's PC application overcame this incorrect output order by introducing an extra layer of synchronization around setSharedChar()/System.out.println() and an extra layer of synchronization around getSharedChar()/System.out.println(). The next section shows you an alternative in the form of locks.

Locks

The java.util.concurrent.locks package provides interfaces and classes for locking and waiting for conditions in a manner that is distinct from built-in synchronization and monitors.

This package's most basic lock interface is Lock, which provides more extensive locking operations than can be achieved via the synchronized reserved word. Lock also supports a wait/notification mechanism through associated Condition objects.

NOTE: The biggest advantage of Lock objects over the implicit locks that are obtained when threads enter critical sections (controlled via the synchronized reserved word) is their ability to back out of an attempt to acquire a lock. For example, the tryLock() method backs out if the lock is not available immediately or before a timeout expires (if specified). Also, the lockInterruptibly() method backs out when another thread sends an interrupt before the lock is acquired.

ReentrantLock implements Lock, describing a reentrant mutual exclusion Lock implementation with the same basic behavior and semantics as the implicit monitor lock accessed via synchronized, but with extended capabilities.

Listing 9–6 demonstrates Lock and ReentrantLock in a version of Listing 9–5 that ensures that the output is never shown in incorrect order (a consumed message appearing before a produced message).

Listing 9–6. *Achieving synchronization in terms of locks*

```
import java.util.concurrent.ArrayBlockingQueue;
import java.util.concurrent.BlockingQueue;
import java.util.concurrent.ExecutorService;
import java.util.concurrent.Executors;

import java.util.concurrent.locks.Lock;
import java.util.concurrent.locks.ReentrantLock;

public class PC
{
   public static void main(String[] args)
   {
      final Lock lock = new ReentrantLock();
      final BlockingQueue<Character> bq;
      bq = new ArrayBlockingQueue<Character>(26);
      final ExecutorService executor = Executors.newFixedThreadPool(2);
      Runnable producer;
      producer = new Runnable()
```

```
      {
         public void run()
         {
            for (char ch = 'A'; ch <= 'Z'; ch++)
            {
               try
               {
                  lock.lock();
                  try
                  {
                     while (!bq.offer(ch))
                     {
                        lock.unlock();
                        Thread.sleep(50);
                        lock.lock();
                     }
                     System.out.println(ch + " produced by producer.");
                  }
                  catch (InterruptedException ie)
                  {
                     assert false;
                  }
               }
               finally
               {
                  lock.unlock();
               }
            }
         }
      };
executor.execute(producer);
Runnable consumer;
consumer = new Runnable()
      {
         public void run()
         {
            char ch = '\0';
            do
            {
               try
               {
                  lock.lock();
                  try
                  {
                     Character c;
                     while ((c = bq.poll()) == null)
                     {
                        lock.unlock();
                        Thread.sleep(50);
                        lock.lock();
                     }
                     ch = c; // unboxing behind the scenes
                     System.out.println(ch + " consumed by consumer.");
                  }
                  catch (InterruptedException ie)
                  {
                     assert false;
```

```
                    }
                  }
                  finally
                  {
                      lock.unlock();
                  }
                }
                while (ch != 'Z');
                executor.shutdownNow();
              }
            };
       executor.execute(consumer);
     }
}
```

Listing 9–6 uses Lock's lock() and unlock() methods to obtain and release a lock. When a thread calls lock() and the lock is unavailable, the thread is disabled (and cannot be scheduled) until the lock becomes available.

This listing also uses BlockingQueue's offer() method instead of put() to store an object in the blocking queue, and its poll() method instead of take() to retrieve an object from the queue. These alternative methods are used because they do not block.

If I had used put() and take(), this application would have deadlocked in the following scenario:

1. The consumer thread acquires the lock via its lock.lock() call.

2. The producer thread attempts to acquire the lock via its lock.lock() call and is disabled because the consumer thread has already acquired the lock.

3. The consumer thread calls take() to obtain the next Character object from the queue.

4. Because the queue is empty, the consumer thread must wait.

5. The consumer thread does not give up the lock that the producer thread requires before waiting, so the producer thread also continues to wait.

NOTE: If I had access to the private lock used by BlockingQueue implementations, I would have used put() and take(), and also would have called Lock's lock() and unlock() methods on that lock. The resulting application would then have been identical (from a lock perspective) to Listing 7-13's PC application, which used synchronized twice for each of the producer and consumer threads.

Run this application and you will discover that it generates the same output as Listing 7-13's PC application.

Atomic Variables

The java.util.concurrent.atomic package provides Atomic-prefixed classes (such as AtomicLong) that support lock-free, thread-safe operations on single variables. Each class declares methods such as get() and set() to read and write this variable without the need for external synchronization.

Listing 7-9 declared a small utility class named ID for returning unique long integer identifiers via ID's getNextID() method. Because this method was not synchronized, multiple threads could obtain the same identifier. Listing 9–7 fixes this problem by including reserved word synchronized in the method header.

Listing 9–7. *Returning unique identifiers in a thread-safe manner via* synchronized

```
public class ID
{
   private static long nextID = 0;
   public static synchronized long getNextID()
   {
      return nextID++;
   }
}
```

Although synchronized is appropriate for this class, excessive use of this reserved word in more complex classes can lead to deadlock, starvation, or other problems. Listing 9–8 shows you how to avoid these assaults on a concurrent application's *liveness* (the ability to execute in a timely manner) by replacing synchronized with an atomic variable.

Listing 9–8. *Returning unique IDs in a thread-safe manner via* AtomicLong

```
public class ID
{
   private static AtomicLong nextID = new AtomicLong(0);
   public static long getNextID()
   {
      return nextID.getAndIncrement();
   }
}
```

In Listing 9–8, I have converted nextID from a long to an AtomicLong instance, initializing this object to 0. I have also refactored the getNextID() method to call AtomicLong's getAndIncrement() method, which increments the AtomicLong instance's internal long integer variable by 1 and returns the previous value in one indivisible step.

Internationalization APIs

We tend to write software that reflects our cultural backgrounds. For example, a Spanish developer's application might present Spanish text, an Arabic developer's application might present a Hijri (Islamic) calendar, and a Japanese developer's application might display its currencies using the Japanese Yen currency symbol. Because cultural biases restrict the size of an application's audience, you might consider internationalizing your Android and Java SE applications to reach a larger audience (and make more money).

Internationalization is the process of creating an application that automatically adapts to its current user's culture so that the user can read the application's text, hear audio clips in the user's language (if audio is supported), and so on. Java simplifies internationalization by supporting *Unicode* (a universal character set that encodes the various symbols making up the world's written languages) via char (see Chapter 2) and java.lang.Character (see Chapter 6), and by offering the APIs discussed in this section.

Locales

The java.util.Locale class is the centerpiece of the various internationalization APIs. Instances of this class represent *locales*, which are geographical, political, or cultural regions.

> **NOTE:** Java version 6 introduced the Locale-Sensitive Services SPI (Service Provider Interface) to let third parties support unsupported locales by introducing new implementations of various locale-sensitive classes located in the java.text and java.util packages. For example, you can use this SPI to provide new implementations of the java.util.BreakIterator class (discussed later in this chapter). To learn about Locale-Sensitive Services, and to explore an example that introduces a new currency, check out this topic in my book *Beginning Java SE 6 Platform: From Novice to Professional* (Apress, 2007; ISBN: 159059830).

Locale declares constants (such as CANADA) that describe some common locales. This class also declares three constructors for initializing Locale objects, in case you cannot find an appropriate Locale constant for a specific locale:

- Locale(String language) initializes a Locale instance to a language code; for example, "fr" for French.

- Locale(String language, String country) initializes a Locale instance to a language code and a country code; for example, "en" for English and "US" for United States.

- Locale(String language, String country, String variant) initializes a Locale instance to a language code, a country code, and a vendor- or browser-specific variant code; for example, "de" for German, "DE" for Germany, and "WIN" for Windows (or "MAC" for Macintosh).

The International Standards Organization (ISO) defines language and country codes. ISO 639 (http://ftp.ics.uci.edu/pub/ietf/http/related/iso639.txt) defines language codes. ISO 3166 (http://userpage.chemie.fu-berlin.de/diverse/doc/ISO_3166.html) defines country codes. Locale works with both standards.

NOTE: ISO 639 is not a stable standard and some language codes have changed; specifically, iw, ji, and in have changed to he, yi, and id, respectively.

Variant codes are useful for dealing with computing platform differences. For example, font differences may force you to use different characters on Windows-, Linux-, and Unix-based operating systems (such as Solaris). Unlike language and country codes, variant codes are not standardized.

Although applications can create their own Locale objects (perhaps to let users choose from similar locales), they will often call API methods that work with the *default locale*, which is the locale made available to the virtual machine at startup. An application can call Locale's static Locale getDefault() method if it needs to access this locale.

For testing or other purposes, the application can override the default locale by calling Locale's static void setDefault(Locale locale) method. setDefault() sets the default locale to locale. However, passing null to locale causes setDefault() to throw NullPointerException.

Listing 9–9 demonstrates getDefault() and setDefault().

Listing 9–9. *Viewing and changing the default locale*

```
import java.util.Locale;

public class MyLocale
{
    public static void main(String[] args)
    {
        System.out.println(Locale.getDefault());
        Locale.setDefault(Locale.CANADA);
        System.out.println(Locale.getDefault());
    }
}
```

When I run this application, I observe the following output:

```
en_US
en_CA
```

You can change the default locale that is made available to the virtual machine by assigning appropriate values to the user.language and user.country system properties when you launch the application via the java tool. For example, the following java command line changes the default locale to fr_FR:

```
java -Duser.language=fr -Duser.country=FR MyLocale
```

As you continue to explore Locale, you will discover additional useful methods. For example, static String[] getISOLanguages() returns an array of ISO 639 language codes (including former and changed codes), and static String[] getISOCountries() returns an array of ISO 3166 country codes.

> **NOTE:** Read John O'Conner's "Internationalization: Understanding Locale in the Java Platform" article (`http://java.sun.com/developer/technicalArticles/J2SE/locale/`) for more information on `Locale`.

Resource Bundles

An internationalized application contains no hard-coded text or other locale-specific elements (such as a specific currency format). Instead, each supported locale's version of these elements is stored outside of the application.

> **NOTE:** Creating a set of locale-specific elements is known as *localization*.

Java is responsible for storing each locale's version of certain elements, such as currency formats. In contrast, it is your responsibility to store each supported locale's version of other elements, such as text, audio clips, and locale-sensitive images.

Java facilitates this element storage by providing *resource bundles*, which are containers that hold one or more locale-specific elements, and which are each associated with one and only one locale.

Many applications work with one or more resource bundle families. Each family consists of resource bundles for all supported locales and typically contains one kind of element (perhaps text, or audio clips that contain language-specific verbal instructions).

Each family also shares a common *family name* (also known as a *base name*); each of its resource bundles has a unique locale designation that is appended to the family name, to differentiate one resource bundle from another within the family.

Consider an internationalized text-based game application for English and French users. After choosing game as the family name, and en and fr as the English and French locale designations, you end up with the following complete resource bundle names:

- game_en is the complete resource bundle name for English users.
- game_fr is the complete resource bundle name for French users.

Although you can store all of your game's English text in the game_en resource bundle, you might want to differentiate between American and British text (such as elevator versus lift). This differentiation leads to the following complete resource bundle names:

- game_en_US is the complete resource bundle name for users who speak the United States version of the English language.
- game_en_GB is the complete resource bundle name for users who speak the British version of the English language.

An application loads its resource bundles by calling the various getBundle() utility methods that are located in the abstract java.util.ResourceBundle class. For example, the application might call the following getBundle() factory methods:

- static ResourceBundle getBundle(String baseName) loads a resource bundle using the specified baseName and the default locale. For example, ResourceBundle resources = ResourceBundle.getBundle("game"); attempts to load the resource bundle whose base name is game, and whose locale designation matches the default locale. If the default locale is en_US, getBundle() attempts to load game_en_US.

- static ResourceBundle getBundle(String baseName, Locale locale) loads a resource bundle using the specified baseName and locale. For example, ResourceBundle resources = ResourceBundle.getBundle("game", new Locale("zh", "CN", "WIN")); attempts to load the resource bundle whose base name is game, and whose locale designation is Chinese with a Windows variant. In other words, getBundle() attempts to load game_zh_CN_WIN.

NOTE: ResourceBundle is an example of a pattern that you will discover throughout the internationalization APIs. With few exceptions, each API is architected around an abstract entry-point class whose factory methods return instances of concrete subclasses.

If the resource bundle identified by the base name and locale designation does not exist, the getBundle() methods search for the next closest bundle. For example, if the locale is en_US and game_en_US does not exist, getBundle() looks for game_en.

The getBundle() methods first generate a sequence of candidate bundle names for the specified locale (language1, country1, and variant1) and the default locale (language2, country2, and variant2) in the following order:

- baseName + "_" + language1 + "_" + country1 + "_" + variant1
- baseName + "_" + language1 + "_" + country1
- baseName + "_" + language1
- baseName + "_" + language2 + "_" + country2 + "_" + variant2
- baseName + "_" + language2 + "_" + country2
- baseName + "_" + language2
- baseName

Candidate bundle names in which the final component is an empty string are omitted from the sequence. For example, if country1 is an empty string, the second candidate bundle name is omitted.

The getBundle() methods iterate over the candidate bundle names to find the first name for which they can instantiate an actual resource bundle. For each candidate bundle name, getBundle() attempts to create a resource bundle as follows:

- It first attempts to load a class that extends the abstract java.util.ListResourceBundle class using the candidate bundle name. If such a class can be found and loaded using the specified class loader, is assignment compatible with ResourceBundle, is accessible from ResourceBundle, and can be instantiated, getBundle() creates a new instance of this class and uses it as the result resource bundle.

- Otherwise, getBundle() attempts to locate a properties file. It generates a pathname from the candidate bundle name by replacing all "." characters with "/" and appending ".properties." It attempts to find a "resource" with this name using java.lang.ClassLoader. getResource(). (Note that a "resource" in the sense of getResource() has nothing to do with the contents of a resource bundle; it is just a container of data, such as a file.) If getResource() finds a "resource," it attempts to create a new java.util.PropertyResourceBundle instance from its contents. If successful, this instance becomes the result resource bundle.

If no result resource bundle is found, getBundle() throws an instance of the java.util.MissingResourceException class; otherwise, getBundle() instantiates the bundle's parent resource bundle chain.

NOTE: The parent resource bundle chain makes it possible to obtain fallback values when resources are missing. The chain is built by using ResourceBundle's protected void setParent(ResourceBundle parent) method.

getBundle() builds the chain by iterating over the candidate bundle names that can be obtained by successively removing variant, country, and language (each time with the preceding "_") from the complete resource bundle name of the result resource bundle.

NOTE: Candidate bundle names where the final component is an empty string are omitted.

With each candidate bundle name, getBundle() tries to instantiate a resource bundle, as just described. If it succeeds, it calls the previously instantiated resource bundle's setParent() method with the new resource bundle, unless the previously instantiated resource bundle already has a nonnull parent.

NOTE: getBundle() caches instantiated resource bundles and may return the same resource bundle instance multiple times.

ResourceBundle declares various methods for accessing a resource bundle's resources. For example, Object getObject(String key) gets an object for the given key from this resource bundle or one of its parent bundles.

getObject() first tries to obtain the object from this resource bundle using the protected abstract handleGetObject() method, which is implemented by concrete subclasses of ResourceBundle (such as PropertyResourceBundle).

If handleGetObject() returns null, and if a nonnull parent resource bundle exists, getObject() calls the parent's getObject() method. If still not successful, it throws MissingResourceException.

Two other resource-access methods are String getString(String key) and String[] getStringArray(String key). These convenience methods are wrappers for (String) getObject(key) and (String[]) getObject(key).

> **NOTE:** Java version 6 introduced numerous ResourceBundle enhancements. Enhancements range from new clearCache() methods for removing resource bundles from the cache to a new nested Control class whose methods let you take control of the resource bundle search order, and even load resource bundles from another source (such as an XML file). Although Android does not support these enhancements at the time of writing, this may change in a future release of Android. I explore the enhancements to ResourceBundle in *Beginning Java SE 6 Platform: From Novice to Professional.*

Property Resource Bundles

A *property resource bundle* is a resource bundle that is backed by a *properties file*, a text file (with a .properties extension) that stores textual elements as a series of *key=value* entries. The *key* is a nonlocalized identifier that an application uses to obtain the localized *value*.

> **NOTE:** Properties files are accessed via instances of the java.util.Properties class. In Chapter 8, I mentioned that the Preferences API (discussed later in this chapter) has made Properties largely obsolete. Property resource bundles prove that the Properties class is not entirely obsolete.

PropertyResourceBundle, a concrete subclass of ResourceBundle, manages property resource bundles. You should rarely (if ever) need to work with this subclass. Instead, for maximum portability, you should only work with ResourceBundle, as Listing 9–10 demonstrates.

Listing 9–10. *Accessing a localized* elevator *entry in* game *resource bundles*

```
import java.util.ResourceBundle;

public class PropertyResourceBundleDemo
{
   public static void main(String[] args)
   {
      ResourceBundle resources = ResourceBundle.getBundle("game");
      System.out.println("elevator = " + resources.getString("elevator"));
   }
}
```

Listing 9–10 refers to ResourceBundle instead of PropertyResourceBundle, which lets you easily migrate to ListResourceBundle as necessary. I use getString() instead of getObject() for convenience; text resources are stored in textual properties files.

When you run this application, it generates the following output:

```
Exception in thread "main" java.util.MissingResourceException: Can't find bundle for
base name game, locale en_US
        at java.util.ResourceBundle.throwMissingResourceException(Unknown Source)
        at java.util.ResourceBundle.getBundleImpl(Unknown Source)
        at java.util.ResourceBundle.getBundle(Unknown Source)
        at PropertyResourceBundleDemo.main(PropertyResourceBundleDemo.java:7)
```

This exception is thrown because no property resource bundles exist. You can easily remedy this situation by copying Listing 9–11 into a game.properties file, which is the basis for a property resource bundle.

Listing 9–11. *A fallback* game.properties *resource bundle*

```
elevator=elevator
```

Assuming that game.properties is located in the same directory as PropertyResourceBundleDemo.class, execute java PropertyResourceBundleDemo and you will see the following output:

```
elevator = elevator
```

Because my locale is en_US, getBundle() first tries to load game_en_US.properties. Because this file does not exist, getBundle() tries to load game_en.properties. Because this file does not exist, getBundle() tries to load game.properties, and succeeds.

Copy Listing 9–12 into a game_en_GB.properties file.

Listing 9–12. *A* game *resource bundle for the en_GB locale*

```
elevator=lift
```

Execute java -Duser.language=en -Duser.country=GB PropertyResourceBundleDemo. This time, you should see the following output:

```
elevator = lift
```

With the locale set to en_GB, getBundle() first tries to load game_en_GB.properties, and succeeds.

Comment out elevator = lift by prepending a # character to this line (as in #elevator = lift). Then execute java -Duser.language=en -Duser.country=GB PropertyResourceBundleDemo and you should see the following output:

```
elevator = elevator
```

Although getBundle() loaded game_en_GB.properties, getString() (via getObject()) could not find an elevator entry. As a result, getString()/getObject() searched the parent resource bundle chain, encountering game.properties' elevator=elevator entry, whose elevator value was subsequently returned.

> **NOTE:** A common reason for getString() throwing MissingResourceException in a property resource bundle context is forgetting to append .properties to a properties file's name.

List Resource Bundles

A *list resource bundle* is a resource bundle that is backed by a classfile, which describes a concrete subclass of ListResourceBundle (an abstract subclass of ResourceBundle). As a result, list resource bundles can store binary data (such as images or audio) as well as text. In contrast, property resource bundles can only store text.

> **NOTE:** If a property resource bundle and a list resource bundle have the same complete resource bundle name, the list resource bundle takes precedence over the property resource bundle. For example, when getBundle() is confronted with game_en.properties and game_en.class, it loads game_en.class instead of game_en.properties.

Listing 9–13 demonstrates a list resource bundle by presenting a flags_en_CA class that extends ListResourceBundle.

Listing 9–13. *A resource bundle containing a small Canadian flag image and English/French text*

```
import java.awt.Toolkit;

import java.util.ListResourceBundle;

public class flags_en_CA extends ListResourceBundle
{
    private byte image[] =
    {
        (byte) 137,
        (byte) 80,
        (byte) 78,
        (byte) 71,
        (byte) 13,
        (byte) 10,
        (byte) 26,
        (byte) 10,
```

```
         (byte) 0,
         (byte) 0,
// ...
         (byte) 0,
         (byte) 0,
         (byte) 73,
         (bytc) 69,
         (byte) 78,
         (byte) 68,
         (byte) 174,
         (byte) 66,
         (byte) 96,
         (byte) 130
      };
      private Object[][] contents =
      {
         { "flag", Toolkit.getDefaultToolkit().createImage(image) },
         { "msg", "Welcome to Canada! | Bienvenue vers le Canada !" },
         { "title", "CANADA | LA CANADA" }
      };
      public Object[][] getContents()
      {
         return contents;
      }
}
```

Listing 9–13's flags_en_CA class describes a list resource bundle whose base name is flags and whose locale designation is en_CA. This class's image array stores a Portable Network Graphics (PNG)-based sequence of byte integers that describes an image of the Canadian flag, contents stores key/value pairs, and getContents() returns contents.

NOTE: For brevity, Listing 9–13 does not present the complete image array with Canadian flag image data. You must obtain flags_en_CA.java from this book's companion code file (see the book's introduction for instructions on how to obtain this file) to get the complete listing.

The first key/value pair consists of a key named flag (which will be passed to ResourceBundle's getObject() method) and an instance of the java.awt.Image class. This instance represents the flag image and is obtained with the help of the java.awt.Toolkit class and its createImage() utility method.

NOTE: AWT stands for *Abstract Window Toolkit*, a windowing toolkit that makes it possible to create crude user interfaces consisting of windows, buttons, text fields, and so on. The AWT was released as part of Java version 1.0 in 1995, and continues to be part of Java's standard class library. The AWT is not supported by Android.

Listing 9–14 shows you how to load the default flags_en_CA list resource bundle (or another list resource bundle via command-line arguments) and display its flag and text.

Listing 9–14. *Obtaining and displaying a list resource bundle's flag image and text*

```java
import java.awt.EventQueue;
import java.awt.Image;

import java.util.Locale;
import java.util.ResourceBundle;

import javax.swing.ImageIcon;
import javax.swing.JOptionPane;

public class ListResourceBundleDemo
{
    public static void main(String[] args)
    {
        Locale l = Locale.CANADA;
        if (args.length == 2)
            l = new Locale(args[0], args[1]);
        final ResourceBundle resources = ResourceBundle.getBundle("flags", l);
        Runnable r = new Runnable()
                     {
                         public void run()
                         {
                             Image image = (Image) resources.getObject("flag");
                             String msg = resources.getString("msg");
                             String title = resources.getString("title");
                             ImageIcon ii = new ImageIcon(image);
                             JOptionPane.showMessageDialog(null,
                                                           msg,
                                                           title,
                                                           JOptionPane.PLAIN_MESSAGE,
                                                           ii);
                         }
                     };
        EventQueue.invokeLater(r);
    }
}
```

Listing 9–14's `main()` method begins by selecting `CANADA` as its default `Locale`. If it detects that two arguments were passed on the command line, `main()` assumes that the first argument is the language code and the second argument is the country code, and creates a new `Locale` object based on these arguments as its default locale.

`main()` next attempts to load a list resource bundle by passing the `flags` base name and the previously chosen `Locale` object to `ResourceBundle`'s `getBundle()` method. Assuming that `MissingResourceException` is not thrown, `main()` creates a runnable task on which to load resources from the list resource bundle and display them graphically.

`main()` relies on a windowing toolkit known as *Swing* to present a simple user interface that displays the flag and text. Because Swing is single threaded, where everything runs on a special thread known as the *event-dispatching thread*, it is important that all Swing-based operations occur on this thread. `EventQueue.invokeLater()` makes this happen.

> **NOTE:** Swing is built on top of the AWT and provides many sophisticated features. This windowing toolkit was officially released as part of Java version 1.2, and continues to be part of Java's standard class library. Swing is not supported by Android.
>
> If you would like to learn more about Swing, I recommend the definitive *Java Swing, Second Edition*, by Marc Loy, Robert Eckstein, David Wood, James Elliott, and Brian Cole (O'Reilly Media, 2002; ISBN: 0596004087).

Shortly after EventQueue.invokeLater() is executed on the main thread, the event-dispatching thread starts running and executes the runnable task. This task first obtains the Image object from the list resource bundle by passing flag to getObject() and casting this method's return value to Image.

The task then obtains the msg and title strings by passing these keys to getString(), and converts the Image object to a javax.swing.ImageIcon instance. This instance is required by the subsequent JOptionPane.showMessageDialog() method call, which presents a simple message-oriented dialog box.

> **NOTE:** JOptionPane is a Swing component that makes it easy to display a standard dialog box that prompts the user to enter a value or informs the user of something important.

Now that you understand how ListResourceBundleDemo works, obtain the complete flags_en_CA.java source file, compile this source code (javac flags_en_CA.java) and Listing 9–14 (javac ListResourceBundleDemo.java), and execute the application (java ListResourceBundleDemo). Figure 9–1 shows the resulting user interface on Windows XP.

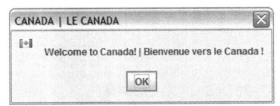

Figure 9–1. *An almost completely localized dialog box (OK is not localized) displaying Canada-specific resources on Windows XP*

> **NOTE:** I obtained the language translations for this section's examples from Yahoo! Babel Fish (http://babelfish.yahoo.com/), an online text translation service.

This book's accompanying code file also contains flags_fr_FR.java, which presents resources localized for the France locale. After compiling this source file, execute java ListResourceBundleDemo fr FR and you will see Figure 9–2.

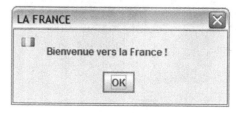

Figure 9–2. *An almost completely localized dialog box displaying France-specific resources on Windows XP*

Finally, this book's accompanying code file also contains `flags_ru_RU.java`, which presents resources localized for the Russia locale. After compiling this source file, execute `java ListResourceBundleDemo ru RU` and you will see Figure 9–3.

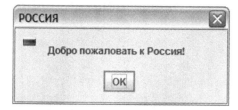

Figure 9–3. *An almost completely localized dialog box displaying Russia-specific resources on Windows XP*

> **NOTE:** You will need to ensure that appropriate Cyrillic fonts are installed to view the Russian text. Also, because I stored Russian characters verbatim (and not as Unicode escape sequences, such as `'\u0041'`), `flags_ru_RU.java` is a Unicode file and must be compiled via `javac -encoding Unicode flags_ru_RU.java`.

Break Iterators

Internationalized text-processing applications (such as word processors) need to detect logical boundaries within the text they are manipulating. For example, a word processor needs to detect these boundaries when highlighting a character, selecting a word to cut to the clipboard, moving the *caret* (text insertion point indicator) to the start of the next sentence, and wrapping a word at the end of a line.

Java provides the Break Iterator API with its abstract `java.text.BreakIterator` entry-point class to detect text boundaries.

`BreakIterator` declares the following factory methods for obtaining break iterators that detect character, word, sentence, and line boundaries:

- `static BreakIterator getCharacterInstance()`
- `static BreakIterator getWordInstance()`
- `static BreakIterator getSentenceInstance()`
- `static BreakIterator getLineInstance()`

Each of these factory methods returns a break iterator for the default locale. If you need a break iterator for a specific locale, you can call the following factory methods:

- static BreakIterator getCharacterInstance(Locale locale)

- static BreakIterator getWordInstance(Locale locale)

- static BreakIterator getSentenceInstance(Locale locale)

- static BreakIterator getLineInstance(Locale locale)

Each of these factory methods throws NullPointerException when its locale argument is null.

BreakIterator's locale-sensitive factory methods might not support every locale. For this reason, you should only pass Locale objects that are also stored in the array returned from this class's static Locale[] getAvailableLocales() method (which is also declared in other entry-point classes) to the aforementioned factory methods—this array contains at least Locale.US. Check out Listing 9–15.

Listing 9–15. *Obtaining* BreakIterator*'s supported locales and passing the first locale (possibly* Locale.US*) to* getCharacterInstance(Locale)

```
Locale[] supportedLocales = BreakIterator.getAvailableLocales();
BreakIterator bi = BreakIterator.getCharacterInstance(supportedLocales[0]);
```

A BreakIterator instance has an imaginary cursor that points to the current boundary within a text string. This cursor position can be interrogated and the cursor moved from boundary to boundary with the help of the following BreakIterator methods:

- abstract int current() returns the text boundary that was most recently returned by next(), next(int), previous(), first(), last(), following(int), or preceding(int). If any of these methods returns BreakIterator.DONE because either the first or the last text boundary has been reached, current() returns the first or last text boundary depending on which one was reached.

- abstract int first() returns the first text boundary. The iterator's current position is set to this boundary.

- abstract int following(int offset) returns the first text boundary following the specified character offset. If offset equals the last text boundary, following(int) returns BreakIterator.DONE and the iterator's current position is unchanged. Otherwise, the iterator's current position is set to the returned text boundary. The value returned is always greater than offset or BreakIterator.DONE.

- abstract int last() returns the last text boundary. The iterator's current position is set to this boundary.

- abstract int next() returns the text boundary following the current boundary. If the current boundary is the last text boundary, next() returns BreakIterator.DONE and the iterator's current position is unchanged. Otherwise, the iterator's current position is set to the boundary following the current boundary.

- abstract int next(int n) returns the nth text boundary from the current boundary. If either the first or the last text boundary has been reached, next(int) returns BreakIterator.DONE and the current position is set to either the first or last text boundary depending on which one is reached. Otherwise, the iterator's current position is set to the new text boundary.

- int preceding(int offset) returns the last text boundary preceding the specified character offset. If offset equals the first text boundary, preceding(int) returns BreakIterator.DONE and the iterator's current position is unchanged. Otherwise, the iterator's current position is set to the returned text boundary. The returned value is always less than offset or equals BreakIterator.DONE. (This method was added to BreakIterator in Java version 1.2. It could not be declared abstract because abstract methods cannot be added to existing classes; such methods would also have to be implemented in subclasses that might be inaccessible.)

- abstract int previous() returns the text boundary preceding the current boundary. If the current boundary is the first text boundary, previous() returns BreakIterator.DONE and the iterator's current position is unchanged. Otherwise, the iterator's current position is set to the boundary preceding the current boundary.

Figure 9–4 reveals that characters are located between boundaries, boundaries are zero-based, and the last boundary is the length of the string.

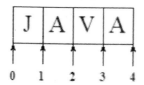

Figure 9–4. *JAVA's character boundaries as reported by the* next() *and* previous() *methods*

BreakIterator also declares a void setText(String newText) method that identifies newText as the text to be iterated over. This method resets the cursor position to the beginning of this string.

Listing 9–16 shows you how to use a character-based break iterator to iterate over a string's characters in a locale-independent manner.

Listing 9–16. *Iterating over English/US and Arabic/Saudi Arabia strings*

```
import java.text.BreakIterator;

import java.util.Locale;

public class BreakIteratorDemo
```

```
{
   public static void main(String[] args)
   {
      BreakIterator bi = BreakIterator.getCharacterInstance(Locale.US);
      bi.setText("JAVA");
      dumpPositions(bi);
      bi = BreakIterator.getCharacterInstance(new Locale("ar", "SA"));
      bi.setText("\u0631\u0641\u0651");
      dumpPositions(bi);
   }
   static void dumpPositions(BreakIterator bi)
   {
      int boundary = bi.first();
      while (boundary != BreakIterator.DONE)
      {
         System.out.print(boundary + " ");
         boundary = bi.next();
      }
      System.out.println();
   }
}
```

The main() method first obtains a character-based break iterator for the United States locale. main() then calls the iterator's setText() method to specify JAVA as the text to be iterated over.

Iteration occurs in the dumpPositions() method. After calling first() to obtain the first boundary, this method uses a while loop to output the boundary and move to the next boundary (via next()) while the current boundary does not equal BreakIterator.DONE.

Because character iteration is straightforward for English words, main() next obtains a character-based break iterator for the Saudi Arabia locale, and uses this iterator to iterate over the characters in Figure 9–5's Arabic version of "shelf" (as in shelf of books).

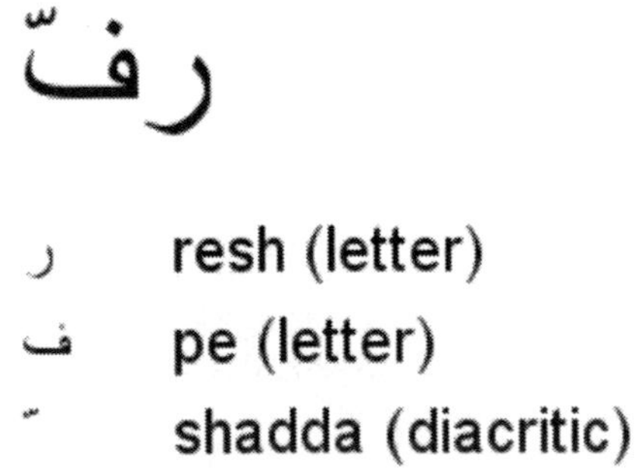

ر   resh (letter)

ف   pe (letter)

ّ   shadda (diacritic)

Figure 9–5. *The letters and diacritic making up the Arabic equivalent of "shelf" are written from right to left.*

In Arabic, the word "shelf" consists of letters resh and pe, and diacritic shadda. A *diacritic* is an ancillary *glyph*, or mark on paper or other writing medium, added to a letter, or basic glyph. Shadda, which is shaped like a small written Latin w, indicates *gemination* (consonant doubling or extra length), which is *phonemic* (the smallest identifiable discrete unit of sound employed to form meaningful contrasts between utterances) in Arabic. Shadda is written above the consonant that is to be doubled, which happens to be pe in this example.

When you run this application, it generates the following output:

```
0 1 2 3 4
0 1 3
```

The first output line reveals Figure 9–4's character boundaries for the word JAVA. The second output line (0 comes before resh, 1 comes before pe) implies that you cannot move an Arabic word processor's caret on the screen once for every Unicode character. Instead, it is moved once for every *user character*, a logical character that can be composed of multiple Unicode characters, such as pe (\u0641) and shadda (\u0651).

> **NOTE:** For examples of break iterators that iterate over words, sentences, and lines, check out the "Detecting Text Boundaries" section (http://download.oracle.com/docs/cd/E17409_01/javase/tutorial/i18n/text/boundaryintro.html) in *The Java Tutorials*' Internationalization trail.

Collators

Applications perform string comparisons while sorting text. When an application targets English-oriented users, String's compareTo() method is probably sufficient for comparing strings. However, this method's binary comparison of each string's Unicode characters is not reliable for languages where the relative order of their characters does not correspond to the Unicode values of these characters. French is one example.

Java provides the Collator API with its abstract java.text.Collator entry-point class for making reliable comparisons.

Collator declares the following factory methods for obtaining collators:

- static Collator getInstance()
- static Collator getInstance(Locale locale)

The first factory method obtains a collator for the default locale; the second factory method throws NullPointerException when its locale argument is null. As with BreakIterator, you should only pass Locale objects that are also stored in the array returned from Collator's static Locale[] getAvailableLocales() method to the second factory method.

Listing 9–17 shows you how to use a collator to perform comparisons so that French words that differ only in terms of accented characters are sorted into the correct order.

Listing 9–17. *Using a collator to correctly order French words in the France locale*

```
import java.text.Collator;

import java.util.Arrays;
import java.util.Locale;
```

```
public class CollatorDemo
{
    public static void main(String[] args)
    {
        Collator en_USCollator = Collator.getInstance(Locale.US);
        Collator fr_FRCollator = Collator.getInstance(Locale.FRANCE);
        String[] words =
        {
            "côte", "coté", "côté", "cote"
        };
        Arrays.sort(words, en_USCollator);
        for (String word: words)
            System.out.println(word);
        System.out.println();
        Arrays.sort(words, fr_FRCollator);
        for (String word: words)
            System.out.println(word);
    }
}
```

In Listing 9–17, each of the four words being sorted has a different meaning. For example, côte means coast and coté means side.

When you run this application, it generates the following output (I am showing this output as it appears in the Windows XP Notepad editor):

```
cote
coté
côte
côté

cote
côte
coté
côté
```

The first four output lines show the order in which these words are sorted according to the en_US locale. This ordering is not correct because it does not account for accents. In contrast, the final four output lines show the correct order when the words are sorted according to the fr_FR locale. Words are compared as if none of the characters contain accents, and then equal words are compared from right to left for accents.

> **NOTE:** Learn about Collator's java.text.RuleBasedCollator subclass for creating custom collators when predefined collation rules do not meet your needs, and about improving collation performance via java.text.CollationKey and Collator's CollationKey getCollationKey(String source) method by reading the "Comparing Strings" section (http://download.oracle.com/docs/cd/E17409_01/javase/tutorial/i18n/text/collationintro.html) in *The Java Tutorials'* Internationalization trail.

Dates, Time Zones, and Calendars

Internationalized applications must properly handle dates, time zones, and calendars. A *date* is a recorded temporal moment, a *time zone* is a set of geographical regions that share a common number of hours relative to Greenwich Mean Time (GMT), and a *calendar* is a system of organizing the passage of time.

> **NOTE:** GMT identifies the standard geographical location from where all time is measured. UTC, which stands for Coordinated Universal Time, is often specified in place of GMT.

Java version 1.0 introduced the `java.util.Date` class as its first attempt to describe calendars. However, `Date` was not amenable to internationalization because of its English-oriented nature, and because of its inability to represent dates prior to midnight January 1, 1970 GMT, which is known as the *Unix epoch*.

`Date` was eventually refactored to make it more useful by allowing `Date` instances to represent dates prior to the epoch as well as after the epoch, and by deprecating most of this class's constructors and methods—deprecated methods have been replaced by more appropriate API classes. Table 9–3 describes the more useful `Date` class.

Table 9–3. *Date Constructors and Methods*

Method	Description
`Date()`	Allocate a `Date` object and initialize it to the current time by calling `System.currentTimeMillis()`.
`Date(long date)`	Allocate a `Date` object and initialize it to the time represented by `date` milliseconds. A negative value indicates a time before the epoch, 0 indicates the epoch, and a positive value indicates a time after the epoch.
`boolean after (Date date)`	Return true when this date occurs after `date`. This method throws `NullPointerException` when `date` is null.
`boolean before (Date date)`	Return true when this date occurs before `date`. This method throws `NullPointerException` when `date` is null.
`Object clone()`	Return a copy of this object.
`int compareTo (Date date)`	Compare this date with `date`. Return 0 when this date equals `date`, a negative value when this date comes before `date`, and a positive value when this date comes after `date`. This method throws `NullPointerException` when `date` is null.
`boolean equals (Object obj)`	Compare this date with the `Date` object represented by `obj`. Return true if and only if `obj` is not null and is a `Date` object that represents the same point in time (to the millisecond) as this date.

Method	Description
long getTime()	Return the number of milliseconds that must elapse before the epoch (a negative value) or have elapsed since the epoch (a positive value).
int hashCode()	Return this date's hash code. The result is the exclusive OR of the two halves of the long integer value returned by getTime(). That is, the hash code is the value of expression (int) (this.getTime()^(this.getTime()>>>32)).
void setTime (long time)	Set this date to represent the point in time specified by time milliseconds (a negative value refers to before the epoch; a positive value refers to after the epoch).
String toString()	Return a String object containing this date's representation as dow mon dd hh:mm:ss zzz yyyy, where dow is the day of the week (Sun, Mon, Tue, Wed, Thu, Fri, Sat), mon is the month (Jan, Feb, Mar, Apr, May, Jun, Jul, Aug, Sep, Oct, Nov, Dec), dd is the two decimal digit day of the month (01 through 31), hh is the two decimal digit hour of the day (00 through 23), mm is the two decimal digit minute within the hour (00 through 59), ss is the two decimal digit second within the minute (00 through 61, where 60 and 61 account for leap seconds), zzz is the (possibly empty) time zone (and may reflect daylight saving time), and yyyy is the four decimal digit year.

Listing 9–18 provides a small demonstration of the Date class.

Listing 9–18. *Exploring the Date class*

```
import java.util.Date;

class DateDemo
{
   public static void main(String[] args)
   {
      Date now = new Date();
      System.out.println(now);
      Date later = new Date(now.getTime()+86400);
      System.out.println(later);
      System.out.println(now.after(later));
      System.out.println(now.before(later));
   }
}
```

Listing 9–18's main() method creates a pair of Date objects (now and later) and outputs their dates, formatted according to Date's implicitly called toString() method. main() then demonstrates after() and before(), proving that now comes before later, which is one second in the future.

When you run this application, it generates output similar to the following:

```
Sun Jul 25 18:36:20 CDT 2010
Sun Jul 25 18:37:47 CDT 2010
false
true
```

The toString() method's description and Listing 9–18's output reveal that a time zone is part of a date. Java provides the abstract java.util.TimeZone entry-point class for obtaining TimeZone instances. This class declares a pair of factory methods for obtaining TimeZone instances:

- static TimeZone getDefault()

- static TimeZone getTimeZone(String ID)

The latter method returns a TimeZone instance for the time zone whose String identifier (such as "CST") is passed to ID.

> **NOTE:** Some time zones take into account *daylight saving time*, the practice of temporarily advancing clocks so that afternoons have more daylight and mornings have less; for example, Central Daylight Time (CDT). Check out Wikipedia's "Daylight saving time" entry (http://en.wikipedia.org/wiki/Daylight_saving_time) to learn more about daylight saving time.
>
> If you need to introduce a new time zone or modify an existing time zone, perhaps to deal with changes to a time zone's daylight saving time policy, you can work directly with TimeZone's java.util.SimpleTimeZone concrete subclass. SimpleTimeZone describes a raw offset from GMT and provides rules for specifying the start and end of daylight saving time.

Java version 1.1 introduced the Calendar API with its abstract java.util.Calendar entry-point class as a replacement for Date. Calendar is intended to represent any kind of calendar. However, time constraints meant that only the Gregorian calendar could be implemented (via the concrete java.util.GregorianCalendar subclass) for version 1.1.

> **NOTE:** Java version 1.4 introduced support for the Thai Buddhist calendar via an internal class that subclasses Calendar. Java version 6 introduced support for the Japanese Imperial Era calendar via the package-private java.util.JapaneseImperialCalendar class, which also subclasses Calendar. For an in-depth look at the Japanese Imperial Era calendar, and to explore an example that presents this calendar graphically, check out this topic in *Beginning Java SE 6 Platform: From Novice to Professional.*

Calendar declares the following factory methods for obtaining calendars:

- static Calendar getInstance()

- static Calendar getInstance(Locale locale)

- static Calendar getInstance(TimeZone zone)

- static Calendar getInstance(TimeZone zone, Locale locale)

The first and third methods return calendars for the default locale; the second and fourth methods take the specified locale into account. Also, calendars returned by the first two methods are based on the current time in the default time zone; calendars returned by the last two methods are based on the current time in the specified time zone.

Calendar declares various constants, including YEAR, MONTH, DAY_OF_MONTH, DAY_OF_WEEK, LONG, and SHORT. These constants identify the year (four digits), month (0 represents January), current month day (1 through the month's last day), and current weekday (1 represents Sunday) calendar fields, and display styles (such as January versus Jan).

The first four constants are used with Calendar's various set() methods to set calendar fields to specific values (set the year field to 2010, for example). They are also used with Calendar's int get(int field) method to return field values, along with other field-oriented methods, such as void clear(int field) (unset a field).

The latter two constants are used with Calendar's String getDisplayName(int field, int style, Locale locale) and Map<String,Integer> getDisplayNames(int field, int style, Locale locale) methods, which return short (Jan, for example) or long (January, for example) localized String representations of various field values.

Listing 9–19 shows you how to use various Calendar constants and methods to output calendar pages according to the en_US and fr_FR locales.

Listing 9–19. *Outputting calendar pages*

```
import java.util.Calendar;
import java.util.Iterator;
import java.util.Locale;
import java.util.Map;
import java.util.Set;

public class CalendarDemo
{
    public static void main(String[] args)
    {
        if (args.length < 2)
        {
            System.err.println("usage: java CalendarDemo yyyy mm [f|F]");
            return;
        }
        try
        {
            int year = Integer.parseInt(args[0]);
            int month = Integer.parseInt(args[1]);
            Locale locale = Locale.US;
            if (args.length == 3 && args[2].equalsIgnoreCase("f"))
                locale = Locale.FRANCE;
            showPage(year, month, locale);
        }
        catch (NumberFormatException nfe)
        {
            System.err.print(nfe);
        }
    }
    static void showPage(int year, int month, Locale locale)
    {
        if (month < 1 || month > 12)
            throw new IllegalArgumentException("month [" + month + "] out of " +
```

```
                                             "range [1, 12]");
      Calendar cal = Calendar.getInstance(locale);
      cal.set(Calendar.YEAR, year);
      cal.set(Calendar.MONTH, --month);
      cal.set(Calendar.DAY_OF_MONTH, 1);
      displayMonthAndYear(cal, locale);
      displayWeekdayNames(cal, locale);
      int daysInMonth = cal.getActualMaximum(Calendar.DAY_OF_MONTH);
      int firstRowGap = cal.get(Calendar.DAY_OF_WEEK)-1; // 0 = Sunday
      for (int i = 0; i < firstRowGap; i++)
         System.out.print("   ");
      for (int i = 1; i <= daysInMonth; i++)
      {
         if (i < 10)
            System.out.print(' ');
         System.out.print(i);
         if ((firstRowGap+i)%7 == 0)
            System.out.println();
         else
            System.out.print(' ');
      }
      System.out.println();
   }
   static void displayMonthAndYear(Calendar cal, Locale locale)
   {
      System.out.println(cal.getDisplayName(Calendar.MONTH, Calendar.LONG,
                                      locale) + " " +
                                      cal.get(Calendar.YEAR));
   }
   static void displayWeekdayNames(Calendar cal, Locale locale)
   {
      Map<String, Integer> weekdayNamesMap;
      weekdayNamesMap = cal.getDisplayNames(Calendar.DAY_OF_WEEK,
                                      Calendar.SHORT, locale);
      String[] names = new String[weekdayNamesMap.size()];
      int[] indexes = new int[weekdayNamesMap.size()];
      Set<Map.Entry<String, Integer>> weekdayNamesEntries;
      weekdayNamesEntries = weekdayNamesMap.entrySet();
      Iterator<Map.Entry<String, Integer>> iter;
      iter = weekdayNamesEntries.iterator();
      while (iter.hasNext())
      {
         Map.Entry<String, Integer> entry = iter.next();
         names[entry.getValue()-1] = entry.getKey();
         indexes[entry.getValue()-1] = entry.getValue();
      }
      for (int i = 0; i < names.length; i++)
         for (int j = i; j < names.length; j++)
            if (indexes[j] == i+1)
            {
               System.out.print(names[j].substring(0, 2) + " ");
               continue;
            }
      System.out.println();
   }
}
```

Listing 9–19 is pretty straightforward, with the exception of displayWeekdayNames(). This method calls Calendar's getDisplayNames() method to return a map of localized weekday names. Instead of returning a map where the keys are Integers and the values are localized Strings, this map's keys are the localized Strings.

This would be fine if the keys were ordered (as in Sunday first and Saturday last, or lundi first and dimanche last). However, they are not ordered. To output these names in order, it is necessary to obtain a set of map entries, iterate over these entries and populate parallel arrays, and then iterate over these arrays to output the weekday names.

> **NOTE:** A French calendar begins the week on lundi (Monday) and ends it on dimanche (Sunday). However, Calendar does not take this ordering into account.

Specify java CalendarDemo 2010 7 and you will see the following calendar page for the en_US locale:

```
July 2010
Su Mo Tu We Th Fr Sa
             1  2  3
 4  5  6  7  8  9 10
11 12 13 14 15 16 17
18 19 20 21 22 23 24
25 26 27 28 29 30 31
```

If you would like to see this page in the fr_FR locale, specify java CalendarDemo 2010 7 f or java CalendarDemo 2010 7 F:

```
juillet 2010
di lu ma me je ve sa
             1  2  3
 4  5  6  7  8  9 10
11 12 13 14 15 16 17
18 19 20 21 22 23 24
25 26 27 28 29 30 31
```

> **NOTE:** Calendar declares a Date getTime() method that returns a calendar's time representation as a Date instance. Calendar also declares a void setTime(Date date) method that sets a calendar's time representation to the specified date.
>
> *Joda Time* (http://joda-time.sourceforge.net/), the Java date and time API, offers a high-quality replacement for Java's date and time classes. You might prefer to use these classes as an alternative.

Formatters

Internationalized applications do not present unformatted numbers (including currencies and percentages), dates, and messages to the user. These items must be formatted according to the user's locale so they appear meaningful to the user. To help with formatting, Java provides the abstract `java.text.Format` class and various subclasses.

> **NOTE:** Format defines the programming interface for formatting locale-sensitive objects into `Strings` via its `format()` methods, and for parsing `Strings` back into objects via its `parseObject()` methods. For brevity, I ignore the `parseObject()` methods.

Number Formatters

The abstract `java.text.NumberFormat` entry-point class (a `Format` subclass) declares the following factory methods to return formatters that format numbers as currencies, integers, numbers with decimal points, and percentages (and also to parse such values):

- `static NumberFormat getCurrencyInstance()`
- `static NumberFormat getCurrencyInstance(Locale locale)`
- `static NumberFormat getIntegerInstance()`
- `static NumberFormat getIntegerInstance(Locale locale)`
- `static NumberFormat getInstance()`
- `static NumberFormat getInstance(Locale locale)`
- `static NumberFormat getNumberInstance()`
- `static NumberFormat getNumberInstance(Locale locale)`
- `static NumberFormat getPercentInstance()`
- `static NumberFormat getPercentInstance(Locale locale)`

The `getInstance()` and `getInstance(Locale)` factory methods are equivalent to `getNumberInstance()` and `getNumberInstance(Locale)`. They are present as a shorthand convenience to the longer-named `getNumberInstance()` methods.

Listing 9–20 shows you how to obtain and use number formatters to format numbers as currencies, integers, numbers with decimals points, and percentages for various locales.

Listing 9–20. *Formatting numbers as currencies, integers, numbers with decimal points, and percentages*

```
import java.text.NumberFormat;

import java.util.Locale;

public class NumberFormatDemo
{
```

```
public static void main(String[] args)
{
    System.out.println("Unformatted: " + 9875432.25);
    formatCurrencies(Locale.US, 98765432.25);
    formatCurrencies(Locale.FRANCE, 98765432.25);
    formatCurrencies(Locale.GERMANY, 98765432.25);
    System.out.println();
    System.out.println("Unformatted: " + 123456789.0);
    formatIntegers(Locale.US, 123456789.0);
    formatIntegers(Locale.FRANCE, 123456789.0);
    formatIntegers(Locale.GERMANY, 123456789.0);
    System.out.println();
    System.out.println("Unformatted: " + 6751.326);
    formatNumbers(Locale.US, 6751.326);
    formatNumbers(Locale.FRANCE, 6751.326);
    formatNumbers(Locale.GERMANY, 6751.326);
    System.out.println();
    System.out.println("Unformatted: " + 0.85);
    formatPercentages(Locale.US, 0.85);
    formatPercentages(Locale.FRANCE, 0.85);
    formatPercentages(Locale.GERMANY, 0.85);
}
static void formatCurrencies(Locale locale, double amount)
{
    NumberFormat nf = NumberFormat.getCurrencyInstance(locale);
    System.out.println(locale + ": " + nf.format(amount));
}
static void formatIntegers(Locale locale, double amount)
{
    NumberFormat nf = NumberFormat.getIntegerInstance(locale);
    System.out.println(locale + " : " + nf.format(amount));
}
static void formatNumbers(Locale locale, double amount)
{
    NumberFormat nf = NumberFormat.getNumberInstance(locale);
    System.out.println(locale + ": " + nf.format(amount));
}
static void formatPercentages(Locale locale, double amount)
{
    NumberFormat nf = NumberFormat.getPercentInstance(locale);
    System.out.println(locale + ": " + nf.format(amount));
}
}
```

Listing 9–20 uses a double instead of a BigDecimal object to represent 9875432.25 as a currency, for simplicity and because this value can be represented exactly as a double.

When you run this application, it generates output that is shown with the Windows XP Notepad editor window (so that the Euro currency symbol can be seen) in Figure 9–6.

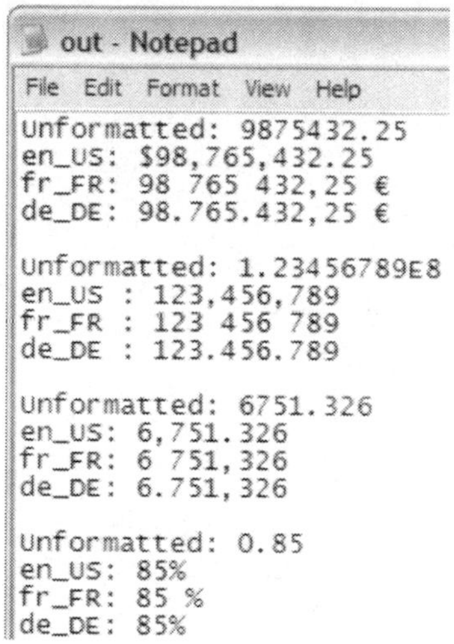

Figure 9–6. *Unformatted and formatted numeric output for the US, France, and Germany locales*

NumberFormat declares void setMaximumFractionDigits(int newValue), void setMaximumIntegerDigits(int newValue), void setMinimumFractionDigits(int newValue), and void setMinimumIntegerDigits(int newValue) methods to limit the number of digits that are allowed in a formatted number's integer or fraction. These methods are helpful for aligning numbers, as Listing 9–21 demonstrates.

Listing 9–21. *Aligning numbers*

```
NumberFormat nf = NumberFormat.getInstance();
System.out.println(nf.format(123.4567)); // Output: 123.457
nf.setMaximumIntegerDigits(10);
nf.setMinimumIntegerDigits(6);
nf.setMaximumFractionDigits(2);
nf.setMinimumFractionDigits(2);
System.out.println(nf.format(123.4567)); // Output: 000,123.46
System.out.println(nf.format(80978.3)); // Output : 080,978.30
```

This code fragment specifies that a number's integer portion cannot exceed ten digits, but must have a minimum of six digits. Leading zeros are output to meet the minimum. The code fragment reveals that the fraction is rounded.

A concrete subclass of NumberFormat might enforce an upper limit on the value passed to setMaximumFractionDigits(int), setMaximumIntegerDigits(int), setMinimumFractionDigits(int), or setMinimumIntegerDigits(int). Call getMaximumFractionDigits(), getMaximumIntegerDigits(), getMinimumFactionDigits(), or getMinimumIntegerDigits() to find out if the value you specified has been accepted.

> **NOTE:** If you ever need to create customized number formatters, you will find yourself working with NumberFormat's java.text.DecimalFormat subclass and this subclass's java.text.DecimalFormatSymbols companion class. The "Customizing Formats" section (http://download.oracle.com/docs/cd/E17409_01/javase/tutorial/i18n/format/decimalFormat.html) in *The Java Tutorials'* Internationalization trail introduces you to these classes.

Date Formatters

The abstract java.text.DateFormat entry-point class (a Format subclass) provides access to formatters that format Date instances as dates or time values (and also to parse such values). This class declares the following factory methods:

- static DateFormat getDateInstance()
- static DateFormat getDateInstance(int style)
- static DateFormat getDateInstance(int style, Locale locale)
- static DateFormat getDateTimeInstance()
- static DateFormat getDateTimeInstance(int dateStyle, int timeStyle)
- static DateFormat getDateTimeInstance(int dateStyle, int timeStyle, Locale locale)
- static DateFormat getInstance()
- static DateFormat getTimeInstance()
- static DateFormat getTimeInstance(int style)
- static DateFormat getTimeInstance(int style, Locale locale)

The getDateInstance() factory methods' formatters generate only date information, the getTimeInstance() factory methods' formatters generate only time information, and the getDateTimeInstance() factory methods' formatters generate date and time information.

The dateStyle and timeStyle fields determine how that information will be presented according to the following DateFormat constants:

- SHORT is completely numeric, such as 12.13.52 or 3:30pm
- MEDIUM is longer, such as Jan 12, 1952
- LONG is longer, such as January 12, 1952 or 3:30:32pm
- FULL is pretty completely specified, such as Tuesday, April 12, 1952 AD or 3:30:42pm PST.

Listing 9–22 shows you how to format a Date instance that represents the Unix epoch according to the local time zone and the UTC time zone.

Listing 9–22. *Formatting the Unix epoch*

```java
import java.text.DateFormat;

import java.util.Date;
import java.util.Locale;
import java.util.TimeZone;

public class DateFormatDemo
{
   public static void main(String[] args)
   {
      Date d = new Date(0); // Unix epoch
      System.out.println(d);
      DateFormat df = DateFormat.getDateTimeInstance(DateFormat.LONG,
                                                     DateFormat.LONG,
                                                     Locale.US);
      System.out.println("Default format: " + df.format(d));
      df.setTimeZone(TimeZone.getTimeZone("UTC"));
      System.out.println("Taking UTC into account: " + df.format(d));
   }
}
```

When you run this application, it generates the following output for the CST time zone:

```
Wed Dec 31 18:00:00 CST 1969
Default format: December 31, 1969 6:00:00 PM CST
Taking UTC into account: January 1, 1970 12:00:00 AM UTC
```

The Unix epoch, which is represented by passing 0 to the Date(long) constructor, is defined as January 1, 1970 00:00:00 UTC, but the first output line does not indicate this fact. Instead, it shows the epoch in my CST time zone, which is six hours away from GMT/UTC. To show the epoch correctly, I need to obtain the UTC time zone, which I accomplish by passing "UTC" to TimeZone's getTimeZone(String) factory method, and install this time zone instance into the date formatter with the help of DateFormat's void setTimeZone(TimeZone zone) method.

> **NOTE:** If you ever need to create customized date formatters, you will find yourself working with DateFormat's java.text.SimpleDateFormat subclass and this subclass's java.text.DateFormatSymbols companion class. The "Customizing Formats" section (http://download.oracle.com/docs/cd/E17409_01/javase/tutorial/i18n/format/decimalFormat.html) and the "Changing Date Format Symbols" section (http://download.oracle.com/docs/cd/E17409_01/javase/tutorial/i18n/format/dateFormatSymbols.html) in *The Java Tutorials'* Internationalization trail introduce you to these classes.

Message Formatters

Applications often display simple and/or compound status and error messages to the user. A *simple message* consists of static (unchanging) text, whereas a *compound message* consists of static text and variable (changeable) data. For example, consider the following compound messages, where the underlined text identifies variable data:

```
10,536 visitors have visited your website since June 16, 2010.
Warning: 25 files have been modified in a suspicious manner.
Account balance is $10,567.00!
```

For a simple message, you obtain its text from a resource bundle and then display this text to the user. For a compound message, you obtain a *pattern* (template) for the message from a property resource bundle, pass this pattern along with the variable data to a message formatter to create a simple message, and display this message's text.

A *message formatter* is an instance of the concrete java.util.MessageFormat class (a Format subclass). (Unlike other APIs, the Message Format API does not have an abstract entry-point class with factory methods for obtaining instances of subclasses.) This class declares the following constructors:

- MessageFormat(String pattern) initializes a MessageFormat instance to the specified pattern and the default locale. This constructor throws IllegalArgumentException when pattern is invalid.

- MessageFormat(String pattern, Locale locale) initializes a MessageFormat instance to the specified pattern and locale. This constructor throws IllegalArgumentException when pattern is invalid.

A pattern consists of static text and placeholders for variable data. Each placeholder is a brace-delimited sequence of a zero-based integer identifier, an optional format type, and an optional format style. Examples include {0} (insert text between braces), {1, date} (insert a date in default style), and {2, number, currency} (insert a currency).

For example, the previous set of compound messages can be converted into Listing 9–23's patterns for the en_US locale.

Listing 9–23. *Patterns in an example_en_US.properties file*

```
p1 = {0, number, integer} visitors have visited your website since {1, date, long}.
p2 = Warning: {0, number, integer} files have been modified in a suspicious manner.
p3 = Account balance is {0, number, currency}!
```

The same placeholders can be used in equivalent compound messages localized to another locale, such as Listing 9–24's fr_FR locale.

Listing 9–24. *Patterns in an example_fr_FR.properties file*

```
p1 = {0, number, integer} visiteurs ont visité votre site Web depuis le {1, date, long}.
p2 = Avertissement : {0, number, integer} dossiers ont été modifiés d'une façon↵
  soupçonneuse.
p3 = L''équilibre de compte est {0, number, currency} !
```

> **NOTE:** An apostrophe (also known as a single quote) in a pattern starts a quoted string, in which, for example, `'{0, number, currency}` is treated as a literal string and is not interpreted as a placeholder by the formatter. To ensure that this placeholder is not treated as a literal string in Listing 9–24, L'équilibre's single quote must be doubled, which is why L''équilibre appears.

After instantiating a MessageFormat instance, where the pattern is obtained from a resource bundle, you typically create an array of Objects and call Message's inherited String format(Object obj) method (from Format) with this array—passing an array of Objects to a method whose parameter type is Object works because arrays are Objects.

When format() is called, it scans the pattern, replacing each placeholder with the corresponding entry in the Objects array. For example, if format() finds a placeholder with integer identifier 0, it causes the zeroth entry in the Objects array to be formatted and then the formatted results to be output.

> **TIP:** You might find MessageFormat's static String format(String pattern, Object... arguments) method convenient for one-time formatting operations. This method is equivalent to executing new MessageFormat(pattern).format(arguments, new StringBuffer(), null).toString() on the default locale.

Listing 9–25 demonstrates message formatting in the context of Listings 9–23's and 9–24's properties files and their localized patterns.

Listing 9–25. *Formatting and outputting compound messages according to the en_US and fr_FR locales*

```java
import java.text.MessageFormat;

import java.util.Calendar;
import java.util.Locale;
import java.util.ResourceBundle;

public class MessageFormatDemo
{
   public static void main(String[] args)
   {
      dumpMessages(Locale.US);
      System.out.println();
      dumpMessages(Locale.FRANCE);
   }
   static void dumpMessages(Locale locale)
   {
      ResourceBundle rb = ResourceBundle.getBundle("example", locale);
      MessageFormat mf = new MessageFormat(rb.getString("p1"), locale);
      Calendar cal = Calendar.getInstance(locale);
      cal.set(Calendar.YEAR, 2010);
      cal.set(Calendar.MONTH, Calendar.JUNE);
      cal.set(Calendar.DAY_OF_MONTH, 16);
      Object[] args = new Object[] { 10536, cal.getTime() };
```

```
        System.out.println(mf.format(args));
        mf.applyPattern(rb.getString("p2"));
        args = new Object[] { 25 };
        System.out.println(mf.format(args));
        mf.applyPattern(rb.getString("p3"));
        args = new Object[] { 10567.0 };
        System.out.println(mf.format(args));
    }
}
```

Listing 9–25 takes advantage of MessageFormat's void applyPattern(String pattern) method to override a previous pattern with a new pattern.

When you run this application, it generates output that is shown with the Windows XP Notepad editor window (so that the Euro currency symbol can be seen) in Figure 9–7.

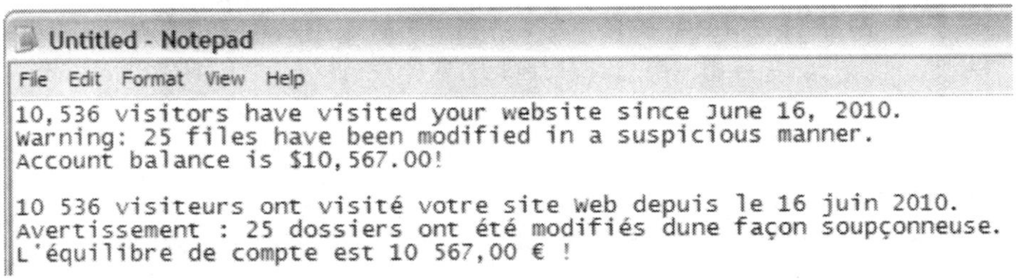

Figure 9–7. *Compound messages formatted for the en_US and fr_FR locales*

> **NOTE:** Some compound messages contain singular and plural words. For example, Logging 1 message to x.log and Logging 2 messages to x.log reveal singular and plural messages. Although you could specify pattern Logging {0} message(s) to {1}, it is not grammatically correct to state Logging 2 message(s) to x.log. The solution to this problem is to use the concrete java.text.ChoiceFormat class, a subclass of NumberFormat and a partner of MessageFormat, so that you can output Logging 1 message to x.log or Logging 2 messages to x.log depending on the numeric value passed to {0}. To learn how to use ChoiceFormat, check out the "Handling Plurals" section (http://download.oracle.com/docs/cd/E17409_01/javase/tutorial/i18n/format/choiceFormat.html) in *The Java Tutorials*' Internationalization trail.

Preferences API

Significant applications have *preferences*, which are configuration items. Examples include the location and size of the application's main window, and the locations and names of files that the application most recently accessed. Preferences are persisted to a file, to a database, or to some other storage mechanism so that they will be available to the application the next time it runs.

The simplest approach to persisting preferences is to use the Properties API, which consists of the `Properties` class. This class persists preferences as a series of *key=value* entries to text-based properties files. Although properties files are ideal for simple applications with few preferences, they have proven to be problematic with larger applications:

- Properties files tend to grow in size and the probability of name collisions among the various keys increases. This problem could be eliminated if properties files stored preferences in a hierarchy, but they are nonhierarchical in nature.

- As an application grows in size and complexity, it tends to acquire numerous properties files with each part of the application associated with its own properties file. The names and locations of these properties files must be hard-coded in the application's source code.

Additionally, someone could directly modify these text-based properties files (perhaps inserting gibberish), causing the application that depends upon the modified properties file to crash unless it is properly coded to deal with this possibility. Also, properties files cannot be used on diskless computing platforms. Because of these problems, the Preferences API has been introduced as a replacement for the Properties API.

The Preferences API lets you store preferences in a hierarchical manner so that you can avoid name collisions. Because this API is backend-neutral, it does not matter where the preferences are stored (a file, a database, or [on Windows platforms] the registry); you do not have to hardcode file names and locations. Also, there are no text-based files that can be modified, and Preferences can be used on diskless platforms.

This API uses trees of nodes to manage preferences. These nodes are the analogue of a hierarchical filesystem's directories. Also, preference name/value pairs stored under these nodes are the analogues of a directory's files. You navigate these trees in a similar manner to navigating a filesystem: specify an absolute path starting from the root node (/) to the node of interest; for example, `/window/location` and `/window/size`.

There are two kinds of trees: system and user. All users share the *system preference tree*, whereas the *user preference tree* is specific to a single user, which is generally the person who logged into the underlying operating system. (The precise description of "user" and "system" varies from implementation to implementation of the Preferences API.)

Although the Preferences API's `java.util.prefs` package contains three interfaces (`NodeChangeListener`, `PreferencesChangeListener`, and `PreferencesFactory`), four regular classes (`AbstractPreferences`, `NodeChangeEvent`, `PreferenceChangeEvent`, and `Preferences`), and two exception classes (`BackingStoreException` and `InvalidPreferencesFormatException`), you mostly work with the `Preferences` class.

The `Preferences` class describes a node in a tree of nodes. To obtain a `Preferences` node, you must call one of the following utility methods:

- static Preferences systemNodeForPackage(Class<?> c): Return the node whose path corresponds to the package containing the class represented by c from the system preference tree.

- static Preferences systemRoot(): Return the root preference node of the system preference tree.

- static Preferences userNodeForPackage(Class<?> c): Return the node whose path corresponds to the package containing the class represented by c from the current user's preference tree.

- static Preferences userRoot(): Return the root preference node of the current user's preference tree.

Listing 9–26 demonstrates systemNodeForPackage(), along with Preferences' abstract void put(String key, String value) and abstract String get(String key, String def) methods for storing String-based preferences to and retrieving String-based preferences from the system preference tree. A default value must be passed to get() in case no value is associated with the key (which should not happen in this example).

Listing 9–26. *Storing a single preference to and retrieving a single preference from the system preference tree*

```
package ca.mb.javajeff.examples;

import java.util.prefs.Preferences;

public class PrefsDemo
{
   public static void main(String[] args)
   {
      Preferences prefs = Preferences.systemNodeForPackage(PrefsDemo.class);
      prefs.put("version", "1.0");
      System.out.println(prefs.get("version", "unknown"));
   }
}
```

When you run this application (java ca.mb.javajeff.examples.PrefsDemo), it generates the following output:

```
1.0
```

More interestingly, Figure 9–8 reveals how this preference is stored in the Windows XP registry.

Figure 9–8. *Listing 9–26's version key in a Windows XP registry context*

My Computer\HKEY_LOCAL_MACHINE\SOFTWARE\JavaSoft\Prefs is the path to the Windows XP registry area for storing system preferences. Under Prefs, you will find a node for each package stored in this area. For example, ca identifies Listing 9–26's ca package. Continuing, a hierarchy of nodes is stored under ca. Within the bottommost node (examples), you find an entry consisting of version (the key) and 1.0 (the value).

Listing 9–27 provides a second example that works with the user preference tree and presents a more complex key.

Listing 9–27. *Storing a single preference to and retrieving a single preference from the current user's preference tree*

```java
import java.util.prefs.Preferences;

public class PrefsDemo
{
   public static void main(String[] args)
   {
      Preferences prefs = Preferences.userNodeForPackage(PrefsDemo.class);
      prefs.put("SearchEngineURL", "http://www.google.com");
      System.out.println(prefs.get("SearchEngineURL", "http://www.bing.com"));
   }
}
```

When you run this application (java PrefsDemo), it generates the following output:

```
http://www.google.com
```

More interestingly, Figure 9–9 reveals how this preference is stored in the Windows XP registry.

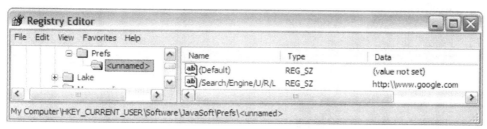

Figure 9–9. *Listing 9–27's* SearchEngineURL *key in a Windows XP registry context*

The Windows XP registry encodes the SearchEngineURL key into /Search/Engine/U/R/L because Preferences regards keys and node names as case sensitive but the Windows XP registry does not.

> **NOTE:** Check out Ray Djajadinataz's "Sir, What Is Your Preference?" article (http://www.javaworld.com/javaworld/jw-08-2001/jw-0831-preferences.html) to learn more about the Preferences API.

Random Number Generation

Chapter 6 formally introduced you to the java.lang.Math class's random() method. If you were to investigate this method's source code, you would discover Listing 9–28's implementation (for Java SE 6 Update 16).

Listing 9–28. *Implementing* Math's random() *method*

```
public static double random()
{
   if (randomNumberGenerator == null)
      initRNG();
   return randomNumberGenerator.nextDouble();
}
private static Random randomNumberGenerator;
private static synchronized void initRNG()
{
   if (randomNumberGenerator == null)
      randomNumberGenerator = new Random();
}
```

Listing 9–28 shows you that Math's random() method is implemented in terms of a class named Random, which is located in the java.util package. Random instances generate sequences of random numbers and are known as *random number generators*.

> **NOTE:** These numbers are not truly random because they are generated from a mathematical algorithm. As a result, they are often referred to as pseudorandom numbers. However, it is often convenient to drop the "pseudo" prefix and refer to them as random numbers.
>
> Also, delaying object creation (new Random(), for example) until the first time the object is needed is known as *lazy initialization*.

Random generates its sequence of random numbers by starting with a special 48-bit value that is known as a *seed*. This value is subsequently modified by a mathematical algorithm, which is known as a *linear congruential generator*.

> **NOTE:** Check out Wikipedia's "Linear congruential generator" entry (http://en.wikipedia.org/wiki/Linear_congruential_generator) to learn about this algorithm for generating random numbers.

Random declares a pair of constructors:

- Random() creates a new random number generator. This constructor sets the seed of the random number generator to a value that is very likely to be distinct from any other call to this constructor.

- Random(long seed) creates a new random number generator using its seed argument. This argument is the initial value of the internal state of the random number generator, which is maintained by the `protected int next(int bits)` method.

Because `Random()` does not take a `seed` argument, the resulting random number generator always generates a different sequence of random numbers. This explains why `Math.random()` generates a different sequence each time an application starts running.

> **TIP:** `Random(long seed)` gives you the opportunity to reuse the same seed value, allowing the same sequence of random numbers to be generated. You will find this capability useful when debugging a faulty application that involves random numbers.

`Random(long seed)` calls the `void setSeed(long seed)` method to set the seed to the specified value. If you call `setSeed()` after instantiating `Random`, the random number generator is reset to the state that it was in immediately after calling `Random(long seed)`.

Listing 9–28 demonstrates `Random`'s `double nextDouble()` method, which returns the next pseudorandom, uniformly distributed double precision floating-point value between 0.0 and 1.0 in this random number generator's sequence.

`Random` also declares the following methods for returning other kinds of values:

- `boolean nextBoolean()` returns the next pseudorandom, uniformly distributed Boolean value in this random number generator's sequence. Values true and false are generated with (approximately) equal probability.

- `void nextBytes(byte[] bytes)` generates pseudorandom byte integer values and stores them in the `bytes` array. The number of generated bytes is equal to the length of the `bytes` array.

- `float nextFloat()` returns the next pseudorandom, uniformly distributed floating-point value between 0.0 and 1.0 in this random number generator's sequence.

- `double nextGaussian()` returns the next pseudorandom, Gaussian ("normally") distributed double precision floating-point value with mean 0.0 and standard deviation 1.0 in this random number generator's sequence.

- `int nextInt()` returns the next pseudorandom, uniformly distributed integer value in this random number generator's sequence. All 2^{32} possible integer values are generated with (approximately) equal probability.

- `int nextInt(int n)` returns a pseudorandom, uniformly distributed integer value between 0 (inclusive) and the specified value (exclusive), drawn from this random number generator's sequence. All n possible integer values are generated with (approximately) equal probability.

- long nextLong() returns the next pseudorandom, uniformly distributed long integer value in this random number generator's sequence. Because Random uses a seed with only 48 bits, this method will not return all possible 64-bit long integer values.

The java.util.Collections class declares a pair of shuffle() methods for shuffling the contents of a list. In contrasl, the java.util.Arrays class does not declare a shuffle() method for shuffling the contents of an array. Listing 9–29 addresses this omission.

Listing 9–29. *Shuffling an array of integers*

```java
import java.util.Random;

public class Shuffler
{
   public static void main(String[] args)
   {
      Random r = new Random();
      int[] array = { 0, 1, 2, 3, 4, 5, 6, 7, 8, 9 };
      for (int i = 0; i < array.length; i++)
      {
         int n = r.nextInt(array.length);
         // swap array[i] with array[n]
         int temp = array[i];
         array[i] = array[n];
         array[n] = temp;
      }
      for (int i = 0; i < array.length; i++)
         System.out.print(array[i] + " ");
      System.out.println();
   }
}
```

Listing 9–29 presents a simple recipe for shuffling an array of integers—this recipe could be generalized. For each array entry from the start of the array to the end of the array, this entry is swapped with another entry whose index is chosen by int nextInt(int n).

When you run this application, you will observe a shuffled sequence of integers that is similar to the following sequence that I observed:

5 8 3 4 0 2 7 6 9 1

Regular Expressions API

Text-processing applications often need to match text against *patterns*. For example, an application might need to locate all occurrences of a word in a text file so that it can replace those occurrences with another word. Java provides regular expressions to help text-processing applications perform pattern matching.

A *regular expression* (also known as a *regex* or *regexp*) is a string-based pattern that represents the set of strings that match this pattern. The pattern consists of literal characters and *metacharacters*, which are characters with special meanings instead of literal meanings.

The Regular Expressions API provides the java.util.regex.Pattern class to represent patterns via compiled regexes. Regexes are compiled for performance reasons; pattern matching via compiled regexes is much faster than if the regexes were not compiled. Table 9–4 describes Pattern's methods.

Table 9–4. *Pattern Methods*

Method	Description
static Pattern compile (String regex)	Compile regex and return its Pattern object. This method throws java.util.regex.PatternSyntaxException when regex's syntax is invalid.
static Pattern compile (String regex,int flags)	Compile regex according to the given flags (a bitset consisting of some combination of Pattern's CANON_EQ, CASE_INSENSITIVE, COMMENTS, DOTALL, LITERAL, MULTILINE, UNICODE_CASE, and UNIX_LINES constants) and return its Pattern object. This method throws PatternSyntaxException when regex's syntax is invalid, and IllegalArgumentException when bit values other than those corresponding to the defined match flags are set in flags.
int flags()	Return this Pattern object's match flags. This method returns 0 for Pattern instances created via compile(String), and the bitset of flags for Pattern instances created via compile(String, int).
Matcher matcher (CharSequence input)	Return a Matcher that will match input against this Pattern's compiled regex.
static boolean matches (String regex, CharSequence input)	Compile regex and attempt to match input against the compiled regex. Return true if there is a match; otherwise, return false. This convenience method is equivalent to Pattern.compile(regex).matcher(input).matches(), and throws PatternSyntaxException when regex's syntax is invalid.
String pattern()	Return this Pattern's uncompiled regex.
static String quote (String s)	Quote s using "\Q" and "\E" so that all other metacharacters lose their special meaning. If the returned String is later compiled into a Pattern instance, it can only be matched literally.
String[] split (CharSequence input)	Split input around matches of this Pattern's compiled regex and return an array containing the matches.
String[] split (CharSequence input, int limit)	Split input around matches of this Pattern's compiled regex; limit controls the number of times the compiled regex is applied and thus affects the length of the resulting array.
String toString()	Return this Pattern's uncompiled regex.

Table 9–4 reveals the java.lang.CharSequence interface, which describes a readable sequence of char values. Instances of any class that implements this interface (such as String, StringBuffer, and StringBuilder) can be passed to Pattern methods that take CharSequence arguments (such as split(CharSequence)).

> **NOTE:** CharSequence declares methods char charAt(int index) (return the character at location index within this sequence), int length() (return the length of this sequence), CharSequence subSequence(int start, int end) (return a subsequence of this sequence ranging from location start, inclusive, to location end, exclusive), and String toString() (return a string containing this sequence's characters in the same order and having the same length as this sequence).

Table 9–4 also reveals that each of Pattern's compile() methods and its matches() method (which calls the compile(String) method) throws PatternSyntaxException when a syntax error is encountered while compiling the pattern argument. Table 9–5 describes PatternSyntaxException's methods.

Table 9–5. *PatternSyntaxException Methods*

Method	Description
String getDescription()	Return a description of the syntax error.
int getIndex()	Return the approximate index of where the syntax error occurred in the pattern, or -1 if the index is not known.
String getMessage()	Return a multiline string containing the description of the syntax error and its index, the erroneous pattern, and a visual indication of the error index within the pattern.
String getPattern()	Return the erroneous pattern.

Finally, Table 9–4's Matcher matcher(CharSequence input) method reveals that the Regular Expressions API also provides the java.util.regex.Matcher class, whose *matchers* attempt to match compiled regexes against input text. Matcher declares the following methods to perform matching operations:

- boolean matches() attempts to match the entire region against the pattern. If the match succeeds, more information can be obtained by calling Matcher's start(), end(), and group() methods. For example, int start() returns the start index of the previous match, int end() returns the offset of the first character following the previous match, and String group() returns the input subsequence matched by the previous match. Each method throws java.lang.IllegalStateException when a match has not yet been attempted or the previous match attempt failed.

■ boolean lookingAt() attempts to match the input sequence, starting at the beginning of the region, against the pattern. As with matches(), this method always starts at the beginning of the region. Unlike matches(), lookingAt() does not require that the entire region be matched. If the match succeeds, more information can be obtained by calling Matcher's start(), end(), and group() methods.

■ boolean find() attempts to find the next subsequence of the input sequence that matches the pattern. It starts at the beginning of this matcher's region, or, if a previous call to this method was successful and the matcher has not since been reset (by calling Matcher's Matcher reset() or Matcher reset(CharSequence input) method), at the first character not matched by the previous match. If the match succeeds, more information can be obtained by calling Matcher's start(), end(), and group() methods.

NOTE: A matcher finds matches in a subset of its input called the *region*. By default, the region contains all of the matcher's input. The region can be modified by calling Matcher's Matcher region(int start, int end) method (set the limits of this matcher's region), and queried by calling Matcher's int regionStart() and int regionEnd() methods.

I have created a simple application that demonstrates Pattern, PatternSyntaxException, and Matcher. Listing 9–30 presents this application's source code.

Listing 9–30. *Playing with regular expressions*

```
import java.util.regex.Matcher;
import java.util.regex.Pattern;
import java.util.regex.PatternSyntaxException;

public class RegExDemo
{
   public static void main(String[] args)
   {
      if (args.length != 2)
      {
         System.err.println("usage: java RegExDemo regex input");
         return;
      }
      try
      {
         System.out.println("regex = " + args[0]);
         System.out.println("input = " + args[1]);
         Pattern p = Pattern.compile(args[0]);
         Matcher m = p.matcher(args[1]);
         while (m.find())
            System.out.println("Located [" + m.group() + "] starting at "
                               + m.start() + " and ending at " + (m.end()-1));
      }
      catch (PatternSyntaxException pse)
      {
```

```
            System.err.println("Bad regex: " + pse.getMessage());
            System.err.println("Description: " + pse.getDescription());
            System.err.println("Index: " + pse.getIndex());
            System.err.println("Incorrect pattern: " + pse.getPattern());
         }
      }
   }
}
```

After compiling this source code, execute java RegExDemo ox ox. You will discover the following output:

```
regex = ox
input = ox
Located [ox] starting at 0 and ending at 1
```

find() searches for a match by comparing regex characters with the input characters in left-to-right order, and returns true because o equals o and x equals x.

Continuing, execute java RegExDemo box ox. This time, you will discover the following output:

```
regex = box
input = ox
```

find() begins by comparing regex character b with input character o. Because these characters are not equal, and because there are not enough characters in the input to continue the search, find() does not output a "Located" message to indicate a match. However, if you execute java RegExDemo ox box, you will discover a match:

```
regex = ox
input = box
Located [ox] starting at 1 and ending at 2
```

The ox regex consists of literal characters. More sophisticated regexes combine literal characters with metacharacters (such as the period [.]) and other regex constructs.

> **TIP:** To specify a metacharacter as a literal character, precede the metacharacter with a backslash character (as in \.), or place the metacharacter between \Q and \E (as in \Q.\E). In either case, make sure to double the backslash character when the escaped metacharacter appears in a string literal; for example, "\\." or "\\Q.\\E".

The period metacharacter matches all characters except for the *line terminator* (a one- or two-character sequence designating the end of the line). For example, each of java RegExDemo .ox box and java RegExDemo .ox fox report a match because the period matches the b in box and the f in fox.

> **NOTE:** `Pattern` recognizes the following line terminators: carriage return (\r), newline (line feed) (\n), carriage return immediately followed by newline (\r\n), next line (\u0085), line separator (\u2028), and paragraph separator (\u2029). The period metacharacter can be made to also match these line terminators by specifying the `Pattern.DOTALL` flag when calling `Pattern.compile(String, int)`.

A *character class* is a set of characters appearing between [and]. There are six kinds of character classes:

- A *simple character class* consists of literal characters placed side by side, and matches only these characters. For example, [abc] consists of characters a, b, and c. Also, java RegExDemo t[aiou]ck tack reports a match because a is a member of [aiou]. It also reports a match when the input is tick, tock, or tuck because i, o, and u are members.

- A *negation character class* consists of a circumflex metacharacter (^), followed by literal characters placed side by side, and matches all characters except for the characters in the class. For example, [^abc] consists of all characters except for a, b, and c. Also, java RegExDemo "[^b]ox" box does not report a match because b is not a member of [^b], whereas java RegExDemo "[^b]ox" fox reports a match because f is a member. (The double quotes surrounding [^b]ox are necessary on my Windows XP platform because ^ is treated specially at the command line.)

- A *range character class* consists of successive literal characters expressed as a starting literal character, followed by the hyphen metacharacter (-), followed by an ending literal character, and matches all characters in this range. For example, [a-z] consists of all characters from a through z. Also, java RegExDemo [h-l]ouse house reports a match because h is a member of the class, whereas java RegExDemo [h-l]ouse mouse does not report a match because m lies outside of the range and is therefore not part of the class. You can combine multiple ranges within the same range character class by placing them side by side; for example, [A-Za-z] consists of all uppercase and lowercase Latin letters.

- A *union character class* consists of multiple nested character classes, and matches all characters that belong to the resulting union. For example, [abc[u-z]] consists of characters a, b, c, u, v, w, x, y, and z. Also, java RegExDemo [[0-9][A-F][a-f]] e reports a match because e is a hexadecimal character. (I could have alternatively expressed this character class as [0-9A-Fa-f] by combining multiple ranges.)

- An *intersection character class* consists of multiple &&-separated nested character classes, and matches all characters that are common to these nested character classes. For example, [a-c&&[c-f]] consists of character c, which is the only character common to [a-c] and [c-f]. Also, java RegExDemo "[aeiouy&&[y]]" y reports a match because y is common to classes [aeiouy] and [y].

- A *subtraction character class* consists of multiple &&-separated nested character classes, where at least one nested character class is a negation character class, and matches all characters except for those indicated by the negation character class/classes. For example, [a-z&&[^x-z]] consists of characters a through w. (The square brackets surrounding ^x-z are necessary; otherwise, ^ is ignored and the resulting class consists of only x, y, and z.) Also, java RegExDemo "[a-z&&[^aeiou]]" g reports a match because g is a consonant and only consonants belong to this class. (I am ignoring y, which is sometimes regarded as a consonant and sometimes regarded as a vowel.)

A *predefined character class* is a regex construct for a commonly specified character class. Table 9–6 identifies Pattern's predefined character classes.

Table 9–6. *Predefined Character Classes*

Predefined Character Class	Description
\d	Match any digit character. \d is equivalent to [0-9].
\D	Match any non-digit character. \D is equivalent to [^\d].
\s	Match any whitespace character. \s is equivalent to [\t\n\x0B\f\r].
\S	Match any non-whitespace character. \S is equivalent to [^\s].
\w	Match any word character. \w is equivalent to [a-zA-Z0-9].
\W	Match any non-word character . \W is equivalent to [^\w].

For example, java RegExDemo \wbc abc reports a match because \w matches the word character a in abc.

A *capturing group* saves a match's characters for later recall during pattern matching, and is expressed as a character sequence surrounded by parentheses metacharacters (and). All characters within a capturing group are treated as a unit. For example, the (Android) capturing group combines A, n, d, r, o, i, and d into a unit. It matches the Android pattern against all occurrences of Android in the input. Each match replaces the previous match's saved Android characters with the next match's Android characters.

Capturing groups can appear inside other capturing groups. For example, capturing groups (A) and (B(C)) appear inside capturing group ((A)(B(C))), and capturing group (C) appears inside capturing group (B(C)). Each nested or nonnested capturing group receives its own number, numbering starts at 1, and capturing groups are numbered from left to right. For example, ((A)(B(C))) is assigned 1, (A) is assigned 2, (B(C)) is assigned 3, and (C) is assigned 4.

A capturing group saves its match for later recall via a *back reference*, which is a backslash character followed by a digit character denoting a capturing group number. The back reference causes the matcher to use the back reference's capturing group number to recall the capturing group's saved match, and then use that match's characters to attempt a further match. The following example uses a back reference to determine if the input consists of two consecutive Android patterns:

```
java RegExDemo "(Android) \1" "Android Android"
```

RegExDemo reports a match because the matcher detects Android, followed by a space, followed by Android in the input.

A *boundary matcher* is a regex construct for identifying the beginning of a line, a word boundary, the end of text, and other commonly occurring boundaries. See Table 9-7.

Table 9-7. *Boundary Matchers*

Boundary Matcher	Description
^	Match beginning of line.
$	Match end of line.
\b	Match word boundary.
\B	Match non-word boundary.
\A	Match beginning of text.
\G	Match end of previous match.
\Z	Match end of text except for line terminator (if present).
\z	Match end of text.

For example, java RegExDemo \b\b "I think" reports several matches, as revealed in the following output:

```
regex = \b\b
input = I think
Located [] starting at 0 and ending at -1
Located [] starting at 1 and ending at 0
Located [] starting at 2 and ending at 1
Located [] starting at 7 and ending at 6
```

This output reveals several *zero-length matches*. When a zero-length match occurs, the starting and ending indexes are equal, although the output shows the ending index to be one less than the starting index because I specified end()-1 in Listing 9–30 (so that a match's end index identifies a non-zero-length match's last character, not the character following the non-zero-length match's last character).

> **NOTE:** A zero-length match occurs in empty input text, at the beginning of input text, after the last character of input text, or between any two characters of that text. Zero-length matches are easy to identify because they always start and end at the same index position.

The final regex construct I present is the *quantifier*, a numeric value implicitly or explicitly bound to a pattern. Quantifiers are categorized as greedy, reluctant, or possessive:

- A *greedy quantifier* (?, *, or +) attempts to find the longest match. Specify *X*? to find one or no occurrences of *X*, *X** to find zero or more occurrences of *X*, *X*+ to find one or more occurrences of *X*, *X*{*n*} to find *n* occurrences of *X*, *X*{*n*,} to find at least *n* (and possibly more) occurrences of *X*, and *X*{*n*,*m*} to find at least *n* but no more than *m* occurrences of *X*.

- A *reluctant quantifier* (??, *?, or +?) attempts to find the shortest match. Specify *X*?? to find one or no occurrences of *X*, *X**? to find zero or more occurrences of *X*, *X*+? to find one or more occurrences of *X*, *X*{*n*}? to find *n* occurrences of *X*, *X*{*n*,}? to find at least *n* (and possibly more) occurrences of *X*, and *X*{*n*,*m*}? to find at least *n* but no more than *m* occurrences of *X*.

- A *possessive quantifier* (?+, *+, or ++) is similar to a greedy quantifier except that a possessive quantifier only makes one attempt to find the longest match, whereas a greedy quantifier can make multiple attempts. Specify *X*?+ to find one or no occurrences of *X*, *X**+ to find zero or more occurrences of *X*, *X*++ to find one or more occurrences of *X*, *X*{*n*}+ to find *n* occurrences of *X*, *X*{*n*,}+ to find at least *n* (and possibly more) occurrences of *X*, and *X*{*n*,*m*}+ to find at least *n* but no more than *m* occurrences of *X*.

For an example of a greedy quantifier, execute java RegExDemo .*end "wend rend end". You will discover the following output:

```
regex = .*end
input = wend rend end
Located [wend rend end] starting at 0 and ending at 12
```

The greedy quantifier (.*) matches the longest sequence of characters that terminates in end. It starts by consuming all of the input text, and then is forced to back off until it discovers that the input text terminates with these characters.

For an example of a reluctant quantifier, execute java RegExDemo .*?end "wend rend end". You will discover the following output:

```
regex = .*?end
input = wend rend end
Located [wend] starting at 0 and ending at 3
Located [ rend] starting at 4 and ending at 8
Located [ end] starting at 9 and ending at 12
```

The reluctant quantifier (.*?) matches the shortest sequence of characters that terminates in end. It begins by consuming nothing, and then slowly consumes characters until it finds a match. It then continues until it exhausts the input text.

For an example of a possessive quantifier, execute java RegExDemo .*+end "wend rend end". You will discover the following output:

```
regex = .*+end
input = wend rend end
```

The possessive quantifier (.*+) does not detect a match because it consumes the entire input text, leaving nothing left over to match end at the end of the regex. Unlike a greedy quantifier, a possessive quantifier does not back off.

While working with quantifiers, you will probably encounter zero-length matches. For example, execute java RegExDemo 1? 101101:

```
regex = 1?
input = 101101
Located [1] starting at 0 and ending at 0
Located [] starting at 1 and ending at 0
Located [1] starting at 2 and ending at 2
Located [1] starting at 3 and ending at 3
Located [] starting at 4 and ending at 3
Located [1] starting at 5 and ending at 5
Located [] starting at 6 and ending at 5
```

The result of this greedy quantifier is that 1 is detected at locations 0, 2, 3, and 5 in the input text, and that nothing is detected (a zero-length match) at locations 1, 4, and 6.

This time, execute java RegExDemo 1?? 101101:

```
regex = 1??
input = 101101
Located [] starting at 0 and ending at -1
Located [] starting at 1 and ending at 0
Located [] starting at 2 and ending at 1
Located [] starting at 3 and ending at 2
Located [] starting at 4 and ending at 3
Located [] starting at 5 and ending at 4
Located [] starting at 6 and ending at 5
```

This output might look surprising, but remember that a reluctant quantifier looks for the shortest match, which (in this case) is no match at all.

Finally, execute java RegExDemo 1+? 101101:

```
regex = 1+?
input = 101101
Located [1] starting at 0 and ending at 0
Located [1] starting at 2 and ending at 2
Located [1] starting at 3 and ending at 3
```

Located [1] starting at 5 and ending at 5

This possessive quantifier only matches the locations where 1 is detected in the input text. It does not perform zero-length matches.

> **NOTE:** Refer to the JDK documentation on the `Pattern` class to learn about additional regex constructs.

Most of the previous regex examples have not been practical, except to help you grasp how to use the various regex constructs. In contrast, the following examples reveal a regex that matches phone numbers of the form (ddd) ddd-dddd or ddd-dddd. A single space appears between (ddd) and ddd; there is no space on either side of the hyphen.

```
java RegExDemo "(\(\d{3}\))?\s*\d{3}-\d{4}" "800 555-1212"
regex = (\(\d{3}\))?\s*\d{3}-\d{4}
input = (800) 555-1212
Located [(800) 555-1212] starting at 0 and ending at 13
java RegExDemo "(\(\d{3}\))?\s*\d{3}-\d{4}" 555-1212
regex = (\(\d{3}\))?\s*\d{3}-\d{4}
input = 555-1212
Located [555-1212] starting at 0 and ending at 7
```

> **NOTE:** To learn more about regular expressions, check out my *JavaWorld* article "Regular Expressions Simplify Pattern-Matching Code" (http://www.javaworld.com/javaworld/jw-02-2003/jw-0207-java101.html). Also, you should check out "Lesson: Regular Expressions" (http://download-llnw.oracle.com/javase/tutorial/essential/regex/index.html) in *The Java Tutorials'* Essential Classes trail.

EXERCISES

The following exercises are designed to test your understanding of this chapter's additional utility APIs:

1. Define task.
2. Define executor.
3. Identify the `Executor` interface's limitations.
4. How are `Executor`'s limitations overcome?
5. What differences exist between `Runnable`'s `run()` method and `Callable`'s `call()` method?
6. True or false: You can throw checked and unchecked exceptions from `Runnable`'s `run()` method but can only throw unchecked exceptions from `Callable`' `call()` method?
7. Define future.

8. Describe the `Executors` class's `newFixedThreadPool()` method.

9. Define synchronizer.

10. Identify and describe four commonly used synchronizers.

11. What concurrency-oriented extensions to the collections framework are provided by the concurrency utilities?

12. Define lock.

13. What is the biggest advantage that `Lock` objects hold over the implicit locks that are obtained when threads enter critical sections (controlled via the `synchronized` reserved word)?

14. Define atomic variable.

15. Define internationalization.

16. Define locale.

17. What are the components of a `Locale` object?

18. Define resource bundle.

19. True or false: If a property resource bundle and a list resource bundle have the same complete resource bundle name, the list resource bundle takes precedence over the property resource bundle.

20. Define break iterator.

21. What kinds of break iterators does the Break Iterator API support?

22. True or false: You can pass any `Locale` object to any of `BreakIterator`'s factory methods that take `Locale` arguments.

23. What is a collator?

24. Define date, time zone, and calendar.

25. True or false: `Date` instances can represent dates prior to or after the Unix epoch.

26. How would you obtain a `TimeZone` object that represents Central Standard Time?

27. Assuming that `cal` identifies a `Calendar` instance and `locale` identifies a specific locale, how would you obtain a localized name for the month represented by `cal`?

28. Define formatter.

29. What kinds of formatters does `NumberFormat` return?

30. True or false: `DateFormat`'s `getInstance()` factory method is a shortcut to obtaining a default date/time formatter that uses the `MEDIUM` style for both the date and the time.

31. What does a message formatter let you accomplish?

32. Define preference.

33. Why is the Properties API problematic for persisting preferences?

34. How does the Preferences API persist preferences?

35. What does the `Random` class accomplish?

36. Define regular expression.

37. What does the `Pattern` class accomplish?

38. What do `Pattern`'s `compile()` methods do when they discover illegal syntax in their regular expression arguments.

39. What does the `Matcher` class accomplish?

40. What is the difference between `Matcher`'s `matches()` and `lookingAt()` methods?

41. Define character class.

42. Identify the various kinds of character classes.

43. Define capturing group.

44. What is a zero-length match?

45. Define quantifier.

46. What is the difference between a greedy quantifier and a reluctant quantifier?

47. How do possessive and greedy quantifiers differ?

48. Create a `SpanishCollation` application that outputs Spanish words ñango (weak), llamado (called), lunes (monday), champán (champagne), clamor (outcry), cerca (near), nombre (name), and chiste (joke) according to this language's current collation rules followed by its traditional collation rules. According to the current collation rules, the output order is as follows: cerca, **champán**, **chiste**, **clamor**, **llamado**, **lunes**, nombre, and ñango. According to the traditional collation rules, the output order is as follows: cerca, **clamor**, **champán**, **chiste**, **lunes**, **llamado**, nombre, and ñango. Use the `RuleBasedCollator` class to specify the rules for traditional collation. Also, construct your `Locale` object using only the es (Spanish) language code.

> **NOTE:** The Spanish alphabet consists of 29 letters: a, b, c, ch, d, e, f, g, h, i, j, k, l, ll, m, n, ñ, o, p, q, r, s, t, u, v, w, x, y, z. (Vowels are often written with accents, as in tablón [plank or board], and u is sometimes topped with a dieresis or umlaut, as in vergüenza [bashfulness]. However, vowels with these diacritical marks are not considered separate letters.) Prior to April 1994's voting at the X Congress of the Association of Spanish Language Academies, ch was collated after c, and ll was collated after l. Because this congress adopted the standard Latin alphabet collation rules, ch is now considered a sequence of two distinct characters, and dictionaries now place words starting with ch between words starting with ce and ci. Similarly, ll is now considered a sequence of two characters.

49. Create a `RearrangeText` application that takes a single text argument of the form *x, y* and outputs *y x*. For example, `java RearrangeText "Gosling, Dr. James"` outputs `"Dr. James Gosling"`.

50. Create a `ReplaceText` application that takes input text, a pattern that specifies text to replace, and replacement text command-line arguments, and uses `Matcher`'s `String replaceAll(String replacement)` method to replace all matches of the pattern with the replacement text (passed to replacement). For example, java ReplaceText "too   many   embedded   spaces" "\s+" " " should output too many embedded spaces with only a single space character between successive words.

Summary

Java version 5 introduced the concurrency utilities to simplify the development of concurrent applications. The concurrency utilities are organized into executor, synchronizer, concurrent collection, lock, and atomic variable categories, and leverage the low-level Threading API in their implementations.

An executor decouples task submission from task-execution mechanics and is described by the Executor, ExecutorService, and ScheduledExecutorService interfaces. A synchronizer facilitates common forms of synchronization: countdown latches, cyclic barriers, exchangers, and semaphores are commonly used synchronizers.

A concurrent collection is an extension to the collections framework. A lock supports high-level locking and can associate with conditions in a manner that is distinct from built-in synchronization and monitors. Finally, an atomic variable encapsulates a single variable, and supports lock-free, thread-safe operations on that variable.

We tend to write software that reflects our cultural backgrounds. Internationalization is the process of creating an application that automatically adapts to its current user's culture so that the user can read the application's text, hear audio clips in the user's language (if audio is supported), and so on.

Java encourages internationalization by supporting Unicode via the char reserved word and the Character class, and by offering the Locale class and additional APIs, including Break Iterator, Calendar, and Collator. Locale is the centerpiece of the internationalization APIs.

Significant applications have preferences that must be persisted to a file, to a database, or to some other storage mechanism so that they are available to the application the next time it runs. The simplest approach to persisting preferences is to use the Properties API, but this API has proven to be problematic with larger applications.

These problems are solved with the Preferences API, which lets you store preferences in a hierarchical manner so that you can avoid name collisions. This API uses trees of nodes to manage preferences. All users share the system preference tree, whereas the user preference tree is specific to a single user.

The Math class's random() method is implemented in terms of the Random class, whose instances are known as random number generators. Random generates a sequence of random numbers by starting with a special 48-bit seed. This value is subsequently modified via a mathematical algorithm that is known as a linear congruential generator.

Text-processing applications often match text against patterns. Java provides the Regular Expressions API to help text-processing applications perform pattern matching.

This API's `Pattern` class represents patterns via compiled regexes. Its `Matcher` class describes matchers that attempt to match compiled regexes against input text.

Meaningful applications perform input and output operations. Java supports these I/O operations in part through classic I/O APIs such as `File`, `RandomAccessFile`, streams, and writers/readers. It also supports I/O operations through modern I/O APIs such as bytes, channels, and selectors. I introduce you to Java's classic I/O APIs in Chapter 10.

Chapter 10

Performing I/O

Applications often input data for processing and output processing results. Data is input from a file or some other source, and is output to a file or some other destination. Java supports I/O via the classic I/O APIs located in the java.io package. This chapter introduces you to java.io's File, RandomAccessFile, stream, and writer/reader classes.

File

File-oriented I/O activities often interact with a *filesystem*, which is typically expressed as a hierarchy of files and directories starting from a *root directory*. The underlying platform on which a Java virtual machine runs may support zero or more filesystems.

For example, a Unix or Linux platform combines all *mounted* (attached and prepared) disks into a single virtual filesystem. In contrast, a Windows platform associates a separate filesystem with each active disk drive.

Java offers access to the underlying platform's available filesystem(s) via its concrete File class. File declares the static File[] listRoots() utility method to return the root directories (roots) of available filesystems as an array of File objects.

> **NOTE:** The set of available filesystem roots is affected by various system-level operations, such as the insertion or ejection of removable media, and the disconnecting or unmounting of physical or virtual disk drives.

Listing 10–1 presents a DumpRoots application that uses listRoots() to obtain an array of available filesystem roots and then outputs the array's contents.

Listing 10–1. *Dumping available filesystem roots to the standard output device*

```
import java.io.File;

public class DumpRoots
{
    public static void main(String[] args)
    {
```

```
        File[] roots = File.listRoots();
        for (File root: roots)
            System.out.println(root);
    }
}
```

When I run this application on my Windows XP platform, I receive the following output, which reveals four available roots:

```
A:\
C:\
D:\
E:\
```

If I happened to run DumpRoots on a Unix or Linux platform, I would receive one line of output that consists of the virtual filesystem root (/).

Instances of the File class contain the pathnames of files and directories that may or may not exist in their filesystems. For example, a File object containing pathname C:\ identifies the root directory on the C: drive (and this pathname most likely exists).

> **NOTE:** A *path* is a hierarchy of directories that must be traversed to locate a file or a directory. A *pathname* is a string representation of a path; a platform-dependent *separator character* (such as the Windows backslash [\] character) appears between consecutive names. File's constructors convert these separator characters to the correct platform separator character; I discuss this conversion later in this section.

Apart from listRoots(), the easiest way to instantiate File is to use the File(String pathname) constructor, which creates a File instance that stores the pathname string. The following assignment statements demonstrate this constructor:

```
File file1 = new File("/x/y");
File file2 = new File("C:\\temp\\x.dat");
```

The first statement assumes a Unix or Linux platform, starts the pathname with root directory symbol /, and continues with directory name x, separator character /, and file or directory name y.

The second statement assumes a Windows platform, starts the pathname with drive specifier C:, and continues with root directory symbol \, directory name temp, separator character \, and filename x.dat (although x.dat might refer to a directory).

> **CAUTION:** Always double backslash characters that appear in a string literal, especially when specifying a pathname; otherwise, you run the risk of bugs or compiler error messages. For example, I doubled the backslash characters in the second statement to denote a backslash and not a tab (\t), and to avoid a compiler error message (\x is illegal).

Each statement's pathname is an *absolute pathname*, which is a pathname that starts with the root directory symbol. In contrast, a *relative pathname* does not start with the root directory symbol; it is interpreted via information taken from some other pathname.

> **NOTE:** The java.io package's classes default to resolving relative pathnames against the current user (also known as working) directory, which is identified by system property user.dir, and which is typically the directory in which the virtual machine was launched. (In Chapter 7, I show you how to read system properties via System's getProperty() method.)

File offers additional constructors for instantiating this class. For example, the following constructors merge parent and child pathnames into combined pathnames that are stored in File objects:

- File(String parent, String child) creates a new File instance from a parent pathname string and a child pathname string.

- File(File parent, String child) creates a new File instance from a parent pathname File instance and a child pathname string.

Each constructor's parent parameter is passed a *parent pathname*, a string that consists of all pathname components except for the last name, which is specified by child. The following statement demonstrates this concept via File(String, String):

```
File file3 = new File("prj/books/", "ljfad");
```

The constructor merges parent pathname prj/books/ with child pathname ljfad into pathname prj/books/ljfad. (If I had specified prj/books as the parent pathname, the constructor would have added the separator character after books.)

All three constructors *normalize* their pathname arguments by replacing separator characters with the default name-separator character so that the pathname is compliant with the underlying filesystem.

> **NOTE:** The default name-separator character is obtainable from system property file.separator, and is also stored in File's separator and separatorChar static fields. The first field stores the character as a char and the second field stores it as a String. Neither field name follows the convention of appearing entirely in uppercase.

For example, if you pass argument "/x/y" to a File constructor on a Unix or Linux platform, the constructor normalizes this pathname to "/x/y". However, if you pass this same argument on a Windows platform, the constructor normalizes it to "\x\y".

Because these constructors do not detect invalid pathname arguments (and throw exceptions), you must be careful when specifying pathnames. You should strive to only specify pathnames that are valid for all platforms on which the application will run.

> **NOTE:** If you plan to create applications exclusively for Android devices, which are based on a Linux kernel, you probably do not need to worry about platform independence for pathnames and can specify them according to Unix/Linux conventions. However, you never know what changes might arrive in the future.

For example, instead of hard-coding a drive specifier (such as C:) in a pathname, use the roots that are returned from listRoots(). Even better, keep your pathnames relative to the current user/working directory (returned from the user.dir system property).

After you obtain a File object, you can interrogate it to learn about its stored pathname by calling the methods that are described in Table 10–1.

Table 10–1. *File Methods for Learning About a Stored Pathname*

Method	Description
File getAbsoluteFile()	Return the absolute form of this File object's pathname. This method is equivalent to new File(this.getAbsolutePath()), which is roughly how File implements this method.
String getAbsolutePath()	Return the absolute pathname string of this File object's pathname. If this File object's pathname is already absolute, the pathname string is returned as if by calling getPath().
File getCanonicalFile()	Return the *canonical* (simplest possible) form of this File object's pathname. This method is equivalent to new File(this.getCanonicalPath()), which is roughly how File implements this method. It throws IOException when an I/O error occurs (constructing the canonical pathname may require filesystem queries).
String getCanonicalPath()	Return the canonical pathname string of this File object's pathname. A canonical pathname is absolute and unique. This method throws IOException when an I/O error occurs (constructing the canonical pathname may require filesystem queries).
String getName()	Return the name of the file or directory denoted by this File object's pathname. The returned value is the last name in the pathname's name sequence.
String getParent()	Return the parent pathname string of this File object's pathname, or return null when this pathname does not name a parent directory.
File getParentFile()	Return a File object containing the parent pathname of this File object's pathname, or return null when this File object's pathname does not name a parent directory.
String getPath()	Return this File object's pathname.

Method	Description
boolean isAbsolute()	Return true when this File object's pathname is absolute; otherwise, return false when it is relative.
String toString()	A synonym for getPath().

Table 10-1 refers to IOException, which is the common exception superclass for those exception classes that describe various kinds of I/O errors.

Listing 10–2 instantiates File with its pathname command-line argument, and calls some of the File methods described in Table 10–1 to learn about this pathname.

Listing 10–2. *Obtaining abstract pathname information*

```java
import java.io.File;
import java.io.IOException;

public class PathnameInfo
{
   public static void main(final String[] args) throws IOException
   {
      if (args.length != 1)
      {
         System.err.println("usage: java PathnameInfo pathname");
         return;
      }
      File file = new File(args[0]);
      System.out.println("Absolute path = " + file.getAbsolutePath());
      System.out.println("Canonical path = " + file.getCanonicalPath());
      System.out.println("Name = " + file.getName());
      System.out.println("Parent = " + file.getParent());
      System.out.println("Path = " + file.getPath());
      System.out.println("Is absolute = " + file.isAbsolute());
   }
}
```

For example, when I specify java PathnameInfo . (the period represents the current directory on my XP platform), I observe the following output:

```
Absolute path = C:\prj\dev\ljfad\c10\code\PathnameInfo\.
Canonical path = C:\prj\dev\ljfad\c10\code\PathnameInfo
Name = .
Parent = null
Path = .
Is absolute = false
```

This output reveals that the canonical pathname does not include the period. It also shows that there is no parent pathname and that the pathname is relative.

Continuing, I now specify java PathnameInfo c:\reports\2010\..\2009\February. This time, I observe the following output:

```
Absolute path = c:\reports\2010\..\2009\February
Canonical path = C:\reports\2009\February
Name = February
```

```
Parent = c:\reports\2010\..\2009
Path = c:\reports\2010\..\2009\February
Is absolute = true
```

This output reveals that the canonical pathname does not include 2010. It also shows that the pathname is absolute.

For my final example, suppose I specify java PathnameInfo "" to obtain information for the empty pathname. In response, this application generates the following output:

```
Absolute path = C:\prj\dev\ljfad\c10\code\PathnameInfo
Canonical path = C:\prj\dev\ljfad\c10\code\PathnameInfo
Name =
Parent = null
Path =
Is absolute = false
```

The output reveals that getName() and getPath() return the empty string ("") because the empty pathname is empty.

You can interrogate the filesystem to learn about the file or directory represented by a File object's stored pathname by calling the methods that are described in Table 10–2.

Table 10–2. *File Methods for Learning About a File or Directory*

Method	Description
boolean canRead()	Return true when this File object's pathname represents an existing readable file.
boolean canWrite()	Return true when this File object's pathname represents an existing file that can be modified.
boolean exists()	Return true if and only if the file or directory that is denoted by this File object's pathname exists.
boolean isDirectory()	Return true when this File object's pathname refers to an existing directory.
boolean isFile()	Return true when this File object's pathname refers to an existing normal file. (A file is *normal* when it is not a directory and satisfies other platform-dependent criteria: it is not a symbolic link or named pipe, for example. Any non-directory file created by a Java application is guaranteed to be a normal file.)
boolean isHidden()	Return true when the file denoted by this File object's pathname is hidden. The exact definition of *hidden* is platform dependent. On Unix/Linux platforms, a file is hidden when its name begins with a period character. On Windows platforms, a file is hidden when it has been marked as such in the filesystem.

Method	Description
`long lastModified()`	Return the time that the file denoted by this `File` object's pathname was last modified, or 0 when the file does not exist or an I/O error occurred during this method call. The returned value is measured in milliseconds since the Unix epoch (00:00:00 GMT, January 1, 1970).
`long length()`	Return the length of the file denoted by this `File` object's pathname. The return value is unspecified when the pathname denotes a directory.

Listing 10–3 instantiates `File` with its pathname command-line argument, and calls all of the `File` methods described in Table 10–2 to learn about the pathname's file/directory.

Listing 10–3. *Obtaining file/directory information*

```
import java.io.File;
import java.io.IOException;

import java.util.Date;

public class FileDirectoryInfo
{
   public static void main(final String[] args) throws IOException
   {
      if (args.length != 1)
      {
         System.err.println("usage: java FileDirectoryInfo pathname");
         return;
      }
      File file = new File(args[0]);
      System.out.println("About " + file + ":");
      System.out.println("Can read = " + file.canRead());
      System.out.println("Can write = " + file.canWrite());
      System.out.println("Exists = " + file.exists());
      System.out.println("Is directory = " + file.isDirectory());
      System.out.println("Is file = " + file.isFile());
      System.out.println("Is hidden = " + file.isHidden());
      System.out.println("Last modified = " + new Date(file.lastModified()));
      System.out.println("Length = " + file.length());
   }
}
```

For example, suppose I have a three-byte read-only file named x.dat. When I specify java FileDirectoryInfo x.dat, I observe the following output:

```
About x.dat:
Can read = true
Can write = false
Exists = true
Is directory = false
Is file = true
Is hidden = false
Last modified = Wed Aug 04 16:58:32 CDT 2010
Length = 3
```

> **NOTE:** Java version 6 extended `File` with new boolean `canExecute()`, long
> `getFreeSpace()`, long `getTotalSpace()`, and long `getUsableSpace()` methods that
> return additional information about the file, the directory, or the *partition* (an operating system–
> specific portion of storage for a filesystem; for example, C:\) described by the `File` instance's
> pathname. At time of writing, Android's `File` documentation (see
> `http://developer.android.com/reference/java/io/File.html`) indicated that
> Android does not support these methods. However, Android might support them in the future.

`File` declares five methods that return the names of files and directories located in the
directory identified by a `File` object's pathname. Table 10–3 describes these methods.

Table 10–3. *File Methods for Obtaining Directory Content*

Method	Description
`String[] list()`	Return an array of strings naming the files and directories in the directory denoted by this `File` object's pathname. If the pathname does not denote a directory, or if an I/O error occurs, this method returns null. Otherwise, it returns an array of strings, one string for each file or directory in the directory. Names denoting the directory itself and the directory's parent directory are not included in the result. Each string is a filename rather than a complete path.
	There is no guarantee that the name strings in the resulting array will appear in any specific order; they are not, in particular, guaranteed to appear in alphabetical order.
`String[] list (FilenameFilter filter)`	Return an array of strings naming the files and directories in the directory denoted by this `File` object's pathname that satisfy the specified `filter`. If the pathname does not denote a directory, or if an I/O error occurs, this method returns null. Otherwise, it returns an array of strings, one string for each file or directory that is accepted by `filter`. If `filter` is null, all names are accepted. Otherwise, a name is accepted only when `filter`'s `accept(File, String)` method returns true for the file or directory whose `File` object is passed to `accept()`. Names denoting the directory itself and the directory's parent directory are not included in the result. Each string is a filename rather than a complete path.
	There is no guarantee that the name strings in the resulting array will appear in any specific order; they are not, in particular, guaranteed to appear in alphabetical order.
`File[] listFiles()`	A synonym for calling `list()` and converting its array of `Strings` to an array of `Files`.

Method	Description
`File[] listFiles (FileFilter filter)`	A synonym for calling `list()` and converting its array of Strings to an array of Files, but only for those Strings that satisfy filter.
`File[] listFiles (FilenameFilter filter)`	A synonym for calling `list()` and converting its array of Strings to an array of Files, but only for those Strings that satisfy filter.

The overloaded `list()` methods return arrays of Strings. The second method lets you return only those names of interest (such as only those names that end with extension .txt) via a FilenameFilter-based filter object.

The FilenameFilter interface declares a single boolean `accept(File dir, String name)` method that is called for each file/directory located in the directory identified by the File object's pathname:

- `dir` identifies the parent portion of the pathname (the directory path).

- `name` identifies the name portion of the pathname (the final directory name or the filename).

The `accept()` method uses these arguments to determine whether or not the file or directory satisfies its criteria for what is acceptable. It returns true when the file/directory name should be included in the returned array; otherwise, this method returns false.

Listing 10–4 presents a Dir(ectory) application that uses `list(FilenameFilter)` to obtain only those names that end with a specific extension.

Listing 10–4. *Listing specific names*

```java
import java.io.File;
import java.io.FilenameFilter;

public class Dir
{
    public static void main(final String[] args)
    {
        if (args.length != 2)
        {
            System.err.println("usage: java Dir dirpath ext");
            return;
        }
        File file = new File(args[0]);
        FilenameFilter fnf = new FilenameFilter()
                             {
                                 public boolean accept(File dir, String name)
                                 {
                                     return name.endsWith(args[1]);
                                 }
                             };
        String[] names = file.list(fnf);
        for (String name: names)
            System.out.println(name);
    }
}
```

When I, for example, specify java Dir c:\windows exe on my XP platform, Dir outputs only those \windows directory filenames that have the exe extension:

```
explorer.exe
hh.exe
IsUninst.exe
notepad.exe
NuNinst.exe
regedit.exe
slrundll.exe
twunk_16.exe
twunk_32.exe
uninst.exe
winhelp.exe
winhlp32.exe
```

The overloaded listFiles() methods return arrays of Files. For the most part, they are symmetrical with their list() counterparts. However, listFiles(FileFilter) introduces an asymmetry.

The FileFilter interface declares a single boolean accept(String pathname) method that is called for each file/directory located in the directory identified by the File object's pathname:

- pathname identifies the complete path of the file or directory.

The accept() method uses this argument to determine whether or not the file or directory satisfies its criteria for what is acceptable. It returns true when the file/directory name should be included in the returned array; otherwise, this method returns false.

> **NOTE:** Because each interface's accept() method accomplishes the same task, you might be wondering which interface to use. If you prefer a path broken into its directory and name components, use FilenameFilter. However, if you prefer a complete pathname, use FileFilter; you can always call getParent() and getName() to get these components.

File also declares several methods for creating files and manipulating existing files. Table 10–4 describes these methods.

Table 10-4. *File Methods for Creating Files and Manipulating Existing Files*

Method	Description
`boolean createNewFile()`	Atomically create a new, empty file named by this `File` object's pathname if and only if a file with this name does not yet exist. The check for file existence and the creation of the file if it does not exist are a single operation that is atomic with respect to all other filesystem activities that might affect the file. This method throws `IOException` when an I/O error occurs.
`static File createTempFile (String prefix, String suffix)`	Create an empty file in the default temporary file directory using the given `prefix` and `suffix` to generate its name. This overloaded method calls its three-parameter variant, passing `prefix`, `suffix`, and `null` to this other method, and returning this other method's return value.
`static File createTempFile (String prefix, String suffix, File directory)`	Create an empty file in the specified `directory` using the given `prefix` and `suffix` to generate its name. The name begins with the character sequence specified by `prefix` and ends with the character sequence specified by `suffix`; `.tmp` is used as the suffix when `suffix` is `null`. This method returns the created file's pathname when successful. It throws `java.lang.IllegalArgumentException` when `prefix` contains fewer than three characters, and `IOException` when the file could not be created.
`boolean delete()`	Delete the file or directory denoted by this `File` object's pathname. Return true when successful; otherwise, return false. If the pathname denotes a directory, the directory must be empty in order to be deleted.
`void deleteOnExit()`	Request that the file or directory denoted by this `File` object's pathname be deleted when the virtual machine terminates. Once deletion has been requested, it is not possible to cancel the request. Therefore, this method should be used with care.
`boolean mkdir()`	Create the directory named by this `File` object's pathname. Return true when successful; otherwise, return false.
`boolean mkdirs()`	Create the directory and any necessary intermediate directories named by this `File` object's pathname. Return true when successful; otherwise, return false.

Method	Description
boolean renameTo (File dest)	Rename the file denoted by this File object's pathname to dest. Return true when successful; otherwise, return false. Throw java.lang.NullPointerException when dest is null.
	Many aspects of this method's behavior are platform dependent. For example, the rename operation might not be able to move a file from one filesystem to another, the operation might not be atomic, or it might not succeed if a file with the destination pathname already exists. The return value should always be checked to make sure that the rename operation was successful.
boolean setLastModified (long time)	Set the last-modified time of the file or directory named by this File object's pathname. Return true when successful; otherwise, return false. This method throws IllegalArgumentException when time is negative.
	All platforms support file-modification times to the nearest second, but some provide more precision. The time value will be truncated to fit the supported precision. If the operation succeeds and no intervening operations on the file take place, the next call to lastModified() will return the (possibly truncated) time value passed to this method.
boolean setReadOnly()	Mark the file or directory denoted by this File object's pathname so that only read operations are allowed. After calling this method, the file or directory is guaranteed not to change until it is deleted or marked to allow write access. Whether or not a read-only file or directory can be deleted depends upon the filesystem.

Suppose you are designing a text-editor application that a user will use to open a text file and make changes to its content. Until the user explicitly saves these changes to the file, you want the text file to remain unchanged.

Because the user does not want to lose these changes when the application crashes or the computer loses power, you design the application to save these changes to a temporary file every few minutes. This way, the user has a backup of the changes.

You can use the overloaded createTempFile() methods to create the temporary file. If you do not specify a directory in which to store this file, it is created in the directory identified by the java.io.tmpdir system property.

You probably want to remove the temporary file after the user tells the application to save or discard the changes. The deleteOnExit() method lets you register a temporary file for deletion; it is deleted when the virtual machine ends without a crash/power loss.

Listing 10–5 presents a TempFileDemo application that lets you experiment with the createTempFile() and deleteOnExit() methods.

Listing 10–5. *Experimenting with temporary files*

```
import java.io.File;
import java.io.IOException;

public class TempFileDemo
{
   public static void main(String[] args) throws IOException
   {
      System.out.println(System.getProperty("java.io.tmpdir"));
      File temp = File.createTempFile("text", ".txt");
      System.out.println(temp);
      temp.deleteOnExit();
   }
}
```

After outputting the location where temporary files are stored, TempFileDemo creates a temporary file whose name begins with text and which ends with the .txt extension. TempFileDemo next outputs the temporary file's name and registers the temporary file for deletion upon the successful termination of the application.

After compiling the source code, run this application. During one run of TempFileDemo, I observed the following output (and the file did not hang around after application exit):

```
C:\DOCUME~1\JEFFFR~1\LOCALS~1\Temp\
C:\DOCUME~1\JEFFFR~1\LOCALS~1\Temp\text3010913241139161364.txt
```

> **NOTE:** Java version 6 extended File with new boolean setExecutable(boolean executable), boolean setExecutable(boolean executable, boolean ownerOnly), boolean setReadable(boolean readable), boolean setReadable(boolean readable, boolean ownerOnly), boolean setWritable(boolean writable), and boolean setWritable(boolean writable, boolean ownerOnly) methods that let you set the owner's or everybody's execute, read, and write permissions (respectively) for the file identified by the File object's pathname. At time of writing, Android's File documentation indicated that Android does not support these methods. However, Android might support them in the future.

Finally, File implements the java.lang.Comparable interface's compareTo() method, and overrides equals() and hashCode(). Table 10–5 describes these miscellaneous methods.

Table 10–5. *File's Miscellaneous Methods*

Method	Description
int compareTo (File pathname)	Compare two pathnames lexicographically. The ordering defined by this method depends upon the underlying platform. On Unix/Linux platforms, alphabetic case is significant when comparing pathnames; on Windows platforms, alphabetic case is not significant. Return zero when pathname equals this File object's pathname, a negative value when this File object's pathname is less than pathname, and a positive value when this File object's pathname is greater than pathname.
boolean equals (Object obj)	Compare this File object with obj for equality. Pathname equality depends upon the underlying platform. On Unix/Linux platforms, alphabetic case is significant when comparing pathnames; on Windows platforms, alphabetic case is not significant. Return true if and only if obj is not null and is a File object whose pathname denotes the same file/directory as this File object's pathname.
int hashCode()	Calculate and return a hash code for this pathname. This calculation depends upon the underlying platform. On Unix/Linux systems, a pathname's hash code equals the exclusive OR of its pathname string's hash code and decimal value 1234321. On Windows systems, the hash code equals the exclusive OR of the lowercased pathname string's hash code and decimal value 1234321. The current locale is not taken into account when lowercasing the pathname string.

TIP: To accurately compare two File objects, first call getCanonicalFile() on each File object and then compare the returned File objects.

RandomAccessFile

Files can be created and/or opened for *random access* in which a mixture of write and read operations can occur until the file is closed. Java supports this random access by providing the concrete RandomAccessFile class.

RandomAccessFile declares the following constructors:

- RandomAccessFile(File file, String mode) creates and opens a new file if it does not exist, or opens an existing file. The file is identified by file's pathname and is created and/or opened according to the mode that is specified by mode.

- RandomAccessFile(String pathname, String mode) creates and opens a new file if it does not exist, or opens an existing file. The file is identified by pathname and is created and/or opened according to the mode that is specified by mode.

> **CAUTION:** Be careful when specifying a pathname for either constructor. You should strive to specify only pathnames that are valid for all platforms on which the application will run, unless you are creating your application to run on a single platform.

Either constructor's mode argument must be one of "r", "rw", "rws", or "rwd"; otherwise, the constructor throws IllegalArgumentException. These string literals have the following meanings:

- "r" informs the constructor to open an existing file for reading only. Any attempt to write to the file results in a thrown instance of the IOException class.

- "rw" informs the constructor to create and open a new file if it does not exist for reading and writing, or open an existing file for reading and writing.

- "rwd" informs the constructor to create and open a new file if it does not exist for reading and writing, or open an existing file for reading and writing. Furthermore, each update to the file's content must be written synchronously to the underlying storage device.

- "rws" informs the constructor to create and open a new file if it does not exist for reading and writing, or open an existing file for reading and writing. Furthermore, each update to the file's content or metadata must be written synchronously to the underlying storage device.

> **NOTE:** A file's *metadata* is data about the file and not actual file contents. Examples of metadata include the file's length and the time the file was last modified.

The "rwd" and "rws" modes ensure than any writes to a file located on a local storage device are written to the device, which guarantees that critical data is not lost when the system crashes. No guarantee is made when the file does not reside on a local device.

> **NOTE:** Operations on a random access file opened in "rwd" or "rws" mode are slower than these same operations on a random access file opened in "rw" mode.

These constructors throw FileNotFoundException (a subclass of IOException) when mode is "r" and the file identified by pathname cannot be opened (it might not exist or might be a directory), or when mode is "rw" and pathname is read-only or a directory.

The following example demonstrates the second constructor by attempting to open an existing random access file via the "r" mode string:

```
RandomAccessFile raf = new RandomAccessFile("employee.dat", "r");
```

A random access file is associated with a *file pointer*, a cursor that identifies the location of the next byte to write or read. When an existing file is opened, the file pointer is set to its first byte, at offset 0. The file pointer is also set to 0 when the file is created.

Write or read operations start at the file pointer and advance it past the number of bytes written or read. Operations that write past the current end of the file cause the file to be extended. These operations continue until the file is closed.

RandomAccessFile declares a wide variety of methods. I present a representative sample of these methods in Table 10–6.

Table 10–6. *RandomAccessFile Methods*

Method	Description
void close()	Close the file and release any associated system resources. Subsequent writes or reads result in IOException. Also, the file cannot be reopened with this RandomAccessFile object. This method throws IOException when an I/O error occurs.
FileDescriptor getFD()	Return the file's associated file descriptor object. This method throws IOException when an I/O error occurs.
long getFilePointer()	Return the file pointer's current zero-based byte offset into the file. This method throws IOException when an I/O error occurs.
long length()	Return the length (measured in bytes) of the file. This method throws IOException when an I/O error occurs.
int read()	Read and return (as an int in the range 0 to 255) the next byte from the file, or return -1 when the end of the file is reached. This method blocks if no input is available, and throws IOException when an I/O error occurs.
int read (byte[] b)	Read up to b.length bytes of data from the file into byte array b. This method blocks until at least one byte of input is available. It returns the number of bytes read into the array, or returns -1 when the end of the file is reached. It throws NullPointerException when b is null, and IOException when an I/O error occurs.
char readChar()	Read and return a character from the file. This method reads two bytes from the file starting at the current file pointer. If the bytes read, in order, are b1 and b2, where 0 <= b1, b2 <= 255, the result is equal to (char) ((b1<<8)|b2). This method blocks until the two bytes are read, the end of the file is detected, or an exception is thrown. It throws EOFException (a subclass of IOException) when the end of the file is reached before reading both bytes, and IOException when an I/O error occurs.

Method	Description
int readInt()	Read and return a 32-bit integer from the file. This method reads four bytes from the file starting at the current file pointer. If the bytes read, in order, are b1, b2, b3, and b4, where 0 <= b1, b2, b3, b4 <= 255, the result is equal to (b1<<24)|(b2<<16)+(b3<<8)+b4. This method blocks until the four bytes are read, the end of the file is detected, or an exception is thrown. It throws EOFException when the end of the file is reached before reading all four bytes, and IOException when an I/O error occurs.
void seek (long pos)	Set the file pointer's current offset to pos (which is measured in bytes from the beginning of the file). If the offset is set beyond the end of the file, the file's length does not change. The file length will only change by writing after the offset has been set beyond the end of the file. This method throws IOException when the value in pos is negative, or when an I/O error occurs.
void setLength (long newLength)	Set the file's length. If the present length as returned by length() is greater than newLength, the file is truncated. In this case, if the file offset as returned by getFilePointer() is greater than newLength, the offset will be equal to newLength after setLength() returns. If the present length is smaller than newLength, the file is extended. In this case, the contents of the extended portion of the file are not defined. This method throws IOException when an I/O error occurs.
int skipBytes (int n)	Attempt to skip over n bytes. This method skips over a smaller number of bytes (possibly zero) when the end of file is reached before n bytes have been skipped. It does not throw EOFException in this situation. If n is negative, no bytes are skipped. The actual number of bytes skipped is returned. This method throws IOException when an I/O error occurs.
void write (byte[] b)	Write b.length bytes from byte array b to the file starting at the current file pointer position. This method throws IOException when an I/O error occurs.
void write(int b)	Write the lower eight bits of b to the file at the current file pointer position. This method throws IOException when an I/O error occurs.
void writeChars (String s)	Write string s to the file as a sequence of characters starting at the current file pointer position. This method throws IOException when an I/O error occurs.
void writeInt (int i)	Write 32-bit integer i to the file starting at the current file pointer position. The four bytes are written with the high byte first. This method throws IOException when an I/O error occurs.

Most of Table 10–6's methods are fairly self-explanatory. However, the getFD() method requires further enlightenment.

> **NOTE:** RandomAccessFile's read-prefixed methods and skipBytes() originate in the DataInput interface, which this class implements. Furthermore, RandomAccessFile's write-prefixed methods originate in the DataOutput interface, which this class also implements.

When a file is opened, the underlying platform creates a platform-dependent structure to represent the file. A handle to this structure is stored in an instance of the FileDescriptor class, which getFD() returns.

> **NOTE:** A *handle* is an identifier that Java passes to the underlying platform to identify, in this case, a specific open file when it requires that the underlying platform perform a file operation.

FileDescriptor is a small class that declares three FileDescriptor constants named in, out, and err. These constants let System.in, System.out, and System.err provide access to the standard input, standard output, and standard error streams.

FileDescriptor also declares a pair of methods:

- void sync() tells the underlying platform to *flush* (empty) the contents of the open file's output buffers to their associated local disk device. sync() returns after all modified data and attributes have been written to the relevant device. It throws SyncFailedException when the buffers cannot be flushed, or because the platform cannot guarantee that all the buffers have been synchronized with physical media.

- boolean valid() determines whether or not this file descriptor object is valid. It returns true when the file descriptor object represents an open file or other active I/O connection; otherwise, it returns false.

Data that is written to an open file ends up being stored in the underlying platform's output buffers. When the buffers fill to capacity, the platform empties them to the disk. Buffers improve performance because disk access is slow.

However, when you write data to a random access file that has been opened via mode "rwd" or "rws", each write operation's data is written straight to the disk. As a result, write operations are slower than if the random access file was opened in "rw" mode.

Suppose you have a situation that combines writing data through the output buffers and writing data directly to the disk. Listing 10–6 addresses this hybrid scenario by opening the file in mode "rw" and selectively calling FileDescriptor's sync() method.

Listing 10–6. *Selectively calling sync()*

```
RandomAccessFile raf = new RandomAccessFile("employee.dat", "rw");
FileDescriptor fd = raf.getFD();
// Perform a critical write operation.
raf.write(...);
// Synchronize with underlying disk by flushing platform's output buffers to disk.
```

```
fd.sync();
// Perform non-critical write operation where synchronization is not necessary.
raf.write(...);
// Do other work.
// Close file, emptying output buffers to disk.
raf.close();
```

RandomAccessFile is useful for creating a *flat file database*, a single file organized into records and fields. A *record* stores a single entry (such as a part in a parts database) and a *field* stores a single attribute of the entry (such as a part number).

A flat file database typically organizes its content into a sequence of fixed-length records. Each record is further organized into one or more fixed-length fields. Figure 10–1 illustrates this concept in the context of a parts database.

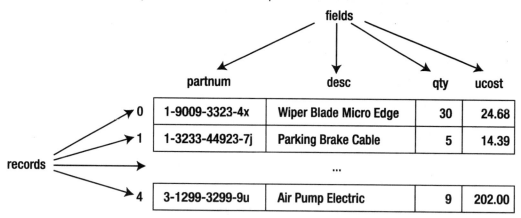

Figure 10–1. *A flat file database of automotive parts*

According to Figure 10–1, each field has a name (partnum, desc, qty, and ucost). Also, each record is assigned a number starting at 0. This example consists of five records, of which only three are shown for brevity.

> **NOTE:** The term *field* is also used to refer to a variable declared within a class. To avoid confusion with this overloaded terminology, think of a field variable as being analogous to a record's field attribute.

To show you how to implement a flat file database in terms of RandomAccessFile, I have created a simple PartsDB class to model Figure 10–1. Check out Listing 10–7.

Listing 10–7. *Implementing the parts flat file database*

```java
import java.io.IOException;
import java.io.RandomAccessFile;

public class PartsDB
{
    public final static int PNUMLEN = 20;
    public final static int DESCLEN = 30;
```

```java
   public final static int QUANLEN = 4;
   public final static int COSTLEN = 4;

   private final static int RECLEN = 2*PNUMLEN+2*DESCLEN+QUANLEN+COSTLEN;
   private RandomAccessFile raf;

   public PartsDB(String pathname) throws IOException
   {
      raf = new RandomAccessFile(pathname, "rw");
   }
   public void append(String partnum, String partdesc, int qty, int ucost)
      throws IOException
   {
      raf.seek(raf.length());
      write(partnum, partdesc, qty, ucost);
   }
   public void close()
   {
      try
      {
         raf.close();
      }
      catch (IOException ioe)
      {
         System.err.println(ioe);
      }
   }
   public int numRecs() throws IOException
   {
      return (int) raf.length()/RECLEN;
   }
   public Part select(int recno) throws IOException
   {
      if (recno < 0 || recno >= numRecs())
         throw new IllegalArgumentException(recno + " out of range");
      raf.seek(recno*RECLEN);
      return read();
   }
   public void update(int recno, String partnum, String partdesc, int qty,
                      int ucost) throws IOException
   {
      if (recno < 0 || recno >= numRecs())
         throw new IllegalArgumentException(recno + " out of range");
      raf.seek(recno*RECLEN);
      write(partnum, partdesc, qty, ucost);
   }
   private Part read() throws IOException
   {
      StringBuffer sb = new StringBuffer();
      for (int i = 0; i < PNUMLEN; i++)
         sb.append(raf.readChar());
      String partnum = sb.toString().trim();
      sb.setLength(0);
      for (int i = 0; i < DESCLEN; i++)
         sb.append(raf.readChar());
      String partdesc = sb.toString().trim();
      int qty = raf.readInt();
```

```
            int ucost = raf.readInt();
            return new Part(partnum, partdesc, qty, ucost);
        }
        private void write(String partnum, String partdesc, int qty, int ucost)
            throws IOException
        {
            StringBuffer sb = new StringBuffer(partnum);
            if (sb.length() > PNUMLEN)
                sb.setLength(PNUMLEN);
            else
            if (sb.length() < PNUMLEN)
            {
                int len = PNUMLEN-sb.length();
                for (int i = 0; i < len; i++)
                    sb.append(" ");
            }
            raf.writeChars(sb.toString());
            sb = new StringBuffer(partdesc);
            if (sb.length() > DESCLEN)
                sb.setLength(DESCLEN);
            else
            if (sb.length() < DESCLEN)
            {
                int len = DESCLEN-sb.length();
                for (int i = 0; i < len; i++)
                    sb.append(" ");
            }
            raf.writeChars(sb.toString());
            raf.writeInt(qty);
            raf.writeInt(ucost);
        }
    }
    public static class Part
    {
        private String partnum;
        private String desc;
        private int qty;
        private int ucost;
        public Part(String partnum, String desc, int qty, int ucost)
        {
            this.partnum = partnum;
            this.desc = desc;
            this.qty = qty;
            this.ucost = ucost;
        }
        String getDesc()
        {
            return desc;
        }
        String getPartnum()
        {
            return partnum;
        }
        int getQty()
        {
            return qty;
        }
        int getUnitCost()
```

```
      {
          return ucost;
      }
   }
}
```

PartsDB first declares constants that identify the lengths of the string and 32-bit integer
fields. It then declares a constant that calculates the record length in terms of bytes. The
calculation takes into account the fact that a character occupies two bytes in the file.

These constants are followed by a field named raf that is of type RandomAccessFile.
This field is assigned an instance of the RandomAccessFile class in the subsequent
constructor, which creates/opens a new file or opens an existing file because of "rw".

The public interface continues with append(), close(), numRecs(), select(), and
update(). These methods append a record to the file, close the file, return the number of
records in the file, select and return a specific record, and update a specific record.

The append() method first calls length() and seek(). Doing so ensures that the file
pointer is positioned to the end of the file before calling the private write() method to
write a record containing this method's arguments.

RandomAccessFile's close() method can throw IOException. Because this is a rare
occurrence, I chose to handle this exception in PartDB's close() method, which keeps
that method's signature simple. However, I print a message when IOException occurs.

The numRecs() method returns the number of records in the file. These records are
numbered starting with 0 and ending with numRecs()-1. Each of the select() and
update() methods verifies that its recno argument lies within this range.

The select() method calls the private read() method to return the record identified by
recno as an instance of the Part static member class. Part's constructor initializes a
Part object to a record's field values, and its getter methods return these values.

The update() method is equally simple. As with select(), it first positions the file pointer
to the start of the record identified by recno. As with append(), it calls the write()
method to write out its arguments, but replaces a record instead of adding one.

Fields must have exact sizes. write() pads String-based values that are shorter than a
field size with spaces on the right, and truncates these values to the field size if needed.
read() removes the padding before saving a String-based field value in the Part object.

By itself, PartsDB is useless. We need an application that lets us experiment with this
class, and Listing 10–8 fulfills this requirement.

Listing 10–8. *Experimenting with the parts flat file database*

```java
import java.io.IOException;

public class UsePartsDB
{
    public static void main(String[] args)
    {
        PartsDB pdb = null;
        try
```

```
      {
         pdb = new PartsDB("parts.db");
         if (pdb.numRecs() == 0)
         {
            // Populate the database with records.
            pdb.append("1-9009-3323-4x", "Wiper Blade Micro Edge", 30, 2468);
            pdb.append("1-3233-44923-7j", "Parking Brake Cable", 5, 1439);
            pdb.append("2-3399-6693-2m", "Halogen Bulb H4 55/60W", 22, 813);
            pdb.append("2-599-2029-6k", "Turbo Oil Line O-Ring ", 26, 155);
            pdb.append("3-1299-3299-9u", "Air Pump Electric", 9, 20200);
         }
         dumpRecords(pdb);
         pdb.update(1, "1-3233-44923-7j", "Parking Brake Cable", 5, 1995);
         dumpRecords(pdb);
      }
      catch (IOException ioe)
      {
         System.err.println(ioe);
      }
      finally
      {
         if (pdb != null)
            pdb.close();
      }
   }
   static String format(String value, int maxWidth, boolean leftAlign)
   {
      StringBuffer sb = new StringBuffer();
      int len = value.length();
      if (len > maxWidth)
      {
         len = maxWidth;
         value = value.substring(0, len);
      }
      if (leftAlign)
      {
         sb.append(value);
         for (int i = 0; i < maxWidth-len; i++)
            sb.append(" ");
      }
      else
      {
         for (int i = 0; i < maxWidth-len; i++)
            sb.append(" ");
         sb.append(value);
      }
      return sb.toString();
   }
   static void dumpRecords(PartsDB pdb) throws IOException
   {
      for (int i = 0; i < pdb.numRecs(); i++)
      {
         PartsDB.Part part = pdb.select(i);
         System.out.print(format(part.getPartnum(), PartsDB.PNUMLEN, true));
         System.out.print(" | ");
         System.out.print(format(part.getDesc(), PartsDB.DESCLEN, true));
```

```
            System.out.print(" | ");
            System.out.print(format("" + part.getQty(), 10, false));
            System.out.print(" | ");
            String s = part.getUnitCost()/100 + "." + part.getUnitCost()%100;
            if (s.charAt(s.length()-2) == '.') s += "0";
            System.out.println(format(s, 10, false));
         }
         System.out.println("Number of records = " + pdb.numRecs());
         System.out.println();
      }
}
```

The `main()` method begins by instantiating `PartsDB`, with `parts.db` as the name of the database file. If this file has no records, `numRecs()` returns 0 and several records are appended to the file via the `append()` method.

`main()` next dumps the five records stored in `parts.db` to the standard output device, updates the unit cost in the record whose number is 1, once again dumps these records to the standard output device to show this change, and closes the database.

> **NOTE:** I store unit cost values as integer-based penny amounts. For example, I specify literal 1995 to represent 1995 pennies, or $19.95. If I were to use `BigDecimal` objects to store currency values, I would have to refactor `PartsDB` to take advantage of object serialization, and I am not prepared to do that right now. (I discuss object serialization later in this chapter.)

`main()` relies on a `dumpRecords()` helper method to dump these records, and `dumpRecords()` relies on a `format()` helper method to format field values so that they can be presented in properly aligned columns. The following output reveals this alignment:

```
1-9009-3323-4x      | Wiper Blade Micro Edge   |       30 |     24.68
1-3233-44923-7j     | Parking Brake Cable      |        5 |     14.39
2-3399-6693-2m      | Halogen Bulb H4 55/60W   |       22 |      8.13
2-599-2029-6k       | Turbo Oil Line O-Ring    |       26 |      1.55
3-1299-3299-9u      | Air Pump Electric        |        9 |    202.00
Number of records = 5

1-9009-3323-4x      | Wiper Blade Micro Edge   |       30 |     24.68
1-3233-44923-7j     | Parking Brake Cable      |        5 |     19.95
2-3399-6693-2m      | Halogen Bulb H4 55/60W   |       22 |      8.13
2-599-2029-6k       | Turbo Oil Line O-Ring    |       26 |      1.55
3-1299-3299-9u      | Air Pump Electric        |        9 |    202.00
Number of records = 5
```

And there you have it: a simple flat file database. Despite its lack of support for advanced database features such as indexes and transaction management, a flat file database might be all that your Android application requires.

> **NOTE:** Check out Wikipedia's "Flat file database" entry
> (`http://en.wikipedia.org/wiki/Flat_file_database`) to learn more about flat file
> databases.

Streams

Along with `File` and `RandomAccessFile`, Java uses streams to perform I/O operations. A *stream* is an ordered sequence of bytes of arbitrary length. Bytes flow over an *output stream* from an application to a destination, and flow over an *input stream* from a source to an application. Figure 10–2 illustrates these flows.

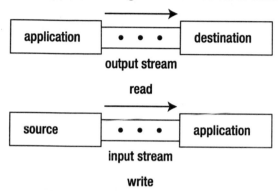

Figure 10–2. *Conceptualizing output and input streams*

> **NOTE:** Java's use of the word *stream* is analogous to other uses that refer to a flow of water or a
> flow of electrons.

Java recognizes various stream destinations; for example, byte arrays, files, screens, *sockets* (network endpoints), and thread pipes. Java also recognizes various stream sources. Examples include byte arrays, files, keyboards, sockets, and thread pipes. (I do not discuss sockets in this chapter.)

Stream Classes Overview

The `java.io` package provides several output stream and input stream classes that are descendents of the abstract `OutputStream` and `InputStream` classes. In the following list of classes, output stream classes (except for `PrintStream`) are denoted by their `OutputStream` suffixes and input stream classes are denoted by their `InputStream` suffixes:

- BufferedOutputStream
- BufferedInputStream
- ByteArrayOutputStream
- ByteArrayInputStream
- DataOutputStream
- DataInputStream
- FileOutputStream
- FileInputStream
- FilterOutputStream
- FilterInputStream
- ObjectOutputStream
- ObjectInputStream
- PipedOutputStream
- PipedInputStream
- PrintStream
- PushbackInputStream
- SequenceInputStream

Additionally, `java.io` offers `LineNumberInputStream` and `StringBufferInputStream` classes. However, these classes have been deprecated because they do not support different character encodings, a topic I discuss later in this chapter. `LineNumberReader` and `StringReader` are their replacements. (I discuss readers later in this chapter.)

> **NOTE:** `PrintStream` is another class that should be deprecated because it does not support different character encodings; `PrintWriter` is its replacement. However, it is doubtful that Oracle will deprecate this class because `PrintStream` is the type of the `java.lang.System` class's `out` and `err` class fields, and too much legacy code depends upon this fact.

Other Java packages provide additional output stream and input stream classes. For example, `java.util.zip` provides four output stream classes that compress uncompressed data into various formats, and four matching input stream classes that uncompress compressed data from the same formats:

- CheckedOutputStream
- CheckedInputStream
- DeflaterOutputStream
- GZIPOutputStream

- GZIPInputStream

- InflaterInputStream

- ZipOutputStream

- ZipInputStream

> **NOTE:** For an example of ZipOutputStream, check out Kode Java's "How do I create a zip file?" example (http://www.kodejava.org/examples/119.html). For an example of ZipInputStream, check out Kode Java's "How do I decompress a zip file using ZipInputStream?" example (http://www.kodejava.org/examples/334.html).

Also, the java.util.jar package provides a pair of stream classes for writing content to a JAR file and for reading content from a JAR file:

- JarOutputStream

- JarInputStream

The next several sections take you on a tour of most of java.io's output stream and input stream classes, beginning with OutputStream and InputStream.

OutputStream and InputStream

Java provides the OutputStream and InputStream classes for performing stream I/O. OutputStream is the superclass of all output stream subclasses. Table 10–7 describes OutputStream's methods.

Table 10–7. OutputStream Methods

Method	Description
void close()	Close this output stream and release any system resources associated with the stream. This method throws IOException when an I/O error occurs.
void flush()	Flush this output stream by writing any buffered output bytes to the destination. If the intended destination of this output stream is an abstraction provided by the underlying platform (for example, a file), flushing the stream only guarantees that bytes previously written to the stream are passed to the underlying platform for writing; it does not guarantee that they are actually written to a physical device such as a disk drive. This method throws IOException when an I/O error occurs.
void write(byte[] b)	Write b.length bytes from byte array b to this output stream. In general, write(b) behaves as if you specified write(b, 0, b.length). This method throws NullPointerException when b is null, and IOException when an I/O error occurs.

Method	Description
void write(byte[] b, int off, int len)	Write len bytes from byte array b starting at offset off to this output stream. This method throws NullPointerException when b is null; java.lang.IndexOutOfBoundsException when off is negative, len is negative, or off+len is greater than b.length; and IOException when an I/O error occurs.
void write(int b)	Write byte b to this output stream. Only the 8 low-order bits are written; the 24 high-order bits are ignored. This method throws IOException when an I/O error occurs.

The flush() method is useful in a long-running application where you need to save changes every so often; for example, the previously mentioned text-editor application that saves changes to a temporary file every few minutes.

> **NOTE:** The close() method automatically flushes the output stream. If an application ends before close() is called, the output stream is automatically closed and its data is flushed.

InputStream is the superclass of all input stream subclasses. Table 10–8 describes InputStream's methods.

Table 10–8. *InputStream Methods*

Method	Description
int available()	Return an estimate of the number of bytes that can be read from this input stream via the next read() method call (or skipped over via skip()) without blocking the calling thread. This method throws IOException when an I/O error occurs.
	It is never correct to use this method's return value to allocate a buffer for holding all of the stream's data because a subclass may not return the total size of the stream.
void close()	Close this input stream and release any system resources associated with the stream. This method throws IOException when an I/O error occurs.
void mark (int readlimit)	Mark the current position in this input stream. A subsequent call to reset() repositions this stream to the last marked position so that subsequent read operations reread the same bytes. The readlimit argument tells this input stream to allow that many bytes to be read before invalidating this mark (so that the stream cannot be reset to the marked position).
boolean markSupported()	Return true when this input stream supports mark() and reset(); otherwise, return false.

Method	Description
`int read()`	Read and return (as an `int` in the range 0 to 255) the next byte from this input stream, or return -1 when the end of the stream is reached. This method blocks until input is available, and throws `IOException` when an I/O error occurs.
`int read(byte[] b)`	Read some number of bytes from this input stream and store them in byte array b. Return the number of bytes actually read (which might be less than b's length but is never more than this length), or return -1 when the end of the stream is reached (no byte is available to read). This method blocks until input is available. It throws `NullPointerException` when b is `null`, and `IOException` when an I/O error occurs.
`int read(byte[] b, int off, int len)`	Read no more than `len` bytes from this input stream and store them in byte array b, starting at the offset specified by `off`. Return the number of bytes actually read (which might be less than `len` but is never more than `len`), or return -1 when the end of the stream is reached (no byte is available to read). This method blocks until input is available. It throws `NullPointerException` when b is `null`; `IndexOutOfBoundsException` when `off` is negative, `len` is negative, or `len` is greater than `b.length-off`; and `IOException` when an I/O error occurs.
`void reset()`	Reposition this input stream to the position at the time `mark()` was last called. This method throws `IOException` when this input stream has not been marked or the mark has been invalidated.
`long skip(long n)`	Skip over and discard n bytes of data from this input stream. This method may skip over some smaller number of bytes (possibly zero); for example, when the end of the file is reached before n bytes have been skipped. The actual number of bytes skipped is returned. If n is negative, no bytes are skipped. This method throws `IOException` when this input stream does not support skipping or when some other I/O error occurs.

`InputStream` subclasses such as `ByteArrayInputStream` support marking the current read position in the input stream via the `mark()` method, and later return to that position via the `reset()` method.

> **CAUTION:** Do not forget to call `markSupported()` to find out if the subclass supports `mark()` and `reset()`.

ByteArrayOutputStream and ByteArrayInputStream

Byte arrays are occasionally useful as stream destinations and sources. The concrete `ByteArrayOutputStream` class lets you write a stream of bytes to a byte array; the concrete `ByteArrayInputStream` class lets you read a stream of bytes from a byte array.

ByteArrayOutputStream declares a pair of constructors. Each constructor creates a byte array output stream with an internal byte array; a copy of this array can be returned by calling ByteArrayOutputStream's byte[] toByteArray() method:

- ByteArrayOutputStream() creates a byte array output stream with an internal byte array whose initial size is 32 bytes. This array grows as necessary.

- ByteArrayOutputStream(int size) creates a byte array output stream with an internal byte array whose initial size is specified by size, and which grows as necessary. This constructor throws IllegalArgumentException when size is less than zero.

The following example uses ByteArrayOutputStream() to create a byte array output stream with an internal byte array set to a default size:

ByteArrayOutputStream baos = new ByteArrayOutputStream();

ByteArrayInputStream also declares a pair of constructors. Each constructor creates a byte array input stream based on the specified byte array, and also keeps track of the next byte to read from the array and the number of bytes to read:

- ByteArrayInputStream(byte[] ba) creates a byte array input stream that uses ba as its byte array (ba is used directly; a copy is not created). The position is set to 0 and the number of bytes to read is set to ba.length.

- ByteArrayInputStream(byte[] ba, int offset, int count) creates a byte array input stream that uses ba as its byte array (no copy is made). The position is set to offset and the number of bytes to read is set to count.

The following example uses ByteArrayInputStream(byte[]) to create a byte array input stream whose source is a copy of the previous byte array output stream's byte array:

ByteArrayInputStream bais = new ByteArrayInputStream(baos.toByteArray());

ByteArrayOutputStream can be useful in a scenario where an image file is converted to an array of bytes, perhaps as a prelude to storing the image in a database. Listing 10–9's Android-specific example provides a demonstration.

Listing 10–9. *Decoding a file into an Android-specific* BitMap *instance, compressing this instance into a* ByteArrayOutputStream *instance, and obtaining a copy of the byte array output stream's array*

```
String pathname = ... ; // Assume a legitimate pathname to an image.
Bitmap bm = BitmapFactory.decodeFile(pathname);
ByteArrayOutputStream baos = new ByteArrayOutputStream();
If (bm.compress(Bitmap.CompressFormat.PNG, 100, baos))
{
   byte[] imageBytes = baos.toByteArray();
   // Do something with imageBytes.
}
```

Listing 10–9 obtains a pathname of an image file and then calls the concrete android.graphics.BitmapFactory class's static Bitmap decodeFile(String pathname) method. This method decodes the image file identified by `pathname` into a bitmap, and returns an `android.graphics.Bitmap` instance that represents this bitmap.

After creating a `ByteArrayOutputStream` object, Listing 10–9 uses the returned `Bitmap` instance to call `BitMap`'s `boolean compress(Bitmap.CompressFormat format, int quality, OutputStream stream)` method to write a compressed version of the bitmap to the byte array output stream:

- `format` identifies the format of the compressed image. I have chosen to use the popular Portable Network Graphics (PNG) format.

- `quality` hints to the compressor as to how much compression is required. This value ranges from 0 through 100, where 0 means maximum compression at the expense of quality and 100 means maximum quality at the expense of compression. Formats such as PNG ignore `quality` because they employ lossless compression.

- `stream` identifies the stream on which to write the compressed image data.

If `compress()` returns true, which means that it successfully compressed the image onto the byte array output stream in the PNG format, the `ByteArrayOutputStream` object's `toByteArray()` method is called to create and return a byte array with the image's bytes.

FileOutputStream and FileInputStream

Files are common stream destinations and sources. The concrete `FileOutputStream` class lets you write a stream of bytes to a file; the concrete `FileInputStream` class lets you read a stream of bytes from a file.

`FileOutputStream` subclasses `OutputStream` and declares five constructors for creating file output streams. For example, `FileOutputStream(String pathname)` creates a file output stream to the existing file identified by `pathname`. This constructor throws `FileNotFoundException` when the file does not exist and cannot be created, it is a directory rather than a normal file, or there is some other reason for why the file cannot be opened for output.

The following example uses `FileOutputStream(String pathname)` to create a file output stream with `employee.dat` as its destination:

```
FileOutputStream fos = new FileOutputStream("employee.dat");
```

> **TIP:** `FileOutputStream(String pathname)` overwrites an existing file. To append data instead of overwriting existing content, call a `FileOutputStream` constructor that includes a `boolean` append parameter and pass `true` to this parameter.

`FileInputStream` subclasses `InputStream` and declares three constructors for creating file input streams. For example, `FileInputStream(String pathname)` creates a file input stream from the existing file identified by `pathname`. This constructor throws

FileNotFoundException when the file does not exist, it is a directory rather than a normal file, or there is some other reason for why the file cannot be opened for input.

The following example uses FileInputStream(String pathname) to create a file input stream with employee.dat as its source:

```
FileInputStream fis - ncw FileInputStream("employee.dat");
```

> **CAUTION:** Be careful when specifying a pathname for these classes' constructors. You should strive to only specify pathnames that are valid for all platforms on which the application will run, unless you are creating your application to run on a single platform.

Listing 10–10 presents the source code to a DumpFileInHex application, which uses this FileInputStream constructor to create a file input stream from a *binary* (nontextual) file, reads this stream's bytes, and outputs them to standard output in hexadecimal format.

Listing 10–10. *Outputting a file input stream's bytes to standard output in hexadecimal format*

```java
import java.io.FileInputStream;
import java.io.IOException;

public class DumpFileInHex
{
    public static void main(String[] args) throws IOException
    {
        if (args.length != 1)
        {
            System.err.println("usage: java DumpFileInHex pathname");
            return;
        }
        FileInputStream fis = new FileInputStream(args[0]);
        StringBuffer sb = new StringBuffer();
        int offset = 0;
        int ch;
        while ((ch = fis.read()) != -1)
        {
            if ((offset % 16) == 0)
                System.out.printf("%08X ", offset);
            System.out.printf("%02X ", ch);
            if (ch < 32 || ch > 127)
                sb.append('.');
            else
                sb.append((char) ch);
            if ((++offset % 16) == 0)
            {
                System.out.println(sb.toString());
                sb.setLength(0);
            }
        }
        if (sb.length() != 0)
        {
            for (int i = 0; i < 16-sb.length(); i++)
                System.out.printf("   ");
            System.out.println(sb.toString());
```

```
        }
        fis.close();
    }
}
```

After establishing a file input stream and storing its reference in local variable fis, the main thread enters a loop that reads each byte from this stream and outputs the byte to standard output as part of a formatted hexadecimal listing.

The source code uses System.out.printf() method calls to output the eight-character hex equivalent of the offset argument and the two-character hex equivalent of the ch argument. (I will discuss printf() when I explore PrintStream later in the chapter.)

> **NOTE:** If the application throws IOException, fis.close(); is not executed. This is not a problem because the file input stream is automatically closed when the application exits.

Suppose you want to see a hexadecimal listing of DumpFileInHex.class. Execute java DumpFileInHex DumpFileInHex.class and this command line generates the following output, which I have abbreviated because the listing is extensive:

```
00000000 CA FE BA BE 00 00 00 32 00 53 0A 00 0C 00 24 09 .......2.S....$.
00000010 00 25 00 26 08 00 27 0A 00 28 00 29 07 00 2A 0A .%.&..'..(.)..*.
00000020 00 05 00 2B 07 00 2C 0A 00 07 00 24 0A 00 05 00 ...+..,....$....
00000030 2D 09 00 25 00 2E 08 00 2F 07 00 30 0A 00 31 00 -..%..../..0..1.
00000040 32 0A 00 28 00 33 08 00 34 0A 00 07 00 35 0A 00 2..(.3..4....5..
00000050 07 00 36 0A 00 07 00 37 0A 00 07 00 38 08 00 39 ..6....7....8..9
00000060 0A 00 05 00 3A 07 00 3B 01 00 06 3C 69 6E 69 74 ....:..;...<init
00000070 3E 01 00 03 28 29 56 01 00 04 43 6F 64 65 01 00 >...()V...Code..
00000080 0F 4C 69 6E 65 4E 75 6D 62 65 72 54 61 62 6C 65 .LineNumberTable
00000090 01 00 04 6D 61 69 6E 01 00 16 28 5B 4C 6A 61 76 ...main...([Ljav
000000A0 61 2F 6C 61 6E 67 2F 53 74 72 69 6E 67 3B 29 56 a/lang/String;)V
000000B0 01 00 0D 53 74 61 63 6B 4D 61 70 54 61 62 6C 65 ...StackMapTable
000000C0 07 00 2A 07 00 2C 01 00 0A 45 78 63 65 70 74 69 ..*..,...Excepti
000000D0 6F 6E 73 07 00 3C 01 00 0A 53 6F 75 72 63 65 46 ons..<...SourceF
000000E0 69 6C 65 01 00 12 44 75 6D 70 46 69 6C 65 49 6E ile...DumpFileIn
000000F0 48 65 78 2E 6A 61 76 61 0C 00 17 00 18 07 00 3D Hex.java.......=
```

> **NOTE:** Chapter 4 presents a pair of FileInputStream/FileOutputStream binary file-copying examples, which I located there to demonstrate the try statement's finally clause.

PipedOutputStream and PipedInputStream

Threads often need to communicate. One communication approach involves using shared variables. Another approach involves using piped streams courtesy of Java's PipedOutputStream and PipedInputStream classes.

The concrete PipedOutputStream class lets a sending thread write a stream of bytes to an instance of the concrete PipedInputStream class, which a receiving thread uses to subsequently read those bytes.

> **CAUTION:** Attempting to use a `PipedOutputStream` object and a `PipedInputStream` object from a single thread is not recommended because it may deadlock the thread.

`PipedOutputStream` declares a pair of constructors for creating piped output streams:

- `PipedOutputStream()` creates a piped output stream that is not yet connected to a piped input stream. It must be connected to a piped input stream, either by the receiver or the sender, before being used.

- `PipedOutputStream(PipedInputStream dest)` creates a piped output stream that is connected to piped input stream `dest`. Bytes written to the piped output stream can be read from `dest`. This constructor throws `IOException` when an I/O error occurs.

`PipedOutputStream` declares a **void connect(PipedInputStream dest)** method that connects this piped output stream to `dest`. This method throws `IOException` when this piped output stream is already connected to another piped input stream.

`PipedInputStream` declares four constructors for creating piped input streams:

- `PipedInputStream()` creates a piped input stream that is not yet connected to a piped output stream. It must be connected to a piped output stream before being used.

- `PipedInputStream(int pipeSize)` creates a piped input stream that is not yet connected to a piped output stream and uses `pipeSize` to size the piped input stream's buffer. It must be connected to a piped output stream before being used. This constructor throws `IllegalArgumentException` when `pipeSize` is less than or equal to 0.

- `PipedInputStream(PipedOutputStream src)` creates a piped input stream that is connected to piped output stream `src`. Bytes written to `src` can be read from this piped input stream. This constructor throws `IOException` when an I/O error occurs.

- `PipedInputStream(PipedOutputStream src, int pipeSize)` creates a piped input stream that is connected to piped output stream `src` and uses `pipeSize` to size the piped input stream's buffer. Bytes written to `src` can be read from this piped input stream. This constructor throws `IOException` when an I/O error occurs, and `IllegalArgumentException` when `pipeSize` is less than or equal to 0.

`PipedInputStream` declares a **void connect(PipedOutputStream src)** method that connects this piped input stream to `src`. This method throws `IOException` when this piped input stream is already connected to another piped output stream.

The easiest way to create a pair of piped streams is in the same thread, and in either order. For example, you can first create the piped output stream:

```
PipedOutputStream pos = new PipedOutputStream();
PipedInputStream pis = new PipedInputStream(pos);
```

Alternatively, you can first create the piped input stream:

```
PipedInputStream pis = new PipedInputStream();
PipedOutputStream pos = new PipedOutputStream(pis);
```

You can leave both streams unconnected and later connect them to each other using the appropriate piped stream's connect() method, as follows:

```
PipedOutputStream pos = new PipedOutputStream();
PipedInputStream pis = new PipedInputStream();
// ...
pos.connect(pis);
```

Listing 10–11 presents a PipedStreamsDemo application whose sender thread streams a sequence of randomly generated byte integers to a receiver thread, which outputs this sequence.

Listing 10–11. *Piping randomly generated bytes from a sender thread to a receiver thread*

```java
import java.io.IOException;
import java.io.PipedOutputStream;
import java.io.PipedInputStream;

public class PipedStreamsDemo
{
    public static void main(String[] args) throws IOException
    {
        final PipedOutputStream pos = new PipedOutputStream();
        final PipedInputStream pis = new PipedInputStream(pos);
        Runnable senderTask = new Runnable()
                            {
                                final static int LIMIT = 10;
                                public void run()
                                {
                                    try
                                    {
                                        for (int i = 0 ; i < LIMIT; i++)
                                            pos.write((byte)(Math.random()*256));
                                    }
                                    catch (IOException ioe)
                                    {
                                        ioe.printStackTrace();
                                    }
                                    finally
                                    {
                                        try
                                        {
                                            pos.close();
                                        }
                                        catch (IOException ioe)
                                        {
                                            ioe.printStackTrace();
                                        }
                                    }
                                }
                            };
```

```
                                        };
            Runnable receiverTask = new Runnable()
                                       {
                                          public void run()
                                          {
                                             try
                                             {
                                                int b;
                                                while ((b = pis.read()) != -1)
                                                   System.out.println(b);
                                             }
                                             catch (IOException ioe)
                                             {
                                                ioe.printStackTrace();
                                             }
                                             finally
                                             {
                                                try
                                                {
                                                   pis.close();
                                                }
                                                catch (IOException ioe)
                                                {
                                                   ioe.printStackTrace();
                                                }
                                             }
                                          }
                                       };
            Thread sender = new Thread(senderTask);
            Thread receiver = new Thread(receiverTask);
            sender.start();
            receiver.start();
      }
}
```

When you run this application, you will discover output similar to the following:

```
7
23
131
177
138
143
130
117
139
37
```

Perhaps you are wondering why I did not also declare pos and pis volatile? After all,
each variable is accessed by the main thread and its sender or receiver thread. I did not
declare these variables volatile for the following reasons:

- The compiler outputs a "modifier volatile not allowed here" error message whenever you attempt to declare a local variable volatile (only fields can be declared volatile).

- The compiler outputs an "illegal combination of modifiers: final and volatile" error message whenever you combine final with volatile in a field declaration (final fields are immutable; they are not volatile).

FilterOutputStream and FilterInputStream

Byte array, file, and piped streams pass bytes unchanged to their destinations. Java also supports *filter streams* that buffer, compress/uncompress, encrypt/decrypt, or otherwise manipulate an input stream's byte sequence before it reaches its destination.

A *filter output stream* takes the data passed to its write() methods (the input stream), filters it, and writes the filtered data to an underlying output stream, which might be another filter output stream or a destination output stream such as a file output stream.

Filter output streams are created from subclasses of the concrete FilterOutputStream class, an OutputStream subclass. FilterOutputStream declares a single FilterOutputStream(OutputStream out) constructor that creates a filter output stream built on top of out, the underlying output stream.

> **NOTE:** FilterOutputStream's constructor was originally declared protected because it does not appear to make sense to instantiate FilterOutputStream. However, this constructor's access was later changed to public for reasons unknown to me.

Listing 10–12 reveals that it is easy to subclass FilterOutputStream. At minimum, you declare a constructor that passes its OutputStream argument to FilterOutputStream's constructor and override FilterOutputStream's write(int) method.

Listing 10–12. *Scrambling a stream of bytes*

```
import java.io.FilterOutputStream;
import java.io.IOException;
import java.io.OutputStream;

public class ScrambledOutputStream extends FilterOutputStream
{
    private int[] map;
    public ScrambledOutputStream(OutputStream out, int[] map)
    {
        super(out);
        if (map == null)
            throw new NullPointerException("map is null");
        if (map.length != 256)
            throw new IllegalArgumentException("map.length != 256");
        this.map = map;
    }
    @Override
```

```
    public void write(int b) throws IOException
    {
        out.write(map[b]);
    }
}
```

Listing 10–12 presents a ScrambledOutputStream class that performs trivial encryption on its input stream by scrambling the input stream's bytes via a remapping operation. This constructor takes a pair of arguments:

-   out identifies the output stream on which to write the scrambled bytes.

-   map identifies an array of 256 byte integer values to which input stream bytes map.

The constructor first passes its out argument to the FilterOutputStream parent via a super(out); call. It then verifies its map argument's integrity (map must be nonnull and have a length of 256—a byte stream offers exactly 256 bytes to map) before saving map.

The write(int) method is trivial: it calls the underlying output stream's write(int) method with the byte to which argument b maps. FilterOutputStream declares out to be protected (for performance), which is why I can directly access this field.

> **NOTE:** It is only essential to override write(int) because FilterOutputStream's other two write() methods are implemented via this method.

Listing 10–13 presents the source code to a Scramble application, which lets us experiment with ScrambledOutputStream by scrambling a source file's bytes and writing these scrambled bytes to a destination file.

Listing 10–13. *Scrambling a file's bytes*

```java
import java.io.FileInputStream;
import java.io.FileOutputStream;
import java.io.IOException;

import java.util.Random;

public class Scramble
{
    public static void main(String[] args)
    {
        if (args.length != 2)
        {
            System.err.println("usage: java Scramble srcpath destpath");
            return;
        }
        FileInputStream fis = null;
        ScrambledOutputStream sos = null;
        try
        {
            fis = new FileInputStream(args[0]);
            FileOutputStream fos = new FileOutputStream(args[1]);
            sos = new ScrambledOutputStream(fos, makeMap());
```

```
            int b;
            while ((b = fis.read()) != -1)
                sos.write(b);
        }
        catch (IOException ioe)
        {
            ioe.printStackTrace();
        }
        finally
        {
            if (fis != null)
                try
                {
                    fis.close();
                }
                catch (IOException ioe)
                {
                    ioe.printStackTrace();
                }
            if (sos != null)
                try
                {
                    sos.close();
                }
                catch (IOException ioe)
                {
                    ioe.printStackTrace();
                }
        }
    }
    static int[] makeMap()
    {
        int[] map = new int[256];
        for (int i = 0; i < map.length; i++)
            map[i] = i;
        // Shuffle map.
        Random r = new Random(0);
        for (int i = 0; i < map.length; i++)
        {
            int n = r.nextInt(map.length);
            int temp = map[i];
            map[i] = map[n];
            map[n] = temp;
        }
        return map;
    }
}
```

Scramble's main() method first verifies the number of command-line arguments: the first argument identifies the source path of the file with unscrambled content; the second argument identifies the destination path of the file that stores scrambled content.

Assuming that two command-line arguments have been specified, main() instantiates FileInputStream, creating a file input stream that is connected to the file identified by args[0].

Continuing, `main()` instantiates `FileOutputStream`, creating a file output stream that is connected to the file identified by `args[1]`. It then instantiates `ScrambledOutputStream`, passing the `FileOutputStream` instance to `ScrambledOutputStream`'s constructor.

> **NOTE:** When a stream instance is passed to another stream class's constructor, we say that the two streams are *chained together*. For example, the scrambled output stream is chained to the file output stream.

`main()` now enters a loop, reading bytes from the file input stream and writing them to the scrambled output stream by calling `ScrambledOutputStream`'s `write(int)` method. This loop continues until `FileInputStream`'s `read()` method returns -1 (end of file).

The finally clause closes the file input stream and scrambled output stream by calling their `close()` methods. It does not call the file output stream's `close()` method because `FilterOutputStream` automatically calls the underlying output stream's `close()` method.

The `makeMap()` method is responsible for creating the map array that is passed to `ScrambledOutputStream`'s constructor. The idea is to populate the array with all 256 byte integer values, storing them in random order.

> **NOTE:** I pass 0 as the seed argument when creating the `Random` object in order to return a predictable sequence of random numbers. I need to use the same sequence of random numbers when creating the complementary map array in the `Unscramble` application, which I will present shortly. Unscrambling will not work without the same sequence.

Suppose you have a simple 15-byte file named `hello.txt` that contains "Hello, World!" (followed by a carriage return and a line feed). If you execute `java Scramble hello.txt hello.out` on an XP platform, you will observe Figure 10–3's scrambled output.

Figure 10–3. *Different fonts yield different-looking scrambled output.*

A *filter input stream* takes the data obtained from its underlying input stream, which might be another filter input stream or a source input stream such as a file input stream, filters it, and makes this data available via its `read()` methods (the output stream).

Filter input streams are created from subclasses of the concrete `FilterInputStream` class, an InputStream subclass. `FilterInputStream` declares a single `FilterInputStream(InputStream in)` constructor that creates a filter input stream built on top of in, the underlying input stream.

Listing 10–14 reveals that it is easy to subclass `FilterInputStream`. At minimum, declare a constructor that passes its `InputStream` argument to `FilterInputStream`'s constructor and override `FilterInputStream`'s `read()` and `read(byte[], int, int)` methods.

Listing 10–14. *Unscrambling a stream of bytes*

```java
import java.io.FilterInputStream;
import java.io.InputStream;
import java.io.IOException;

public class ScrambledInputStream extends FilterInputStream
{
    private int[] map;
    public ScrambledInputStream(InputStream in, int[] map)
    {
        super(in);
        if (map == null)
            throw new NullPointerException("map is null");
        if (map.length != 256)
            throw new IllegalArgumentException("map.length != 256");
        this.map = map;
    }
    @Override
    public int read() throws IOException
    {
        int value = in.read();
        return (value == -1) ? -1 : map[value];
    }
    @Override
    public int read(byte[] b, int off, int len) throws IOException
    {
        int nBytes = in.read(b, off, len);
        if (nBytes <= 0)
            return nBytes;
        for (int i = 0; i < nBytes; i++)
            b[off+i] = (byte) map[off+i];
        return nBytes;
    }
}
```

Listing 10–14 presents a `ScrambledInputStream` class that performs trivial decryption on its underlying input stream by unscrambling the underlying input stream's scrambled bytes via a remapping operation.

The `read()` method first reads the scrambled byte from its underlying input stream. If the returned value is -1 (end of file), this value is returned to its caller. Otherwise, the byte is mapped to its unscrambled value, which is returned.

The `read(byte[], int, int)` method is similar to `read()`, but stores bytes read from the underlying input stream in a byte array, taking an offset into this array and a length (number of bytes to read) into account.

Once again, -1 might be returned from the underlying `read()` method call. If so, this value must be returned. Otherwise, each byte in the array is mapped to its unscrambled value, and the number of bytes read is returned.

> **NOTE:** It is only essential to override read() and read(byte[], int, int) because FilterInputStream's read(byte[]) method is implemented via the latter method.

Listing 10–15 presents the source code to an Unscramble application, which lets us experiment with ScrambledInputStream by unscrambling a source file's bytes and writing these unscrambled bytes to a destination file.

Listing 10–15. *Unscrambling a file's bytes*

```java
import java.io.FileInputStream;
import java.io.FileOutputStream;
import java.io.IOException;

import java.util.Random;

public class Unscramble
{
   public static void main(String[] args)
   {
      if (args.length != 2)
      {
         System.err.println("usage: java Unscramble srcpath destpath");
         return;
      }
      ScrambledInputStream sis = null;
      FileOutputStream fos = null;
      try
      {
         FileInputStream fis = new FileInputStream(args[0]);
         sis = new ScrambledInputStream(fis, makeMap());
         fos = new FileOutputStream(args[1]);
         int b;
         while ((b = sis.read()) != -1)
            fos.write(b);
      }
      catch (IOException ioe)
      {
         ioe.printStackTrace();
      }
      finally
      {
         if (sis != null)
            try
            {
               sis.close();
            }
            catch (IOException ioe)
            {
               ioe.printStackTrace();
            }
         if (fos != null)
            try
            {
               fos.close();
```

```
            }
            catch (IOException ioe)
            {
                ioe.printStackTrace();
            }
        }
    }
    static int[] makeMap()
    {
        int[] map = new int[256];
        for (int i = 0; i < map.length; i++)
            map[i] = i;
        // Shuffle map.
        Random r = new Random(0);
        for (int i = 0; i < map.length; i++)
        {
            int n = r.nextInt(map.length);
            int temp = map[i];
            map[i] = map[n];
            map[n] = temp;
        }
        int[] temp = new int[256];
        for (int i = 0; i < temp.length; i++)
            temp[map[i]] = i;
        return temp;
    }
}
```

Unscramble's `main()` method first verifies the number of command-line arguments: the first argument identifies the source path of the file with scrambled content; the second argument identifies the destination path of the file that stores unscrambled content.

Assuming that two command-line arguments have been specified, `main()` instantiates `FileInputStream`, creating a file input stream that is connected to the file identified by `args[0]`.

Continuing, `main()` instantiates `ScrambledInputStream`, passing the `FileInputStream` instance to `ScrambledInputStream`'s constructor. It then instantiates `FileOutputStream`, creating a file output stream that is connected to the file identified by `args[1]`.

> **NOTE:** When a stream instance is passed to another stream class's constructor, we say that the two streams are *chained together*. For example, the scrambled input stream is chained to the file input stream.

`main()` now enters a loop, reading bytes from the scrambled input stream and writing them to the file output stream. This loop continues until `ScrambledInputStream`'s `read()` method returns -1 (end of file).

The finally clause closes the scrambled input stream and file output stream by calling their `close()` methods. It does not call the file input stream's `close()` method because `FilterOutputStream` automatically calls the underlying input stream's `close()` method.

The makeMap() method is responsible for creating the map array that is passed to ScrambledInputStream's constructor. The idea is to duplicate Listing 10–13's map array and then invert it so that unscrambling can be performed.

Continuing from the previous hello.txt/hello.out example, execute java Unscramble hello.out hello.bak and you will see the same unscrambled content in hello.bak that is present in hello.txt.

> **NOTE:** For an additional example of a filter output stream and its complementary filter input stream, check out the "Extending Java Streams to Support Bit Streams" article (http://www.drdobbs.com/184410423) on the Dr. Dobb's website. This article introduces BitStreamOutputStream and BitStreamInputStream classes that are useful for outputting and inputting bit streams. The article then demonstrates these classes in a Java implementation of the Lempel-Zif-Welch (LZW) data compression and decompression algorithm. (Click the *Next Page* >> link at the bottom of the article page to access the listings.)

BufferedOutputStream and BufferedInputStream

FileOutputStream and FileInputStream have a performance problem. Each file output stream write() method call and file input stream read() method call results in a call to one of the underlying platform's native methods, and these native calls slow down I/O.

> **NOTE:** A *native method* is an underlying platform API function that Java connects to an application via the *Java Native Interface (JNI)*. Java supplies reserved word native to identify a native method. For example, the RandomAccessFile class declares a private native void open(String name, int mode) method. When either of RandomAccessFile's constructors calls this method, Java asks the underlying platform (via the JNI) to open the specified file in the specified mode on Java's behalf.

The concrete BufferedOutputStream and BufferedInputStream filter stream classes improve performance by minimizing underlying output stream write() and underlying input stream read() method calls. Instead, calls to BufferedOutputStream write() and BufferedInputStream read() methods take Java buffers into account:

- When a write buffer is full, write() calls the underlying output stream write() method to empty the buffer. Subsequent calls to BufferedOutputStream write() methods store bytes in this buffer until it is once again full.

- When the read buffer is empty, read() calls the underlying input stream read() method to fill the buffer. Subsequent calls to BufferedInputStream read() methods return bytes from this buffer until it is once again empty.

BufferedOutputStream declares the following constructors:

- BufferedOutputStream(OutputStream out) creates a buffered output stream that streams its output to out. An internal buffer is created to store bytes written to out.

- BufferedOutputStream(OutputStream out, int size) creates a buffered output stream that streams its output to out. An internal buffer of length size is created to store bytes written to out.

Listing 10–16 chains a BufferedOutputStream instance to a FileOutputStream instance. Subsequent write() method calls on the BufferedOutputStream instance buffer bytes and occasionally result in internal write() method calls on the encapsulated FileOutputStream instance.

Listing 10–16. *Chaining a buffered output stream to a file output stream*

```
FileOutputStream fos = new FileOutputStream("employee.dat");
BufferedOutputStream bos = new BufferedOutputStream(fos); // Chain bos to fos.
bos.write(0); // Write to employee.dat through the buffer.
// Additional write() method calls.
bos.close(); // This method call internally calls fos's close() method.
```

BufferedInputStream declares the following constructors:

- BufferedInputStream(InputStream in) creates a buffered input stream that streams its input from in. An internal buffer is created to store bytes read from in.

- BufferedInputStream(InputStream in, int size) creates a buffered input stream that streams its input from in. An internal buffer of length size is created to store bytes read from in.

Listing 10–17 chains a BufferedInputStream instance to a FileInputStream instance. Subsequent read() method calls on the BufferedInputStream instance unbuffer bytes and occasionally result in internal read() method calls on the encapsulated FileInputStream instance.

Listing 10–17. *Chaining a buffered input stream to a file input stream*

```
FileInputStream fis = new FileInputStream("employee.dat");
BufferedInputStream bis = new BufferedInputStream(fis); // Chain bis to fis.
int ch = bis.read(); // Read employee.dat through the buffer.
// Additional read() method calls.
bis.close(); // This method call internally calls fis's close() method.
```

DataOutputStream and DataInputStream

FileOutputStream and FileInputStream are useful for writing and reading bytes and arrays of bytes. However, they provide no support for writing and reading primitive type values (such as integers) and strings.

For this reason, Java provides the concrete DataOutputStream and DataInputStream filter stream classes. Each class overcomes this limitation by providing methods to write or read primitive type values and strings in a platform-independent way:

- Integer values are written and read in *big-endian format* (the most significant byte comes first). Check out Wikipedia's "Endianness" entry (http://en.wikipedia.org/wiki/Endianness) to learn about the concept of *endianness*.

- Floating-point and double precision floating-point values are written and read according to the IEEE 754 standard, which specifies four bytes per floating-point value and eight bytes per double precision floating-point value.

- Strings are written and read according to a modified version of *UTF-8*, a variable-length encoding standard for efficiently storing two-byte Unicode characters. Check out Wikipedia's "UTF-8" entry (http://en.wikipedia.org/wiki/Utf-8) to learn more about UTF-8.

DataOutputStream declares a single DataOutputStream(OutputStream out) constructor. Because this class implements the DataOutput interface, DataOutputStream also provides access to the same-named write methods as provided by RandomAccessFile.

DataInputStream declares a single DataInputStream(InputStream in) constructor. Because this class implements the DataInput interface, DataInputStream also provides access to the same-named read methods as provided by RandomAccessFile.

Listing 10–18 presents the source code to a DataStreamsDemo application that uses a DataOutputStream instance to write multibyte values to a FileOutputStream instance, and uses DataInputStream to read multibyte values from a FileInputStream instance.

Listing 10–18. *Outputting and then inputting a stream of multibyte values*

```java
import java.io.DataInputStream;
import java.io.DataOutputStream;
import java.io.FileInputStream;
import java.io.FileOutputStream;
import java.io.IOException;

public class DataStreamsDemo
{
   final static String FILENAME = "values.dat";
   public static void main(String[] args)
   {
      DataOutputStream dos = null;
      DataInputStream dis = null;
      try
      {
         FileOutputStream fos = new FileOutputStream(FILENAME);
         dos = new DataOutputStream(fos);
         dos.writeInt(1995);
         dos.writeUTF("Saving this String in modified UTF-8 format!");
         dos.writeFloat(1.0F);
         dos.close(); // Close underlying file output stream.
```

```
          // The following null assignment prevents another close attempt on
          // dos (which is now closed) should IOException be thrown from
          // subsequent method calls.
          dos = null;
          FileInputStream fis = new FileInputStream(FILENAME);
          dis = new DataInputStream(fis);
          System.out.println(dis.readInt());
          System.out.println(dis.readUTF());
          System.out.println(dis.readFloat());
          dis.close(); // Close underlying file input stream.
       }
       catch (IOException ioe)
       {
          System.err.println(ioe.getMessage());
          try
          {
             if (dos != null)
                dos.close();
          }
          catch (IOException ioe2) // Cannot redeclare local variable ioe.
          {
             System.err.println(ioe2.getMessage());
          }
          try
          {
             if (dis != null)
                dis.close();
          }
          catch (IOException ioe2) // Cannot redeclare local variable ioe.
          {
             System.err.println(ioe2.getMessage());
          }
       }
    }
}
```

DataStreamsDemo creates a file named values.dat, calls DataOutputStream methods to write an integer, a string, and a floating-point value to this file, and calls DataInputStream methods to read back these values. Unsurprisingly, it generates the following output:

```
1995
Saving this String in modified UTF-8 format!
1.0
```

CAUTION: When reading a file of values written by a sequence of DataOutputStream method calls, make sure to use the same method-call sequence. Otherwise, you are bound to end up with erroneous data and, in the case of the readUTF() methods, thrown instances of the UTFDataFormatException class (a subclass of IOException).

Object Serialization and Deserialization

Although you can use the data stream classes to stream primitive type values and String objects, you cannot use these classes to stream non-String objects. Instead, you must use object serialization and deserialization to stream objects of arbitrary types.

Object serialization is a virtual machine mechanism for *serializing* object state into a stream of bytes. Its *deserialization* counterpart is a virtual machine mechanism for *deserializing* this state from a byte stream.

> **NOTE:** An object's state consists of instance fields that store primitive type values and/or references to other objects. When an object is serialized, the objects that are part of this state are also serialized (unless you prevent them from being serialized). Furthermore, the objects that are part of those objects' states are serialized (unless you prevent this), and so on.

Java supports three forms of serialization and deserialization: default serialization and deserialization, custom serialization and deserialization, and externalization.

Default Serialization and Deserialization

Default serialization and deserialization is the easiest form to use but offers little control over how objects are serialized and deserialized. Although Java handles most of the work on your behalf, there are a couple of tasks that you must perform.

Your first task is to have the class of the object that is to be serialized implement the Serializable interface (directly, or indirectly via the class's superclass). The rationale for implementing Serializable is to avoid unlimited serialization.

> **NOTE:** Serializable is an empty marker interface that a class implements to tell the virtual machine that it is okay to serialize the class's objects. When the serialization mechanism encounters an object whose class does not implement Serializable, it throws an instance of the NotSerializableException class (an indirect subclass of IOException).

Unlimited serialization is the process of serializing an entire *object graph* (all objects that are reachable from a starting object). Java does not support unlimited serialization for the following reasons:

- *Security*: If Java automatically serialized an object containing sensitive information (such as a password or a credit card number), it would be easy for a hacker to discover this information and wreak havoc. It is better to give the developer a choice to prevent this from happening.

- *Performance*: Serialization leverages the Reflection API, introduced in Chapter 7. In that chapter, you learned that reflection slows down application performance. Unlimited serialization could really hurt an application's performance.

- *Objects not amenable to serialization*: Some objects exist only in the context of a running application and it is meaningless to serialize them. For example, a file stream object that is deserialized no longer represents a connection to a file.

Listing 10–19 declares an Employee class that implements the Serializable interface to tell the virtual machine that it is okay to serialize Employee objects.

Listing 10–19. *Implementing* Serializable

```
public class Employee implements java.io.Serializable
{
   private String name;
   private int age;
   public Employee(String name, int age)
   {
      this.name = name;
      this.age = age;
   }
   public String getName() { return name; }
   public int getAge() { return age; }
}
```

Because Employee implements Serializable, the serialization mechanism will not throw a NotSerializableException instance when serializing an Employee object. Not only does Employee implement Serializable, the String class also implements this interface.

Your second task is to work with the ObjectOutputStream class and its writeObject() method to serialize an object, and the OutputInputStream class and its readObject() method to deserialize the object.

> **NOTE:** Although ObjectOutputStream extends OutputStream instead of FilterOutputStream, and although ObjectInputStream extends InputStream instead of FilterInputStream, these classes behave as filter streams.

Java provides the concrete ObjectOutputStream class to initiate the serialization of an object's state to an object output stream. This class declares an ObjectOutputStream(OutputStream out) constructor that chains the object output stream to the output stream specified by out.

When you pass an output stream reference to out, this constructor attempts to write a serialization header to that output stream. It throws NullPointerException when out is null, and IOException when an I/O error prevents it from writing this header.

ObjectOutputStream serializes an object via its void writeObject(Object obj) method. This method attempts to write information about obj's class followed by the values of obj's instance fields to the underlying output stream.

writeObject() does not serialize the contents of static fields. In contrast, it serializes the contents of all instance fields that are not explicitly prefixed with the transient reserved word. For example, consider the following field declaration.

```
public transient char[] password;
```

This declaration specifies transient to avoid serializing a password for some hacker to encounter. The virtual machine's serialization mechanism ignores any instance field that is marked transient.

writeObject() throws IOException or an instance of an IOException subclass when something goes wrong. For example, this method throws NotSerializableException when it encounters an object whose class does not implement Serializable.

> **NOTE:** Because ObjectOutputStream implements DataOutput, it also declares methods for writing primitive type values and strings to an object output stream.

Java provides the concrete ObjectInputStream class to initiate the deserialization of an object's state from an object input stream. This class declares an ObjectInputStream(InputStream in) constructor that chains the object input stream to the input stream specified by in.

When you pass an input stream reference to in, this constructor attempts to read a serialization header from that input stream. It throws NullPointerException when in is null, IOException when an I/O error prevents it from reading this header, and StreamCorruptedException (an indirect subclass of IOException) when the stream header is incorrect.

ObjectInputStream deserializes an object via its Object readObject() method. This method attempts to read information about obj's class followed by the values of obj's instance fields from the underlying input stream.

readObject() throws java.lang.ClassNotFoundException, IOException, or an instance of an IOException subclass when something goes wrong. For example, this method throws OptionalDataException when it encounters primitive values instead of objects.

> **NOTE:** Because ObjectInputStream implements DataInput, it also declares methods for reading primitive type values and strings from an object input stream.

Listing 10–20 presents an application that uses these classes to serialize and deserialize an instance of Listing 10–19's Employee class to and from an employee.dat file.

Listing 10–20. *Serializing and deserializing an* Employee *object*

```java
import java.io.FileInputStream;
import java.io.FileOutputStream;
import java.io.IOException;
import java.io.ObjectInputStream;
import java.io.ObjectOutputStream;

public class SerializationDemo
{
   final static String FILENAME = "employee.dat";
   public static void main(String[] args)
   {
      ObjectOutputStream oos = null;
      ObjectInputStream ois = null;
      try
      {
         FileOutputStream fos = new FileOutputStream(FILENAME);
         oos = new ObjectOutputStream(fos);
         Employee emp = new Employee("John Doe", 36);
         oos.writeObject(emp);
         oos.close();
         emp = null;
         FileInputStream fis = new FileInputStream(FILENAME);
         ois = new ObjectInputStream(fis);
         emp = (Employee) ois.readObject(); // (Employee) cast is necessary.
         ois.close();
         System.out.println(emp.getName());
         System.out.println(emp.getAge());
      }
      catch (ClassNotFoundException cnfe)
      {
         System.err.println(cnfe.getMessage());
         closeFiles(oos, ois);
      }
      catch (IOException ioe)
      {
         System.err.println(ioe.getMessage());
         closeFiles(oos, ois);
      }
   }
   static void closeFiles(ObjectOutputStream oos, ObjectInputStream ois)
   {
      try
      {
         if (oos != null)
            oos.close();
      }
      catch (IOException ioe)
      {
         System.err.println(ioe.getMessage());
      }
      try
      {
         if (ois != null)
            ois.close();
      }
```

```
      catch (IOException ioe)
      {
         System.err.println(ioe.getMessage());
      }
   }
}
```

Most of the source code is taken up with exception handling and closing the underlying file streams. The crucial code (shown in bold) is much briefer and demonstrates the tasks of default serialization and deserialization.

When you run this application, you will discover a file named `employee.dat` and observe the following output:

```
John Doe
36
```

There is no guarantee that the same class will exist when a serialized object is deserialized (perhaps an instance field has been deleted). During deserialization, this mechanism causes `readObject()` to throw an instance of `InvalidClassException` (an indirect subclass of `IOException`) when it detects a difference between the deserialized object and its class.

Every serialized object has an identifier. The deserialization mechanism compares the identifier of the object being deserialized with the serialized identifier of its class (all serializable classes are automatically given unique identifiers unless they explicitly specify their own identifiers) and causes `InvalidClassException` to be thrown when it detects a mismatch.

Perhaps you have added an instance field to a class, and you want the deserialization mechanism to set the instance field to a default value rather than have `readObject()` throw an `InvalidClassException` instance. (The next time you serialize the object, the new field's value will be written out.)

You can avoid the thrown `InvalidClassException` instance by adding a `static final long serialVersionUID = long integer value;` declaration to the class. The *long integer value* must be unique and is known as a *stream unique identifier (SUID)*.

During deserialization, the virtual machine will compare the deserialized object's SUID to its class's SUID. If they match, `readObject()` will not throw `InvalidClassException` when it encounters a *compatible class change* (such as adding an instance field). However, it will still throw this exception when it encounters an *incompatible class change* (such as changing an instance field's name or type).

NOTE: Whenever you change a class in some fashion, you must calculate a new SUID and assign it to `serialVersionUID`.

The JDK provides a `serialver` tool for calculating the SUID. For example, to generate an SUID for Listing 10–19's `Employee` class, change to the directory containing `Employee.class` and execute `serialver Employee`. In response, `serialver` generates the following output, which you paste (except for `Employee:`) into `Employee.java`:

Employee: static final long serialVersionUID = 1517331364702470316L;

The Windows version of serialver also provides a graphical user interface that you might find more convenient to use. To access this interface, specify the -show command-line option. For example, Figure 10–4 reveals this user interface in the context of the Employee class.

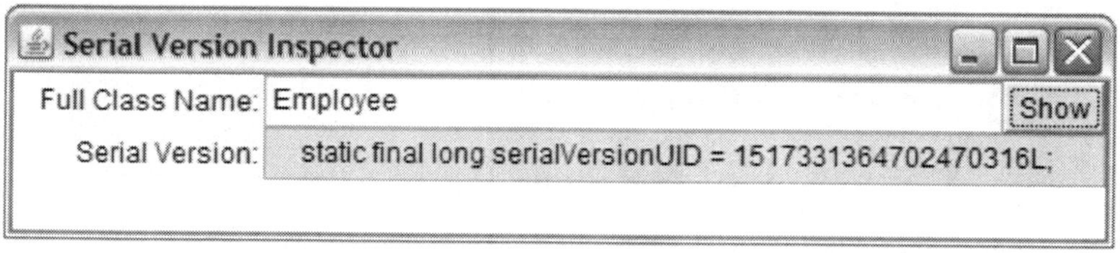

Figure 10–4. *The* serialver *graphical user interface*

Custom Serialization and Deserialization

My previous discussion focused on default serialization and deserialization (with the exception of marking an instance field transient to prevent it from being included during serialization). However, situations arise where you need to customize these tasks.

For example, suppose you want to serialize instances of a class that does not implement Serializable. As a workaround, you subclass this other class, have the subclass implement Serializable, and forward subclass constructor calls to the superclass.

Although this workaround lets you serialize subclass objects, you cannot deserialize these serialized objects when the superclass does not declare a noargument constructor, which is required by the deserialization mechanism.

Consider java.util.StringTokenizer. This concrete class does not implement Serializable and does not declare a noargument constructor. Listing 10–21 subclasses StringTokenizer and proves that serialized subclass instances cannot be deserialized.

Listing 10–21. *Problematic deserialization*

```
import java.io.ByteArrayInputStream;
import java.io.ByteArrayOutputStream;
import java.io.ObjectInputStream;
import java.io.ObjectOutputStream;
import java.io.Serializable;

import java.util.StringTokenizer;

class SerializableStringTokenizer extends StringTokenizer
   implements Serializable
{
   SerializableStringTokenizer(String str)
   {
      super(str);
   }
   SerializableStringTokenizer(String str, String delim)
   {
```

```
            super(str, delim);
        }
        SerializableStringTokenizer(String str, String delim,
                                             boolean returnDelims)
        {
            super(str, delim, returnDelims);
        }
    }
public class SerializationDemo
{
    public static void main(String[] args)
    {
        try
        {
            SerializableStringTokenizer sst;
            sst = new SerializableStringTokenizer("The quick brown fox");
            System.out.println("Number of tokens = " + sst.countTokens());
            System.out.println("First token = " + sst.nextToken());
            ByteArrayOutputStream baos = new ByteArrayOutputStream();
            ObjectOutputStream oos = new ObjectOutputStream(baos);
            oos.writeObject(sst); // Line 40
            oos.close();
            System.out.println("sst object written to byte array");
            ByteArrayInputStream bais;
            bais = new ByteArrayInputStream(baos.toByteArray());
            ObjectInputStream ois = new ObjectInputStream(bais);
            Object o = ois.readObject(); // Line 46
            System.out.println("sst object read from byte array");
        }
        catch (Exception e)
        {
            e.printStackTrace();
        }
    }
}
```

Listing 10–21's main() method instantiates SerializableStringTokenizer with a sample string argument. SerializableStringTokenizer(String) passes this argument to its StringTokenizer counterpart, which assumes that tokens are delimited with spaces.

main() next calls StringTokenizer's countTokens() method to return the number of tokens in the string, and its nextToken() method to return the first token. Both values are output to the standard output device.

Continuing, main() works with the ByteArrayOutputStream and ByteArrayInputStream classes to provide a byte array as a stream destination and source. An instance of the SerializableStringTokenizer class is serialized to and deserialized from this array.

When you run this application, it generates the following output:

```
Number of tokens = 4
First token = the
sst object written to byte array
java.io.InvalidClassException: SerializableStringTokenizer; 
 SerializableStringTokenizer; no valid constructor
        at java.io.ObjectStreamClass.checkDeserialize(Unknown Source)
        at java.io.ObjectInputStream.readOrdinaryObject(Unknown Source)
```

```
        at java.io.ObjectInputStream.readObject0(Unknown Source)
        at java.io.ObjectInputStream.readObject(Unknown Source)
        at SerializationDemo.main(SerializationDemo.java:46)
Caused by: java.io.InvalidClassException: SerializableStringTokenizer; no valid↵
   constructor
        at java.io.ObjectStreamClass.<init>(Unknown Source)
        at java.io.ObjectStreamClass.lookup(Unknown Source)
        at java.io.ObjectOutputStream.writeObject0(Unknown Source)
        at java.io.ObjectOutputStream.writeObject(Unknown Source)
        at SerializationDemo.main(SerializationDemo.java:40)
```

This output reveals a thrown instance of the InvalidClassException class. This exception object was thrown during deserialization because StringTokenizer does not possess a noargument constructor.

We can overcome this problem by taking advantage of the wrapper class pattern that I presented in Chapter 3. Furthermore, we declare a pair of private methods in the subclass that the serialization and deserialization mechanisms look for and call.

Normally, the serialization mechanism writes out a class's instance fields to the underlying output stream. However, you can prevent this from happening by declaring a private void writeObject(ObjectOutputStream oos) method in that class.

When the serialization mechanism discovers this method, it calls the method instead of automatically outputting instance field values. The only values that are output are those explicitly output via the method.

Conversely, the deserialization mechanism assigns values to a class's instance fields that it reads from the underlying input stream. However, you can prevent this from happening by declaring a private void readObject(ObjectInputStream ois) method.

When the deserialization mechanism discovers this method, it calls the method instead of automatically assigning values to instance fields. The only values that are assigned to instance fields are those explicitly assigned via the method.

Because SerializableStringTokenizer does not introduce any fields, and because StringTokenizer does not offer access to its internal fields, what would a serialized SerializableStringTokenizer object include?

Although we cannot serialize StringTokenizer's internal state, we can serialize the argument(s) passed to its constructors, such as the string being tokenized. The deserialized StringTokenizer object is then primed to being tokenizing.

Listing 10–22 reveals the refactored SerializableStringTokenizer and SerializationDemo classes.

Listing 10–22. *Solving problematic deserialization*

```
import java.io.ByteArrayInputStream;
import java.io.ByteArrayOutputStream;
import java.io.IOException;
import java.io.ObjectInputStream;
import java.io.ObjectOutputStream;
import java.io.Serializable;
```

```java
import java.util.StringTokenizer;

class SerializableStringTokenizer implements Serializable
{
   private StringTokenizer st;
   private String str, delim;
   private boolean returnDelims;
   SerializableStringTokenizer(String str)
   {
      this(str, null, false);
   }
   SerializableStringTokenizer(String str, String delim)
   {
      this(str, delim, false);
   }
   SerializableStringTokenizer(String str, String delim,
                                          boolean returnDelims)
   {
      this.str = str;
      this.delim = delim;
      this.returnDelims = returnDelims;
      st = new StringTokenizer(str, delim, returnDelims);
   }
   private void writeObject(ObjectOutputStream oos) throws IOException
   {
      oos.writeUTF(str);
      oos.writeUTF(delim);
      oos.writeBoolean(returnDelims);
   }
   private void readObject(ObjectInputStream ois)
      throws ClassNotFoundException, IOException
   {
      str = ois.readUTF();
      delim = ois.readUTF();
      returnDelims = ois.readBoolean();
      st = new StringTokenizer(str, delim, returnDelims);
   }
   public int countTokens()
   {
      return st.countTokens();
   }
   public String nextToken()
   {
      return st.nextToken();
   }
}
public class SerializationDemo
{
   public static void main(String[] args)
   {
      try
      {
         SerializableStringTokenizer sst;
         sst = new SerializableStringTokenizer("A,B,C,D", ",", true);
         System.out.println("Number of tokens = " + sst.countTokens());
         System.out.println("First token = " + sst.nextToken());
         System.out.println("Second token = " + sst.nextToken());
```

```
            ByteArrayOutputStream baos = new ByteArrayOutputStream();
            ObjectOutputStream oos = new ObjectOutputStream(baos);
            oos.writeObject(sst);
            oos.close();
            System.out.println("sst object written to byte array");
            ByteArrayInputStream bais;
            bais = new ByteArrayInputStream(baos.toByteArray());
            ObjectInputStream ois = new ObjectInputStream(bais);
            sst = (SerializableStringTokenizer) ois.readObject();
            System.out.println("sst object read from byte array");
            System.out.println("Number of tokens = " + sst.countTokens());
            System.out.println("First token = " + sst.nextToken());
            System.out.println("Second token = " + sst.nextToken());
        }
        catch (Exception e)
        {
            e.printStackTrace();
        }
    }
}
```

SerializableStringTokenizer's writeObject(ObjectOutputStream) and
readObject(ObjectInputStream) methods rely on DataOutput and DataInput methods:
they do not need to call writeObject() and readObject() to perform their tasks.

When you run this application, it generates the following output, which reveals that the
deserialized SerializableStringTokenizer object is ready to extract tokens:

```
Number of tokens = 7
First token = A
Second token = ,
sst object written to byte array
sst object read from byte array
Number of tokens = 7
First token = A
Second token = ,
```

The writeObject(ObjectOutputStream) and readObject(ObjectInputStream) methods
can be used to serialize/deserialize data items beyond the normal state (non-transient
instance fields); for example, serializing/deserializing the contents of a static field.

However, before serializing or deserializing the additional data items, you must tell the
serialization and deserialization mechanisms to serialize or deserialize the object's
normal state. The following methods help you accomplish this task:

- ObjectOutputStream's defaultWriteObject() method outputs the
  object's normal state. Your writeObject(ObjectOutputStream) method
  first calls this method to output that state, and then outputs additional
  data items via ObjectOutputStream methods such as writeUTF().

- ObjectInputStream's defaultReadObject() method inputs the object's
  normal state. Your readObject(ObjectInputStream) method first calls
  this method to input that state, and then inputs additional data items
  via ObjectInputStream methods such as readUTF().

Externalization

In addition to default serialization/deserialization and custom serialization/deserialization, Java supports externalization. Unlike default/custom serialization/deserialization, *externalization* offers complete control over the serialization and deserialization tasks.

> **NOTE:** Externalization helps you improve the performance of the reflection-based serialization and deserialization mechanisms by giving you complete control over what fields are serialized and deserialized.

Java supports externalization via its `Externalizable` interface. This interface declares the following pair of `public` methods:

- `void writeExternal(ObjectOutput out)` saves the calling object's contents by calling various methods on the out object. This method throws IOException when an I/O error occurs. (`ObjectOutput` is a subinterface of `DataOutput` and is implemented by `ObjectOutputStream`.)

- `void readExternal(ObjectInput in)` restores the calling object's contents by calling various methods on the in object. This method throws IOException when an I/O error occurs, and `ClassNotFoundException` when the class of the object being restored cannot be found. (`ObjectInput` is a subinterface of `DataInput` and is implemented by `ObjectInputStream`.)

If a class implements `Externalizable`, its `writeExternal()` method is responsible for saving all field values that are to be saved. Also, its `readExternal()` method is responsible for restoring all saved field values and in the order they were saved.

Listing 10–23 presents a refactored version of Listing 10–19's `Employee` class to show you how to take advantage of externalization.

Listing 10–23. *Refactoring Listing 10–19's* Employee *class to support externalization*

```java
import java.io.Externalizable;
import java.io.IOException;
import java.io.ObjectInput;
import java.io.ObjectOutput;

public class Employee implements Externalizable
{
   private String name;
   private int age;
   public Employee()
   {
      System.out.println("Employee() called");
   }
   public Employee(String name, int age)
   {
      this.name = name;
      this.age = age;
```

```
    }
    public String getName() { return name; }
    public int getAge() { return age; }
    @Override
    public void readExternal(ObjectInput in) throws
      IOException, ClassNotFoundException
    {
      System.out.println("readExternal() called");
      name = in.readUTF();
      age = in.readInt();
    }
    @Override
    public void writeExternal(ObjectOutput out) throws IOException
    {
      System.out.println("writeExternal() called");
      out.writeUTF(name);
      out.writeInt(age);
    }
}
```

Employee declares a public Employee() constructor because each class that participates in externalization must declare a public noargument constructor. This constructor is called during deserialization to instantiate the object.

> **CAUTION:** The deserialization mechanism throws InvalidClassException with a "no valid constructor" message when it does not detect a public noargument constructor.

You initiate externalization by instantiating ObjectOutputStream and calling its writeObject(Object) method, or by instantiating ObjectInputStream and calling its readObject() method.

> **NOTE:** When passing an object whose class (directly/indirectly) implements Externalizable to writeObject(), the writeObject()-initiated serialization mechanism writes only the identity of the object's class to the object output stream.

Suppose you compiled Listing 10–20's SerializationDemo.java source code and Listing 10–23's Employee.java source code in the same directory. Now suppose you executed java SerializationDemo. In response, you would observe the following output:

```
writeExternal() called
Employee() called
readExternal() called
John Doe
36
```

Before serializing an object, the serialization mechanism checks the object's class to see if it implements Externalizable. If so, the mechanism calls writeExternal(). Otherwise, it looks for a private writeObject(ObjectOutputStream) method, and calls this method if present. If this method is not present, the mechanism performs default serialization, which includes only non-transient instance fields.

Before deserializing an object, the deserialization mechanism checks the object's class to see if it implements `Externalizable`. If so, the mechanism attempts to instantiate the class via the public noargument constructor. Assuming success, it calls `readExternal()`.

If the object's class does not implement `Externalizable`, the deserialization mechanism looks for a private `readObject(ObjectInputStream)` method. If this method is not present, the mechanism performs default deserialization, which includes only non-transient instance fields.

PrintStream

Of all the stream classes, `PrintStream` is an oddball: it should have been named `PrintOutputStream` for consistency with the naming convention. This filter output stream class writes string representations of input data items to the underlying output stream.

> **NOTE:** `PrintStream` uses the default character encoding to convert a string's characters to bytes. (I will discuss character encodings in the next section.) Because `PrintStream` does not support different character encodings, you should use the equivalent `PrintWriter` class instead of `PrintStream`. However, you need to know about `PrintStream` when working with `System.out` and `System.err` because these class fields are of type `PrintStream`.

`PrintStream` instances are print streams whose various `print()` and `println()` methods print string representations of integers, floating-point values, and other data items to the underlying output stream. Unlike the `print()` methods, `println()` methods append a line terminator to their output.

> **NOTE:** The line terminator (also known as line separator) is not necessarily the newline (also commonly referred to as line feed). Instead, to promote portability, the line separator is the sequence of characters defined by system property `line.separator`. On Windows platforms, `System.getProperty("line.separator")` returns the actual carriage return code (13), which is symbolically represented by `\r`, followed by the actual newline/line feed code (10), which is symbolically represented by `\n`. In contrast, `System.getProperty("line.separator")` returns only the actual newline/line feed code on Unix and Linux platforms.

The `println()` methods call their corresponding `print()` methods followed by the void `println()` method, which outputs `line.separator`'s value. For example, void `println(int x)` outputs x's string representation and calls `println()` to output the line separator.

CAUTION: Never hard-code the \n escape sequence in a literal string that you are going to output via a print() or println() method. Doing so is not portable. For example, when Java executes System.out.print("first line\n"); followed by System.out.println("second line");, you will see first line on one line followed by second line on a subsequent line when this output is viewed at the Windows command line. In contrast, you will see first linesecond line when this output is viewed in the Windows Notepad application (which requires a carriage return/line feed sequence to terminate lines). When you need to output a blank line, the easiest way to do this is to call System.out.println();, which is why you find this method call scattered throughout my book. I confess that I do not always follow my own advice, so you might find instances of \n in literal strings being passed to System.out.print() or System.out.println() elsewhere in this book.

The PrintStream class also declares a pair of printf() methods that let you achieve formatted output in a manner similar to that performed by the C language's printf() function:

- PrintStream printf(Locale l, String format, Object... args) creates a formatted string using format specifier string format and the args array according to the locale specified by l (null indicates the default locale), and writes the formatted string to the output stream.

- PrintStream printf(String format, Object... args) creates a formatted string using format specifier string format and the args array according to the default locale, and writes the formatted string to the output stream.

Each method throws NullPointerException when format is null, and IllegalArgumentException when format contains an illegal syntax, format contains a format specifier that is incompatible with the given arguments, there are insufficient arguments to match the format string, or some other illegal condition applies.

NOTE: The printf() methods are convenience methods for specifying out.format(l, format, args) and out.format(format, args), respectively. Behind the scenes, they call PrintStream's PrintStream format(Locale l, String format, Object... args) and PrintStream format(String format, Object... args) methods to write the formatted string to the output stream. Internally, these methods instantiate the java.util.Formatter class, which serves as an interpreter for printf()-style strings and performs the actual formatting.

The format string consists of literal text and *format specifiers*, %-prefixed character sequences that offer instructions on how to format an argument. For example, %x indicates that an integer argument is to be formatted as a hexadecimal string with lowercase letters (a–f), whereas %X indicates that uppercase letters (A–F) are to be used.

> **CAUTION:** You must specify one argument for each format specifier appearing in the format specifier string. Fail to do that and `printf()` throws `IllegalArgumentException`.

Each `printf()` method returns a reference to the print stream so that you can create a chain of `printf()` method calls. (This is an example of chained instance method calls, which I discussed in Chapter 2.) Listing 10–24 demonstrates chained `printf()` method calls along with various format specifier strings.

Listing 10–24. *Formatting and outputting formatted values via* `System.out.printf()`

```
import java.util.Calendar;
import java.util.Locale;

public class FormattingDemo
{
    public static void main(String[] args)
    {
        String name = "John Doe";
        int age = 36;
        System.out.printf("Name = %s, age = %d%n", name, age);
        System.out.printf(Locale.FRANCE, "e = %10.4f%n", Math.E);
        System.out.printf("e = %10.4f%n", Math.E);
        Calendar cal = Calendar.getInstance();
        System.out.printf("Current time = %tR, ", cal).printf("%tT%n", cal);
        System.out.printf("Current date = %tD%n", cal);
    }
}
```

The first `System.out.printf()` method call's format specifier string demonstrates the %s (string) and %d (decimal integer) format specifiers. It also demonstrates format specifier %n, which is equal to the value of the `line.separator` system property.

The second `System.out.printf()` method call's format specifier string demonstrates the %f (floating-point) format specifier. This format specifier is preceded by 10.4, where 10 specifies that at least ten characters must be written (the width), and 4 specifies that exactly four characters must be written after a decimal point (the precision).

The second `System.out.printf()` method call also demonstrates localizing the output according to a specific locale. In the example, `Locale.FRANCE` is passed, which indicates that numbers must be written out with commas instead of decimal points.

The third `System.out.printf()` method call is similar to the second call, except that it does not pass a locale. As a result, the default locale is used. On my platform, that locale is en_US, which results in decimal points being output.

The fourth and fifth `System.out.printf()` method calls are chained together. The fourth method call uses format specifier %tR to format a `Calendar` object's time as HH:MM, according to the 24-hour clock. In contrast, the fifth method call uses format specifier %tT to format a `Calendar` object's time as HH:MM:SS, according to the 24-hour clock.

The final `System.out.println()` method call's format specifier string demonstrates the `%tD` format specifier, which formats the date portion of a `Calendar` object's time value as mm/dd/yy.

When you run this application, it generates the following output:

```
Name = John Doe, age = 36
e =     2,7183
e =     2.7183
Current time = 19:52, 19:52:13
Current date = 08/11/10
```

NOTE: The `Formatter` class's Java documentation provides a detailed reference on all supported format specifiers.

`PrintStream` offers two other features that you will find useful:

- Unlike other output streams, a print stream never rethrows an `IOException` instance thrown from the underlying output stream. Instead, exceptional situations set an internal flag that can be tested by calling `PrintStream`'s `boolean checkError()` method, which returns true to indicate a problem.

- `PrintStream` objects can be created to automatically flush their output to the underlying output stream. In other words, the `flush()` method is automatically called after a byte array is written, one of the `println()` methods is called, or a newline is written. The `PrintStream` instances assigned to `System.out` and `System.err` automatically flush their output to the underlying output stream.

Writers and Readers

Java's stream classes are good for streaming sequences of bytes, but they are not good for streaming sequences of characters because bytes and characters are two different things: a byte represents an 8-bit data item and a character represents a 16-bit data item. Also, Java's char and String types naturally handle characters instead of bytes.

More importantly, byte streams have no knowledge of *character sets* (sets of mappings between integer values [known as *code points*] and symbols, such as Unicode) and their *character encodings* (mappings between the members of a character set and sequences of bytes that encode these characters for efficiency, such as UTF-8).

If you need to stream characters, you should take advantage of Java's writer and reader classes, which were designed to support character I/O (they work with char instead of byte). Furthermore, the writer and reader classes take character encodings into account.

A BRIEF HISTORY OF CHARACTER SETS AND CHARACTER ENCODINGS

Early computers and programming languages were created mainly by English-speaking programmers in countries where English was the native language. They developed a standard mapping between code points 0 through 127 and the 128 commonly used characters In the English language (such as A–Z). The resulting character set/encoding was named *American Standard Code for Information Interchange (ASCII)*.

The problem with ASCII is that it is inadequate for most non-English languages. For example, ASCII does not support diacritical marks such as the cedilla used in the French language. Because a byte can represent a maximum of 256 different characters, developers around the world started creating different character sets/encodings that encoded the 128 ASCII characters, but also encoded extra characters to meet the needs of languages such as French, Greek, or Russian. Over the years, many legacy (and still important) files have been created whose bytes represent characters defined by specific character sets/encodings.

The International Organization for Standardization (ISO) and the International Electrotechnical Commission (IEC) have worked to standardize these eight-bit character sets/encodings under a joint umbrella standard called ISO/IEC 8859. The result is a series of substandards named ISO/IEC 8859-1, ISO/IEC 8859-2, and so on. For example, ISO/IEC 8859-1 (also known as Latin-1) defines a character set/encoding that consists of ASCII plus the characters covering most Western European countries. Also, ISO/IEC 8859-2 (also known as Latin-2) defines a similar character set/encoding covering Central and Eastern European countries.

Despite ISO's/IEC's best efforts, a plethora of character sets/encodings is still inadequate. For example, most character sets/encodings only allow you to create documents in a combination of English and one other language (or a small number of other languages). You cannot, for example, use an ISO/IEC character set/encoding to create a document using a combination of English, French, Turkish, Russian, and Greek characters.

This and other problems are being addressed by an international effort that has created and is continuing to develop *Unicode*, a single universal character set. Because Unicode characters are twice as big as ISO/IEC characters, Unicode uses one of several variable-length encoding schemes known as *Unicode Transformation Format (UTF)* to encode Unicode characters for efficiency. For example, UTF-8 encodes every character in the Unicode character set in one to four bytes (and is backward compatible with ASCII).

The terms *character set* and *character encoding* are often used interchangeably. They mean the same thing in the context of ISO/IEC character sets, where a code point is the encoding. However, these terms are different in the context of Unicode, where Unicode is the character set and UTF-8 is one of several possible character encodings for Unicode characters.

Writer and Reader Classes Overview

The java.io package provides several writer and reader classes that are descendents of the abstract Writer and Reader classes. In the following list, writer classes are denoted by their Writer suffixes and reader classes are denoted by their Reader suffixes:

- BufferedWriter
- BufferedReader
- CharArrayWriter

- CharArrayReader
- FileWriter
- FileReader
- FilterWriter
- FilterReader
- InputStreamReader
- LineNumberReader
- OutputStreamWriter
- PipedWriter
- PipedReader
- PrintWriter
- PushbackReader
- StringWriter
- StringReader

Because many of these classes have equivalent stream classes (BufferedWriter is equivalent to BufferedOutputStream, for example), upcoming sections take you on a tour of only a few of these writer and reader classes, beginning with Writer and Reader.

Writer and Reader

Java provides the Writer and Reader classes for performing character I/O. Writer is the superclass of all writer subclasses. The following list identifies differences between Writer and OutputStream:

- Writer declares several append() methods for appending characters to this writer. These methods exist because Writer implements the java.lang.Appendable interface, which is used in partnership with the Formatter class to output strings that are created in a manner similar to using the C language's printf() function.

- Writer declares additional write() methods, including a convenient void write(String str) method for writing a String object's characters to this writer.

Reader is the superclass of all reader subclasses. The following list identifies differences between Reader and InputStream:

- Reader declares read(char[]) and read(char[], int, int) methods instead of read(byte[]) and read(byte[], int, int) methods.

- Reader does not declare an available() method.

- Reader declares a boolean ready() method that returns true when the next read() call is guaranteed not to block for input.

- Reader declares an int read(CharBuffer target) method for reading characters from a character buffer. (I discuss CharBuffer in Chapter 11—see "The Road Goes Ever On" at the end of this chapter for more information about Chapter 11 and the other chapters that I am posting on my website.)

OutputStreamWriter and InputStreamReader

The concrete OutputStreamWriter class (a Writer subclass) is a bridge between an incoming sequence of characters and an outgoing stream of bytes. Characters written to this writer are encoded into bytes according to the default or specified character encoding.

NOTE: The default character encoding is accessible via the file.encoding system property.

Each call to an OutputStreamWriter write() method causes an encoder to be called on the given character(s). The resulting bytes are accumulated in a buffer before being written to the underlying output stream. The characters passed to the write() methods are not buffered.

OutputStreamWriter declares four constructors, including the following:

- OutputStreamWriter(OutputStream out) creates a bridge between an incoming sequence of characters (passed to OutputStreamWriter via its append() and write() methods) and underlying output stream out. The default character encoding is used to encode characters into bytes.

- OutputStreamWriter(OutputStream out, String charsetName) creates a bridge between an incoming sequence of characters (passed to OutputStreamWriter via its append() and write() methods) and underlying output stream out. charsetName identifies the character encoding used to encode characters into bytes. This constructor throws UnsupportedEncodingException when the named character encoding is not supported.

NOTE: OutputStreamWriter depends on the abstract java.nio.charset.Charset and java.nio.charset.CharsetEncoder classes to perform character encoding.

Listing 10–25 uses the second constructor to create a bridge to an underlying file output stream so that Polish text can be written to an ISO/IEC 8859-2-encoded file.

Listing 10–25. *Outputting Polish text*

```
FileOutputStream fos = new FileOutputStream("polish.txt");
OutputStreamWriter osw = new OutputStreamWriter(fos, "8859_2");
char ch = '\u0323'; // Accented N.
osw.write(ch);
```

The concrete InputStreamReader class (a Reader subclass) is a bridge between an incoming stream of bytes and an outgoing sequence of characters. Characters read from this reader are decoded from bytes according to the default or specified character encoding.

Each call to an InputStreamReader read() method may cause one or more bytes to be read from the underlying input stream. To enable the efficient conversion of bytes to characters, more bytes may be read ahead from the underlying stream than are necessary to satisfy the current read operation.

InputStreamReader declares four constructors, including the following:

- InputStreamReader(InputStream in) creates a bridge between underlying input stream in and an outgoing sequence of characters (returned from InputStreamReader via its read() methods). The default character encoding is used to decode bytes into characters.

- InputStreamReader(InputStream in, String charsetName) creates a bridge between underlying input stream in and an outgoing sequence of characters (returned from InputStreamReader via its read() methods). charsetName identifies the character encoding used to decode bytes into characters. This constructor throws UnsupportedEncodingException when the named character encoding is not supported.

NOTE: InputStreamReader depends on the abstract Charset and java.nio.charset.CharsetDecoder classes to perform character decoding.

Listing 10–26 uses the second constructor to create a bridge to an underlying file input stream so that Polish text can be read from an ISO/IEC 8859-2-encoded file.

Listing 10–26. *Inputting Polish text*

```
FileInputStream fis = new FileInputStream("polish.txt");
InputStreamReader isr = new InputStreamReader(fis, "8859_2");
char ch = isr.read(ch);
```

NOTE: OutputStreamWriter and InputStreamReader declare a String getEncoding() method that returns the name of the character encoding in use. If the encoding has a historical name, that name is returned; otherwise, the encoding's canonical name is returned.

You may not be aware of all the character encodings supported by your Java virtual machine. However, you can use the Charset class to find out. Listing 10–27 presents a DumpEncodings application that shows you how to accomplish this task.

Listing 10–27. *Dumping the default and all supported character encodings to standard output*

```java
import java.nio.charset.Charset;

import java.util.Iterator;
import java.util.Set;
import java.util.SortedMap;

public class DumpEncodings
{
   public static void main(String[] args)
   {
      System.out.println("Default file encoding = " +
                          System.getProperty("file.encoding"));
      SortedMap<String, Charset> map = Charset.availableCharsets();
      Set<String> keys = map.keySet();
      System.out.println("=============================================" +
                         "=======");
      System.out.printf("%-20s %-20s %-5s%n", "Canonical name",
                        "Display name", "Encode?");
      System.out.println("=============================================" +
                         "=======");
      Iterator<String> iter = keys.iterator();
      while (iter.hasNext())
      {
         String canonicalName = iter.next();
         Charset charset = map.get(canonicalName);
         String displayName = charset.displayName();
         boolean canEncode = charset.canEncode();
         System.out.printf("%-20s %-20s %-5b%n", canonicalName,
                           displayName, canEncode);
         Set<String> aliases = charset.aliases();
         Iterator<String> iter2 = aliases.iterator();
         System.out.println("ALIASES");
         while (iter2.hasNext())
            System.out.println("- " + iter2.next());
         System.out.println("---------------------------------------------" +
                            "-------");
      }
   }
}
```

After outputting file.encoding's value, main() obtains a sorted map from *canonical* (standard) charset names to Charset objects by calling Charset's static SortedMap<String,Charset> availableCharsets() method.

> **NOTE:** An instance of a concrete `Charset` subclass is an implementation of a character encoding and is often referred to as a *charset.* In addition to providing methods that return useful information about the charset, the instance provides methods to obtain an encoder and a decoder associated with the charset.

`main()` next calls the sorted map's `keySet()` method to return a set of canonical charset name keys. After calling this set's `iterator()` method to return an `Iterator` instance for looping over the set of names, `main()` performs this iteration.

For each iteration, `main()` uses the returned canonical name to obtain its associated `Charset` object from the map. It then calls `Charset`'s `String displayName()` method on this object to return this charset's human-readable name for the default locale.

> **NOTE:** The intent of `displayName()` is to provide a localized version of the character encoding name for display to the user. The default (`Charset`) implementation of this method returns the nonlocalized canonical name, which is also returned from `Charset`'s `String name()` method.

After outputting the display name, `main()` calls `Charset`'s `boolean canEncode()` method to find out if this charset supports encoding. Most character sets can be encoded, and this method returns true. However, this method returns false for auto-detect charsets.

> **NOTE:** An *auto-detect charset* is a charset whose decoder can determine which of several possible encoding schemes is in use by examining the input byte sequence. Such a charset does not support encoding because there is no way to determine which encoding should be used on output.

After outputting `canEncode()`'s value, `main()` calls `Charset`'s `Set<String> aliases()` method to return a nonnull (but possibly empty) set of strings that serve as aliases for the canonical name. It then iterates over this set, outputting each alias.

When I run this application on my XP platform, it generates the following output (which I have abbreviated for brevity):

```
Default file encoding = Cp1252
=================================================
Canonical name      Display name        Encode?
=================================================
Big5                Big5                true
ALIASES
- csBig5
-------------------------------------------------
Big5-HKSCS          Big5-HKSCS          true
ALIASES
- big5-hkscs:unicode3.0
- Big5_HKSCS
- big5-hkscs
```

```
- big5hkscs
- big5hk
-------------------------------------------------------
EUC-JP                  EUC-JP                  true
ALIASES
- eucjis
- Extended_UNIX_Code_Packed_Format_for_Japanese
- x-eucjp
- eucjp
- csEUCPkdFmtjapanese
- euc_jp
- x-euc-jp
```

> **NOTE:** You can pass a charset's canonical name or alias to the aforementioned
> `OutputStreamWriter` or `InputStreamReader` constructors that present `charsetName`
> parameters.

FileWriter and FileReader

`FileWriter` is a convenience class for writing characters to files. It subclasses
`OutputStreamWriter`, and its constructors call `OutputStreamWriter(OutputStream)`. An
instance of this class is equivalent to the following code fragment:

```
FileOutputStream fos = new FileOutputStream(pathname);
OutputStreamWriter osw;
osw = new OutputStreamWriter(fos, System.getProperty("file.encoding"));
```

In Chapter 4, I presented a logging library with a `File` class (Listing 4-19) that did not
incorporate file-writing code. Listing 10–28 addresses this situation by presenting a
revised `File` class that uses `FileWriter` to log messages to a file.

Listing 10–28. *Logging messages to an actual file*

```java
package logging;

import java.io.FileWriter;
import java.io.IOException;

class File implements Logger
{
   private final static String LINE_SEPARATOR = System.getProperty("line.separator");
   private String dstName;
   private FileWriter fw;
   File(String dstName)
   {
      this.dstName = dstName;
   }
   public boolean connect()
   {
      if (dstName == null)
         return false;
      try
      {
```

```
         fw = new FileWriter(dstName);
      }
      catch (IOException ioe)
      {
         return false;
      }
      return true;
   }
   public boolean disconnect()
   {
      if (fw == null)
         return false;
      try
      {
         fw.close();
      }
      catch (IOException ioe)
      {
         return false;
      }
      return true;
   }
   public boolean log(String msg)
   {
      if (fw == null)
          return false;
      try
      {
         fw.write(msg + LINE_SEPARATOR);
      }
      catch (IOException ioe)
      {
         return false;
      }
      return true;
   }
}
```

Listing 10–28 refactors Listing 4-19 to support FileWriter by making changes to each
of the connect(), disconnect(), and log() methods:

- connect() attempts to instantiate FileWriter, whose instance is saved
  in fw upon success; otherwise, fw continues to store its default null
  reference.

- disconnect() attempts to close the file by calling FileWriter's close()
  method, but only when fw does not contain its default null reference.

- log() attempts to write its String argument to the file by calling
  FileWriter's void write(String str) method, but only when fw does
  not contain its default null reference.

connect()'s catch clause specifies IOException instead of FileNotFoundException
because FileWriter's constructors throw IOException when they cannot connect to
existing normal files; FileOutputStream's constructors throw FileNotFoundException.

log()'s write(String) method appends the line.separator value (which I assigned to a constant for convenience) to the string being output instead of appending \n, which would violate portability.

FileReader is a convenience class for reading characters from files. It subclasses InputStreamReader, and its constructors call InputStreamReader(InputStream). An instance of this class is equivalent to the following code fragment:

```
FileInputStream fis = new FileInputStream(pathname);
InputStreamReader isr;
isr = new InputStreamReader(fis, System.getProperty("file.encoding"));
```

Unix introduced a command-line utility called *grep* (global regular expression print) that searches files or standard input globally for those lines matching a given regex, and prints matching lines to the standard output device.

To demonstrate FileReader, Listing 10–29 presents a FindAll application as a vastly scaled down version of grep. FindAll is useful for identifying the paths and names of those files that contain content matching the specified regex, and that is it.

Listing 10–29. *Finding all files that contain content matching a regex*

```
import java.io.BufferedReader;
import java.io.File;
import java.io.FileReader;
import java.io.IOException;

import java.util.regex.Matcher;
import java.util.regex.Pattern;
import java.util.regex.PatternSyntaxException;

public class FindAll
{
   static Matcher m;
   public static void main(String[] args)
   {
      if (args.length == 0 || args.length > 2)
      {
         System.err.println("usage: java FindAll regex [pathname]");
         return;
      }
      try
      {
         Pattern p = Pattern.compile(args[0]);
         m = p.matcher("");
         String cwd = System.getProperty("user.dir");
         findAll(new File(args.length == 2 ? args[1] : cwd), p);
      }
      catch (PatternSyntaxException pse)
      {
         pse.printStackTrace();
      }
   }
   static void findAll(File file, Pattern p)
   {
      if (!file.isDirectory())
      {
```

```
         System.err.println(file + " is not a directory");
         return;
      }
      File[] files = file.listFiles();
      if (files == null)
      {
         System.err.println("unable to access " + file + "'s contents");
         return;
      }
      for (int i = 0; i < files.length; i++)
         if (files[i].isDirectory())
            findAll(files[i], p);
         else
         if (find(files[i].getPath(), p))
            System.out.println(files[i].getPath());
   }
   static boolean find(String pathname, Pattern p)
   {
      BufferedReader br = null;
      try
      {
         FileReader fr = new FileReader(pathname);
         br = new BufferedReader(fr);
         String line;
         while ((line = br.readLine()) != null)
         {
            m.reset(line);
            if (m.find())
               return true;
         }
      }
      catch (IOException ioe)
      {
         ioe.printStackTrace();
      }
      finally
      {
         if (br != null)
            try
            {
               br.close();
            }
            catch (IOException ioe)
            {
               ioe.printStackTrace();
            }
      }
      return false;
   }
}
```

After compiling the regex into a Pattern object, creating a Matcher object, and obtaining the current working directory (also known as the current user directory), main() calls the recursive findAll() method with the starting search path and Pattern object.

> **NOTE:** The Apache Commons IO library (http://commons.apache.org/io/) includes a
> FileUtils class (http://commons.apache.org/io/api-
> 1.4/org/apache/commons/io/FileUtils.html) that provides methods for recursively
> listing the contents of all subdirectories of a directory while applying a filter (and more).

findAll() verifies that its File argument is a directory and then calls listFiles() on
this object to obtain an array of File objects for all directory entries. For each File
object that is a directory, findAll() calls itself with the File and Pattern objects.
However, if the entry is a file, findAll() calls find() with the File object's pathname
string and Pattern object.

find() attempts to open the pathname for input via the FileReader(String pathname)
constructor. Assuming success, it chains a BufferedReader object to the file reader in
order to speed up file reading through fewer calls to the file reader's read() methods.

BufferedReader declares a handy String readLine() method for reading a line of text
(not including line-termination characters) into a String object. readLine() returns null
when the end of the input is reached; it throws IOException when an I/O error occurs.

When a line is read, the Matcher object's reset() method is called with the line's String
object as an argument. The matcher is reset so that the same Matcher object can be
reused (to avoid creating unnecessary Matcher objects).

Finally, Matcher's find() method is called to look for a match between the Pattern
object's compiled regex and the line. If a match is found, find() returns true and the
loop ends by returning true from find(); otherwise, the next line is read and searched.

Now that you know how FindAll works, you will probably want to try it out. The
following examples show you how I might use this application on my XP platform:

```
java FindAll Emboss \prj\dev
```

This example searches my \prj\dev directory on my default drive (C:) for all files that
contain the word Emboss (case is significant) and generates the following output:

```
\prj\dev\ebooks\javase\mj2dipq\c04\code\IP\Emboss.java
\prj\dev\ebooks\javase\mj2dipq\c04\code\IP\EmbossOp.java
\prj\dev\ebooks\javase\mj2dipq\c04\code\IP\IP.java
\prj\dev\ljfad\c10\1-4302-3156-1_Friesen_Ch10.doc
\prj\dev\ws\java\java.html
\prj\dev\wsold\java\java.html
```

If I now specify java FindAll emboss \prj\dev, I observe the following slightly different
output:

```
\prj\dev\ebooks\javase\mj2dipq\c04\code\IP\Emboss.java
\prj\dev\ebooks\javase\mj2dipq\c04\code\IP\EmbossOp.java
\prj\dev\ljfad\c10\1-4302-3156-1_Friesen_Ch10.doc
\prj\dev\ws\java\java.html
\prj\dev\wsold\java\java.html
```

At the end of Chapter 9, I presented a useful demonstration of RegExDemo for matching phone numbers with or without area codes. Suppose I have a file named withareacodes.txt that contains (800) 555-1212, and a file named withoutareacodes.txt that contains 555-1212 in my current directory. When I execute java FindAll "(\(\d{3}\))?\s*\d{3}-\d{4}", I observe the following output:

```
C:\prj\dev\ljfad\c10\code\FindAll\withareacodes.txt
C:\prj\dev\ljfad\c10\code\FindAll\withoutareacodes.txt
```

This output reveals that regex (\(\d{3}\))?\s*\d{3}-\d{4} matched (800) 555-1212 in withareacodes.txt and 555-1212 in withoutareacodes.txt. I can now identify all files in a starting directory/subdirectories containing phone numbers with/without area codes.

EXERCISES

The following exercises are designed to test your understanding of Java's classic I/O APIs:

1. What is the purpose of the File class?
2. What do instances of the File class contain?
3. What does File's listRoots() method accomplish?
4. What is a path and what is a pathname?
5. What is the difference between an absolute pathname and a relative pathname?
6. How do you obtain the current user (also known as working) directory?
7. What is a parent pathname?
8. File's constructors normalize their pathname arguments. What does *normalize* mean?
9. How do you obtain the default name-separator character?
10. What is a canonical pathname?
11. What is the difference between File's getParent() and getName() methods?
12. True or false: File's exists() method only determines whether or not a file exists.
13. What is a normal file?
14. What does File's lastModified() method return?
15. True or false: File's list() method returns an array of Strings where each entry is a filename rather than a complete path.
16. What is the difference between the FilenameFilter and FileFilter interfaces?
17. True or false: File's createNewFile() method does not check for file existence and create the file if it does not exist in a single operation that is atomic with respect to all other filesystem activities that might affect the file.
18. File's createTempFile(String, String) method creates a temporary file in the default temporary directory. How can you locate this directory?

19. Temporary files should be removed when no longer needed after an application exits (to avoid cluttering the filesystem). How do you ensure that a temporary file is removed when the virtual machine ends normally (it does not crash or the power is not lost)?

20. How would you accurately compare two File objects?

21. What is the purpose of the RandomAccessFile class?

22. What is the purpose of the "rwd" and "rws" mode arguments?

23. What is a file pointer?

24. True or false: When you call RandomAccessFile's seek(long) method to set the file pointer's value, and if this value is greater than the length of the file, the file's length changes.

25. What is a flat file database?

26. What is a stream?

27. What is the purpose of OutputStream's flush() method?

28. True or false: OutputStream's close() method automatically flushes the output stream.

29. What is the purpose of InputStream's mark(int) and reset() methods?

30. How would you access a copy of a ByteArrayOutputStream instance's internal byte array?

31. True or false: FileOutputStream and FileInputStream provide internal buffers to improve the performance of write and read operations.

32. Why would you use PipedOutputStream and PipedInputStream?

33. What is a filter stream?

34. What does it mean for two streams to be chained together?

35. How do you improve the performance of a file output stream or a file input stream?

36. How do DataOutputStream and DataInputStream support FileOutputStream and FileInputStream?

37. What is object serialization and deserialization?

38. What three forms of serialization and deserialization does Java support?

39. What is the purpose of the Serializable interface?

40. What does the serialization mechanism do when it encounters an object whose class does not implement Serializable?

41. Identify the three stated reasons for Java not supporting unlimited serialization.

42. How do you initiate serialization? How do you initiate deserialization?

43. True or false: Class fields are automatically serialized.

44. What is the purpose of the transient reserved word?

45. What does the deserialization mechanism do when it attempts to deserialize an object whose class has changed?

46. How does the deserialization mechanism detect that a serialized object's class has changed?

47. How can you add an instance field to a class and avoid trouble when deserializing an object that was serialized before the instance field was added? What JDK tool can you use to help with this task?

48. How do you customize the default serialization and deserialization mechanisms without using externalization?

49. How do you tell the serialization and deserialization mechanisms to serialize or deserialize the object's normal state before serializing or deserializing additional data items?

50. How does externalization differ from default and custom serialization and deserialization?

51. How does a class indicate that it wishes to support externalization?

52. True or false: During externalization, the deserialization mechanism throws `InvalidClassException` with a "no valid constructor" message when it docs not detect a `public` noargument constructor.

53. What is the difference between `PrintStream`'s `print()` and `println()` methods?

54. What does `PrintStream`'s noargument `void println()` method accomplish?

55. True or false: `PrintStream`'s `%tR` format specifier is used to format a `Calendar` object's time as HH:MM.

56. Why are Java's stream classes not good at streaming characters?

57. What does Java provide as the preferred alternative to stream classes when it comes to character I/O?

58. True or false: `Reader` declares an `available()` method.

59. What is the purpose of the `OutputStreamWriter` class? What is the purpose of the `InputStreamReader` class?

60. How do you identify the default character encoding?

61. What is the purpose of the `FileWriter` class? What is the purpose of the `FileReader` class?

62. Create a Java application named Touch for setting a file's or directory's timestamp to the current or specified time. This application has the following usage syntax: `java Touch [-d timestamp] pathname`. If you do not specify `[-d timestamp]`, *pathname*'s timestamp is set to the current time; otherwise, it is set to the specified *timestamp* value, which has the format *yyyy-MM-dd HH:mm:ss z* (2010-08-13 02:37:45 UTC and 2006-04-22 12:35:45 EST are examples). Hints: The Date class has a `getTime()` method whose return value can be passed to File's `setLastModified()` method. Also, you will find `Date date = new SimpleDateFormat("yyyy-MM-dd HH:mm:ss z").parse(args[1]);` and `System.err.println("invalid option: " + args[0]);` to be helpful.

NOTE: Wikipedia's "touch (Unix)" entry
(http://en.wikipedia.org/wiki/Touch_%28Unix%29) introduces you to a standard Unix program named touch. In addition to changing a file's access and modification timestamps, touch is used to create a new empty file.

63. Suppose you are creating a Media class whose static methods perform various media-oriented utility tasks; for example, a getID3Info() method returns an object containing information about an MP3 file (such as song title and artist). This information is typically stored in a 128-byte block at the end of the file according to a format known as ID3. The block begins with ASCII sequence TAG.

Listing 10–30 reveals the skeletal contents of the Media class and this method, and begins with a description of the ID3v1.1 format that getID3Info() targets (there are several versions of this format).

Listing 10–30. *The Media class and its getID3Info() method*

```
/*

In 1996, Eric Kemp devised ID3, a small file format for storing metadata in
MP3 files. This metadata consisted of song title, artist, album, year,
comments, and genre; and was organized into a 128-byte block stored at the
end of the file.

The following table describes the format of ID3 version 1 (ID3v1):

Offset (decimal) Field Name        Field Size (byte)
================ ==========        =================
0                Signature (TAG)   3
3                Song title        30
33               Artist            30
63               Album             30
93               Year              4
97               Comment           30
127              Genre             1

Each field except for Genre is a string of ASCII characters. Strings are
padded on the right with zeros or spaces. An uninitialized field is
equivalent to the empty string ("").

In 1997, Michael Mutschler made a small improvement to ID3. Because the
Comment field is too small to write anything of use, he trimmed this field by
two bytes and used those bytes to store the CD track number where the song is
located.

If a track number is stored, the second-last byte of the Comment field is set
to 0 and the subsequent byte stores the track number. The resulting format is
known as ID3v1.1.

Offset (decimal) Field Name        Field Size (byte)
================ ==========        =================
0                Signature (TAG)   3
3                Song title        30
33               Artist            30
```

```
63          Album        30
93          Year         4
97          Comment      29 (last byte must be a binary 0)
126         Track (0-255) 1
127         Genre (0-255) 1  (255 means no genre)
```

Unlike most of the fields, Track and Genre are single-byte integer fields.
The legal values that can appear in the Genre field and their descriptions
Are described in the following table:

```
 0 Blues          20 Alternative      40 AlternRock       60 Top 40
 1 Classic Rock   21 Ska              41 Bass             61 Christian Rap
 2 Country        22 Death Metal      42 Soul             62 Pop/Funk
 3 Dance          23 Pranks           43 Punk             63 Jungle
 4 Disco          24 Soundtrack       44 Space            64 Nat American
 5 Funk           25 Euro-Techno      45 Meditative       65 Cabaret
 6 Grunge         26 Ambient          46 Instrumental Pop 66 New Wave
 7 Hip-Hop        27 Trip-Hop         47 Instrumental Rock 67 Psychadelic
 8 Jazz           28 Vocal            48 Ethnic           68 Rave
 9 Metal          29 Jazz+Funk        49 Gothic           69 Showtunes
10 New Age        30 Fusion           50 Darkwave         70 Trailer
11 Oldies         31 Trance           51 Techno-Industrial 71 Lo-Fi
12 Other          32 Classical        52 Electronic       72 Tribal
13 Pop            33 Instrumental     53 Pop-Folk         73 Acid Punk
14 R&B            34 Acid             54 Eurodance        74 Acid Jazz
15 Rap            35 House            55 Dream            75 Polka
16 Reggae         36 Game             56 Southern Rock    76 Retro
17 Rock           37 Sound Clip       57 Comedy           77 Musical
18 Techno         38 Gospel           58 Cult             78 Rock & Roll
19 Industrial     39 Noise            59 Gangsta          79 Hard Rock
```

WinAmp expanded this table with the following Genre codes:

```
80 Folk            92 Progressive Rock 104 Chamber Music  116 Ballad
81 Folk-Rock       93 Psychedelic Rock 105 Sonata         117 Power Ballad
82 National-Folk   94 Symphonic Rock   106 Symphony       118 Rhythmic Soul
83 Swing           95 Slow Rock        107 Booty Brass    119 Freestyle
84 Fast Fusion     96 Big Band         108 Primus         120 Duet
85 Bebob           97 Chorus           109 Porn Groove    121 Punk Rock
86 Latin           98 Easy Listening   110 Satire         122 Drum Solo
87 Revival         99 Acoustic         111 Slow Jam       123 A cappella
88 Celtic          100 Humour          112 Club           124 Euro-House
89 Bluegrass       101 Speech          113 Tango          125 Dance Hall
90 Avantgarde      102 Chanson         114 Samba
91 Gothic Rock     103 Opera           115 Folklore
```

Although there are probably additional defined codes, treat any other value
stored in the Genre field as Unknown.

To learn more about ID3 and new versions, visit the official site at id3.org.

```
*/

import java.io.IOException;
import java.io.RandomAccessFile;

public class Media
```

```
{
   public static class ID3
   {
      private String songTitle, artist, album, year, comment, genre;
      private int track; // -1 if track not present
      public ID3(String songTitle, String artist, String album, String year,
                 String comment, int track, String genre)
      {
         this.songTitle = songTitle;
         this.artist = artist;
         this.album = album;
         this.year = year;
         this.comment = comment;
         this.track = track;
         this.genre = genre;
      }
      String getSongTitle() { return songTitle; }
      String getArtist() { return artist; }
      String getAlbum() { return album; }
      String getYear() { return year; }
      String getComment() { return comment; }
      int getTrack() { return track; }
      String getGenre() { return genre; }
   }
   public static ID3 getID3Info(String mp3path) throws IOException
   {
      return null;
   }
}
```

Your job is to fill in the getID3Info() method by using the RandomAccessFile
class to obtain the data from the 128-byte block, and then create and populate an ID3
object with this data. getID3Info() subsequently returns this object.

After completing getID3Info(), you will want to test this method. Listing 10–31
presents the source code to a TestMedia application that you can use for this
purpose.

Listing 10–31. *The* TestMedia *class*

```
import java.io.IOException;

public class TestMedia
{
   public static void main(String[] args)
   {
      if (args.length != 1)
      {
         System.err.println("usage: java TestMedia mp3path");
         return;
      }
      try
      {
         Media.ID3 id3Info = Media.getID3Info(args[0]);
         if (id3Info == null)
         {
            System.err.printf("%s not MP3 or has no ID3 block%n", args[0]);
            return;
```

```
      }
      System.out.println("Song title = " + id3Info.getSongTitle());
      System.out.println("Artist = " + id3Info.getArtist());
      System.out.println("Album = " + id3Info.getAlbum());
      System.out.println("Year = " + id3Info.getYear());
      System.out.println("Comment = " +id3Info.getComment());
      System.out.println("Track = " + id3Info.getTrack());
      System.out.println("Genre = " + id3Info.getGenre());
    }
    catch (IOException ioe)
    {
      ioe.printStackTrace();
    }
  }
}
```

Suppose you have ripped a track from a CD that contains Tom Jones' "She's a Lady" into a file called Lady.mp3. When you execute java TestMedia Lady.mp3, you should see output similar to the following:

```
Song title = She's A Lady
Artist = Tom Jones
Album = Billboard Top Soft Rock Hits -
Year = 1998
Comment =
Track = 2
Genre = Rock
```

64. Create a Java application named Split for splitting a large file into a number of smaller partx files (where x starts at 0 and increments; for example, part0, part1, part2, and so on). Each partx file (except possibly the last partx file, which holds the remaining bytes) will have the same size. This application has the following usage syntax: java Split *pathname*. Furthermore, your implementation must use the BufferedInputStream, BufferedOutputStream, File, FileInputStream, and FileOutputStream classes.

NOTE: I find Split helpful for storing huge files that do not fit onto a single CD/DVD across multiple CDs/DVDs, and also for emailing huge files to friends. To recombine the part files on a Windows platform, I use the copy command and its /B binary option. When recombining the part files, recombine them in order: part0, part1 ... part9, part10, and so on.

65. It is often convenient to read lines of text from standard input, and the InputStreamReader and BufferedReader classes make this task possible. Create a Java application named CircleInfo that, after obtaining a BufferedReader instance that is chained to standard input, presents a loop that prompts the user to enter a radius, parses the entered radius into a double value, and outputs a pair of messages that report the circle's circumference and area based on this radius.

Summary

Applications often input data for processing and output processing results. Data is input from a file or some other source, and is output to a file or some other destination. Java supports I/O via the classic I/O APIs located in the `java.io` package.

File I/O activities often interact with a filesystem. Java offers access to the underlying platform's available filesystem(s) via its concrete `File` class. `File` instances contain the pathnames of files and directories that may or may not exist in their filesystems.

Files can be opened for random access in which a mixture of write and read operations can occur until the file is closed. Java supports this random access by providing the concrete `RandomAccessFile` class.

Java uses streams to perform I/O operations. A stream is an ordered sequence of bytes of arbitrary length. Bytes flow over an output stream from an application to a destination, and flow over an input stream from a source to an application.

The `java.io` package provides several output stream and input stream classes that are descendents of the abstract `OutputStream` and `InputStream` classes. Examples of subclasses include `BufferedOutputStream` and `FileInputStream`.

Java's stream classes are good for streaming sequences of bytes, but are not good for streaming sequences of characters because bytes and characters are two different things, and because byte streams have no knowledge of character sets and encodings.

If you need to stream characters, you should take advantage of Java's writer and reader classes, which were designed to support character I/O (they work with `char` instead of `byte`). Furthermore, the writer and reader classes take character encodings into account.

The `java.io` package provides several writer and reader classes that are descendents of the abstract `Writer` and `Reader` classes. Examples of subclasses include `OutputStreamWriter`, `FileWriter`, `InputStreamReader`, `FileReader`, and `BufferedReader`.

The Road Goes Ever On

Although this book is finished from Apress's perspective, it is not finished from my perspective because the physical limitations of a paperback book prevented me from covering additional topics that are important to Android app developers; networking is one example.

Accordingly, I am writing six more chapters (with the same organization as this book's chapters, but not necessarily with the same style) that you will be able to freely download from my website (javajeff.mb.ca) as PDF files:

- Chapter 11: Performing I/O Redux
- Chapter 12: Parsing and Creating XML Documents
- Chapter 13: Accessing Networks
- Chapter 14: Accessing Databases

- Chapter 15: Working with Security

- Chapter 16: Odds and Ends

Chapter 11 focuses on New I/O in terms of buffers, channels, and selectors. Furthermore, it discusses additional New I/O APIs being introduced by Java version 7. The `Paths` and `Path` classes are examples.

Chapter 12 focuses on XML, beginning with an abbreviated introduction to this technology. It continues by exploring Java's support for parsing XML documents via its DOM, SAX, and StAX APIs, and for creating these documents via its DOM and StAX APIs.

Chapter 13 explores Java's support for networking in terms of various API classes that range from `URL` and `URLConnection`, to `Socket` and `ServerSocket`. I have planned exciting examples for this chapter, including one example that involves HTML 5.

Chapter 14 explores Java's support for database access in terms of JDBC, which is Java's API for accessing databases. However, before exploring JDBC, this chapter briefly introduces you to SQLite, which is the database supported by Android.

Chapter 15 discusses various aspects of security, ranging from security managers and access controllers, to HTTP authentication and XML digital signatures. This chapter will also introduce `jarsigner` and additional security-oriented JDK tools.

Chapter 16 wraps up my extended book by exploring Java version 7 language features not covered (such as closures) because they were not available at time of writing, native methods, additional APIs not covered (such as Logging), and other odds and ends.

These six chapters will not be available immediately but will slowly emerge over the next several months. I will also make available an appendix that contains solutions to each chapter's exercises, and a `code.zip` file that contains the additional source code.

Solutions to Exercises

Chapters 1 through 10 close with an "Exercises" section that tests your understanding of the chapter's material through various exercises. Solutions to these exercises are presented in this appendix.

Chapter 1: Getting Started with Java

1. *Java* is a language and a platform. The language is partly patterned after the C and C++ languages to shorten the learning curve for C/C++ developers. The platform consists of a virtual machine and associated execution environment.

2. A *virtual machine* is a software-based processor that presents its own instruction set.

3. The purpose of the Java compiler is to translate source code into instructions (and associated data) that are executed by the virtual machine.

4. The answer is true: a classfile's instructions are commonly referred to as bytecode.

5. When the virtual machine's interpreter learns that a sequence of bytecode instructions is being executed repeatedly, it informs the virtual machine's Just In Time (JIT) compiler to compile these instructions into native code.

6. The Java platform promotes portability by providing an abstraction over the underlying platform. As a result, the same bytecode runs unchanged on Windows-based, Linux-based, Mac OS X–based, and other platforms.

7. The Java platform promotes security by providing a secure environment in which code executes. It accomplishes this task in part by using a bytecode verifier to make sure that the classfile's bytecode is valid.

8. The answer is false: Java SE is the platform for developing applications and applets.

9. The JRE implements the Java SE platform and makes it possible to run Java programs.

10. The difference between the public and private JREs is that the public JRE exists apart from the JDK, whereas the private JRE is a component of the JDK that makes it possible to run Java programs independently of whether or not the public JRE is installed.

11. The JDK provides development tools (including a compiler) for developing Java programs. It also provides a private JRE for running these programs.

12. The JDK's javac tool is used to compile Java source code.

13. The JDK's java tool is used to run Java applications.

14. The purpose of the JDK's jar tool is to create new JAR files, update existing JAR files, and extract files from existing JAR files.

15. *Standard I/O* is a mechanism consisting of Standard Input, Standard Output, and Standard Error that makes it possible to read text from different sources (keyboard or file), write nonerror text to different destinations (screen or file), and write error text to different definitions (screen or file).

16. An IDE is a development framework consisting of a project manager for managing a project's files, a text editor for entering and editing source code, a debugger for locating bugs, and other features.

17. Two popular IDEs are NetBeans and Eclipse.

18. *Pseudocode* is a compact and informal high-level description of the problem domain.

19. You would use the jar tool along with its t (table of contents) and f (JAR file's name) options to list FourOfAKind.jar's table of contents; for example, jar tf FourOfAKind.jar.

20. Listing 1 presents the FourOfAKind application's refactored FourOfAKind class that was called for in Chapter 1.

Listing 1. *Letting the human player pick up the top card from the discard pile or the deck*

```
/**
 *  <code>FourOfAKind</code> implements a card game that is played between two
 *  players: one human player and the computer. You play this game with a
 *  standard 52-card deck and attempt to beat the computer by being the first
 *  player to put down four cards that have the same rank (four aces, for
 *  example), and win.
 *
 *  @author Jeff Friesen
 *  @version 1.0
 */
public class FourOfAKind
{
```

```java
/**
 *  Human player
 */
final static int HUMAN = 0;
/**
 *  Computer player
 */
final static int COMPUTER = 1;
/**
 *  Application entry point.
 *
 *  @param args array of command-line arguments passed to this method
 */
public static void main(String[] args)
{
   System.out.println("Welcome to Four of a Kind!");
   Deck deck = new Deck(); // Deck automatically shuffled
   DiscardPile discardPile = new DiscardPile();
   Card hCard;
   Card cCard;
   while (true)
   {
      hCard = deck.deal();
      cCard = deck.deal();
      if (hCard.rank() != cCard.rank())
         break;
      deck.putBack(hCard);
      deck.putBack(cCard);
      deck.shuffle(); // prevent pathological case where every successive
   }                  // pair of cards have the same rank
   int curPlayer = HUMAN;
   if (cCard.rank().ordinal() > hCard.rank().ordinal())
      curPlayer = COMPUTER;
   deck.putBack(hCard);
   hCard = null;
   deck.putBack(cCard);
   cCard = null;
   Card[] hCards = new Card[4];
   Card[] cCards = new Card[4];
   if (curPlayer == HUMAN)
      for (int i = 0; i < 4; i++)
      {
         cCards[i] = deck.deal();
         hCards[i] = deck.deal();
      }
   else
      for (int i = 0; i < 4; i++)
      {
         hCards[i] = deck.deal();
         cCards[i] = deck.deal();
      }
   while (true)
   {
      if (curPlayer == HUMAN)
      {
         showHeldCards(hCards);
         if (discardPile.topCard() != null)
```

```
                    {
                        System.out.println("Discard pile top card: " +
                                           discardPile.topCard());
                        System.out.println();
                    }
                    int choice = 0;
                    while (choice < 'A' || choice > 'D')
                    {
                        choice = prompt("Which card do you want to throw away (A, B, " +
                                        "C, D)? ");
                        switch (choice)
                        {
                            case 'a': choice = 'A'; break;
                            case 'b': choice = 'B'; break;
                            case 'c': choice = 'C'; break;
                            case 'd': choice = 'D';
                        }
                    }
                    Card card = null;
                    if (discardPile.topCard() != null)
                    {
                        int dest = 0;
                        while (dest != 'D' && dest != 'P')
                        {
                            dest = prompt("Pick up top card from deck or discard pile " +
                                          "(D, P)? ");
                            switch (dest)
                            {
                                case 'd': dest = 'D';
                                case 'p': dest = 'P';
                            }
                        }
                        card = (dest == 'D') ? deck.deal() : discardPile.getTopCard();
                    }
                    else
                        card = deck.deal();
                    discardPile.setTopCard(hCards[choice-'A']);
                    hCards[choice-'A'] = card;
                    card = null;
                    if (isFourOfAKind(hCards))
                    {
                        System.out.println();
                        System.out.println("Human wins!");
                        System.out.println();
                        putDown("Human's cards:", hCards);
                        System.out.println();
                        putDown("Computer's cards:", cCards);
                        return; // Exit application by returning from main()
                    }
                    curPlayer = COMPUTER;
                }
                else
                {
                    int choice = leastDesirableCard(cCards);
                    discardPile.setTopCard(cCards[choice]);
                    cCards[choice] = deck.deal();
```

```java
            if (isFourOfAKind(cCards))
            {
                System.out.println();
                System.out.println("Computer wins!");
                System.out.println();
                putDown("Computer's cards:", cCards);
                return; // Exit application by returning from main()
            }
            curPlayer = HUMAN;
        }
        if (deck.isEmpty())
        {
            while (discardPile.topCard() != null)
                deck.putBack(discardPile.getTopCard());
            deck.shuffle();
        }
    }
}
/**
 * Determine if the <code>Card</code> objects passed to this method all
 * have the same rank.
 *
 * @param cards array of <code>Card</code> objects passed to this method
 *
 * @return true if all <code>Card</code> objects have the same rank;
 * otherwise, false
 */
static boolean isFourOfAKind(Card[] cards)
{
    for (int i = 1; i < cards.length; i++)
        if (cards[i].rank() != cards[0].rank())
            return false;
    return true;
}
/**
 * Identify one of the <code>Card</code> objects that is passed to this
 * method as the least desirable <code>Card</code> object to hold onto.
 *
 * @param cards array of <code>Card</code> objects passed to this method
 *
 * @return 0-based rank (ace is 0, king is 13) of least desirable card
 */
static int leastDesirableCard(Card[] cards)
{
    int[] rankCounts = new int[13];
    for (int i = 0; i < cards.length; i++)
        rankCounts[cards[i].rank().ordinal()]++;
    int minCount = Integer.MAX_VALUE;
    int minIndex = -1;
    for (int i = 0; i < rankCounts.length; i++)
        if (rankCounts[i] < minCount && rankCounts[i] != 0)
        {
            minCount = rankCounts[i];
            minIndex = i;
        }
    for (int i = 0; i < cards.length; i++)
        if (cards[i].rank().ordinal() == minIndex)
```

```
              return i;
          return 0; // Needed to satisfy compiler (should never be executed)
    }
    /**
     *  Prompt the human player to enter a character.
     *
     *  @param msg message to be displayed to human player
     *
     *  @return integer value of character entered by user.
     */
    static int prompt(String msg)
    {
        System.out.print(msg);
        try
        {
            int ch = System.in.read();
            // Erase all subsequent characters including terminating \n newline
            // so that they do not affect a subsequent call to prompt().
            while (System.in.read() != '\n');
            return ch;
        }
        catch (java.io.IOException ioe)
        {
        }
        return 0;
    }
    /**
     *  Display a message followed by all cards held by player. This output
     *  simulates putting down held cards.
     *
     *  @param msg message to be displayed to human player
     *  @param cards array of <code>Card</code> objects to be identified
     */
    static void putDown(String msg, Card[] cards)
    {
        System.out.println(msg);
        for (int i = 0; i < cards.length; i++)
            System.out.println(cards[i]);
    }
    /**
     *  Identify the cards being held via their <code>Card</code> objects on
     *  separate lines. Prefix each line with an uppercase letter starting with
     *  <code>A</code>.
     *
     *  @param cards array of <code>Card</code> objects to be identified
     */
    static void showHeldCards(Card[] cards)
    {
        System.out.println();
        System.out.println("Held cards:");
        for (int i = 0; i < cards.length; i++)
            if (cards[i] != null)
                System.out.println((char) ('A'+i) + ". " + cards[i]);
        System.out.println();
    }
}
```

Chapter 2: Learning Language Fundamentals

1. A class declaration contains field declarations, method declarations, constructor declarations, and other initializer (instance and class) declarations.

2. Identifier `transient` is a reserved word in Java. Identifier `delegate` is not a reserved word in Java.

3. A *variable* is a memory location whose value can change.

4. Character is Java's only unsigned primitive type. It is represented in source code via the `char` reserved word.

5. The difference between an instance field and a class field is that each object (instance) gets its own copy of an instance field, whereas all objects share a single copy of a class field.

6. An *array* is a multivalued variable in which each element holds one of these values.

7. You declare a one-dimensional array variable with a single set of square brackets, as in `String[] cities;`. You declare a two-dimensional array variable with two sets of square brackets, as in `double[][] temperatures;`.

8. *Scope* refers to a variable's accessibility. For example, the scope of a `private` field is restricted to the class in which it is declared. Also, the scope of a parameter is restricted to the method in which the parameter is declared. Another word for scope is *visibility*.

9. String literal `"The quick brown fox \jumps\ over the lazy dog."` is illegal because, unlike `\"`, `\j` and `\` (a backslash followed by a space character) are not valid escape sequences. To make this string literal legal, you must escape these backslashes, as in `"The quick brown fox \\jumps\\ over the lazy dog."`.

10. The purpose of the cast operator is to convert from one type to another type. For example, you can use this operator to convert from floating-point type to 32-bit integer type.

11. The `new` operator is used to create an object.

12. You cannot nest multiline comments.

13. The answer is true: when declaring a method that takes a variable number of arguments, you must specify the three consecutive periods just after the rightmost parameter's type name.

14. Given a two-dimensional array x, x`.length` returns the number of rows in the array.

15. The difference between the while and do-while statements is that a while statement performs zero or more iterations, whereas a do-while statement performs one or more iterations.

16. Initializing the sines array using the new syntax yields double[] sines = new double[360];. Initializing tho cosines array using the new syntax yields double[] cosines = new double[360];.

17. It is okay for an expression assigned to an instance field to access a class field that is declared after the instance field because all class fields are initialized before any instance fields are initialized. The compiler knows that the virtual machine will know about the class fields before an object is created. As a result, this situation does not result in an illegal forward reference.

18. Creating an array of objects requires that you first use new to create the array, and then assign an object reference to each of the array's elements.

19. You prevent a field from being shadowed by changing the name of a same-named local variable or parameter, or by qualifying the local variable's name or a parameter's name with this or the class name followed by the member access operator.

20. You chain together instance method calls by having each participating method specify the name of the class in which the method is declared as the method's return type, and by having the method return this.

21. Calculating the greatest common divisor of two positive integers, which is the greatest positive integer that divides evenly into both positive integers, provides another example of tail recursion. Listing 2 presents the source code.

Listing 2. *Recursively calculating the greatest common divisor*

```
public static int gcd(int a, int b)
{
   // The greatest common divisor is the largest positive integer that
   // divides evenly into two positive integers a and b. For example,
   // GCD(12,18) is 6.

   if (b == 0) // Base problem
      return a;
   else
      return gcd(b, a%b);
}
```

As with the Math class's various static methods, the gcd() method is declared to be static because it does not rely on any instance fields.

22. Merging the various CheckingAccount code fragments into a complete application results in something similar to Listing 3.

Listing 3. *A* CheckingAccount *class that is greater than the sum of its code fragments*

```java
public class CheckingAccount
{
    private String owner;
    private int balance;
    public static int counter;
    public CheckingAccount(String acctOwner, int acctBalance)
    {
        owner = acctOwner;
        balance = acctBalance;
        counter++; // keep track of created CheckingAccount objects
    }
    public CheckingAccount(String acctOwner)
    {
        this(acctOwner, 100); // New account requires $100 minimum balance
    }
    public CheckingAccount printBalance()
    {
        System.out.println(owner+"'s balance:");
        int magnitude = (balance < 0) ? -balance : balance;
        String balanceRep = (balance < 0) ? "(" : "";
        balanceRep += magnitude;
        balanceRep += (balance < 0) ? ")" : "";
        System.out.println(balanceRep);
        return this;
    }
    public CheckingAccount deposit(int amount)
    {
        if (amount <= 0.0)
            System.out.println("cannot deposit a negative or zero amount");
        else
            balance += amount;
        return this;
    }
    public CheckingAccount withdraw(int amount)
    {
        if (amount <= 0.0)
            System.out.println("cannot deposit a negative or zero amount");
        else
        if (balance-amount < 0)
            System.out.println("cannot withdraw more funds than are available");
        else
            balance -= amount;
        return this;
    }
    public static void main(String[] args)
    {
        new CheckingAccount("Jane Doe", 1000).withdraw(2000).printBalance();
        CheckingAccount ca = new CheckingAccount("John Doe");
        ca.printBalance().withdraw(50).printBalance().deposit(80).printBalance();
        System.out.println ("Number of created CheckingAccount objects = "+
                            ca.counter);
    }
}
```

Chapter 3: Learning Object-Oriented Language Features

1. *Implementation inheritance* is inheritance through class extension.

2. Java supports implementation inheritance by providing reserved word extends.

3. A subclass can have only one superclass because Java does not support multiple implementation inheritance.

4. You prevent a class from being subclassed by declaring the class final.

5. The answer is false: the super() call can only appear in a constructor.

6. If a superclass declares a constructor with one or more parameters, and if a subclass constructor does not use super() to call that constructor, the compiler reports an error because the subclass constructor attempts to call a nonexistent noargument constructor in the superclass.

7. An *immutable class* is a class whose instances cannot be modified.

8. The answer is false: a class cannot inherit constructors.

9. Overriding a method means to replace an inherited method with another method that provides the same signature and the same return type, but provides a new implementation.

10. To call a superclass method from its overriding subclass method, prefix the superclass method name with reserved word super and the member access operator in the method call.

11. You prevent a method from being overridden by declaring the method final.

12. You cannot make an overriding subclass method less accessible than the superclass method it is overriding because subtype polymorphism would not work properly if subclass methods could be made less accessible.

    Suppose you upcast a subclass instance to superclass type by assigning the instance's reference to a variable of superclass type. Now suppose you specify a superclass method call on the variable. If this method is overridden by the subclass, the subclass version of the method is called. However, if access to the subclass's overriding method's access could be made private, calling this method would break encapsulation—private methods cannot be called directly from outside of their class.

13. You tell the compiler that a method overrides another method by prefixing the overriding method's header with the @Override annotation.

14. Java does not support multiple implementation inheritance because this form of inheritance can lead to ambiguities.

15. The name of Java's ultimate superclass is `Object`. This class is located in the `java.lang` package.

16. The purpose of the `clone()` method is to duplicate an object without calling a constructor.

17. `Object`'s `clone()` method throws `CloneNotSupportedException` when the class whose instance is to be shallowly cloned does not implement the `Cloneable` interface.

18. The difference between shallow copying and deep copying is that *shallow copying* copies each primitive or reference field's value to its counterpart in the clone, whereas *deep copying* creates, for each reference field, a new object and assigns its reference to the field. This deep copying process continues recursively for these newly created objects.

19. The `==` operator cannot be used to determine if two objects are logically equivalent because this operator only compares object references, not the contents of these objects.

20. `Object`'s `equals()` method compares the current object's `this` reference to the reference passed as an argument to this method. (When I refer to `Object`'s `equals()` method, I am referring to the `equals()` method in the `Object` class.)

21. Expression `"abc" == "a" + "bc"` returns true. It does so because the `String` class contains special support that allows literal strings and string-valued constant expressions to be compared via `==`.

22. You can optimize a time-consuming `equals()` method by first using `==` to determine if this method's reference argument identifies the current object (which is represented in source code via reserved word `this`).

23. The purpose of the `finalize()` method is to provide a safety net for calling an object's cleanup method in case that method is not called.

24. You should not rely on `finalize()` for closing open files because file descriptors are a limited resource and an application might not be able to open additional files until `finalize()` is called, and this method might be called infrequently (or perhaps not at all).

25. A *hash code* is a small value that results from applying a mathematical function to a potentially large amount of data.

26. The answer is true: you should override the `hashCode()` method whenever you override the `equals()` method.

27. Object's toString() method returns a string representation of the current object that consists of the object's class name, followed by the @ symbol, followed by a hexadecimal representation of the object's hash code. (When I refer to Object's toString() method, I am referring to the toString() method in the Object class.)

28. You should override toString() to provide a concise but meaningful description of the object in order to facilitate debugging via System.out.println() method calls. It is more informative for toString() to reveal object state than to reveal a class name, followed by the @ symbol, followed by a hexadecimal representation of the object's hash code.

29. *Composition* is a way to reuse code by composing classes out of other classes, based upon a has-a relationship between them.

30. The answer is false: composition is used to implement "has-a" relationships and implementation inheritance is used to implement "is-a" relationships.

31. The fundamental problem of implementation inheritance is that it breaks encapsulation. You fix this problem by ensuring that you have control over the superclass as well as its subclasses, by ensuring that the superclass is designed and documented for extension, or by using a wrapper class in lieu of a subclass when you would otherwise extend the superclass.

32. *Subtype polymorphism* is a kind of polymorphism where a subtype instance appears in a supertype context, and executing a supertype operation on the subtype instance results in the subtype's version of that operation executing.

33. Subtype polymorphism is accomplished by upcasting the subtype instance to its supertype, by assigning the instance's reference to a variable of that type, and, via this variable, calling a superclass method that has been overridden in the subclass.

34. You would use abstract classes and abstract methods to describe generic concepts (such as shape, animal, or vehicle) and generic operations (such as drawing a generic shape). Abstract classes cannot be instantiated and abstract methods cannot be called because they have no code bodies.

35. An abstract class can contain concrete methods.

36. The purpose of downcasting is to access subtype features. For example, you would downcast a Point variable that contains a Circle instance reference to the Circle type so that you can call Circle's getRadius() method on the instance.

37. The three forms of RTTI are the virtual machine verifying that a cast is legal, using the instanceof operator to determine if an instance is a member of a type, and reflection.

38. A *covariant return type* is a method return type that, in the superclass's method declaration, is the supertype of the return type in the subclass's overriding method declaration.

39. You formally declare an interface by specifying at least reserved word `interface`, followed by a name, followed by a brace-delimited body of constants and/or method headers.

40. The answer is true: you can precede an interface declaration with the `abstract` reserved word.

41. A *marker interface* is an interface that declares no members.

42. *Interface inheritance* is inheritance through interface implementation or interface extension.

43. You implement an interface by appending an implements clause, consisting of reserved word `implements` followed by the interface's name, to a class header, and by overriding the interface's method headers in the class.

44. You might encounter one or more name collisions when you implement multiple interfaces.

45. You form a hierarchy of interfaces by appending reserved word `extends` followed by an interface name to an interface header.

46. Java's interfaces feature is so important because it gives developers the utmost flexibility in designing their applications.

47. Interfaces and abstract classes describe abstract types.

48. Interfaces and abstract classes differ in that interfaces can only declare abstract methods and constants, and can be implemented by any class in any class hierarchy. In contrast, abstract classes can declare constants and nonconstant fields, can declare abstract and concrete methods, and can only appear in the upper levels of class hierarchies, where they are used to describe abstract concepts and behaviors.

49. Listings 4 through 10 declare the `Animal`, `Bird`, `Fish`, `AmericanRobin`, `DomesticCanary`, `RainbowTrout`, and `SockeyeSalmon` classes that were called for in Chapter 3.

Listing 4. *The `Animal` class abstracting over birds and fish (and other organisms)*

```
public abstract class Animal
{
    private String kind;
    private String appearance;
    public Animal(String kind, String appearance)
    {
        this.kind = kind;
        this.appearance = appearance;
```

```
    }
    public abstract void eat();
    public abstract void move();
    @Override
    public final String toString()
    {
        return kind + "    " + appearance;
    }
}
```

Listing 5. *The* Bird *class abstracting over American robins, domestic canaries, and other kinds of birds*

```
public abstract class Bird extends Animal
{
    public Bird(String kind, String appearance)
    {
        super(kind, appearance);
    }
    @Override
    public final void eat()
    {
        System.out.println("eats seeds and insects");
    }
    @Override
    public final void move()
    {
        System.out.println("flies through the air");
    }
}
```

Listing 6. *The* Fish *class abstracting over rainbow trout, sockeye salmon, and other kinds of fish*

```
public abstract class Fish extends Animal
{
    public Fish(String kind, String appearance)
    {
        super(kind, appearance);
    }
    @Override
    public final void eat()
    {
        System.out.println("eats krill, algae, and insects");
    }
    @Override
    public final void move()
    {
        System.out.println("swims through the water");
    }
}
```

Listing 7. *The* AmericanRobin *class denoting a bird with a red breast*

```
public final class AmericanRobin extends Bird
{
    public AmericanRobin()
    {
        super("americanrobin", "red breast");
    }
}
```

Listing 8. *The DomesticCanary class denoting a bird of various colors*

```
public final class DomesticCanary extends Bird
{
    public DomesticCanary()
    {
        super("domestic canary", "yellow, orange, black, brown, white, red");
    }
}
```

Listing 9. *The RainbowTrout class denoting a rainbow-colored fish*

```
public final class RainbowTrout extends Fish
{
    public RainbowTrout()
    {
        super("rainbowtrout", "bands of brilliant speckled multicolored " +
            "stripes running nearly the whole length of its body");
    }
}
```

Listing 10. *The SockeyeSalmon class denoting a red-and-green fish*

```
public final class SockeyeSalmon extends Fish
{
    public SockeyeSalmon()
    {
        super("sockeyesalmon", "bright red with a green head");
    }
}
```

Animal's toString() method is declared final because it does not make sense to override this method, which is complete in this example. Also, each of Bird's and Fish's overriding eat() and move() methods is declared final because it does not make sense to override these methods in this example, which assumes that all birds eat seeds and insects; all fish eat krill, algae, and insects; all birds fly through the air; and all fish swim through the water.

The AmericanRobin, DomesticCanary, RainbowTrout, and SockeyeSalmon classes are declared final because they represent the bottom of the Bird and Fish class hierarchies, and it does not make sense to subclass them.

50. Listing 11 declares the Animals class that was called for in Chapter 3.

Listing 11. *The Animals class letting animals eat and move*

```
public class Animals
{
    public static void main(String[] args)
    {
        Animal[] animals = { new AmericanRobin(), new RainbowTrout(),
                            new DomesticCanary(), new SockeyeSalmon() };
        for (int i = 0; i < animals.length; i++)
        {
            System.out.println(animals[i]);
            animals[i].eat();
            animals[i].move();
            System.out.println();
```

```
        }
      }
    }
```

51. Listings 12 through 14 declare the Countable interface, the modified Animal class, and the modified Animals class that were called for in Chapter 3.

Listing 12. *The Countable interface for use in taking a census of animals*

```java
public interface Countable
{
    String getID();
}
```

Listing 13. *The refactored Animal class for help in census taking*

```java
public abstract class Animal implements Countable
{
    private String kind;
    private String appearance;
    public Animal(String kind, String appearance)
    {
        this.kind = kind;
        this.appearance = appearance;
    }
    public abstract void eat();
    public abstract void move();
    @Override
    public final String toString()
    {
        return kind + " -- " + appearance;
    }
    @Override
    public final String getID()
    {
        return kind;
    }
}
```

Listing 14. *The modified Animals class for carrying out the census*

```java
public class Animals
{
    public static void main(String[] args)
    {
        Animal[] animals = { new AmericanRobin(), new RainbowTrout(),
                             new DomesticCanary(), new SockeyeSalmon(),
                             new RainbowTrout(), new AmericanRobin() };
        for (int i = 0; i < animals.length; i++)
        {
            System.out.println(animals[i]);
            animals[i].eat();
            animals[i].move();
            System.out.println();
        }

        Census census = new Census();
        Countable[] countables = (Countable[]) animals;
        for (int i = 0; i < countables.length; i++)
```

```
            census.update(countables[i].getID());

        for (int i = 0; i < Census.SIZE; i++)
            System.out.println(census.get(i));
    }
}
```

Chapter 4: Mastering Advanced Language Features Part 1

1. A *nested class* is a class that is declared as a member of another class or scope.

2. The four kinds of nested classes are static member classes, nonstatic member classes, anonymous classes, and local classes.

3. Nonstatic member classes, anonymous classes, and local classes are also known as inner classes.

4. The answer is false: a static member class does not have an enclosing instance.

5. You instantiate a nonstatic member class from beyond its enclosing class by first instantiating the enclosing class, and then prefixing the new operator with the enclosing class instance as you instantiate the enclosed class. Example: new EnclosingClass().new EnclosedClass().

6. It is necessary to declare local variables and parameters final when they are being accessed by an instance of an anonymous class or a local class.

7. The answer is true: an interface can be declared within a class or within another interface.

8. A *package* is a unique namespace that can contain a combination of top-level classes, other top-level types, and subpackages.

9. You ensure that package names are unique by specifying your reversed Internet domain name as the top-level package name.

10. A *package statement* is a statement that identifies the package in which a source file's types are located.

11. The answer is false: you cannot specify multiple package statements in a source file.

12. An *import statement* is a statement that imports types from a package by telling the compiler where to look for unqualified type names during compilation.

13. You indicate that you want to import multiple types via a single import statement by specifying the wildcard character (*).

14. During a runtime search, the virtual machine reports a "no class definition found" error when it cannot find a classfile.

15. You specify the user classpath to the virtual machine via the `-classpath` option used to start the virtual machine or, if not present, the `CLASSPATH` environment variable.

16. A *constant interface* is an interface that only exports constants.

17. Constant interfaces are used to avoid having to qualify their names with their classes.

18. Constant interfaces are bad because their constants are nothing more than an implementation detail that should not be allowed to leak into the class's exported *interface*, because they might confuse the class's users (what is the purpose of these constants?). Also, they represent a future commitment: even when the class no longer uses these constants, the interface must remain to ensure binary compatibility.

19. A *static import statement* is a version of the import statement that lets you import a class's static members so that you do not have to qualify them with their class names.

20. You specify a static import statement as `import`, followed by `static`, followed by a member access operator–separated list of package and subpackage names, followed by the member access operator, followed by a class's name, followed by the member access operator, followed by a single static member name or the asterisk wildcard; for example, `import static java.lang.Math.cos;` (import the `cos()` static method from the `Math` class).

21. An *exception* is a divergence from an application's normal behavior.

22. Objects are superior to error codes for representing exceptions because error code Boolean or integer values are less meaningful than object names, and because objects can contain information about what led to the exception. These details can be helpful to a suitable workaround.

23. A *throwable* is an instance of `Throwable` or one of its subclasses.

24. The `getCause()` method returns an exception that is wrapped inside another exception.

25. `Exception` describes exceptions that result from external factors (such as not being able to open a file) and from flawed code (such as passing an illegal argument to a method). `Error` describes virtual machine–oriented exceptions such as running out of memory or being unable to load a classfile.

26. A *checked exception* is an exception that represents a problem with the possibility of recovery, and for which the developer must provide a workaround.

27. A *runtime exception* is an exception that represents a coding mistake.

28. You would introduce your own exception class when no existing exception class in Java's class library meets your needs.

29. The answer is false: you use a throws clause to identify exceptions that are thrown from a method by appending this clause to a method's header.

30. The purpose of a try statement is to provide a scope (via its brace-delimited body) in which to present code that can throw exceptions. The purpose of a catch clause is to receive a thrown exception and provide code (via its brace-delimited body) that handles that exception by providing a workaround.

31. The purpose of a finally clause is to provide cleanup code that is executed whether an exception is thrown or not.

32. Listing 15 presents the G2D class that was called for in Chapter 3.

Listing 15. *The G2D class with its* Matrix *nonstatic member class*

```java
public class G2D
{
    private Matrix xform;
    public G2D()
    {
        xform = new Matrix();
        xform.a = 1.0;
        xform.e = 1.0;
        xform.i = 1.0;
    }
    private class Matrix
    {
        double a, b, c;
        double d, e, f;
        double g, h, i;
    }
}
```

33. To extend the logging package to support a null device in which messages are thrown away, first introduce Listing 16's NullDevice package-private class.

Listing 16. *Implementing the proverbial "bit bucket" class*

```java
package logging;

class NullDevice implements Logger
{
    private String dstName;
    NullDevice(String dstName)
    {
    }
    public boolean connect()
    {
        return true;
    }
    public boolean disconnect()
```

```
    {
        return true;
    }
    public boolean log(String msg)
    {
        return true;
    }
}
```

Continue by introducing, into the LoggerFactory class, a NULLDEVICE constant and code that instantiates NullDevice with a null argument—a destination name is not required—when newLogger()'s dstType parameter contains this constant's value. Check out Listing 17.

Listing 17. *A refactored* LoggerFactory *class*

```
package logging;

public abstract class LoggerFactory
{
    public final static int CONSOLE = 0;
    public final static int FILE = 1;
    public final static int NULLDEVICE = 2;
    public static Logger newLogger(int dstType, String...dstName)
    {
        switch (dstType)
        {
            case CONSOLE    : return new Console(dstName.length == 0 ? null
                                                                      : dstName[0]);
            case FILE       : return new File(dstName.length == 0 ? null
                                                                  : dstName[0]);
            case NULLDEVICE: return new NullDevice(null);
            default         : return null;
        }
    }
}
```

34. Modifying the logging package so that Logger's connect() method throws a CannotConnectException instance when it cannot connect to its logging destination, and the other two methods each throw a NotConnectedException instance when connect() was not called or when it threw a CannotConnectException instance, results in Listing 18's Logger interface.

Listing 18. *A* Logger *interface whose methods throw exceptions*

```
package logging;

public interface Logger
{
    void connect() throws CannotConnectException;
    void disconnect() throws NotConnectedException;
    void log(String msg) throws NotConnectedException;
}
```

Listing 19 presents the CannotConnectException class.

Listing 19. *An uncomplicated CannotConnectException class*

```
package logging;

public class CannotConnectException extends Exception
{
}
```

The NotConnectedException class has a similar structure.

Listing 20 presents the Console class.

Listing 20. *The Console class satisfying Logger's contract without throwing exceptions*

```
package logging;

class Console implements Logger
{
   private String dstName;
   Console(String dstName)
   {
      this.dstName = dstName;
   }
   public void connect() throws CannotConnectException
   {
   }
   public void disconnect() throws NotConnectedException
   {
   }
   public void log(String msg) throws NotConnectedException
   {
      System.out.println(msg);
   }
}
```

Listing 21 presents the File class.

Listing 21. *The File class satisfying Logger's contract by throwing exceptions as necessary*

```
package logging;

class File implements Logger
{
   private String dstName;
   File(String dstName)
   {
      this.dstName = dstName;
   }
   public void connect() throws CannotConnectException
   {
      if (dstName == null)
         throw new CannotConnectException();
   }
   public void disconnect() throws NotConnectedException
   {
      if (dstName == null)
         throw new NotConnectedException();
   }
   public void log(String msg) throws NotConnectedException
```

```
   {
      if (dstName == null)
         throw new NotConnectedException();
      System.out.println("writing " + msg + " to file " + dstName);
   }
}
```

35. When you modify TestLogger to respond appropriately to thrown
CannotConnectException and NotConnectedException objects, you end up with
something similar to Listing 22.

Listing 22. *A* TestLogger *class that handles thrown exceptions*

```
import logging.*;

public class TestLogger
{
   public static void main(String[] args)
   {
      try
      {
         Logger logger = LoggerFactory.newLogger(LoggerFactory.CONSOLE);
         logger.connect();
         logger.log("test message #1");
         logger.disconnect();
      }
      catch (CannotConnectException cce)
      {
         System.err.println("cannot connect to console-based logger");
      }
      catch (NotConnectedException nce)
      {
         System.err.println("not connected to console-based logger");
      }

      try
      {
         Logger logger = LoggerFactory.newLogger(LoggerFactory.FILE, "x.txt");
         logger.connect();
         logger.log("test message #2");
         logger.disconnect();
      }
      catch (CannotConnectException cce)
      {
         System.err.println("cannot connect to file-based logger");
      }
      catch (NotConnectedException nce)
      {
         System.err.println("not connected to file-based logger");
      }

      try
      {
         Logger logger = LoggerFactory.newLogger(LoggerFactory.FILE);
         logger.connect();
         logger.log("test message #3");
         logger.disconnect();
```

```
      }
      catch (CannotConnectException cce)
      {
         System.err.println("cannot connect to file-based logger");
      }
      catch (NotConnectedException nce)
      {
         System.err.println("not connected to file-based logger");
      }
   }
}
```

Chapter 5: Mastering Advanced Language Features Part 2

1. An *assertion* is a statement that lets you express an assumption of program correctness via a Boolean expression.

2. You would use assertions to validate internal invariants, control-flow invariants, preconditions, postconditions, and class invariants.

3. The answer is false: specifying the -ea command-line option with no argument enables all assertions except for system assertions.

4. An *annotation* is an instance of an annotation type and associates metadata with an application element. It is expressed in source code by prefixing the type name with the @ symbol.

5. Constructors, fields, local variables, methods, packages, parameters, and types (annotation, class, enum, and interface) can be annotated.

6. The three compiler-supported annotation types are Override, Deprecated, and SuppressWarnings.

7. You declare an annotation type by specifying the @ symbol, immediately followed by reserved word interface, followed by the type's name, followed by a body.

8. A *marker annotation* is an instance of an annotation type that supplies no data apart from its name—the type's body is empty.

9. An *element* is a method header that appears in the annotation type's body. It cannot have parameters or a throws clause. Its return type must be primitive (such as int), String, Class, an enum type, an annotation type, or an array of the preceding types. It can have a default value.

10. You assign a default value to an element by specifying default followed by the value, whose type must match the element's return type. For example, String developer() default "unassigned";.

11. A *meta-annotation* is an annotation that annotates an annotation type.

12. Java's four meta-annotation types are `Target`, `Retention`, `Documented`, and `Inherited`.

13. *Generics* can be defined as a suite of language features for declaring and using type-agnostic classes and interfaces.

14. You would use generics to ensure that your code is typesafe by avoiding `ClassCastExceptions`.

15. The difference between a generic type and a parameterized type is that a *generic type* is a class or interface that introduces a family of parameterized types by declaring a formal type parameter list, and a *parameterized type* is an instance of a generic type.

16. Anonymous classes cannot be generic because they have no names.

17. The five kinds of actual type arguments are concrete types, concrete parameterized types, array types, type parameters, and wildcards.

18. The answer is true: you cannot specify a primitive type name (such as `double` or `int`) as an actual type argument.

19. A *raw type* is a generic type without its type parameters.

20. The compiler reports an unchecked warning message when it detects an explicit cast that involves a type parameter. The compiler is concerned that downcasting to whatever type is passed to the type parameter might result in a violation of type safety.

21. You suppress an unchecked warning message by prefixing the constructor or method that contains the unchecked code with the `@SuppressWarnings("unchecked")` annotation.

22. The answer is true: `List<E>`'s E type parameter is unbounded.

23. You specify a single upper bound via reserved word extends followed by a type name.

24. The answer is false: `MyList<E super Circle>` does not specify that the E type parameter has a lower bound of `Circle`. In contrast, `MyList<? super Circle>` specifies that `Circle` is a lower bound.

25. A *recursive type bound* is a type parameter bound that includes the type parameter.

26. Wildcard type arguments are necessary because, by accepting any actual type argument, they provide a typesafe workaround to the problem of polymorphic behavior not applying to multiple parameterized types that differ only in regard to one type parameter being a subtype of another type parameter.

For example, because List<String> is not a kind of List<Object>, you cannot pass an object whose type is List<String> to a method parameter whose type is List<Object>. However, you can pass a List<String> object to List<?> provided that you are not going to add the List<String> object to the List<?>.

27. *Reification* is the process or result of treating the abstract as if it was concrete.

28. The answer is false: type parameters are not reified.

29. *Erasure* is the throwing away of type parameters following compilation so that they are not available at runtime. Erasure also involves replacing uses of other type variables by the upper bound of the type variable (such as Object), and inserting casts to the appropriate type when the resulting code is not type correct.

30. A *generic method* is a static or non-static method with a type-generalized implementation.

31. Although you might think otherwise, Listing 5-43's methodCaller() generic method calls someOverloadedMethod(Object o). This method, instead of someOverloadedMethod(Date d), is called because overload resolution happens at compile time, when the generic method is translated to its unique bytecode representation, and erasure (which takes care of that mapping) causes type parameters to be replaced by their leftmost bound or Object (if there is no bound). After erasure, we are left with Listing 23's nongeneric methodCaller() method.

Listing 23. *The nongeneric methodCaller() method that results from erasure*

```
public static void methodCaller(Object t)
{
    someOverloadedMethod(t);
}
```

32. An *enumerated type* is a type that specifies a named sequence of related constants as its legal values.

33. Three problems that can arise when you use enumerated types whose constants are int-based are lack of compile-time type safety, brittle applications, and the inability to translate int constants into meaningful string-based descriptions.

34. An *enum* is an enumerated type that is expressed via reserved word enum.

35. You use a switch statement with an enum by specifying an enum constant as the statement's selector expression and constant names as case values.

36. You can enhance an enum by adding fields, constructors, and methods—you can even have the enum implement interfaces. Also, you can override toString() to provide a more useful description of a constant's value, and subclass constants to assign different behaviors.

37. The purpose of the abstract Enum class is to serve as the common base class of all Java language–based enumeration types.

38. The difference between Enum's name() and toString() methods is that name() always returns a constant's name, but toString() can be overridden to return a more meaningful description instead of the constant's name.

39. The answer is true: Enum's generic type is Enum<E extends Enum<E>>.

40. Listing 24 presents a ToDo marker annotation type that annotates only type elements, and that also uses the default retention policy.

Listing 24. *The ToDo annotation type for marking types that need to be completed*

```
import java.lang.annotation.ElementType;
import java.lang.annotation.Target;

@Target(ElementType.TYPE)
public @interface ToDo
{
}
```

41. Listing 25 presents a rewritten StubFinder application that works with Listing 5-15's Stub annotation type (with appropriate @Target and @Retention annotations) and Listing 5-16's Deck class.

Listing 25. *Reporting a stub's ID, due date, and developer via a new version of StubFinder*

```
import java.lang.reflect.*;

public class StubFinder
{
    public static void main(String[] args) throws Exception
    {
        if (args.length != 1)
        {
            System.err.println("usage: java StubFinder classfile");
            return;
        }
        Method[] methods = Class.forName(args[0]).getMethods();
        for (int i = 0; i < methods.length; i++)
            if (methods[i].isAnnotationPresent(Stub.class))
            {
                Stub stub = methods[i].getAnnotation(Stub.class);
                System.out.println("Stub ID = " + stub.id());
                System.out.println("Stub Date = " + stub.dueDate());
                System.out.println("Stub Developer = " + stub.developer());
                System.out.println();
            }
    }
}
```

42. Listing 26 presents the generic Stack class and the StackEmptyException and StackFullException helper classes that were called for in Chapter 5.

Listing 26. *Stack and its* StackEmptyException *and* StackFullException *helper classes proving that not all helper classes need to be nested*

```java
class StackEmptyException extends Exception
{
}
class StackFullException extends Exception
{
}
public class Stack<E>
{
   private E[] elements;
   private int top;
   @SuppressWarnings("unchecked")
   public Stack(int size)
   {
      elements = (E[]) new Object[size];
      top = -1;
   }
   public void push(E element) throws StackFullException
   {
      if (top == elements.length-1)
         throw new StackFullException();
      elements[++top] = element;
   }
   E pop() throws StackEmptyException
   {
      if (isEmpty())
         throw new StackEmptyException();
      return elements[top--];
   }
   public boolean isEmpty()
   {
      return top == -1;
   }
   public static void main(String[] args)
      throws StackFullException, StackEmptyException
   {
      Stack<String> stack = new Stack<String>(5);
      assert stack.isEmpty();
      stack.push("A");
      stack.push("B");
      stack.push("C");
      stack.push("D");
      stack.push("E");
      // Uncomment the following line to generate a StackFullException.
      //stack.push("F");
      while (!stack.isEmpty())
         System.out.println(stack.pop());
      // Uncomment the following line to generate a StackEmptyException.
      //stack.pop();
      assert stack.isEmpty();
   }
}
```

43. Listing 27 presents the Compass enum that was called for in Chapter 5.

Listing 27. *A Compass enum with four direction constants*

```
public enum Compass
{
   NORTH, SOUTH, EAST, WEST
}
```

Listing 28 presents the UseCompass class that was called for in Chapter 5.

Listing 28. *Using the Compass enum to keep from getting lost*

```
public class UseCompass
{
   public static void main(String[] args)
   {
      int i = (int)(Math.random()*4);
      Compass[] dir = { Compass.NORTH, Compass.EAST, Compass.SOUTH,
                        Compass.WEST };
      switch(dir[i])
      {
         case NORTH: System.out.println("heading north"); break;
         case EAST : System.out.println("heading east"); break;
         case SOUTH: System.out.println("heading south"); break;
         case WEST : System.out.println("heading west"); break;
         default   : assert false; // Should never be reached.
      }
   }
}
```

Chapter 6: Exploring the Basic APIs Part 1

1.   Math declares double constants E and PI that represent, respectively, the natural logarithm base value (2.71828...) and the ratio of a circle's circumference to its diameter (3.14159...). E is initialized to 2.718281828459045 and PI is initialized to 3.141592653589793.

2.   Math.abs(Integer.MIN_VALUE) equals Integer.MIN_VALUE because there does not exist a positive 32-bit integer equivalent of MIN_VALUE. (Integer.MIN_VALUE equals -2147483648 and Integer.MAX_VALUE equals 2147483647.)

3.   Math's random() method returns a pseudorandom number between 0.0 (inclusive) and 1.0 (exclusive).

4.   The five special values that can arise during floating-point calculations are +infinity, -infinity, NaN, +0.0, and -0.0.

5.   Math and StrictMath differ in the following ways:

   ■   StrictMath's methods return exactly the same results on all platforms. In contrast, some of Math's methods might return values that vary ever so slightly from platform to platform.

■ Because StrictMath cannot utilize platform-specific features such as an extended-precision math coprocessor, an implementation of StrictMath might be less efficient than an implementation of Math.

6. The purpose of strictfp is to restrict floating-point calculations to ensure portability. This reserved word accomplishes portability in the context of intermediate floating-point representations and overflows/underflows (generating a value too large or small to fit a representation). Furthermore, it can be applied at the method level or at the class level.

7. BigDecimal is an immutable class that represents a signed decimal number (such as 23.653) of arbitrary *precision* (number of digits) with an associated *scale* (an integer that specifies the number of digits after the decimal point). You might use this class to accurately store floating-point values that represent monetary values, and properly round the result of each monetary calculation.

8. The RoundingMode constant that describes the form of rounding commonly taught at school is HALF_UP.

9. BigInteger is an immutable class that represents a signed integer of arbitrary precision. It stores its value in *two's complement format* (all bits are flipped—1s to 0s and 0s to 1s—and 1 has been added to the result to be compatible with the two's complement format used by Java's byte integer, short integer, integer, and long integer types).

10. The purpose of Package's isSealed() method is to indicate whether or not a package is *sealed* (all classes that are part of the package are archived in the same JAR file). This method returns true when the package is sealed.

11. The answer is true: getPackage() requires at least one classfile to be loaded from the package before it returns a Package object describing that package.

12. The two main uses of the primitive wrapper classes are to store objects containing primitive values in the collections framework's lists, sets, and maps; and to provide a good place to associate useful constants (such as MAX_VALUE and MIN_VALUE) and class methods (such as Integer's parseInt() methods and Character's isDigit(), isLetter(), and toUpperCase() methods) with the primitive types.

13. You should avoid coding expressions such as ch >= '0' && ch <= '9' (test ch to see if it contains a digit) or ch >= 'A' && ch <= 'Z' (test ch to see if it contains an uppercase letter) because it is too easy to introduce a bug into the expressions, the expressions are not very descriptive of what they are testing, and the expressions are biased toward Latin digits (0–9) and letters (A–Z, a–z).

14. The four kinds of reachability are strongly reachable, softly reachable, weakly reachable, and phantom reachable.

15. A *referent* is the object whose reference is stored in a SoftReference, WeakReference, or PhantomReference object.

16. The References API's PhantomReference class is the equivalent of Object's finalize() method. Both entities are used to perform object cleanup tasks.

17. Listing 29 presents the Circle application that was called for in Chapter 6.

Listing 29. *Using asterisks to display a circle shape*

```java
public class Circle
{
   final static int NROWS = 22;
   final static int NCOLS = 22;
   final static double RADIUS = 10.0;
   public static void main(String[] args)
   {
      // Create the screen array for storing the cardioid image.
      char[][] screen = new char[NROWS][];
      for (int row = 0; row < NROWS; row++)
         screen[row] = new char[NCOLS];

      // Initialize the screen array to space characters.
      for (int col = 0; col < NCOLS; col++)
         screen[0][col] = ' ';
      for (int row = 1; row < NROWS; row++)
         System.arraycopy(screen[0], 0, screen[row], 0, NCOLS);

      // Create the circle shape.
      for (int angle = 0; angle < 360; angle++)
      {
         int x = (int)(RADIUS*Math.cos(Math.toRadians(angle)))+NCOLS/2;
         int y = (int)(RADIUS*Math.sin(Math.toRadians(angle)))+NROWS/2;
         screen[y][x] = '*';
      }

      // Output the screen array.
      for (int row = 0; row < NROWS; row++)
         System.out.println(screen[row]);
   }
}
```

18. Listing 30 presents the PrimeNumberTest application that was called for in Chapter 6.

Listing 30. *Checking a positive integer argument to discover if it is prime*

```java
public class PrimeNumberTest
{
   public static void main(String[] args)
   {
      if (args.length != 1)
      {
         System.err.println("usage: java PrimeNumberTest integer");
         System.err.println("integer must be 2 or higher");
         return;
      }
      try
      {
```

```
            int n = Integer.parseInt(args[0]);
            if (n < 2)
            {
                System.err.println(n + " is invalid because it is less than 2");
                return;
            }
            for (int i = 2; i <= Math.sqrt(n); i++)
                if (n % i == 0)
                {
                    System.out.println (n + " is not prime");
                    return;
                }
            System.out.println(n + " is prime");
        }
        catch (NumberFormatException nfe)
        {
            System.err.println("unable to parse " + args[0] + " into an int");
        }
    }
}
```

Chapter 7: Exploring the Basic APIs Part 2

1. *Reflection* is a third form of runtime type identification. Applications use reflection to learn about loaded classes, interfaces, enums (a kind of class), and annotation types (a kind of interface); and to instantiate classes, call methods, access fields, and perform other tasks reflectively.

2. The difference between Class's getDeclaredFields() and getFields() methods is as follows: getDeclaredFields() returns an array of Field objects representing all public, protected, default (package) access, and private fields declared by the class or interface represented by this Class object while excluding inherited fields, whereas getFields() returns an array of Field objects representing public fields of the class or interface represented by this Class object, including those public fields inherited from superclasses and superinterfaces.

3. You would determine if the method represented by a Method object is abstract by calling the object's getModifiers() method, bitwise ANDing the return value with Modifier.ABSTRACT, and comparing the result with Modifier.ABSTRACT. For example, ((method.getModifiers() & Modifier.ABSTRACT) == Modifier.ABSTRACT) evaluates to true when the method represented by the Method object whose reference is stored in method is abstract.

4. The three ways of obtaining a Class object are to use Class's forName() method, Object's getClass() method, and a class literal.

5. The answer is true: a string literal is a String object.

6. The purpose of String's intern() method is to store a unique copy of a String object in an internal table of String objects. intern() makes it possible to compare strings via their references and == or !=. These operators are the fastest way to compare strings, which is especially valuable when sorting a huge number of strings.

7. String and StringBuffer differ in that String objects contain immutable sequences of characters, whereas StringBuffer objects contain mutable sequences of characters.

8. StringBuffer and StringBuilder differ in that StringBuffer methods are synchronized, whereas StringBuilder's equivalent methods are not synchronized. As a result, you would use the thread-safe but slower StringBuffer class in multithreaded situations and the nonthread-safe but faster StringBuilder class in single-threaded situations.

9. System's arraycopy() method copies all or part of one array's elements to another array.

10. A *thread* is an independent path of execution through an application's code.

11. The purpose of the Runnable interface is to identify those objects that supply code for threads to execute via this interface's solitary public void run() method.

12. The purpose of the Thread class is to provide a consistent interface to the underlying operating system's threading architecture. It provides methods that make it possible to associate code with threads, as well as to start and manage those threads.

13. The answer is false: a Thread object associates with a single thread.

14. A *race condition* is a scenario in which multiple threads update the same object at the same time or nearly at the same time. Part of the object stores values written to it by one thread, and another part of the object stores values written to it by another thread.

15. *Synchronization* is the act of allowing only one thread at time to execute code within a method or a block.

16. Synchronization is implemented in terms of monitors and locks.

17. Synchronization works by requiring that a thread that wants to enter a monitor-controlled critical section first acquire a lock. The lock is released automatically when the thread exits the critical section.

18. The answer is true: variables of type long or double are not atomic on 32-bit virtual machines.

19. The purpose of reserved word volatile is to let threads running on multiprocessor or multicore machines access a single copy of an instance field or class field. Without volatile, each thread might access its cached copy of the field and will not see modifications made by other threads to their copies.

20. The answer is false: Object's wait() methods cannot be called from outside of a synchronized method or block.

21. *Deadlock* is a situation where locks are acquired by multiple threads, neither thread holds its own lock but holds the lock needed by some other thread, and neither thread can enter and later exit its critical section to release its held lock because some other thread holds the lock to that critical section.

22. The purpose of the ThreadLocal class is to associate per-thread data (such as a user ID) with a thread.

23. InheritableThreadLocal differs from ThreadLocal in that the former class lets a child thread inherit a thread-local value from its parent thread.

24. Listing 31 presents a more efficient version of Listing 6-14's image names loop.

Listing 31. *A more efficient image names loop*

```
String[] imageNames = new String[NUM_IMAGES];
StringBuffer sb = new StringBuffer();
for (int i = 0; i < imageNames.length; i++)
{
   sb.append("image");
   sb.append(i);
   sb.append(".gif");
   imageNames[i] = sb.toString();
   sb.setLength(0); // Erase previous StringBuffer contents.
}
```

25. Listing 32 presents the Classify application that was called for in Chapter 7.

Listing 32. *Classifying a command-line argument as an annotation type, enum, interface, or class*

```
public class Classify
{
   public static void main(String[] args)
   {
      if (args.length != 1)
      {
         System.err.println("usage: java Classify pkgAndTypeName");
         return;
      }
      try
      {
         Class<?> clazz = Class.forName(args[0]);
         if (clazz.isAnnotation())
            System.out.println("Annotation");
         else
         if (clazz.isEnum())
            System.out.println("Enum");
         else
```

```
         if (clazz.isInterface())
            System.out.println("Interface");
         else
            System.out.println("Class");
      }
      catch (ClassNotFoundException cnfe)
      {
         System.err.println("could not locate " + args[0]);
      }
   }
}
```

Specify java Classify java.lang.Override and you will see Annotation as the output. Also, java.Classify java.math.RoundingMode outputs Enum, java Classify java.lang.Runnable outputs Interface, and java Classify java.lang.Class outputs Class.

26. Listing 33 presents the revised ExploreType application that was called for in Chapter 7.

Listing 33. *An improved ExploreType application*

```
public class ExploreType
{
   public static void main(String[] args)
   {
      if (args.length != 1)
      {
         System.err.println("usage: java ExploreType pkgAndTypeName");
         return;
      }
      try
      {
         Class<?> clazz = Class.forName(args[0]);
         if (clazz.isAnnotation())
            dumpAnnotation(clazz);
         else
         if (clazz.isEnum())
            dumpEnum(clazz);
         else
         if (clazz.isInterface())
            dumpInterface(clazz);
         else
            dumpClass(clazz);
      }
      catch (ClassNotFoundException cnfe)
      {
         System.err.println("could not locate " + args[0]);
      }
   }
   public static void dumpAnnotation(Class clazz)
   {
      // Left blank as an exercise for you to complete.
   }
   public static void dumpClass(Class clazz)
   {
      // Output class header.
```

```
         int modifiers = clazz.getModifiers();
         if ((modifiers & Modifier.PUBLIC) == Modifier.PUBLIC)
            System.out.print("public ");
         if ((modifiers & Modifier.ABSTRACT) == Modifier.ABSTRACT)
            System.out.print("abstract ");
         System.out.println("class " + clazz.getName());
         System.out.println("{");

         // Output fields.
         System.out.println ("   // FIELDS");
         Field[] fields = clazz.getDeclaredFields();
         for (int i = 0; i < fields.length; i++)
         {
            System.out.print("   ");
            System.out.println(fields[i]);
         }
         System.out.println();

         // Output constructors.
         System.out.println ("   // CONSTRUCTORS");
         Constructor[] constructors = clazz.getDeclaredConstructors();
         for (int i = 0; i < constructors.length; i++)
         {
            System.out.print("   ");
            System.out.println(constructors[i]);
         }
         System.out.println();

         // Output methods.
         System.out.println ("   // METHODS");
         Method[] methods = clazz.getDeclaredMethods();
         for (int i = 0; i < methods.length; i++)
         {
            System.out.print("   ");
            System.out.println(methods[i]);
         }

         // Output class trailer.
         System.out.println("}");
      }
      public static void dumpEnum(Class clazz)
      {
         // Left blank as an exercise for you to complete.
      }
      public static void dumpInterface(Class clazz)
      {
         // Left blank as an exercise for you to complete.
      }
   }
```

I have deliberately written this application so that it can be expanded to output annotation types, enums, and interfaces.

27. Listing 34 presents the revised CountingThreads application that was called for in Chapter 7.

Listing 34. *Counting via daemon threads*

```java
public class CountingThreads
{
   public static void main(String[] args)
   {
      Runnable r = new Runnable()
                   {
                      @Override
                      public void run()
                      {
                         String name = Thread.currentThread().getName();
                         int count = 0;
                         while (true)
                            System.out.println(name + ": " + count++);
                      }
                   };
      Thread thdA = new Thread(r);
      thdA.setDaemon(true);
      Thread thdB = new Thread(r);
      thdB.setDaemon(true);
      thdA.start();
      thdB.start();
   }
}
```

When you run this application, the two daemon threads start executing and you will probably see some output. However, the application will end as soon as the default main thread leaves the `main()` method and dies.

28. Listing 35 presents the `StopCountingThreads` application that was called for in Chapter 7.

Listing 35. *Stopping the counting threads when Enter is pressed*

```java
public class StopCountingThreads
{
   private static volatile boolean stopped = false;

   public static void main(String[] args)
   {
      Runnable r = new Runnable()
                   {
                      @Override
                      public void run()
                      {
                         String name = Thread.currentThread().getName();
                         int count = 0;
                         while (!stopped)
                            System.out.println(name + ": " + count++);
                      }
                   };
      Thread thdA = new Thread(r);
      Thread thdB = new Thread(r);
      thdA.start();
      thdB.start();
      try { System.in.read(); } catch (IOException ioe) {}
      stopped = true;
```

```
    }
}
```

Chapter 8: Discovering the Collections Framework

1. A *collection* is a group of objects that are stored in an instance of a class designed for this purpose.

2. The *collections framework* is a standardized architecture for representing and manipulating collections.

3. The collections framework largely consists of core interfaces, implementation classes, and utility classes.

4. A *comparable* is an object whose class implements the Comparable interface.

5. You would have a class implement the Comparable interface when you want objects to be compared according to their *natural ordering*.

6. A *comparator* is an object whose class implements the Comparator interface. Its purpose is to allow objects to be compared according to an order that is different from their natural ordering.

7. The answer is false: a collection uses a *comparable* (an object whose class implements the Comparable interface) to define the natural ordering of its elements.

8. The Iterable interface describes any object that can return its contained objects in some sequence.

9. The Collection interface represents a collection of objects that are known as *elements*.

10. A situation where Collection's add() method would throw an instance of the UnsupportedOperationException class is an attempt to add an element to an unmodifiable collection.

11. Iterable's iterator() method returns an instance of a class that implements the Iterator interface. This interface provides a hasNext() method to determine if the end of the iteration has been reached, a next() method to return a collection's next element, and a remove() method to remove the last element returned by next() from the collection.

12. The purpose of the enhanced for loop statement is to simplify collection or array iteration.

13. The enhanced for loop statement is expressed as for (*type id*: *collection*) or for (*type id*: *array*) and reads "for each *type* object in *collection*, assign this object to *id* at the start of the loop iteration" or "for each *type* object in *array*, assign this object to *id* at the start of the loop iteration."

14. The answer is true: the enhanced for loop works with arrays. For example, int [] x = { 1, 2, 3 }; for (int i: x) System.out.println(i); declares array x and outputs all of its int-based elements.

15. *Autoboxing* is the act of wrapping a primitive value in an object of a primitive wrapper class type whenever a primitive type is specified but a reference is required. This feature saves the developer from having to explicitly instantiate a wrapper class when storing the primitive value in a collection.

16. *Unboxing* is the act of unwrapping a primitive value from its wrapper object whenever a reference is specified but a primitive type is required. This feature saves the developer from having to explicitly call a method on the object (such as intValue()) to retrieve the wrapped value.

17. A *list* is an ordered collection, which is also known as a *sequence*. Elements can be stored in and accessed from specific locations via integer indexes.

18. A ListIterator instance uses a *cursor* to navigate through a list.

19. A *view* is a list that is backed by another list. Changes that are made to the view are reflected in this backing list.

20. You would use the subList() method to perform *range-view* operations over a collection in a compact manner. For example, list.subList(fromIndex, toIndex).clear(); removes a range of elements from list where the first element is located at fromIndex and the last element is located at toIndex-1.

21. The ArrayList class provides a list implementation that is based on an internal array.

22. The LinkedList class provides a list implementation that is based on linked nodes.

23. A *node* is a fixed sequence of value and link memory locations.

24. The answer is false: ArrayList provides slower element insertions and deletions than LinkedList.

25. A *set* is a collection that contains no duplicate elements.

26. The TreeSet class provides a set implementation that is based on a tree data structure. As a result, elements are stored in sorted order.

27. The HashSet class provides a set implementation that is backed by a hashtable data structure.

28. The answer is true: to avoid duplicate elements in a hashset, your own classes must correctly override equals() and hashCode().

29. The difference between HashSet and LinkedHashSet is that LinkedHashSet uses a linked list to store its elements, resulting in its iterator returning elements in the order in which they were inserted.

30. The EnumSet class provides a Set implementation that is based on a bitset.

31. A *sorted set* is a set that maintains its elements in ascending order, sorted according to their natural ordering or according to a comparator that is supplied when the sorted set is created. Furthermore, the set's implementation class must implement the SortedSet interface.

32. The answer is false: HashSet is not an example of a sorted set. However, TreeSet is an example of a sorted set.

33. A sorted set's add() method would throw ClassCastException when you attempt to add an element to the sorted set because the element's class does not implement Comparable.

34. A *queue* is a collection in which elements are stored and retrieved in a specific order. Most queues are categorized as "first-in, first out," "last-in, first-out," or priority.

35. The answer is true: Queue's element() method throws NoSuchElementException when it is called on an empty queue.

36. The PriorityQueue class provides an implementation of a *priority queue*, which is a queue that orders its elements according to their natural ordering or by a comparator provided when the queue is instantiated.

37. A *map* is a group of key/value pairs (also known as *entries*).

38. The TreeMap class provides a map implementation that is based on a red-black tree. As a result, entries are stored in sorted order of their keys.

39. The HashMap class provides a map implementation that is based on a hashtable data structure.

40. A hashtable uses a *hash function* to map keys to integer values.

41. Continuing from the previous exercise, the resulting integer values are known as *hash codes*; they identify hashtable array elements, which are known as *buckets* or *slots*.

42. A hashtable's *capacity* refers to the number of buckets.

43. A hashtable's *load factor* refers to the ratio of the number of stored entries divided by the number of buckets.

44. The difference between HashMap and LinkedHashMap is that LinkedHashMap uses a linked list to store its entries, resulting in its iterator returning entries in the order in which they were inserted.

45. The IdentityHashMap class provides a Map implementation that uses reference equality (==) instead of object equality (equals()) when comparing keys and values.

46. The WeakHashMap class provides a Map implementation that is based on weakly reachable keys.

47. The EnumMap class provides a Map implementation whose keys are the members of the same enum.

48. A *sorted map* is a map that maintains its entries in ascending order, sorted according to the keys' natural ordering or according to a comparator that is supplied when the sorted map is created. Furthermore, the map's implementation class must implement the SortedMap interface.

49. The answer is true: TreeMap is an example of a sorted map.

50. The purpose of the Arrays class's static <T> List<T> asList(T... array) method is to return a fixed-size list backed by the specified array. (Changes to the returned list "write through" to the array.)

51. The answer is false: binary search is faster than linear search.

52. You would use Collections' static <T> Set<T> synchronizedSet(Set<T> s) method to return a synchronized variation of a hashset.

53. The seven legacy collections-oriented types are Vector, Enumeration, Stack, Dictionary, Hashtable, Properties, and BitSet.

54. Listing 36 presents the JavaQuiz application's JavaQuiz source file that was called for in Chapter 8.

Listing 36. *How much do you know about Java? Take the quiz and find out!*

```
public class JavaQuiz
{
   static QuizEntry[] quizEntries =
   {
      new QuizEntry("What was Java's original name?",
                    new String[] { "Oak", "Duke", "J", "None of the above" },
                    'A'),
      new QuizEntry("Which of the following reserved words is also a literal?",
                    new String[] { "for", "long", "true", "enum" },
                    'C'),
      new QuizEntry("The conditional operator (?:) resembles which statement?",
                    new String[] { "switch", "if-else", "if", "while" },
                    'B')
   };
   public static void main(String[] args)
```

```
    {
        // Populate the quiz list.
        List<QuizEntry> quiz = new ArrayList<QuizEntry>();
        for (QuizEntry entry: quizEntries)
            quiz.add(entry);
        // Perform the quiz.
        System.out.println("Java Quiz");
        System.out.println("---------\n");
        Iterator<QuizEntry> iter = quiz.iterator();
        while (iter.hasNext())
        {
            QuizEntry qe = iter.next();
            System.out.println(qe.getQuestion());
            String[] choices = qe.getChoices();
            for (int i = 0; i < choices.length; i++)
                System.out.println("   " + (char) ('A'+i) + ": " + choices[i]);
            int choice = -1;
            while (choice < 'A' || choice > 'A'+choices.length)
            {
                System.out.print("Enter choice letter: ");
                try
                {
                    choice = System.in.read();
                    // Remove trailing characters up to and including the newline
                    // to avoid having these characters automatically returned in
                    // subsequent System.in.read() method calls.
                    while (System.in.read() != '\n');
                    choice = Character.toUpperCase((char) choice);
                }
                catch (java.io.IOException ioe)
                {
                }
            }
            if (choice == qe.getAnswer())
                System.out.println("You are correct!\n");
            else
                System.out.println("You are not correct!\n");
        }
    }
}
```

JavaQuiz first creates a list of quiz entries. In a more sophisticated application, I would obtain quiz data from a database and dynamically create the entries. JavaQuiz then performs the quiz with the help of iterator() and its returned Iterator instance's hasNext() and next() methods.

Listing 37 reveals the companion QuizEntry class.

Listing 37. *A helper class for storing a quiz's data*

```
class QuizEntry
{
    private String question;
    private String[] choices;
    private char answer;
    QuizEntry(String question, String[] choices, char answer)
    {
```

```
        this.question = question;
        this.choices = choices;
        this.answer = answer;
    }
    String[] getChoices()
    {
        // Demonstrate returning a copy of the choices array to prevent clients
        // from directly manipulating (and possibly screwing up) the internal
        // choices array.
        String[] temp = new String[choices.length];
        System.arraycopy(choices, 0, temp, 0, choices.length);
        return temp;
    }
    String getQuestion()
    {
        return question;
    }
    char getAnswer()
    {
        return answer;
    }
}
```

QuizEntry is a reusable class that stores quiz data. I did not nest QuizEntry in JavaQuiz because QuizEntry is useful for all kinds of quizzes. However, I made this class package-private by not declaring QuizEntry to be a public class because it is a helper class to a quiz's main class (such as JavaQuiz).

55. (int) (f^(f>>>32)) is used instead of (int) (f^(f>>32)) in the hash code generation algorithm because >>> always shifts a 0 to the right, which does not affect the hash code, whereas >> shifts a 0 or a 1 to the right, which affects the hash code when a 1 is shifted.

56. Listing 38 presents the FrequencyDemo application that was called for in Chapter 8.

Listing 38. *Reporting the frequency of last command-line argument occurrences in the previous command-line arguments*

```
import java.util.LinkedList;
import java.util.Collections;
import java.util.List;

public class FrequencyDemo
{
    public static void main(String[] args)
    {
        List<String> listOfArgs = new LinkedList<String>();
        String lastArg = (args.length == 0) ? null : args[args.length-1];
        for (int i = 0; i < args.length-1; i++)
            listOfArgs.add(args[i]);
        System.out.println("Number of occurrences of " + lastArg + " = " +
                           Collections.frequency(listOfArgs, lastArg));
    }
}
```

Chapter 9: Discovering Additional Utility APIs

1. A *task* is an object whose class implements the `Runnable` interface (a runnable task) or the `Callable` interface (a callable task).

2. An *executor* is an object whose class directly or indirectly implements the `Executor` interface, which decouples task submission from task-execution mechanics.

3. The `Executor` interface focuses exclusively on `Runnable`, which means that there is no convenient way for a runnable task to return a value to its caller (because `Runnable`'s `run()` method does not return a value); `Executor` does not provide a way to track the progress of executing runnable tasks, cancel an executing runnable task, or determine when the runnable task finishes execution; `Executor` cannot execute a collection of runnable tasks; and `Executor` does not provide a way for an application to shut down an executor (much less to properly shut down an executor).

4. `Executor`'s limitations are overcome by providing the `ExecutorService` interface.

5. The differences existing between `Runnable`'s `run()` method and `Callable`'s `call()` method are as follows: `run()` cannot return a value whereas `call()` can return a value, and `run()` cannot throw checked exceptions whereas `call()` can throw checked exceptions.

6. The answer is false: you can throw checked and unchecked exceptions from `Callable`'s `call()` method but can only throw unchecked exceptions from `Runnable`'s `run()` method.

7. A *future* is an object whose class implements the `Future` interface. It represents an asynchronous computation and provides methods for cancelling a task, for returning a task's value, and for determining whether or not the task has finished.

8. The `Executors` class's `newFixedThreadPool()` method creates a thread pool that reuses a fixed number of threads operating off of a shared unbounded queue. At most, `nThreads` threads are actively processing tasks. If additional tasks are submitted when all threads are active, they wait in the queue for an available thread. If any thread terminates because of a failure during execution before the executor shuts down, a new thread will take its place when needed to execute subsequent tasks. The threads in the pool will exist until the executor is explicitly shut down.

9. A *synchronizer* is a class that facilitates a common form of synchronization.

10. Four commonly used synchronizers are countdown latches, cyclic barriers, exchangers, and semaphores. A *countdown latch* lets one or more threads wait at a "gate" until another thread opens this gate, at which point these other threads can continue. A *cyclic barrier* lets a group of threads wait for each other to reach a common barrier point. An *exchanger* lets a pair of threads exchange objects at a synchronization point. A *semaphore* maintains a set of permits for restricting the number of threads that can access a limited resource.

11. The concurrency-oriented extensions to the collections framework provided by the concurrency utilities are BlockingQueue (a subinterface of java.util.Queue that describes a first-in, first-out data structure, and provides additional operations that wait for the queue to become nonempty when retrieving an element, and wait for space to become available in the queue when storing an element); the ArrayBlockingQueue, LinkedBlockingQueue, PriorityBlockingQueue, and SynchronousQueue classes that implement BlockingQueue; ConcurrentMap (a subinterface of java.util.Map that declares additional atomic putIfAbsent(), remove(), and replace() methods); the ConcurrentHashMap class that implements ConcurrentMap; and the ConcurrentLinkedQueue class (an unbounded thread-safe FIFO implementation of the Queue interface).

12. A *lock* is an instance of a class that implements the Lock interface, which provides more extensive locking operations than can be achieved via the synchronized reserved word. Lock also supports a wait/notification mechanism through associated Condition objects.

13. The biggest advantage that Lock objects hold over the implicit locks that are obtained when threads enter critical sections (controlled via the synchronized reserved word) is their ability to back out of an attempt to acquire a lock.

14. An *atomic variable* is an instance of a class that encapsulates a single variable, and supports lock-free, thread-safe operations on that variable; for example, AtomicInteger.

15. *Internationalization* is the process of creating an application that automatically adapts to its current user's culture so that the user can read the application's text, hear audio clips in the user's language (if audio is supported), and so on. This word is commonly abbreviated to *i18n*, with 18 representing the number of letters between the initial *i* and the final *n*.

16. A *locale* is a geographical, political, or a cultural region.

17. The components of a Locale object are a language code, an optional country code, and an optional variant code.

18. A *resource bundle* is a container that holds one or more locale-specific elements, and which is associated with one and only one locale.

19. The answer is true: if a property resource bundle and a list resource bundle have the same complete resource bundle name, the list resource bundle takes precedence over the property resource bundle.

20. A *break iterator* is an object that detects logical boundaries within a section of text.

21. The Break Iterator API supports character, word, sentence, and line break iterators.

22. The answer is false: you cannot pass any Locale object to any of BreakIterator's factory methods that take Locale arguments. Instead, you can only pass Locale objects for locales that are identified by BreakIterator's getAvailableLocales() method.

23. A *collator* is a Collator instance that performs locale-specific comparisons for sorting purposes. For example, a Collator for the fr_FR locale takes into account accented characters by first comparing words as if none of the characters contain accents, and then comparing equal words from right to left for accents.

24. A *date* is a recorded temporal moment, a *time zone* is a set of geographical regions that share a common number of hours relative to Greenwich Mean Time (GMT), and a *calendar* is a system of organizing the passage of time.

25. The answer is true: Date instances can represent dates prior to or after the Unix epoch.

26. You would obtain a TimeZone object that represents Central Standard Time by calling TimeZone's static TimeZone getTimeZone(String ID) factory method with argument "CST".

27. Assuming that cal identifies a Calendar instance and locale identifies a specific locale, you would obtain a localized name for the month represented by cal by calling cal.getDisplayName(Calendar.MONTH, Calendar.LONG, locale) to return the long form of the month name, or by calling cal.getDisplayName(Calendar.MONTH, Calendar.SHORT, locale) to return the short form of the month name.

28. A *formatter* is an instance of a class that subclasses Format.

29. NumberFormat returns formatters that format numbers as currencies, integers, numbers with decimal points, and percentages (and also to parse such values).

30. The answer is false: DateFormat's getInstance() factory method is a shortcut to obtaining a default date/time formatter that uses the SHORT style for both the date and the time.

31. A *message formatter* lets you convert a *compound message pattern* (a template consisting of static text and brace-delimited placeholders) along with the variable data required by the pattern's placeholders into a localized message.

32. A *preference* is a configuration item.

33. The Properties API is problematic for persisting preferences because properties files tend to grow in size and the probability of name collisions among the various keys increases; a growing application tends to acquire numerous properties files with each part of the application associated with its own properties file (and the names and locations of these properties files must be hard-coded in the application's source code); someone could directly modify these text-based properties files (perhaps inserting gibberish) and cause the application that depends upon the modified properties file to crash unless it is properly coded to deal with this possibility; and properties files cannot be used on diskless computing platforms.

34. The Preferences API persists preferences by storing them in platform-specific storage facilities (such as the Windows registry). Preferences are stored in trees of nodes, which are the analogue of a hierarchical filesystem's directories. Also, preference name/value pairs stored under these nodes are the analogues of a directory's files. There are two kinds of trees: system and user. All users share the *system preference tree*, whereas the *user preference tree* is specific to a single user, which is generally the person who logged into the underlying operating system.

35. Instances of the `Random` class generate sequences of random numbers by starting with a special 48-bit value that is known as a *seed*. This value is subsequently modified by a mathematical algorithm, which is known as a *linear congruential generator*.

36. A *regular expression* (also known as a *regex* or *regexp*) is a string-based pattern that represents the set of strings that match this pattern.

37. Instances of the `Pattern` class represent patterns via compiled regexes. Regexes are compiled for performance reasons; pattern matching via compiled regexes is much faster than if the regexes were not compiled.

38. `Pattern`'s `compile()` methods throw instances of the `PatternSyntaxException` class when they discover illegal syntax in their regular expression arguments.

39. Instances of the `Matcher` class attempt to match compiled regexes against input text.

40. The difference between `Matcher`'s `matches()` and `lookingAt()` methods is that, unlike `matches()`, `lookingAt()` does not require the entire region to be matched.

41. A *character class* is a set of characters appearing between [and].

42. There are six kinds of character classes: simple, negation, range, union, intersection, and subtraction.

43. A *capturing group* saves a match's characters for later recall during pattern matching.

44. A *zero-length match* is a match of zero length in which the start and end indexes are equal.

45. A *quantifier* is a numeric value implicitly or explicitly bound to a pattern. Quantifiers are categorized as greedy, reluctant, or possessive.

46. The difference between a greedy quantifier and a reluctant quantifier is that a greedy quantifier attempts to find the longest match, whereas a reluctant quantifier attempts to find the shortest match.

47. Possessive and greedy quantifiers differ in that a possessive quantifier only makes one attempt to find the longest match, whereas a greedy quantifier can make multiple attempts.

48. Listing 39 presents the `SpanishCollation` application that was called for in Chapter 9.

Listing 39. *Outputting Spanish words according to this language's current collation rules followed by its traditional collation rules*

```java
import java.text.Collator;
import java.text.ParseException;
import java.text.RuleBasedCollator;

import java.util.Arrays;
import java.util.Locale;

public class SpanishCollation
{
    public static void main(String[] args)
    {
        String[] words =
        {
            "ñango",   // weak
            "llamado", // called
            "lunes",   // monday
            "champán", // champagne
            "clamor",  // outcry
            "cerca",   // near
            "nombre",  // name
            "chiste",  // joke
        };
        Locale locale = new Locale("es", "");
        Collator c = Collator.getInstance(locale);
        Arrays.sort(words, c);
        for (String word: words)
            System.out.println(word);
        System.out.println();
        // Define the traditional Spanish sort rules.
```

```java
String upperNTilde = new String ("\u00D1");
String lowerNTilde = new String ("\u00F1");
String spanishRules = "< a,A < b,B < c,C < ch, cH, Ch, CH < d,D < e,E " +
                      "< f,F < g,G < h,H < i,I < j,J < k,K < l,L < ll, " +
                      "lL, Ll, LL < m,M < n,N < " + lowerNTilde + "," +
                      upperNTilde + " < o,O < p,P < q,Q < r,R < s,S < " +
                      "t,T < u,U < v,V < w,W < x,X < y,Y < z,Z";

try
{
    c = new RuleBasedCollator(spanishRules);
    Arrays.sort(words, c);
    for (String word: words)
        System.out.println(word);
}
catch (ParseException pe)
{
    System.err.println(pe);
}
    }
}
```

49. Listing 40 presents the RearrangeText application that was called for in Chapter 9.

Listing 40. *Rearranging a single text argument of the form x, y into the form y x*

```java
import java.util.regex.Matcher;
import java.util.regex.Pattern;
import java.util.regex.PatternSyntaxException;

public class RearrangeText
{
    public static void main(String[] args)
    {
        if (args.length != 1)
        {
            System.err.println("usage: java RearrangeText text");
            return;
        }
        try
        {
            Pattern p = Pattern.compile("(.*), (.*)");
            Matcher m = p.matcher(args[0]);
            if (m.matches())
                System.out.println(m.group(2)+" " + m.group(1));
        }
        catch (PatternSyntaxException pse)
        {
            System.err.println(pse);
        }
    }
}
```

50. Listing 41 presents the ReplaceText application that was called for in Chapter 9.

Listing 41. *Replacing all matches of the pattern with replacement text*

```java
import java.util.regex.Matcher;
import java.util.regex.Pattern;
import java.util.regex.PatternSyntaxException;
```

```
public class ReplaceText
{
    public static void main(String[] args)
    {
        if (args.length != 3)
        {
            System.err.println("usage: java ReplaceText text oldText newText");
            return;
        }
        try
        {
            Pattern p = Pattern.compile(args[1]);
            Matcher m = p.matcher(args[0]);
            String result = m.replaceAll(args[2]);
            System.out.println(result);
        }
        catch (PatternSyntaxException pse)
        {
            System.err.println(pse);
        }
    }
}
```

Chapter 10: Performing I/O

1. The purpose of the `File` class is to offer access to the underlying platform's available filesystem(s).

2. Instances of the `File` class contain the pathnames of files and directories that may or may not exist in their filesystems.

3. `File`'s `listRoots()` method returns an array of `File` objects denoting the root directories (roots) of available filesystems.

4. A *path* is a hierarchy of directories that must be traversed to locate a file or a directory. A *pathname* is a string representation of a path; a platform-dependent *separator character* (such as the Windows backslash [\] character) appears between consecutive names.

5. The difference between an absolute pathname and a relative pathname is as follows: an *absolute pathname* is a pathname that starts with the root directory symbol, whereas a *relative pathname* is a pathname that does not start with the root directory symbol; it is interpreted via information taken from some other pathname.

6. You obtain the current user (also known as working) directory by specifying `System.getProperty("user.dir")`.

7. A *parent pathname* is a string that consists of all pathname components except for the last name.

8. *Normalize* means to replace separator characters with the default name-separator character so that the pathname is compliant with the underlying filesystem.

9. You obtain the default name-separator character by accessing File's separator and separatorChar static fields. The first field stores the character as a char and the second field stores it as a String.

10. A *canonical pathname* is a pathname that is absolute and unique.

11. The difference between File's getParent() and getName() methods is that getParent() returns the parent pathname and getName() returns the last name in the pathname's name sequence.

12. The answer is false: File's exists() method determines whether or not a file or directory exists.

13. A *normal file* is a file that is not a directory and satisfies other platform-dependent criteria: it is not a symbolic link or named pipe, for example. Any nondirectory file created by a Java application is guaranteed to be a normal file.

14. File's lastModified() method returns the time that the file denoted by this File object's pathname was last modified, or 0 when the file does not exist or an I/O error occurred during this method call. The returned value is measured in milliseconds since the Unix epoch (00:00:00 GMT, January 1, 1970).

15. The answer is true: File's list() method returns an array of Strings where each entry is a filename rather than a complete path.

16. The difference between the FilenameFilter and FileFilter interfaces is as follows: FilenameFilter declares a single boolean accept(File dir, String name) method, whereas FileFilter declares a single boolean accept(String pathname) method. Either method accomplishes the same task of accepting (by returning true) or rejecting (by returning false) the inclusion of the file or directory identified by the argument(s) in a directory listing.

17. The answer is false: File's createNewFile() method checks for file existence and creates the file if it does not exist in a single operation that is atomic with respect to all other filesystem activities that might affect the file.

18. The default temporary directory where File's createTempFile(String, String) method creates temporary files can be located by reading the java.io.tmpdir system property.

19. You ensure that a temporary file is removed when the virtual machine ends normally (it does not crash or the power is not lost) by registering the temporary file for deletion through a call to File's deleteOnExit() method.

20. You would accurately compare two `File` objects by first calling `File`'s `getCanonicalFile()` method on each `File` object and then comparing the returned `File` objects.

21. The purpose of the `RandomAccessFile` class is to create and/or open files for *random access* in which a mixture of write and read operations can occur until the file is closed.

22. The purpose of the `"rwd"` and `"rws"` mode arguments is to ensure than any writes to a file located on a local storage device are written to the device, which guarantees that critical data is not lost when the system crashes. No guarantee is made when the file does not reside on a local device.

23. A *file pointer* is a cursor that identifies the location of the next byte to write or read. When an existing file is opened, the file pointer is set to its first byte, at offset 0. The file pointer is also set to 0 when the file is created.

24. The answer is false: when you call `RandomAccessFile`'s `seek(long)` method to set the file pointer's value, and if this value is greater than the length of the file, the file's length does not change. The file length will only change by writing after the offset has been set beyond the end of the file.

25. A *flat file database* is a single file organized into records and fields. A *record* stores a single entry (such as a part in a parts database) and a *field* stores a single attribute of the entry (such as a part number).

26. A *stream* is an ordered sequence of bytes of arbitrary length. Bytes flow over an *output stream* from an application to a destination, and flow over an *input stream* from a source to an application.

27. The purpose of `OutputStream`'s `flush()` method is to write any buffered output bytes to the destination. If the intended destination of this output stream is an abstraction provided by the underlying platform (for example, a file), flushing the stream only guarantees that bytes previously written to the stream are passed to the underlying platform for writing; it does not guarantee that they are actually written to a physical device such as a disk drive.

28. The answer is true: `OutputStream`'s `close()` method automatically flushes the output stream. If an application ends before `close()` is called, the output stream is automatically closed and its data is flushed.

29. The purpose of `InputStream`'s `mark(int)` and `reset()` methods is to reread a portion of a stream. `mark(int)` marks the current position in this input stream. A subsequent call to `reset()` repositions this stream to the last marked position so that subsequent read operations reread the same bytes. Do not forget to call `markSupported()` to find out if the subclass supports `mark()` and `reset()`.

30. You would access a copy of a `ByteArrayOutputStream` instance's internal byte array by calling `ByteArrayOutputStream`'s `toByteArray()` method.

31. The answer is false: `FileOutputStream` and `FileInputStream` do not provide internal buffers to improve the performance of write and read operations.

32. You would use `PipedOutputStream` and `PipedInputStream` to communicate data between a pair of executing threads.

33. A *filter stream* is a stream that buffers, compresses/uncompresses, encrypts/decrypts, or otherwise manipulates an input stream's byte sequence before it reaches its destination.

34. Two streams are chained together when a stream instance is passed to another stream class's constructor.

35. You improve the performance of a file output stream by chaining a `BufferedOutputStream` instance to a `FileOutputStream` instance and calling the `BufferedOutputStream` instance's `write()` methods so that data is buffered before flowing to the file output stream. You improve the performance of a file input stream by chaining a `BufferedInputStream` instance to a `FileInputStream` instance so that data flowing from a file input stream is buffered before being returned from the `BufferedInputStream` instance by calling this instance's `read()` methods.

36. `DataOutputStream` and `DataInputStream` support `FileOutputStream` and `FileInputStream` by providing methods to write and read primitive type values and strings in a platform-independent way. In contrast, `FileOutputStream` and `FileInputStream` provide methods for writing/reading bytes and arrays of bytes only.

37. *Object serialization* is a virtual machine mechanism for *serializing* object state into a stream of bytes. Its *deserialization* counterpart is a virtual machine mechanism for *deserializing* this state from a byte stream.

38. The three forms of serialization and deserialization that Java supports are default serialization and deserialization, custom serialization and deserialization, and externalization.

39. The purpose of the `Serializable` interface is to tell the virtual machine that it is okay to serialize objects of the implementing class.

40. When the serialization mechanism encounters an object whose class does not implement `Serializable`, it throws an instance of the `NotSerializableException` class.

41. The three stated reasons for Java not supporting unlimited serialization are as follows: security, performance, and objects not amenable to serialization.

42. You initiate serialization by creating an `ObjectOutputStream` instance and calling its `writeObject()` method. You initialize deserialization by creating an `ObjectInputStream` instance and calling its `readObject()` method.

43. The answer is false: class fields are not automatically serialized.

44. The purpose of the `transient` reserved word is to mark instance fields that do not participate in default serialization and default deserialization.

45. The deserialization mechanism causes `readObject()` to throw an instance of the `InvalidClassException` class when it attempts to deserialize an object whose class has changed.

46. The deserialization mechanism detects that a serialized object's class has changed as follows: Every serialized object has an identifier. The deserialization mechanism compares the identifier of the object being deserialized with the serialized identifier of its class (all serializable classes are automatically given unique identifiers unless they explicitly specify their own identifiers) and causes `InvalidClassException` to be thrown when it detects a mismatch.

47. You can add an instance field to a class and avoid trouble when deserializing an object that was serialized before the instance field was added by introducing a `long serialVersionUID = ` *long integer value*`;` declaration into the class. The *long integer value* must be unique and is known as a *stream unique identifier (SUID)*. You can use the JDK's `serialver` tool to help with this task.

48. You customize the default serialization and deserialization mechanisms without using externalization by declaring private void `writeObject(ObjectOutputStream)` and void `readObject(ObjectInputStream)` methods in the class.

49. You tell the serialization and deserialization mechanisms to serialize or deserialize the object's normal state before serializing or deserializing additional data items by first calling `ObjectOutputStream`'s `defaultWriteObject()` method in `writeObject(ObjectOutputStream)` and by first calling `ObjectInputStream`'s `defaultReadObject()` method in `readObject(ObjectInputStream)`.

50. Externalization differs from default and custom serialization and deserialization in that it offers complete control over the serialization and deserialization tasks.

51. A class indicates that it supports externalization by implementing the `Externalizable` interface instead of `Serializable`, and by declaring void `writeExternal(ObjectOutput)` and void `readExternal(ObjectInput in)` methods instead of void `writeObject(ObjectOutputStream)` and void `readObject(ObjectInputStream)` methods.

52. The answer is true: during externalization, the deserialization mechanism throws `InvalidClassException` with a "no valid constructor" message when it does not detect a public noargument constructor.

53. The difference between PrintStream's print() and println() methods is that the print() methods do not append a line terminator to their output, whereas the println() methods append a line terminator.

54. PrintStream's noargument void println() method outputs the line.separator system property's value to ensure that lines are terminated in a portable manner (such as a carriage return followed by a newline/line feed on Windows, or only a newline/line feed on Unix/Linux).

55. The answer is true: PrintStream's %tR format specifier is used to format a Calendar object's time as HH:MM.

56. Java's stream classes are not good at streaming characters because bytes and characters are two different things: a byte represents an 8-bit data item and a character represents a 16-bit data item. Also, byte streams have no knowledge of character sets and their character encodings.

57. Java provides writer and reader classes as the preferred alternative to stream classes when it comes to character I/O.

58. The answer is false: Reader does not declare an available() method.

59. The purpose of the OutputStreamWriter class is to serve as a bridge between an incoming sequence of characters and an outgoing stream of bytes. Characters written to this writer are encoded into bytes according to the default or specified character encoding. The purpose of the InputStreamReader class is to serve as a bridge between an incoming stream of bytes and an outgoing sequence of characters. Characters read from this reader are decoded from bytes according to the default or specified character encoding.

60. You identify the default character encoding by reading the value of the file.encoding system property.

61. The purpose of the FileWriter class is to conveniently connect to the underlying file output stream using the default character encoding. The purpose of the FileReader class is to conveniently connect to the underlying file input stream using the default character encoding.

62. Listing 42 presents the Touch application that was called for in Chapter 10.

Listing 42. *Setting a file or directory's timestamp to the current or specified time*

```
import java.io.File;

import java.text.ParseException;
import java.text.SimpleDateFormat;

import java.util.Date;

public class Touch
{
```

```java
public static void main(String[] args)
{
   if (args.length != 1 && args.length != 3)
   {
      System.err.println("usage: java Touch [-d timestamp] pathname");
      return;
   }
   long time = new Date().getTime();
   if (args.length == 3)
   {
      if (args[0].equals("-d"))
      {
         try
         {
            SimpleDateFormat sdf;
            sdf = new SimpleDateFormat("yyyy-MM-dd HH:mm:ss z");
            Date date = sdf.parse(args[1]);
            time = date.getTime();
         }
         catch (ParseException pe)
         {
            pe.printStackTrace();
         }
      }
      else
      {
         System.err.println("invalid option: " + args[0]);
         return;
      }
   }
   new File(args[args.length == 1 ? 0 : 2]).setLastModified(time);
}
}
```

63. Listing 43 presents the `Media` class that was called for in Chapter 10.

Listing 43. *Obtaining the data from an MP3 file's 128-byte ID3 block, and creating/populating/returning an ID3 object with this data*

```java
import java.io.IOException;
import java.io.RandomAccessFile;

public class Media
{
   public static class ID3
   {
      private String songTitle, artist, album, year, comment, genre;
      private int track; // -1 if track not present
      public ID3(String songTitle, String artist, String album, String year,
                 String comment, int track, String genre)
      {
         this.songTitle = songTitle;
         this.artist = artist;
         this.album = album;
         this.year = year;
         this.comment = comment;
         this.track = track;
         this.genre = genre;
```

```java
        }
        String getSongTitle() { return songTitle; }
        String getArtist() { return artist; }
        String getAlbum() { return album; }
        String getYear() { return year; }
        String getComment() { return comment; }
        int getTrack() { return track; }
        String getGenre() { return genre; }
    }
    public static ID3 getID3Info(String mp3path) throws IOException
    {
        RandomAccessFile raf = null;
        try
        {
            raf = new RandomAccessFile(mp3path, "r");
            if (raf.length() < 128)
                return null; // Not MP3 file (way too small)
            raf.seek(raf.length()-128);
            byte[] buffer = new byte[128];
            raf.read(buffer);
            raf.close();
            if (buffer[0] != (byte) 'T' && buffer[1] != (byte) 'A' &&
                buffer[2] != (byte) 'G')
                return null; // No ID3 block (must start with TAG)
            String songTitle = new String(buffer, 3, 30);
            String artist = new String(buffer, 33, 30);
            String album = new String(buffer, 63, 30);
            String year = new String(buffer, 93, 4);
            String comment = new String(buffer, 97, 28);
            // buffer[126]&255 converts -128 through 127 to 0 through 255
            int track = (buffer[125] == 0) ? buffer[126]&255 : -1;
            String[] genres = new String[]
                                {
                                    "Blues",
                                    "Classic Rock",
                                    "Country",
                                    "Dance",
                                    "Disco",
                                    "Funk",
                                    "Grunge",
                                    "Hip-Hop",
                                    "Jazz",
                                    "Metal",
                                    "New Age",
                                    "Oldies",
                                    "Other",
                                    "Pop",
                                    "R&B",
                                    "Rap",
                                    "Reggae",
                                    "Rock",
                                    "Techno",
                                    "Industrial",
                                    "Alternative",
                                    "Ska",
                                    "Death Metal",
                                    "Pranks",
```

```
                "Soundtrack",
                "Euro-Techno",
                "Ambient",
                "Trip-Hop",
                "Vocal",
                "Jazz+Funk",
                "Fusion",
                "Trance",
                "Classical",
                "Instrumental",
                "Acid",
                "House",
                "Game",
                "Sound Clip",
                "Gospel",
                "Noise",
                "AlternRock",
                "Bass",
                "Soul",
                "Punk",
                "Space",
                "Meditative",
                "Instrumental Pop",
                "Instrumental Rock",
                "Ethnic",
                "Gothic",
                "Darkwave",
                "Techno-Industrial",
                "Electronic",
                "Pop-Folk",
                "Eurodance",
                "Dream",
                "Southern Rock",
                "Comedy",
                "Cult",
                "Gangsta",
                "Top 40",
                "Christian Rap",
                "Pop/Funk",
                "Jungle",
                "Native American",
                "Cabaret",
                "New Wave",
                "Psychedelic",
                "Rave",
                "Showtunes",
                "Trailer",
                "Lo-Fi",
                "Tribal",
                "Acid Punk",
                "Acid Jazz",
                "Polka",
                "Retro",
                "Musical",
                "Rock & Roll",
                "Hard Rock",
                "Folk",
```

```
                              "Folk-Rock",
                              "National-Folk",
                              "Swing",
                              "Fast Fusion",
                              "Bebob",
                              "Latin",
                              "Revival",
                              "Celtic",
                              "Bluegrass",
                              "Avantegarde",
                              "Gothic Rock",
                              "Progressive Rock",
                              "Psychedelic Rock",
                              "Symphonic Rock",
                              "Slow Rock",
                              "Big Band",
                              "Chorus",
                              "Easy Listening",
                              "Acoustic",
                              "Humour",
                              "Speech",
                              "Chanson",
                              "Opera",
                              "Chamber Music",
                              "Sonata",
                              "Symphony",
                              "Booty Brass",
                              "Primus",
                              "Porn Groove",
                              "Satire",
                              "Slow Jam",
                              "Club",
                              "Tango",
                              "Samba",
                              "Folklore",
                              "Ballad",
                              "Power Ballad",
                              "Rhythmic Soul",
                              "Freestyle",
                              "Duet",
                              "Punk Rock",
                              "Drum Solo",
                              "A cappella",
                              "Euro-House",
                              "Dance Hall"
                          };
        assert genres.length == 126;
        String genre = (buffer[127] < 0 || buffer[127] > 125)
                        ? "Unknown" : genres[buffer[127]];
        return new ID3(songTitle, artist, album, year, comment, track, genre);
    }
    catch (IOException ioe)
    {
        if (raf != null)
            try
            {
                raf.close();
```

```
            }
            catch (IOException ioe2)
            {
                ioe2.printStackTrace();
            }
            throw ioe;
        }
    }
}
```

64. Listing 44 presents the `Split` application that was called for in Chapter 10.

Listing 44. *Splitting a large file into numerous smaller part files*

```java
import java.io.BufferedInputStream;
import java.io.BufferedOutputStream;
import java.io.File;
import java.io.FileInputStream;
import java.io.FileOutputStream;
import java.io.IOException;

public class Split
{
    static final int FILESIZE = 1400000;
    static byte[] buffer = new byte[FILESIZE];
    public static void main(String[] args)
    {
        if (args.length != 1)
        {
            System.err.println("usage: java Split pathname");
            return;
        }
        File file = new File(args[0]);
        long length = file.length();
        int nWholeParts = (int) (length/FILESIZE);
        int remainder = (int) (length%FILESIZE);
        System.out.printf("Splitting %s into %d parts%n", args[0],
                        (remainder == 0) ? nWholeParts : nWholeParts+1);
        BufferedInputStream bis = null;
        BufferedOutputStream bos = null;
        try
        {
            FileInputStream fis = new FileInputStream(args[0]);
            bis = new BufferedInputStream(fis);
            for (int i = 0; i < nWholeParts; i++)
            {
                bis.read(buffer);
                System.out.println("Writing part " + i);
                FileOutputStream fos = new FileOutputStream("part" + i);
                bos = new BufferedOutputStream(fos);
                bos.write(buffer);
                bos.close();
                bos = null;
            }
            if (remainder != 0)
            {
                int br = fis.read(buffer);
                if (br != remainder)
```

```
            {
                System.err.println("Last part mismatch: expected " + remainder
                                   + " bytes");
                System.exit(0);
            }
            System.out.println("Writing part " + nWholeParts);
            FileOutputStream fos = new FileOutputStream("part" + nWholeParts);
            bos = new BufferedOutputStream(fos);
            bos.write(buffer, 0, remainder);
            bos.close();
            bos = null;
        }
    }
    catch (IOException ioe)
    {
        ioe.printStackTrace();
        if (bis != null)
            try
            {
                bis.close();
            }
            catch (IOException ioe2)
            {
                ioe2.printStackTrace();
            }
        if (bos != null)
            try
            {
                bos.close();
            }
            catch (IOException ioe2)
            {
                ioe2.printStackTrace();
            }
    }
  }
}
```

65. Listing 45 presents the `CircleInfo` application that was called for in Chapter 10.

Listing 45. *Reading lines of text from standard input that represent circle radii, and outputting circumference and area based on the current radius*

```
import java.io.BufferedReader;
import java.io.InputStreamReader;
import java.io.IOException;

public class CircleInfo
{
    public static void main(String[] args) throws IOException
    {
        InputStreamReader isr = new InputStreamReader(System.in);
        BufferedReader br = new BufferedReader(isr);
        while (true)
        {
            System.out.print("Enter circle's radius: ");
            String str = br.readLine();
            double radius;
```

```
        try
        {
           radius = Double.valueOf(str).doubleValue();
           if (radius <= 0)
              System.err.println("radius must not be 0 or negative");
           else
           {
              System.out.println("Circumference: " + Math.PI*2.0*radius);
              System.out.println("Area: " + Math.PI*radius*radius);
           }
        }
        catch (NumberFormatException nfe)
        {
           nfe.printStackTrace();
        }
     }
   }
}
```

Index

ReferenceQueue class, 260
Short class, 255
SoftReference class, 260
SortedSet interface, 340
String class, 278, 280
StringBuffer class, 282
ThreadLocal class, 309
Throwable class, 163
TreeMap class, 355
TreeSet class, 332
WeakReference class, 263
contains method, Collection, 319
containsAll method, Collection, 319, 321
containsKey/containsValue methods, Map,
    351
continue reserved word, 71
continue statement, 71
    labeled continue statement, 72
Control class, 403
control-flow invariants, 184–185
conversions
    byte cast, 56
    cast operator, 56
    operands of different types in operator,
        56
Coordinated Universal Time see UTC
copy method, 176
copying
    deep copying/cloning, 105
    shallow copying/cloning, 104
copylist method, generics, 209, 210, 212,
    213
core interfaces, collections framework, 315,
    316
cos method, Math, 228
countdown latches, 390
countDown method, 390, 391
CountDownLatch class, 390
countTokens method, StringTokenizer, 502
covariance, arrays, 211
covariant return type, 123–124
createImage method, Toolkit, 406
createNewFile method, 459
createTempFile method, 459, 460
currency
    formatting numbers as, 421
    NumberFormat class, 235
current method, BreakIterator, 410
currentThread method, 288, 289, 290
currentTimeMillis method, 285, 286, 415
cursor position, ListIterator, 328

cyclic barriers, 390
CyclicBarrier class, 390

D

\d predefined character class, 440
daemon thread, 289
Dalvik virtual machine
    Android platform, 5
data I/O, 449
data stream classes see stream classes
database driver
    loading via class initializer, 77
databases
    accessing, 530
    creating flat file database, 467–472
DataInputStream class, 494
DataOutputStream class, 494
Date class, 415–416
    methods, 415–416
date formatters, 424–425
DateFormat class, 424
    setTimeZone method, 425
DateFormatSymbols class, 425
dates
    internationalization, 415
    Unix epoch, 425
daylight saving time, 417
deadlock, 306–308
deal method, Four of a Kind game, 28
decimal format, integer literals, 49
decimal numbers
    formatting numbers as, 421
DecimalFormat class, 424
DecimalFormatSymbols class, 424
decimals
    BigDecimal class, 234–239
Deck class, Four of a Kind game, 26, 28
    methods, 28
decodeFile method, BitmapFactory, 479
Decorator design pattern, 115
deep copying/cloning, 105
default reserved word
    switch statement, 65
defaultReadObject method, 505
defaultWriteObject method, 505
delete method, File, 459
deleteOnExit method, File, 459, 460
delimiters, 44
    Javadoc comments, 34
Deprecated annotation type, 191

O

Y

Z

CPSIA information can be obtained at www.ICGtesting.com

227919LV00004B/20/P